TREASURE HOUSE

THE STEWART DAWSON STORY

Author Bio

Geoff Nadin is a retired business consultant who wrote too many dry-as-dust reports for too many indifferent readers. Seeking an outlet for his unacknowledged talents, he turned over a stone and found, right on his doorstep, a whole world hidden in plain sight: the long-forgotten saga of the Stewart Dawsons. The path it took him on was long and winding, the goal sometimes out of reach. But the reward was worth the effort, he thinks. With several short stories already published, poems, and a possible novel in the pipeline, he's playing the literary field, enjoying every minute of it. Geoff lives in a Stewart Dawson house in the Blue Mountains.

TREASURE HOUSE

THE STEWART DAWSON STORY

AN AUSTRALASIAN FORTUNE BUILT ON JEWELLERY, CELEBRATED IN JAZZ STYLE, SQUANDERED IN SCANDAL AND VIOLENCE.

GEOFF NADIN

This is an IndieMosh book

brought to you by MoshPit Publishing
an imprint of Mosher's Business Support Pty Ltd

PO Box 4363
Penrith NSW 2750

indiemosh.com.au

A catalogue record for this work is available from the National Library of Australia

https://www.nla.gov.au/collections

Title:	Treasure House
Subtitle:	The Stewart Dawson Story
Author:	Nadin, Geoff (1945–)
ISBNs:	9781922812582 (paperback) 9781922812599 (ebook – epub) 9781922812605 (ebook – Kindle)
Subjects:	BIOGRAPHY & AUTOBIOGRAPHY /Business; Historical; Rich and Famous

The author has made every effort to ensure that the information in this book was correct at the time of publication. However, the author and publisher accept no liability for any errors of fact, omission or otherwise.

Cover design and layout by Ally Mosher at allymosher.com
Cover photos from Geoff Nadin's personal collections
Other cover images used under licence from Envato elements.

To Val, both of you

'Than the Stewart Dawson family there is perhaps no better-known people in Australia'

Truth (Sydney) 22nd May 1938

Table of Contents

Author's Note

To the best of my knowledge, every event in this narrative is factual, based on contemporary reports, first-person accounts and recollections, letters and pronouncements by the protagonists and official documents such as birth, marriage and death certificates, travel, and immigration records, and title deeds. Historical background to the story, spanning as it does over 150 years, was gleaned from accredited sources, newspaper reports, and so on. In all cases, I have endeavoured to provide a source reference, and have sought copyright clearance. This includes all images used in the book.

Having lived with the personal history of the Stewart Dawsons, particularly David and Harriet, for more than seventeen years I'm confident I have not misrepresented them. If I have, mea culpa, David.

GN

Family tree

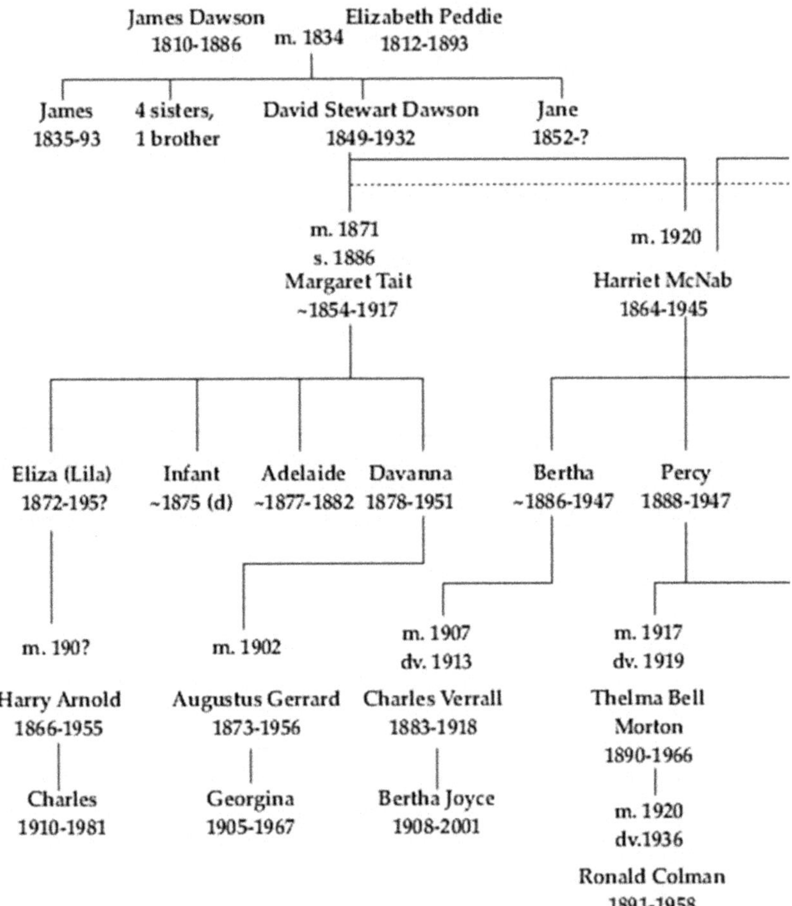

James Dawson
1810-1886
m. 1834
Elizabeth Peddie
1812-1893
James
1835-93
4 sisters,
1 brother
David Stewart Dawson
1849-1932
Jane
1852-?
m. 1871
s. 1886
Margaret Tait
~1854-1917
m. 1920
Harriet McNab
1864-1945
Eliza (Lila)
1872-195?
Infant
~1875 (d)
Adelaide
~1877-1882
Davanna
1878-1951
Bertha
~1886-1947
Percy
1888-1947
m. 190?
Harry Arnold
1866-1955
m. 1902
Augustus Gerrard
1873-1956
m. 1907
dv. 1913
Charles Verrall
1883-1918
m. 1917
dv. 1919
Thelma Bell
Morton
1890-1966
Charles
1910-1981
Georgina
1905-1967
Bertha Joyce
1908-2001
m. 1920
dv.1936
Ronald Colman
1891-1958

Family tree

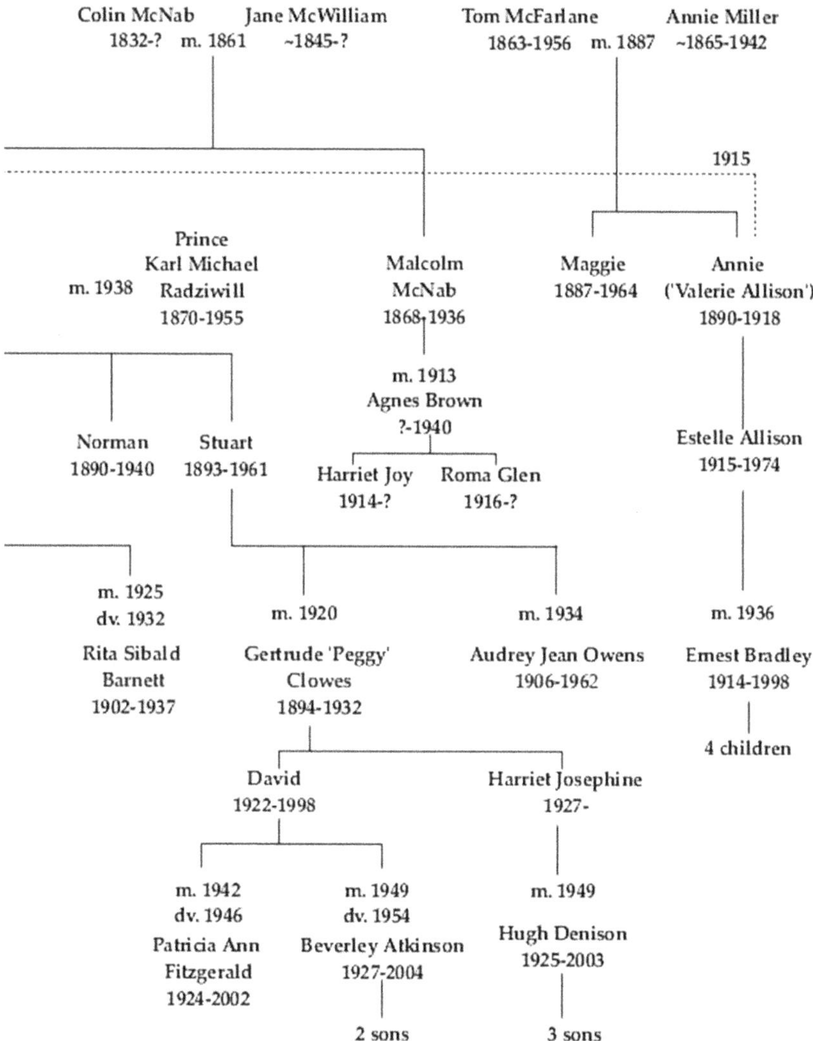

Colin McNab
1832-? m. 1861
Jane McWilliam
~1845-?
Tom McFarlane
1863-1956 m. 1887
Annie Miller
~1865-1942
1915
Prince
Karl Michael
m. 1938 Radziwill
1870-1955
Malcolm
McNab
1868-1936
Maggie
1887-1964
Annie
('Valerie Allison')
1890-1918
m. 1913
Agnes Brown
?-1940
Norman
1890-1940
Stuart
1893-1961
Harriet Joy
1914-?
Roma Glen
1916-?
Estelle Allison
1915-1974
m. 1925
dv. 1932
Rita Sibald
Barnett
1902-1937
m. 1920
Gertrude 'Peggy'
Clowes
1894-1932
m. 1934
Audrey Jean Owens
1906-1962
m. 1936
Ernest Bradley
1914-1998
4 children
David
1922-1998
Harriet Josephine
1927-
m. 1942
dv. 1946
Patricia Ann
Fitzgerald
1924-2002
m. 1949
dv. 1954
Beverley Atkinson
1927-2004
2 sons
m. 1949
Hugh Denison
1925-2003
3 sons

Introduction: Heights and Depths

In February 1998, the death occurred in South Kensington, London of David Stewart Dawson.[1] The passing of the 75-year-old retired taxi driver went unremarked. There is no record of a funeral notice. He departed in obscurity. This was the same David who, fifty years earlier had inherited a life of privilege and luxury in Australia, lived at Sydney's best addresses, married two beautiful women, owned a hotel, and gambled millions, only to lose it all in scandal and shame.

In 1849 his grandfather and namesake was born in equal obscurity but relative poverty on a farm in Scotland. In the next 150 years, a dynasty was founded and foundered, a fortune built and squandered, the family name became a byword for style and luxury then faded from memory just as quickly. This is the story of the Stewart Dawsons, watchmakers, and jewellers extraordinaires, roaring twenties Australian pioneers of sophisticated popular entertainment, property tycoons and philanthropists, doyens of society who counted royalty among their connections. It's also a story of marital duplicity and deception, hubris and abuse of privilege, hedonism, fraud, and criminal violence leaving a trail of victims and damaged lives, where there were few happy endings.

This story was inspired when my wife and I purchased our house in Springwood, New South Wales, in 2002. After 23 years in Sydney's suburbia, we knew it was time to escape the traffic congestion that was strangling our once quiet enclave in leafy Pennant Hills. No one can deny the beauty of Australia's magnificent coastline, but it was the interior that drew us away for weekend drives and holidays, so our bolt hole from Greater Sydney was always going to be somewhere westward. I was still working at the time, so commuting had to be factored in; no point in exchanging a couple of hours stuck in Sydney traffic for even longer droning along a motorway or squeezed into a train. We knew the Blue Mountains well from many happy day trips to the spectacular views and quirky towns and villages, so our search began for a home with "character" to replace our comfortable but bland 70's project house in Pennant Hills. We set our search limit at Springwood, based on access to rail commuting and a good range of amenities, but several months and many depressing "open house" viewings later we were losing hope of finding the home of our planned retirement. Then, driving back south along Hawkesbury Road into the town from another fruitless inspection, Val grabbed my arm and pointed to a "For Sale" sign half hidden in the dense trees of a property on our left. "What about that place? It's worth a look, pull in along here." Peering through the overgrown vegetation we could see a large old weatherboard cottage with an impressive pillared veranda and a steeply pitched, tiled roof. It looked tired and neglected but a peek round the side revealed a much larger building than it appeared from the sidewalk. "Looks out of our price range," Val observed, "but worth a call to the agent." I rang on my cell phone and requested the asking price (there were few auctions those days in the Mountains). When Val saw the look on my face, she figured we were either way out of the money or about to strike a bargain. I reassured her it was the latter and within days we had inspected "The Spinney", confirming our initial impressions of neglect and poor maintenance. Nevertheless, the place oozed character and the large, sloping grounds offered enormous potential for a dedicated gardener like Val. Our offer was accepted, and we took a deep breath as we prepared to move. Four months later we were still at Pennant Hills, driving the 40 miles to the Mountains most days to clean and refurbish The Spinney. Stained carpets were ripped up, revealing honey-coloured floorboards desperately in need of a polish; years of soot from the never-cleaned fireplace were swabbed from walls and ceilings; the 1960s horror that was the main bathroom was gutted and refitted; chipped and splintered woodwork was restored and finally the whole exterior received a fresh coat of paint, reviving the faded weatherboard siding and stained ionic pillars on the veranda. We moved in, cleared out the resident possum in the chimney, and set our minds to enjoying our new home.

This was our first move to a home that wasn't brand new, but just how old was The Spinney? A visit to the local historian in Springwood revealed that the house dated from the 1920s, though its architecture was from an earlier era. The original owner was a Mrs Valerie Allison. Beyond that nothing was known, except that the lady was buried in Springwood cemetery, the other side of the golf course opposite The Spinney. A five-minute walk took us to the quiet corner of the Presbyterian section where one grave stood apart from the rest. Surrounded by a low stuccoed wall, it had a neglected look, weeds and brambles encroaching on the gravel surface. The plain headstone read: "In loving memory of Valerie A. Allison, died 28th November 1918, loved by all." "Same names as mine," exclaimed Val, whose middle name is Ann. "I knew we were meant to have this house!"

A couple of months later we visited an open garden not far down Hawkesbury Road. Chatting to the owner, the redoubtable and late-lamented Wilma Leech-Larson, we complimented her on her impressive garden and compared it to the challenge we faced on our own overgrown plot. She asked where we lived and when we told her, exclaimed: "Oh, the Stewart Dawson house!" Perplexed, we protested that, no, its original owner was a Mrs Allison. Wilma, however, was adamant and went on to relate a story of high society scandal that involved a family of rich Sydneysiders who had made Springwood their second home. On returning home we checked the reference from the historical society again and saw we had overlooked something; Mrs Valerie Allison was indeed the original registered owner, but her address was "C/- Stewart Dawson, Pitt Street, Sydney", whoever that was. If Wilma was to be believed, this Stewart Dawson must have been well known in Sydney and Springwood, but all our follow up enquiries came to a dead end. The Historical Society had a few sketchy notes about the man and references to another large house in Springwood that was no longer standing. An internet search revealed some jewellery stores by that name in New Zealand but none in Australia. There was a Wikipedia entry that seemed to support the story of wealth and influence over the late 19th and early 20th centuries. The article mentioned large property holdings and a night club or restaurant called "Ambassadors" that we recalled hearing about, but the trail didn't lead very far. Though we asked many, including a centenarian friend, the name "Stewart Dawson" meant nothing to older residents of Springwood. What about descendants? There were no subscribers by that name in any Australian telephone directories, on social media sites or, apart from the aforesaid entries, turned up by search engines. It was almost as if he had been airbrushed from history. As for the connection with Mrs Valerie A. Allison and who she may have been, we drew a complete blank. Surely someone as prominent as this man must have been would have left more of a mark, particularly in Australia where larger than life individuals are celebrated, if not revered. What could have led to the obliteration of a well-known family name within a couple of generations?

And so, the search began to uncover the mystery. It has taken nearly seventeen years to piece together the story, aided more recently by online services such as Ancestry and the extensive newspaper archives of Australia, Great Britain, and New Zealand. We also received valuable assistance from members of Springwood Historical Society including John Low and John Merriman, Susan Hamill, who supplied photographs of the Springwood houses, and Pamela Smith. Special thanks are due to Alexis Dailey for providing photographs of the McFarlane family and much of the background to the story of Maggie and Annie. Anne Norman, Managing Director of James Pascoe (New Zealand) kindly presented us with a complete history of the Stewart Dawson business in that country. Anne Worthington and husband, Simon, who are restoring the terraced gardens on the site of the former "Davesta" have given much advice and encouragement. New South Wales Land Titles Office were most helpful with access to title deeds for the Hawkesbury Road properties and staff at Sydney's Mitchell Library allowed us full access to David Stewart Dawson's "The Boy and the Wheelbarrow 1858, The Man and The Ambassadors 1924". The State Library of Western Australia in Perth supplied copies of Harriet Stewart Dawson's letters to Kathleen O'Connor. Staff at the Hydro Majestic Hotel, Medlow Bath, gave permission for us to photograph parts of the hotel not publicly accessible. Fraser Bradley offered personal memories of his mother, Estelle; Tom Clarke filled in many gaps in the chequered history of Norman Stewart Dawson, and John Maclurcan was a mine of information on Hannah Maclurcan and the Wentworth Hotel. Thanks to Joy Morrison, Rosemary Madeley, Paola Kistner, Shirley and Ian King, Steve Nicholson, Geoff Reynolds, Alex Okunew, and Janice Freelander for critical feedback and some very useful insights.

Thanks to IndieMosh; to Ally, for a cover Baz Luhrmann might envy, and Astrid, for guiding me through final editing and layout, and navigating the shoals of publishing.

Finally, my patient and very thorough wife, Val, deserves special thanks for her painstaking research of land titles, library references (it was she who discovered "The Boy and the Wheelbarrow …", a key to understanding David Stewart Dawson's character), and obscure family relationships. Without her critical insights and constant support this book would not have been written.

Springwood
November 2019

Part 1: 1849 – 1929.

A Self-Made Man

A Long Way from Scotland

The slim, black hull of the ship cut easily through the gentle swells of the Indian Ocean as the sun rose high on the port side. The sky was bluer here, the air warmer day by day; could it really be February? Was it only two weeks since they had clung fast to anything solid to remain standing, shouting to each other above the howling wind, praying to maintain control of their heaving stomachs? Under Captain Ruthven's stewardship they had weathered what some were now calling the worst storm in the Channel in living memory. But this was no creaking, straining, sailing barque of yesteryear, at the mercy of the elements; this was 1884, after all. The pounding engine, streaming its reassuring sooty smoke, confirmed their confidence in the might of engineering and man's inexorable progress. Few other vessels, it was said, would have survived the titanic gale that swept up the English Channel as the SS Chimborazo departed Plymouth. What tales they would tell, forgetting the fear they had shared.[2] Now they skimmed along a favourable current, the south easterly breeze a mere vesper in comparison. Aden, with its colourful, shouting markets, the smells of spices and a bewildering array of silver, brass, and gold trinkets to tempt the naïve traveller, was days astern; the marvel of Suez,* a picture book memory. No land broke the horizon on any side, nor would it for almost a fortnight. The two hundred passengers and crew might well have been the sole inhabitants of a watery planet.

The stylishly attired gentleman taking a turn around the upper deck greeted fellow passengers: "Morning, Mr Basnett, Miss Basnett," "Good morning, Mr Stewart Dawson;" "Doctor Parker!" "Morning, Mr Stewart Dawson." [3] In the weeks since leaving London he had made the acquaintance, indeed, sought the company, of many. He had been surprised to see how young they all were; scarcely one of them looked over forty. Almost without exception, they were first-time

---

* The Suez Canal opened in 1869 but was not fully operational for larger vessels such as the Chimborazo until the late 1870s. It was still a great novelty and wonder for international travellers at the time of David's voyage.

voyagers like him, bound for a new life or seeking adventure in the colonies. As he took out his watch for the hundredth time (was he overplaying his hand?) he reflected that, despite any initial disappointment he may have felt at their relative youth and corresponding lack of means, the odds were that these mostly single people would prosper beyond their dreams in their new homeland.

The things he had heard about Melbourne and Sydney back in the Liverpool public house and at the exchange! The torrent of money that had already poured in from just these two young cities! And it wasn't abating. Day after day orders arrived in the post and by cable so that his workers hardly kept pace. Contrary to what some said, this was not too good to be true. His smile as he saluted another promenading couple was as much a reflection of his inner self-satisfaction as of his pleasure at the encounter; at the age of only 34 he was, by any standard, a rich man, a success in business, a maestro of the persuasive art. And he was on his way to conquer a continent! He leant on the rail, the steady breeze in his face, squinting at the empty horizon. He had come a long way in the past few weeks, a longer way since the scrabbling years in Liverpool; soon, a whole world away from Scotland. His mother, that "wise philosopher", would be proud of him if she knew where he was heading, all that he had achieved. If his brother, James and the girls ever wondered what became of the laddie with the wheelbarrow they would be in for the surprise of their lives. Whatever would they make of him now? As the ship drove on and his eyes closed against the dazzling sun, his mind returned, as it had so often in the past twenty years, to the place where, as he would put it, his destiny was forged.

"Cairnie" (he rolled the "r" as he silently spoke it, as no Sassenach would), was there ever a more authentic, Celtic name to call home? In the Lowlands of Scotland, up near the border of Aberdeenshire and Banffshire in the district of Strathbogie, sits the tiny hamlet. The forty-eight square miles of Strathbogie, in sight of the Cairngorm highlands is part of the Duke of Richmond's vast land holdings. The small streams and rivulets that flow into larger rivers such as the Spey and Isla, fed by abundant rain and snowmelt from the nearby mountains, are a source of the unique, peaty water used in the production of Scotch whisky. The famous "Strathisla" whisky distillery where Chivas Regal is made is no more than five miles north-west at Keith.

The road from Aberdeen to Inverness passes through the parish, with no more than a hamlet to mark its geographical identity. In 1850 the population of the entire parish numbered less than 1700, scattered among the many smallholdings or crofts. The livelihood of a crofter family could be precarious. Highland landowners, as a feature of their so-called improvement programmes, leased land to tenant farmers who then either farmed it themselves, often with the help of cottars or agricultural labourers, or rented it out in smaller lots to crofters and cottars. Crofters subsisted on their small holdings, growing vegetables, and having a few stock, with their income often augmented by a trade such as weaving or blacksmithing. In 1884, as the Chimborazo's passengers sailed for the land of unlimited plenty, Scottish landlords were still entitled to terminate the crofter's tenancy at the end of any year and recover possession of the land, together with any buildings and other permanent improvements that might have been on the croft.*

James Dawson married Elizabeth Peddie in 1834. Together they farmed a landholding in Cairnie, growing oats, with a few cattle on the rougher, more stony pasture. Life in the parish was not for the weak-willed. Biting winds and driving rain sweep in from the North Sea. With little high land to break the gales, the countryside around Cairnie is a challenge for the hardiest farm labourer. Add to the wind the frequent rain, and the winter sleet and snow, and the picture emerges of an often bleak, if beautiful environment. James and Elizabeth occasionally had a teenage farm hand, son of a neighbour, to help with animal and land care and perform menial work around the house. Otherwise, they relied on children of the family who were old enough to harness a horse, carry a basket, clear the many stones, or scrub out weeds.

By the late 1840s the two-roomed cottage had welcomed five children. The first born, James, had completed his education at the parish school and at the age of fifteen, was preparing himself for the teaching profession. Still at home were James' four sisters, the

* It would be another two years before the Crofters' Act was passed, granting a degree of tenure and a modicum of control to the tenant farmers.

youngest, Mary, born in 1847. Their mother looked forward to the day when they would all be old enough to lend a hand about the farm or leave for paid work or marriage. It was into this household that, on a bitterly cold night on November 25th, 1849, she gave birth to her second son. They christened him David. Tradition held that the first-born son took the name of his father, as James had done. Their second son honoured his paternal grandfather. The elder David Dawson had married Margaret Stewart, now many years a widow and in service to a local farmer.

In his infancy, David's care was shared among his sisters, when he wasn't left alone to crawl and stumble about the croft or play in the dirt outside. Then, at the age of four he was accepted at the parish school in Cairnie, where James was now the teacher. His earliest memory was of walking the muddy lanes from the croft to the hamlet where the one room school stood at the western end of the single street. He remembered how proud he was of his elder brother but wryly recalled the stern warning from his parents that there would be no filial favouritism bestowed on him. School was for learning and that demanded obedience and acceptance of sometimes harsh discipline. With James in front of the class attendance was never an issue for David, but in other respects his experience matched that of many of his peers. In 1859, when he was a mere nine-and-a-half, the family was uprooted by the landlord, forcing a move west to Kininvie, near Dufftown, the home to the Glen Fiddich Distillery. It wasn't a bad farm as such but for David and his younger sisters it meant the end of their formal education. The nearest parish school was over six miles away with no practical means for David to reach it. He was left with basic skills in reading, writing and arithmetic and a sound knowledge of the catechism, but very little else to equip him for life.

So, how had it come to this? What was an under-educated Scots farm-lad doing on the promenade deck of an ocean liner, a cabin all to himself, sporting a well-cut suit and all the accoutrements of a gentleman? "It's a good question, I suppose, a good story," he mused, "I must write it down some day. Lord knows, I've told it often enough to those who'll listen." His mind returned to the draughty croft in Kininvie, indistinguishable from his old home, in which he now found himself.

His grandmother was back in the family home, in her seventies still able to assist her daughter-in-law and administer discipline around the house when called upon. Apart from Mary, now eleven, and six-year-old Jane, his other sisters were long gone, in service to various farms and households. Mary helped with the cooking and cleaning, Jane was too young to be of much use, leaving David the heavier, outdoor chores. He sensed he was a disappointment to his father, not through any fault of his own but because emulating his elder brother was now out of the question. Or was it? He had to find something to alleviate his boredom, prove his worth, earn his keep until the day when he would find paying work elsewhere. Shooed from the house by his mother one morning, he spotted among the ferns and thistles the beginnings of a garden, its beds overgrown. A previous occupant must have started and abandoned it. Now, there was a challenge; he could go one better and complete the work. It would please his mother and maybe persuade his father that he was no idle layabout. A few minutes' prodding about with a stick as his kilt swirled and lifted in the blustering wind was all that was needed to convince him why his predecessor had given up: this was the windward side of the house; nothing bar thistles and ferns could survive long in the frigid blast. "I need a dyke, like the one by the vegetable patch. It doesn't have to be more than an enclosure a couple of feet high and I can leave a gap on the side facing the house." He would never forget the look his father gave him when he asked permission; part mild surprise, part dismissive, but not entirely discouraging, as he answered: "Certainly, but you have nothing to build it with," before turning away to his own work. The busy farmer was not a man to waste time discussing what he considered trivial matters with a nine-year-old, and anyway, what was the point? Even if the lad succeeded, they stood to gain little benefit if, as had already happened, they were moved on yet again without compensation for improvements made. "Well, I have my arms and the old wheelbarrow", thought David, "it can't be that hard to build a wee stone wall."

How naïve he had been! He felt again the ache in his puny frame, the bruises and cuts from heavy, sharp stones as if it were yesterday. He'd had no more desire for hard work, as such, than the next boy but, he supposed, the rudiments of a high purpose, the will to achieve, determination to accomplish something, anything to show what he could do. Lord! that old wheelbarrow was heavy! Even empty, it took most of his strength to lift the rough shafts. Pushing it over the stony ground, the iron wheel grating and slipping, jamming against a protruding rock, might well have been a penance for his sins. His mother could always find a pertinent bible verse to encourage his efforts, but it soon became clear to him that he had taken on more than he had bargained for. Collecting the best stones from the fields and digging a trench for the foundation was only the start; now he had to determine how to erect a wall that would stand against the wind. He took a walk around the vegetable garden and along local lanes where for the first time he examined the sturdy structures built by hands much older than his. He saw that what he had taken for dry-stone was in fact bound together with mortar. There was no way he could obtain or mix the real stuff; to start with, he had no lime. Could he accomplish anything with clay? There was plenty of this free resource in the boggy hollows, so he dug down to expose the dun-coloured layer. "Just add water and, 'presto!' we have our mortar," he figured. Several failed attempts later, as he once again collected the tumbled stones, the realisation dawned that some sort of bonding material was needed. Once more he headed for the fields and hillsides, grass hook in hand, to harvest barrow-loads of heather. Layering it into the puddled clay, he spread the mix over the joints between the stones and, sure enough, the beginnings of the wall stood strong. His hopes were buoyed by the glorious weather, for it was now high summer, when the rain kept off for a while and the sun shone.

The wall slowly grew, a kind of plan emerging as he went, but with only a vague notion of when it would be complete. He had started, and, by golly, he would finish. His mother and grandmother, glancing up from their housework through the side window, could catch his eye and nod their approval and encouragement. Even his father gruffly acknowledged his progress, noting the additional benefit of keeping his son out of mischief with the other boys of the parish. It would be a year before David stood back to admire the finished enclosure, by which time word had got around and more than one neighbour had stepped over to appraise his work. It felt good; he still remembered the glow of pride when others, older and wiser than he, congratulated him and praised the quality of his endeavours. He had "gone one better" and if he could do it once to such good effect, then he would do it again.

And here he was, doing it yet again. There was no point in false modesty, by now most of his fellow voyagers knew of his name and fame, a few of them even sporting his wares. He was gracious, of course, but seldom missed an opportunity to initiate discussion of commerce, fashion, and the incidental promotion of his business. It was in his nature and, by now, he was adept at steering the conversation his way, he didn't mind admitting.

Such discussions sooner or later turned to comparing the life and conditions in the old country with the exciting prospects ahead in Australia. Though many of the young folks on board came from large cities such as London, Manchester, Birmingham and Liverpool, they all shared a desire for the new, the opportunity to make a better life where the streets, if not paved with gold, were lined with bold buildings that spoke of wealth and endless possibilities for creating their own future. David's personal experience, which he shared with his eager listeners, reinforced their expectations.

In 1863, at fourteen, it was time to leave the farm to find work. He was to take a position as a farm servant, some twenty miles east at Mr Mellis' farm in Smallburn.[4] Neither the Mellises nor his own parents deluded themselves that this would be more than a temporary engagement. The industrial revolution had for decades drained the countryside of its stock of young farm labourers with the lure of secure employment and real wages in the cities. David read the newspapers, mixed with other young men more experienced than he. The stories they told excited his imagination, filling his mind with dreams of wealth, fame, and success. "Boy wanted", "Young man needed for growing business" advertisements filled the columns of the classified section of the papers. In short order he gave notice to Mr Mellis and set off for the nearest city, Aberdeen, confident of finding a trade or other form of paid employment. His shock and excitement upon arriving in the port city was extreme. The crowded streets were paved! Buildings as high as four storeys lined them as far as he could see. The din of the markets, the ceaseless clatter of horses' hooves on the manure-smeared cobble stones and the grating of iron carriage wheels were like some sort of Bedlam. Unfamiliar and not always pleasant smells filled the air and down at the quayside he had his first sight of a real steamship, belching sulphurous fumes from its tall smokestack. How quaint that seemed twenty years on; the stubby coastal steamer would be dwarfed by the nearly four-thousand-ton iron behemoth on which he stood, creaming along faster than any horse could run. No mind, Aberdeen was a revelation, and he could hardly wait to dive into its untidy streets. His apprenticeship as a messenger boy, if it could be so called, taught him survival lessons in the competitive world. He had to be quick on his feet, it went without saying; polite and deferential to his superiors, a trait instilled in him at home and school; but also, a good listener: he was here to learn, make good the lost school years. He observed the ways of business and commerce, the winners and losers. In and out of shops and offices, meeting shopkeepers, clerks, buyers, agents, and wholesalers, he listened and learned the language of persuasion, heard the catchphrases that brought in the customers, witnessed the effects of the printed word on posters and in newspapers. The pace of life was so much faster here than back on the land and he had energy to spare. So much so that he soon found the limits of Aberdeen, where the wind was even worse than at home, whistling round his draughty room and along the narrow streets, and his feet itched. If he was to get on, he must venture further away, preferably south, where the weather was more forgiving and where he could exploit his new-found skills in a bigger arena.

So, it was on to Edinburgh, over ninety miles away. His time here was to be short, however. The capital city was certainly bigger than Aberdeen, and commercial life more sophisticated but, at seventeen, bursting with confidence but restless as seldom before, he set his sights on the bigger prize: nearby Glasgow,[5] already Scotland's fastest growing city, a place of exceptional economic buoyancy and urban growth. Here was a prosperous middle class, dominated by businessmen and many well-paid skilled workers in engineering and shipbuilding. Servicing this was a vibrant retail trade in which David, parlaying his charm and social skills, found work as a draper's salesman. At a time before ready-made clothes were common, there was abundant work for tailors, dressmakers and seamstresses making garments to order. The retail drapery trade employed many of them as outworkers, showcasing fabrics in high street drapery stores or in the new "department" stores then emerging in the larger cities. Wholesale drapers were the middlemen with the exclusive right to buy fabric from the manufacturers. They, in turn, employed travelling salesmen to service the retail outlets.

Thrown into this highly competitive environment, David soon built a web of connections among his many customers. Up early six days a week, he would tote his catalogues and his samples of silks, wool cloth, and fine cottons through the busy streets, dodging through the streams of carriages, carts and horse-drawn omnibuses, to greet his customers or make the all-important first call to capture the business from a competitor. The days were long, the weather often bitter, the busy streets always a danger for pedestrians who failed to keep a watchful eye for runaway horses or unsecured loads on passing carts. He revelled in the life, bursting with energy and confidence, and he was making more than enough money to pay his bills, send a regular remittance to his parents and put some aside in the savings bank. But his immediate concern on reaching the metropolis had been finding somewhere to live. In overcrowded cities such as Glasgow affordable accommodation was scarce, and it was common practice for single men to find lodgings with families eager to supplement their income. The community of wholesale and retail drapers provided many leads and connections for its busy young salesmen and it was a matter of days before David joined two other young men at the home of Margaret Tait, a widowed dressmaker, at 157 Eglinton Street, in the Gorbals district.[6] The building was one of the hundreds of brand new four storey sandstone terraces that lined the streets south of the river Clyde.

David's fellow lodgers were Lachlan McIntosh, another draper's salesman, and young Joseph Cameron, who served behind the counter in one of their customers' shops. The three lads shared a room, but long working hours and a busy social life meant they imposed no great burden on their landlady. With the exception of the Sabbath, when attendance at kirk was the only organised activity available or permitted to God fearing folk, and a quiet stroll in the park or by the river was the limit of social intercourse, most evenings the threesome were out at the pubs in Saltmarket, laughing at the skits and shows at the Penny Geggies* or singing to the rowdy crowd at one of the Free and Easies† in the back room of The Shakespeare or the Baillie Nicholl Jarvie. There they could meet young ladies, not all of spotless reputation. David had first encountered this demi-monde around the docksides of Aberdeen, his boyish innocence confronted by the sometimes-open licentiousness. By the time he landed in the teeming back streets of Glasgow the constraints of a rural upbringing in the parish were long behind him. He had real money to spend, dressed well and fashionably, thanks to his employer and the need to impress his clients, and had developed a fine line of conversation and persuasion. He was far away from prying eyes at home and in the company of ambitious young men out to challenge and impress each other. It was an easy step to initiation into adult life by willing and experienced ladies, especially when egged on by his boisterous companions. Those were hectic days, he recalled. He had been free to be reckless with time, there seemed to be no limit to the ways to indulge in drink, song, women. In some ways, might Australia, this young country overflowing with hope and prosperity, be a portal to that fondly remembered time of his life?

It had lasted no more than a couple of years before he took the fateful step that was the cause of so much pain and regret, a decision that still puzzled and annoyed him. How could he have been so impetuous, so careless of his own interests? He, whose motto was to go one better, had risked squandering his advantage as a free and single man for, what? Well, perhaps this few months on the other side of the world would be a taste of that lost freedom while giving him time to think, plan and scheme. Come to think of it, Margaret might benefit from the separation too, and come to her senses; you never knew. If only he'd found other lodgings in Glasgow, if only he'd waited or kept his respectful distance, but he hadn't, the deed was

---

* The Geggies were originally temporary theatres staged at travelling fairs. By mid-century they were often more equivalent to a music hall or sketch comedy theatre.

† The "Free and Easy", in the back room of the pub, was the forerunner of the modern-day karaoke, where anybody could get up and sing.

done, the milk spilt. He supposed it had been Margaret's innocence, her unspoilt prettiness and her constant presence in the cramped house that had beguiled him. For his landlady, Margaret Tait, had a young daughter at home, also Margaret, a seamstress, like her mother She was a mere fourteen when David joined the household. Born in Stromness, Orkney, she had moved with her mother to the mainland upon the death of her father, as the widow sought employment to keep them from the workhouse. Her schooling had been as brief as David's, but she could read and write and had patiently learned the sewing and finishing skills that kept them gainfully employed. The two women worked from home, though Margaret senior walked out to collect fabric and notions from the shops they serviced and to deliver the finished goods. It would not be long before some of the larger stores commissioned their own work rooms, equipped with the latest sewing machines: so much in everyday life was changing. Margaret's early years in Stomness had not prepared her for this, but though, like David, she viewed the world through youthful eyes, eager for experience, unlike him she retained much of her childish reticence.

Nevertheless, perhaps she dreamed of a time when she could break the bonds of home-based outwork and see more of the big world outside, more so when she listened to the carefully censored tales of the three young lodgers. As she grew and matured, she gained confidence through familiarity and joined in the conversation around the dinner table. David, by this time, was the most self-assured and assertive of the trio. His vision of future success far exceeded the limited ambitions of Lachlan and Joseph. David's polished patter and, if he might say so, his ready wit, beguiled mother and daughter and it was a matter of pride and satisfaction to him to grasp and hold the attention of the two women while his roommates looked on and, he supposed, learned from him.

Inevitably, David and Margaret grew closer and, in part encouraged by her mother (it must have been at her mother's instigation, mustn't it?) he took up with the seventeen-year-old. If only he'd kept the relationship casual. If only … If only. In the end, it all seemed to happen very quickly. Before he knew it, he'd proposed to the starry-eyed, innocent maid and been accepted, with her mother's blessing. On

September 18th, 1871, he and Margaret were married.[7] The wedding took place not in church but in Margaret's home, as was the custom then in Scotland even for "regular", religiously sanctioned marriages.* What with the wedding party, the witnesses, the guests and the local Presbyterian minister, there was a mighty crowd in the tiny parlour. David was sorry his mother couldn't be there, but it was a long journey for her to make from Kininvie and she had more than enough on her hands. He'd write a letter telling her all about it. She'd like that.

So, there they were, the twenty-one-year-old and his child bride, with the world at their feet and, if David were to be believed, great expectations of wealth and success. Now their priority was finding a place of their own to live on a single income. Margaret would not be expected to earn a living. It was not proper for a married woman, and in any case, David had a lot to prove, and it wasn't to be in Glasgow.

---

* Margaret's young age was by no means unusual; it was not until 1929 that the legal minimum age for marriage in Scotland was raised from twelve.

"Watches! Watches! Watches!"

The sun was now higher in the clear sky. Someone cried out that they could see flying fish skimming over the troughs in the swells and he walked over to the other side of the ship to join the excited travellers. What a sight it was! He'd heard about these fantastic creatures but until now they had belonged with sea monsters and two-headed men, in the realms of fantasy. But here they were, more than keeping pace with the swift vessel, their flight enduring for many seconds before they slipped with barely a splash into the next rising wave, to emerge a moment later with another soaring leap. He reflected that, sooner or later, if a man put his mind to it, he too could break free of supposed natural bounds. A man of vision, such as he, never hesitated, understood the serendipity of the circumstances, and boldly made his move. He had done this when he left Glasgow and now he was the flying fish, skimming above the shoals below.

Though Glasgow was often at that time referred to as "the second city of the empire" a southern rival competed for that title. Liverpool, with its magnificent port, excellent railway and canal connections to the cotton mills of Manchester and the coalfields of Lancashire and the Black Country, was now the fastest growing city of all.* Moreover, its location on the west side of the country made it the port of choice for the great majority of international sea trade, surpassing even London. If David was to make his mark, he had to be where commerce was burgeoning at a pace that suited his need to compete and prove himself.

In early 1872 he and Margaret packed their bags, boarded the train and it seemed, in the blink of an eye, found themselves being swept along by the moving mass of people on the platform of Liverpool's

---

* Liverpool University: "*... the city's pre-eminent position at the turn of the 19th century resulted from the port's willingness to handle a very wide range of cargo (including millions of migrants to the new world). Liverpool was second only to London in this respect – and this, together with its great ethnic diversity, was the basis of its claim to be the 'second city of empire'.*"

towering Lime Street Station. In short order, he rented a house in the Toxteth district, a couple of miles south of the city centre and within strolling distance of newly opened Sefton Park. His movement up the social ladder from grimy Glasgow had begun. Their first child, Eliza (soon and ever after known as Lila) was born in July that year.[8] Now Margaret had fulfilled her role in life, though a son might have been preferred.

David did not come unprepared. He had £50 in savings* and a head full of ideas. He was now the local agent for wholesale drapery in a far larger market, with time, space, and funds to plan for a greater future. Much of the fabric on sale in Scotland was made in and around Lancashire and Cheshire; he'd sold many bolts of it in his time. He'd also learned that success was not inevitable; there had been plenty of bankruptcies among his customers who'd overreached themselves. As a middleman who spread his custom the risks were lower but the rewards (though he couldn't complain) were marginal. In the bigger market down south, he could spread the risk wider and, he hoped, increase rewards correspondingly. He could bide his time, learning the local market, building his relationships and customers, and saving every spare penny until he could establish his own wholesale business and sit at the top of the pyramid.

Five years of hard work later he was forced to acknowledge that breaking into the fabric market in his own right was not as straightforward as he had expected. Control of supply was tightly held and profit margins not as large as they once had been. He would have to persuade cloth manufacturers and importers to grant him a share of the business dominated by, among others, his own employer. Securing favourable prices would not be easy and he would face strong competition. It was then that he concluded that in his new hometown there could be a faster path to riches than hawking fabric. He wondered why he hadn't taken the leap sooner. Liverpool was more than a transport hub and entrepot; manufacturing employed significant numbers of people, and they appeared to be doing very well. You only had to spend a short time in the commercial centre or

* Fifty years later, he claimed to have saved £50 (about £30,000 in 2016) from his earnings in Glasgow.

around the docks that stretched for miles along the riverside to see the throngs of workers, clerks, shopkeepers, and professional men displaying their relative wealth. They dressed well, wore good shoes, fine cravats, and ties. To be sure, there was poverty, principally among the poor wretches who had streamed over to escape the Irish famines, and despite the phenomenal number of new houses there were too many overcrowded tenements, reminiscent of Glasgow. But overall, there was money to spend wherever you looked. Alert to new opportunities, David perused his daily newspaper. In his business he had made a habit of scanning the classified advertisements, checking that those placed by his employer had appeared on time and free of typographical errors, looking for competitors' promotions and taking the temperature of the market. His eye would be caught by the more compelling advertisements, the boldest typefaces, the loudest messages. Those that stood out were not promoting drapery but something much more appealing: watches, especially the ones placed by successful watch manufacturers such as Edward Kaltenbach of Cardiff,[9] F Woodstock and Anthony and Louis White of Liverpool.[10] Here was a market with enormous demand and a ready local supply. Moreover, pocket watches were more profitable than bolts of fabric, they were robust and cheap to transport individually and, most importantly, brandable. He could literally make his name on the face of every watch sold.* Watches were made in Liverpool and nearby Prescot from components made by hundreds of skilled craftsmen† and women. Prized for their quality, reliability and accurate time keeping,

---

* David claimed late in life that his start in watch manufacturing came in 1871 when the Liverpool Police invited tenders to supply pocket watches to the constabulary. The story told was that he bid for and won the tender and later exploited his purported success with advertisements using the catch phrase: "Who watches the police?". This is almost certainly a myth. He was still in Glasgow in 1871 and there is no record of the Liverpool police inviting tenders for watches any time in the 1870s. The watch maker who won a police tender in 1876 and used the catch phrase in advertisements in the Dundee Evening Telegraph was HJ Norris of Coventry (ref: Bury Free Press 30th December 1876).

† The author's own ancestor, Frances Eden, was a Liverpool watchmaker (an outworker) in the 1830s.

these English Lever timepieces had dominated world markets since the end of the 18th century.

Until the decade of David's birth, only the rich could afford a watch, but then two things changed everything. First, the railway network grew to cover the entire country in a matter of decades. Costs of travel plummeted as speed and ease grew. The move to the cities accelerated, spurring even more growth in jobs and wealth for the common people. Second, and partly because of the railways, Britain introduced what was called Railway (or Standard) Time. David had never known anything different. If he ever thought of time by the clock in his childhood, it was as a means of regulating his school days. It would never have occurred to him and he would not have been taught that only in his lifetime had Inverness, say, kept the same time as Orkney. In the days of horse-drawn coach travel it didn't matter much that Bristol kept local time 20 minutes behind London. Trains moving at 40-50 miles an hour however brought a new challenge. In November 1840 the Great Western Railway first applied Railway time[11] in England, and it was progressively taken up by all railway companies in Great Britain over the following two to three years. The schedules by which trains were organised and the times station clocks displayed were brought in line with "London Time".[*] A possibly unforeseen consequence was to encourage greater precision in daily tasks and the demand for punctuality. Now every working person needed a watch.[†]

Inspired by the advertisements, and finally finding a use for his capital, David decided to ride the crest of a new wave. In late 1877 he set up at premises in Park Road, Toxteth, with a team of workers assembling lever watches from bought in components.[12] He was no longer somebody's middleman, now he had his own company: "David Dawson & Company" would be the new name in watches. Except that, when he came to register the company, he found to his dismay that there already existed a firm by that name, in Stamford, Lincolnshire. There was also a "Dawson Ltd & Sons", in London,

* "London Time" was otherwise known as Greenwich Mean Time.

† As late as 1929 David was advertising a "Railway Lever" pocket watch.

further limiting his choices. He cast about for something that promoted his name with distinction. Then it came to him; Dawson was, it was fair to say, a common English name. Though many Scots families bore the name, particularly in Aberdeenshire, it was more associated with folks south of the border. He was proud of his Scots heritage, more so in this strangely cosmopolitan city with its growing Irish population, and if he was to become nationally famous he might as well play to that strength and further distinguish himself from his competitors. Many successful firms were partnerships, combining the names of their principals. He had no room for financial backers or partners; he would be beholden to no-one. But that shouldn't prevent him from putting on the cloak of a consortium of like-minded and, by inference, experienced gentlemen. He was only twenty-eight, but the world was not to know that. Add a "partner" and doors would open that otherwise might have remained closed. "So," he reasoned, "Dawson needs another name beside it that is distinctly Scottish without offending southern sensibilities and that lends special gravitas to the company." The one that came to mind was "Stewart", his grandmother's maiden name. Unmistakably Scottish, it avoided reviving historical English antipathy towards the papist Scottish royal family, which had adopted the French spelling, "Stuart" during the reign of Mary, Queen of Scots. He experimented with variations: "Dawson & Stewart", "Stewart and Dawson", until he lit upon the one that would work: "Stewart, Dawson & Company Limited". He had his business cards printed.

What he avoided for the time being was opening a retail shop. His experience in the wholesale drapery business taught him that he could be more profitable without the overheads of renting and fitting out premises, employing sales staff and wearing the costs of insurance, unsold inventory, and theft. After all, he thought, he would have to raise capital, possibly even borrow some: anathema! Why not sell directly to the public from his manufactory and cut out the middleman altogether by exploiting another recent innovation: mail order? David's own employer in Glasgow had made effective use of catalogues to advertise his range of fabrics, following the example of the Welsh entrepreneur Pryce Pryce-Jones,[13] who set up the world's first mail order business in 1861. Pryce-Jones distributed catalogues of his wares across the country, allowing people to choose the items they wished and order them via post, making payment by money order; he would then dispatch the goods to the customer via the railways. It was an ideal way of meeting the needs of customers in isolated rural locations who were either too busy or unable to shop directly.

David took the plunge. For the time being he didn't bother with a catalogue. His range of watches was still small, and it was cheaper to place sixpenny advertisements in many regional and local newspapers that listed the entire range in a few lines than to print and distribute multi-page catalogues. In this he followed the likes of the White brothers and Edward Kaltenbach, even copying their tag line: "Watches! Watches! Watches!" He placed his first advertisement, not in a local Liverpool newspaper, but in The Aberdeen People's Journal in March 1878. It was best to keep a low local profile for the time being, in order to gain a footing without alerting the established competitors. By the end of 1878 he was advertising almost daily in newspapers as far apart as Dundee, Dublin, Bradford, York, Somerset, Lincolnshire and even, for a short time, London. A further advantage for a start-up such as he was that he could exploit geographical gaps in the market. Surveying the coverage of the established manufacturers he observed that they each had their own regions, towns, and cities in whose newspapers they placed their advertisements and that there was little, if any overlap between one seller and another. They had segmented the market, but there were still plenty of gaps to fill, which he proceeded to do. He had virtually no competition in his chosen markets and if sales proved him wrong, as happened with his brief foray into London, he could always find another untouched town.

In order to compete against established names, David chose a new business model: wholesale prices to the public. As a long-term middleman himself he was aware of the mark-up between wholesale and retail, much of which had gone into his own pocket. What if he offered his wares at prices that he could claim undercut his competitors by cutting out the middleman? He did the sums, figuring that, if his order book turned over quickly and he could rely on his workers to fulfil the orders, he could make a more than healthy profit. He'd have little if any idle stock, however his reputation would depend upon how promptly he responded to orders. At the start, he had high expectations but little certainty of the volumes of orders. If business remained slow, he could lay off workers and he had few fixed overheads, but he had sunk all his capital into the business and still had a family to feed. On the other hand, should the world flock to his door with orders, he would have to be quick on his feet to expand the workforce and equip his manufactory. Thankfully, there was no shortage of skilled labour in and around Liverpool and he was willing to pay well to attract the best.*

Drafting the copy for his first advertisements, he added a further hook that had appealed to him as he scanned the classifieds: a coupon that had to be clipped and sent with the order, to guarantee the low price. Watches would be delivered at no cost to the customer, he offered to refund dissatisfied customers and guaranteed his watches for three years. Truth be told, Stewart, Dawson & Co's business model was little different from most of his competitors'. White, Kaltenbach and others all sold directly to the public, though they also wholesaled to retailers. David's prices were not significantly lower than theirs but that didn't prevent him from claiming that they were. Orders streamed in and by the end of 1878 his advertisements included glowing testimonials, some of which looked suspiciously similar from one newspaper to another, despite being attributed to different customers. He trumpeted the "unparalleled success" of his first year in business and celebrated it with more gimmicks. Now he offered a "free" gold watch to the first 50 customers ordering with a coupon. No testimonials existed to prove that anyone benefited from this generous offer but again, it had its effect and sales continued to climb. Kaltenbach and the Whites may have shaken their heads at some of his more outrageous claims, but the fact was that Stewart, Dawson & Co. had taken a share of their market, whether they liked it or not.

---

* Despite his propensity at social gatherings to heavy-handed parody of the stereotypical parsimonious Scotsman, David was a generous and caring employer, inspiring loyalty from his workers throughout his life.

Catching the Second Wave

The flying fish were gone now, the breeze picking up and whipping occasional white tops to the swells. Some less-hardy passengers had quit the upper deck for the comfort of the saloon but for the time being he preferred his own company; it had been a while since he had time alone to reflect, reminisce and regain lost equilibrium. Once again, he indulged in a moment of silent satisfaction. It was hard not to smile when casting his mind back to the moment when fate and his own vision had combined to launch him above and far beyond the parochial Whites and Kaltenbachs. Had the business continued to compete solely in the British market, he had no doubt he would have enjoyed further success and wealth. His cash flow was prodigious, overheads minimal and the market still buoyant, despite the lingering depression that the UK then suffered.[14]

A gregarious and astute businessman even at the age of 31, David was constantly on the alert for new opportunities and mixed with a large community of entrepreneurs and merchants. The "Stewart, Dawson" calling card was by now in many hands and his reputation around Liverpool was established. So much so that he started to notice, with amusement and not a little pride, that many of his newer acquaintances and business associates would refer to him as "Mr Stewart Dawson". When he reflected on this, it occurred to him that the apparently double-barrelled name did have a certain cachet that plain and simple "Dawson" lacked, and he ceased correcting his interlocutors. Before long, he omitted the comma from the company name and the "silent partner" was no more.

The great leap into a higher world of prosperity and esteem came in 1880. No small part of Liverpool's trade was with Australia. The port handled almost all imports of Australian wheat and wool and exported shiploads of British manufactured goods in return.[15] In pursuit of business and pleasure, David frequented public houses and hotels in the city centre. Here he mingled with importers and exporters, and he recalled how enthusiastically they would promote the tremendous business opportunities in the exploding colonial markets. Far away in Australia and New Zealand were green fields, ripe for exploitation. Across Australia's eastern seaboard, the discovery of gold had generated great wealth and population expansion, especially in Melbourne, a young city that would soon become the cosmopolitan centre of Australian cultural life. The seafarers and merchants David met spoke of "Marvellous Melbourne", as it had come to be known, marked by teeming boulevards like Elizabeth and Collins Street, where banks and trading companies built a financial capital, where jewellers and luxury stores supplied the growing needs of their middle and upper-class patrons. But Australia's small jewellery-making industry could not cope with demand. Along with many other luxuries, jewellery and watches were largely imported from Britain and Europe.

"What a market!" thought David, "but how will I conquer the distance? By the time I receive the order it will already be several weeks, if not months after it's been placed, then perhaps an even longer period before the goods are in the hands of the customer. Nobody will be prepared to wait that long." "No," he was assured, "We have the international telegraph link throughout Australia. Your orders will be in your office the day they are placed." Of course, he should have known; only eight years before, Australia had been linked via telegraph to Britain. He could be confident of fulfilling orders as speedily as if they were from Edinburgh or Hastings, faster, perhaps, since most local orders still arrived by post. Taking a chance, he placed one of his standard advertisements in "The Melbourne Leader" on January 3rd, 1880.[16]

Despite his hopes, he was not prepared for the deluge that followed. He received 51 orders almost immediately.[17] Local, established watch retailers in Australia couldn't compete on price or range. The boldness of his advertising copy stood in stark contrast with their bland efforts. They were caught off guard and the new player seized a share of the market. What a time that had been! The days and long nights planning, putting in place a whole new office to deal with exports, casting about for even more workers and suppliers. He foresaw the day when locally made watches might surrender their primacy to the exploding foreign competition, so, despite his antipathy toward anything not of Imperial origin, he extended his range with "Defiance" watches from US manufacturer, Star. Fulfilling Australian orders from far off Liverpool was still a concern, however. There was no "international telegraph" through which to dispatch them, and a typical voyage took anything from seven to ten weeks at best. If he was to capitalise on this unique opportunity he had to stock up in Australia. It wasn't his style and he risked holding many thousands of pounds of unsold stock if the gamble did not pay off, but he could see no alternative. He had put a toe in the water with the first advertisements; now he was about to wade in up to his waist, but he would avoid getting out of his depth too soon: for the time being, there would be no "Stewart Dawson" shop to complicate matters. So, the plan settled on after another late night, whisky-fuelled session with his manager was: send two agents to Australia with £10,000 worth of watches; have them rent temporary premises in Melbourne and Sydney and, using local mail and telegraph services, place new advertisements; stand back and wait for orders, fingers crossed. Off sailed the two men with their crates of watches stowed in the ship's hold. The weeks followed with only the odd telegraph message reporting arrival at or departure from a foreign port, each one closer to the island continent, until first Melbourne, then Sydney, reported safe arrival of the consignment, rental of premises and placement of the advertisements.

The entire stock sold out in weeks. The whoops of joy in his office as the news streamed in still rang in his ears. It was "cigars all round and another toast to Mr Stewart Dawson!" He took a further £50,000 of mail orders before the stock was exhausted and was soon shipping crate loads of watches to Melbourne and Sydney, where he contracted with local agents for receipt and forwarding.[18] This antipodean business could soon outstrip all sales in the homeland. He employed more clerks to process orders, increased his supplies from Star and recruited every watchmaker he could find in town. He spread the word. By 1881 his adverts were a familiar sight in newspapers in all Australian colonies.

David's wealth was now assured. It was time to invest some of it and become a man of property. Around Sefton Park land was being sold, streets laid out for the flourishing middle class. The "Groves", as they were called, radiated from the perimeter of the fashionable park.

Pelham Grove,[19] close to the north-west corner, meandered towards the city centre, a curve of genteel, two-storey red-brick terraces fronted by shady trees. The man of property was not content to purchase number 15, the best-situated dwelling, for his family, he bought another eleven houses in the street,[20] all of which immediately found tenants willing to rent. He named their house "Strathisla", after the river valley of his birthplace.

The location suited David: almost equidistant from his manufactory in Toxteth and the city centre, close to the park and well served by cabs and omnibuses. Margaret could walk the children and perhaps meet the right kind of people on her promenades. She needed something to occupy her, get her out of the house and spark some life into her. She had her servants, three of them by now,[21] and all the clothes she could want, but Lord! she was a misery to live with. Unlike him, she seemed never to have adjusted to the move south, pining for her mother and unwilling, or too withdrawn, to share his enthusiasm for society. It hadn't been helped by the children. She'd not got over the loss of their second child so young; four-year-old Adelaide was sickly, and she must have sensed his disappointment when their fourth, born in '78, had also turned out to be a girl.[22] When it appeared that it was unlikely Margaret would bear any more children, David had found it hard to conceal his frustration. No son to carry his name! How could she do this to him? He had taken for granted that one day, "Stewart Dawson & Son Ltd." would be proudly displayed on marquees and across newspapers; now he faced a future without legacy. Well, he'd have to improvise, he thought. He had composed so many advertisements, beguiled so many customers that he, the lad with less than five years' formal education, had become the wizard of eloquence, the bard of business. He would conjure a name for their new-born that would honour him, despite the misfortune of her sex. And so, Davanna Stewart Dawson was christened. The name combined "David" and Margaret's middle name, "Anna", and while unambiguously female, it would remind all who heard it of her paternal heritage, regardless of her future married status. But it was not to be; before he knew it, Margaret and the two older children, abetted by the servants, had thwarted his clever ambition by shortening the name to "Vanna" and the child herself, knowing no better, followed their example when she began to speak.

It was too much! The nerve of them to defy him! He was, after all, the head of the house. He provided everything for their needs, and more, but he was not receiving his due. Margaret, of all people, knew that he lived life at a frantic pace, on the road more often than at home, juggling manufacturing, suppliers, his own agencies both in Britain and now Australia and latterly New Zealand, not to mention the complexities of cash collection, accounting and investment, all of which came under his direct control. He even wrote his own advertising copy and liaised with newspapers. A man such as he who had achieved so much deserved a more respectful, spirited wife than drab Margaret. He needed an outlet for his boundless energy and libido and Margaret, for one, had not provided it for some time past. If that was how she wanted it, then so be it; there were plenty of attractive, available women in the saloons of the public houses, around the merchants' and even among his own employees to flatter and impress with his ready supply of trinkets and jewellery. The way they succumbed to his charm recalled his carefree days in the Glasgow Free and Easies, except that now he had more money than most of them had ever seen and the confidence of a winner. It was on one of his many forays into the smoke-filled, noisy taverns around Lime Street in September 1879 that he met Jennie Cohen. She was special, he thought, vivacious and amusing; he still thought so, five years later, and he missed her as he sailed ever further away. Their first meeting was one of the few in public. David's perambulations around Liverpool had uncovered many convenient hideaways: hotels aplenty, private rooms for rent or borrowed from understanding friends. It was to these that the couple escaped for afternoons in curtained privacy.

It had started to fall apart when, shortly before Christmas, 1880, Margaret confronted him. Despite her failing attraction, he continued to exercise his conjugal rights, as any husband would. It was more than a duty; he couldn't be with Jennie every day. Now, Margaret revealed, with reticence and shame, that she had contracted what her doctor told her was a "venereal disease". David had had his own suspicions for several weeks but was caught by surprise by his wife's implied accusation. It wasn't embarrassment that he felt, rather annoyance that the control he exercised over every aspect of their life had not been as thorough as he supposed. He knew the risks of promiscuity of course, those nights in the back rooms of Glasgow and the many occasions since in Liverpool had been a lesson in life. He'd been confident Jennie did not harbour anything he could catch but now, he wasn't so sure. On the other hand, it could have been one of the several other women he'd met casually, you just never knew. Now, he would have to break the uncomfortable news to Jennie, presenting him with a further dilemma: if she had infected him then he'd be obliged to leave her for the sake of his own dignity and reputation; but, if she had been untainted, innocent, then he would not only be accusing her falsely, worse than that, he himself might have passed the infection to her, would be the guilty party. He would deserve to lose her affection and trust. He decided to bluff his way out and hope that nature would take its course; the infection was only minor, and they did go away, didn't they? He refused to answer Margaret's questions, defied her to impugn him, dismissed her effrontery. She was to speak no more of it, remember her place.

Margaret retreated and, recovering his dignity, he resumed his affair with Jennie. As far as he could tell she had not been the cause of the infection and he was able to avoid the painful confrontation he had feared. He would be more careful from now on, though, take the necessary precautions and confine his affections to the one girl whom he could trust. Christmas came and went, the familiar routine of business, pleasure and domestic obligations resumed, but something was not right. Margaret's demeanour had changed. She withdrew even further, eyed him with suspicion, showed less respect than formerly. By February he'd had enough of her cold shouldering. He felt irritable and short-tempered around her and, as they prepared for bed one evening, he challenged her to buck up, show more respect and affection. Something broke in her. The look on her face remained imprinted on his memory even now. Then she spoke, pouring out her anger and bitterness, naming Jennie. How had she come to know this? Who had told her? How dare she pry into his private life and accuse him so blatantly? He was not a violent man; on the contrary, self-control was his watchword, but this was a step too far. Margaret, not content with having made her accusation, persisted in whining about his lack of affection for her, his supposed dereliction of his marital responsibilities, and on, and on. His frustration and anger overwhelmed him, and he pushed her backwards onto the bed. For God's sake, would she just shut up! Enraged beyond endurance, he threw himself onto her, pressing his knee into her chest and grasping her by the throat. "Shut up! Shut up or I'll choke you!"* He could still see the terror in her eyes as he pressed down upon her, still feel his own heart pounding, see the whiteness of his clenched fingers around her neck. Did he think she would submit? "Of course, I did", he assured himself, "she was the one who lost control, overstepped the bounds of marital fealty. Hadn't she vowed to honour and obey?" Cowed and fearing for her life, Margaret submitted, and he relinquished his hold. There would be no more accusations in his house if she knew what was best for her. David was now confident he had a licence to continue the affair. Henceforth, Margaret was to confine herself to raising their children and maintaining a household fit for a gentleman.

Domestic affairs settled for the time being, he was able to concentrate his attention on the pressing matter of relocating his manufactory to larger premises. The business had outgrown the Toxteth building in less than four years, and he had his eye on a newer, airier edifice where he could seat more workers and install the latest machines and tools. Ranelagh Place was much closer to the centre of the city, serviced by trams and trains and within a mile of the docks where his cargoes of watches would be shipped. The five-storey corner building had good natural light, space for scores more workbenches and excellent high ceilings from which to suspend the pulleys and belts that drove the precision lathes and stamping

---

* Divorce petition May 1882. Court for Divorce and Matrimonial Causes, later Supreme Court of Judicature: Divorce and Matrimonial Causes Files; Class: J 77; Piece: 278; Item: 8177. Margaret's account of the events leading to the petition includes a full description of the confrontations and assaults on her, as well as a detailed list of the places at which David conducted his adulterous relationship with Jennie Cohen. The narrative in this account is based on Margaret's testimony.

machines. Other floors could be used for offices and storerooms and there was space at street level for a reception vestibule. Proximity to the centre endowed the building with one other advantage: it could be connected to the telephone exchange. David would be able to speak instantly and directly with suppliers and dispatchers as far away as London and Leeds. The move accomplished, his advertisements now claimed S.D & Co. was "supplying constant employment in its manufactory for 700 hands."[23] The range now included chronograph watches, priced at £6.15.* These were the first stop watches, with an outer engraved dial often marked in fifths of a second and were the "must have" for sporting gentlemen.

Throughout 1881 and into the early months of the next year, when he wasn't occupied in the city, he spent more time with Jennie than at home, though he always provided generously for his family. This convenient arrangement might have continued indefinitely, he believed. But his complacency misled him and, almost a year to the day after the first misunderstanding Margaret once more confronted him. It was clear that her patience was exhausted, but what shocked and dismayed him most was that the damned woman must have employed a detective to snoop on him. She was able to list all the places he and Jennie met, as far back as '79: the houses in Lodge Lane, Admiral Street and Grove Street, Tyler's Hotel, even their weekend hideaways in Cheshire, at Sandbach and Frodsham, miles away from Pelham Grove. She never learned, did she? This very day she must have had him followed to Admiral Street, for those had been her immediate, accusing words as he closed the front door. "Damnation, woman! I'll kill you if you don't keep your nose out of my business!" he swore. But the cat was out of the bag and running around the room. As the weeks passed, the home became a battleground that he fled whenever possible until the final straw drove him once more to violence. It was at the end of February, when he returned tired but exhilarated from a day of business dealings, that she provoked another argument, this time raising the threat of divorce. Divorce! Was she mad? Didn't she realise the consequences, the shame she

---

* Approximately £400 or $700 at today's values.

would bring upon his name? She'd lost her mind, that was clear. Grasping her by the shoulders he tried to shake some sense into her. No longer passive, emboldened by desperation, she resisted, repeating her threat. Something snapped. He clutched at her hair, pulling her head back as he felt his anger and fury boil to the surface, but that failed to silence her. She broke free and turned her back on him. Frustrated to breaking point, he rained punches on her as she cowered against the wall, finally throwing her bodily into the hard surface, where she crumpled, whimpering, to the floor. Whenever he recalled that awful scene, he regretted his intemperance, the loss of control that made him no better than a drunken brawler. But the damage was done, though he was still surprised when, on May 24th, 1882, he was served with a petition for divorce on the grounds of persistent adultery and cruelty.

All the sordid details of his affair, the assaults, even the embarrassing episode of the sexual infection were laid out for the court. Margaret sought custody of the children and alimony for their support. He had moved out of the family home to rooms he kept at Ranelagh Place and delayed responding. He needed time to consider his position. Margaret's timing of the petition had been fortuitous and, should it succeed, could devastate his fortune. As his solicitor explained, under the Married Women's Property Act, which had this very year become law, if Margaret divorced him or was granted legal separation, alimony conditions would be legally enforceable and would be on her and the court's terms, not his. His assets, including the twelve houses in Pelham Grove, could be threatened and he could lose control over much of what he had built.[24] On the other hand, if he persuaded her to withdraw the petition, regardless of whether they continued to cohabit he could afford to keep her in the style to which she had become accustomed, scandal would be avoided, and she would be permanently dependent upon him without posing a threat to his capital. She might have "rights" to his property but would never be able to exercise them. It turned out to be easier said than done. Margaret stubbornly resisted his blandishments and in June she submitted her detailed petition for alimony, to which he was obliged to respond. Once more he delayed and there was a second round of petitioning and a new deadline for his response, which he again ignored.

David's waiting game could have continued indefinitely. He would never submit to Margaret's petition, and he knew that she knew it. He could outlast her and in any case he had far more important matters to deal with than this exasperating woman. He was in the middle of negotiations to expand the Australian and New Zealand business, which required his personal attention to the numerous telegraph messages arriving from Sydney, leaving no time to waste on tiresome court appearances. He took solace and respite from business matters, not at home but in the arms of ever-understanding Jennie. But then, fate took a hand. Little Adelaide had always been a feeble child, subject to fevers and every childhood ailment. Now, in October, the chills of late autumn overtook her. He and Margaret called a truce as the child weakened daily, but it soon became clear that nothing more could be done, and they watched, helpless, as the five-year-old was taken from them.[25] Their mutual grief at the death served to revive if only for a while, their affection for each other. Though they did not fully reconcile, David felt sufficiently constrained by grief and guilt to end his affair with Jennie, a fact he was able to communicate to Margaret. He submitted his affidavit in response in January 1883, as a formality. It seemed to break the deadlock; the petition petered out. He'd outlasted his wife through the legal process, as he knew he could. He'd encouraged her to believe that all should be forgiven now that Jennie was out of the picture, she dropped the case and he moved back into the family home. His relief was intense. This had been a close-run thing and an outrageous distraction. He swore he would never again permit himself such a lapse in concentration. He had to regain control of family life while he got on with the business of growing his wealth, prestige, and influence. There was another business development demanding his attention. Time enough for affairs on the side when he had dealt with that.

The Plunge into Retail

Though he'd established agencies in Sydney and Melbourne, David accepted that, sooner or later, and contrary to all his "direct from manufacturer to customer" rhetoric, a more permanent local presence in the colony would be necessary. He was at risk of becoming too removed from control of the transport and final sale of his goods and, worse, losing some of his profit to his own middlemen. It was early in 1882, at the height of his distraction over the divorce proceedings that he opened his own retail shop, his first ever, at 79 Goulburn Street, Sydney.[26] Not for one moment did he contemplate a similar step in Britain; Australia and soon New Zealand were where his future lay; it was so much easier to compete there. Scarcely had the shop opened its doors, however, when news from his Sydney manager alerted him to a more attractive alternative a mere block away, so before the year's end he relocated the business to new, larger and more prestigious premises at 27 Royal Arcade, off Pitt Street,[27] thus starting a life-long connection with the fashionable precinct. "I suppose that was when my education in salesmanship reached a new level," he reflected. Until then, he'd relied on the power of the written word to entice customers, and very successful it had been. Those days, many outrageous claims could be made without fear of challenge. With not a qualm, David peppered his advertisements with superlatives, repeated words, and phrases to drive the message and keep the attention of skimming readers. His was:

> *the largest and most varied stock of English watches in the colonies, Stewart Dawson's [were] one of the largest manufacturing firms in the world, the English Silver Hunting Lever watch (£3.10) [was] acknowledged by every buyer to be the best lever watch ever worn.*

and so on. David's "unique business model" had brought success to himself and to his customers but now he'd noticed upstart competitors attempting to steal his thunder. Even as he voyaged south, he'd had to place strongly worded advertisements to defend his hard-won place in commerce:

> *A wonderful discovery, a system of business adopted by S.D. & Co in the sale of their world wide celebrated English Lever Watches has at last had the effect of awaking the watchmakers of [insert the town, county or Australian colony] to the startling fact that they no longer have the power to levy blackmail wholesale upon the public, that the days of exorbitant profits are past and that a Firm exists … who are determined to throw open the portals of their manufactory to the public direct and at once and forever banish the enormous profits grasped by the Merchant, Importer and the Retail Shopkeeper.*

He continued, now fully on the attack:

> *In this extremity there are not wanting unprincipled persons who do not scruple to the cowardly resort of barefaced imitation in the hope of intercepting some at least of the orders for the well known house of S.D. & Co, the pioneers of that great revolution in the watch trade.* [28]

That would show them! But now that he had bricks and mortar retail premises in which to display and market his watches and the new range of jewellery, he knew that it would take more than a sixpenny advertisement to draw customers in from the sidewalk. A stroller down Lord Street or around Ranelagh Place in Liverpool, along Regent or Oxford Streets in London, would soon be diverted to the latest, most appealing shop fronts that were supplanting traditional establishments. Customers were being enticed into these new establishments through attractive displays, plate-glass windows, and bright lighting and, instead of having to request assistance across a counter and wait for goods to be selected from a hidden drawer, they were encouraged to browse. David embraced this modern approach with his Sydney outlet, lavishly furnishing it and filling the windows with artful displays. With the move to the Royal Arcade he went a step further, selecting a corner site that doubled his exposure to passing traffic. This was to become the model for many of his subsequent establishments. He'd also extended his range of watches and added jewellery items such as necklaces, bracelets and rings and began to characterise the business as "Jewellers and Watchmakers". He had been obliged to publish a catalogue as early as 1879 when his range of watches grew too large for listing in the advertisements and now the latest editions, 100 pages of them, were bursting with illustrations of every kind of watch and jewellery piece.[29]

One last touch to the launch of the new Royal Arcade shop was to bestow upon it a fitting title for the exciting establishment. Stewart Dawson's was no run-of-the-mill watch seller or hawker of a paltry selection of trinkets. His shelves, showcases and windows would overflow with shimmering, sparkling delights, an Aladdin's cave beyond compare. Just as he had skittled the local traders with his first Australian advertisements, now he was about to deal the knockout blow with incontrovertible evidence of his superiority. While his so-called competitors dared not claim to be more than shopkeepers, gilded letters above his doorway welcomed customers to "The Treasure House", to marvel, to be entranced and never to depart empty-handed.

Not so successful was his brief venture across the Atlantic. Shortly after the Goulburn Street outlet commenced business in Sydney, he opened a shop in Toronto, Canada,[30] only to close it after less than a year. Though he would never admit it in public, David grudgingly accepted that he had misunderstood the market. Proximity to the powerhouse US economy meant there was an abundant supply of cheap watches from across the border with which Stewart Dawson's could not compete. This setback coloured his opinion of American business: henceforth he seldom missed an opportunity to denigrate American commercial practices, consistently and publicly rating them inferior to those of Britain and the colonies.

Business in the United Kingdom continued to thrive. David stepped up his advertising and catalogue sales. Newspapers throughout the nation carried adverts proclaiming the "unprecedented success" of his business, which was expanding ever faster thanks in part to the introduction of the over-the-counter postal order a mere three years before.* It was becoming hard to keep up with modern

* Postal orders were the brainchild of the President of the Birmingham Chamber of Commerce, John Skirrow Wright. The rich had bank accounts and could write cheques. The mass market David was targeting was unlikely to have bank accounts but could now buy goods and services more easily by post.

progress. First, the marvel of railways spreading to every corner of the land and bringing prosperity to the cities, then the cheap postal service, followed by the magic of the telegraph and telephone, facilitating communications in the blink of an eye, and to top it all, just when he could take greatest advantage of it, a secure and simple way to receive payment. He abhorred giving any form of credit, therein lay the road to ruin for customer and merchant alike, but thanks to postal orders, payment now need be nothing more than a short step to the post office, a stamp on the envelope and money in the bank with no fuss. If he believed in luck he would have to admit, in private, to having been born at the right time. Publicly, he ascribed his success to sheer hard work and his vision to go one better. Perhaps there was a little of both.

David was by this time floating on a river of cash, his every ambition being realised. It was time to celebrate and where better than in Australia? He just had to witness at first hand the splendour of his Sydney establishment and meet his loyal, hard-working staff. Then there was Melbourne and New Zealand to deal with. His agents had been busy surveying vacancies in Melbourne's centre from not long after he'd opened the first Sydney shop. If it hadn't been for the easy availability of the lease in Goulburn Street, he would have chosen the younger southern city to make his mark.[31] But Sydney was more established, and so far, things seemed to be going well, particularly since the move to Royal Arcade. From that shop alone orders from both Melbourne and the whole of New Zealand were being supplied, so successfully that he now found ample justification for extending the Sydney experiment to Victoria. As for New Zealand, he hadn't quite worked out whether to go north or south. On the one hand, the north island was more populated; Auckland and Wellington alone were already significant cities. On the other, he was receiving a lot of orders from Otago, in the south. Centred on Dunedin, the country's single largest urban area, thanks to its own version of the gold rush, the province was home to thousands of Scots immigrants. The very name: "Dunedin", "The Edinburgh of the South" appealed to his Scottish nationalism and he was tempted to follow his instincts and go where the new money was. The problem was, just as he had been obliged to postpone the Melbourne opening due to an immediate lack of suitable premises, it seemed he would face a similar barrier in Dunedin, so he revised his itinerary and booked onward passage from Sydney to Auckland instead.

So, here he was, somewhere in the Indian Ocean, on the good ship Chimborazo. He'd be in Sydney by the middle of March, after brief visits to Adelaide and Melbourne.[32] He looked at his watch: "Good gracious! Time for lunch." His reverie interrupted, he joined other passengers on their way to the dining saloon. He would use his post-prandial resting time to refine his plans for the arrival of The Great Man. For, like a generous missionary, he came bearing gifts. In thanks to the Australian public for having bought £25,000 worth of watches* from the Sydney store alone he would give a present to the first 1,000 patrons who purchased a watch there. Every gentleman who bought a watch worth £3† or more would receive:

> *a splendid full suite of fine gold fronted studs and patent solitaires, each suite in velvet case, full value half a guinea.‡ For the ladies, an elegant set of earrings and brooch, horse shoe or fern leaf pattern at choice, each set also in velvet case.*[33]

He would have time to telegraph the details from Adelaide to his Sydney manager, leaving a good week in hand for advertisements to be placed in the Sydney papers. The crates of new watches and jewellery in the hold contained a good supply of the gift items and he'd learned that local jewellery makers in Sydney were eager to gain extra business from this sophisticated entrepreneur from the mother country. They could take on some of the brooches, perhaps.

---

* £25,000 in 1884 is roughly £1,500,000 or $2,500,000 today. This was less than two years' sales from a single outlet. David claimed that it exceeded the combined sales of all other Australian watch sellers. He was probably right.

† About $300 today.

‡ $30 today.

A New Albion

The first sight of land was at once exciting and disappointing. The call had come down from the crow's nest high on the foremast and was repeated among the expectant passengers. Those few for whom this was a return home exhibited a mixture of pride and insouciance, they had seen it all before, but it was their land of plenty. For David and the other first-timers, the low, featureless smudge on the horizon gave little hint of the promises that lay beyond. As the days passed and the Chimborazo cruised closer to the coast, their interest in the monotonous, endless line of dunes, rocky outcrops and treeless low hills evaporated. No sign of human habitation, not even a fishing boat or coaster to be seen, until the port of Fremantle was spotted far on the port bow, only to dip below the horizon as the ship slowly turned eastward towards Adelaide. Once into the Bight, the winds favoured the vessel and for the first time on the voyage sails were raised, supplementing the power of the engine. David wasn't the only one to ponder this anachronism, even in the Chimborazo's short lifetime ships had crossed oceans with not a square yard of canvas aloft. All the same, the romance and reassurance of the snapping, billowing sails couldn't be denied, as the passengers made way for the crew scaling the ratlines, hauling the rough sheets, and spread like acrobats along the swaying yards.

Not two days later, Adelaide hove into sight. They had made up much of the time lost fighting the gale in the Channel and the Bay of Biscay. Sails were lowered, a tugboat manoeuvred alongside, cabin trunks and suitcases appeared from below. At half past four in the afternoon of March 9th they made fast against the quay. David wished "farewell" to the Brandts and the trio of young ladies, Misses Wright, Hayes, and Fitch. As the last porter carried away their bags, he stepped down the gangplank to set foot on the Great Southern Land. The city of Adelaide was to be no more than a stop-over, the ship departing the very next day, but its significance was not lost on David. If not in this outpost of European civilisation, then in the powerhouses of Melbourne and Sydney, his vision of success would be realised. His feet planted on this vast continent, he was ready to stride where few had had the courage and imagination to go. There was also the practical objective of getting up to date with events and plans in Sydney and Melbourne. He headed for the port authority office. Here, he found a waiting telegraph assuring him that his Sydney shop prospered and supervised the transmission of his own message containing the all-important advertisement promoting his visit.

It was a similar story in Melbourne when they docked at Williamstown. Here, David watched the unloading of one of his cases of watches and jewellery and met with his local representative. The ship would spend another night in port, leaving time for him to explore the city's commercial centre, before departing on the last leg of the journey. Shaking the hand of the man who was so diligently carrying out his mission gave him special pleasure, and the two enjoyed a welcoming drink at a city hostelry before getting down to business. The wide, straight streets were at once familiar and strange. The facades of the buildings could have been in Oxford Street or maybe a European capital such as Paris or Vienna, but they were too regular and far too clean to belong in one of those northern cities. He had to remind himself that most of what he saw was less than twenty years old, rigorously planned and too new to have accumulated a grimy patina. Shown the vista down Collins Street, he congratulated his agent on the excellent choice of location for the proposed store. Just a few yards from the corner of Elizabeth Street, Number 3 presented a bold front of classical arches, beneath which were large plate-glass windows of the latest design. The owners of the building were willing to discuss leasing conditions and had already shown their inclination towards a prestigious business such as his. With little time to do more than inspect the premises, David left for Williamstown, promising to return for the opening of the store and confident that his agent could follow his instructions for completion of the contract, fit-out and stocking.

After the trials and stresses of the oceans, the last leg of the voyage to Sydney felt more like a cruise. David's spirits were high, the weather fair and the coastline, now close by on the port side, no longer threatened or repelled as had the distant shore first encountered. Dense woodland covered the hinterland, in which low ranges of mountains or solitary hills broke the skyline. High sandstone cliffs marched forward as the ship neared Sydney until, late on Saturday, the lighthouse high on the headland drew them close inshore. The run into the harbour, crossing the heavy swells between the Heads, would forever remain in his memory. The afternoon sun lay directly ahead, turning the surface of the water into a blinding shimmer almost too brilliant to bear. Seagulls swooped and screeched above and low alongside, fighting for scraps flung out by the excited voyagers on deck. The many coves on either side revealed stone and timber dwellings, dozens of small boats darted about or swung at moorings and several miles away the tall masts of sea-going vessels bristled on the skyline. This was no Liverpool, to be sure; he'd become used to the forests of spars and rigging along Merseyside and the frantic congestion of the docksides. It would take more than a few score ships at anchor to impress him. Perhaps it was the air that was different, the scent of something exotic on the breeze, the warmth even at this late hour of the day, the persistent brightness of the light. There was a promise of greatness, a feeling of vast, untapped potential ahead. Hidden behind the last headland lay the source of so much of his wealth.

If he thought to disembark like some latter-day Queen of Sheba upon arrival, he was to be disappointed. As the ship slowed on approach to Circular Quay the congestion of the inner harbour became apparent. Vessels lay two-, three-deep alongside the wharfs, lighters jostled and bumped around them, and the quayside was crammed with carts, piles of cargo and hundreds of labourers. Behind the quay, along the two arms, tall warehouses disgorged bales of wool, stacks of timber and anonymous crates and bundles. Beyond that again rose a dense conglomeration of buildings, some in the modern classical style seen in Melbourne, others clearly from a different, more primitive era. There was little of Melbourne's pristine order here, but in the disorder there was a dynamic energy that he yearned to capture. Finally, the announcement came: they would anchor across the harbour in Neutral Bay until a suitable berth was available. So near and yet, so far!

Saturday night and all day, Sunday the passengers fretted as the ship swung around the buoy. They were not alone; crewmen looking forward to a few days' rest ashore were occupied stoking the ship's auxiliary boiler to keep the new-fangled refrigeration plant in the hold operating. Many tons of frozen mutton had been taken on board in Melbourne for export to London on the return voyage and it would only take a couple of days in these warm conditions for it to spoil.* It was early Monday morning before they cast off from the buoy for the tugboat to tow them the couple of furlongs to their berth and, with relief and thanks to their popular captain and crew, disembark on the hard cobbles of the quay. David was impatient to get down to work. Once more he oversaw the unloading of his crate of watches and trinkets but now, he could accompany them through the packed streets to the Royal Arcade, just a few blocks from the quay. His manager, James Lyons Duncan,[34] and staff waited to greet him in the store, where introductions were made, and he graciously accepted their hospitality. As the carter unloaded the watch-crate he had time to admire the sumptuous furnishings and well-stocked shelves. It was even better than he'd been led to believe. Dozens of carefully wound and perfectly synchronised watches ticked softly, clusters of diamonds flashed and shimmered in rings and bracelets lying on velvet cushions. Everywhere was light and opulence. Early customers were introduced by the deferential staff, and he witnessed the first sales and the giving of gifts. The word must have spread, for now a queue had formed outside.

Pleasantries over, he retired with Mr Lyons Duncan to his hotel, for the serious business of reviewing sales, assessing the prospects for further growth and expansion of the range of stock, and preparing orders for the next batch from England. David's preoccupation with the coverage Stewart Dawson's had received in local and national

---

* The SS Chimborazo was one of the first ships to be fitted with a crude refrigeration plant for storage of frozen meat. The trade started experimentally in 1879 from Argentina, Australia and New Zealand to the United Kingdom and by 1883 the concept was generally proven, as meat arrived in good condition for London markets after several months at sea. The Chimborazo had delivered 4,000 carcasses of frozen mutton on her previous voyage, leaving Sydney on November 17th, 1883. Geelong Advertiser 3rd January 1884 P.3.

press might have surprised his manager at first but he soon understood the central role that advertising played in David's world and learned not to question his proprietor's judgement. New and repeat advertisements had to be placed in every newspaper and journal in the colony, heralding the arrival of The Great Man and hammering home the message of quality and unbeatable value. Nothing was to be left to chance, every superlative brought to bear. Most importantly, scoundrels who shamelessly dared to imitate Stewart Dawson's had to be fought off, smashed, and defeated. David drafted some of his most aggressively worded advertisements to sound the trumpets of battle:

Beware of interested trade jealousy! Beware of Piracy! Bribery! And Base Calumny! Uphold Truth! Honour! And Integrity!!! Stewart, Dawson & Co.'s World Wide Business which has stood and will stand as solid as the granite rock when the exorbitant profit dealer's malignant vindictiveness and jealousy is crumbled to the dust!

The challenge was then thrown down:

£1,000 REWARD! £1,000 will be paid by Stewart, Dawson and Co., Watch Manufacturers, Ranelagh Place, Liverpool, Eng., to any firm either of watch manufacturers or watch dealers in the Colonies or in the Wide-World, who can produce the same amount of genuine testimony and unsolicited testimonials from their customers in proof of the qualities of their watches, as can Stewart, Dawson and Co.

He was in full flight by now. Mr Lyons Duncan shook his head in wonder at the audacity and outright intemperance of the concluding words, the like of which he could be certain had never been published in Australia:

Let those who have a reputation at stake take up S. & D. Co.'s challenge or forever keep silent. The gigantic operations of Stewart, Dawson & Co. have spread from pole to pole … and have scattered to the winds the profits of the Merchant, Importer and Retail Dealer. This great work has not been effected without feeling the Truth of that historical line – the anger of the Protectionist, the jealousy of the weak, the calumny of the vicious, the vindictiveness of the exposed, have flown like a turgid stream across their onward path, still they pressed victoriously to the front, and now they have their reward from a grateful public, who daily show that, in Stewart Dawson and Co. they have found the real champions of their rights![35]

The instruction given to the manager was to postpone the release of the advertisement until after David had left and the impact of his promotional visit had provoked competitors to attempt to match his winning formula for success. The new advertisement would be his crushing riposte to their impudence. Mr Lyons Duncan was quickly reassured that he need not make provision for paying rash challengers a thousand pounds. The Great Man's stock of Stewart Dawson testimonials was inexhaustible and would overwhelm any competitor foolish enough to consider claiming the reward.

In the weeks that followed, David made daily appearances in Royal Arcade, dispensing largesse to eager customers, but his most profitable efforts were in the back office of the shop, dealing with telegraphs from Melbourne, Dunedin, and Auckland. All seemed to be in order for opening the Collins Street shop by June and he was confident that premises would be leased in Auckland, thus settling the question of where first to launch the business in New Zealand. When not thus occupied, he was at leisure to explore Sydney and make the acquaintance of men of influence in commerce. A walk around the block in which the Royal Arcade stood revealed a mix of businesses, including other jewellers. The established firm of Sinnets[36] was just a few doors from Stewart Dawson's but not a real competitor; rather, it complemented David's store with its range of more expensive, custom jewellery. He made a mental note to follow up some of his contacts in the local jewellery manufacturing trade and fill gaps in his trinket and novelty range before his departure. Along Pitt Street the impressive front of Hoffnung and Company stood tall. David could have chosen them or rivals, T & W Willis, in York Street, as wholesale import agents for his own products. Both had earned a reputation for efficient handling of everything from drapery to kitchenware and could have smoothed the way for delivering his first stocks of watches. However, he'd preferred from the outset to go his own way and the proof of his judgement was there for all to see.

He couldn't help comparing the narrow Sydney streets with Melbourne's boulevards. The alignment north and south of George

Street, Pitt, Castlereagh and so on meant there were few hours in the day when traffic along them was exposed to the full glare of the sun. He took a steam tram* along George Street towards Circular Quay. Away from the central grid the streets were even narrower, recalling the lanes and alleys he'd frequented in Aberdeen, until they squeezed into the peninsular on the western edge they called "The Rocks". Some had warned him to avoid this dense warren of decaying cottages and terraces where, only a furlong or so from the harbour, poverty and unsanitary conditions were said to be the bed mates of crime. He shrugged off their concerns; Sydney had a long way to go before it compared with his old Glasgow haunts. Reaching the shoreline, he could see down the harbour in both directions and his eye was drawn to the prominent villas and mansions gracing the headlands to the east. So, that was where Sydney's society lived. It certainly put Pelham Grove in the shade. He'd observed from his obligatory habit of scanning the newspapers that many of the more influential families who belonged to the merchant class to which he aspired occupied addresses in these eastern districts. He'd also noted the generosity of spirit they exhibited, with their frequent charitable events and donations to worthy causes. Liverpool and, he knew, London society were fundamentally no less caring but here perhaps it was the enormous concentration of new wealth and optimism for the future that opened hearts and wallets. Every evening it seemed, there was a charity ball at one of the several town halls. Society ladies oversaw the committees raising funds for hospitals, children's welfare, education, and poor relief. Vice-regal patronage guaranteed prestige and a high turnout to fancy dress balls, dances, and concerts, where captains of industry and merchants mingled with politicians and artists. He'd find it easier here than back home to make useful connections in furtherance of his business, though he couldn't imagine Margaret supporting him with her presence. On the contrary, she would embarrass him in the company of the confident, cultured

* Steam trams were introduced in Sydney in 1879, supplementing but not yet replacing horse-drawn trams.

wives of the likes of Dymock, Penfold, the Horderns or the Fairfaxes.* He sighed: one way or another he would have to confront reality upon his return to Liverpool.

The days passed all too quickly before he found himself embarking for the short voyage to Auckland. As the ship left Sydney astern his emotions were mixed; the whole of New Zealand was, in effect, his for the taking and should have his full attention over the coming weeks, but his heart was already captive to Sydney, and he counted the days until he would return to the harbour city once more. It was almost with a sense of déjà vu therefore, that he first set eyes on Auckland harbour, for its general aspect was eerily similar to Sydney's: the headlands and inlets close on either side, the narrows immediately before and beyond the quay, a dense green backdrop to the cluster of buildings before him. Once more, he stepped ashore in a new land, as far away as one could journey from the seat of Empire and yet familiar and reassuring in its very Englishness.

He needn't spend too long in the city; as he had done in Sydney, he had been advertising his impending arrival in the country since the beginning of April, foreshadowing the opening of the first local branch,[37] and he had promised rewards and gifts to his New Zealand customers to celebrate his arrival and the opening of the Auckland shop. Within the first week after he arrived, he was relieved to be able to sign the lease on No. 195 Queen Street, under the Theatre Royal. The grand opening sale was announced with great fanfare:

> *Special and Important Announcement – Stewart Dawson & Co. of Liverpool, the Champion Watchmakers of England, have arrived in Auckland from Liverpool, England with a magnificent stock of the World-renowned English Lever Watches!*

---

* William Dymock opened his first bookstore in 1879 in Sydney's Market Street. WC Penfold, stationers, was founded in 1830 by the English bookbinder, William Moffit, who had been sentenced to seven years' transportation for stealing tea. The Penfold brothers took over the business in 1880 and quickly grew it into the largest stationers in the colony. The Hordern family were the founders and proprietors of Australia's and, at one time, the world's largest department store. John Fairfax was the owner of The Sydney Morning Herald.

1,000 "magnificent presents" were to be given away as Stewart Dawson & Co.

have much pleasure in announcing that they have opened a permanent Branch Establishment for New Zealand at 195 Queen Street ...[38]

He announced his own presence, as he had done for the grand event at the Royal Arcade shop:

Mr. D. S. Dawson, of the Firm, is now in Auckland, and in order to commemorate his visit, by his Firm's desire, will present to every purchaser of a Watch in price from £3 and upwards a Splendid Present gratis, worth half a guinea, suitable for Ladies' or Gentlemen's wear.

Out came the box of trinkets and in flowed the customers. The bonus for David was that he now had a base in New Zealand from which to distribute mail-ordered watches, relieving some of the burden on the Sydney establishment. All that was needed now was patience and application to the task of finding the elusive Dunedin premises, after which he had somewhere like Christchurch in his sights. In the meantime, Queen Street could suffice while he got back to settling the Melbourne acquisition.

April over, he returned to Sydney, where he found that negotiations for the Collins Street lease had been concluded, allowing him to take possession of the premises in preparation for a June opening. He could relax, enjoying more local hospitality and renewing recent acquaintances in the business community. By the end of May, the Melbourne shop was fitted out, staff had been hired and stock delivered. Now he raised expectations through a barrage of advertisements, proclaiming:

Victory! Victory! Triumphant victory declared throughout the world![39]

As it happened, he missed the opening of the store in the first week of the month,[40] but, by all accounts it went as well as he had expected. On June 17th he boarded the express train at Sydney Central and headed south through New South Wales. He reached Melbourne that evening, and it was only a brief cab ride from Flinders Street station to his hotel for a good night's rest before he made his entrance in Collins Street. Up early, he made his way to the new store, where once again he was struck by the sheer opulence of his window displays and the tall glass cases inside. Until this visit, he could only imagine the final product of his efforts, contenting himself with envious glimpses of competitors' establishments; but Sydney, Auckland and now, Melbourne, were concrete proof of the realisation of his vision. He need not be falsely modest; he had gone one better both in preparing the way and in delivering to the public more than he or anyone could have hoped for. He telegraphed instructions to his head office in Liverpool to place his "Victory! Victory!" advertisements as widely as possible and to increase production, pending fresh orders from the colonies.

His business in the antipodes was now done, for the time being. Dunedin was only a matter of time; Sydney and Melbourne were flourishing, and he was confident in the abilities of the local managers and staff. From what he had learned, Sydney, rather than the southern capital, would be his preferred base for overseeing the two colonies, but he could now afford to export to all three cities and, he hoped, to Dunedin. If, in addition he could tap into local jewellery manufacturers he could broaden the appeal of his wares without incurring long distance transport expenses. All in all, a satisfactory conclusion. He sailed for England, triumphant.

Reality Bites

The voyage home gave David time to think, and he welcomed the weeks of enforced inactivity. The weather was kind, the sunsets over the ocean still as blood red as those that had amazed the outward-bound passengers. They said it had something to do with the volcano that had exploded the previous year in the Indies, Krakatoa, was it? Something like that.* But, as the home country drew daily closer, David's initial high spirits waned. The success of his endeavours in the colonies was undeniable and the possibilities for the future were endless but he was about to surrender his personal freedom once more. The months away from Margaret had increased his restlessness. Returning to Pelham Grove would be at best a duty; he, they, had to face reality sooner or later.

The air was chill, the early twilight closing in, and gusts of rain spattered his umbrella as he alighted from the London train. The cab splashed through the Liverpool streets. His mood was grim but, best get it over with, see how the children had grown, unpack his bags. Margaret's greeting was polite but cautious; it was as if there were a stone wall between them. For the sake of the children they maintained a decorous façade but, as soon as decency allowed, he left. He offered no explanation, nor did Margaret expect one. He could make better use of his time at his chambers in Ranelagh Place and, when he was not occupied with business, other arms would be there to embrace him. Not long before he left for Australia, he had met Fanny Lyon, a nineteen-year-old who, like so many others, had been seduced by his easy charm and magnanimity. One of his several pieds à terre was a nondescript terrace at 59 Crown Street, not far from the railway

* The eruption of Krakatoa, or Krakatau, in August 1883 was one of the deadliest volcanic eruptions of modern history. It is estimated that more than 36,000 people died. The initial blast of the eruption sent a cloud of gas and debris an estimated 15 miles into the air, darkening skies up to 275 miles from the volcano. The atmospheric effects made for spectacular sunsets all over Europe and the United States.

station. It was here that he'd entertained her in the months preceding his departure and now he renewed the relationship. It was an easy, short cab ride from Ranelagh Place to Crown Street and a convenient walk from the station, whence he arrived from his visits to Manchester and other business centres. To provide Fanny with some variety and indulge their mutual need to escape Liverpool now and then, it was a matter of purchasing a couple of train tickets and in no time at all they could register as a married couple at a hotel where no questions would be asked. With Fanny, he favoured Lancaster, to the north, now that Margaret had discovered his bolt holes in Cheshire, south of the city.

David's periods of absence from the family home lengthened. He no longer bothered to offer excuses. It wasn't as if his behaviour was unusual; many in his circle maintained similar "arrangements". Provided they followed the code of public respectability, gentlemen's private affairs were off limits and sanctioned and men of good standing ensured that their wives lacked nothing in home comforts. The problem was that Margaret didn't seem to understand the rules and now, in April 1885, she confronted him with evidence of his affair with Fanny. She knew about Crown Street and even the hotel in Lancaster. She must have once more employed a detective to spy on him. It looked as if she had been squirreling away the housekeeping money (his own money!) to pay the fellow, and clearly, he had done his job. How dare she! They were supposed to have an understanding. Wasn't that what they'd agreed back in '82? There was no reasoning with this woman, and here she was whining and complaining again. This time, he passed his threshold of tolerance with ease, cuffing her about the head to drum some sense into her. Margaret's resilience had also grown and though she quietened, it was clear to both that they had reached a point of no return. The battle lines were drawn. Any time they spent together from now on would be at arms' length, another argument only a breath away.

The annoying consequence of the April confrontation was the end of David's affair with Fanny. The frisson of risk evaporated with the revelation of the work of the detective, and they went their separate ways. It was almost as an act of defiance therefore that David sought new amorous encounters. Among the many taverns and public houses in the city centre one of the closest to Ranelagh Place was at the lower end of Old Haymarket, just a few hundred yards away. He'd often dropped in and was by now almost a regular customer. He knew the landlord, Colin McNab. As fellow Scots, they were drawn into friendly conversation across the mahogany bar. Colin's three older daughters, Sidney, Harriet, and Rebecca, helped behind the bar and cleared tables.[41] Twenty-one-year-old Harriet caught David's eye. A flattering comment, a flirtatious response later and he had secured an assignation with the dark-haired ingénue. Harriet was instantly attracted to the older man, with his piercing blue eyes and luxuriant Bismarck moustache, but she was no fool. She persuaded a friend, Mary Walker, to accompany her to Crown Street. David was becoming careless, perhaps he was beyond caring about his marriage, for it was here, on April 24th, that Margaret's detective again tracked him and observed the two women entering the house and emerging several hours later.

Margaret had her evidence, or so she believed. After another shouting match during which he again threatened to kill her, and in which she reminded him of the divorce petition so recently fought, she took the final step. On May 5th she served him with a petition for judicial separation.* Separation, eh? She must have had a more realistic expectation than formerly of the outcome of the case. She had learned that he wouldn't be pushed into an absolute divorce. It seemed she was prepared to negotiate. Well, he might be able to accommodate her. This second time around, they had both learned a lesson and much of the heat had gone out of their argument by the time the court considered the petition. He was somewhat dismayed when he read the petition to see her rake over the old affair with Jennie and the embarrassing infection and she'd overdone the descriptions of the so-called assaults. She claimed that he had committed adultery with both Harriet and Mary at Crown Street on the same day. What

* Divorce Petition, 5th May 1885 Court for Divorce and Matrimonial Causes, later Supreme Court of Judicature: Divorce and Matrimonial Causes Files; Class: J 77; Piece: 337; Item: 147. The account in this narrative of David's affairs with Fanny Lyon and Harriet McNab, and of the assaults on Margaret, is taken directly from Margaret's deposition in this petition.

did she expect the court to think: that he was some sort of perverted Lothario? Yes, the two women had entered and left together, but she'd no right to infer from that what went on behind the closed door. But what was the point of disputing her assertion? He'd have to provide a convincing argument and that would mean admitting more than he wanted and testing his word against hers. He was no longer interested in saving the marriage, it had gone far past that point, so he would have been wasting his time for no reward. He decided instead to confine his response to practical matters of alimony.

The more he looked at the matter, however, the less inclined he was to formalise the financial arrangements. If there was one thing he could not abide it was someone else taking control, however slight, of his finances. He had no problem giving away money, any of his friends or associates would attest to his largesse, but it had to be on his terms, always. It was intolerable to think that some court could sequestrate even a part of his income, possibly for the rest of his life. He played for time, submitting formal responses to avoid official sanction but conceding nothing to Margaret. Privately, he approached his wife with a new version of the undertaking he had made in '82. He would guarantee her and the girls' financial future and would restrain his impulse to conduct open affairs with other women. They would maintain the proprieties of married life for the time being but concede that a conjugal relationship was no longer possible. It was a de facto separation that allowed him to retain full control of his fortune while granting him (her, too, he supposed) the freedom to pursue a separate life. The façade would be preserved, Margaret need feel no pressure to fulfil more than domestic duties and he could get on with building the business and his fortune. Margaret was exhausted and persuaded. She withdrew the petition on October 31st, just as she had done in 1882.

In the end, he reasoned, he had devised the ideal solution to their problems. Margaret and the girls were settled in Pelham Grove, seldom venturing far from the quiet street, certainly not into his favourite haunts or anywhere near his place of business. He resumed his relationship with Harriet McNab, and such was his infatuation with the younger woman that he abandoned promiscuity for a more monogamous existence. Harriet was the opposite of Margaret, worldly-wise, outgoing, and passionate. Her education behind the bar at the pub had taught her to put aside girlish reticence when in company and, though always polite, she sparkled where others held back. She was also ambitious, understanding his need for social esteem and aware of the important role of a woman in building social connections, something Margaret had never been able or willing to take on. Despite David's promise to Margaret, he set up house for Harriet in one of his other properties and divided his time between the two dwellings.

He was learning to juggle time and responsibilities, but before long he faced a new challenge: Harriet was with child. Damn! Now he had to manage two families and sooner or later decide which to favour. He loved his two girls; Lila was now thirteen and showing a degree of independence and maturity, seven-year-old Vanna was her mother's darling but a sweet child all the same. But what if Harriet bore him a son? Legitimate or not, the boy would carry his name forward and, if Harriet were any model for it, the lad could be a worthy torch bearer for the Stewart Dawson name and fortune. This could turn into a conundrum if he didn't organise matters soon. Then it came to him: he had kept his family life private, few even knew he was married; it had suited him to play the bachelor. He could present anyone as his wife, and nobody would question him. Harriet would be the public Mrs Stewart Dawson as he allowed Margaret to fade into anonymity.

And thus it was that Mr and Mrs David Stewart Dawson welcomed their first child into the world in the summer of 1886: a girl. Ah, well, there would be more of this "marriage" and sooner or later his luck would change. The dark-haired child had her mother's looks and if she grew to inherit Harriet's lively spirit, she could yet make him proud. They gave her the name of Harriet's youngest sister, Bertha, a name that had become popular during the life of the late Prince Consort. Harriet's parents and her siblings were informed of the happy event and David's warm relationship with Colin McNab assured their acceptance. It took little effort to convince the McNabs that Harriet would enjoy a life befitting the wife of a man of means. Harriet, for her part, could not believe her luck. She was in thrall to David and had now been inducted into his world of wealth and privilege. Doors that might have been forever closed to her would open, she could dream of meeting, dining, and dancing with society gentlemen and ladies, perhaps even accompanying David on his travels, and of becoming his worthy helpmate.

London Calling

By 1887 Stewart Dawson & Co. had outgrown its Liverpool roots. The Australasian business consumed ever more production. Sydney and Melbourne were well established, the Dunedin branch had opened in September '84, and plans were advanced to open branches in Brisbane and Perth. Ranelagh Place, so recently the acme of modernity, was straining to keep up with production and running short of space in its warehouse. More than that, he was now a Jeweller and Watchmaker, and he could foresee the day when his original source of wealth might be eclipsed by the sheer variety and appeal of cut stones and worked silver and gold. Already the competition from the Americans was cutting into his sales and profits on watches and now even the Swiss were adopting American mass production methods and showing signs of improving the poor quality of their timepieces.* He could always compete on quality in that market but, at what cost? While in Sydney, he couldn't help noticing the reports of sporting and cultural events that were sponsored by local businesses. There was a silver cup for yachting, an engraved plate for tennis, a cask of wine for the best rifle shot; the list was endless. He'd seen the like here in England but not on the scale of the Australians. They seemed to be obsessed with sporting and other outdoor competitions; then again, they did have the weather for it. So, here was another avenue to promote his name, whether through watches (still a favourite with the gentlemen) or with a more ostentatious trophy to be displayed by its proud winner. It was time to mobilise his local managers in the colony, make use of some of those connections he'd established and add the name of Stewart Dawson to the list of prize-givers. Time to acknowledge that he just wasn't set up for jewellery and silverware manufacture in Liverpool. He would have to consider moving to London.

---

* Swiss watch production far exceeded the British by the mid-nineteenth century, but the overall quality was poor until they adopted American technology and mass production methods. By the end of the century the once-dominant English industry had virtually disappeared.

He'd passed through the capital many times on visits to suppliers. The jewellery centre of Hatton Garden was now a familiar stamping ground, and he'd made some solid business connections among the diamond merchants and goldsmiths. He scouted for a suitable establishment and in October he announced the opening of a "new London Depot" at 96 Newgate Street, on the eastern edge of Hatton Garden, close enough to his new suppliers and a good base from which to establish his name in the city.[42] For the time being, watch manufacturing would continue at Ranelagh Place, but the jewellery business could only flourish in London. It meant even more of his time spent on trains between the two cities, but what was the alternative? However, as the months passed, the burden of travel grew. Four hours on the train, plus half an hour or so in cabs at each end, two or three times a week was wearing him down and keeping him from both business and pleasure. Margaret and the girls were coping quite well, as far as he knew, but as time passed, he found it harder to keep the gossips quiet about his domestic arrangements. Liverpool was a big city but not so big that word could not spread and upturn his applecart. As if that weren't enough, Harriet was expecting their second child and would, rightly, demand more of his time. The answer, as he saw it, was to get Margaret away from the source of her unhappiness once and for all, so, as soon as he was satisfied that the Newgate Street depot was in operation, he moved her and the girls to London.

The new home was in Ullathorne Road, Streatham in the borough of Wandsworth.[43] Like Pelham Grove, it was close to a park, but unlike the Liverpool house, this was a detached villa with established gardens. Margaret was impressed. In case she needed reminding of his proprietorship, he named the house "Cairn Gorm", another reference to his birthplace. He maintained a room for himself, convenient for when he was in town, and provided the usual complement of servants. Margaret and he could for the most part avoid each other's company, which suited them both. His two families were now separated by 200 miles, as good as a world away. In Liverpool, he was free to lead a more open life with Harriet and it was there on January 1st, 1888, that she gave birth to their second child. And what a New Year's present for them! She had honoured him with a son! He skipped for joy; more toasts were drunk. Now the name could be carried forward as Stewart Dawson's cemented their place in the world of commerce. The child was on the small side, but he looked healthy and would lack for nothing. The nurse employed to care for Bertha could be relied upon to protect and nurture the new-born. They christened him, Percy,[44] a popular name very much in fashion in recent years, and appropriate for a go-ahead young man, he thought.

If Harriet expected any kind of settled home life with David and the children, she was to be disappointed, at least in the short term. He was still shuttling between the two cities and, lately, spending more time in London than her hometown. The growth of the Australasian business was beyond belief. Plans were advanced to relocate the Melbourne branch to 97 Swanston Street,[45] an excellent corner site opposite the Town Hall, and in Sydney soon, Stewart Dawson's would move to no. 456 George Street, opposite the busy Queen Victoria Markets.[46] In New Zealand he'd added to the Dunedin and Auckland branches with an establishment in Wellington.[47] Now both north and south islands were covered, and he was considering Australian operations in Brisbane and Perth. The demands on his time were made all the heavier by his reluctance, or inability, to delegate authority to any of his managers in England. While he was obliged to grant a degree of autonomy to store managers on the other side of the world, and was rewarded with dedication and loyalty, there were few among his local staff to whom he ceded control. As he was fond of saying:

> *Life is full of opportunity; all that is required is depth of insight and work, work, work.*[48]

It wasn't that others were lazy, he conceded, it was just that none of them could match his acumen, his insights, and his attention to detail in all things. Margaret had heard this sort of talk almost since they first met and by now it elicited no more than a roll of her eyes, but Harriet was still in awe of this dynamo of a man. However, though she had been willing to accept his absences until now, Percy's arrival had bestowed a higher rank upon her and, as the months passed, she came to resent her isolation and was emboldened to prevail upon him.

In the end, it was easier than she might have expected. Though it was contrary to his better judgement, he accepted that his expedient separation of the two households was no longer practical or necessary. Margaret had settled well in Streatham and the tension that had caused them so much pain had subsided. They could hold a civil conversation once more and a new realism lay on the relationship. Margaret seemed content with her lot, perhaps due to a realisation that she exercised a degree of control over David that he could never escape, so long as they both played their part. For all she knew or cared, this current infatuation would pass, and he would be back at her door or in pursuit of a new jade. So, in 1890 he cut his ties with Liverpool, moving Harriet and their children to London and selling the twelve houses in Pelham Grove for a good profit, as they were all "well let" and still relatively new.[49] Rather than purchase another London house, he rented a terrace for them at 8 Priory Villas, Wandsworth,[50] not a mile north of Margaret. There just wasn't time to secure a permanent residence before Harriet's confinement and furthermore he wanted to keep his options open: he was planning a much more radical move for his second family. On 11th December, his second son, Norman, came into the world.[51] The line of succession was secure. Some might have said that the gods were showing favour; he preferred to say:

> *Success is what the world pays a man for discovering and developing himself.*[52]

Life for David and the two families during those years in South London was, on the surface, mundane and, after the stresses of Liverpool, calm and pleasant. Though less than a mile separated them, Margaret was kept in ignorance of Harriet's exact whereabouts even as David continued to visit and stay at "Cairn Gorm" from time to time. Harriet fretted less over his forced absences, now that travelling to and from his office in Hatton Garden was a matter of half an hour, at most. But he was unsettled; his mind strayed to memories of the great southern lands he had visited. The daily routine of breakfast in a suburban terrace, the walk through the uninspiring streets, the cramped, draughty tram clattering north across the river, the cold and dampness that pervaded everything; was this what he was working for? Where was the buzz of excitement he'd felt in Sydney and Auckland? London might be the centre of the world and he might be making his way well enough in Hatton Garden, but he had been brought down to earth rather more than he would have liked since his arrival in the great city. In Sydney he was still a small player, but there, in just a few months he'd met, mixed with, and felt welcome in the company of some of its great businessmen and politicians. In the colony there was space for him to grow and possibly dominate in his chosen field. He could be a flag-bearer for the Empire in Australia. In London, he foresaw a struggle through the ranks of the hundreds of established jewellers, doubtless earning respect for his commercial acumen, but going one better could be a challenge too far in this company. The more he thought about it, the more orders he despatched to Melbourne, Wellington, Brisbane, the greater his restlessness and resolve to accompany those crates of watches and silverware to their destination. He determined that, once he was satisfied that the Newgate Street manufactory could be left in safe hands, he would quit London with Harriet and the children and establish a new, personal base in a warmer, younger country. All was in place by 1892 but before the year was out, Harriet announced that she was expecting another child, further postponing their voyage. Their third son, Stuart, was born on 22nd June 1893.[53] David's mind was now made up; the family was complete, it was time for Harriet to escape the parlour and the nursery and take her rightful place beside him in the new world.

Harriet's Debut

Throughout eighteen ninety-four, the call of the distant shore grew louder. David was impatient to see the littlest child weaned but Harriet would not countenance the risks of a sea voyage with a babe in arms and they hadn't yet settled young Percy into his boarding school. Until then, he had no trouble keeping busy, checking the order books, dropping in on the silversmiths preparing cups and plate for sale and presentation, and driving the advertising that was the lifeblood of the business. The months passed but Harriet resisted his urging to make the journey. Anticipating her assent, he booked passage in July on the SS Himalaya[54] but at the last moment she made another excuse for delay. So be it. He had committed to being in Sydney before the end of August;[55] she could follow when it suited her, as he knew she would.

By God, it was good to be back on Australian soil! James Dempster, the manager of the Sydney store, was on the dockside to welcome him. David congratulated him on his recent marriage[56] and on the coup they had struck with the latest removal in the city. At the end of 1891, the magnificent Strand Arcade had opened. Sydney's largest and most luxurious shopping precinct, it was one of the first buildings in the city designed to take account of the Australian climate. The roof was made of glass, tinted to reduce glare, and the access gallery of the top floor was projected to shade the lower levels. Delicate ironwork brackets supported the galleries and railings. Finely carved cedar balustrades and shopfronts, marble columns and richly tiled floors featured. The lighting was innovative, a combined gas and electric system was used in combination fittings designed by the architect; the concourse was lit by two huge central chandeliers suspended from the crown of the roof trusses and having 50 gas jets and 50 electric lamps in each. There were also two state-of-the-art hydraulic lifts.[57] Stewart Dawson's now occupied number 412 George Street, another corner site right at the entrance to the arcade. David inspected the custom-built, hermetically sealed cases displaying the huge selection of watches now on sale. To his own brand he had added the American Waltham and Rotherham's of Coventry. There was everything from a boy's first watch to luxury chronographs, even a fine range of ladies' wristlet watches. How right he had been to advertise:

> *A peep at our George Street window will leave a picture in your mind not to be forgotten as to the extent of our watch stock, certainly more colossal than the total stocks of any 10 Retail Shops in Sydney put together.*

Scarcely had he settled into his hotel and taken in the sights along Pitt and George Street once more, when news arrived that Harriet had set sail to join him. He had a month to arrange an itinerary for her and the children that would most convince her of the virtues of this great new land. He would show her the sights, acclimatise her to the warmer weather, introduce her in local society. He felt sure she would find her feet among the ladies who formed Sydney's tight knit but growing monied class. Here, she could leave her humble beginnings once and for all, just as many of the well-dressed socialites gracing the balls and vice-regal garden parties must have done. She had already, to her credit, cultivated a more refined London accent, masking the provincial Liverpool voice of her childhood, she had excellent taste in dress and bore herself with confidence in any company. She made friends easily and could be relied upon to lend her quite acceptable singing voice to any soirée.

She would arrive in October, not long before Melbourne Cup Day. The great horse race, so popular that it "stopped a nation", seized David's imagination. Harriet, from her earliest days in Liverpool, had witnessed the fever and excitement of wagering on every-day and important races. The Grand National, England's premier steeplechase, was held only five miles away from Old Haymarket. Illegal, off-course betting was rife, and most publicans turned a blind eye to the activities of the many bookmakers who mingled with their customers. Young Harriet, ducking between the noisy patrons to collect empty glasses and full ashtrays, had fallen into the habit of placing a few pence from her tips onto a fancied nag and of counting her unrealised winnings. She would be in Melbourne for race day, and he could join her to celebrate her arrival with the crowds on the course. Announcing a bumper "Melbourne Cup Sale" for all his Australian shops, he took the southbound train.[58]

He'd just enough time to call in and show the flag at Swanston Street, before heading across to Williamtown to greet the family. Harriet had brought Bertha and the two younger boys, leaving Percy in the care of his boarding school. David would have preferred to see his oldest son with them on this side of the world, but Harriet had resisted, hedging her bet that the trip would be a short one. Their reunion had a special flavour: for the first time, he presented Harriet as Mrs Stewart Dawson. Until now he'd had to be circumspect in London and Liverpool, where there was always a chance that the real Mrs Stewart Dawson might be remembered. But here the risks of embarrassing exposure were negligible. Though his employees and some of his business contacts knew he was married, none had met his "wife". Harriet's secret was safe and now she had been elevated, formally, to the status to which she felt entitled.

November 6th marked the Stewart Dawsons' debut into society as a couple. Leaving the children in the care of the nurse who had accompanied Harriet, they joined the throng at Flemington Racecourse. The weather was cool, and clouds covered the south-west sky as the guests entered the enclosure for the day's racing carnival. Harriet wore a brown and pink plaid silk bodice over her full skirt, topped with a hat of Italian Leghorn woven straw, which was decorated with bunches of pink daisies and black plumes. The distinctive hat, bought in London, won the admiration of bystanders.[59] Rain threatened to dampen the excitement of the day but when the riders aligned their skittish mounts at the start all thoughts of the weather were put aside. David and Harriet were intrigued by the sight of a wire stretched the width of the field along the chalk starting line, at the level of the horses' heads. It was explained that this was a new experiment, tried for the first time at a major race this very day. The traditional method of starting, with which the London couple were familiar, was at the drop of a flag at one end of the start line. As they all knew, some to their cost, more than one race had been ruined when nervous thoroughbreds bolted or threw their riders at the sight of the fluttering flag. In a bid to reduce the risk, a Mr Gray, from Sydney, had recently invented what he called the Strand Start. As they watched, a steward moved a lever, the wire sprang up and away from the horses, and they were off! There was no time to marvel at the success of the simple device as the field thundered into the distance. The favourite, Ruenalf, took an early lead and looked certain of breaking the hearts of the bookmakers, but a couple of furlongs from the finish, as the cheers from the crowd grew loud and shrill, he was bumped into the rails, almost unseating his jockey. A mighty groan arose in the enclosure. The five-year-old Devon, and Ruenalf's younger brother, Patron, challenged for the lead, Patron finally running down Devon, to win by three-quarters of a length in front of the yelling crowd. Betting slips fluttered to the ground, more champagne was poured, parties drifted together in marquees or watched the presentation of the cup by the Governor of Victoria. Harriet had never experienced the like of it. Her "husband" was at ease in this company and soon, so was she, as he introduced her to acquaintances down from Sydney or from among his Melbourne circle.

It was to be the start of a round of balls, race meetings, theatre, and opera evenings. When David was occupied with business, he arranged outings for her and the children to see the sights of Melbourne and, upon their arrival in Sydney, to enjoy the hospitality of new friends in his favourite city. The months passed, cool, dry winter came and went, and she felt once more the oppressive heat and humidity of the southern summer. Only on the harbour shores or, they said, in the mountains away to the west of the city, could one find cooling breezes. Stewart Dawson's had been sponsoring races in the Balmain Regatta on the river upstream from the harbour for several years and it was with relief that the couple watched from the bank or on board one of the committee boats, before presenting yet another trophy. Harriet was delighted to fill the role of guest of honour and presenter of prizes to strapping young yachtsmen and rowers. In the evenings, perspiring gentlemen surreptitiously loosened their collars or made excuses to step outside for another cigar, while the ladies counted the hours until they could be free of their stays. As the parties dispersed, David and Harriet to their hotel while others took cabs to their mansions around the bays and headlands, David reflected on the life that he had led and on his hopes for a second chance with his new family. So long as Harriet could be occupied and entertained, he believed she would be open to persuasion that Sydney offered more than she could ever aspire to in London. They, like their dinner companions, could at this very moment be standing on the terrace of some crenelated villa overlooking the lights on the harbour. Would she really prefer to be peering through the London fog across a narrow street at an unbroken row of identical yellow brick townhouses? In Wandsworth, they had lived an unsettled life, never two consecutive Christmases in the same house, the wrong side of the Thames for easy access to the kind of society that was on their doorstep here in Sydney. True, he had the means now to join the Mayfair set if he chose, but he preferred not to raise Harriet's expectations, fearing an even greater challenge to his judgement and authority. It was going to be a long game and he had to be patient.

As their first Christmas in the colony approached, David's pride was crowned when an article appeared in the Sydney paper, "The Australian Star" of December 13th, titled: "Growth and Change in Sydney".[60] The journalist celebrated the success of the many flourishing retail businesses, listing department stores, David Jones, Anthony Hordern, and Mark Foy, Gowing Brothers' drapers, together with the likes of music publisher, Palings, and the premier brewer, Tooth & Co. In this illustrious company the writer effused:

> *Jewellery, the love of glitter, which enables South Africa to prosper and Australia to live her high and progressive life, is very well exemplified in some of the best establishments of Sydney ... we have examples of firms which stand out and cannot be missed in any account of the life of our city. Stewart Dawson & Company stands high among these, a jeweller's shop which would not need to blush in any comparison with Regent Street or the Rue de Rivoli, a reputable and renowned firm whose name is, throughout Australia, regarded as equivalent to a hallmark of good taste and honest worth.*

To gain this reputation in only a decade was an outstanding achievement by any measure. The George Street store was now lit by electricity and above the shop were spacious workrooms in which twelve men were employed, setting diamond jewellery. Silverware decorated with Australian flora and fauna was another local offering and the full range of goods on offer swamped the limited stock of David's remaining rivals. Besides the Waltham, Rotherham, and

Stewart Dawson watches there were handsome clocks in oak and marble, cups, and trophies, first quality field-glasses, Sheffield cutlery, leather goods and Doulton fine china. Bangles, brooches, lockets, necklets, tiaras, scarfpins and gentlemen's studs competed for shelf space or dangled above cases of signet, wedding, and engagement rings.[61]

Eager to put some of his enormous capital to work and swept up by the Victorian gold rush, David joined a group of potential investors in a Gippsland gold mine. The Alice Gold Mine, in Rokeby, was one of hundreds of leases in the colony following the dykes and reefs of the precious ore. David and his partners were encouraged to invest but prudence won out. John Complin, manager of the South Warragul Mine, an experienced and hard-headed engineer, was appointed to inspect the Alice Mine. He valued the work done at no more than a few pounds and stated that none of it was of any use to future mining operations. Relieved that they had not risked thousands of pounds, the investors withdrew, and the lease was abandoned.[62] But David's appetite had been whetted and having put one foot into the world of precious metals, he took another step a month later, joining a syndicate led by one Augustus Gross. Mr Gross was a fellow merchant, in the small circle of entrepreneurs to which David had been admitted. In January 1895, now styling himself "Mechanical Consulting Engineer", he formed the syndicate, announcing his intention to re-work an abandoned reef at Box Ridge, in the Hill End district, west of Sydney.[63] Some of the miners who had worked in the old mine joined the syndicate, paying for their share in alluvial gold, from the only workings still active in the district. To promote the venture David undertook to display samples of this gold in Stewart Dawson's George Street window. Unsurprisingly, nothing further was heard of the syndicate, and Gross returned to his first love, inventing, and patenting a diving suit that he promoted to the pearl-diving industry, a device for lacing shoes and boots, and an improved pump for pneumatic tyres.

Undeterred, David bought shares in a Kalgoorlie gold mine after a side trip to the West Australian gold fields during a visit to Perth. This turned into another disappointment when a hostile takeover without notice deprived him and other shareholders of most of their investment. His letters of protest to the newspapers exhibited sophisticated understanding of the complexities of equity raising,[64] but his advocacy on behalf of the minority shareholders was ignored and he was obliged to write off his losses. His personal losses were trivial by David's standards, but he'd learned a lesson: for the time being, it was best to stick to his core business. As he wrote:

> *Cherished schemes may occasionally fail, but earnest thoughts abide with you forever.*[65]

So well-known was David that he became the potential victim of a criminal kidnapping in January 1895. Buck Millidge, a Melbourne criminal notorious for his bold and brazen behaviour, was reported to have planned to kidnap David on his way home from the Swanston Street shop and hold him captive while Millidge used his keys to the shop to make off with the contents. David, unaware of the plot, learned of it when evidence was led in another case against Millidge. The plot was foiled when one of the gang members was arrested on another matter and spilled the beans to the police.[66] Millidge was executed in Sydney in May of that year for shooting at a policeman.

In the same month, David received an anonymous tip off. The letter alleged that a sales employee at the Swanston Street shop, one Herbert Crisp, was living a fast life beyond his means and pointed to his position of trust with the stock at the shop. David passed the letter to the police, and Detective Macmanamy was soon on the case. He entered the shop during the lunch hour, when Crisp was in charge and purchased a brooch with a marked sovereign. Macmanamy left the shop and took a position across the street from where he could observe the front door. He didn't have long to wait; when Crisp emerged from the shop for his lunch break in the nearby park, Macmanamy strode across the street and confronted the surprised assistant. A brief search of Crisp's pockets revealed the incriminating marked sovereign. As the youth protested his innocence, Macmanamy marched him back into the shop and instructed him to open the sales book. Crisp's face told it all; there was no entry of the sale of the brooch. To everyone's consternation, it turned out that Crisp had been very active from the day he had been employed, purloining between £60 and £70 worth of jewellery, which he pawned, squandering the money on a life of dissipation.[67] David gave evidence at the trial, where he was affronted when the defence counsel admonished him that if he cared to take the risk of leaving a youth at 15 shillings a week in charge of the valuable contents of his shop he should bear the consequences. Seeking mitigation, Counsel "referred to the custom of wealthy employers placing young boys in positions of trust at miserable salaries."[68] His effort was unrewarded, Crisp was sentenced to 18 months in Castlemaine Jail.

Had the Counsel taken the trouble to enquire, he might have been surprised to learn that David was one of several merchants prepared to accept unionisation of his business.[69] The Mercantile Employees' Union, founded shortly after the trial concluded, provided employee benefits including unemployment and sickness payments, support for job seekers and relief to employee dependants. It was based on the model of the Liverpool Clerks' Union, with which David was familiar. Despite his middle-class aspirations, he never forgot his roots and the effort required to make a living. He showed a degree of care for his staff and customers that belied his hard-nosed attitude to business. Many of his staff had served since the opening of the first shop and Crisp himself had been taken on to save him from hardship after his retrenchment from a previous position.[70]

David was once more in court in July 1895,[71] giving evidence in a much more serious case. Employees at his George Street shop had stolen 43 diamond rings and one sapphire and diamond ring valued at £1,500* and fenced them through a criminal gang. David gave evidence of a further deficiency of £1,650. As the case continued over the next five months more thefts came to light and the so-called "gang" turned out to be a group of boys as young as fourteen. Inept amateurs, they all eventually pleaded guilty and were sentenced to terms of several years in the local reformatory. David had offered a £100 reward for a successful conviction but baulked at paying it to the two detectives who apprehended the culprits, claiming they were just doing the job they were paid for. They sued him and, ever the realist, he paid.[72]

---

* about $180,000

Harriet was ignorant of these criminal and commercial events and David was content to keep her so. His mission was to convince her of the benefits of life in high society in Australia. The less she knew of the inner workings of the men's world in which he moved, the better. He doubled his efforts to keep her entertained and supplied with the accoutrements of wealth. Her wardrobe expanded weekly, there was a bottomless pot of jewels with which to adorn herself, and few evenings without the company of glittering ladies and distinguished gentlemen. At weekends, a day at the races became de rigueur, whether at Sydney's Rosehill or Canterbury, or for the season in Melbourne. Harriet's flutters with the bookmakers amused David. It couldn't have been for the money alone, could it? She had and could ask for any amount from him. Ah, well, let it serve his purpose to seduce her away from the old life back in the home country.

By 1896 he was no more confident that Harriet would submit to his inducement, since he had not been able to persuade her to call for young Percy to join them. The absence of the now eight-year-old was a constant reminder of her determination to retain a living connection to England. David's hopes were encouraged from time to time that she would allow him to bring the child over to join them but there was always an excuse for delay and another social commitment to divert them. On June 15th they joined Mr and Mrs Mark Foy and hundreds of other guests at a French charity ball in Sydney's Paddington Town Hall.[73] The guest of honour was Lord Hampden, the Governor of New South Wales, and the cream of Sydney's society mixed with French diplomats and expatriates. Harriet was swept away by the European sophistication and élan of the French contingent, to David's mild consternation. This wasn't part of his plan at all.

For his part, David made the most of his time with the Foys. Mark Foy, fifteen years his junior, was head of the eponymous department store that he had founded with his older brother, Francis. Their common business origins in the drapery trade were a good conversation starter, as David regaled Foy with tales of his early days in Glasgow and Liverpool. They'd also met at regattas on the river, where Foy, a keen sportsman, raced sailing skiffs. Foy's flamboyance and sheer energy appealed to David. The younger man's imaginative daring and willingness to break with tradition exemplified David's "going one better" philosophy. Above all, it jolted him out of his complacency; while he had been squiring Harriet around, he had let his attention drift from the need to take the next step in building his commercial empire. He now had a jewellery establishment in Brisbane (another good corner site) and the Wellington store was doing excellent business. All in all, he was close to dominating the Australasian market, but though there was still enormous potential for growth here he couldn't foresee many opportunities for further expansion. There might be a case for opening a store in Perth, he supposed; his visit to the gold fields at Kalgoorlie had opened his eyes to the wealth of Western Australia, but, beyond that, the colonies' population was too concentrated in their respective capitals to justify premises in, say, Newcastle or Ballarat. His strategy would be to improve the quality and appeal of the existing stores or take advantage of better locations becoming available. There was so much new construction in progress in Melbourne and Sydney that he was constantly on the lookout for the ideal corner location in the best shopping precincts. Eighteen ninety-seven was to be the year of consolidation of Stewart Dawson's primacy in the market. He fixed on Melbourne, where he'd long had his eye on the premises adjoining the Swanston Street store that would bring him a step closer to the coveted corner position. His spies had informed him that the lease was about to expire so he opened negotiations and within weeks the deal was done. The store now featured a thirty-foot frontage to Swanston Street, its walnut-framed windows encased in marble. Melbourne's Traveller newspaper was persuaded to print another of David's promotional articles, where he boasted:

> *Needless to say, everything has been done in the most modern London style, and if a block were extracted from Bond Street, and wedged into the present site, the effect could not be more metropolitan.*[74]

More than by sheer size, the store made a deep impression on Melbourne's cultural and artistic elite. David had commissioned the artist, John Ford Paterson, to decorate the walls with four Australian landscapes. Paterson was a Scottish-born near contemporary of his patron. He was influenced by the Swiss artist, Louis Buvelot, himself a member of the Australian Heidelberg school of landscape painters and embraced the "en plein air" method in his dreamy landscapes. The Melbourne Age was one of many journals moved to comment upon Stewart Dawson's enterprise in artistic promotion:

Besides being a novelty in shop decoration in Melbourne, the painted interior of Messrs. Stewart Dawson and Co.'s show room ... is of noteworthy merit as a work of art. In panels of the walls are cameo paintings by Mr. John Ford Paterson, after the style of the great French artist, De Chavannes.[75]

Melbourne's "Table Talk" went as far as describing the store as "Melbourne's Tiffany's". The article described the interior, much as The Age had done, offering the opinion:

It is called a showroom; but it is handsomer, and those wares are more artistically arranged than in most art museums. ...[76]

David could not have been more pleased. He had, of course, provided much of the copy for the articles, having learned the value of supposed independent commentary in the press, versus unambiguously paid advertising. Though he was by no means alone in this practice, he had perfected the art of embedding promotional material in the "news" columns, usually with a telling reference to a paid advertisement elsewhere in the journal but now and again masquerading as journalistic or editorial comment. But behind the glowing (self)praise was a deeper message, an expression of his vision for Australasia and his personal mission to overcome Harriet's resistance to leaving England. He had spared no expense with the Sydney and Melbourne store fit outs to create the image of an antipodean Tiffany's that Table Talk described. He believed that his example would, first, demonstrate the innate superiority and sophistication of Stewart Dawson's and, second, provide an example that others could follow, thus raising the tone of otherwise provincial cities to something approaching the ideal European model. In this Jubilee year, the Victorian age had reached its zenith. All the colonies, not least the Australian ones, joined the celebrations of the might and power of the British Empire. How grateful the New South Welshmen, the Queenslanders, the Victorians, the New Zealanders were for the privilege of belonging to this great family of nations, whose capital was a modern-day Mecca for all its members. Yes, Melbourne, Sydney, Auckland had their own monuments to modern progress and style, but who could pretend to the magnificence and sheer good taste of a London, New York, or Paris? Now, here was a modern prophet, come from these very realms of beauty, to show that they need not remain mere country cousins. He had even celebrated the emerging strengths of local artists in commissioning the painted panels in Swanston Street. This was not merely an aesthetic gesture, however. David recognised and acknowledged the rise in Australian nationalism that had been growing since before his first visit all those years ago and by now saw its expression in a concerted push towards federation of the colonies. His association with Augustus Gross had been an education that had nurtured his own belief in the future of the nation as the premier imperial colony.

As to Harriet, he reasoned that the more like "home" Australia became, the easier it should be to persuade her to settle there. She could always escape the extremes of the Australian climate in the northern hemisphere if she wished, refresh her wardrobe in Paris or London, and renew her family ties from time to time. Bertha and the two boys would be reunited with their absent brother, whom Harriet must miss after three years. He redoubled his efforts, exhausting as the social round had become, to occupy and overwhelm her senses with the gaiety and glamour of life among the cream of colonial society. To escape the summer heat of Sydney, he organised an excursion in January 1898 to the Southern Highlands of New South Wales.[77] Taking the train from Sydney's Central Station, they bundled the children and their nurse on board and set off to the town of Bowral. The cooler, drier air was a welcome relief for all. They repaired to The Grand Hotel to change and refresh. If Harriet feared rustication in the charming town she was quickly enlightened. Half of Sydney's finest seemed to be there, enjoying the relief this "Indian Hill Station" provided. There were tennis parties, soirées, dances and long walks through the gardens and parks to enjoy. The children could explore the lower slopes of Mount Gibraltar, towering over the eastern side of the town, while their parents settled into comfortable settees for extended afternoon teas or aperitifs before dinner. The Grand Hotel, a mere decade old and well appointed, offered fine wines and well-prepared meals using the best local produce. David had bought time yet again, but the game was not over, for he had one further venture to pursue that year, one more opportunity to expand Stewart Dawson's business and incidentally engage and impress his "wife". On April 15th, 1898, Sydney's Evening News announced:

To Westralians and others it will be a matter of interest to know that on June 1 next Messrs. Stewart Dawson and Company, the well-known jewellers, watch manufacturers, silversmiths, and diamond merchants, of George-street and the Strand, Sydney, will open their splendid new premises at Perth.[78]

David had secured another prime corner spot at 395 Hay Street, Perth, and as he had done in Sydney and Melbourne, remodelled the premises, which would be "fitted throughout in an artistic manner." As work progressed on the store, he and Harriet once more boarded the train for Melbourne in April, sailing from there to Albany, the port city of the western colony. The early start, some six weeks before the official opening of the Hay Street establishment, was to give the couple time to explore the fertile southern quarter of the colony and for David to follow up local mining contacts. He still harboured ambitions, which had been encouraged by his Sydney circle, to invest in the mineral riches that abounded this side of the continent. Meanwhile, he could entertain Harriet with visits to vineyards in the Swan Valley or introduce her to Perth's merchant class. He officiated at the opening of the store, which, like the Swanston Street branch, was admired for its artistry and design. The West Australian Sunday Times[79] sent a reporter, whom David escorted around the premises. After admiring the precision engineering of the display windows, the reporter entered the shop, where David gave him a guided tour:

Well, this superb showroom is fitted up with a series of air-tight containers and wall show cases. There is a great deal of significance in the arrangements, and one cannot fail to be struck with the idea that it was the result of the experience of a master in the art. …

A detailed description of the elegant fittings followed, before the account moved to the artistic decoration of the establishment, executed by one J. Ross Anderson:

... The whole of the arrangements were designed by Mr. Dawson ... He is evidently endowed with a large amount of constructive ability and organisation, and, moreover, believes in doing everything well.

The final paragraphs extolled the beauty of the décor on the ceiling and cornices, which were in David's favoured colours of turquoise blue, pale amber, and cream. With the three stores, David had cemented his position as the premier purveyor of luxury and style in Australia, while acknowledging and showcasing local artistic talent and motifs. J. Ross Anderson was a leading interior designer, based in Perth, who was much in demand for ecclesiastical, commercial, and domestic assignments. In choosing him, as he had done with Ford Paterson in Melbourne, David signalled that, in his view, Australia could be culturally the equal of any nation. It was a timely move, calculated to forge a real local identity for Stewart Dawson's just as the wave of nationalism and the push for federation reached a new level. Stewart Dawson's would be Australia's own Tiffany's, with a British pedigree to honour the imperial connection.

Harriet's introduction to Perth society followed the opening of the store. She was a guest at a mayoral reception for the visiting English actor, Wilson Barrett, and shortly after, made her singing debut in the home of a prominent hostess, Mrs. Greene.[80]

A musical interlude took place between the dances. Mrs. Stewart Dawson, the possessor of a sympathetic light soprano voice, charmed her hearers by the rendering of the two songs she was entrusted with ... Mrs. Stewart Dawson wore an elegant evening toilette of black moiré, bodice relieved with edging of pink cream silk folds, showing under zouaves, brilliant necklet of diamonds, with diamond hair ornaments en suite.*

Harriet even had a taste of the frontier life when she accompanied David on a brief trip to Kalgoorlie. The gold rush that had commenced there in 1894 was still drawing thousands of hopeful prospectors and investors. In five years, the population had grown from nothing to

---

* Zouaves were a jacket modelled on the uniform of French North African infantry soldiers, featuring loose three-quarter sleeves.

over 25,000, temporary tents and shacks had given way to solid buildings of timber and local stone, telegraph wires festooned the wide streets, which were lit by electricity.[81] Though David had learned some lessons from his earlier abortive ventures into mining, he could not resist another close inspection of some of the leases on offer. They stayed at Kalgoorlie's newest and finest hotel, The Palace. Opened only months before their arrival, the two-storey building, with its shady balconies decorated with intricate iron lacework and its sumptuous interiors, boasted electric lighting throughout and fresh water piped to all forty-four bedrooms. Though the town had a "wild west" air, Harriet could enjoy the company of other, wealthy out-of-towners taking tea. From their vantage point on the balcony they overlooked the wide, dusty streets where gigs and traps criss-crossed, and carters rumbled their heavy loads of supplies to the mine workings. Upon retiring to their room, which was furnished with the best that Melbourne and Perth could supply, they could imagine themselves back in one of the eastern metropolises, rather than this isolated outpost of civilisation. Nevertheless, for Harriet it was no more than a brief adventure; she counted the days before their return to Sydney and, as she hoped, before they would be back home once more in London. David was more preoccupied with business and, though he made no immediate commitment, he was moved to comment upon his departure that they had both enjoyed their stay and that he intended to take the first possible opportunity to revisit Kalgoorlie, which he described as "the largest gold factory I have been shown over."[82]

By the beginning of September, they were back in Sydney. With all the talk of federation Sydney's population continued to grow faster than any might have predicted at the beginning of the decade. On George Street alone, there were several long-established jewellers and watch businesses: T.F. Wiesener's, William Kerr, A. Saunders, and The London Watch and Jewellery Company among them. Around the corner in Hunter Street were William Farmer and Fairfax & Roberts, the latter advertising itself as "Vice-regal Jewellers", a sore point for David. Scattered along Castlereagh and Park Street were the lesser businesses, most of them importers or specialist watch repairers. Some had come and gone in the blink of an eye; others, like William

Kerr and Saunders, had workshops that rivalled David's, but none quite matched Stewart Dawson's for the breadth of their range or the opulence of their premises.

There was to be one last Christmas in the colony before the inevitable return home. David conceded that Harriet's homesickness would not be cured by another season of colonial hospitality. Furthermore, there were pressing business reasons for at least a temporary stint in London so, after celebrating his forty-ninth birthday and seeing in the new year, David and family took the train to Melbourne. There, the colossal German liner, GMS Bremen, awaited them. Staff from Swanston Street gathered on board to drink a farewell toast to them, reflecting on the goodwill that prevailed within the company.* David "feelingly responded and deeply regretted leaving so many friends, among whom was his trusted and popular manager." With a last, fond look over the shoulder, he shepherded Harriet and the children on board ship, and they sailed northwards.

---

* Table Talk (Melbourne) 13th January 1899 P.10 "*The manager of the firm – Mr. A.E. Snappere – in proposing the health of Mr. Dawson, touched upon the entente cordiale which existed between Mr. Dawson and the firm's employees, and in wishing Mr. and Mrs. Dawson a pleasant trip home trusted that a speedy return would again give their friends the opportunity of according them a hearty welcome.*"

London or Sydney?

The family arrived in London in July 1899,[83] where David wasted little time executing some well-planned moves. On the domestic front, he relocated from South London to the West End, taking a luxury apartment in Ridgmount Gardens, St Giles in the Fields.[84] Harriet could not have been more pleased. Her patience had been rewarded, she was back, not in unfashionable Wandsworth, but in the heart of London society. She had been reunited with ten-year-old Percy, who had gained a degree of independence in his years apart from the family. But he had paid the price of isolation from his parents and siblings. Unlike his confident younger brother, Norman, Percy was a reserved, serious boy. He'd also been outgrown by Norman, who though two years his junior, was almost his equal in height and sturdier. Though David disapproved of favouritism in the family, it soon became clear to him that Norman had displaced Percy in Harriet's affections. He'd have to keep an eye on them, though he was reluctant to intervene, recalling his own boyhood lessons of resilience and perseverance in the face of paternal indifference.

David's other initiative was to arrange for Margaret to move to an equally impressive apartment at Sloane Court, Chelsea, where he provided for her and 22-year-old Vanna, a housekeeper and a cook.[85] The years of separation had dimmed the memories of their troubled time together. Margaret kept her counsel but, by all accounts she was content to live her life quietly, with the two girls for company when she needed it. David's conscience still troubled him so, after a brief visit to Ullathorne Road, he persuaded Margaret that a move across the river would brighten her life. She would be going up in the world and there would be better social opportunities for Lila and Vanna in busy Chelsea. He avoided mention of his second family, and there was no sign that Margaret maintained any interest in them. She still styled herself "Mrs Stewart Dawson", as was her right, so there were now two women of that name living no more than a couple of miles apart. He no longer cared. The passage of time had erased local memories of David's former family relationships, no questions would be asked.*

While they were away fashions had changed in Europe. David capitalised on this, and the Australian stores were soon promoting new styles. Bird brooches were the latest thing; swallows on the wing, birds on the bough, songsters with jewels for feathers; the "lucky bean" appeared in pendants and charms, the always fashionable duchesse chain was now free of trinkets and plain or studded at intervals with gems.[86] Sydney, Melbourne and Perth loved it and sales took off once more.

But David's principal reason for being in London was to organise yet another relocation of his business premises. Just as he had been obliged to move from Liverpool's Ranelagh Place to Newgate Street, he was now casting an eye on a building right at the heart of the jewellery centre of Hatton Garden, and as the new century dawned he announced that Stewart Dawson's London headquarters' address would henceforth be number 20 Hatton Garden.[87] The workshops and administrative offices would now be within easy walking distance of the world's greatest concentration of diamond merchants, goldsmiths and silversmiths and, perhaps more importantly, he could boast of this premier address in his many advertisements. In Australia and New Zealand, the prestige of the address would resonate with local customers. Twenty Hatton Garden was a modest building, and he foresaw the day when he would again be on the move but, for now, it would serve his purpose. His ultimate target was the site directly opposite, at 19-21 Hatton Garden, an older building divided into many small workshops and offices, whose landlord might be persuaded to sell for the right price. He could afford to wait a couple of years.

He was also having to grapple with the problems of growth; Stewart Dawson's was by now a major international concern with

---

* In the days before centralised personal identification records, radio or TV there was little risk of Harriet's status being questioned and the fact that both women identified themselves as Mrs Stewart Dawson on the 1901 census would have gone unnoticed. David's name was next to Harriet's, absent from Margaret's census record.

seven overseas branches, the still thriving mail order business, the Hatton Garden manufacturing facility and headquarters, and several warehouses scattered across the world. He was now 52 with six children and two households to manage in addition to the hundreds of sales and production staff he employed. He controlled it all. There was no board of directors, no general managers; the highest-level executives were his shop and factory managers; everyone reported directly to him. Moreover, the legal structure of the company left him personally liable for all and any losses or penalties incurred by the business. His immense fortune was vulnerable to the whims of the market, which had experienced some rough times during the Australian recession of the early '90s. It was time to consider restructuring. He set the wheels in motion but, drawn to what he now considered his alternative homeland, he delayed acting until he had settled a few matters back in Australia. The lease on the premises adjacent to the Swanston Street shop in Melbourne had expired, and the landlord had invited tenders for its renewal or transfer. David could have left negotiations to his local manager, but this was too important a deal to delegate; he needed to take control on the spot. All in all, a perfect excuse for a return to the new Federation of Australia.

Overcoming Harriet's objections, he booked passage from Southampton in July 1901. This time, they were accompanied only by Bertha. All three boys, including eight-year-old Stuart, were boarded at school for the duration of their visit. They arrived in Sydney in October. The arrival date was perfect for the start of the racing season and Harriet hurried down to Melbourne for Derby Day, where she was observed wearing "white silk muslin over silk, elaborately tucked and lace inserted, and a lilac hat trimmed with flowers."[88] Though David escorted her he didn't rate a mention in the gossip column; outside of the vice-regal party few men did. Harriet's costume was the height of fashion, much sought after for the summer season and promoted by the likes of Anthony Hordern in their vast department store. Upright and slender, she could carry off even the most daring fashions. As "Euphrosnye", fashion columnist of the Australian Town and Country Journal observed:

Charming and distinguished though these [tucks and lace] undoubtedly are, I do not advise anyone to wear one, unless her entire costume is of the most perfect, and even then, they are only suitable for an occasion when dressiness is permissible.[89]

The season was now in full swing, leading to another Melbourne Cup, not to be missed at any cost. Since David and Harriet's last attendance, the race had gained an even greater prominence in the Australian racing calendar and with the advent of Federation was being billed as "The Greatest Festival in Australia". After the brief interval of fine weather on Derby Day, Tuesday November 5th was cool and wet ("unfavourable conditions," noted the form guides), but the crowds were undiminished. Harriet was spotted wearing "duck egg blue and white satin foulard, with cream lace and a floral hat."[90] Sydney's sporting journal, "The Referee", observed:

It is all ... very grand and impressive as a spectacle, and suggests that it costs lots more money to dress the fashionable people to be seen in thousands than many of them will be able to afford if the Federal Tariff makes them poor.[91]

The "Tariff" was the brainchild of the Protectionist group within the ranks of Federal Parliament, as a quid pro quo for the elimination of internal tariffs between the former colonies, now states of Australia. The rival Free-Traders, who included many of David's business associates, saw it as a barrier to international trade, with possibly dire consequences for domestic prices. Thanks to his local manufacturing workshops and sources of raw materials, David was confident that Stewart Dawson's would ride out the worst of any trade war. As with the Derby, the Cup race was won by the red-hot favourite, in this case, "Revenue". Few betting slips landed in the wet grass as punters swamped the bookmakers, though at odds of 6 to 4 on, the "revenue" returned amounted to pocket money for most.

While Harriet indulged her passion for wagering and displayed her jewels in the now-familiar circles – back in Sydney, she attended the Boxing Day races at Randwick ("white muslin and lace insertions, blue toque")[92] – David had not been idle, as he concluded the business that had brought him back down under. The Howey family estate, owners of the freehold of the block at the corner of Collins and

Swanston Streets, had decided to invite tenders for a building lease of the site known as "Germain Nicholson's Corner". This was the very corner that David had long coveted for the extension of Stewart Dawson's and now it was being offered for 21 years with permission to remodel all five shops, including his own existing premises. It was too good to miss, and he was prepared to outbid the competition.[93] Melbourne would have its Stewart Dawson's Corner at long last, which he would endow with the beauty and style that only he could afford. Not one to rest on his laurels, he took ship to New Zealand, where he supervised the acquisition of the final Treasure House in Christchurch, another monument to affluence and artistry. He now had North and South Island covered, though he would remain alert for better locations wherever possible, particularly the vital corner sites. Wellington and Dunedin looked the best prospects, according to his local agents, and he would without hesitation relocate once more if the opportunity arose.

~/~/~

The summer of 1901-2 was hot in Southeast Australia and Sydney's Freeman's Journal observed just after Christmas:

> *With the beginning of the year numbers of well-known people quit the city for Hobart, New Zealand, The Mountains and Southern Line, to escape the hot months.*[94]

It was just at this time that David's old acquaintance, Mark Foy began to purchase the site in the Blue Mountains of what was to become the Hydro Majestic Hotel. Since the opening of the western railway from Sydney through the mountains, Sydneyites had filled weekend trains in search of recreation, adventure and reinvigoration in the clear, fresh air. Along the way, they could alight at Springwood, with its two popular and comfortable hotels and nearby walks through the forests to clear streams and pools, or further up at Wentworth Falls. Here they could walk in the steps of Charles Darwin, taking in the view of the spectacular falls cascading hundreds of feet down the sheer sandstone cliff, or venturing to the very edge of the rocky escarpment to gaze upon mysterious and largely unexplored valleys and more precipitous sandstone walls, as far as the eye could see. For a truly memorable experience, they could take the train as far as Blackheath, three and a half thousand feet above sea level. They could look with wonder at the chasm of Govett's Leap or, on the southern side, the majestic sweep of the Megalong Valley disappearing into the blue haze that gave the mountains their name. Foy, the sportsman, held strong views about health and fitness, and had for many years frequented European spa towns such as Matlock Bath, in Derbyshire, England. Inspired by these experiences and always one to take up a challenge, he fixed on the township of Medlow, one station below Blackheath and perched at the very edge of the escarpment. They said there was a mineral spring here, close by the country retreat of W.H. Hargraves, Registrar in Equity, and trustee of the Australian Museum in Sydney. Foy snapped up the property and soon thereafter mounted a campaign to acquire the adjacent Belgravia Hotel, which had been operating as a health resort for the past decade. Between visits to Derbyshire and his beloved Smedley's Hydropathic Establishment, Foy shuttled to and from Medlow, keen to promote what he now called the Hotel Hargravia to his affluent and influential friends, among whom were the Stewart Dawsons. For David, it was the start of a love affair. The Mountains invoked nostalgia for his far-off birthplace yet were within a half day's ride from the heart of the city where his fortune lay. He and Harriet could afford to enjoy the best of both worlds if he chose: a town and country life to suit any mood or occasion. If the likes of Mark Foy could do it, then why not the Stewart Dawsons? Meantime, however, there were other, more pressing matters to deal with. As he was to write:

> *Remember, there is no such word as "finality." Minds made resourceful by thought leap forward at each succeeding stage.*[95]

Back in London, things had started to move, and it looked certain that the property at 19-21 Hatton Garden would soon be on the market. This could be the opportunity of a lifetime if he timed his bid, not for a lease, but for outright ownership. The more he took stock of his financial position, the more he was convinced of the need for a solid base in equity to protect his liquid assets. It was all very well to have a lot of money in the bank and still reassuring to add up the figures each month and confirm the stupendous cash-flow of the retail business, but capital could and should be put to better use. Moreover, it would only take one more depression like that of the early nineties to expose Stewart Dawson's to risks that he was no longer prepared to accept. In bricks and mortar, he would have a haven for his capital. Hadn't he learned that from the success of the investment in Pelham Grove all those years ago? And why pay rent to a landlord when he could be one himself? David had not planned an early return to London, expecting a wait of several years before the property came on the market, but this news trumped all his Australian endeavours for the time being. After one last season at the races in November 1902 David, Harriet and Bertha boarded the RMS Sierra in Sydney bound for Auckland on the 11th of the month.[96] They spent Christmas and New Year in New Zealand, giving David the opportunity to see how his by now customary Christmas specials were boosting sales and to thank his hard-working employees for another good year. Newspapers reported:

> *The name of Stewart Dawson & Co. has become almost a household word … As progressive jewellers par excellence, their Christmas catalogue is replete with every design known to the jeweller's art …*[97]

The family returned to Melbourne in February 1903 before sailing for England via Perth, where they were the guests of honour at another "at home". Harriet once again sang, and Bertha performed on piano.[98] As they boarded ship for the long voyage home, and loyal staff again toasted David, he responded:

> *Unless I launch out in England in the same manner as I have done in the colonies I trust to soon be among those friends whom I now feel a strain in parting from, whilst Mrs and Miss Dawson will always remember the days spent in the colonies.*[99]

If Harriet and Bertha were keen to return to the old country, he was ambivalent at best.

London Fame

Upon arriving in London, and still in celebratory mood, David commissioned the artist John Longstaff to paint a full-length portrait of Harriet. Longstaff was Australian Society's painter of choice.* Among David and Harriet's friends were the JC Williamsons. James Cassius Williamson was an American-born actor who had become Australia's foremost theatrical manager. At the time the Stewart Dawsons met him he was the lessee of the Theatre Royal in Sydney and Her Majesty's in Melbourne and Sydney and had staged some of the biggest and most successful productions the colonies had ever seen, including "Ben Hur", in Sydney, for a reputed record-breaking cost of £14,000. In 1901 Williamson commissioned Longstaff to paint his younger daughter, Marjorie, and the painting was displayed at the Sydney Society of Artists' exhibition to much acclaim. JC was delighted and celebrated by printing a photograph of the portrait on his Christmas cards,[100] one of which would have been received by the Stewart Dawsons. Even if they had missed the exhibition, they must get the message now. And indeed, David got the message: if JC could do it, he could go one better. But Longstaff had moved to London after painting the Williamson portrait, so David lost his opportunity. Now that he was back there too, he swooped on the artist, who had just completed portraits of King Edward VII and Queen Alexandra,[101] and the painting was complete before the end of the year. By 1905 Longstaff's reputation was such that he confidently submitted the portrait to the Royal Academy's annual exhibition, where it was one of only five Australian works accepted. Critical comment was favourable and a London gossip columnist covering the exhibition swooned:

> *I discovered … the full length portrait of a very pretty woman, wearing a very pretty dress, 'not' too much off the shoulders. A delightful picture, delightfully painted, hanging in a delightful light.*

---

* John Longstaff was to become Australia's official World War One artist and be rewarded with a knighthood.

The lady has warm-coloured chestnut hair, pretty eyes, charming expression, pretty background, a screen in panels of old gold and brown leaves, the chiffon dress absolutely translucent, falling on the feet in graceful waves, curves, many roses, rosettes, frills and a general 'Frou' effect. I turn over my catalogue. Let me see. Oh, here it is; number 779, 'Mrs Stewart Dawson' – J Longstaff. Australia should be proud of her artists.[102]

Though it was gratifying for David and Harriet to revel in their celebrity it was time to get down to business. Australia and New Zealand were saturated and beyond Adelaide and Hobart there was nowhere of any size to grow the business. London was now the obvious next step, but it would take more than a shop fit and opening sale to break into this market. He needed to establish the Stewart Dawson brand anew before risking another Toronto failure. He took the first step in 1906. After acquiring 19-21 Hatton Garden he had collected rents for a while, progressively giving notice to the many small tenants, and now he commissioned a new building on the site. The architects were the Scottish firm of Niven and Wigglesworth,[103] whose recently completed Courier Building in Dundee[104] had drawn praise for its construction technique employing steel and concrete, an early example of the emerging "skyscraper" architecture. Nineteen to twenty-one Hatton Garden was to be a similar, if smaller building. The choice of architect may have also been influenced by the personality of its leading partner. Of him it was said:

David Barclay Niven was one of those militant beings whose ardent and earnest enthusiasm contributed generously to architecture. His energy was untiring, he worked at high pressure and at furious speed … Complacency and inability, he incontinently brushed aside. The physical and mental fatigue that ensued were to him a small price to pay for the exhilaration so thoroughly enjoyed.[105]

Here was a man who met David Stewart Dawson's own high standards. There was no hesitation, no sparing of cash or resources, and the building went ahead, being completed in record time for its opening on November 29th, 1907.[106]

The Treasure House, as it was named, had four storeys and though its style appeared conservative it was decorated by bas relief stone carvings in art nouveau style of figures portraying different aspects of the mining, production, display and enjoyment of gems and precious metals. Inside was electrified, including the lifts. Above the ground floor showroom and below two floors of offices and workrooms was a luxurious lounge equipped with writing desks, a tearoom and areas for reading provided with copies of Australian newspapers for homesick visitors. David even arranged for visitors' correspondence to be addressed to the building for collection on arrival and during their stay in Britain. The Treasure House was a sensation and soon attracted the attention David sought in London. The Daily Mail reported:

To wander about these rooms and examine the dazzling objects with which they abound is as instructive as it is fascinating.

The Daily Express enthused:

The Stewart Dawson Treasure House must be added to the list of "sights" which no visitor to London should miss.[107]

True to his fashion, David extracted maximum publicity from the opening. He announced that he had ordered "the largest parcel of gems ever in the history of Hatton Garden."[108] He threw a sumptuous luncheon at the Hotel Cecil, where he addressed 150 guests including the agents general of Australia and New Zealand, expatiating on why he had opened what he called "the largest and finest jewellery store in Europe" in this part of London:

*My building marks a new era in the history of this time-honoured locality, by creating in the heart of the world's chief wholesale centre for precious stones and jewellery, a retail establishment of stately proportions and of an architectural significance which casts its surroundings into the shade.**

He bought half a page of the Pall Mall Gazette to expound once more on "The Philosophy of Business Success".[109] After retelling the

---

* Evening News (Sydney) 1st January 1908 P.9 Op. Cit. For once he didn't exaggerate; to this day The Treasure House is regarded as one of the premier architectural examples in the jewellery quarter.

history of Stewart Dawsons, from its Liverpool beginnings to its current level of international fame, he answered his own question: "Why open business in London?"

> *Because London is to me, as to every patriotic Briton, the world's centre and chief point of human concentration. It is the nerve centre of civilisation …*

He finished the article with a flourishing facsimile of his signature and an invitation to inspect the premises prior to its official opening.

David's other initiative that year was to restructure the business by incorporation. In July 1907, he registered Stewart Dawson & Co Ltd at Somerset House with a capital of £100,000. He was appointed permanent Governing Director with 5% of the capital and remuneration of a similar percent of the company's earnings. Among the shareholders was Captain Augustus (Gus) Jerrard, his son-in-law who had married Vanna five years before. Another shareholder and director was mining engineer Harry Hoffman, an old crony of David's from his West Australian mining venture who was now living in London. Harry's remuneration and that of all other directors was to be determined by David.[110] Six months later Stewart Dawson & Co Australasia Ltd was registered in New South Wales and later in other states with a capital of £150,000. Managing director was J McWilliam, long-time manager of the Sydney store and David's most trusted employee.*

The timing of the Treasure House opening was no accident. In May 1908, the great Franco-British Exhibition opened at Shepherds Bush, west London. The exhibition was to celebrate the Entente Cordiale signed in 1904 between the two imperial powers and would showcase the best and latest from their respective empires. The fair was the largest exhibition of its kind in Britain, and the first international exhibition co-organised and sponsored by two countries. It covered an area of some 140 acres, including an artificial lake, surrounded by an immense network of white buildings in elaborate, often Oriental styles. The buildings, though only temporary, inspired the name by

---

* Evening News (Sydney) 20th January 190 P.6. The shareholders weren't named but there can be no doubt who was the principal one.

which the area became known: White City. The 1908 Olympic Games were staged on the same site.

Stewart Dawson's had a large "Treasure House" stand in the Applied Arts pavilion, laid out like an extended version of one of their shops. Full height glass cases framed in mahogany displayed practically every item in the range. Australian opals set in silver were a favourite with visitors, among whom was the Prince of Wales, who spent many minutes at the exhibit. It was "one in the eye" for Fairfax and Roberts, with their "vice-regal" connections back in Sydney. The exhibit won four gold medals for watches, jewellery, silverware, and leather goods: in other words, the entire range. Brisbane's "Truth" commented:

> *Several Queensland firms have won honors at the Franco-British Exhibition, but it has been reserved for Stewart Dawson and Co., the well-known jewellers, to, in ordinary parlance, scoop the pool. No less than four gold medals fell to their lot ... "Truth" heartily congratulates this enterprising firm – which has now become quite an Australasian institution by virtue of its numerous business places in every town of note – upon its well-deserved and fully-merited distinctions, which should go far to assure the public that Stewart Dawsons make no idle boast when they lay out that they defy competition.* [111]

David's pride and self-confidence reached a new peak. Emboldened, he fired off articles in the press and lectured anyone who would listen about his vision for the British Empire.[112] He advocated for colonial migration and a federal model of the empire, partly as a counter to the growing power of the USA. He deprecated the mass migration of working-class British to the US when there were jobs, living space and underdeveloped economies begging for them, particularly in Australia. He promoted a stronger Colonial Service and decried the apparent lack of political will that undermined it, though he made exceptions for mavericks like Winston Churchill and Joseph Chamberlain, the great Colonial Secretary who was his inspiration in this. His credibility was aided by his magnificent track record and unchallenged experience in the markets he promoted, but he was on shaky ground. The problem with the idea of the imperial federation was that it implied an imperial parliament that would be superior to the British Parliament at Westminster, and to the Australian, Canadian and New Zealand Parliaments. It would not just be the British Parliament dominating decisions. The British were not going to accept decisions possibly made against their wishes by an imperial parliament. The New Zealanders, the Australians and the Canadians had gained practical independence – they ran their own domestic affairs without any interference from Westminster. They were not going to give that up either; the idea went against the trend of colonial self-government.

Five long years had now passed since David had left Australia, and it seemed that though his passion for the country had not abated, the success and fame occasioned by the opening of the Treasure House and the grand splash of the exhibition had set him on a new course. The long-postponed opening of his first retail establishment in England was now a reality. In 1909 he leased extensive frontage on Regent Street. As if to emphasise the new direction in which Stewart Dawson's was headed, David wrote:

> *Just two years ago, on the site of our export offices in Hatton Garden, we erected the Treasure House, the first of the Great Jewellery Houses we propose building in England. We knew that the methods that had built and made a success of the eight great Stewart Dawson stores in Australasia would be a success here, but we had no idea that the success would be so big, and that additional premises in London would be necessary in so short a time. We are fortunate in securing the full term of the Crown lease of the magnificent premises, 73, 75, 77 and 79, Regent Street, on exceptional terms, and in December will open there what may truly be called a Jewellery Palace which, in fittings, arrangement and stock will, jointly with the Treasure House, form the two finest, largest and most complete Jewellery Houses in the world.* [113]

It was at the time the second largest of his shops and in perhaps the best location anywhere. The fit out was beyond luxurious, with the very latest in crystal display cases and elaborate décor to seduce patrons.[114] Unstinting praise was lavished:[115]

Both establishments leave the visitor almost breathless amid the wonders that are shown (Westminster Gazette)

The Regent Street establishment is already accepted as being one of the pleasantest shopping rendezvous in London (Observer)

The spacious salons with their inspiring selection of presents are almost as fashionable a rendezvous just now as the showrooms of a Rue de la Paix dress artist (Standard)

The whole place is of a splendour and beauty quite unique (Pall Mall Gazette).

Though absent from Australia, David had managed the extension and complete redevelopment of the Melbourne shop around the corner of Swanston Street.[116] Having long rented the corner site at the entrance to Sydney's Strand Arcade, he now occupied perhaps the prime retail locations in both Melbourne and Sydney. The good times were here to stay.

Success also lifted David's profile in London, just as it had done in Australia. He was soon being quoted in newspapers, promoting his cash only, direct from the manufacturer to the customer business model. He was moving in illustrious company; in 1910 he addressed an advertising conference at Olympia, alongside Sir Thomas Dewar of whisky fame and Gordon Selfridge, whose own magnificent shop had also opened for business in 1909.[117] All speakers emphasised the importance of newspaper advertising. Gordon Selfridge's opinion was that "the best and surest results were to be obtained through the columns of widely circulated journals." He added, however that this medium did not produce results commensurate with the enormous number of newspapers printed and distributed. Papers, he thought, owed it to their advertising clients to help make the advertisements read. David concurred: the editors of newspapers should, he thought, publish articles explaining to the public why they should read advertised articles. In this he was ahead of Selfridge. For years, he had been paying for articles in British and Australian papers that promoted his brand and pointed readers to his paid advertisements elsewhere in the same paper. He also co-opted friendly journalists to interview him whenever he needed an outlet for his opinions, as he had done with his current pet project to federalise the British Empire.

He was always on these occasions able to inject references to his business success and by inference to his products and shops. The greater his fame the easier it became to find cheap or free publicity, it seemed.

Hints of Mortality, Changing Times

In 1911, at twenty-three, Percy was ready for his entry into the business. David had apprenticed him in the Regent Street store but now he gave him his first solo challenge; Percy was to become his representative in Australia. The young man landed in Sydney in the middle of the year[118] and, under the tutelage of MD, McWilliam, he acted as travelling ambassador for the firm, promoting Stewart Dawson's with newspaper interviews in the capital cities. His target audience was the fashionable and aspiring middle class women of Australia, so he courted the gossip columnists of popular journals. He talked a fine line, showing the confidence he had inherited from his father and exploiting the ever-present cultural cringe that saw superior value in all things British, with his evident broad knowledge of northern hemisphere jewellery trends, including the popularity of the lucky swastika emblem in brooches, necklaces and bracelets. It looked as if his father had found a worthy successor. As "Table Talk" wrote:

> *One learns a lot by a visit to an up-to-date jewellery establishment of this kind, especially from one who is thoroughly in touch with the latest ideas both in Europe and here as is Mr. Dawson.*

But though David was grooming Percy, it was not by any means as his immediate or even proximate successor. He was now 62 and at the peak of his success and fame. Percy's apprenticeship was to be a long one with no guarantee of promotion. In the meantime, David did need some form of insurance because his health was suffering from the prodigious workload he continued to impose upon himself. His complicated family life wasn't helping; daughter, Bertha had married Charles Royston Verrall in 1907[119] and within a year the marriage was over.[120] Verrall was a violent alcoholic, a "perpetual student" with no career nor any prospect of one. Bertha gave birth to a daughter, Joyce, in July 1908[121] but soon after left him. He had abandoned her and the child to live with another woman* and Bertha returned to the family home, now at Hyde Park Place.[122] It was in 1911 that David fell ill and withdrew from day to day business to recover. Harriet, now settled in London society and confidently in charge of domestic matters, took him to Monte Carlo for an extended convalescence in a warmer climate, where he spent several months in early 1912.[123] The couple were spotted at the Café de Paris with Zeb Lane, another gold mining friend, who was recovering from an abdominal operation. The years since their return from Australia had opened Harriet's eyes and heart to the glamour of Europe and already the Riviera felt like a second home. Her darling, Norman had been schooled in Paris and was now at Heidelberg University, living the life of a Student Prince. Though he showed little sign of academic prowess, he delighted his mother by excelling at sporting endeavours, something Percy could never claim. Monte Carlo was followed by a spell taking the waters at Wiesbaden, once more in the company of the dying Lane and old friend JC Williamson.[124] JC was also in poor health, suffering a heart condition that had forced his retirement from active theatre management.† It was a sobering occasion for David. JC was a mere four years older than he and Zeb was seven years his junior, and here were the three of them laid up together like so many sacks of oats. Well, he wasn't ready to throw in the towel, there was too much left to do and the lad who had braved the icy winds of Aberdeenshire had a lot more years left in him.‡ As soon as he could, he prevailed upon Harriet to let him return to London, no matter that she preferred to extend her sojourn another couple of months. In any case, he had plans for their financial future that could not be delayed whiling away the time with princes and playboys.

---

* Verrall descended to a life of crime, serving time for forgery, theft and conspiracy to swindle bookmakers.

† JC Williamson died in Paris in 1913 of heart failure.

‡ Whatever it was that laid David low, he seems never to have fully recovered his previous vigour, though his active life was by no means over and he would hold onto the reins of power until the very end.

Before he could act, he was confronted with the realities of a changing world. The death of Edward VII in 1910 marked the end of a continuous period of growth and prosperity for the United Kingdom, though few would have foreseen it at the time. Stewart Dawson's rode high, winning acclaim for their style and value. The Regent Street store had rapidly gained popularity with London's elite and The Treasure House could barely cope with the burgeoning Australasian trade. But change was coming, and an era was dawning where baubles for the well-off would take a back seat to more mundane and utilitarian objects and women would realise a new place in a society that valued them for more than their adornments.

While David had been building his London empire, he had paid little attention to matters of social justice, least of all, women's issues. But social unrest had reached breaking point by 1910, when a wave of strikes stunned the government. On 21st November 1911 the first mass window breaking took place, mainly of government offices but including a few shops. This had such an impact that the suffragettes decided to repeat it, this time concentrating on the most fashionable spots in the West End. On 1st March 1912, for the first time, they struck without warning: about 150 women were given hammers, told which windows to break, when to break them, and how to hit panes low so that glass would not fall from above. At 5.45 p.m. in Oxford Street, Regent Street, the Strand, and other prominent thoroughfares, well-dressed women produced hammers from handbags and began to smash windows.[125] Not all stores were targeted, one notable exclusion being Selfridges, where Gordon Selfridge had been one of the first owners to acknowledge the needs of women shoppers by installing rest rooms for their convenience. Stewart Dawson's, however, were not spared; most of their windows were smashed. David was unprepared and still unwell. Norman, now graduated from Heidelberg, was nominally in charge of the shop. The physical damage was repaired but the shop's reputation had suffered. Women did not need to be declared suffragettes to sympathise with the activists, and it would be many months before custom returned to former levels. David's "jewel in the crown" had been tainted and he never recovered his enthusiasm for it.

In November 1912, a curious family group sailed for Melbourne. David and 22-year-old Norman were accompanied by Bertha, her daughter Joyce and Harry Hoffman.[126] Harriet remained in Monte Carlo. Bertha's divorce from Charles Verrall was not final and would only become absolute the following year but upon arriving in Australia she and Harry were introduced as Mr and Mrs Hoffman, Joyce as their daughter. Here, once again, were all the hallmarks of David's need for control of the family image and his propensity for expedient deception. He had passed off Harriet as his wife for 26 years while keeping Margaret out of sight. Why not repeat the practice for Bertha and Harry?*

The group spent time in Melbourne before sailing for Sydney, arriving in January 1913. Interviewed by Sydney's Evening News, David stated that he was making the trip "purely for health-recruiting purposes,"[127] which was borne out by his subsequent progress and actions. He took the opportunity to visit his shops in both cities, checking Percy's progress and introducing Norman as a prospective second string to Percy in Sydney. Here, David joined the summer exodus of Sydney's elite to the Blue Mountains. On 26th January, they motored to Medlow Bath where they were guests of Mark Foy at the Hydro Majestic.[128] Foy had extended his hold on the property in 1903, when he prevailed upon New South Wales Railways to add "Bath" to the town's name. In 1904 he announced the Medlow Bath Hydropathic Establishment. Guests at the opening on July 4th, having motored to the mountains in a raging snowstorm, were greeted by the sight of the resort lit up by electricity. Foy had beaten the City of

---

* It's possible that Bertha and Harry had been conducting their own affair for some time, probably not long after Verrall's behaviour drove her away from him. Though Verrall did not contest the divorce, probably because he was serving 12 months hard labour in Wormwood Scrubs for drunkenness and false pretences, evidence was cited of his belief that Bertha was unfaithful to him. Was Harry a safe haven, source of solace and comfort for Bertha or even proof of Verrall's assertion? Regardless, he and Bertha were to all intents man and wife during their two year stay in Australia; but despite Bertha's becoming free in 1913 the relationship was never formalised, and they appear to have separated during the war years as Bertha reverted to her former married name after the war. She never remarried.

Sydney by four days in this momentous event. In the years since, the local stream having dried up and the foul taste of the imported spa water having lost its appeal, Foy abandoned the idea of a health spa in favour of a luxury resort for weekend and extended visits from the city, and its success was assured.

On the way, the party stopped at some of the growing communities along the Great Western Highway for refreshments and to refuel the vehicle. It was then that David was able to take in the attractions of Springwood, the first significant mountain settlement 50 miles from Sydney and no more than 90 minutes' travel by train.* It was already an established town with two comfortable hotels and a reputation for its ideal climate – cooler in summer than the sometimes steamy coastal plain but seldom as cold in winter as the higher parts of the Mountains. If he were to consider his health, maybe here was his future retreat. And his health was still a concern; David had to cut short his stay at the Hydro Majestic to return to Sydney for "a slight operation."[129] The surgery was minor and within a week he, Norman and the Hoffmans made a brief visit to Auckland.[130] There was always a need to show the flag at the local establishments and in this case, to expose Norman to the wider Stewart Dawson world, not that he showed any real inclination to play any sort of active role, to David's dismay and disappointment. By mid-March they were back in Sydney.[131] The Hoffmans returned to their holiday at the Hydro Majestic, where they had left little Joyce in the care of a nurse.[132] David remained at the Wentworth Hotel, catching up with many of his Australian friends. A week later the working holiday was over. The party left Sydney on the Orama on 9th April, bound for London.[133]

The 1906 purchase and development of 19-21 Hatton Garden was proving more astute than he might have foreseen. At a time when London residential property prices were stable if not declining in real terms due to the steady release of suburban land, developed urban areas such as the West End were holding value along with the still buoyant economy. His purchase was protecting his capital as well as paying dividends in operating efficiencies. The Australian market was

---

* Travel time by rail from Sydney to Springwood is only ten minutes less today than it was in 1900.

similarly skewed toward commercial property. Now was the time to act. Back in London, where he had been joined by Percy, he made his move. Having leased the shops on Swanston and Collins Streets and redeveloped them in 1907, he had now persuaded the Howey estate trustees to sell. Though he could have delegated the task of consummating the deal to his Melbourne manager and saved himself five months of travel, David elected to return to Australia for the final negotiations and contract signing. He took Percy back to Melbourne in December 1913 and within a month the sale was complete; Stewart Dawson & Co acquired the property for £90,000, a near record for the city but almost pocket money for David.[134] The deal done, he was back in London by April, leaving Percy to mind the shop.

Harriet was still relaxing on the Riviera. She was in no hurry to return to London and Australia was the last place on her mind. Norman had joined her on his return and then gone on to St Moritz, where he competed in the "Ragtime Cup" bobsleigh event on the famous Cresta Run, crashing, and sustaining minor injuries.[135] Newspapers reported:

> *it is the custom of the superintendent of Stewart Dawson's Regent Street branch to visit St Moritz every year about this time. Last year he won practically all the prizes for bob-sleighing.*[136]

If Percy was the budding executive, Norman was the apprentice playboy.

It was to be Norman and Harriet's last taste of continental hedonism for five years. On 28th June 1914 Archduke Franz Ferdinand of Austria was assassinated in Sarajevo, precipitating Austria-Hungary's declaration of war on Serbia and the start of World War 1.

~/~/~

A Tangled Web

David made his way briskly to the upper deck of the liner. The shimmering surface of the sea triggered memories of another voyage, when he had taken the first leap into an unknown land, hopes high for his future. For a moment, he imagined himself again at thirty-four, no more than half his age, full of ambition and brimming with confidence. He recalled the confused emotions of his younger self, the frustration over his complicated personal life and the dumb intransigence of his benighted wife. What was Margaret up to these days? He'd lost touch with her since she had left the expensive townhouse he kept for her in London. Down on the south coast, he'd heard, in the care of Vanna and her husband. So much the better for everyone, really; he had more than enough on his plate and re-hashing past embarrassments was the last thing he needed.

Speaking of tangled personal lives, Annie would be joining him soon on deck. Annie, Valerie, he'd have to remember the new name. More to the point, so must she, if they were to carry this off once ashore in Sydney; there was too much at stake. It had been a close-run affair but, now that he considered it, leaving England could not have come at a better time. In truth, he probably would have made the decision regardless of the compelling personal circumstances. Another year of confinement in London, more months of trudging to and from Hatton Garden in the damp and cold, more tedious "at homes" for officers back from the front, playing the host while Harriet swooped and dazzled, bless her, would have been more than he could bear.

His reverie was interrupted by a hand on his shoulder. He turned to see Valerie beside him, clutching her hat against the breeze. All thoughts of the mess he had created vanished at the sight of her fresh young face. He offered his arm to promenade around the deck. Passengers circulating towards them or seated in deck chairs nodded and smiled at the handsome couple: he with his distinguished white hair and moustache, his healthy, bronzed complexion and upright bearing; she in her elegant sun-dress, her thick, auburn hair framing a heart-shaped face. More than one male risked a second glance at those full lips, and the dreaming blue-grey eyes.[137] As they walked, he spoke again of the delights that awaited them in Australia, conjuring up visions of limitless space, golden opportunities for living life to the full, wealth unencumbered by old social mores, and a future for Valerie and the child. The frustrations of the war years faded with his every word.

From almost the beginning of the war, David had had to accept that travel to Australia was out of the question for the duration. Within weeks of the declaration, German ships began laying mines in the North Sea and threatened shipping lanes in the English Channel. The Royal Navy was quick to respond, laying its own minefields to deter German commerce raiders, but though transatlantic traffic was soon back to almost pre-war levels the long journey to Australia was more hazardous. This was particularly true in the southern oceans, where armed merchant cruisers and High Seas Fleet vessels such as the notorious Emden roamed. Prudence dictated, and Harriet urged that David remain in London. Initially, there was plenty to keep him occupied, the telegraph lines busy with messages to and from Melbourne, Auckland, Perth, and the other cities of his empire, and very soon the regular business of raising funds to support the troops and their ancillaries. Since the beginning of the century, Stewart Dawson's had been a prominent player in charitable support of war efforts, when nurses and Australian troops fighting in the South African war had benefited from large donations. Once the confusion and false optimism of the opening months of the Great War had faded, and casualties began to rise, a corps of volunteers from all walks of life arose to contribute in cash to funds established by prominent persons, titled dignitaries, and royalty itself. Stewart Dawson's first contributions were as early as September 1914, to The Prince's Fund, the Prince being the heir to the throne.

Norman volunteered for military service soon after the declaration of war and in September was commissioned as 2nd Lieutenant in the 5th Hussars,* but by March the following year he'd transferred to the

---

* Or so says his RNAS military record. In 1914 there was no "5th Hussars"; the regiment had been renamed the 5th Royal Irish Lancers in 1861. Based at Woolwich, it would have been convenient for London-based Norman.

newly formed Royal Naval Air Service, where he was commissioned with the equivalent Naval rank of Sub-Lieutenant. On 17th September 1915, he was awarded his flying certificate and joined active service.[138] His squadron served in East Africa in operations against the Imperial German Army and on 30th May 1916 he earned the Distinguished Service Cross for evading capture after being forced down 40 miles inside enemy territory while on a reconnaissance mission.[139] He had made his way through dense bush, carrying vital equipment salvaged from the downed aircraft and navigating instinctively towards his base. He was not a well man, having contracted malaria in this inhospitable territory, so his efforts were even more remarkable. Repatriated to the homeland to recover, he was now serving the rest of the war in England, from where he flew reconnaissance patrols, earning respect for his flying abilities and initiative. He was considered: "a good pilot with plenty of dash, but not much judgement at present, and is apt to be too self-assertive." His military record included a note that he absented himself from a training course on the grounds of illness (he suffered repeated bouts of malaria once back home) but was seen by one of his superiors in London on the day in question. Norman's casual deception would become second nature to him in his private life, where the line between truth and fiction blurred time and again to suit his purposes.

Harriet was milking every moment of her new-found role as society hostess for officers on leave from the front. She opened their Park Lane apartment for teas and soirées and was starting to acquire a reputation for charitable fund raising in her own right.[140] Stewart Dawson's business was still strong, thanks to the booming market in patriotic trinkets and keepsakes. Every soldier's sweetheart had to have a brooch, pendant or ring to remind them of their boy fighting in the trenches. In Australia boomerang-shaped letter openers and kangaroo handles on ashtrays had revitalised the silverware line. Most importantly, the War boosted sales of wristwatches as they became standard service issue for all branches of the military.[141] The idea that a man would wear what was considered a women's item of jewellery on a bracelet rather than pluck a handsome pocket watch from his vest had for many years deterred manufacturers from serious efforts to broaden the market. But first with the Boer War and now, as trenches stretched along the western front, the call went up for change. Officers leading their men over the top, pistol in one hand and whistle in the other, and trying to time their advance to the second, risked their lives stopping to fumble for and open cumbersome timepieces that were easily lost in the mud. Manufacturers such as Patek Phillipe had pioneered the miniature wristlet watch with its robust screw-on back and hardened glass and soon every watchmaker offered a "military" or "trench" wristlet watch. Stewart Dawson's, ever alert to trends, stocked a large range of "ANZAC Lever Watches" and their advertisements boasted the practical and patriotic advantages of this modern necessity "for the man on active service".

David spent much of his time in his office at The Treasure House overseeing the transition to more local manufacturing in Australia since exports from England were restricted by enemy submarine activity. However, he had little face to face contact with his managers. Though he fulfilled his duty to Harriet in her fundraising activities and gave generously from his own pocket he was for the most part at a loose end and about to lose his heart again. As the war progressed, The Treasure House hosted fewer visiting Australians and New Zealanders. The spacious lounge was almost empty, the writing desks dusted daily but unused. Many of the younger male employees volunteered for military service, as Norman had done, or were conscripted. Those remaining, the older, more experienced workers, continued to occupy their workbenches on the third floor but now it was the women who took on the administrative duties that sustained the business. David's days in town saw him wandering the floors, encouraging the staff, making polite enquiries about the orders they were processing, or appraising the products on display in the workroom or the show room.

On his patrols, his eye was drawn to two young stenographers. The McFarlane sisters, Maggie and Annie, had been with the firm since the opening, a good eight years now.[142] He'd not had cause to deal directly with them, relying on his personal secretary for his own correspondence, but now that they had taken on more responsibility, he found excuses to engage them in conversation, sharing news of the efforts to sustain the business in these troubled times. The girls, at first awed by the attentions of the head of the firm, were soon exchanging pleasantries and volunteering details of their family background in response to his gentle probing. He employed all his charm as he learned of their Scottish origins, something of a surprise despite their name. Though born in Dundee, they had lived most of their lives in London and retained no more than a trace of an accent.* Their father, Tom, a former mariner, was now lock gate keeper on the Thames at Rotherhithe, in the East End, and the family lived in a modest house in nearby Bermondsey. The girls had a good upbringing and a sound education, readily finding employment. To have secured and maintained positions in this prestigious establishment for so long was a credit to their abilities and a feather in the cap of their proud parents.

The friendly chats between the silver-haired patriarch and the bright young women might have continued in this way, a diversion for David and an interlude of privilege for the girls but, in 1915 Maggie, the elder at 27, announced her forthcoming marriage[143] and as was the norm, resigned her employment. Twenty-five-year old Annie was now the focus of David's daily visits. He paid her compliments, offered to show her the new items fresh from the workroom, entertained her with stories of his adventures and conquests in Australia, until the day he invited her into his private office on a pretext. It seemed natural and proper that she should accompany him but, once behind the closed oak-panelled door his intentions were clear. He blushed now as he recalled the moment when he was transported back to the heady days in Liverpool, with Jennie, Fanny, and young Harriet. In an instant, the years fell away, and he was once more the dark-haired young blade, sweeping all before him. As for Annie, how could she refuse? Thinking back on it, David mused that, while she was not exactly "on the shelf" the dearth of eligible men due to the war had left her with fewer opportunities to enjoy the company of the opposite sex. At the same time, and perhaps because of the War and all this feminist business, women were becoming bolder and more independent, not to say, assertive; look at Harriet, for instance. It was easy for him to reason that Annie

---

* Maggie's granddaughter recalls her grandmother's accent as *"refined English, with perhaps the trace of a lilt."* Two years younger, Annie could probably have passed for native-born Londoner.

knew what she wanted and what she was about to do. This would be a brief fling that would rejuvenate him and, he was confident, give the young woman what the French called a "sentimental education". What harm was there in it for either of them?

How wrong he had been! No more than weeks after their first passionate encounter, Annie took him aside to break the news to him: she was expecting a child. David's consternation was profound; he, the master philanderer had managed several simultaneous affairs in his younger days without this unfortunate consequence. But then, he had to remind himself, his youthful encounters had almost all been with "experienced" women able and willing to take the necessary precautions. Annie was by comparison an innocent and David had grown careless. What to do? There was no question of denial, Annie would have to reveal and explain her condition to her parents sooner or later and, in any case, David was no cad; he would never stoop to paying her off and burying the consequences. He applied his own maxim: "The great follow up is alertness of brain, steadiness of nerve, and courage.",* accepted his responsibility and initiated another plan of action, face-saving and deception. First, he informed her parents and took full responsibility for their daughter's welfare, assuring them that they would not only be protected from gossip and calumny, but would be generously compensated. He urged them not to blame Annie, while guaranteeing the welfare and care of the child. The meeting with Tom and Annie Senior, upright Presbyterians as they were, was one of David's great challenges, calling upon all his practised charm and persuasion and, for the first time in many years, a dose of genuine humility, but though they were left with no firm plan for Annie's future they were assured all would be well.

Next, he had to confront Harriet. It was inevitable that she would find out, her grapevine was extensive, so it was important for him to take the initiative with her. She was no Margaret, submitting to his will, accommodating his erratic and imperious behaviour. She had come a long way from the Liverpool pub and worked hard to establish her society credentials, too far to risk harm to her reputation. David

* One of David's many maxims, quoted in "The Boy and the Wheelbarrow, 1858, the Man and The Ambassadors, 1924".

accepted that to an extent he was at her mercy, so she could set the terms that preserved her status quo. While Harriet remained "at home" in Park Lane he moved with Annie into a luxurious apartment at 41 St James Place on the edge of Green Park, no more than half a mile from Buckingham Palace.[144] Frederic Chopin had stayed in the house opposite and Winston Churchill was in residence a few doors away. Here Annie could reside incognito. A plausible story was concocted to explain her sudden disappearance from The Treasure House and from her home in Bermondsey. David's final step to sever all ties with Annie's past was to give her a new identity befitting her pre-maternal status; she was now Mrs Valerie Allison.

On December 14th, 1915, David and Annie's daughter was born.[145] They named her Estelle. Annie registered the birth in her new name and gave the father's name as "David Allison", occupation: jeweller. No questions were asked or checking performed on the veracity of the information. The absent "David Allison" could well have been one of the tens of thousands of men killed in the war. Now all they had to do was extricate themselves from the impending complexities and embarrassments of the London scene; simple, really, if you were David Stewart Dawson. Even simpler if Harriet were to have a hand in the arrangements.

In January 1916, less than a month after Estelle's birth, David placed an advertisement in "The Scotsman"[146] and other newspapers: "Jewellery business: Exceptional Opportunity." Management and effective ownership of the Regent Street branch was on offer to "competent men who have already shown initiative in the jewellery business." He continued: "My health necessitates living abroad, hence this opportunity." For the time being he would retain control of The Treasure House but, after just seven years, he was quitting retail in England.

This was no more than a ruse. David's health wasn't what it had been, but he was still capable of running the business, as evidenced by his retention of control over The Treasure House. In any case, he already had a manager for the Regent Street shop, just as he did for all the Australian and New Zealand outlets. Gone were the days, in fact there never had been a day when David stood behind a counter or occupied a managerial office in a shop. To his relief, Harriet had put her foot down and insisted on remaining in London regardless of his intentions. She had lived there without interruption for twelve years, her portrait had been hung at the Royal Academy, she holidayed on the Riviera and hosted the cream of London society at the Park Lane townhouse. She was also a tireless and high-profile voluntary worker at the Aldwych theatre, the London headquarters of the Australian Y.M.C.A.[147] She was in no mood to surrender this life. On the other hand, David's nostalgia for Australia had increased during his enforced absence. Despite the success and fame he had achieved in London he accepted that, at the age of 66, his best was past and that it would become increasingly difficult for him to compete in this cosmopolitan market. In Australia, he would still be lionised and when the time came, he could retire or at least withdraw from active leadership to enjoy the benign climate and indulge his mistress without fear of disapprobation. It would mean separation from Harriet, but he'd burned a few boats thanks to his dalliance with Valerie and they already led their own lives for the most part. He could no longer maintain the pretence of enjoying the social whirl that consumed her day and night. If she was leaving him behind in that sphere, he reasoned, good luck to her. She was also offering him a way out of his folly that preserved both their reputations.

While the handover of Regent Street was in progress, he arranged his other affairs. Valerie and Estelle were moved out of town to Hove, near Brighton on the south coast.[148] He decided not to abandon Valerie's parents or merely pay them off. They would become part of his extended and ever more complex family. David recalled the uncomfortable conversation with Tom when he spelled out the choices ahead for them. It came down to what was best for Valerie and the child and, as far as David could see, the solution was a complete break with the past and the start of a new life in Australia. The problem was, though his own passion for the antipodean life was unquenchable and made more urgent by the current circumstances, he was asking Tom and Annie senior to take a leap into the unknown. He took it for granted that Valerie shared his enthusiasm, though now he thought about it, he conceded that he might have relied on her youthful naivety and pliability somewhat. But her parents were not starry-eyed. Tom's job at the Rotherhithe lock was assured and they were settled in their middle years. What guarantee was there of gainful or worthwhile employment for him in far off Sydney? What about their ties to family in England? Older daughter Maggie had moved north upon her marriage but was still within a day's train journey. If Annie (they could not accept their daughter's assumed name) were to sail off to the other side of the world they would soon lose touch. All the more reason, David interjected, to accompany her and enjoy seeing their granddaughter grow up in the new world. And he remembered assuring Tom that he need have no worries about his financial future. On the contrary, he could live the life of a country squire with never a moment's concern for income, rent or any other expense; David would take care of everything. It was an offer too good to refuse, though he knew that Maggie's opinion was that if it was a matter of the family's welfare, David might just as well afford to keep them all together here at home. After all, he had his own family to think about. Why break up both the McFarlanes and the Stewart Dawsons with this selfish indulgence? Annoying as this was, David was not for turning, and with Valerie as his ally, he prevailed with Tom.

By the end of the year all plans were in place. It was time to leave with his new family.* On November 26th, 1916, David and Valerie sailed from Liverpool for New York on the SS St Louis, a US-registered ship capable of steaming at a handy 20 knots, well beyond the reach of any submarine that might still have been tempted to attack. They travelled first class. In second class were Tom and Annie senior, baby Estelle and a nurse, Lucy Nelson.[149] They arrived in New York on December 3rd. Valerie and the family stepped ashore in the famous city, eyes wide at the sight of the skyline of tall buildings, so unlike any seen before. Here was a golden opportunity for him to impress them with his cosmopolitan knowledge. Instead, he felt flat

---

* Oceanic travel was less hazardous from September 18th, 1915, when Germany halted the campaign of unrestricted submarine warfare after the US, then neutral, threatened to suspend diplomatic relations. From that date until February 1st, 1917, when the German High Command resumed its campaign to starve Great Britain by sinking without warning any merchant ship in the surrounding waters, fast passenger liners on the transatlantic run could sail with relative confidence of a safe voyage.

and uninspired. The past months must have taken more out of him than he'd bargained for. Over the next few days, while they waited for the train to carry them across the continent, the family took in the sights of Manhattan, the famous park, the ridiculously tall skyscrapers, and the colossal Statue of Liberty out in the bay. David escorted them while nursing his growing unease. He couldn't put his finger on it but gradually his irritation and resentment crystallised. For perhaps the first time in his life he sensed regret. What had he given up for the sake of this bold gesture? Had he been too hasty in handing over Regent Street? Was this a sign of things to come, when he would cede primacy to younger, more energetic rivals?

But it wasn't as simple as that. Now that he stood on the busy New York street, taking in the glittering shop-fronts decorated for the Christmas season, and the lobbies of luxurious hotels, the antipathy towards all things American that he had harboured since the Toronto fiasco, his sole failure in all these years, rose to the surface. He'd been here once before, in 1901, when the family returned to Sydney, but that was at the height of his business success, when he had conquered Australia and had Hatton Garden in his sights.[150] In the meantime, American commerce had boomed, as many saw it, at the expense of Britain and the Europeans. David's strong free-trade beliefs were offended by American imposition of heavy tariffs and blatant disdain for hard-won intellectual property rights. Now they were sitting out the war as Europe bled and the British Empire groaned under the burden of endless conflict. The evidence was all around of what he could only characterise as taking advantage of others' misfortunes while copying the best of their ideas with impunity. Perhaps it was because his recent folly left him feeling vulnerable or maybe the years had simply caught up with him, but he needed to vent his ill-temper. While the McFarlanes enjoyed his hospitality and the best that New York could offer in food, drink, and entertainments, he retired to his hotel room to commit his thoughts to paper. Even as the family took the cross-continental train to San Francisco, and thence onward to Hawaii, he brooded in silence. By the time the SS Sierra docked in Honolulu, he was ready to deliver his message to America. The journalist whom he contacted at The Honolulu Star Bulletin was unprepared for what landed on his desk but had no hesitation in publishing it on January 20th.[151] Titled: "How Stands United States of America?" the sub-headline of the article read:

Noted merchant of London and Australia gives frank view of Uncle Sam's country, people and business, as he sees them – some disappointments noted.

This was a gross understatement of the splenetic and pompous diatribe recorded over three columns. All of David's long-held resentment of America and its business practices was on display. He railed against the flagrant disregard of copyright and patent protection, the imposition of extreme tariff barriers and the pursuit of profit at the expense of quality and good taste. Little escaped his wrath: department stores, skyscrapers, restaurant décor, were all excoriated.* America, in his view, was:

That land of vaunted progress, where passing events have proved that hereditary blood does not fill the adage of being thicker than water, and where the soul of all that should count as representing the highest instincts of humanity seemingly has stood for nothing …

Claiming that "perhaps I arrived in New York with too high expectations," he continued:

… It is perfectly apparent to me … that the United States has been the great expert assembling emporium in getting together and using the pick of all the valuable unprotected ideas of the world … Therefore today in America the prevailing condition throughout industry is that invariably every person appears to be working on a copy – eternal copy – always copy …

Architecture and the skyscraper were his next targets:

[when] only buildings that will pay dividends, although devoid of art and character, are asked for, the soulless skyscraper is the sequel … They are all practically alike … These skyscrapers in a sense proclaim the stereotyped spirit of the country …

---

* His comments would have found an echo in present-day American criticism of China.

Hotels, restaurants, and department stores were not exempted from criticism, as he compared them unfavourably with their European counterparts:

The restaurant decorations, even in some of the newest of them, form spectacles of dismay. Anyone who has visited our "Carlton", London, can picture its appearance by changing its ivory white and gold, Adam's decoration, into chocolate brown and placing overhead extremely heavy copper-colored electroliers, which to add to the tragedy are only faintly lighted during dinner …

… The department store in America taking its best points offers attractive merchandise and service, but there is nothing novel or wonderful in its environment …

Returning to his theme of protectionism versus free trade, he concluded:

If Great Britain has remained mildly insane in her free-trade policy … America tops the list in reckless protective insanity, she pampers her capitalists, stuffs their banking accounts, pads her industrial artisans with tariff, in plain words announcing to all the world, that without this padding her artisans' competitive ability is such that they could not survive in the stress of personal effort.

He reserved his final criticism for the jewellery trade, disdaining what he saw as the abandonment of quality in pursuit of profit:

… on the whole the country is poorly represented in the jewellery line. The production of jewellery and silverware is limited in character and in the class of goods produced, their diamonds and gem set articles are mostly copies of Parisian and Continental productions. The shop windows and shop interiors present a meagre soulless expression, and reveal an entire absence of any artistic ability in displaying their wares … Even the best shops are all fitted up in the so much per yard style of abiding dreary sameness …

He concluded on a personal note:

The modern distractions of big cities like New York, Chicago and London in my way of thinking destroy the concerted purpose and continuity of youth, no getting along in an original way. I therefore admit I had a great natural advantage. The invigorating, peaceful bracing air of the heather hills of Scotland enforced me with that kind of vigor and enthusiasm that make study and work a recreation and lift a man lightly over many every-day difficulties. Life on a farm lays a foundation entirely different to that over-shadowed by the glare and hustle of electrically lighted big city streets.

In this he revealed his profound resentment of the unfair advantages, as he saw them, bestowed on formally educated men. In his world, "self-made" meant what it said. There was no substitute for hard work and hands-on experience. No amount of book-learning could prepare a man for the competitive world of commerce. On the contrary, formal education suffocated creativity and imagination. As he reflected on this now, he conceded that he might have gone a bit overboard and confused or diffused the message he wished to convey to the Americans, but he was glad all the same to have got it off his chest. He wondered what American readers would make of the article, but in the end, he no longer cared. They could think what they liked, he had a record second to none and a fresh start to life ahead of him. New Zealand was no more than a week away over the horizon and after that, the shores of the land of plenty where he could spend his remaining years indulging his extended family, watching his daughter grow. He took another opportunity to describe the beauty of the promised land to Valerie. Though she'd heard it many times before, he never tired of embellishing his memories of the landscape, the welcoming people, and the benign climate. What kind of life lay ahead for Valerie he knew not, but he was certain it would bring out the best in her and earn her eternal gratitude and friendship.

The Fatal Shore

Once ashore in Auckland, despite his relief at being on familiar soil, or perhaps because being back in Imperial territory reminded him of his recent observations, David's agitation revived, and he gave another copy of his "How stands America?" opinion piece to "The Dominion", which was delighted to print this example of pro-imperial polemic.[152] The newspaper also dutifully reported in its social column that Mr Stewart Dawson, in the country to inspect all his shops, was accompanied by his daughter, for that was how he had decided to explain his relationship to Valerie.[153] Tom's objections to David's appropriation of his flesh and blood were overridden with assurances that this was no more than a ruse for convenience in public outings. Of course, Tom was still her father! He just had to be discreet about it. Tom could as easily argue that it was David who had to practise discretion. Having previously introduced his real daughter, Bertha, and her siblings to Australian society it would seem odd now to produce another long-lost daughter, wouldn't it? Not to mention that he had two sons still in Sydney, whose reaction to the new "married sister" could not be predicted. Why complicate matters unnecessarily and incidentally relegate the real parents to irrelevant obscurity? Maintain the fiction of the late "David Allison" to explain little Estelle's existence, but why couldn't he introduce the McFarlanes as the real family they were, all three generations and "long-time" friends from the old country? David shrugged off Tom's concerns; it was a little late to tell that story now that the newspapers had hold of the Stewart Dawson version. His real motive, unspoken by any of them, was his unchaperoned escorting of Valerie out and about, in public and to the hotels of his choice.

The stay in New Zealand was brief before the party landed in Melbourne in March 1917. David was looking forward to seeing Percy and Stuart after five years of forced separation. Percy had made a name for himself overseeing the Australian business. Stuart, at twenty-four, was somewhat of an enigma; David had no idea what the young man wanted to make of his life. He showed no inclination to follow his older brother into the business, preferring to spend his time in not always desirable company at the racetrack and in dubious city establishments, if rumours were to be believed. Until a few months ago, neither of them had followed Norman's example and volunteered for the armed services. Considering the appalling casualty lists now filling daily newspaper columns, David could understand their reticence until he had learned out of the blue that Percy was about to leave to join an Australian regiment in England, bound for the western front. Not only that, but he was also getting married.

In October 1916, just as David was completing preparations to leave England, Percy had made his patriotic contribution when he enlisted in the 8th Field Artillery Brigade, 3rd Division AIF.[154] His departure date for Europe had been uncertain but David was confident he would see his son once again in Sydney to give his blessing. Now it seemed that Percy was leaving for the front a married man, without waiting for his father's attendance at the wedding. On March 21st, 1917, three weeks before he left for England, he married Thelma Bell Morton at St Stephens Church in Sydney. They honeymooned at the Hydro Majestic. Thelma Raye, as she was known, was a sultry actress whom Percy had met in 1915 when JC Williamson brought her to Australia. In 1913, while in England, she had given birth to daughter, Dawn Beatrice Mary. By the time that Percy met her, Thelma had chosen to legitimise Dawn by presenting her as the child of a previous marriage. How he came to marry Thelma was a mystery. Unlike his two younger brothers, Percy was unprepossessing in appearance, at 5′ 5½″ tall, 121lbs and with a chest measurement of less than 34″. But he did have a lot of money and more than a little charm, thanks to his public relations efforts with Australian gossip columnists.

> *Those who have eyes to see,* wrote "Celia", in her "Ladies' Letter" in Melbourne's "Table Talk", *were not much surprised at the news of Thelma Raye's marriage to Percy Dawson, one of the young sons of the well-known Stewart Dawson family. He has squired her about for a long time past, and recently folks have wondered who was the young soldier who has been with her everywhere. He looks so very boyish in his khaki: it seems to have had the effect of knocking several years off*

> *his age. He is a nice boy and popular. … [Thelma's] second marriage was very quietly celebrated in Sydney, where the bridegroom was having his final leave before departing for the front. During his absence the bride will retain her position with the Tivoli Follies. Afterwards – well, their plans "lie in the lap of the gods."*

David, had he known, would have cut short his stay in New Zealand to attend the wedding. His disappointment mingled with irritation and anger when gossip reached him that he might be perceived to have slighted Percy and Thelma by his failure to grace the ceremony. Brisbane's "Truth" reported snippily, "The Stewart Dawson family were conspicuously absent."[155] As it was, he had the briefest opportunity to meet the bride and groom in Sydney before Percy's departure.

At first it was easy to keep the McFarlanes occupied in and around Sydney. They visited the Zoo[156] and the Royal Botanical Gardens[157] and enjoyed ferry trips across the harbour to Manly. The city itself was exciting and Tom found much to interest his critical eye at the harbourside. They stayed variously at the Carlton[158] and Ushers Hotels and there were plenty of shops to divert the women, especially when David was footing the bill and owned one of the most prestigious. There were also the now obligatory trips to the Blue Mountains. It was on one of these that David's plans for the family began to take form. Despite the arrangements he had agreed with her he knew there could come a day when Harriet would return to claim her place, though in 1917 with no end in sight for the war and the U-boats back on patrol she was still established at Park Lane. There was no question of Valerie supplanting Harriet to become the next Mrs Stewart Dawson, but David was still infatuated with her and beset with enough guilt to oblige him to provide long term support for her, Estelle, and her parents. For the time being he needed to be in the city during the week, but why not find a home for them out of town yet within easy reach for weekend visits? Moreover, Harriet was an urbanite never more at home than in high society gatherings. Should she return to Australia she would crave the world of charity balls and vice-regal receptions that only Sydney residence could offer. Separation of his love interests sounded like the perfect answer to his dilemma: he would be back in control.

It was while he mulled over the possibilities that the news arrived from England in June of the death of Margaret.[159] She had been living with Vanna and Gus Jerrard at Mudeford, in Hampshire on the south coast. The Jerrards had a family connection with the locality and "Haven Cottage" had been Gus' home. This could change everything: David was now officially free to marry again. If indeed he was tempted it was only for a moment; Valerie was "out" as his daughter and as far as the world knew Harriet had been his legal wife for over thirty years, even if she had been off the Australian scene for half that time. His plan to establish Harriet in the city and Valerie in the mountains had to stand.

He needed somewhere close enough to Sydney to minimise his journey time but also within reach of his favourite watering hole at the Hydro Majestic. Springwood fit the bill, an hour and a half by train from Sydney Central and less than an hour from Medlow Bath, with spectacular Katoomba in between. There was good cheap land to be had right outside the township with views all the way to the coast on a clear day. He had no shortage of advice from his new acquaintance, Hugh McIntosh. Hugh Donald McIntosh, nicknamed "Huge Deal", was at the time the most successful promoter of theatrical and sporting events in Australia's short history.[160] Born in Sydney's inner suburb of Surry Hills in 1876, he was a self-made man, like David. After hustling his way around the country, at the age of 23 he took over Thomas Helmore's catering company, supplying pies to racetracks and prize-fights from the Masonic Hall, North Sydney, where he lived; here he also ran a physical-culture club and managed a few boxers. In 1908, "Mack", as his friends called him, made a fortune staging a bout between world heavyweight boxing champion Tommy Burns and Australian Bill Squires. In August 1912 he bought Harry Rickards' Australasia-wide Tivoli circuit. It was as the owner of this chain of vaudeville theatres that he staged performances by the JC Williamson Company, including "The Marriage Market" in 1915, that saw Thelma's first appearance on the Australian stage.[161] When Thelma and Percy married it was Mack who gave the bride away,[162] and it was through Percy that David was introduced to the brash promoter.

Mack had long been friends of the artists, Lionel, and Norman Lindsay, enthusiastically promoting their work in Australia and Europe. When Norman fell ill (tuberculosis was suspected), his model and wife, Rose, found a cottage in the upper Blue Mountains at Leura, then another lower down at Faulconbridge, after which they bought the house at Springwood, formerly owned by Mark Foy's brother, Francis, that became their permanent home.[163] Mack was a frequent visitor and would have had no difficulty persuading David of the health and scenic benefits of this potential country hideaway.

On February 21st, 1918, David purchased two adjacent lots totalling over 13 acres on Hawkesbury Road, less than a mile from Springwood village centre and a similar distance from Lindsay's home across the rolling fields to the west. The land, bought from Francis Poke Ryland, was undeveloped. Hawkesbury Road is one of only two arterial roads running generally north along one of the many ridges joined to the spine of the Great Western Highway. It descends from Springwood for six miles before winding down the escarpment at Hawkesbury Heights to the plain of the Nepean River and thence to the Macquarie towns of Richmond and Castlereagh. In 1918 there were scattered dairy farms and orchards and even a nine-hole golf course on the west side of the road, but the east side, especially nearer to Springwood where David bought, was too steep and incised with gullies to offer much for the farmer or horticulturist. What it did have were excellent views over the forested slopes and enough level land adjacent to the road for building residential properties. This was to be the future home of the McFarlanes and David's first venture in domestic building. However, David didn't acquire the land in his own name; the transfer was from Francis Poke Ryland to "Valerie Allison of Springwood, Widow."[164] He was making a gift of thirteen acres of prime building land to Valerie.

She was indeed already "of Springwood" because in late 1917 David found accommodation for the McFarlanes, Valerie, Estelle, and the nurse no more than half a mile from the railway station. "Warrah" was an early 20th century Federation style bungalow then used as a guest house. Its shaded verandas and wooden construction were a novelty for the erstwhile Londoners, and they were sufficiently impressed to send a picture postcard of their new residence to sister Maggie in England.*

It was while the family settled in to Warrah that an illuminating incident occurred that resulted in David's appearance in court.[165] He spent his weekdays in Sydney, escaping via the Friday afternoon train to the mountains. He would enjoy weekends with Valerie at the Hydro Majestic, collecting her on the way as the train stopped in Springwood. On Friday 15th February, just a week before he completed the land purchase, he arrived at Medlow Bath railway station across the road from the Hydro, accompanied by Valerie with Estelle and Lucy, the nurse.† He was looking forward to another two days luxuriating with his lover in a closed community where few questions were asked, for the Hydro had for years been favoured by gentlemen seeking privacy for their illicit liaisons. As the porter unloaded their luggage the night officer, a Mr Vincent, observed that the luggage exceeded the allowed weight for a first-class carriage and that there was an item for which insufficient freight had been paid, namely, a perambulator. In his evidence before the court, Vincent stated:

> *I asked Mr Dawson for 5/7 extra freight for luggage, and 5/- for the perambulator. Mr Dawson objected and said to me, "You 'sanguinary' swank, you d----- insolent cur." He repeated these words within the hearing of witnesses.*

Francis Donohoe, the porter, corroborated Vincent's evidence, adding that David had been very angry at being detained. Two other independent witnesses, a waiter, and a domestic servant, agreed with Donohoe. David of course denied being the aggressor. This was the first time, he testified, he had been summoned to court. He arrived from Sydney with his daughter and nurse. When the night officer

---

* Warrah exists today, now a veterinary surgery sheltered behind tall trees on one of Springwood's busier roads.

† Perhaps they were there to celebrate the impending property acquisition, or maybe it was just another weekend of dalliance for the couple with Lucy as "chaperone".

questioned his luggage, which had been passed in Sydney, he referred to it as "a bit of a d-----d swank." He claimed the night officer was offensive in both manner and language. Until then the case might have gone either way, but poor Vincent hadn't a chance when Valerie and then Lucy were called to the stand.

Valerie Allison (daughter) also swore her father never used the words, at least, "she never heard Pa make use of them." Lucy Nelson (nurse) said ditto. She was there when the goods were weighed, but never heard Mr Dawson say the naughty words.

The conclusion was inevitable:

Mr McIntosh (counsel) made a lengthy address to the bench which, boiled down, was to the effect that the railway official (who is a man of high repute) and all his witnesses lied damnably and that Mr Dawson and his domestic group were paragons of propriety and Washingtonians of the first water. It went well and, after a little homily, the PM (magistrate) dismissed the case. On the decision being voiced, Mr Dawson excitedly shook the hand of his solicitor and enthusiastically patted him on the back, evidently in appreciation and admiration of the capital fight he had made.*

David was never quite sure what Valerie made of this distasteful affair. To be sure, she'd played her part well (he loved "at least, I never heard Pa make use of them."), but she had seen the blunter side of his personality. No matter that the blessed Vincent fellow had been made to look a fool and a liar, that came with the job; he, David, had been caught off guard. He'd lost control for a precious moment when he should have brushed the man aside and left. It had spoiled the start of what should have been a happy weekend together celebrating the land purchase, a case of bad timing at best, a weakening of his authority at worst.†

---

* After the Washington Temperance Movement i.e. paragons of sobriety and good behaviour.

† What was most likely to have been the cause of the incident is that Valerie or Lucy had overlooked paying for the perambulator when loading it onto the train at Springwood.

Once the Hawkesbury Road land purchase was complete David wasted no time in commissioning his own houses, for there were to be more than one on Valerie's property. First up was a weatherboard cottage of three bedrooms and generous living areas located near the eastern end of the property line, down the hill, where the land levelled out somewhat. Though it boasted a veranda like Warrah's that wrapped partly around the house, it substituted a more expensive terracotta tiled roof for the corrugated iron one of Warrah. The house, named "Bonnie Doon", was completed in less than six months. The second house was bigger and more lavishly finished. Situated closer to Springwood at the top of the hill, it was to have five bedrooms and be more European in style. Its estimated cost of building was £3,000, about three times as much as Bonnie Doon.* Construction started in September. David decided to call this home "Davesta", another of his confected names. As he had done with daughter Davanna, he combined his own name with another, but this time it was his new daughter, Estelle, who provided the second part of the name. It would be his and Valerie's secret, though he felt sure that Harriet would not be fooled.

As soon as Bonnie Doon was complete the McFarlanes moved from Warrah and Tom took on the life of a country squire, just as David had promised him. He acquired a shotgun and potted rabbits for the table[166] and the family explored the unspoilt countryside around Springwood. They all missed the hurly burly of London life, the familiar faces of friends and colleagues left behind. Valerie pined for the freedom of the modern single woman she had so recently taken for granted, but fate had dealt her an unusual hand and she had to play it. Estelle was her daily reminder of her responsibilities, past, present, and future. Sooner or later the services of the nurse would be dispensed with, and she would return to the homeland but there would be no return, not for many years, for mother and daughter. No matter what became of her relationship with David, about which she harboured fewer illusions as time passed, she would have to make her own way in this beautiful yet strange

---

* Blue Mountains Echo 23rd August 1918. £3,000 would be equivalent to about $260,000 today.

country. In the meantime, there were still the weekend trysts to enjoy, the frisson had not yet gone. Father, Tom had been promised a job managing David's future estate up the hill, but for the time being it could have been one long vacation for them all.

The winter months passed, milder than any Britisher would ever have believed. Strolling to and from the village centre or down the hill to the dairy farm for milk and butter, they inserted themselves into the local community, where there was always a friendly greeting, a helpful shopkeeper, or a welcoming congregation at the lovely gothic Fraser Memorial Church on the main street. Across Hawkesbury Road, weekend golfers could be seen toting their bags of clubs down the long fairways and Tom had become used to retrieving wayward balls from their front garden, even if Annie was more concerned with protecting their windows from the consequences of wild slices. Then, in about September, Valerie's health began to fail. At first the symptoms were vague and diffuse. She was losing weight and lacking her usual energy, there was a general feeling of malaise but nothing that could not be explained by the turn of the season from the cool of winter to what was to be an unusually warm spring and summer. By October it was clear that she was suffering more than a spring chill. Chest and abdominal pains were more frequent, and Valerie was running a fever. She was constantly fatigued and had now developed a cough. David was concerned; he might have expected the family to take a while acclimatising but they had now been in Australia for 18 months, time enough for all to adjust; Valerie was suffering exceptionally. As mid-October temperatures climbed to record highs, exceeding 91°F in Sydney[167] on the 21st, he accepted that she needed professional care that couldn't be provided in Springwood and brought her down to Sydney, where he had access to his own doctors. She was admitted to Kirketon private hospital in Darlinghurst, but the decline continued. By the middle of November her condition was critical. She was bed-ridden, running a high fever and her organs were failing. On November 28th, her physician, Dr John McPherson, who had attended her the past five days, declared there was nothing more he could do. She succumbed that day with David at her bedside.

Dr McPherson confirmed the cause of death: septic endocarditis, an almost always fatal infection of the interior of the heart. He explained that the bacterial infection could have started with a minor wound, dental problems, or the like,* but Valerie might still have avoided the ensuing septicaemia. The normal heart is relatively resistant to infection. Bacteria and fungi do not easily adhere to the endocardial surface and constant blood flow helps prevent them from settling on endocardial structures. Perhaps Valerie had a congenital defect or had suffered a bout of rheumatic fever in her youth? Tom and Annie could recall no such episode but, what did it matter? Here was a life cut tragically short at 28 years, a child orphaned at three and bereft parents with no close family to comfort them.

David was distraught, was this divine punishment for his sins? In the space of less than two years he had lost Margaret, for whom he retained an affection and an abiding guilt over his treatment of her, and the young lover who had revitalised his spirit. He had committed not only Valerie but her parents to abandoning their familiar life and friends in London and knew that the abrupt separation had embittered sister Maggie. Tom, Annie, and Estelle were now marooned in a strange land in a place that would forever remind David of his loss. He, like Tom and Annie, had no immediate family close by for comfort, even if he had ventured to seek it. Percy and Norman were at the front and Harriet remained in London with Bertha. Lila† and Vanna, daughters of his first marriage, had lived in England for many years, the latter caring for her mother long after David had lost interest, and though they kept in contact could not be expected to rally to him now. Stuart was in Sydney, but he had already proved to be feckless and irresponsible, not David's first choice for support.

David took charge of funeral arrangements. He was the informant for Valerie's death certificate on November 30th. It was a document that told as much about his emotional state as the

---

* These days septic endocarditis would be treatable with antibiotics.

† Lila may have been in Australia but there is no evidence of any material contact between father and daughter at this time.

distressing facts about the event.[168] David was conflicted about his relationship with Valerie. He started to write "Stepfather" but had second thoughts and replaced this with "Friend". He stated that her mother's name was Mary, when he must have known it was Annie, the same as Valerie's real name. Stumbling on, he perpetuated the forgery of Estelle's birth certificate, writing that Valerie had married David Allison four years previously in England. His ornate signature, as steady and confident as ever, completed the sorry epitaph to his lost love.

Valerie was buried at Springwood on December 2nd after a ceremony at the Fraser Memorial Presbyterian Church. The cortège, black plumes quivering on the horses' heads, wove its melancholy way out of town, past the towering gum trees and hidden gullies along Hawkesbury Road until, with the incomplete Davesta in view on the right, it made the left turn towards the cemetery.* David had selected and paid for the burial plot in the Presbyterian section. It stood apart from the rest, as close as possible to the boundary, where it could be glimpsed among the trees from the front garden of Davesta. The grave was surrounded by a low, stuccoed, brick wall with an iron gate, the only such in the cemetery. David commissioned a simple slab for the headstone, engraved: "In loving memory of Valerie A. Allison, died 28th November 1918, loved by all."

David could not face the McFarlanes for long after the funeral and retreated to his Sydney hotel. Tom and Annie sat alone in the darkened rooms of Bonnie Doon nursing their grief, penning letters to England and wondering what to do with the rest of their lives. Now little Estelle would be in their sole care, as good as a daughter in their middle age. Thankful for the presence of Lucy, on whom Estelle had become dependent, they drifted between mourning, homesickness, and anger over their powerlessness in the face of David's authority. Two weeks after the burial Tom first saw the death certificate and determined to set the record straight and reclaim his daughter. He made the painful train journey to Sydney, where he presented the certificate to the Registrar of Births, Deaths

---

* The road to the cemetery is now named "Davesta Road", though the origins of the name have never been documented by local historians.

and Marriages and demanded amendments. For "Valerie Allison" he wanted "Annie McFarlane, known as Valerie Allison". For "Mary" he insisted on "Ann" and he instructed the Registrar to remove all reference to the fictional marriage to "David Allison".* There would be justice and some sort of return to decency for their private memory of a lost daughter.

* Whether David learned of Tom's amendments to the death certificate is not known but he could have made no objection without compromising himself and eternally offending the bereaved father. He kept silent and the record stood. If Tom retained a copy of the certificate, he never shared it with other family members. Estelle grew up shielded from all mention of her mother, as de facto daughter of her grandparents. Her own children were to know nothing of the history of her birth, which was never spoken of in the family. The name on the headstone in Springwood cemetery was no more than a marker for what became the family grave site in future years. Valerie/Annie might never have existed. (Based on a conversation with Fraser Bradley, Estelle's surviving son, in 2016.)

1. *Young David builds the wall. Illustration from 'The Boy and the Wheelbarrow…'*

2. *Buchanan Street, Glasgow, David's "Patch" in the 1860s.*

3. *Two Stewart Dawson watches from the 1880s. Left, a gold double minute chronograph, right, a large sterling silver open face, Liverpool made.*

4. *Prescot watch factory workers. Conditions were excellent by the standards of the time, with good wages and will-lit workplaces.*

5. *SS Chimborazo, on which David sailed to Australia in 1884.*

The Best Five-Guinea Lever

IN ENGLAND

FOR THREE POUNDS.

GUARANTEED THE BEST TIMEKEEPER IN THE WORLD!

Direct from the Manufacturers.

Over 5000 Testimonials from Delighted Purchasers!

Cannot be Purchased in the Colonies under 7 or 8 Guineas.

WATCHES! WATCHES! WATCHES!

Most Important to the Readers of the TOWN AND COUNTRY.

In answer to the many inquiries and hundreds of orders from the British Colonies, and all parts of the world, from those who have seen in the English Press the advantages we offer the British Public; we are glad to announce that we have now arranged to give every reader of this paper an opportunity of obtaining one of these splendid English Levers *at less than half the price* for which a similar watch can be purchased abroad. The Open-Faced English Levers, specially offered by us for £3, are the same as those sold abroad for £7 7s. and the Hunters the same as those sold at £8 8s, the Gold Watches being in the same proportion.

A LIMITED Number of the very best ENGLISH SILVER PATENT LEVER WATCHES that money can buy will be sold to the readers of the TOWN AND COUNTRY for £3 each; but only (at this price) to those who send the Coupon Voucher below, along with their order. Messrs. Stewart, Dawson, and Co., Wholesale Watch Manufacturers, 121. Park Road, Liverpool, beg to assure every reader of this paper, that this is a *BONA FIDE* TRADE ANNOUNCEMANT, and to prove those statements absolutely, to those who desire so, the watches will be supplied exactly on the same conditions as in England.

CONDITIONS.

1st.—That no Watch will be supplied but to those who produce a Voucher Coupon for the same.

2nd.—That any purchaser, not fully satisfied with his purchase, on receipt thereof, may return it to us, when we will refund the amount paid, and pay carriage both ways.

3rd.—That we deliver them solely at our own risk.

4th.—That with every watch we will give a written guarantee to clean and repair, free of charge, for three years

5th.—That we positively guarantee them in every respect as good, or better, than anything sold in the regular colonial trade at £7 7s, and that they cannot possibly be bought in the usual retail way under that price.

6. Part of the first known advertisement in an Australian newspaper (Melbourne Leader. 3rd January 1880). It features the catch line: 'Watches! Watches! Watches!', together with the 'conditions' including the voucher or coupon to be completed in order to secure the order.

CAUTION! CAUTION!

BEWARE OF INTERESTED TRADE JEALOUSY!
BEWARE OF
PIRACY! BRIBERY! and BASE CALUMNY!
UPHOLD TRUTH! HONOUR!! and INTEGRITY!!!
THE FOUNDATION OF.

STEWART, DAWSON & CO.'S

WORLD-WIDE BUSINESS,

Which has stood and will stand as solid as the granite rock when the exorbitant profit dealer's malignant vindictiveness and jealousy is crumbled to the dust!

The unanimous voice of the public and the verdict of the world has proved

STEWART, DAWSON, & CO'S

English Lever Watches

TO BE THE BEST EVER MADE!

£1000 REWARD! £1000

WILL BE PAID BY
STEWART, DAWSON, AND CO.,
WATCH MANUFACTURERS,
RANELAGH PLACE, LIVERPOOL, ENG.,

To any firm of either Watch Manufacturers or Watch Dealers in the Colonies or in the Wide-world, who can produce the same amount of genuine testimony and unsolicited testimonials from their customers in proof of the qualities of their Watches as can

STEWART, DAWSON, AND CO.

NOTICE. NOTICE.

THIS CHALLENGE of £1,000 is Open to the Whole World!

Let those who have a reputation at stake take up S. D., and Co.'s Challenge or for ever keep silent

The gigantic operations of STEWART, DAWSON and Co. have spread from pole to pole; several years ago they threw open the portals of their manufactory to the General Public, and have scattered to the winds the Profits of the Merchant, Importer and Retail Dealer. This great work has not been effected without feeling the truth of that historical line—The sneer of the Protectionist, the jealousy of the weak, the calumny of the vicious, the vindictiveness of the exposed, have flown like a turgid stream across their onward path, still they pressed victoriously to the front, and now they have their reward from a grateful public, who daily show that in STEWART, DAWSON, and Co. they have found the real champions of their rights!

7. Over-the-top advertisement from 1884. David, under challenge, warned off competitors

8. 1908 Franco-British Exhibition at white City. From a postcard in public domain.

9. 'The Treasure House', 19-21 Hatton Garden, 1907.

10. David in 1908, aged 59

11. 1905 Portrait of Harriet by John Longstaff, hung at the Royal Academy

12. Interior of Stewart Dawson's Regent Street shop, opened 1909.

13. Norman Stewart Dawson in 1915, shortly after his commission in the Royal Naval Air Service.

14. Thelma Raye (Bell-Morton) about the time she married Percy (1917)

15. Percy Stewart Dawson

16. Annie McFarlane ('Valerie Allison') in 1916.

17. David, aged 72, in 1923.

18. Annie McFarlane Sr., Tom. Estelle, Annie (Valerie) at Sydney's Taronga Zoo in 1917.

19. Annie's Grave in Springwood Cemetery.

Loose Ends

Valerie died less than three weeks after the Armistice that ended the Great War. The years that followed were a period of profound adjustment to a new world order where old class divisions blurred, women who had held the home front together asserted and were granted new rights and young colonies such as Australia came of age. The immediate public response in Australia, after the euphoria of anticipating the defeat of the Imperial German forces, was somewhat muted, as indeed it was in the home country. One the one hand there were public displays of jingoistic triumph from the elected and elite, celebrating the success of the armies they had committed to the conflict.[169] On the other, there was a sense of emptiness, of waiting for the fighting men to come home and a vague expectation of a return to the status quo ante. But too much had changed in those awful four and a half years and though it took a year or so for the reality to dawn things would never be the same again.

David himself had little to celebrate as he coped with his grief. In addition, he was having to come to terms with the fact that his two younger sons would never be suitable successors in the business. Norman already had a reputation as a playboy from pre-war days and the public adulation of his dashing exploits as an airman had further inflated his arrogance. As early as 1915 he had been apprehended in England for driving a motor vehicle without a licence.[170] It was a minor offence but Norman, according to police evidence, lied that he had left the licence at Bournemouth (it had expired some months earlier), gave a false name (easily checked) and address (also easily checked) and "caused no end of trouble." He was described as "gentleman, of London". He was fined £5 but did not appear in court to answer the charge. As the war ended, any hopes that David or Harriet may have harboured of Norman's return to civilian life and adult responsibilities were put aside, when they learned that he had volunteered for the British expeditionary force supporting the White Russian counter-revolution against the Bolsheviks. Sent to the Murmansk peninsula, he served with Royal Naval and Royal Air

Force squadrons performing reconnaissance and bombing raids on Red Army troops. Norman's service in the confused and ultimately futile conflict was unremarkable, though he did make use of his East African experience when he led a party to recover navigation and photographic equipment from a downed spotter plane.*

Stuart was if possible, more useless than Norman. At the very time that David might have called upon him for support or advice as he gathered the unravelling threads of his life, Stuart was facing his creditors in the bankruptcy court of New South Wales. This was a man of twenty-six who had had an expensive education and enjoyed all the privileges of membership of one of the wealthiest families in Australia. He had avoided war service without, it seemed, pursuing any worthwhile occupation, even a token job in a Stewart Dawson shop.† While Norman risked his life in fragile seaplanes and Percy manned heavy guns behind the trenches, the youngest brother divided his time between the Tivoli, the racetrack and society parties. On October 20th, 1918, as his father tended to the dying Valerie, Percy's exhausted battalion rested after the battle of Amiens and Norman flew his last missions over the English Channel, Stuart made up the numbers at a grand celebration of the marriage of music hall singer, Muriel Starr.[171] Like Norman he relied entirely on his father for his income, which was more than adequate, if intermittent. His problem, like Norman's, was that he didn't like paying his debts. On February 27th, 1919, a Mrs Dorothy Vera de Rivière sued Stuart in the Bankruptcy Court for non-payment of a debt.[172] Dorothy de Rivière was the daughter of well-known Melbourne bookmaker, Barney

---

* From "Tracing Your Air Force Ancestors", Phil Tomaselli, Pen and Sword Books Ltd 2007. Phil Tomaselli believes that Norman was part of the second contingent sent out as reinforcements. Their presence was somewhat resented by the first group, who tended to relegate them to support roles, not Norman's style at all.

† There is no evidence of Stuart doing a single day's paid work his entire life. In later years he styled himself "Company Director" and may well have attended board meetings of the moribund Stewart Dawson empire in the 1940s and 50s, but his sole purpose seems to have been to maintain his considerable income from director's fees.

Allen. David was in no mood to bail Stuart out of court. It could have been a gambling debt or loan to cover a debt; he no longer cared. The likely reason for Mrs de Rivière's suing Stuart was that she herself was facing bankruptcy. In a case that made headlines across the country a few months later[173] Dorothy and her husband, Gerald de Rivière, were exposed as spendthrifts and gamblers on an eye-watering scale. Gerald had been banned from several racecourses for failure to meet gambling debts and the couple had spent over £10,000 in five years, living on credit after running through Dorothy's own substantial inheritance. Questioned about his intentions to repay debts, Gerald de Rivière said[174] that he "was of the opinion that his mother would always meet any just debt contracted by him." He was also of the opinion that "she would not meet any debt incurred by him fecklessly through gambling." They were perfect models for young Stuart, whose debt to them was never admitted or paid; he was declared bankrupt just as their case came to court in August. Stuart's acceptance of this fate and more importantly David's failure to bail him out could only be ascribed to Stuart's arrogance or insouciance and David's determination to follow the example of de Rivière's mother. In any event, Stuart turned his status as a bankrupt to his advantage. Before long, his father resumed payment of his allowance and his lifestyle suffered not a whit. He owned no assets on which his creditors could claim and his income from his allowance could be kept private and secure, being counted as "enough to cover expenses". And those expenses remained high. He continued to dine at the best restaurants, live in a suite at the Carlton Hotel, drive an expensive motor car and gamble extravagantly.

David was not in a state of paralysis, however. Depressed though he might have been there was too much momentum in his life for even a personal tragedy to divert him for long. On the domestic front, he accelerated the construction of Davesta in Springwood, completing it in early 1919 and starting an ambitious programme of landscaping around the house. Taking advantage of the sloping ground to the rear of the dwelling he had sweeping terraces cut into the hillside, built paths and steps, retaining walls, fountains and formal flower beds.* The flurry of activity diverted his mind even as he faced the still-mourning McFarlanes on his mountains visits. While directing the busy landscapers and gardeners, he called on Tom for advice and support, encouraging him to take over the care and maintenance of the finished estate. He owed the younger man (Tom was fourteen years David's junior) more than money could ever pay.

Back in the city, there was another change of emphasis. The Treasure House in Hatton Garden had been a leap of faith for David, not only as a symbol of his commercial bravado but because it committed him not for the first time to investment in prime real estate, now on a grand scale. His first venture had been the row of houses in Pelham Grove, at the start of his career. He had received a good, steady income from rents on the eleven "well let" houses, better than bank interest or speculating in the stock market. Inspired by this and the return he earned from The Treasure House he had followed up with the outright purchase of the Swanston Street premises in Melbourne in 1913 (£90,000), which was also proving successful. He had also been accumulating a Sydney property portfolio. While he continued to lease the George Street shop in Sydney, he had his sights on the entire city block between George Street on the west side and Pitt Street on the east, bounded by Market Street to the south side and King Street to the north. This immense section of the best commercial real estate in the country comprised several multi-storey Victorian-era buildings housing shops, offices, and professional chambers. David commenced by purchasing all the frontage along Pitt Street from No. 183 at the corner of Market to No. 191, next to the Strand Arcade, at the George Street end of which his store was located. These premises housed such well-known businesses as W.C. Penfold, the printers and stationers and one of his competitors, Proud's Jewellers. He also bought No. 105 King Street at the northern end of the block, in a preliminary encircling movement. He then bided his time while collecting increasing amounts of rent.

---

* In years to come, as Davesta's gardens matured they became a showpiece of style and culture in the lower Blue Mountains.

His instincts hitherto had been always to trust in cash flow from the retail business to fund future expansion of that same business. He never borrowed and such capital as he raised from incorporation of the Australian and United Kingdom businesses was trivial, most of it coming from his own pocket. The purpose of each incorporation was defensive. But the retail business was not expanding at the rate it once had. In fact, since Regent Street opened he had made no more attempts to break into the British market. The Australasian business had opened its last outlet as far back as 1890. There had been several re-locations to bigger and better premises along the way, including the major expansion and redevelopment of the Swanston Street site, and David anticipated further moves in the coming decade, but he now had competition where none had existed when he first launched into the Australian market. While he had been building The Treasure House and branching out in Regent Street, he'd taken his eye off Australasia. Apart from his brief visit in 1912, he'd been away for over thirteen years. Newcomers such as Angus & Coote (founded 1895) and Proud's (1903) had established a customer base in Sydney and Melbourne, and over in New Zealand the family firm of James Pascoe (1906) was gaining a reputation for quality and service that rivalled them all. Stewart Dawson's volume-based business model was under challenge as it had never been. He could increase expenditure on marketing to protect his cash flow but that would be a short-term expedient at best; his competitors could and did soon match him in that game. An article in the Melbourne Age on January 6th 1920[175] titled "Jewellery Trade Boom" asked: "Are wage earners extravagant?" It continued:

> *The suggestion has been made that an unduly large proportion of the increased wages of Australian workers generally is being expended in the purchase of jewellery.*

The newspaper surveyed jewellery businesses in Melbourne where, in one suburb alone (working class Brunswick) four new jewellery establishments had opened in the past year. Expenditure on gifts the previous Christmas had reached new highs, with wristwatches and diamond rings among the most popular items. Price seemed not to be an obstacle to purchasers, who preferred paying cash to the alternative of time payments being offered by some businesses. Mr H Bright, President of the Retail Jewellers' Association of Victoria, stated:

> *It can be said with absolute truth that over 25 per cent more money is being spent in Victoria than 2 or 3 years ago. That is not on account of increased prices. It is due to the increased prosperity of average wage earners ...*

Mr Bright also expressed the opinion that the soldier who had been to England and the Continent and seen the high prices paid for jewellery there was quite prepared to buy expensive items on his return to Australia. David was one of the business owners surveyed. He endorsed Mr Bright's view but then offered a further insight. He believed that people were not so much buying more jewellery but that they were displaying a keener appreciation of finish and good workmanship than formerly, and were prepared to pay in proportion. This arose, he went on, not from more extravagant tendencies but from a better taste.

All this may have been true but in his heart, David knew that his words were no more than a rear-guard action designed to differentiate Stewart Dawson's from the mass market competitors who he feared would ultimately swamp it. Angus & Coote was already innovating, offering optician services as well as their familiar watch and jewellery lines.[176] Proud's advertisements were almost indistinguishable from Stewart Dawson's' except that the claims of vast savings were more muted. Bill Proud and E. J. Coote went so far as to collaborate in the founding of the trade journal "The Commonwealth Jeweller and Watchmaker" in 1914,[177] while David was in London. While David continued to claim that Stewart Dawson's were "the largest jewellers in the Empire," Angus & Coote's adverts proclaimed them to be "the largest Jewellers and Opticians in Sydney"[178] and as if to taunt the old man their premises were only a block away from Stewart Dawson's, where anyone could make the comparison.

He had to have another iron in the fire if the business was to continue to sustain him and his family in the way to which they had become accustomed. That iron was property, so he turned his attention to consolidating his already substantial portfolio. At the end of 1919 he moved on the Pitt Street precinct, purchasing the Pitt Street end of the magnificent Strand Arcade for an Australian record price of £100,000,* a full 120 feet of frontage with a depth of 180 feet. The Stewart Dawson property, three storeys with a basement, contained two large shops fronting Pitt Street, while there were thirteen shops on the ground floor of the arcade, fifteen on the second floor, four on the third and two on the fourth. Topping it was a photographic gallery on the fifth level. He announced plans to "build a commercial establishment which will be run on modern methods new to Sydney." His own firm would "fill all the jewellery section." The newspaper reporting this[179] was keen to point out, no doubt prompted by David:

> *Mr Dawson is a great enthusiast on business possibilities, and also on the subject of architecture and its adaptation to commercial services – matters to which he has devoted close study during his 40 years of business life.*

So, after all, he was planning to open another shop, (to "fill all the jewellery section"), on the other side of the block from his existing George Street outlet. On the face of it, this made no sense. Why risk cannibalising your own trade? Why this contrarian behaviour when all the signs were that David's retail career had passed its peak? David's answer was, because, regardless of any plans for redevelopment, he would be guaranteed a return of over 10% on his investment from day one. The "rent-roll", or gross rental yield, was estimated at £11,000 per annum,† a tidy sum to offset any decline in retail sales he might suffer. Privately, he intended in the medium term to replace the leased George Street premises with what was to be a premium store in Pitt Street. He hinted at this in the January Melbourne Age article, when he opined that customers were becoming more discerning and willing to pay more for quality.

Before he could consider stepping away, however, he was jolted out of any sense of complacency he may have been enjoying when Harriet announced her intention to return to Australia. It was time again to face domestic reality.

---

* £100,000 in 1919 is worth about $100m today.

† £11,000 per annum in 1919 had an equivalent purchasing power of $11m in 2017.

Harriet Takes Charge

Harriet arrived in Melbourne on Boxing Day of 1919, accompanied by Bertha and eleven-year-old Joyce Verrall.* David journeyed down from Sydney to meet the women at the Menzies Hotel, where they spent a few days before returning north. It was an uncomfortable reunion for David, as he and Harriet gathered the threads of the past four years. He sensed a new assertiveness in Harriet, a determination to live by a new set of rules, against which he could offer little resistance. She could at any time remind him of his foolish romance, bringing him to heel if she wished. It was a power she withheld, of course, signalled only by a turn of the head or, as in their first meeting, a telling condolence on his loss. Harriet, for her part, let it be known that she

> *would have arrived in Australia much sooner, but that she deferred her departure from London until her second son (Major† Norman Stewart Dawson) returned from Russia. After the armistice he had volunteered to take a flying squadron out to Russia, and did so well that he was awarded the DSO, besides which the Russian Commander in Chief personally decorated him with the Order of St. Anne with Crossed Swords.*[180]

The newspaper report after further extolling Norman's valour added in passing that Percy, after three years' service with the A.I.F. in Europe, had returned himself the previous week. Harriet's

---

* Though her mother could afford to board her at a private school Joyce had been Bertha's companion through the years of separation and divorce from the now-deceased Charles Verrall (he died on March 12th, 1918, in a Dublin military hospital).

† Norman adopted the rank of Major for the rest of his life. His final rank in the RNAS was Flight Commander. There was no rank of "Major" in either the RNAS or the Royal Flying Corps (later Royal Air Force). Either the Russians bestowed it upon him as part of the irregular forces or he appropriated it for social purposes.

explanation for her delay was plausible because Norman was and ever would be her favourite while Percy appeared to be worth no more than a footnote. Her timing revealed that she was not speeding to her husband's side so much as descending upon the family to supervise its post-war reunion.

Back in Sydney the couple established themselves at the Carlton Hotel on the corner of Castlereagh and Elizabeth Streets. One of David's first priorities was to show Harriet the new country retreat in Springwood, but all did not go to plan. After dining at the hotel on Friday evening, January 16th, they set off from Sydney Central by train on Saturday morning for the trip up the mountains. Sometime later, Harriet asked David if he had seen her diamond earrings and a diamond and emerald pendant necklace that she had been wearing the previous evening and thought to bring with her. She remembered seeing them on the toilet table at 9 o'clock that morning before giving them to him to mind, as she usually did. He re-joined that he was sure he hadn't seen them and that they hadn't been given to him. After what must have been a typical married couple's futile argument: "I thought you did." "No, I thought it was your job …" they feared the worst and informed the Hotel authorities at one of the stops on the way. What should have been David's grand gesture of reconciliation to Harriet at Davesta turned into three days of anxiety over what they both suspected had occurred. They returned to Sydney on Tuesday, where the loss was confirmed. David circulated a description of the jewels to all city and suburban pawnbrokers, offering a large reward. He had had both pieces made in London to his own design expressly for Harriet and they were valued at the staggering sum of £5,000 (yet another record, according to police reports). David, as was his custom, could not resist hyperbole in describing the earrings and heart-shaped pendant: "So brilliant are they that they could not, at certain angles, be looked at for any length of time."*

While the police conducted their enquiries, Harriet found her feet with remarkable composure, bringing her now well-honed skills as hostess to the Sydney scene. On Friday March 12th JC Williamson's

* Sun (Sydney) 2nd January 1920 P.5 *"Then search for blind burglars"*, quipped Smith's Weekly.

wife, Maggie, sailed from Sydney for America and England accompanied by her daughter, Aimée (known to all as "Tootles"). They were to tour England, Ireland, and Scotland before going on to Paris, where Tootles was to study art.[181] Before leaving, Maggie presented to the National Gallery Longstaff's portrait of her other daughter, Marjorie, the very painting that had inspired David's commissioning Harriet's portrait back in 1905. The ladies of her circle entertained the couple at several dinner parties in the week preceding the departure, one of the hostesses of note being Harriet. She was in her natural element once more.

At about the same time she suffered yet another loss to a thief. It was beginning to look like carelessness on her part. Samuel van Enbergen, who described himself as an importer, was charged in Sydney Criminal Court on April 9th with stealing several articles of clothing and jewellery valued at £83, the property of Mrs. Stewart Dawson, from the Hotel Australia. The newspaper reported:

> *The accused stated that ten years ago he used to stay at the hotel; he then possessed £54,000 but lost everything, owing to the war, most of the money being invested in Russian shares. He went to the hotel but they refused to give him money. He had been starving and he went mad.*[182]

The wretched man was committed for trial and once again Harriet's possessions were returned to her.

Then, a strange episode occurred that shed a new light on the earlier theft from the Carlton and ultimately led to its resolution. On April 8th, 1920, Stuart was once again summoned to the Supreme Court in Bankruptcy to answer a proof of debt application on behalf of one Anthony Aliette. It seemed that being declared bankrupt had failed to deter him from incurring new debts. On April 10th he admitted the debt in full, so perhaps he had learned a lesson of sorts. Aliette followed this with an application for costs: Stuart was not getting off lightly this time. Had the matter ended there it would soon have been forgotten, buried in the back pages of the law reports. But on May 7th a veritable posse of detectives (seven of them) followed a man to City Tattersalls Club in Pitt Street, where they arrested him and, after a short search, recovered a diamond that was identified as belonging to one of Harriet's missing earrings. City Tattersalls was founded in 1895 by a group of bookmakers dissatisfied with their treatment by race-track officials and was the meeting place for serious punters, as well as the bookmakers themselves and their clerks and runners. The arrested man was none other than Anthony Aliette, bookmaker's clerk. At his trial, evidence was given that he had approached a George Street jeweller named Isadore Adams offering a packet of diamonds for sale. After inspecting the gems, which he saw were of the highest quality, Adams asked: "Is that from the Stewart Dawson robbery?" which Aliette confirmed. Adams feigned interest but after Aliette left the packet with him he approached the police, and a sting was arranged. On the day of the arrest Adams and Aliette met by arrangement in Pitt Street, where Adams passed the diamonds back to the clerk. The police then witnessed them walking towards Tattersalls, but Aliette grew suspicious and ducked inside the club to avoid them. It was to no avail as they pursued him indoors. He had put one of the diamonds in his mouth, having told Adams: "It's so handy, in the event of being caught in the street by the police, one can always swallow them." Perhaps he panicked because, instead of swallowing the stone he spat it onto the floor of the club, where it was recovered some time after during the police search. Over the next few days most of the remaining haul turned up, though some pieces had already been broken up, the better to dispose of the stones. Aliette's trial heard that he was also accused of a lesser theft from another man and though he attempted to provide an alibi the jury found him guilty.

It seemed like the classic "open and shut" case where the accused would receive a severe sentence, given the extraordinarily high value of the stolen goods. However, on the jury's recommendation, the court handed down only a two-year sentence, fully suspended, on the grounds that Aliette was "the tool of others". It was never made clear who the "others" were, but it was not a great stretch of the imagination to picture the likely culprits. He was, after all, the agent of a Sydney bookmaker at a time when off-course betting was rife. Enforcement of debt collecting was a rough and ready business and Aliette could have been under extreme pressure to deliver to his boss. There was a grey line between legitimate gambling and criminals in Sydney's underworld. Reckless gamblers such as Stuart

Stewart Dawson and the de Rivières drifted in this orbit and inevitably fell afoul of the money men sooner or later. Aliette's suing of Stuart was almost certainly on behalf of his bookmaker and in the end, was unsuccessful: despite Stuart's acknowledgement of the debt he never paid it or the associated costs.* Was there an element of revenge or pay back in the theft of Stuart's mothers' jewels? Worse, could Aliette have exerted pressure on Stuart to reveal where the jewels were kept in the hotel? David shuddered to think of the possibility that his own son had sunk to betraying his parents' trust. Stuart was already beyond the pale but Sydney, especially its merchant class, was a close-knit society, and banishment was out of the question. A stern lecture and a warning of potential reduction or loss of his allowance had to serve.

While Stuart kept a low profile, Norman slipped back into the country from England. It was to be a short visit, during which he did what he knew best: wine and dine with his brothers and fashionable ladies of the town. He was seen at the Wentworth Café with Percy and Stuart on Thursday evening, May 20th, in company with other society couples. The Wentworth was the epitome of chic in Sydney. The Sunday Times enthused:

> *And for the fairy grace of it I'd tramp a thousand leagues. Indeed, who would not? Never was there such a café as the Wentworth, with its light and laughter and flowers. And the music! Each succeeding night displays only too clearly Mrs Maclurcan's unerring taste in perfection ...*[183]

Hannah Maclurcan was the licensee of the hotel near Wynyard Square. Born Hannah Phillips in 1860 near Hill End, New South Wales, she grew up in hotels managed by her father, married another hotelier, Donald Maclurcan, and on his early death in 1903, took over the lease of the then boarding house that she was to grow into the sophisticated venue of the 1920s. Percy and Norman, returned from the high spots of London, looked with a critical eye upon the ballroom newly completed in March. Mrs Maclurcan was

---

* At least, there is no record of payment, though it is possible that David, against his better judgement, made a private payment.

already celebrated as the pioneer in this field. In the previous year, The Mirror (Sydney) had reported:

> *Ballroom dancing is so much the rage in London, and the nightclubs so many, that Australians returning to Sydney from England are astonished at the lack of public amusement here in the form of dancing. Mrs Maclurcan supplied a long felt want when she instituted her dinner-and-dance evenings at the Wentworth Hotel.*[184]

The 100ft ballroom and cafe, with its overlooking balcony, was completed in a record five weeks, and immediately attracted crowds every night. The Stewart Dawson's, both generations, were regular patrons. When the Prince of Wales arrived in Sydney on June 9th on board the battle-cruiser HMS Renown he and his retinue took over the entire hotel for the two-week visit, bestowing an incontestable seal of approval.

Norman appeared twice more at the Wentworth in the company of a married woman, Mrs Gilbert Garlick, before sailing on the RMS Tahiti on July 23rd for London via Vancouver. Harriet was disappointed that her favourite son, whose absence she had so lamented, had chosen to spend so little time with her and was returning without her to the place she now called home.

If Harriet was upset at the sudden departure of her middle son, she was more bemused by Percy's misfortunes. His whirlwind romance and marriage had surprised her even more than David; she admired Percy's determination to learn the family business and his luck in snaring a star like Thelma, but for the life of her she couldn't understand what Thelma saw in her son. The gossips had hinted as much in their reports of the wedding, when they concluded: "their plans lie in the lap of the gods." The gods, as it turned out, were not in a kindly mood. Thelma had planned to follow Percy to England but was persuaded to delay her journey by the lure of the local stage and continuing concerns about the risks on the high seas. Her contract with the Tivoli theatre was renewed but she eventually made the trip, where she remained at a loose end in London while he completed his training at Aldershot and on the firing ranges. Their separation upon Percy's posting to the front led her to seek employment back in the theatre. Despite wartime restrictions, the

London theatre scene remained active and vibrant. Folks at home and weary troops back from France needed every bit of relief and frivolity that the West End could provide. As Percy's brigade fought and died in the mud of Messines, Passchendaele, Villers Bretonneux, and Amiens, Thelma drifted away from the man she had barely known until formal separation became inevitable. After Percy's return, alone, to Australia in early 1919, Thelma continued to tour with the production company. While playing the lead in Cosmo Hamilton's play "Scandal" she met the actor, Ronald Colman. Their affair was everything that the brief, interrupted marriage had not been, and Percy offering no resistance, she divorced him to marry Colman in 1920.

David remained in the background, organising his business affairs. In June he registered two property companies. Stewart Dawson Strand Property Limited, capital: £100,000, was to become the registered owner of the Strand Arcade and Pitt Street frontage. Stewart Dawson Pitt Street Property Limited, capital: £30,000, was open ended "to acquire any freehold or leasehold lands, buildings etc." David appointed himself Managing Director of both companies. He was funding the purchase of the Strand Arcade partly from equity raised from silent partners and inviting other, or the same partners, to invest in future property acquisitions.*

Meanwhile, Harriet executed her own master plan. On Friday, August 6th she and David decamped to Parramatta, a half hour's train journey from the city, where they were married. After thirty-five years of co-habitation and subterfuge, they were making an honest man and woman of each other. Harriet knew that David was emotionally exhausted by the events of the past five years and was in no position to refuse her. Moreover, she had to secure the inheritance of their children and legitimise their status. Not that there was any indication of David's unwillingness to deal less than generously with the next generation. On the contrary, he continued to indulge all his children, including five-year-old Estelle, with regular allowances that should have more than met their needs.

* As with his previous business incorporations, there is no way of knowing how much equity and control he was willing to share, probably not a lot.

Nevertheless, it was better to be safe and a marriage contract was hard to beat if Lila or Vanna ever contested David's will.

The secret wedding was conducted by the Presbyterian minister, John Paterson, not in the church but at the Presbyterian Manse. There were no witnesses except the minister's wife, Jane, and a lady by the name of Helen Thompson, a local member of the church. David, as was his wont, attempted to conceal his identity while meeting the legal requirements of the marriage certificate. He gave his name as "David Dawson", omitting the obvious tell-tale of his adopted middle name, and stated that his occupation was "Merchant" (no mention of "jewellery" or the like). He correctly stated that he was a widower, aged seventy. Harriet's occupation was "domestic duties", and she was a "spinster". Harriet shaved a few years off her age, claiming to be 48 (she was now 56).* The ceremony complete and the certificate in David's pocket, they thanked the minister, strolled the few blocks to the railway station and boarded the Springwood-bound train. When they returned on Monday morning to business-as-usual few would have noticed the look of quiet triumph on Harriet's face or the silent resignation of her aging husband. A new chapter in their complex life, perhaps the final one, had opened.

---

* So secretive were they that it is doubtful whether even their children knew of the event. There is no evidence to show that any of them had the least suspicion of their own illegitimacy to this date. Lila and Vanna, on the other hand, had always known the true state of affairs; Margaret would have made sure of that if only to reinforce their rights. But the two older women were discreet and in Vanna's case, off the scene in England. They were no threat to the equilibrium of the second family or to David and Harriet's public reputation.

Joining Sydney's Establishment

The wedding may have been a secret but that did not preclude the giving of a present. Harriet received hers from her new husband in short order. Smith's Weekly, in its "Gossip From Here, There and Everywhere" column on October 23rd, reported:

> *Wilga, Potts Point, Sydney, the historic spot where James Martin lived, is to be saved from the hands of the builders. It is to be the Sydney home of Mr and Mrs Stewart Dawson; the property having been recently purchased by them.*

Wilga was the former Clarens, the home of Sir James Martin, the man who became Premier of New South Wales. It stood near the end of Potts Point in one of the best locations anywhere in the world, let alone Sydney. The views across the harbour were uninterrupted, encompassing to the west the bays of Woolloomooloo and Farm Cove, the city skyline, and the inner harbour as far as Lane Cove, and to the east past Garden Island across Elizabeth Bay as far as the Heads four miles away. Clarens, dating from 1847, had been a wedding gift to Martin from his father-in-law, W.A. Long, in 1861, when it was little more than a cottage. It was reported that Martin "had the building mania and spent a fortune (said to be £100,000) in adding to and altering it."[185] Aside from its impressive Romanesque facade and sumptuous interiors, Martin indulged his passion for classical Europe by constructing extensive terraced gardens on the slopes below. With its profusion of classical statuary, this "garden falling down to the sea was like fairyland" for visiting English novelist Anthony Trollope. The house had welcomed many other famous guests, including King George V, the Dukes of Clarence and Edinburgh, and the ill-fated Admiral Tryon, lost in the collision of his battleship in 1893.[186] Harriet could not have asked for more as she cemented her position among the doyennes of Sydney society. David, proud as he was of this evidence of his financial and social success, noted the irony of the asymmetric fulfilment of his great plan of 1917.

Wilga was a bargain purchase since it was a somewhat hasty sale. The owner, Will Moses, was downsizing to move across Elizabeth Bay to an apartment at Darling Point. The house had only been in Moses' name for two years, after he bought it from Dr Robert Faithfull (it was he who renamed the house in 1896), but in that time the Moses daughters had married and left home. Though Will Moses cherished the gardens, a love he shared with his brother, Henry, a noted rose grower, he and his wife were finding it hard to justify keeping such a large house as their Sydney pied à terre. Commenting on the sale, Smith's Weekly feared, "It will be a thousand pities if the Government allows such a place to pass into the hands of the builders."

Already in 1920, the march of the property developers was threatening to destroy the hard-won heritage of the built environment. Grand houses such as Wilga were viewed as obsolete relics of the Victorian era, tempting targets for demolition and replacement with multiple smaller dwellings or apartments. Smith's was somewhat reassured when the identity of the new owners was revealed. No sooner had David taken ownership than he announced he was dividing the house into two flats. One half of the house would be the Stewart Dawson family home while the other would be rented to a suitable tenant. He recognised that his situation was similar to the Moses', but his solution was to occupy a smaller portion of Wilga rather than settle for yet another apartment; he'd had more than enough of them in London over the years and now that he had Davesta in the Mountains half of Wilga was a fair equivalent.

The builders moved in to carry out the internal work, plumbing in new marble-finished bathrooms (three in the rented flat, four in the family half) and kitchens[187] and installing partition walls, but the exterior of the building was untouched, preserving its character. Though the property continued to be known as Wilga, David could not resist the urge to put his stamp on it and the half he and Harriet were to live in became "Strathisla", recalling the first home in Pelham Grove. He found a tenant for the rented half, for which he charged £1,000 per annum, supplementing the already stupendous rental income from his commercial interests. The lady willing and able to pay this amount was Mrs Jane Hordern, widow of Samuel Hordern of the prominent family of merchants and retailers, and another of Harriet's inner circle of friends.

While alterations were in progress, David spent more time up in Springwood. He was now more active in civic affairs, anxious to bring the town into the twentieth century with modern facilities and infrastructure befitting its status as "The Riviera of the Southern Hemisphere", as he loved to call it. Chronically short of funds, the local council squabbled constantly over allocation of money to road maintenance, provision of utilities and general delivery of services. Hawkesbury Road was a regular topic of debate due to its poor state, which reduced it to a barely navigable track after rain. Now that David had a home fronting the road, he became a vocal advocate of upgrading it. Councillors agreed with him but there were many competing projects. In November 1920, the Blue Mountains Echo reported:

Hawkesbury Lookout Road is in a deplorable condition, so bad that it is "the last rut that gives the chauffeur the bump". Mr Stewart Dawson, with customary generosity, has agreed to contribute £1 for every £1 on all money collected locally for the improvement and the Blue Mountains Shire Council has also agreed to subsidise the work to a like amount.[188]

The appeal was successful and by April 1921 the Echo reported:

Great improvements are being made on the Hawkesbury Road, immediately facing Mr Stewart Dawson's property. The road is being re-graded and formed at an estimated cost of £240, of which sum Mr Dawson contributed £140. Before regrading, the hill had a mean grade of 1 in 10 but now the steepest pinch will not be more than 1 in 16.[*]

[*] Blue Mountains Echo 29th April 1921. David had won the day; the cutting through the hill near the entrance to Springwood Golf Club is evidence, to this day of the work done. However, it would be many years before the rest of the 6-mile road matched the standard opposite Davesta. Some claimed that he had the line of the road moved because it passed too close to his front garden at Davesta. (Sunday Times, 9th July 1922 P.1)

The location of the road works was of course no coincidence. Access to and from Davesta and Bonnie Doon down the hill was improved but now there were to be two more dwellings between the earlier houses. The one closer to Bonnie Doon was a direct copy of the earlier house while its neighbour, closer to Davesta and higher up the hill, took advantage of the steeper fall of land to the rear to include a large understory, almost doubling its number of rooms. Though there were no tall trees close by to obscure the extensive views, the name "The Spinney" was bestowed upon it ("spinney" being the English word describing a small cluster of trees, usually on the top of a hill). The houses were completed towards the end of 1920 and received local praise. The Blue Mountains Echo wrote:[189]

The two cottages built for Mr Stewart Dawson at North Springwood are in keeping with the scheme of beautification which Mr Dawson has determined to finalise. In no great while North Springwood should be one of the prettiest spots on the Blue Mountains.

In further consolidation of the Springwood estate, David also purchased the land opposite Davesta, an orchard that backed onto the nine-hole golf course owned by Blue Mountains Councillor, JT Wall, one of David's local acquaintances, who was happy to share his private course. Now visitors to his mountain home could not only enjoy David's hospitality at Davesta, but they could also stroll across the road for a round of the 1920s' most fashionable game.*

David's other campaign had wider-reaching consequences. In 1920 Springwood still lacked proper electric lighting, both public and domestic. He had been lobbying for construction of a power plant and distribution system for some time, but nothing had come of it. While the upper Mountains at Katoomba enjoyed the amenity and safety of a modern lighting system the lower Mountains was locked in the 19th

* With the post-war rise to fame of British and American professional golfers, such as Bobby Jones, Walter Hagen and Gene Sarazen and the inclusion of women in ever increasing numbers, golf became the craze of the middle and upper classes and private courses flourished. There may also have been an ulterior, sentimental motive in David's purchase of the land; its western boundary was metres away from Valerie's grave in the adjacent cemetery.

century. David and several Springwood businessmen and councillors formed a group to raise public awareness of the need and in January 1921 the Shire Council bowed to pressure and convened a public meeting to present a draft agreement. The Echo reported:

> *A public meeting is to be held on Saturday night at Springwood for the purpose of securing the money to erect the plant. The President of the Shire Council (Cllr Savage) and Mr Stewart Dawson, who recently erected a residence in Springwood, will address the meeting.*[190]

David addressed the meeting on Saturday January 8th. As he surveyed the assembled gentlefolk his heart warmed, and he relaxed. For the first time in ages he was part of a real movement for public good. This was not one of those complex and hard-nosed negotiations for property rights or import contracts that had begun to wear him down the past few years. These weren't competitors out to steal his customers or prospectors selling him a worthless hole in the ground. These good people were looking to him for leadership in pursuit of progress, inspiration to widen support for this excellent scheme. They had given him a platform on which to display and share his experience, wit, and wisdom. It was the best medicine for his melancholy. He felt almost euphoric as he started to speak. Notes? What need was there for notes? This would come from the heart. The Echo reported:

> *Mr Stewart Dawson is generally accepted as a hard-headed businessman, one who tackled the scrap for fortune at an early age and made good. At the public meeting held at Springwood on Saturday he delivered a public speech which, in his own words, was "the first in a life of 70 years".*

Even the most naïve among his listeners would have known better, but this odd introduction was explained by what followed. The Echo continued:

> *Had not Mr Dawson amassed a fortune in the jewellery business he would certainly have secured a fair competence on the stage as a Scotch comedian and teller of stories. 'Tween whiles of exhorting the people of Springwood to put their money into the electric light scheme he told many stories of Scotch thrift, many worth repeating.*

The stories were of the stereotypical Scotsman of music hall jokes, ever careful with his last penny, and he won over the audience with his exaggerated highland accent, but he also took the opportunity to inject appropriate homilies into his monologue, capping one story of thrift with the remark:

> *If the boys of Springwood would look more often at the money in their pockets and make up their minds to keep it there they would be better off. They should always get value for money.*

The value on this occasion lay in the investment in the new lighting system. The campaign attracted much publicity and funds flowed in. Realists among the campaigners, including David, knew there would be no overnight success, but momentum was building.* In the meantime, most homes would continue to rely on gas or kerosene lighting or, as was more likely in a house such as Davesta, a private electricity generator. David had staked a claim to being more than a city toff, who merely dropped in for the weekend.

---

* The lights finally came on in Springwood in 1924.

Percy Steps Up

Early in 1921 Bertha returned to England, further depleting Harriet's immediate family in Australia. Only Percy and Stuart remained. In 1920 Stuart had married Gertrude Evangeline ("Peggy") Clowes, daughter of a Queensland resident, English born chemist. He still had no known occupation and remained an undischarged bankrupt. While Stuart wasted his life Percy, the forgotten son, assumed the role of manager of the George Street store. He was now in his thirty third year, single and sobered from his failed marriage and the horrors of the war. David trusted him to look after the showpiece shop while he worked on building his property empire.

Percy was soon put to the test when a fire broke out in the top floor of the shop on the evening of Monday April 11th, 1921, just as he and his staff were preparing to leave. He told the authorities that he made a practice to look around the building after closing time every evening and from what he could learn the fire broke out under the roof in the electric motor that drove the lift.[191]

> *It was a good thing … that the outbreak happened at the time it did, for if it had been five minutes later, all the staff and myself would have been away, and the fire would have had full play in the most dangerous block in the city.*

He did not explain why he thought the block so dangerous, but it came as no surprise that the fire's cause was an electrical fault. Since the adoption of electricity, most domestic fires and those on commercial premises had been the result of poorly installed or maintained wiring or overloading of circuits. Safety and engineering standards were still evolving and often misunderstood, so fires due to electrical failures were common. Insulation would fail, circuit breakers malfunction, or overheat, short circuits from ill-fitting components caused sparking. Percy and the shop survived this literal baptism of fire thanks to his prompt action in calling the fire brigade. Though the roof was partly destroyed the fire was contained and the floors beneath suffered only minor water damage.

The damage to the shop was soon made good and the establishment was back in business. Instead of returning to routine, Percy started to show some of his father's entrepreneurship when, in September of the year, he was invited to become a director of Commercial Air Transport Limited, a newly registered company with a bold ambition to deliver cost-effective air services to the eastern seaboard and inland, regional centres. Despite extensive publicity, the qualifications, experience and bona fides of the putative directors did not pass scrutiny and no more was heard of the venture.

Percy's reputation did not suffer from having his name associated with the failed float and he shrugged off the affair as a life lesson, much as his father had done after his missteps into gold mining ventures. He had, after all, not lost any money (which would probably not have been his to lose) and had demonstrated a willingness to take risks and diversify the business, though an interview David gave to the Brisbane Courier on a visit there in September 1921, at about the time of the failed float, could have been inspired by Percy's close shave:

> *The fault I observe with too many is a lack of continuous application and a considerable desire to subordinate work to the distractions of the city; and enterprise to "get rich quick" methods.*[192] *... a thorough knowledge of a trade or business and a persistency in following it up are maxims on which success is built.*

If he had been honest with himself, he would have conceded that he had enjoyed not a small measure of luck in exploiting rapidly growing markets for established, almost commoditised products. The world was changing faster now than he had ever experienced; innovation and diversification were the new order of the day.

As if to underline his message of "persistence breeding success", in the following month he extended his grasp of the Pitt Street block yet again, with another record-breaking purchase.[193] The price paid was £233,000[194] and for this he acquired most of the rest of the Pitt Street frontage adjoining his recent Strand Arcade purchase and another property on King Street, around the corner. He now owned over two thirds of the entire city block and was one step closer to monopolising control over it. His stated aim was to redevelop and modernise the precinct by, among other things, constructing avenues through the block to increase the shop frontages. The block was already pierced by several such avenues; as well as the Strand and Royal Arcades running between George and Pitt Streets, David had now added the King Street Arcade, but he saw the potential for even more retail exposure to drive up his rental income.

By November contracts were signed with architects and builders for the first stage of the work. To the surprise and consternation of the big city firms, David selected the Leura (Blue Mountains) firm of McLean and Pattie. It was they who had built Davesta and the other Springwood houses, but this project was in another league altogether. The announced budget was between £45,000 and £50,000[195] for unspecified alterations to the Strand Arcade. The architects were Robertson and Marks, a safer choice than the builders since their reputation for quality design was well established in the city. Founded in 1892, they had to their credit the original Challis House (1908), and buildings for the Daily Telegraph, Perpetual Trustees, Farmer and Company and, just the year before, Proud's Limited.[196]

David was overseeing a tremendous number of projects. Domestically, work continued fitting out Wilga and on Davesta's gardens, in which he took a personal interest. He was fighting a long-running dispute with the Blue Mountains Council over property rates[197] while managing the development and promotion of the Springwood golf course. Though the jewellery business continued to delight customers and remained profitable* all of David's business activities from 1916 onward pointed to his waning interest in his traditional core operations. He had walked away from the UK retail scene and had not paid a visit to New Zealand since 1917. Perth and Brisbane were now seldom in his diary and, apart from occasional trips to the races, Melbourne had been left to its own devices. All of Stewart Dawson's investments in that time had been in property, a relatively passive income generator akin to a retirement fund for David and Harriet. His advertising continued to promote value as

* In the last quarter of 1921 Stewart Dawson's imported 25 parcels of watches, silverware, clocks, fancy ware and jewels (rubies), easily matching all their competitors. However, numbers were down on previous years.

much as quality, but Stewart Dawson's was trading on reputation. There would be no more exciting breakthroughs in jewellery or watches, no more triumphant grand openings of glittering stores for David to celebrate and he had long given up any expectation that his sons, even Percy, could carry the torch.

Hand in hand with his realism, if not fatalism, was David's emotional capitulation to Harriet. Everything he did from the day of her return to Sydney seemed to be aimed at pleasing her. Some reports of the purchase of Wilga, the trophy home, named Harriet as the owner. She would not have corrected the record and neither did he. Harriet had wasted little time joining the inner circle of the ladies who lunched and took advantage of the country seat in Springwood perhaps more than David had anticipated, joining Percy and others on their golf course.[198] David had arranged for Harriet's younger brother, Malcolm McNab, and his wife to move to Australia,* employing Malcolm as one of his managers. As he had done with the McFarlanes, he provided not only employment but a home; in 1921 the McNabs moved into The Spinney, from where Malcolm could commute to the city.[199] Only two doors down the road lived the illegitimate offspring of David's affair with Valerie. David wondered if Harriet saw his providing her brother what amounted to a free home almost next door as a further swing of the balance of power in her direction. But it was simpler to think of it as a gesture of reconciliation, an act of pure generosity.

Most of all, Harriet aspired to continue her success as a fund-raiser from her wartime days in London. She had first experienced the excitement and rewards of staging charity events back in the 1890s during their initial visit to Australia. The challenge and thrill of wooing wealthy donors with gay festivities, fancy dress balls, charity auctions and performances by stars of opera, music hall and theatre had appealed to her. This ideal of "women's work" had persisted

---

* Malcolm probably came to Australia before the War. He was certainly in the country from as early as 1913, since his marriage to Agnes Josephine Brown is recorded in that year in Victoria and his two daughters were born in about 1914 and 1916 respectively, in Melbourne. He could have been David's manager at the Melbourne shop until his move to Sydney/Springwood.

from the 19th century through the early decades of the 20th even as the younger generation of women sought to compete in a male-dominated society. The more successful organisers and figureheads were enormously esteemed. Harriet, though, faced an obstacle to her ascendancy in the Sydney fund-raising scene in the person of Hannah Maclurcan. The chatelaine (as she was termed) of the Wentworth Hotel had been the leading light in facilitating fund-raising lunches and dinners at the hotel since the early war years. Her life-long experience in hospitality and her peerless reputation for quality cuisine combined to make her the first choice for hosting these lavish and much publicised events. Since taking over the lease of the hotel she had transformed it into "the Carlton in miniature",[200] a reference to the famous London establishment, with later additions and extensions including the popular Winter Garden. Her crowning achievement at the time of Harriet's re-launching in Sydney society was entertaining the Prince of Wales in the brand-new Ballroom. A tireless self-publicist, Hannah Maclurcan often referred to the visit in the Wentworth Magazine.[201] She never failed to mention the Prince's half-hour chat with her, in which he complimented her on the menu, the music and the Ballroom. "The floor," he said, "was the most perfect [I have] ever danced on," to which Hannah replied, "I had the Ballroom especially built for the coming of your Royal Highness." Gallantly, the Prince responded, "I want you to book the Ballroom for me again tomorrow night and please serve us exactly the same menu." Regardless of whether the Prince made this last request Hannah could be excused for granting herself the Royal imprimatur for her table d'hôte; there was nowhere else in Sydney to compare with The Wentworth Café. If Harriet wanted to make her mark it would have to be on her own territory where she could call the tune, a place that could and should rival The Wentworth in the competition for the hearts and wallets of the rich.

Any doubts David had about the wisdom of this new venture he kept to himself but in August 1921 an event occurred that pushed him over the line. Hannah Maclurcan had a reputation for enforcing strictly moral behaviour on her premises. She would sit at a table on the balcony overlooking the Ballroom, observing the couples and singles dancing and dining below, her Pekinese dogs on her lap.[202] If, according to her judgement any dance frock was permitting too much display of bare skin, the wearer was politely guided to a dressing room, where a deft attendant filled in the upper part of her costume with a wisp of tulle.[203] Unaccompanied young ladies were discouraged from the premises, though the Wentworth was not extreme for the times. Fulminating letter writers to newspapers (always men) tut-tutted over the lax attitudes of "flappers".* The story was that a "slightly drunk" Percy Stewart Dawson had been ejected from The Wentworth over "an indiscretion with a lady in a low-cut dress" and that, vowing he would never be thrown out of a nightclub again, he decided to build his own.[204] This appeared to conflate the stories of Hannah's low tolerance for indiscreet dress and behaviour with an account, which preserved the anonymity of the parties concerned, of a less racy event. Freeman's Journal reported on August 25th, 1921:

> *Rumor hath it that the other evening a young Miss, not long from college, alighted rather late at a popular dancing rendezvous, and was asked by the chatelaine what she was doing there alone at such an hour. The modern Miss responded that she was to "meet a gentleman for a little supper and a dance," but was informed by the chatelaine that she could not remain, as they were within half an hour of closing time.† Soon after her reluctant departure her cavalier arrived on the scene and was highly incensed to find what had happened. He informed the lady that "it was like her, cheek," and that he would never put his nose inside the place again. The proprietress expressed her delight at the resolution, and next morning read a lecture to the young lady's mamma on the evils of too much freedom for little girls who ought still to be under careful chaperonage.‡*

---

* It was only towards the middle of the decade, when the world had not after all ended, that the attitude to youthful exuberance relaxed.

† Closing time was normally 11 p.m. though it was extended on special occasions to 12.30 and even 1 a.m. during the visit of the Prince of Wales.

‡ Whether or not the "cavalier" was indeed Percy, the account supplies no evidence that he was "slightly drunk", a condition the gossip columnist would have gleefully reported. Since he and the "Miss" in question never

Since his divorce, Percy had returned to his bachelor days. His brothers no longer accompanied him about town. Norman was back in England and marriage had done little to moderate Stuart's behaviour; he continued to gamble and both he and Peggy were heavy drinkers. But while the couple were familiar faces in Sydney clubs and restaurants, they were seldom seen in Percy's company. On the night in question, Percy had been looking forward to rounding out another evening on the town with a casual girlfriend, nothing serious or special. He'd done this often, enjoying the dancing on the famous floor of the Wentworth Café and the company of the younger set at the tables set around it. What better way to reward himself for a hard day's work in the shop? What better way, too, to observe the success of this fabulous palace of entertainment, to learn its strengths and weaknesses? For Percy had ambitions beyond minding a shop, even Stewart Dawson's. Knowing and sharing his father's shift in interest away from retail jewellery and his mother's need for social acclaim he hatched a plan, which he revealed to David.

> *Why not build our own cabaret and show Sydney and Australia how it really should be done best? We own and can develop the best part of the Strand Arcade, far better located than The Wentworth, we have excellent connections in the world of entertainment, both here and in London and Europe, and we can afford to outspend anyone in this country.*

It did not take long to persuade David and Harriet. She was to be "chatelaine" of her own domain, David would find a revitalising outlet for his surplus capital and Percy, as manager, would have a lasting role where he made and applied the rules. Provoked by Hannah Maclurcan, he let the cat out of the bag. Neither he nor any member of his family would ever have to put their nose into the Wentworth Café again.

---

even met that evening, at least at the Wentworth, any inference of impropriety between them on the premises is false. However, there is independent evidence that the "cavalier" went further than to aver that "he would never put his nose inside the place again." Maclurcan family lore is that his words amounted to a threat: *"I'll get you! My father will open his own nightclub!"* (conversation with John Maclurcan, 2017) Percy could never have decided independently to "build his own [nightclub]"; that was entirely his father's prerogative.

Birth of The Ambassadors

In early 1922 David registered separate Stewart Dawson companies in New South Wales, Victoria and Western Australia and de-registered Stewart Dawson Australia. He was splitting the assets of the company for greater protection against creditors and to provide him with more options for their future disposal. Though this company restructure was to prove an astute strategic move, it was for another project initiated at that time that David would be acclaimed by the public at large. On April 13th, 1922, Sydney's Daily Commercial News and Shipping List announced the forthcoming registration on March 31st of The Ambassadors Limited, capital: £20,000 in £1 shares, whose objects were: "To carry on the business of amusement proprietors, managers and caterers for public entertainments etc." The first directors were David, Percy, and Stuart Stewart Dawson,* brother-in-law, Malcolm McNab, son-in-law, Harry Arnold, and two others. In May 1922 David dispatched Percy on a mission to the USA and Europe. His instructions were to find the best in musical entertainment, the best chefs and all there was to learn about contemporary style in places for public dining and dancing. David's benchmark was to go one better than the Wentworth Café in every respect. Hannah Maclurcan's kitchen and table service had set the standard as long ago as 1913, when she introduced to Australia à la carte meals available from 11 a.m. to 11 p.m. She constructed a separate grill kitchen to meet the requirements of the Winter Garden. The main kitchen featured the latest in equipment and there was proper refrigeration and cold storage for perishable foods. The Summer Garden "a favorite rendezvous with the Sydney public for luncheon and dinner, and … a fashionable resort for social gatherings and wedding receptions,"

---

* David seems to have overlooked Stuart's ineligibility for the position of company director on the grounds of his bankruptcy. It was probably another attempt to galvanise Stuart into some form of responsibility. There is no evidence that it succeeded.

could seat 500 diners, the internal dining room had a capacity of 250 and private dining rooms took a further 78.[205] When the Ballroom opened in 1920 its basement housed the Wentworth Café, which accommodated another 400 and had yet another set of dedicated kitchens a level lower, with lifts to carry dishes up to the servery and back down to the scullery after the meal.[206]

Mrs Maclurcan's cuisine and service apart, her other major contribution to the modernising of evening entertainment was the introduction in 1913 of cabaret in the Winter Garden. The Sun (Sydney) reported:

> *The word "cabaret" is, of course, a misnomer when used in this respect, but it has come to be applied to entertainments provided in hotels and restaurants in England, the Continent and the United States. So popular has the cabaret idea become in America that no eating house of any repute can afford to be without it ...*

By 1920 the Ballroom offered not only its regular "symphony" orchestra in the early evening but a new jazz band, the Syncopas Band, "organised for modern dance", for when the younger set arrived later. It was an instant success, and the place was packed night after night. Professional dancers were hired to entertain diners and demonstrate the latest dances from America and London. Dance competitions were popular as the Fox-Trot, One-Step, Chicago,* and the modern waltz, described as "the supreme test" due to its stately, gliding measure, supplanted old fashions such as the polka. The dance floor had become so crowded that the Perth Daily News reported, "it is almost impossible to dance".[207]

Such was the popularity of the several places of entertainment that regular gossip columns sprang up in the city newspapers, dedicated to accounts of the parties, balls and charity events held in them. Exhaustive guest lists were published, the pecking order rigorously observed, and the frocks of the ladies meticulously described. Of importance to "those who mattered" was the naming of ad hoc

---

* The "Chicago" was a short-lived early '20s craze. Hannah Maclurcan thought it uncivilised and discouraged it at the Wentworth, but it remained popular in Sydney, nevertheless.

committees formed to organise and manage the many charity events. These groups perpetuated the tradition of ladies taking charge of this important aspect of social and philanthropic life. To be on the committee responsible for an event that could attract upwards of 1200 guests and raise thousands of pounds for a hospital, orphanage, or relief of poverty and to have one's name published for all of Sydney or Melbourne to see was the epitome of social success and esteem. To be a member of successive committees or better, to chair one or more, earned lasting kudos. This was the role to which Harriet aspired and which the lack of an alternative venue to the Wentworth denied her.

While Percy was away, work proceeded excavating and developing the basement of the Strand Arcade, for this was where the new cabaret would be built. It was unused space that would not impinge on the existing retail establishments. The two frontages, on George and Pitt Streets provided excellent exposure and access and there were few constraints on the internal layout. Moreover, there would be no visible impact on the building's impressive exterior. However, the last thing the city needed was another disruption to traffic, so David had a further compelling incentive to finish the work. Since the early war years Sydney had suffered noise, dust and inconvenience from the sporadic work undertaken on the City Railway line from Central Station. This would become the City Circle, looping through the new stations at Town Hall, Wynyard, Circular Quay, St James and Museum, and if all went to plan it would by the end of the twenties connect to what was referred to as "The North Shore Bridge". Traffic along George and Pitt streets from Town Hall (Park Street) northwards had for too long been a nightmare of trams, omnibuses, horse-drawn drays, and cabs and increasing numbers of private motor vehicles. As the commercial centre moved northwards towards the harbour the problem of conveying people almost a mile from the terminus at Central Station to places of business and retail outlets became acute. At peak hours one double-car tram carrying up to 100 passengers passed along George Street every seventeen seconds[208] and congestion often reduced progress to walking pace. The cry went out to replace them with a modern underground rail line linked to Central Station.* If Sydney aspired to be a world city like London or New York, then it was about time it adopted more of their established conveniences. The proposals soon bogged in political arguments, as the inevitable fight for funds between city and country escalated. It was not until the election of 1922, just as David commissioned The Ambassadors, that the City Railway loop finally received the bi-partisan support that ensured its full development. Work commenced excavating the underground station at Hyde Park that would become St James but immediately the long-suffering citizens were subjected to further disruption and inconvenience as a stream of drays carted spoil from the site across town to dump it in Darling Harbour, cutting across the very thoroughfares (George and Pitt Street, among others) whose traffic the railway was intended to relieve.

Now, added to the carts of the railway contractors were those removing hundreds of tons of clay and rock from the basement of the Strand Arcade, while concrete, brick, and steel braced and lined the cavernous space created. The initial budget was soon exceeded, and more capital had to be raised, bringing the total cost to over £100,000 before final fit-out. Five electric lifts were installed to connect the basement with the street level and the vast kitchens two levels up. The kitchens themselves absorbed £10,000. They were equipped with large refrigeration rooms and five cooking ranges, supplied by Metters Ltd, Sydney kitchen engineers. David was proud to proclaim:

> *They [Metters] associate in their immense establishment the highest skill from the celebrated Scotch engineering firms in the neighbourhood of Glasgow, who had done all the big hotel kitchens in England.*[209]

There were facilities for ten chefs and thirty assistants. The servery for the restaurant was 100 feet long, every foot of which would be

---

* Ironically, relief was short-lived. After the last tram line was torn up in 1961 buses and cars soon filled the gaps left by the trams. In 2015 George Street was again a closed building site as the "Light Rail" (modern tram) system was installed to alleviate congestion. History had come full circle.

needed to serve the 700 or more diners. By October 1923, the publicity campaign for the forthcoming opening was in full swing. The Melbourne newspaper, "The Australasian" reported on the 27th of the month, under the headline, "Sydney Topics – City Amusements":

The firm of Stewart Dawson, Pitt Street, Sydney, Property Company, has announced the early completion of a restaurant that will cost about £100,000. For a long time, a tunnel has been going through the bowels of the earth under the buildings in Pitt Street where the Stewart Dawson jewellery shop stands, the entrance bearing the sign "The Ambassadors". Marble staircases, palm courts and all the rest of the accompaniments of costly entertaining are being created, round floors on steel springs for dancing. There will be imported cooks and imported waiters, who probably will receive better pay than many bank managers draw. An imported orchestra will supply the latest fantastic music. As far as mere eating goes a restaurant only has to be opened anywhere in Sydney and it appears to be quickly crowded.[210]

Percy's mission was almost complete. He arrived back in Perth on Tuesday November 13th where he was pleased to announce further details of the ambitious new entertainment Mecca, which the Perth "Daily News" characterised as "The latest in restaurants for the Sydney smart set" and a "gigantic undertaking". Quoting Percy, and pointedly omitting any reference to the Wentworth Café, the paper reported:

The most notable feature is the building and equipment of a modern restaurant, something quite different to what Australia has known up to date, embracing entertainments, such as dancing etc.

Percy's travels had taken him via America, where his goal was to find a distinctive dance band with an international reputation. While in New York he learned that

the best dance music in the world had been taken by Mr Bert Ralton, the conductor and composer, to London, together with his party of instrumentalists, known as the Havana Symphonie Band.

Percy took note but joined briefly by Norman, he continued his search in Europe. Failing to find "musical novelties" that met his and his father's criteria, he tracked down the popular band leader at

London's Savoy Hotel. Ralton, as well as being an outstanding musician, also understood the value of showmanship.[211] Percy had in fact heard the band before he set off from Australia, in recordings and on the early radio stations then gaining in popularity. There was never any other serious contender for The Ambassadors' opening and Percy had a deep wallet to entice Ralton, not to mention a guarantee of further engagements in Australia, thanks to Percy's connections with JC Williamson and the still active Hugh McIntosh. The band was engaged to play at the opening of The Ambassadors and sailed with Percy on the RMS Ormonde to launch their Australian tour at the Melbourne Tivoli.

The final item on his list was the imported cooks and waiters. Once again, Percy picked the plums from the best hotels and restaurants in London and Paris. The Maître d'hôtel was Giovanni Becchio, from the Carlton Hotel and Savoy Restaurant, Director of Services was Orlando Azzalin Romano ("Romano") from the Ritz, London. Head Chef was Fernand Tournes, also from the Carlton and his assistant was a M. de Smet, from Ciros, Paris, who had also worked in Deauville and Monte Carlo.

As the staff assembled from across the world, the construction of The Ambassadors reached its final stage. David dearly wanted to open by Christmas to make the biggest possible impact and to capture the seasonal crowds from the Wentworth. The city was rife with rumour and gossip about the fabulous new palace of entertainment and fine dining, and he fed the newspapers with teasers, exclusive previews and promotional advertisements masquerading as articles.* A sign had been in place at the entrance to the Strand Arcade since the beginning of the year, labelling the excavation of the basement: "The Ambassadors". From mid-year, public curiosity had been piqued by the arrival of marble slabs for stairways, wrought iron railings and cartloads of finished boards for the dance floor. By September advertisements appeared for painters to finish the elaborate plaster mouldings on the ceilings, cornices, and pillars. In October paid promotional articles started to appear in Sydney newspapers. One of

---

* What would be termed "advertorials" today.

the first was in The Sunday Times of October 14th.[212] Headed "To Dance at The Ambassadors – A Privilege in Store," it announced breathlessly:

It won't be long now before Sydney people and their visitors will have a new and delightful diversion to indeed improve the shining hours of the evening. To dancing enthusiasts The Ambassadors holds out the prospect of at least three unique and wonderful delights.

It went on to describe the two state of the art sprung dance floors

such as have few counterparts in the world and the apotheosis of jazz music that would be brought by the world-famous American Savoy Havana Band ... the one band – we have never really heard one like it – that just won't let your feet keep still.

The trifecta of modern wonders was to be completed with "the aid of our stern Lady Science". A form of air-conditioning would ensure that "an even temperature will be maintained for perfect comfort in dancing at all times – whatever the thermometer may say outside." an innovation that would have had instant appeal to Sydney-siders anticipating the sweltering summer season and already suffering what was to be an unusually long drought. After listing several international testimonials to the superiority of the Havana Band, the article stamped David's brand on the venture: "The Ambassadors has been solely planned and executed and is owned by the Stewart Dawson Pitt-street* Property Company, Limited. – Advt." It had all the hallmarks of a David puff-piece but for perhaps the first time in decades, he was not the author. The by-line below read: "Printed and published by Hugh Donald McIntosh". David had enlisted or been persuaded to delegate publicity to his old friend, Mack. He would have had no difficulty placing the advertisements, since Mack happened to be the owner of the paper, which was in a perilous financial state. He followed up with another piece in the Sunday Times on November 4th.[213] Now, The Ambassadors was to be "A New Shrine of Amusement" and Mack laid on the flattery with a heavy hand.

---

* This orthography for street names persisted until the mid-1930s.

Fashionable Sydney, strolling down Pitt-street on shopping or amusement bent, has, for many months been intrigued by the cryptic sign "The Ambassadors" arching over the entrance to one of the Block's most prominent sites. "The Ambassadors", by association of ideas, could not stand for other than something most distinguished and attractive. As a heightened activity of preparation becomes noticeable about that most interesting entry way, it is increasingly evident that Sydney folk, so well equipped by nature and inheritance to appreciate the real graces of living, have never yet been accorded the privilege of dining and dancing in surroundings so ideal as The Ambassadors will make available.

The unspoken message was becoming clear:

Forget that pretentious, old-fashioned, colonial backwater, The Wentworth. If you want to be truly sophisticated (which we know you would …) come and be seen at The Ambassadors!

On November 15th, Norman, back in town from his European interlude, stood in for Percy as the latter travelled with the Havana Band from Perth, showing representatives of various newspapers around the building. It was a consummate public relations exercise. Sydney's Stock and Station Journal, in an article headed: "A New Palace of Beauty" enthused:

The great event in the City of Sydney this Christmas will be the opening of Stewart Dawson's palace of beauty. It would be commonplace to say Café. Right in the centre of Sydney, within a few steps of the big emporiums of fashion, and popular dining de luxe cafés, the finishing touches to an underworld of architectural loveliness are in progress, evidently under pressure of contract time. And this speeding up is to provide a new sensation of what initiative and money can do for the ever-growing need of luxury-loving age, with a good deal of the artistic thrown in.

The article described the lavish use of marble and the tasteful gold and white colour scheme,* the enormous main hall with its sprung

---

* It overlooked mentioning the extensive use of "Asbestolite" fibre in the elaborate plaster mouldings, much ballyhooed elsewhere.

floor of jarrah. The lighting had not yet been installed, the columnist having to "leave it to the imagination." The article concluded:

> *I was merely asked down by Major Dawson to have a look round, and all I could say to myself was: "It is a revelation".*

Despite the avalanche of publicity, David's wish to open as early as November was not fulfilled. By October it was becoming clear that the main ballroom would not be finished before the international staff and the band arrived, though the smaller Palm Court and private rooms would be. Bert Ralton and the band were hastily diverted to the Tivoli circuit in Melbourne and then Sydney to keep them occupied and pay off some of the contracted fee. By December David and Percy could wait no longer and The New York Havana Band moved into the Palm Court, playing for afternoon teas and dinner dances, while doubling at the Sydney Tivoli. It was a softer launch than they would have wanted but it would itself promote the imminent full opening to the excited Sydney populace. Moreover, the lower key operation would give the new staff time to become accustomed to the layout and to work as a professional team under less pressure.

The grand opening was finally announced: it would be on Friday December 21st, just in time for Christmas. The "Cabaret de luxe, à la New York, for which Sydney has been waiting for months and months"[214] would open with a grand ball ("a super de luxe affair!"). Although the price of admission was £3/3/-, a good week's wage for a couple, this would buy a fifteen-course meal and a night's entertainment from both the Havana Band* and The Ambassadors' other orchestra, the so-called Symphony Orchestra, under the baton of Mr Frederick Tacheill (Vienna).

The opening did not disappoint. The Sydney Morning Herald was among the first to publish an account of the gala evening, the next day. Quoting HG Wells, then at the peak of his international fame, the journal opened:

---

* Bert Ralton's band was variously described as the "Royal", "Savoy" and "New York" Havana Band, depending on who had hired it last or what degree of international cachet was to be implied.

It may be that the most serious need of the human race just now is comic relief. At any rate, Mr. H. G. Wells has ventured the confident guess that the world is about to trade its sackcloth for symbols and enter an era of humour. He predicts that "between now and 1940 or 1960, when the nations will be tested by their next bloody tragedy, they will look chiefly for fun." Perhaps it was in the light of Mr. Wells's prophecy that Mr. David Stewart Dawson and his colleagues in the venture conceived the idea of starting The Ambassadors Restaurant, which was officially opened last night. … The Ambassadors will stimulate the laughter of understanding. It will satisfy the connoisseur, for it is no exaggeration to state that it provides facilities for enjoying the best of life on a scale not previously tried in Australasia. Mr. Stewart Dawson … appears to have lavished – almost squandered – money on the appointments, and he has undoubtedly organised a restaurant that for dining and dancing will compare more than favourably with any similar enterprise in the world.

The evening, which was billed as a fund-raiser for The Prince Alfred Hospital, easily raised the £1,000 David had promised.* One eager patron paid as much to secure a table. The Premier of New South Wales, Sir George Fuller, was the guest of honour and the "brilliant company" who "thronged" into the restaurant included many serving members of Parliament, an Admiral, the retail king Sir Samuel Hordern, and tobacco baron and founder of Macquarie Radio, Sir Hugh Denison.† The "brilliant company" sparkled with several hundred of Sydney's brightest and richest. Mack was of course present, hosting his own tables "massed with bon bons" where "each

---

* David was elected a life member of the board of the Benevolent Society of New South Wales, in recognition of the gift of £51 he made to the Royal Hospital for Women, Paddington, from the proceeds.

† Sir Hugh's grandson, also named Hugh, would marry David's granddaughter in 1949.

lady of the party received an amusing mascot doll* and other gifts." David and Harriet's own guests included Mr. and Mrs. Harry Arnold. Lila had married mining engineer Henry William "Harry" Arnold some years before and settled in Australia, the only member of David's original family to do so. David had rewarded Harry with a directorship of The Ambassadors.

If Percy expected public recognition for his efforts in the glowing notices of the evening, he was to be disappointed, and not for the last time. Norman, who had done little more than shepherd visitors around the construction site and who wasn't even on the board of the management company, took centre stage on the opening night. The post-celebration reports told of "Major Stewart Dawson's table guests," listing several eligible young ladies and gentlemen before mentioning "Major (sic) Percy Stewart Dawson." Poor Percy had to suffer the embarrassment of having his younger brother's rank conferred upon him, if only for a day.

Back home at Wilga Harriet floated on air, Percy shrugged off Norman's scene-stealing (he'd learned much from his marriage to Thelma) and celebrated the vindication of his bold challenge to Hannah Maclurcan, while David contemplated facing his own challenge. At seventy-two he had everything a man could wish for, didn't he? More money than almost anyone he knew, all the trappings of wealth, fame and public respect, a loyal and energetic wife, three respectful and by all accounts, happy daughters, at least one worthy son. This decade promised more excitement than ever before: people flying through the air in comfort and safety; motor cars that you could drive at a respectable speed on ever wider, smoother roads; clean, reliable electricity for power and light; wireless broadcasting bringing the world into every home; engineering feats to dwarf all previous accomplishments (this proposed bridge across the harbour would put Sydney on the world map!). He should have been excited, enthused and, yes, he did still have plans for his real estate, but something was missing. Since Valerie's death he had been beset with a sense of

---

* Dolls were a feature gift of many society gatherings at the time. For a while, as private telephone use became more prevalent, kitsch "kewpie" doll covers for "candlestick" phones were a regular item on restaurant tables.

failure; failure to meet his need for control, to take charge of every situation in everyone's best interests. He'd brought unimaginable pain and suffering to the McFarlanes, disappointed Harriet so that he would be forever in her moral debt, embarrassed Percy and, he supposed, the other brothers. Worst of all, he seemed to have lost his touch in the one thing in which he took most pride: innovating and driving new commercial ventures. Of course, The Ambassadors could succeed, and he would be able to take some of the credit, but it was Percy and Harriet who would earn that success. And, when all was said and done, this whole restaurant-cum-cabaret idea might well be just a passing fad. He wasn't banking on it to grow the family fortune. On the contrary, he acknowledged secretly the press's view of his extravagance; The Ambassadors could be a great showpiece for Stewart Dawson's, but it would take a miracle for it to ever earn its keep. Thank goodness he had deep pockets. No, he would grace the place with his presence, support Harriet and Percy, celebrate their successes, enjoy the dancing (he loved to dance) but if he was to have a legacy it would be something more substantial than this. He prepared himself for New Year's 1924.

Happy New Year

The Ambassadors was fully open by New Year's Eve, to welcome 1924 in a blaze of entertainments. Christmas week saw nightly dinner dances and the word soon got around that dining and dancing in Sydney, nay, in Australia, had attained international standard. David's publicity machine changed up a gear, confident in his claims of superiority. The Sunday Times continued to be his preferred channel for shameless self-promotion, and he lost no opportunity to strike favourable comparison with The Wentworth. On December 16th the newspaper published an interview with Louis de Smet, the sous chef at The Ambassadors, which was an unsubtle mix of adulation for David and denigration of Mrs Maclurcan's reputation.[215] Establishing his credentials by reminding readers of the pre-eminence of French cuisine ("the old traditions of renown and superiority"), de Smet praised David effusively:

> *Among the most clever men of Sydney, Mr. Stewart Dawson, who has not only acquired a considerable fortune after many years of consistent work, also a wide experience in business and commerce, having travelled very extensively, visiting in particular, Paris and the South of France, has brought back with him the same impression, which is the wide world opinion of all travellers, that we hold the supremacy in the catering trade in general …*

The flattery and braggadocio continued:

> *More recently the sons* of Mr. Stewart Dawson have been among our foremost and distinguished guests in Paris, and it has given them great pleasure to patronise the best of our restaurants, having greatly appreciated our methods of attending to the needs of our patrons and the manner we conduct our business … Mr. Stewart Dawson must be congratulated and admired … His undertaking is much more to be*

---

* "Sons" implies that Percy was not alone in Paris. If so, it can only have been Norman who accompanied him, perhaps joining him from London. Norman would certainly have taken "great pleasure" but probably left the boring business of negotiating to Percy.

appreciated if anyone considers the importance of this big enterprise, not forgetting that, although Mr. Dawson has nothing better to wish for, we remember that while the weight of age must be felt at times, he might have been enjoying a well deserved and peaceful rest.

The language and tone of the interview were pure David. Frenchman, de Smet could not have used David's verbose and hyperbolic style of English. David was admitting that this was indeed a late life indulgence but what followed confirmed that, more than anything, it was a vanity project calculated to go one better than anyone had ever done in Australia, in particular, his provincial rival, Hannah Maclurcan. The interviewee produced his verbal kitchen knife and proceeded to plunge it into the esteemed chatelaine:

Attracted by a pardonable curiosity of my profession, I have been longing to find out the way Sydneyites are catered for. Therefore, I have found that out for myself by patronising the best known restaurants and hotels in town. Well, without being too strict or severe, I can say that real French culinary kitchens are absolutely unknown in Sydney so far. Nevertheless, my mother language is well displayed in menus but if you choose any dish there is very little of the French culinary mastery about them, only the name of it.

Menus at the Wentworth Café, as was the custom, were in French but it was regrettably true that for the most part the dishes, for all their skilful preparation and presentation, had little of "the Continent" about them and often a distinctly colonial character.

It is almost a pity to stain or violate to a certain extent our long-standing supremacy and to lower the renown of our predecessors, which we very proudly admire …

The interview concluded in the most condescending, not to say, offensive way:

I must conclude by pointing to the fact that the patrons will be the right element we require, and, without any doubt, very easy to please. Why? The great majority of them are still in the dark, and uninitiated to the delicacy and refinements of our work in the composition of a real French menu. Up to now they could not expect it. It is, therefore, our duty to let them know, and we to be tried.

Using the foreign sous chef as a proxy for his views both insulated David from criticism and, in his mind, excused the offensiveness of much of the article on the grounds of unfamiliarity with English idiom or local sensibilities. And the ploy appeared to succeed, as hundreds of patrons queued night after night to dine in the main restaurant, the private rooms and the Palm Court, to dance and be swept away by the kind of music never before heard in the city and to be part of the most exciting, and by a long way the most luxurious milieu of the moment. The sous chef had not exaggerated the quality and presentation of the cuisine and the Havana Band was several classes above the resident workmanlike orchestra of ex-military musicians at the Wentworth. Capitalising on the tremendous publicity that had attended the visit of the Prince of Wales to the Wentworth in 1920 and turning it back on Hannah Maclurcan, David delighted in informing the starry-eyed revellers as often as he could that Bert Ralton's was "the Prince of Wales' favorite dance band."

New Year's Eve was every inch the success he had prayed for. Over 600 turned up for the grand ball, filling the room and overflowing into the smaller chambers. At the entrance, the Scottish note was struck with groups of Scotch thistles and bows of Royal Stuart tartan. Many tables were decorated in purple and gold with full standard rose trees and fragrant stephanotis.* Beds of pansies were strewn over others. David's own table was covered in more thistles, heather, and clan tartan. Balloons and multi-coloured streamers draped between tables and "dainty favors" – little white fans with quaint black silhouettes painted on them – lay at every place. Boxes of bon bons and chocolates were handed round, and elaborate paper hats to suit every guest. After the early evening dining and entertainment by the Symphony Orchestra the jazzing began. As twelve midnight approached,

> *a dramatic hush fell upon The Ambassadors, suddenly darkness descended. A big, luminous clock face shone out of the darkness and*

---

* Stephanotis floribunda: known as Madagascan Jasmine, has starry white blooms and is intensely fragrant.

measured off minute by minute until, with hands on twelve, the lights re-appeared and in the centre of the ballroom floor was a great egg – and Miss 1924 (a six year old child) stepped out. With her silver spear she put Old Father Time to flight ...[216]

A guest complimented David on the magnificent cuisine: "How lucky you were to secure such a chef," to which he replied with predictable hubris, "The luck is always good which follows effort."[217]

But Sydney never abandoned other popular venues in favour of The Ambassadors on that night or any other. Despite a rather depressed economy (retail sales that Christmas were down as drought conditions, broken only in the Christmas week, cut agricultural production that still underpinned the nation) patrons filled restaurants and halls in the city centre, at the Town Hall and nearby Moore Park. The Wentworth suffered no immediate loss, on the contrary, so many turned up (almost 1,000) that

patrons were glad to dance just in any corner they could. At best there was hardly room to turn either in the ball-room, palm court or balcony.[218]

Nearly 2,000 danced the night away in the Palais Royal at Moore Park.* Hannah Maclurcan put on a show that rivalled, and in some ways, outdid David's efforts. Tables were decorated with tall figures of Jack Frost, with wreaths of holly and crimson streamers. The variety of favors exceeded that of The Ambassadors, going as far as powder puffs, scent bottles and "weird dolls". A gossip columnist observed:

We adults are getting so childish the past year or so that we take as much pleasure collecting "souvenirs" at dinner dances as the average small boy or girl at an agricultural show on the hunt for "free samples".[219]

---

* Built in 1913 as the Royal Hall of Industries for the Royal Agricultural Society it was the Showground's largest building, airy and open. In the "Roaring Twenties" it was affectionately known as "The Palais Royal", a popular rendezvous for young Sydneysiders, who flocked to the dances, roller skating and ice skating staged in it. Today it hosts spectacular events such as the annual Mardi Gras Party and MasterChef Live.

The same writer opined, no doubt to David's irritation: "The Wentworth really put up the best entertainment that evening." If David's motto was to "go one better", on this occasion Hannah turned the tables on him. He had had a young child step out of a giant egg but over at the Wentworth:

As the city clocks tolled the midnight hour there was a charming little tableau, for as heralds with a fanfare of trumpets proclaimed the birth of 1924 the curtains of the stage were drawn aside to show Old Father Time blotting out 1923 and as the last figure faded from view a huge egg opened to show within a gilt cradle, with a baby of just a week old very much awake. That infant played its part remarkably well, for its hands and feet were worked quite gleefully. It was not at all perturbed with the noise and it was cheered loudly when Mrs. Maclurcan held it up.

The writer noted, in an aside: "It was rather a pity that the mother could not have been there to have seen her infant's successful debut." A pity indeed: the baby's mother was still "confined", but the sensibilities of new mothers and new-borns were the last thing on the mind of the jazz-age party goers.

The gossip column was notable, not only for its preference for The Wentworth but for its reaction to the sheer ostentation of The Ambassadors, which had already been remarked on in the earlier Sydney Morning Herald article and elsewhere.

The Ambassadors is rather overwhelming in its grandeur, the staff is of infinite variety. Anyone of an economical turn of mind must wonder what they are all doing, for there is a regular retinue of liveried lackeys, page boys, waiters, doorkeepers and attendants ... One wonders how long Sydney folk will be able to pay for the luxury. The expense must be appalling, especially when is added the salaries of the members of the fine band, and also an orchestra. There is at present in Sydney no happier man than Mr. Stewart Dawson, who appears to get 150,000 pounds' worth of pleasure in contemplating what marvels have been done underneath his property in Pitt street.

David was delighted to read the article. An advertisement released at the time read:

Your search for a perfect evening ends at The Ambassadors. A thousand and one items that don't immediately fill the intellect constitute one of the marvels of The Ambassadors, but all heading towards the same object – THE SUPREME ACHIEVEMENT OF AN IDEA. Fancy £165,000 (one hundred and sixty-five thousand pounds) invested to GIVE SYDNEY THE FINEST RESTAURANT AND DANSANT ESTABLISHMENT IN THE WORLD! Admitted you can find in LONDON, PARIS and NEW YORK nooks and corners of Hotels devoted to the same purpose, but all of them are toys compared with THE AMBASSADORS, SYDNEY, the site of which covers in size a greater area than the four biggest hotels in Sydney added together.*

His curious promotional booklet: "The Boy and the Wheelbarrow 1858, The Man and The Ambassadors 1924", published for the opening and distributed to patrons and the press, missed no opportunity to reinforce the message:

Here in Sydney The Ambassadors (produced regardless of cost) stands out as a significant sign of the times, and has placed Sydney at the very top as being in possession of the finest, best, and largest appointed restaurant and dansant establishment in the whole world (vide unanimous verdict of world travellers) … In a casual way, few people readily realise that £10,000 was absorbed in the production of The Ambassadors' kitchens … Two gigantic ventilating plants alone costing over £10,000 … and so on, with little subtlety, for several pages.

He'd been moved to write "The Boy and the Wheelbarrow …" in the months preceding the opening of the restaurant, as his feelings of frustration and depression grew. Much of the content would have been familiar to many from the interviews he had given over several decades. He recounted his origins in Cairnie, making much of the project to build the stone wall in the garden, before leaping forward to the story of his successes in watchmaking and jewellery, including the triumphs of Hatton Garden and Regent Street. Illustrations of The

---

* In case the reader missed the message, he spelt out the amount for them.

Treasure House and the impressive frontage and interior of the Regent Street store were complemented with pages of British press clippings praising his creativity, imagination, and business acumen. The final pages introduced The Ambassadors with detailed descriptions of every room, including the enormous kitchens. Full plate photographs enticed the reader into this "New Palace of Beauty". Sprinkled throughout the book were many of the maxims that comprised David's "Philosophy of Business Success".

There were other insights into David's frame of mind. He had become convinced that Sydney was growing into the premier city of the Empire, if not the world, and that it would sooner or later outstrip London. A feature article in The Sunday Times of February 6th, 1921, entitled; "Personalities of the Week"[220] had photos of six men, including David and one Mohandas Karamchand Gandhi, quoting their recent pronouncements. Edward ("Red Ted") Theodore, Labor Premier of Queensland, and Giovanni Giolitti, Prime Minister of Italy, made disparaging and topical comments about the rampaging Bolsheviks in Soviet Russia, Gandhi stated that three hundred million people of India would oppose British rule. David declared bluntly and more parochially, "Sydney will yet be bigger than London." Now in 1924 he wrote:

> *Sydney, onward and upward. Who shall challenge thy coming power and prestige, or dare try to pervert thy redoubtable inheritance? Australia, the Greater Britain of the future British Empire, glorifying to the full in traditional descent. Men who think, realise how great our inheritance and how marvellous our possibilities! Just a few years hence and Sydney will undoubtedly, in importance, be riding hand in hand alongside London … Sydney, the theme of these remarks, is breathing fast and furious asking for more development … How many cities to-day can boast of putting in hand a five-million-pounds bridge.**

In view of his dismissive opinions of Sydney's provincialism, expressed through de Smet and in his advertisements for The

* Work commenced on the Sydney Harbour Bridge in April 1923, during the construction of The Ambassadors.

Ambassadors, such laudatory words were surprising. However, the praise for Sydney's physical advances was qualified, for he continued:

> *In keeping our hearts, hopes and mentalities aglow, surely what counts in life is how are our thoughts acting in getting us along. How should we all feel or act if we had nothing to enhance the bright side to life.* Despondency and a nameless purpose of doing nothing but waiting for the morrow. What a despondent, lukewarm race we would become – quite unworthy of being sons of the British Empire; but with constructive thoughts, serious work, and happy moments, we hail in sight helpful and significant triumphs.*

And then came the punch line:

> *History has proved that in Sydney there are many thinking men and women. We cordially invite all these capable intellects to visit The Ambassadors one evening and work out in the light of delightful exercise (meaning: dancing) and enlightenment (French dining and service) the role The Ambassadors is quietly filling in adding its quota to the social environment of Sydney.*

There was more in this vein:

> *… taking us away from associations of Australia's hitherto somewhat sombre life …, it is obvious to all who visualise the present tendency of the times that the bygone theory of a joyless existence has been superseded …*

But now David's motives were clearer. Explaining his philosophy of business a few pages on, he listed Ambition, Thoroughness, Value, and Imagination as the keys to success. He could honestly claim all these attributes but might not have admitted their corollaries, impatience with and intolerance of the second rate and an inevitable creeping arrogance. There was a strong sense of frustration in his response to "despondency and a nameless purpose of doing nothing but waiting for tomorrow and associations of Australia's hitherto

---

* For all his ponderous syntax and generally correct grammar, punctuation was not David's strong suit. He seems to have been ignorant of or deliberately avoided question marks.

somewhat sombre life." He had spent ten recent years in London, the very city he celebrated as the paragon for Sydney to emulate and surpass, and enough time "on the Continent" to see how sophisticated society behaved and what it expected by way of cultured entertainment.

He knew, and many in his adopted city acknowledged, that neither Sydney, Melbourne nor any other Australasian metropolitan centre could yet pretend to belong to that illustrious inner circle in the northern hemisphere. At least, they feared to pretend. David was exploiting the deeply felt sense of colonial inferiority versus the culture of the motherland. The Australasian public assumed that anything produced by local dramatists, actors, musicians, artists, and writers was necessarily deficient when compared against the works of their British and European counterparts. The only way local arts professionals could build themselves up in public esteem was either to follow overseas fashions or, more often, to spend time working in Britain. This deference to the supposed superior tastes and skills of the mother countries extended beyond the fine arts to popular culture, emboldening David to challenge local tastes in dining and entertainment. He had two strong allies in the family. Harriet and Norman had never truly adjusted to life in Australia. Harriet's return from London in 1919 had been reluctant at best. Had it not been for David's misadventure with Valerie he suspected that none of them would have made the journey down under ever again. Perhaps there would have been occasional family reunions with Percy and Stuart or short business visits; nothing more. Harriet made no secret of her preference for the "civilised" scene in London and, once the war was over, the opportunity to resume her frequent vacations to Paris and the Riviera. Norman, too, the perpetual bachelor and man about town, found that London and the Continent offered far more than the southern cities for his playboy lifestyle. He would have been happy to bid farewell to his father when David departed in 1917 if his allowance continued to fill his bank account.

And then, there was the dancing. Numerous advertisements and many pages of "The Boy and the Wheelbarrow …" were devoted to promotional rhetoric on the topic. David was eager to attract patrons to fill the dance floor of The Ambassadors, for the straightforward commercial reason that the sheer numbers of people, young and old, who came to trip the floors would be obliged to pay, not only an entry fee but the cost of a meal and drinks, both legal and illegal. But the lengths to which he went, in extolling the virtues of "la vie dansante" were extreme, even by his standards. He wrote:

> *The beneficial effect of exercise has always been recognised and the new improved form of exercise obtained through dancing is merely a befitting sequence to the "has-beens", and at the present moment a universal belief is obtaining that dancing is the best available exercise, combining, as it does, with the highest enjoyment.*

After quoting a Harley Street physician ("Now I advise dancing exercise to all my patients, old and young …") he continued:

> *At the present moment London is enjoying the use of over 500 dancing schools supported by all ranks and conditions of society. This should be enough to impress people, who hitherto have been tied by inclination to home and fireside, that life may be lived to better advantage, and induce them to take in service of that which forms an improvement on accustomed habits.*[221]

He repeated the message, almost verbatim, five pages later in the same publication. This application of sledgehammer to nut was even more curious because if there was one thing for which "Sydneyites" needed no encouragement it was dancing. His instinct for the cutting marketing message seemed to have failed him.* Where he might have sought to differentiate the style, quality or sophistication of the music and dancing at his new mecca to persuade Wentworth or Palais Royal patrons to switch, instead he lectured them on the health benefits of an activity which they took for granted. It was as if he had reverted to his early days of "Watches! Watches! Watches!", where he had been confident of blitzing a naïve market with a novel concept that would sweep all before it, only to find every other person sporting an affordable, quality watch and thinking nothing of it.

---

* Or he had been swept away by his personal enthusiasm for dancing. He was a keen and skilled ballroom dancer even in his later years, taking to the floor late into the evening when other, younger couples would "sit one out".

In the end, his faux pas had little ill effect. Few bothered to read his promotional tract and those that did raised an eyebrow and dismissed it as the ramblings of an out of touch Victorian.

Teething Troubles

The War was five years over and while memories were still fresh for many the massive government investments in infrastructure, coupled with the effects of grants to returned servicemen, engendered a spirit of optimism as cities like Sydney, Melbourne, Brisbane, and Perth enjoyed a new growth spurt. Suburbs filled with California Bungalows, rail networks expanded, and road building reached a new high. In Sydney, the bridge was the most blatant manifestation of this promise of the future as the massive pylons rose and whole streets were demolished in the historic Rocks area on the southern approach to make way for the access ramps. Unemployment remained low,* but real wage growth was almost static, and the country entered a prolonged period of deflation.† As a result, and despite a generally positive outlook, sales in discretionary items declined. Retailers began discounting more aggressively, clearance sales were more frequent.

In Australia, though sales of goods remained mediocre, the nineteen twenties was the decade in which the share of national income spent on services, including popular entertainment, took off, at the expense of the traditional staples, mining, and agriculture, while manufacturing was still to gain full momentum. The young set, now sensing more than ever a freedom to express themselves, flocked to cinemas, restaurants, and dance halls. For the older generation of middle-class city dwellers, it was almost business as usual as they enjoyed what they were now calling The Roaring Twenties.‡ American influence was overtaking the traditional British, witness the excitement generated by the arrival of The Havana Band. Hannah Maclurcan's frequent visits to the USA to

---

* The unemployment rate was around 4 per cent.

† Between 1914 and 1928 the cost of living increased by 70% but the average wage only increased by 82%. A.G.L. Shaw and G.R. Bruns, The Australian Coal Industry (1947), pp.96-7.

‡ 1924 was the year F Scott Fitzgerald wrote "The Great Gatsby" (published 1925)

gain inspiration for her constant updating of the attractions of The Wentworth were given wide coverage in the Sydney press.

Though Australians were aware that Prohibition had been imposed nationwide in the USA since 1920 they also knew, thanks in part to people like Hannah, that it had had little impact on the consumption of alcohol in hotels, restaurants, and clubs. If anything, they envied the Americans their ingenuity in circumventing the draconian laws. Australia had followed the worldwide temperance trend that began at the turn of the century and by 1916 most states* had enacted their version of the early closing regulation, that prohibited the sale or serving of alcohol after 6pm. In restaurants and hotels alcohol could still be consumed after those hours but it had to be ordered and served before 6pm.

While speakeasies in America ran the risk of being raided at any time, it was principally in the evening, when business was briskest, that "Special Squad" police struck in Australia. As in America, restaurant owners tended to shrug off the inconvenience and short-term embarrassment of these raids, pay the fines imposed and hope to be more vigilant (or fortunate) the next time. It was the public houses, which had to close their doors at 6 o'clock, that bore the impact. By the mid-twenties many had either gone out of business (the ultimate objective of the temperance movement) or adapted by converting billiard rooms and lounges to open areas dedicated to the consumption of the greatest possible quantity of beer by the biggest crowd of men in the one hour between the end of normal working hours and the mandated closing time. These comfortless spaces, walls lined with tiles to facilitate the inevitable swab-down most evenings, were a far cry from the sophisticated world that David and his competitors were attempting to create but, perhaps reflecting the proletarian nature of Australia's general population, they were here to stay, unlike many of the up-market venues.†

---

* Western Australia adopted a 9pm. closing time. Queensland retained the old closing times until it introduced 8 o'clock closing in 1923.

† The drinking hour in the converted pubs became known as "The Six-O'clock Swill" in the 1930s. It persisted well into the 60s, when the liquor laws were finally relaxed.

And so it was that, the festive season over, the business of The Ambassadors established a daily rhythm of afternoon teas, early evening wining and dining, and almost every night, an organised, often themed, dance or ball. Percy was the full-time executive manager; his experience running the shops proved invaluable. He and David had a magnificent management team that ensured the best possible service and quality of dining in town. For once, David could step back, confident in his oldest son and the staff below him. Percy was for a while little seen front of house as he established the back-office organisation upstairs in the Strand Arcade. Stuart and his wife, Peggy, dined and danced with friends, recycling David's still generous allowance into the business. Norman, though he had no formal association with The Ambassadors, indulged himself in a prominent role, hosting parties of friends and ensuring they received an even higher level of service and incidentally parted with more money than they might have expected or planned.

Harriet was quick to exploit her position as chatelaine, though she never acknowledged such a title. In January The Ambassadors welcomed the Premier of Queensland and his wife, who "expressed their amazement at seeing, on an entrance from Pitt-street, what appeared to them as an Aladdin's cave."[222] In the same month Harriet entertained the JC Williamsons; threw a bon voyage party for Mrs C G Poole, wife of the representative of the Hupmobile Corporation in Australia, which included the famous Australian cricketer, Harry Musgrove; and staged another farewell party for Mrs George Taylor, wife of the Australian aviation and wireless pioneer.

The Ambassadors now had a regular column in The Sunday Times and frequent mentions in Freeman's Journal's "In the Wintergarden" social column, besides a growing press coverage in other Sydney papers. The Freeman's Journal column was named for the famed indoor-outdoor dining area of The Wentworth and still gave prominence to gossip about Hannah's hotel. It would be a long time before she would be displaced from her pedestal, and she largely ignored the presence of the rival establishment. There appeared to be no immediate impact on the numbers attending The Wentworth Café and though the financial success of the opening season in 1920 was never to be repeated it would be years before Mrs Maclurcan's shareholders saw their dividends decline.

Things were not all going as planned for David and Percy, however. On January 18th Giovanni Becchio resigned[223] after a mere two months as Maître d'hôtel, to return to Europe. Why he left so soon was never explained, but his immediate replacement by Azzalin Romano was a masterstroke, as the younger man assumed the role that would make his name and guarantee the reputation of The Ambassadors for the next few years. In the same week two of the kitchen staff, both Frenchmen, quarrelled over a missing fountain pen, one of them, Roger Phillippin, producing a revolver with which he threatened his adversary. Phillippin was arrested and charged with keeping an unlicensed firearm. He was bound over to keep the peace and fined £5.[224] Less than a month later another kitchen hand was in court. Pablo Ruis was charged with assaulting Vicenti Bau, another employee, occasioning bodily harm. The two had been employed in the scullery, there was bad blood between them, and they quarrelled, Ruis shouting: "You say I don't work like you, I kill you!" and stabbing Bau in the arm with a potato peeler.[225] Ruis was found not guilty on the grounds of acting in self-defence. It seemed that working in the world's most up to date kitchen was small comfort to men homesick for Europe and struggling to understand or be accepted in a land where their "foreignness" was mistrusted, and their accents mocked.

Then the first of several "sly grog" stings hit The Ambassadors. On the afternoon of Friday, February 15th, Constable Cecil Joseph (Joe) Chuck of the Special Squad was given a marked 10-shilling note and some silver coins by his superior, Sergeant Russell and went to The Ambassadors with his brother, Constable AH (Harry) Chuck and two "lady friends". Joe Chuck later told the court that whilst in the Palm Court he heard people call for whiskies and the waiter went to a place where ice-creams and liquors were kept (the Palm Court featured a state-of-the-art soda fountain). He was allotted a table in the main hall and took afternoon tea with his lady companion. About 5.10pm he saw Norman standing a few yards away and signalled brother Harry who had been waiting at a distance. Harry and his lady friend joined Joe and friend and Joe asked them to have a drink. They were served whisky and soda. The sting was then enacted as Joe strode over to where the whisky was served, the ladies left, and Sergeant Russell and other plain clothes police entered. Waiters started to rush about, and other guests made for the doors. Norman was heard to say: "Give them a hand to remove the stuff," but it was too late. Chuck followed the waiter round to a lift where four other waiters were removing wine from a cooling chamber and placing bottles in a basket in the lift. Norman was defiantly defensive. He said he was in charge and wanted to know who sent Chuck and where his warrant was. Chuck, undeterred, inspected the room where the liquor was being deposited, finding wine, lager, and whisky in quantity. Confronted, Norman protested that a liquor licence was not required before 6pm., a nonsensical assertion. Doubling down, he added that he had had King's Counsel's advice on the matter and the police wanted to "be bally careful" of what they were doing. In any case, he concluded, all the liquor on the premises had been ordered (which was legal, if it were true). Despite his protests, Norman was charged with having sold whisky without holding a licence and committed for trial in the Central Police Court.[226]

This first breach of the law illustrated the extreme lengths to which the Special Squads would go in enforcing the liquor and gambling laws. The expense of staging the sting, employing as it did a team of detectives and hired lady friends, not to mention the ensuing court costs must have been difficult to justify when the typical fine imposed would amount to no more than £30. The official police rationale was that the implied threat of closing the business for repeated breaches of the law should deter re-offending, but this was undermined by the mischievous delight they appeared to take in repeatedly targeting the same venues, employing elaborate strategies of concealment and disguise. In the week of The Ambassadors' raid they also swooped on The Wentworth and the Carlton, not for the first time. The Special Squad enjoyed a notoriety around town and played on this, feeding stories to the press, providing tip-offs, and creating a mystique around the trio of the Chuck brothers and Sergeant Russell in particular.

Norman's case was heard on March 7th. His defence followed the classic line of first attacking the credibility of the police witnesses, and then suggesting that since it was common practice for people to purchase liquor at a legal outlet for consumption on unlicensed premises, the police could have brought and planted the whisky. The last resort was to claim that Norman couldn't be held responsible because he was not employed by The Ambassadors. This was true, but Norman hadn't helped his case by claiming to be the Managing Director, according to Sgt Russell. As Norman "reclined leisurely in the dock, playing carelessly with his small moustache" he admitted that he had no official connection with any of his father's companies though he "assisted in the building operations." David, when called to the witness box, confirmed Norman's statement, and went to some trouble distancing himself from the whole affair, making considerable play of the charitable nature of the operations of The Ambassadors. Percy was also called and kept a cool head, offering polite but firm and confident responses to questions. His main defence was that no liquor was kept on the premises and that any orders for whisky and soda were satisfied by sending out for it and serving it at 1s 6d per glass. It was a nice try but the evidence was compelling, and Norman's defence was undermined by his arrogant demeanour at the restaurant, in the police station and in the dock.* The court found him guilty and imposed a fine of £30 in default of six months' imprisonment.[227] In imposing the fine, the Magistrate, Mr Jennings SC,† admonished the police for not taking the names of the customers present on the day: "If this course had been adopted it would have created a tremendous stir in our smartest social set," he remarked, giving weight to the argument that the stings were little more than a game for the Special Squad and that the word was out to protect the reputation of the most prominent citizens regardless of the spirit of the law. His final remarks were reserved for Norman: "I am sorry to

---

* The Police and the courts were familiar with Norman's arrogant and patronising attitude. In September 1923, he was charged with driving without a licence (he had been disqualified for driving dangerously). As he'd done previously, he first denied he had been driving then claimed only to have taken the wheel because the chauffeur didn't know how to drive the car.

† The same Mr Jennings who presided over the 1920 trial of the jewel thief, Anthony Aliette.

say it, but defendant presented a sorry spectacle in the witness box. He failed to impress me in his evidence." – an apt and perceptive observation which Norman's future court appearances would only confirm.

It was a somewhat shaky start but, as "The Australasian" had noted the previous year:

> *Every now and then a police prosecution for selling wine without a licence is noticed in the papers, the defendant being one of the eating houses which charge for meals on the higher scale. The heavy fines imposed do not by any means put an end to the careers of the restaurateurs thus punished.*[228]

And, so it proved as The Ambassadors rearranged its liquor storage and set more staff on alert for the undercover police.

Roaring Along

The dust settled, peace returned to the kitchen and the patrons resumed their seats. Harriet and Norman entertained most evenings and as special occasions approached: Valentine's Day, St Patrick's, April Fools', Sydney's annual Boat Race week on the Parramatta River, the final night of the annual Polo season, and so on, The Ambassadors was there to help celebrate in style. Stars of stage, screen and opera hosted or were fêted at lavish balls where the dancers never tired of the ever-novel tunes and rhythms of The Havana Band. Eileen Castles, dramatic soprano with the Williamson Opera Company, had tea with Harriet and the Williamsons prior to her departure for a tour of the USA.[229] Canadian stage actress, Muriel Starr, who was immensely popular in Australia and who had just rented the Wilga apartment from David and Harriet, staged a grand "theatrical tea party" to raise funds for the Kindergarten Union.* The line-up for the party included Australia's Lady of Song, Gladys Moncrieff; Gilbert and Sullivan star, Nellie Stewart; English actress, Irene Vanbrugh; Dion Boucicault Jr, son of the famous Irish actor and playwright of the same name; Dorothy "Dot" Brunton, the prominent musical comedy performer; and British stage and later movie actor, Charles Heslop. David donated the use of the venue and the services of both the orchestras for the occasion. He would repeat this gesture dozens of times over the coming years, occasionally playing a cameo role himself. He was known to enjoy singing Celtic airs, which he did several times. At the 1924 Shamrock Ball he rendered "The Little Irish Girl" and "My Bonnie Waratah" and received an ovation "as has seldom been the privilege of even a stage star to receive."[230]

The year rolled on, Harriet never tiring of the round of afternoon teas and dinner dances. Norman was her frequent companion if

* Founded in 1895, the Kindergarten Union of New South Wales opened Australia's first preschool aimed at providing education to the community's most disadvantaged children.

David were absent and Percy made one of his rare appearances as Norman's guest in a foursome that included Miss Rita Barnett, daughter of a good family of graziers from the Southern Highlands.[231] Shy Percy was emerging from the shadows of his failed marriage, perhaps with the encouragement of his extrovert brother. For the most part, though, he avoided the bright lights, preferring the company of his able staff, in particular, Romano.

He was also preoccupied with the elaborate arrangements for decorating and preparing the restaurant for festivities and for the quick turnaround from one event to the next, sometimes as many as four to five a week. One such was a "June Revel" hosted by JC Williamson star, Josie Melville. Twenty-seven-year-old Josie was at the height of her fame and popularity, then starring in the musical "Good Morning Dearie" but she was best known and loved as "Sally" in the eponymous Jerome Kern musical that featured the song, "Look for the Silver Lining". Like many others, she was persuaded to help raise funds for St Margaret's Hospital, in Sydney's Surry Hills. The hospital, which provided obstetrical and gynaecological services to mostly single women, had been founded in 1894 by Mrs Gertrude Abbott, a former Sister of Mercy. It subsisted on charitable donations and post war was having difficulty coping with the growing numbers of single or abandoned mothers and children. The June Revel was only the first of several St Margaret's fund-raisers featuring Josie. Heavily promoted in the press, the 700 tickets sold out. Percy and staff should have been better prepared for what ensued on the day; after all, for the Sydney younger set this was their opportunity to meet a famous Star face to face. Josie was more than a talented performer, she was a style icon, with her fashionable wardrobe and as one of the first to have her hair shingled – the must-have cut for any girl under 30 that became the symbol of the flapper. Despite a police cordon in Pitt Street to control the crowds of women, things got out of hand. "An Idle Woman's Diary", syndicated in The Newcastle Morning Herald of June 20th, described the debacle:

I always wondered what a Revel was – now I know. It is thousands of people fighting each other for seats. A June Revel is worse than any other kind, because people seem bigger and wear more clothes. * *Josie Melville was hostess on Monday at a "June Revel" at The Ambassadors in aid of St Margaret's Hospital. Pitt-street was filled with a dense mass of people. Seven hundred had been arranged for, but quite 1000 arrived early in the afternoon, broke down the barriers, and rushed all the tables … When the people who had booked tables arrived, they were crowded out. Mr. Stewart Dawson Jun., a man of slight build, was surrounded by a mob of tall, fur-coated, ear-ringed and be-feathered women, insisting that he throw a thousand people out. "This is no good to us. Where are their manners?" he moaned. "Throw them out." persisted the women. "If it was a theatre and people took seats that didn't belong to them they would be thrown out. Make an example of them for once." "If they don't get off the dance floor, they won't be able to dance, I promise them that," said Mr. Dawson darkly. Mr. Boyce, K.C., M.L.C., said, "I can say all I want in three† words. 'Australia loves Josie Melville'".*

If "An Idle Woman's Diary" had been less focused on making mischief it would have added that Percy and staff rose to the occasion, seating the interlopers in extra chairs behind the booked tables and accommodating almost 1,000 excited women for the show.[232] The event was so successful that Mrs E J Tait, wife of Edward J Tait, the General Manager of JC Williamsons, claimed to have secured Miss Melville's patronage and announced the formation of another committee to hold an evening party to raise even more money for the hospital. Harriet seized her opportunity. Taking her lead from Mrs Tait, she convened a meeting at the Hotel Australia on August 7th to form a committee. Speakers at the meeting included property developer, Sir Arthur Rickard and the esteemed Senator, Sir Albert Gould. Rickard was a man after David's heart. The foundation president of the Millions Club, established in the belief that accelerated British migration would make Sydney the first Australian city to reach a population of one million, he

* June is mid-winter in Australia.

† Four words: Mr. Boyce was a politician.

used the club (whose membership included many leading politicians and businessmen) as a platform for pronouncements on immigration, socialism and the economy. The two men praised Josie Melville, predicting further triumphs for her. The meeting unanimously decided to hold a dinner dance at The Ambassadors on September 2nd "in aid of Miss Melville's effort to raise £500 for the babies of St Margaret's Hospital." A committee was formed, with Harriet as president.

The dance took place on Tuesday September 2nd and was rated "a splendid success." Josie mania divided the women into two sets, defined by their hairstyle: on the one hand were those who sported curls (mostly wigs) impersonating Sally, but they were outnumbered by shingled heads. Sydney's "Truth" reported: "Shingles were cut with utmost chic, and the close clip is apparently the smart flapper's beau ideal."[233] There were prizes for shingled heads, for Pierrots and Pierrettes* lucky jazz caps and Sally sets (tableaux vivants in costume). Josie, performing in "Good Morning Dearie" on the night, arrived after the show to join the Tait party table. Harriet, who "jazzed in a beautiful gown of beaten silver ... wore the gratified air of an entrepreneur who has steered a protégé to financial success."[234]

The evening over, the count of the takings revealed a shortfall on the expected £500 to be raised. Harriet had already organised formal presentation to the hospital at the Carlton Hotel the following week, so someone made up the difference and more. On Friday September 19th Harriet handed over not £500 but £600 in crisp new notes. She, Josie, and David were made life governors of the hospital, as were the McIntoshes, who had made their own contribution with a matinee event the previous year. The ceremony was followed by morning tea at The Ambassadors, hosted by Harriet, where Josie "started on the warpath again with a donation of £15 by Mr Easterbrook for her first art union† ticket for the babes."[235]

---

* The craze for all kinds of fancy dress dating from the 19th century was at its peak in the 1920s and Pierrot/Pierrette were among the favourites.

† Art union: raffle or lottery usually with a non-cash prize. In this case, it was probably an item (silverware etc.) from Stewart Dawson's stock. John Easterbrook CBE was a successful merchant and mayor of Manly.

More Family Business

September 1924 was a busy month for fund raisers. On the 21st Mrs Shand organised a ball in support of Sydney Hospital. Harriet, though not on the committee, attended, wearing a black gown embroidered in gold, in oriental design.[236] The following week, she and David were there to celebrate the success of the Incognitos' ball supporting the Blinded Soldiers' Café.[237] The same afternoon, they had been guests of Hugh McIntosh's wife at a tea party for Lady Smith, the wife of Sir Keith Smith, the famous aviator who, with his brother, Ross, made the first successful flight from England to Australia.[238] Included in the parties at these events were family members such as the Arnolds and close friends, the Barnetts.

Absent were Norman and Stuart, who were also missing in action at Josie's dance. Norman had left the country in August in haste and secrecy and was by the time of the September dances disembarking in London. This sudden decamping had nothing to do with his conviction in April for selling alcohol. Though he considered appealing the verdict he withdrew the action in May.[239] David paid the fine to avoid a jail term for Norman, but he drew the line at what confronted his son in the next few months. Norman's creditors had had enough and collectively sought an action in bankruptcy against him. A company called McWilliam Ltd, who conducted business as land agents in New South Wales, brought the action to recover a debt of £60/10/4.* Despite having an allowance of between £3,000 and £4,000 per annum from David, Norman did not feel disposed to paying the debt. He had also ignored appeals and threats from his bookmaker, Richard Gilbert, a furrier, a wine merchant, a laundry man, a hairdresser, a florist, a costumière and others. He had allowed a lady friend, a Miss Cooper to run up accounts for clothes, including a fur coat, which he never paid. He owed £11 5s 6d† to a barber at the

---

* £60/10/4 – about £3,500 in 2017

† £11 5s 6d in 1924 is worth over £600 today

Australia Hotel, mostly for hair preparation at £2 2s a bottle.* He had not paid for over £31 worth of gramophone records and owed the legal firm Stephen, Jacques and Stephen for expenses incurred when he appealed against a conviction for driving a car on the wrong side of a tram. The car, bought from Percy, had been repossessed because the instalments had not been paid. Faced with that inconvenience, he had rented a vehicle from The Flying Motor Service of Darlinghurst but never paid the £83 11s 8d owed to them.[240] The list seemed endless, the creditors' patience exhausted. Coming so soon after the embarrassing liquor trial, Norman's appearance at a bankruptcy hearing was almost more than David or Harriet could bear. He claimed to have no assets, which was probably true; he spent every penny that came into his hands before it had time to reach the bottom of his wallet and lived perpetually on credit, as a gentleman did.

David was exasperated. All his life he had preached the virtue of a cash-only business model versus the vicissitudes and risks of extending credit. His children had all benefited from his rigorous application of this simple discipline and been given a head start to make their own way, the start David had never enjoyed. And yet, no lesson had been learned, at least not by his two younger sons. Stuart was still an undischarged bankrupt† because David had refused to bail him out. He had left for England in March[241] with his wife and their two-year-old son, David junior, partly to escape his creditors, and now Norman had gone many steps further in this latter-day rake's progress. David was in no mood to set a fresh precedent and was tempted to throw Norman to the wolves but at the last minute he baulked, and Norman escaped court. On Thursday August 14th he sailed from Sydney for London via San Francisco on the RMS Tahiti,‡ his passage paid by David and £300 spending money in his pocket. He was formally declared bankrupt on November 11th.

---

* Norman was losing his hair and there was little left by the mid-twenties.

† In May 1923 the court considered Stuart's release from bankruptcy, but he was not fully discharged until 1950.

‡ The Tahiti was the same vessel in which Percy sailed on his 1922 mission for The Ambassadors.

Harriet's hand in this escapade was evident. Norman the handsome hero could do no wrong in her eyes and she wielded increasing influence over her aging husband. She would do anything to protect her middle son and he, in his turn, could play on her sympathy at will. Stuart had found sanctuary in England, so escape to "home" was the obvious solution in Norman's and her mind. Moreover, she could count on David's accepting the proposal; she could always remind him of his own recourse to exile back in 1917.

Her two younger sons out of harm's way, Harriet resumed the round of parties and balls. The Hallowe'en Ball of 1924 saw David rendering more Scottish airs ("The Waggle o' the Kilt" and "A wee deoch an' doris"). Mashed potato and kilts featured on the night, though once again The Wentworth outdid The Ambassadors, with "witches and sheets and Ku Klux Klan caps (sic)" to help along the party.[242] Percy and staff were now working efficiently and generally without interference from the Special Squad and The Ambassadors' reputation under Maître d', Romano was established, proving that the initial exuberance generated by the launch had been warranted.

The twenties witnessed a massive growth in the number of private motor vehicles throughout the western world, as the benefits of mass production started to be realised in a steady decline in purchase prices. Sydney was no exception, the narrow streets filling with honking, smoking, rumbling motor cars. Competing with trams, omnibuses and the still large numbers of horse drawn vehicles, they were often driven by unskilled people, usually men, with little knowledge of or regard for the rudimentary road rules. Norman's fine for driving on the wrong side of a tram was a typical case in point, though he at least was an experienced driver and should have known better. Stuart had also been an offender, though in this case it was not a moving offence; in December 1923, he left his car parked a good yard away from the kerb in Pitt Street for over two hours, obstructing traffic in the crowded street.[243] He neither noticed nor cared, as he took tea in the Palm Court. Percy was involved in a collision with another vehicle while driving in Darlinghurst but successfully sued for damage, winning £75.[244] This was his only recourse, which he could pursue thanks to his wealth and legal connections; others might not have been so fortunate. David's name was added to the list when his car collided with a taxi in the city. The taxi driver sued him for

£100, alleging that "owing to the negligence of the defendant or his agents, plaintiff was thrown from the cab, and suffered injury and incurred expense." David pleaded not guilty, denied negligence and alleged contributory negligence on the part of the plaintiff.*

He was still spending as much time in Springwood as he could. Davesta's gardens were maturing and already the talk of the town. In August 1924, electric lighting and power came to Springwood, as a result of which local real estate became more attractive to Sydney investors and commuters. The Huntley Grange Estate, bordering Hawkesbury Road on the way to David's property, was the first significant example and was heavily promoted in Sydney newspapers. Land could be had for as little as £25 and there were lucky draw and crossword competitions offering prime lots as incentives. The hand-drawn illustrations featured fashionable California Bungalows,† sporting activities such as golf, tennis and horse riding and emphasised the ease and convenience of road and rail connections for the commuting businessman. To further entice buyers, the promoters described:

> *a beautiful estate … within easy walking distance of the Station … the luxurious residence of Stewart Dawson Esq. on one side of the estate, and the residence of Norman Lindsay Esq. on the other …*[245]

Another advertisement continued this theme:

> *Beautiful mountain ranges form a majestic background for the town, which is within easy reach of Sydney, and lends to it a romance that has hardly been fully appreciated in the past, but it seems now as though Springwood is coming into its own, and many fine places have been built there, including the beautiful home of Stewart Dawson Esq., adding the clinching sales point: Electric light has just been installed there.*[246]

---

* Sydney Morning Herald 19th March 1925 P.6. There is no record of the verdict or whether the action was ever concluded but chances are David succeeded in preserving his spotless character once again.

† California Bungalow was a style that superseded the post-Federation look of David's own houses, Bonnie Doon, Davesta, The Spinney and its neighbour.

On his visits, David took time to look in on his daughter, Estelle, now nearly nine years old, who was growing up in the care of her grandparents at Bonnie Doon. The nurse, latterly nanny, Lucy Nelson, had returned that year to England and Grandmother Annie took on the full-time role of mother while grandfather, Tom, was employed as David's estate manager at Davesta. On October 20th, 1920, as work commenced on The Spinney and its neighbour, David had transferred into his own name all the land on Hawkesbury Road with the exception of the half acre on which Bonnie Doon stood,[247] arranging for Bonnie Doon to be held in trust for Estelle until her maturity.[248] Tom, Annie and Estelle continued to be supported with an allowance in addition to Tom's wages. Though adequate for their needs, it was nothing like the amount David was doling out to his acknowledged sons and daughters: his guilt only extended so far.

Towards the end of 1924 Percy was seen more often in the company of Rita Barnett. Rita Sibald Barnett was the second of three daughters of John Thomas Barnett, dairy farmer, and Ann Ramsey Jackson. She was born in 1902 in Hay, New South Wales. The family moved to Randwick, Sydney, where Rita and her elder sister, Eileen, soon found introductions to the social set. In 1920, Eileen married Oliver Cohen, a banker, whose family was well connected with Sydney's elite, and who was already active in philanthropical ventures. By the end of the year it was clear that romance was in the air and in January 1925 Percy and Rita's engagement was announced. On March 14th, Harriet gave a "kitchen tea" for Rita at The Ambassadors.* The tables were decorated with pink carnations and roses. Harriet presided in a biscuit and green georgette frock.† The guests included Rita's mother and sisters; Bertha; Vanna's daughter, Georgina‡, and Harriet's sister-in-law, Agnes McNab. Agnes was now Harriet's regular companion and fellow committee member. A fortnight later, the celebrations continued. In a week that saw no less than twelve such

* Evening News 14th March 1925 P.8. The kitchen tea was the more decorous predecessor of the modern hen party.

† The dress of the other ladies present did not rate a mention in the gossip column.

‡ Georgina, on her first visit to Australia.

parties at The Ambassadors, Mrs Ross-Soden (oriental frock of flame georgette and grey fox), wife of the Olympic rower, Harry Ross-Soden, gave a "boudoir tea" for Rita.[249] Percy and Rita married at St. Jude's, Randwick, the same church where Eileen had married Oliver Cohen, on Wednesday 22nd April 1925. Rita's younger sister, Jean, was bridesmaid and Percy's best man was Bruce Venn-Brown, an old friend from his army days. The reception was held, naturally, at The Ambassadors, though it was described as "quiet, … only the relatives and a few close friends being invited."250 The couple honeymooned in Melbourne, demonstrating a degree of independence on Percy's part; the expectation would have been that they follow precedence by patronising the Hydro Majestic, as so many did. It could also have been that the Hydro recalled painful memories of Percy's first marriage.

In the months leading up to the wedding, Harriet had been occupied with another charity committee, once more on behalf of St Margaret's Hospital. The star attraction this time was "Dot" Brunton, yet another JC Williamson favourite, who co-opted a troupe of performers for a cabaret afternoon. As had happened when Josie Melville appeared, hundreds of disappointed fans were turned away at the door as over 500 packed the ballroom. Harriet had made a token donation of ten guineas before the event but topped that with a set of Stewart Dawson silverware for auction. The target set by the committee was easily reached, helped by, among others, Mack, whose purse was reported to be "so much lighter for the honour."[251]

David, content to let Harriet build her social reputation, returned to his grand scheme for the Pitt Street precinct. When he first acquired the property, he spoke of his ambition to redevelop much of the site, to "build a commercial establishment which will be run on modern methods new to Sydney" but thus far he had been preoccupied with work on The Ambassadors. Now that the basement of the Strand Arcade was fully operational he could re-examine the possibilities for the rest of the block that he owned. On January 18th, 1925, he placed an advertisement on the front page of The Sunday Times, announcing a competition for "Thinkers, Draughtsmen, Architects, Engineers etc." He was proposing construction of a building of no less than twelve floors fronting Pitt Street, from the Strand Arcade northwards towards King Street and almost the full depth of the block towards

George Street. When complete, it would be the tallest ever erected in Sydney and three times the height of The Treasure House in Hatton Garden. The competition, however, was not to design the building itself. Instead, he canvassed ideas for the types of businesses that would best serve and be served by such a landmark building. The advertisement featured a basic ground plan of the site as might be sketched by an amateur, but the words were all David's, full of the now familiar bombastic and dated prose:

> *Any architect with the usual technical training can make (some sort of) a plan of almost anything in the building line, so can Mr. Stewart Dawson himself, but this phase of the matter does not come into this competitive appeal, which is directed to those who can think out the best services each of the eleven* floors can be used for.*

Having noted that competitors could include ideas for the arrangement of the shops, he added, in bold letters:

> *Now follows the crux of the matter: Mr. Stewart Dawson only desires to have competitive opinions of what business, trades, crafts, professions, socialities, etc., the respective competitors consider will best answer the purpose of the eleven floors for public service.*

There followed more of David's aphorisms reflecting his "self-made with little formal education" ethos:

> *Technical training does not create genius – in fact, it retards genius. Technical training enables any young man to copy that which has been done already, in Mr. Dawson's opinion.*

There was a further paragraph of this, in which David alluded to his, yet unpublished "The Boy and the Wheelbarrow …":

> *One of these days Mr. Dawson will publish the story of The Ambassadors – the greatest basement art scheme Australia has ever seen. Very few people imagine that The Ambassadors covers the whole basement site … entirely schemed and carried out through Mr. Dawson's own initiative.*

---

* The ground floor was to be dedicated to shops.

Three prizes were offered: £100, £50, and £25. Sydney's Construction and Local Government Journal was quick to comment. In an article dated Wednesday 21st January, just three days later, it described David's proposition as "one of the most novel competitions of its kind for the planning of a building." After explaining the background and intentions of the scheme, the Journal raised an eyebrow:

For a building of such magnitude, involving professional fees anywhere in the region of nine thousand pounds, when the scheme is completed, surely Mr. Stewart Dawson could have been more generous with the prize money in his preliminary appeal for suggestions. This is another instance of the low plane upon which architects are placed by the general public ... There is plenty of precedent for a commensurate amount of prize money being offered ... in the Canberra Administrative Buildings ... Here the Government distributed £2,000 in prizes ... In addition, the amount in commission for plans and supervision the successful architect will receive will be about £24,229, with travelling allowances.

It cited other examples, such as the Chicago Tribune (over £20,000 in prizes) and went on to pick apart David's dismissive opinions of the value of a formal education:

The Stewart Dawson advertisement implies that the trained professional mind is at a discount, even if matured by experience, when he places architects third, and the men whom they employ are placed before them ... Allowing that "technical training does not create genius," as he states, surely it would be conceded that a structure of this class, even picturing in the mind to what uses the floors would be best adapted, would stress more than the average man's ability unless he had the trained brain to plot his ideas down with some relation to order.

The demolition continued:

On perusal of the circular advertisement it will be observed that no definite conditions are laid down in respect to the lines on which the suggestions are to be supplied, and this alone is destructive of individual effort for production of the best result. Surely a simple set of conditions could have been evolved asking, say, for single line diagrams to a definite scale and inviting the Council of the Institute of Architects to award augmented prizes.

The Journal's final words were conciliatory and helpful if a little patronising:

The scheme is a great and ambitious one calling for the utilisation of the best brains and it is to be hoped that an amended circular advertisement will be issued with larger prizes, containing definite conditions and a more impartial judging; and if that be done then better results would no doubt be obtained for all concerned.

It was possible that the Journal had missed the point of David's advertisement and that he had already dealt with the commissioning of an architect, but the newspaper was well connected with the profession and would have had notice in advance of any contracts being awarded or competitive tenders invited. Plainly, there had been none such. Whether anybody ever responded to the advertisement nothing came of it, though David found it hard to accept. If he had bothered to confide in Percy he might have paused before committing to the project. He had overreached himself in commercial real estate and was grasping at any half-baked, grandiose concept to justify the enormous investment. Stubborn and arrogant as he was, he still deceived himself that he not only had to go one better, but he also *knew* better; he could yet pull off another stunning coup to impress the world without ceding control to or sharing acclaim with professionals, or anyone, for that matter.

The problem was, he had no idea what he wanted, beyond a vague "grand design" for a building that would ensure his posterity. Percy, powerless to intervene, observed his father's failure. If only he had consulted with experts, as he had done with The Treasure House. Maybe a hotel would have been the best solution for the site, given the location, the shortage of quality hotels in rapidly growing Sydney, and on the doorstep, high end shops and top-class entertainment in the form of The Ambassadors. He could once and for all have gone one better than Hannah Maclurcan and beaten her at her own game with the ultimate vanity project. But, while he dithered and embarrassed himself, others took the professional, business-like route. Only months later, work commenced on the New South Wales Masonic Club building in Castlereagh Street, just a block from his site. Within a year, a twelve-storey building was completed that housed the formal rooms and public areas of the club, plus member accommodation and a roof-top plaza. The building set the record that David could have achieved.

Re-Grouping

Bruised and humiliated by his failure to realise the Stewart Dawson plan for the city centre, David once more retreated. There would be no grand finale to the drama that he had written and acted out over fifty exciting and, ultimately, debilitating years. If he felt cheated, a moment's reflection sufficed to remind him that his destiny still lay in his own hands if he made more realistic choices or accepted his limitations. And indeed, he did just this, reasoning that Sydney was not yet ready for its first skyscraper, that it would not after all attain the sophistication of London, Paris, Berlin, and New York in his lifetime. He had implied as much in his condescending observations of the culinary and entertainment scene. Rather than squander his energy and resources on a commercial venture that risked his reputation and even his fortune, why not indulge his new-found passion for building in something more personal?

His Treasure House in Hatton Garden would be the only permanent monument to his business acumen, but there was still time make his mark with another building, if not one in Sydney. It would be to Springwood that he would turn, but though he could take some pride in the four Springwood houses, especially Davesta, they were not in the league of Wilga or of any of hundreds of Sydney mansions. Even Springwood boasted grander homes dating from Victorian times. On the other hand, he owned plenty of vacant land around Davesta and its location was ideal for visitors to Springwood. Recreational pursuits such as golfing and horse riding were on the doorstep, and it was easy to imagine tennis and even swimming being added. David and Harriet were not the only family members who visited his mountain retreat; Percy, too, often escaped to Davesta, delighting in entertaining guests and showing off the golf course. He was a keen advocate for commercialising the under-used facilities and accommodation and he was someone, perhaps the only one, in whom David could confide. Percy's success in managing The Ambassadors earned him credit from his father. He had learned the hard way, building on his years in the shop. He understood his customers, probably as well as his father did, by now. Moreover, he was forty years younger than David, and far more in tune with the times. He had even negotiated use of The Ambassadors as a location for several scenes of the movie, "Joe".[252] This film,* directed by Frank Beaumont Smith, was based on the Henry Lawson short story, "Joe Wilson's Courtship". As David now turned to him for comfort and advice after the fiasco of the building competition, he was quick to point out the personal and commercial benefits of the Springwood option.

On April 17th, 1925, The Blue Mountains Echo reported:

> *There are extensive alterations going on at Mr. Stewart Dawson's home at North Springwood. There are whispers that a Mountains "Ambassadors" will rear its height in that quarter in the near future, but writer's opinion is that the old Dame is lying as usual.*[253]

The old Dame was not lying. Somebody, possibly Percy, had fed the rumour though no building work had commenced. A broad development application might have been submitted to Council, but details of this project would not be announced prematurely, David did not want to risk another public reproval from so-called experts and Percy urged patience and deference to professional advice. It was to be twenty months before the application was formally approved and work began on David's last plunge into real estate.

In the meantime, he endured and when he could, begged off, a wearying succession of Harriet's charity fund-raising events, for which she retained inexhaustible energy. In the same week as the speculative article published in The Blue Mountains Echo, a cabaret starring Elsa Stralia was staged, breaking more records for the worthy cause of St Margaret's Hospital. Mme Stralia was the former Elsie Moses (née Fischer), an operatic soprano who had performed at Covent Garden and toured with the likes of Dame Clara Butt. Likened to Melba's, her voice was "brilliant of tone, amazing in flexibility."[254] Her appearance at The Ambassadors conferred considerable prestige, coming during a brief tour of Australia between high profile and applauded seasons in the USA and Great Britain. Sir Benjamin Fuller, another theatrical impresario, who was about to open the St James theatre in Sydney,

---

* "Joe", the movie, is now lost.

arranged the programme to include virtuoso violinist, Gregory Ivanoff, and the singer, Oscar Beck. The now familiar faces attended and made their financial contributions, including Mesdames Hugh McIntosh and Harry Musgrave. The social and financial impact of the event warranted the publication of a booklet, entitled "The Lifesaver", which Freeman's Journal promoted enthusiastically:

> *We have to hand a dainty little booklet embodying the work of St. Margaret's Hospital for Women. … Several stars in the theatrical world are working strenuously, including the Hon. Hugh D. McIntosh and Mrs. McIntosh, Madame Elsa Stralia, Miss Dorothy Brunton, Mr. and Mrs. David Stewart Dawson, and many other well-known public citizens; and a glance at this little booklet would be full of enlightenment to the general public.*[255]

Harriet was personally honoured at a special function at The Ambassadors when the Minister for Health, Mr. Oakes, presented her with a scroll of thanks on behalf of the Committee of St. Margaret's.[256] St. Margaret's was not Harriet's sole charity; no sooner had she received her award than she was elected Vice-President of the Lady Mayoress's committee to raise money for the building fund for Sancta Sophia College. In November 1923, the Catholic Archbishop of Sydney, Michael Kelly, and the Bishops of New South Wales had issued a pastoral letter that drew attention to the advantages of university education for the Catholic community and announced that a Catholic Women's College would be built at Sydney University. The cost was to be borne by "all dioceses of the State in exact proportion of the number of Catholics contained in each." Archbishop Kelly asked the Catholic women of New South Wales to assist in the fundraising. The College was to be administered by nuns from the order of the Religious of the Sacred Heart, which had been founded in France in 1800. The founding Mothers sought to establish a residential college that would be a place where women could stand beside men as equals. In 1925 this was a courageous stand, the result of decades of quiet pressure from within the ranks of the faithful.[257]

The foundation stone of the college was laid on March 26th, 1925, but by this time appeals for funds extended and were met far beyond the Catholic community. The post-war feminist movement embraced more than female enfranchisement, seeking opportunities for promoting women's rights in every sphere, where higher education was the great enabler. The first intake of students would study in the fields of medicine, law, arts, science, and education. Harriet's humanitarianism was not only sincere, but it was also focussed and progressive. Since the war years, when she learned the skills of harvesting donations on behalf of wounded soldiers and their families, she had moved determinedly into the world of women's issues with St. Margaret's and now Sancta Sophia.

Despite this, when Harriet presided over a celebration of the success of the St. Margaret's fund-raising drive at a gathering at The Ambassadors on June 11th, she took a back seat to the men. The speakers were Mack and David. The Director, Mr. Fitzpatrick, "paid a warm tribute to the support of Mr. and Mrs. McIntosh, both of whom [were] life governors of the hospital." They had been instrumental in raising between them the best part of £1000 for the babies. Granted, Mack had pulled strings to bring talented stars to attract donations, but it was his wife who, with Harriet and the other committee members, had done the hard work of organising the events. Nevertheless, it was Mack who rose to his feet to respond.

> *… what Mrs. McIntosh had been privileged to do was a real delight. Neither the speaker nor his wife had any children, and the abundant mother-love of Mrs. McIntosh had been generously showered on the babies of St. Margaret's. His wife was proud to be associated with the wonderful work … etc. etc.*

David was the only other speaker apart from the Director. He was briefer than his friend but made essentially the same point:

> *… both he and his wife [had] been interested in the wonderful work of St. Margaret's by the director of the hospital, whom he regarded as an officer of outstanding ability for the particular work in which he was engaged.*

Both speeches were generous and displayed the genuine gratitude of the men towards their wives but nobody, least of all the two women, considered for one moment that they might have been entitled or expected to say a few words on their own or the committee's behalf.

Distant Rumblings

On July 5th, 1925, The Sunday Times published an article in its series: "Wives of our famous men", sub-titled: "Mrs. Stewart Dawson, wife of Mr. Stewart Dawson, who gave Sydney The Ambassadors." This series of interviews ran for many months and included such personalities as Rose Lindsay, Lady Fuller (wife of the Premier of New South Wales), Lady Chauvel (wife of Sir Henry, Inspector-General of the Australian armed forces) and Ethel Curlewis, the former Ethel Turner, author of the beloved children's book, "Seven Little Australians" and now wife of Judge Herbert Curlewis. Harriet was in illustrious company and, taking her cues from the words of some of the wives who had preceded her, spoke frankly and confidently. The interview was revealing in several ways, not least in confirming Harriet's homesickness for the land of her birth and her chronic disappointment with Australian parochialism.

She expounded at length on the virtues of England and The Continent, meanwhile lamenting Australians' lack of appreciation of or exploitation of the natural and man-made attractions of the country:

> *I love Australia, and I think it is a fine country for youth, and people who want to do things. But I can never think of it as home, for my sons [Norman and Stuart] and my people are in England, and my life is wrapped up with them.*

In London, the countryside of Britain, and France she was at home:

> *In the winter in England, we went to the south of France. Everyone goes there, following up the sun. Everything is gay. There women dress exquisitely and play with that lightness of heart which is so charming. In London, too, the parks are never empty of well dressed people. In Paris, and other Continental cities, the boulevards, and gathering places of society are always fascinating. In the South of France, there is beauty everywhere. The lovely Mediterranean, the marvellous palaces, the continual excitement. I do not think you make enough of your lovely parks and gardens. Sometimes in the morning my husband and I stroll through them, and they are always deserted. It is a great pity.*

Harriet's fascination for France and the Riviera dated from the family's pre-war holidays and David's convalescences there, but it would have found many a sympathetic ear in Australian high society. Newspaper columns dedicated to gossip about Australians abroad (meaning, almost always, in Europe) were avidly consumed by aspiring and subscribed members of the right set. A Miss Isabel Ramsay* ("our special correspondent") had a regular "Australians Abroad" column in Mack's Sunday Times. As well as internationally famous names, such as Dame Nellie Melba, the column followed the Continental itineraries of well-connected Australian travellers. In April, Melba's sojourn in Paris before a brief holiday on the Italian Riviera was reported. Pride of place in the column was given to a regular item: "At Monte Carlo". Here were long lists of current and recent visitors from Down Under, but by 1925 the place had become so popular that Miss Ramsay felt bound to observe:

Monte Carlo is attracting so many Australians this season that one is liable to meet as many well-known personalities strolling along the Grande Terrasse as one would walking down the Corso at Manly.†

There followed the names of well-to-do Sydneysiders, familiar to readers. Tootles Williamson was still there, as was a Miss Bebe Robinson, "who has been convalescing from a serious nervous breakdown". Columns such as this were a window into a world of privilege and excess beyond the dreams of most Australians; long distance vacation travel was strictly for the well-to-do. Harriet, in her interview, was taking the opportunity to remind readers of her status and, as she saw it, her right to belong in that world. She continued:

My one hobby is motoring. In England I motored all the time, and I miss my fishing. It was thrilling to go up to Scotland for salmon fishing, and I loved the sport ... My own particular vice is golf. I played a great deal in England, on Walton Heath, where Lloyd George played.

---

* "Isabel Ramsey" was the penname of Mrs. Isabel Foa, Australian journalist who spent much of her working life in Europe.

† The Corso at Manly was Sydney's closest facsimile of a European boulevard, a ferry ride across the harbour from the city centre.

These few sentences encapsulated more messages than even her husband's advertisements could have delivered, and with greater subtlety. Readers would have known that "motoring" in this context did not mean driving a car for the fun of it or for utilitarian purposes. Harriet did not drive herself; she would always have a chauffeur. Her "hobby" of motoring was to enjoy being chauffeured on long road tours or between resorts in Great Britain and Europe, a luxury few could afford. Recreational fishing had been popular in Australia since colonial times, Atlantic salmon were introduced as early as 1864 but did not thrive due to a failure to understand their migratory habits.[258.] Consequently, true salmon fishing was beyond the dreams of most in the country; Harriet's casual reference to her exploits with the rod and line only served to remind readers further of her exclusive lifestyle. As for golf, the game had taken the western world by storm and, except for tennis, was one of the very few sports in which both men and women could jointly participate, at a price. Dropping the name of the revered former Prime Minister of Great Britain was the final turn of the screw.

By 1925 Harriet had been in Australia, uninterrupted, for almost six years, her longest separation from "home" ever. She was restless, and articles such as "At Monte Carlo" intensified her sense of isolation. A trip north of the equator was overdue, but in the meantime, she had duties to perform, causes to support. In September, she presided over the Beaurecaire Ball, a Gladys Moncrieff spectacular inspired by the movie "Monsieur Beaurecaire". The same month saw The Society of Artists' Ball, a mask and fancy-dress affair attended by, among others, the painter, Thea Procter, who wore a hooped Victorian dress. Harriet was elegant, in a beaded frock of fuchsia and crystal. By October, the itch to revisit her beloved Riviera must have been growing, because the theme that night was "The Nice Carnival". The ball reflected the craze for all things Mediterranean.* The Sun reported:

* The Nice Ball was quite possibly Harriet's own concept.

A riot of pink and white blossoms, pink and white snowballs pelting through the air, streamers hurtling and getting tangled around dancers' feet, showers of confetti falling from flower baskets suspended over diners' heads, these were some of the gaieties enjoyed at the Nice carnival at The Ambassadors last night. The carnival spirit of Nice seemed to infect the dancers, for although dancing was made difficult by the litter of streamers, snowballs and confetti, which strewed the floor, there was only cheery laughter as girls stooped down to disentangle the mass from pretty shoes and sandals. A battle of flowers was staged at midnight, and the cabaret girls handed round novel masks, musical toys and caps.[259]

Many of the guests wore fancy dress but Harriet, presiding at her table and transported to the other side of the world by the festivities, preferred to display her taste and affluence with a white georgette gown, beaded all over in silver.

October concluded with another charity event, this time for the Ashfield Infants' Home. By this time, the Twenties were truly beginning to roar. The Sun's "Topics for Women" asked,

Where are the one-steps of yester-year? The jazz band at The Ambassadors unearthed one at the dinner dance given for the Ashfield Infants' Home last night and keeping pace with the music was more strenuous than a relay marathon race. Many people entered, but numbers retired from the fray before the second heat. A couple of years ago the one-step was perhaps even more popular than the fox-trot, but these days the fox-trot is a leisurely minuet by comparison. Dancers gave themselves their heads in the one-step last night and bolted through encores like people trying to elbow their way out of a crowd to catch a tram that wouldn't wait.†*

---

* Bert Ralton's contract had ended in December 1924 but the new band was still promoted as "The New York Band". The departure of the Havana Band seemed not to diminish the attraction of The Ambassadors; local talent had learned much from the Americans.

† Sun 15th October 1925 P.15 "Topics for Women" The Charleston, though it burst onto the scene as early as 1923, in the stage musical, "Running Wild",

There were several more "gay" events in November, but the one that topped them all, confirming Harriet's and Sydney's fascination with The Riviera, was the Grand Monte Carlo Fête, held on December 2nd. Advertised as a "special Riviera dinner", the evening featured Max and Babette,* "World renowned character dancers from Paris, Nice and Monte Carlo," and in case anyone needed to be reminded, it carried the tag-line: "Illustrating to the full a phase of society's enchantment in Monte Carlo." This somewhat clumsy phrase had all the characteristics of a Stewart Dawson marketing puff, though the sentiments embodied in it were more Harriet's than David's. To follow the October carnival in less than six weeks with one so similar in theme was unprecedented and could only be explained by Harriet's melancholic pining for "The lovely Mediterranean, the marvellous palaces, the continual excitement." Also unprecedented, or almost so, was the politely expressed condition of entry: "It is desired that Gentlemen, where convenient, will wear Flannels† on this evening." Black tie was normally de rigueur for evening events but now Sydney was to have a taste of Continental life with this display of casual sophistication so that Harriet could imagine herself one step closer to the world she loved.

As Christmas approached, attention turned to children's causes. Despite the optimistic projections for Australia's future and the visible evidence, day by day, of the construction of that great symbol of progress, the Harbour Bridge, the average family saw little to encourage confidence.‡ As the party-goers danced the night away at

---

and soon spread to US dance spots, had not yet reached Australia. The Charleston and One-Step never completely displaced the Fox-trot.

* Max and Babette had already been performing at The Ambassadors for several weeks. This evening seems to have capitalised on their exotic attraction.

† "Flannels" were smart casual trousers, cut very full, with turn-ups. They were usually cream or light-grey and were coupled with white shirt, cravat and sports coat or blazer. Casual shoes, often two-tone, were also worn.

‡ In the year 1925-6 overall economic growth was negative, a pre-cursor of the years of depression to follow.

The Ambassadors, The Wentworth and other ballrooms around Australia, beneath the very piers of the growing Harbour Bridge hundreds of families were evicted without compensation to make way for the construction. In addition, the legacy of the War left many children orphaned or impoverished their families as disabled fathers struggled to support them. But in the general spirit of charity, those with the means reached out again, as they always had done. The Lady Mayoress of Sydney, Miss Cecilia Walsh, gave a party in the Town Hall on December 15th for over 3,000 children, to which Mr A C Godhard* and his wife donated over 1,000 dolls. David and Harriet's contribution was to lend The Ambassadors, the staff and the band for "The Dream Party", at which 500 children of disabled soldiers and 700 from "the congested areas"† would be entertained at "the largest Xmas tree ever seen" and enjoy a slice of a cake over 5 feet high. An immense tin was donated by confectioner, James Stodman. Out of it popped a fairy to hand out 1500 boxes of sweets, as the squealing children tucked into unlimited servings of ice cream and cakes. A fifteen-foot-high Christmas stocking hung from the ceiling, filled with toys. David organised the screening of a movie for the children and dancer, Phyllis du Barry and her chorus performed as balloons floated down to the awe-struck guests. David donated and handed out prizes for lucky balloons. State Governor, Sir Dudley de Chair, the former Premier, Sir George Fuller, and the Minister for Education all attended, marking the significance of the occasion.

It had been a year to remember. The Ambassadors ("Distinguished throughout the world, the ever-popular restaurant that holds its sway and charm for Sydney's social set"), was now established as "Sydney's greatest achievement in pleasure giving, where appreciation and patronage nightly increase".[260] The New Year's Eve ball broke records for numbers attending, as did the competing celebrations at The

---

* The Godhards were tireless supporters of cancer research, raising hundreds of thousands of pounds through their Shilling Stamp scheme. Mrs Godhard, the former Mona Daley, was awarded the OBE in 1933 for this and for her work as Secretary of Crown Street Women's Hospital.

† The children were under the care of the Welfare Branch of the Department of Education.

Wentworth. Sydneysiders were partying as if there was no tomorrow. Nevertheless, the signs were there for those who looked, and David was one of the first to respond. His advertisements started to hark back to his old "Watches! Watches! Watches!" days, renewing his jewellery business mantra of effort and value before everything. A display advertisement in the Sydney Morning Herald on November 28th carried one of his aphorisms: "To get patronage is to deserve it, hence the daily rising tide of The Ambassadors' popularity", but on December 4th, just days after the smash-hit Monte Carlo carnival, a new note sounded. Below the list of tariffs for meals and entertainment, David* added: "Count total cost elsewhere, make comparison, become a true economist".

In her "Wives of our famous men" interview, Harriet had described The Ambassadors as "my husband's only hobby". She was right; David's interest in the jewellery business had been waning since his return from England in 1917, his venture into property had achieved as much as he could have expected before he over-reached himself with the building competition, and he had created a haven to which they could retire in the mountains. Rents from the commercial property easily covered all expenses. All his pleasures now derived from The Ambassadors and Davesta. As Harriet concluded:

> *My only really happy time is when we go up to our place in the Mountains. We have a little bungalow up there, and we are right away from the noise of the city. I play a little and sing, and at night my husband gets out his flute, and we have a quiet time all to ourselves. These are really his two hobbies, the flute and The Ambassadors. I can hardly get him away from the place. My son and he designed it and did the decoration and the dome. I helped just a weeny bit with the colouring.*

Perhaps she had been disingenuous concerning her own desires and pleasures, but she did not misrepresent David. He could afford to subsidise the costs of The Ambassadors for philanthropy's sake, while

---

* It could have been Percy or Romano (now prominent and confidently managing operations) but the language is pure David, who still called the shots when he chose to.

remaining "one better" than rivals such as Hannah Maclurcan who, unlike him, were answerable to shareholders and for whom entertainment and hospitality was their sole business. While the rents flowed, the patrons received value each night, and the charities benefited he had always been prepared to run The Ambassadors at a loss. David's admonition to "count total cost elsewhere, make comparison, become a true economist" stemmed, in part, from his instinct to promote his brand as he had done for so many years. It was also defensive. Scottish realism urged the old warrior to take the longer view of his cash flow and to consider the sustainability of the venture in the current economic climate. His instincts and timing in business thus far had been impeccable, through painstaking early establishment and periods of phenomenal growth to consolidation of a mature brand. He was realistic about the limits of his retail business and daily monitoring of sales confirmed the gradual flattening in the market for luxury and discretionary goods. In the case of Stewart Dawson's, market conditions were not the sole limiting factor. He now faced aggressive competition from established national brands, and he was starting to suffer the consequences of his stubborn adherence to the cash only model of business. Hire-purchase was attracting many new customers from classes who would formerly have been excluded. The Sydney Morning Herald observed:

> *Of late there has been a tremendous growth in what is popularly known as the time-payment system of buying … and the great portion of the purchases made by its means is not clothing, nor furniture, nor general household goods, but motor cars, player pianos, wireless sets, electric carpet sweepers, and jewellery.*[261]

Except that none of the jewellery so purchased would come from Stewart Dawson's. The writing was on the wall, and he could read it.

Cads and Bricks

As 1926 dawned, David was in his seventy seventh year and feeling his age. He maintained a proprietorial interest in the jewellery shops, though there were no more flying visits outside of Sydney. He was to make a couple of trips to Brisbane and another to Melbourne in 1927, but Perth was too far away, and he was never to see New Zealand again. He kept up his appearances at special events at The Ambassadors, but he could no longer maintain Harriet's hectic pace. His fifteen years younger wife, on the other hand, forged ahead with her afternoon tea parties, fund-raising committees, carnivals, and balls.

Harriet had now encouraged her new daughter-in-law into the fund-raising scene, and Rita soon found her feet. In October 1925, while Harriet busied herself on the committee for The Northern Suburbs Day Nursery, another of her children's causes, Rita was secretary of a committee organising a card party at the Australia Hotel on behalf of the Limbless Soldiers Provident Fund. By Harriet's standards, this was a minor affair, but it was a start. Rita's debut was cut short when her mother died on November 2nd at the age of only fifty. The family was desolated by the loss and Rita stood down from the committee. On December 4th, she felt sufficiently recovered to assist at another Limbless Soldiers' event, albeit in a minor role, handing out flowers to welcome guests at Her Majesty's Theatre.

On March 23rd, 1926, Harriet realised her dream of revisiting her homeland, when she boarded the P&O liner, RMS Comorin in Sydney, and sailed for London.[262] She left her charitable duties in what she hoped were capable hands, as Rita was appointed Acting President of the St. Margaret's committee.[263] Arriving in London on May 8th she rented an apartment in St James Street, and settled into the old, familiar life she craved. David remained in Sydney. He'd no desire to undertake another voyage and trail along in Harriet's wake once in London or on the Riviera. He was discomforted to learn of her intended address in London, no more than a stone's throw from where he had housed Valerie during her time of confinement.

Accompanying Harriet there would have been a step too far. To top it all, he'd been out of sorts for some time; nothing specific, but a good enough excuse to beg off the trip. As the weeks passed, he felt increasingly unwell, finally taking to his bed.[264] Telegrams were dispatched to Harriet, assuring her that he was in good hands, as indeed he was. Percy and Rita, resident in their own rooms at Strathisla, marshalled the best of Sydney's medical specialists to tend to him and he was soon on the road to recovery. But it was a further sign that time was taking its toll. Harriet's resolve strengthened to make a decisive move towards full retirement.

Though Harriet could now reunite with Norman and Stuart, she enjoyed less of their company than she might have expected. Neither man appeared to have learned from his Australian experience. Stuart, despite having Peggy, who was expecting their second child, and young David Jr dependent on him, had achieved the dubious distinction of being declared bankrupt in two countries, when a London court found against him on July 28th, 1925.[265] His sole concern was to extract yet more allowance from his father through the ever-reliable good graces of his mother. Beyond that, he could see little to gain from spending time in her company. Norman was, well, being Norman. Arriving in England in 1924 he had spent the remains of the £300 that David had given him and lapsed into the now-familiar life of irresponsible playboy and unashamed cad. He might have attempted to re-join the social groups of his younger years, but time was not on his side; the comrades of his service life had moved on, married, or left for greener pastures. He remained unemployed and unemployable and drifted in the outer circles of London's society and club life. He lodged with various gullible families, always had a car to drive, and steadfastly avoided paying for goods or services. The very week of Harriet's arrival the General Strike* was called. Norman

---

* The General Strike of Great Britain lasted from 3rd to 12th May 1926. It was called by the General Council of the Trades Union Congress (TUC) in an unsuccessful attempt to force the British government to act to prevent wage reduction and worsening conditions for 1.2 million locked-out coal miners. Some 1.7 million workers went out, especially in transport and heavy

volunteered as a Special Constable, a job that must have appealed to his sense of self-worth and innate authority, and incidentally relieved his boredom. It was during this brief return to uniform that he was fined £2 for bilking a cab driver, the magistrate warning that the next time he did "such a dirty thing" he would send him to jail.* Taking advantage of the authority his Special Constable uniform conferred, he had commandeered a taxi, alighted at his destination and dismissed the driver's demand for payment with a cynical appeal to his patriotism. Stewart Dawson's London Managing Director gave evidence that he often paid fares at Norman's request, "provided the men (the drivers) called."

As if to confirm his recalcitrance, just a year later Norman was in court yet again, this time as the alleged victim of a crime. Rosalie Allen, sixteen-year-old daughter of a doctor, was accused of wilfully destroying £250 worth of Norman's clothing, including dress and lounge suits.[266] Norman had been lodging with the girl's mother, who had lost her husband and was living "in poor circumstances". Evidence was led that he had gone to the house in Clarges Street, Mayfair, with "a woman who took the name Mrs Stewart Dawson,"† paid about two weeks' rent and run up a bill of £55 without disclosing that he was an undischarged bankrupt. He denied concealing this fact from Mrs Allen, or that he took his clothing away from the house "by a trick." Counsel for the defence "suggested that Dawson owed money to several people, including taxi drivers and waiters," which Norman again denied. It appeared that he had absconded from the Allen's residence, taking his clothes with him to another address in Adam Street, near the Savoy Hotel, but young Rosalie, recovering from an attack of the mumps and "greatly incensed by this treatment

---

industry. The government was prepared and enlisted middle-class volunteers to maintain essential services and "Special Constables" to keep order.

* Sun 9th June 1932 P.15. When asked at his bankruptcy hearing in 1932 to confirm that he had been so fined, Norman replied with his customary insolence; *"I suppose you would say so. The word is not correct. I was fined for a technical offence."*

† Harriet, as usual, looked after her wayward son but inevitably he let her down again.

of her mother," tracked him down and "did the damage without properly appreciating what she was doing." The poor girl received little sympathy from the magistrate: "it was a most disgraceful episode, and the girl clearly required control." She was not allowed to stay in London and was ordered to be sent to a school in Switzerland. However, no fine was imposed, nor any order for reparation to Norman; the magistrate had met his kind before.

Fellow Australians visiting London in 1926 included Harriet's old friends, the Jacobsons. Joseph and Estelle Jacobson were frequent guests of the Stewart Dawsons at The Ambassadors. Estelle was a member of many of Harriet's committees and, like Harriet, she also opened their Bellevue Hill* home for meetings and social occasions. Joseph (Jack) Jacobson was Australian principal of SH Lock and Company Limited,[267] merchant bankers with offices throughout the Empire. He was influential in commercial and political circles and generous with his immense wealth. The Jacobsons were in London for an extended vacation with their daughter, Marjorie, who was to be presented at Court and later married. Their vacation was to include several months on the Riviera, and weeks of touring around Britain in their new Daimler limousine, bought upon their arrival in London.[268] Young Marjorie provided a starry-eyed account to Sydney readers in an interview with The Evening News.[269] She described how the family had watched the Test Match, which the Australians lost ("We are all horribly disappointed about it"), and enjoyed "the best musical comedy in London … 'Lady Be Good'. It is a wonderful show, with the two Astaires – brother and sister. They are splendid dancers." They had gone up to Colwyn Bay, North Wales in the Daimler, then "dashed across to Paris to do some shopping," where they "had a gorgeous time." She went on to list the most fashionable restaurants ("most artistic") but noted:

---

* Bellevue Hill was and remains one of Sydney's premier residential enclaves, just a mile or so down the harbour from the Stewart Dawson residence at Potts Point.

One never sees French people dining at these places since the franc dropped. They cannot afford it. One only sees English and Americans everywhere. However, on the whole, I think French people are bricks. They are all so patient, and try so hard to please, despite the bad time they are having.

Nineteen twenty-six had been a bad year for more than one European country. Britain suffered the General Strike, one of whose results was the loss of much of its coal markets to a resurgent Germany, Mussolini's Fascists took complete control of the Italian government, and France saw the final effects of its hyperinflation as the Treasury emptied and the franc collapsed to a rate of 50 to $1 US. Marjorie's sanguine, if patronising description of the French as "bricks" who were "trying so hard to please" was perhaps the blinkered view of a naïve colonial. Because France's reliance on German reparations from the War to fund its debt had been curtailed partly by US reluctance to enforce them, there were French who saw Americans as having plotted the franc's fall, and there were a few attacks on buses filled with American tourists.[270] But in one key regard, Marjorie was right: the Pound or the Dollar went a very long way in France and surrounding countries. There were bargains to be had not only in manufactured goods and services but in real estate, as banks refused to make loans and owners chased after hard currency from foreigners.

The Jacobsons entertained Harriet and were in turn treated to tea and cocktails at the St. James Street apartment. At a gathering in October, guests included Italian painter and miniaturist, Count Mario Grixoni and Princess Hassan, the former Ola Humphrey, who had married and divorced a member of the Egyptian Royal Family but retained her title. Conversation inevitably turned to their mutual interest and experiences in France, and they had Harriet's full attention when the discussion moved to the Jacobson's imminent tour of the Riviera. Harriet was torn between her desire for Europe and her love and duty to her ailing husband. If only she could persuade David to give up his Australian dream and retire with her to the land of their birth all would be well. She knew it would be the challenge of her lifetime and that it could only be accomplished face to face. She had to return to Sydney to confront her husband, for his own good.

First, however, she would avail herself of one last opportunity to visit the Riviera. It was, after all, the season when "everyone goes there, following up the sun," and she could take advantage of the Jacobsons' planned tour in the Daimler to get there, spend a couple of weeks and take ship from Toulon for Australia. If time permitted, she could investigate the market for villas and townhouses to see for herself whether the bargains were as good as everyone claimed. Her stay was short; on the 22nd of October, she boarded the new P&O liner Oronsay* bound for Sydney, her head full of dreams of life on the Riviera and her heart heavy at the prospect of the long voyage to the other side of the world. As the days passed and she idled away the time with cocktails, bridge, and writing postcards and letters to Sydney and London, she sought out sympathetic company. Gregarious and forthright in her opinions, she was attracted to a woman in whom she found an echo of her desires and frustrations. Kathleen O'Connor was a New Zealand born Australian expatriate artist, who had lived in Paris and London since before the war and was now returning to care for her mother in Perth. She called Paris home and, like so many fellow artists from the southern continent, despaired of what was to her an antipodean cultural desert. Her heart would never be in Perth, Sydney, or Melbourne while she could escape to the bohemian circles of the Latin Quarter or famous fashion houses like that of Paul Poiret, for whom she worked. Harriet and Kathleen fascinated each other. They were of a similar age† and while Harriet enthralled Kathleen with tales of parties, famous friends, stylish clothes, luxury cars and lots of servants, she in turn was transported by Kathleen's first-hand accounts of artistic life in what they agreed was the centre of western civilization. Every minute they shared confirmed Harriet's resolve to bring David back home and reunite the family once and for all. By the time the Oronsay berthed at Fremantle on November 16th and Kathleen disembarked they had arranged to meet again, if not in Sydney, where Harriet felt she would be able to help Kathleen make contacts to market her decorative artwork, then certainly in France when they both returned.[271]

---

* The Oronsay was commissioned in 1924.

† Kathleen was born in 1876, though she gave her age as thirty on the ship's passenger manifest. She and Harriet had much in common.

Bon Accord

Harriet's return to Sydney had been anticipated since as early as September. At a meeting of the Ladies' Committee of St. Margaret's Hospital, where Rita presided, plans were discussed to welcome her back.[272] Rita had been busy during her mother-in-law's absence and earned respect for her leadership and imagination. At twenty-four, she was almost the youngest of the organising committee, with no previous experience in planning and organising large social events but schooled by Harriet and supported by Percy and the professional team at the restaurant, she rose to the occasion. By November she had been involved in dozens of successful balls and carnivals at The Ambassadors, including the Spring Carnival on October 15th, where she showed her independence by encouraging Charlestoners to compete for prizes.[273] The Charleston was still frowned upon and discouraged at most dances, but Rita's committee was persuaded that it was time to grant the younger set the freedom to run wild for an evening. The gamble paid, and St. Margaret's babies received another generous contribution to their welfare.

Innovating once more, in November Rita staged a Cup Cabaret to celebrate the by now internationally famous horse race* and to raise more funds. For the first time ever, she arranged for the race call to be broadcast to the assembled guests and punters by wireless.[274] Her youthful and vivacious personality brought a freshness to the scene. In a fancy-dress ball held just after Harriet left, she dared to dress as Rudolf Valentino, winning a prize and the admiration of less adventurous guests.[275] She even coaxed Percy out of his shell, when he impressed partygoers at yet another ball[276] with his impersonation of a cockney engineer.

David, recovering from his illness, made one of his last visits to Queensland in July, in part because he was considering cashing in his investment in the Brisbane Queen Street property occupied by the

* The Melbourne Cup, "The race that stops the nation".

store. In March, the City Valuer, Mr. Ludwig, had announced completion of the valuation of over 90,000 properties in the greater Brisbane area. Asked what was the greatest value yet reached, he responded: "It was the valuation of £700 per foot on Messrs. Stewart Dawson's Queen Street property."[277] After inspecting the shop, David travelled further north than he had ever ventured, to winter in Cairns for a few weeks. The mild weather would ease his ageing body, he hoped, as he relaxed with his companions, Mrs and Miss Drew.*

David still harboured property development ambitions, in November 1926 mentioning a plan to build another arcade in the Pitt Street block.[278] But he had abandoned the skyscraper project and the arcade never went ahead. The Springwood development, however, was still active. In August 1925 he had won a minor but unusual concession from the Blue Mountains Council, when it approved the installation, at his cost, of two additional electric streetlights in front of Davesta.[279] Electric lighting had only come to Springwood the year before, so little had been installed yet. David was in effect paying to jump the queue, and Council accepted his money after some debate, but he was not enhancing the infrastructure merely for his own enjoyment. His plan was for a development on a larger scale than a simple upgrade to Davesta, whose frontage was too short to justify two more streetlights.

Thus, it was that Harriet arrived, on November 25th, David's 77th birthday. Scarcely pausing, she donned her party frock for a combined welcome home and birthday party at The Ambassadors. Dr. Langton, the president of the Board of Management of St. Margaret's, was host of the afternoon tea, whose centrepiece was a huge birthday cake surrounded by flowers. David's present was a miniature of his wife and Harriet received "a handsome card salver in solid silver", as if she needed another one. For all the work she had performed, Rita was thanked and received a posy of flowers. Percy would have empathised. The usual crowd was there; Percy and Rita, the McNabs, and not forgetting Mack, who seemed not to have missed a social gathering in over thirty years. David splashed out with a cheque for £500 for the hospital, on condition that five others subscribed £100.[280]

---

* The Drews were friends from Sydney. The husband, WH Drew, was a well-known lawyer.

Once she had had time to settle back into Sydney life,* Harriet felt able to talk with David about her proposal for their future. She was surprised and encouraged by his prompt acquiescence, perhaps expecting resistance because of his fixation with first the skyscraper, then the arcade and now the Springwood project. Instead, he dismissed the city developments. In November, he had turned down an offer from a British syndicate to buy most of his holdings in the Pitt Street precinct, including The Ambassadors, for a record sum of £700,000. The publicity generated by his aborted development proposals had alerted the syndicate to the potential of the site, and now he played for time, refusing to acknowledge the demise of the arcade scheme, while savouring the prospect of a huge profit on the sale, whenever it came. He also assured her that he no longer viewed the Mountains as his retirement home. He would exploit the natural beauty, the benign climate and growing amenity of Springwood for a grand guest house where they could entertain from time to time without committing to a more permanent move to the country. The building would be a commercial operation, satisfying David's need to derive income wherever possible. To this end, he would turn the whole property over to a company. Percy and he had discussed the project in Harriet's absence and his son had agreed to lead the Board of Management of the new business. For the first time in his life, David was stepping back from governance of an enterprise and Percy was to have unfettered responsibility and control.

Christmas and New Year's Eve over, with another spectacular children's party and more record crowds, Percy and David were relieved to learn that the Blue Mountains Council had granted permission for the erection of a guest house on the Hawkesbury Road. The cost of construction was estimated at £10,124, including provision of 8,000 gallons of water storage.[281] By February, the rumours were spreading in Springwood that something special was about to lift the profile of the town, as the Blue Mountains Echo reported:

---

* There were more "welcome home" parties in those first few weeks, confirming Harriet's popularity and the warm regard she had earned.

It is rumoured that Stewart Dawson contemplates the erection and construction of a mammoth ball-room and recreation hall in Springwood. There should be a fortune in it.[282]

The wheels were turning, if rather slowly. In January, David paid his last visit to Brisbane, where he gave another of his "my life and success in business" interviews to the local paper.[283] It was as usual, a business trip, to open negotiations for the sale of the Queen Street property. While he was away, Harriet busied herself with another of her causes. The long-drawn out case of Mrs Mort was again in the headlines and Harriet had taken a hand in the public campaign to free the imprisoned lady when she learned of it upon her return. Dorothy Mort, wife of a respectable North Shore businessman, had been convicted in 1920 of shooting to death her lover, Doctor Claude Tozer. In a confusing and inconclusive trial, she had been found not guilty on the grounds of insanity and sentenced to detention "at the Governor's pleasure" in Long Bay Jail. Public sympathy for Dorothy grew when the late doctor's womanising lifestyle was revealed and other evidence of his cavalier treatment of his lover came to light. Six years later, however, she was no nearer release despite petitions and appeals. Harriet's efforts led to a petition that gathered many signatures being presented to the State Minister for Justice, Mr McKell, supported by Harriet's personal appeal after she visited Dorothy in Long Bay.* Though the Minister agreed to consider the petition he gave no assurances, and it was not until 1929 that the convicted woman was deemed sane enough for release to the arms of her forgiving husband. Where others feared to intervene Harriet never gave up. As late as November 1928, she made a personal application to the Chief Justice and the Prisons Department for Dorothy's release. Speaking to a journalist from Sydney's "Truth", she confirmed that she had made the application, but added:

---

* Sun 11th January 1927 P.15. After visiting Dorothy, Harriet told the Minister that in her opinion the prisoner was quite rational *"though broken down in health."*

but I am almost afraid to say anything at this stage for fear of prejudicing her chances. I have not met with the sympathy and support from public women that I expected; but then some of them are so timid, and they do not realise that she is a broken woman. Surely she has paid enough for having been betrayed?

She related how each Thursday for many months she had taken along to Long Bay "some little delicacy" for her invalid acquaintance. The journalist described Dorothy's solitary existence in the prison, screened off from others in the hospital wing. The few personal items close to her were photos of her two children and, beside her bed, "the smiling photo of her best champion, Mrs. Stewart Dawson."

Back from Brisbane, David was off to Melbourne, now accompanied by Harriet, to initiate similar discussions about the Swanston Street store. Two Stewart Dawson's Corners were now unofficially on the market. While they were in the southern city, they missed the appearance at The Ambassadors of the greatest star of opera of the early twentieth century, Dame Nellie Melba. Percy and Rita were among the spellbound guests on the evening of February 5th as the diva entered for an after-theatre supper party.[284] It seemed to be a spur of the moment occasion; Harriet would not have missed the opportunity to meet the great lady had she been in town. When she and David did return, she was expected to immerse herself once again in the endless round of organising committees, though by now Rita had earned her spurs and continued to play a prominent role in organising new events. There was the Sunny Ball in February, celebrating the eponymous musical then playing,[285] but then, apart from a minor cabaret in May where Harriet and Agnes McNab sang a duet, nothing; where her diary should have been filled with committee meetings, afternoon teas and meticulously staged cabarets and balls, the pages were blank. True, The Ambassadors remained busy, but it was school reunions, minor charities' and building funds' dances that kept its doors open. It wasn't until July, when Netherlands born actress and singer, Beppie de Vries, lent her name to a "Madame Pompadour" cabaret,[286] that Harriet's St. Margaret's charity once more benefited. Harriet's low profile among the charity queens of Sydney was reflected in the results of the "Hospital Queen" competition, announced at the end of July.

Though she was credited with raising £4,333 for St. Margaret's she was relegated to fifth position, the winner raising £12,500 for St. Vincent's Hospital.[287] Some said she had lost her touch, that her seven-month absence from Australia had disconnected her from the social centre for too long. While she pursued her one-woman campaign on behalf of Dorothy Mort, St. Margaret's and other causes could be passed into other, younger hands in preparation for her eventual departure.

One encounter that did lift Harriet's spirits was her meeting with Kathleen O'Connor in June 1927. A few months in Perth had been more than enough to crush Kathleen's spirit ("I'll die if I stay here") so she sailed for Sydney, thinking that perhaps there she might find a more stimulating and congenial atmosphere, and be able to continue her friendship with Harriet. She had come prepared, should the opportunity arise, to set up as a designer and had printed purple and gold display cards with embossed letters:

KATHLEEN O'CONNOR

OF PARIS

PICTURES AND DECORATION

IN MODERN MOVEMENT

She took rooms in Young Street, in the city, and on June 12th a delighted Harriet invited her to afternoon tea at The Ambassadors, where she joined a select group of artists and musicians, including the Polish piano virtuoso, Ignaz Friedman and the singer, Anita Roma.[288] The very next day Kathleen was receiving commissions from two of Sydney's main emporiums, Grace Brothers and David Jones. Sadly, though connoisseurs appreciated her hand-painted dinner plates, sunshades and fabric, the Australian eye was not accustomed to the vivid colours she used and her success in Sydney was moderate at best. In any event, her stay in the city was curtailed when her hypochondriac mother recalled her to Perth. A short time there was enough to convince her that it was time to return to Paris, whence she sailed later in the year. Harriet, who had expected to see her friend back in Sydney, was distressed. She wrote on December 14th, just before Kathleen left:

My Dear Kathleen,

I am sending these few lines in the hope it will catch you ere you sail for foreign shores. You will be glad I feel sure to get back to your beloved Paris although there is always a little sadness in farewell. I do hope you have a pleasant voyage and that the gods will be good to you when you arrive at your destination. Keep in touch as much as you can dear. I will look forward with pleasure to our meeting on the other side. God bless you my dear friend and put some of the good things in your way. Keep on smiling.

With much love, Harriet Dawson

It was clear from the letter that Harriet had already confided in her friend her intention to return to Europe. It was only a matter of time before she would make the journey herself, but first she had to support her husband's divestment of his Australian interests.

David, for his part, had had to cope with a set-back early in the year, when a fire destroyed the top four floors of the Swanston Street corner building.* His shop occupied the ground floor and suffered only water damage, but the upper storeys housed a collection of other businesses, most of which fared badly. Thanks to several acts of courage all occupants were saved, though lack of a proper fire escape made it a close run and was criticised at the subsequent enquiry, as was the absence of sprinklers. Damage was estimated at between £15,000 and £20,000. Insurance cover was £15,000 so David was personally not out of pocket, though most of his tenants' losses in stock and fittings were not covered. Nevertheless, it meant a delay in

---

* Sun 12th March 1927 P.3, Melbourne Age 14th March 1927 P.9 and 15th March 1927 P.10. The fire resulted in moves to strengthen fire safety regulations for all commercial buildings.

his plans to sell the property. On the other hand, he now had the opportunity to restore and improve the building to new standards that would reward him upon its eventual sale.

In Springwood, he announced plans to develop the land opposite Davesta that he'd purchased in 1921, as another nine-hole course.[289] It was all part of the guest house project, which was proceeding at a leisurely pace by David's standards. The Blue Mountains Echo, reporting the plans, observed that the land adjoined the cemetery. The layout of the proposed course placed the tee-box for what would be the fourth hole* less than ten yards from Valerie's grave.

The same month, April, he granted an option over the Pitt Street property for £770,000, a ten percent premium on the price he had been offered not six months previously. He had waited out his bidders, knowing that market conditions favoured him. Sydney was waking up to the realisation of the tremendous boost to its economy approaching as the Bridge and the associated railway links visibly progressed. The cut and fill work for the rail stations was well past and street traffic was returning to normal. On the eastern side of the city loop St. James and Museum stations had opened the previous December.[290] Tunnelling was progressing northwards towards the Bridge from the underground Wynyard station, the closest to David's shops and The Ambassadors, and buyers were alert to the impact on property values. In March, a small block of shops near what would become Wynyard Station sold for £50,000.[291] Sydney's Construction and Local Government Journal observed on May 18th: "Sydney real estate is winning keen attention where likely to be closely affected by the City Railway."

Plans for the ownership and management of the Springwood guest house saw the October registration of a company "to acquire and sell, or otherwise dispose of real and personal property." Initial capital was £20,000 and the directors would be Percy, Harriet, Malcolm McNab and three others, including a professional accountant.[292] David was not listed as a board member. The company was to be known as "Bon Accord Investment Limited". "Bon Accord" was the motto of

---

* The original fourth hole is today's 13th hole

Aberdeen for "Good Agreement". It dated from the Wars of Scottish Independence in the 14th century, when Robert the Bruce and his men laid siege to Aberdeen Castle, destroying it in 1308 and massacring the English Garrison, retaking Aberdeen for the townspeople. "Bon Accord" was the secret password used during the campaign.[293] The broader meaning of the words is "Good will" or "Good fellowship", and as such it was in wide use in former times. David had himself used the term in advertisements for The Ambassadors as early as 1924: "Afternoon teas, social Bon Accord in an atmosphere of enchantment." He was to appropriate it for his personal motto and watchword in this, the final phase of his life.

Cash is King

Nineteen twenty-seven closed with David taking a back seat, occasionally boring listeners with his well-worn business tales and aphorisms but otherwise leading a quiet life. His major public appearance was in October at the Proud Benefit, in honour of cricketer, Edwin Proud. It was one of Harriet's last fund-raisers, attracting a good crowd of sportsmen and supporters. The famous cricketer and cartoonist, Arthur Mailey, attended and sketched several of the personalities, including David.

He was now truly a "grand old man" and the decline in his physical strength and abilities was evident. The illness that had laid him low in the previous year had left him in some pain and it was now that he became a regular user of A.P.C. pain relievers. Aspirin, Phenacetin, Codeine powders and tablets first appeared in Australia that very year. The two major brands, Bex* and Vincent's, promised immediate relief from pain and, indeed, could be relied upon for the occasional muscular injury or neuralgia brought on by eye strain and the like, but both phenacetin and codeine are highly addictive and the former insidiously attacks internal organs such as the kidneys. However, the cheap, over the counter drug seemed like a miracle cure and David had no hesitation in relying on it for daily relief.

Rita was still the more active of the women, playing the leading role in an important fund raiser on October 10th for the great Trans Pacific Flight.[294] Charles Kingsford Smith ("Smithy") was preparing for the first non-stop flight across the Pacific Ocean. This was the era of record-breaking aviation exploits. Charles Lindbergh had made history in May by crossing the Atlantic and now it was time for the Australians to show the world. Smithy had already been feted in June for completing a round-Australia flight in 10 days, 5 hours, on the strength of which the New South Wales government made him a

* Bex was promoted as "mother's little helper" and many women could not get through the day without their dose. The slogan: *"Have a Bex, a cup of tea and a good lie down"* became part of Australian folklore.

grant of £9,000. Thanks to Rita, the flight received a further handsome donation towards the final total of over £20,000. David and Harriet were not among the guests on the night, nor did they attend Rita's Harlequin Ball, which mixed metaphors with Harlequin/Columbine costumes and Harold Lloyd* spectacles (organisers had made it plain that this event was for the younger set).

David's principal contribution to charity as the year ended was to lend his name to "The Ugly Men's Competition", a fund-raiser for the Limbless Soldiers' Benevolent Fund that was promoted and sponsored by the Sun newspaper. Set a target of £50,000, a group of distinguished businessmen and community leaders agreed to become candidates for the title of Sydney's ugliest man, gathering donations in their support. The "ugliest" tag was a gimmick, as the newspaper made use of distorted photographs to identify the candidates. David joked about his photo:

> *I must protest against the picture of me published in "The Sun". It shows distinct bias in favour of the other competitors. Your artist, for reasons best known to himself, has presented a picture much better-looking than is justified ... many of my friends ... say there are several angles from which I might be shown as much uglier ... One of these is usually obtainable after being interviewed by a traffic "cop".*

The competition stretched over several weeks in November and December. Candidates raised money from supporters by staging events or canvassing for votes which pledged donations to the fund. David, representing the jewellery trade and the Scots community, was an early leader, a clear 10,000 votes ahead of his nearest rival. However, he faded in the straight, beaten into eighth place by a field that was biased towards union leaders but ultimately dominated by the theatrical entrepreneur Stuart Doyle, who won over a million votes, almost ten times David's count. David, though, had made his contribution with good humour and not too much effort, and could end the year satisfied.

---

* Harold Lloyd was an American actor, comedian, and stunt performer who appeared in many silent comedy films. He is considered alongside Charlie Chaplin and Buster Keaton as one of the most influential film comedians of the silent film era. His signature costume included prominent spectacles.

After what had been a long gestation, work commenced on the Springwood building in January 1928. Despite being out of town, it rated a mention in the Construction and Local Government Journal,[295] though it was an inaccurate characterisation of the guest house:

> *The Golf Club House (sic) at Springwood, which is being built by Mr. Stewart Dawson, will be completed in six months. It will have a very spacious ball-room, as well as ample reception rooms.*

As construction advanced, David applied pressure to the Blue Mountains Council to make further improvements to Hawkesbury Road, still notoriously rough and under-maintained. If he was to attract high-status, high-paying guests to Springwood, they could hardly be expected to travel the last mile from Sydney on what he would only describe as a cart track. In a letter to the Council in March[296] he wrote that part of the road fronting his property was not in a satisfactory condition. He stressed the fact that

> *the surface was to have been exactly a duplicate in quality of the new road from the foot of the Mountains … also that there was no sign of tar and that the macadam was uneven, unrolled and potholed.*

The Council's engineer responded, claiming the road was, in effect, as good as could be expected for the amount spent on it. He doubted David had been told it would be a duplicate in quality to the new Mountain road. This road, he stated, "probably cost £13,000 per mile, while the Hawkesbury section cost £750 per mile." So determined was David, however, that he withheld the £75 he had promised towards the cost of road improvements. The argument continued over several months, with the Council's engineers refusing to concede to David's demands. By June, the parties reached stalemate; the Council claiming it had done all the work required, while David refused to pay over the promised contribution. A resolution was passed that the President interview Council's solicitor and give seven days' notice in which the amount must be paid. Otherwise, legal action would be taken.[297] Gritting his teeth, David paid.*

---

* Possibly at the urging of Percy and the other shareholders in Bon Accord Investments. In any event, no more was heard of the dispute.

In a further step towards severing his personal links with Springwood, in September 1928 he transferred ownership of all the property save the excised lot on which Bonnie Doon stood from his own name to Bon Accord Investments. The company, in which he was not a shareholder, now owned all the other dwellings: Davesta, The Spinney and its neighbour, and almost 13 acres of what was now prime residential development land. Work on the extension to Davesta was almost complete and, as if to draw a veil over the tragic origins of the name, the house and its extension were renamed, "Bon Accord". The guest house opened before the end of the year.* It was an impressive addition to the Mountains. The three-storey colonial-style building abutted the original Davesta at an angle of about 30 degrees, following the curve of the property's frontage. It towered over the bungalow and dominated the view across the valley behind. Airy verandas opened the front to the afternoon breeze and an open deck at the rear looked out over the tree-covered slopes below. Two stone lions, the emblem of Aberdeen, squatted beside the steps to the main entrance. Inside, there were thirty bedrooms, all with running hot and cold water, a ballroom, billiards, cards and writing rooms. There was a pianola for guests to entertain themselves, wireless to keep in touch with news and gossip, and first-class dining using the best of local produce. Outside, as well as the golf course, were tennis courts and bicycles for the more adventurous guests keen to explore the local beauty spots. The gardens were by now well-established and a noteworthy attraction for Springwood visitors. A 1927 description in The Sunday Times[298] of the walk from Springwood along Hawkesbury Road read:

> *Continue right into Springwood, and turn to the right across the railway bridge into the Hawkesbury-road ... This takes you past the magnificent residence of Mr. Stewart Dawson, with its beautiful terraced gardens and statuary, facing the Springwood links.*

---

* There is no clear record of the actual opening of Bon Accord, and it does not appear in advertisements until as late as 1933. However, it can be inferred from some of these advertisements that it was operating from late 1928.

By the time of the opening of Bon Accord, hundreds of rose bushes filled the beds surrounding the buildings and fountains played at the intersections of the meticulously groomed pathways. Inspired by the gardens at Wilga, the rear was terraced like a Roman amphitheatre and more fountains, statues and ponds graced the leafy slope. Bon Accord would soon be known as "The Rose Garden Guest House".[299] Percy and company brought their experience of establishing and operating the best in hospitality and entertainment to Bon Accord and introduced many of their friends and acquaintances from the city to this lower-Mountains alternative to the Hydro Majestic.

In January, the lease on the George Street store expired and David announced it would not be renewed. He conceded that, having failed to acquire the freehold of the George Street end of the Strand Arcade back in 1919, it might have been better to vacate the shop there and then, while opening the premium outlet at the Pitt Street end. Instead, for nearly eight years the two shops had competed for business. Now, as trade turned down, he opted to cut his losses. In any case, he needed to clear the decks in preparation for the sale of his holding in the block. He advertised what amounted to a fire sale in both shops, discounting all watches, jewellery, diamond articles and solid silver by 5 shillings in the pound and 8 shillings off all silver plate and fancy goods.* The George Street shop immediately found another tenant. The firm of Lewis' Ltd., drapers, and milliners, announced that they would be retiring from the drapery trade to focus on their Brightlights business. Brightlights was a "five and dime" store with four branches in the city and a wholesale warehouse. Its supplanting of the prestigious jewellery shop at the very end of the fashionable arcade was an embarrassing reminder that the tide was turning against the luxury market.†

Just as Lewis' faced reality and retired from the drapery trade, David's growing acceptance that it might be time to consider exiting the jewellery business altogether was reinforced when, on Friday 13th

---

* Sunday Times 15th January 1928 P.5. 5 shillings in the pound equals a 20% discount, 8 shillings is 40% off.

† Brightlights itself lasted only three years, when Lewis' Ltd. was forced into liquidation as the Depression took hold.

of January Stewart Dawson's, Sydney were the victims of a robbery that netted at least £1,500. Police soon concluded that the theft had to be the work of an organised gang, possibly English, that had entered the country with a well-thought plan to hit major stores. Within the same week jewels and rings worth over twice as much as those lost from David's shop were stolen from Roberts' Jewellers in Melbourne, in similar circumstances.[300] The stolen goods were never recovered, and the thefts soon forgotten by the public as the news broke with alarming frequency of robbery after robbery from jewellers large and small. Most of the crimes were committed by opportunistic amateurs, who were usually apprehended while attempting to fence the loot but, as the police admitted,

> *It is rare for an arrest to follow a big jewellery robbery. The few really "good men" are satisfied with a small number of big hauls in a year.*[301]

The depressing fact that David had to acknowledge was that, as times became harder, paying customers were being replaced by the non-paying variety. If this trend continued, increased insurance premiums and concerns for his employees' safety and well-being could bring an end to the entire business.

At The Ambassadors business was still good, for the time being. Maître d', Romano had left to open his own restaurant and dance hall in December 1927. His loss would be sorely felt as he established an independent and competitive reputation but for now Percy retained control of experienced staff and there was no shortage of patrons if the band played, and the kitchens served. On Tuesday March 13th Harriet presided over the Hinkler Ball. Herbert John (Bert) Hinkler was an Australian aviator who had achieved more successes as a solo flier than any of his countrymen. An ace air-gunner in the war, he had also qualified as a pilot and until 1926 was chief test pilot for the Avro company and found time to compete for several trophies. In 1927 he flew non-stop in an Avro Avian single-engined tourer from London to Riga, Latvia, receiving a Latvian decoration. Buoyed by this achievement, he planned the first solo flight from London to Australia. Only nine years before, Ross and Keith Smith had flown the route for the first time, but their aircraft was a large, twin-engined Vimy bomber and they carried two mechanics with them. Hinkler's flight, by comparison, would be more of a Lindbergh-style exploit. The ball was one of his last public appearances before Hinkler's departure from Australia to collect his aircraft in London. The guest of honour received a hero's welcome. The highlight of the evening, yet another St. Margaret's fundraiser, was the auctioning of a gramophone record of a speech by Hinkler, his "Message to Australia". David led the bidding, securing the record for the staggering price of £100. The recording was considered so historically significant (Hinkler, after all, might not survive the flight) that David promptly donated it to Sydney's Mitchell Library for archival preservation.[302] As Australians were relieved to see, Hinkler did survive, completing the journey in slightly over fifteen days.*

The Hinkler Ball was perhaps the highlight of 1928 for The Ambassadors. As the months passed, Percy faced the fact that Romano's with its more intimate atmosphere, was gaining a share of the declining Sydney market at his expense. He was losing valuable, experienced staff to his new rival. The Wentworth's popularity remained high and with the passing of time even the Stewart Dawsons were seen dining there. Rita, Harriet, granddaughter Georgina† on a visit from England, Agnes McNab and, on at least one occasion, even David, set aside old rivalry with Hannah Maclurcan to take tea or attend celebratory gatherings in the Café.[303] Percy had bought a house at Newport,[304] on the western, Pittwater side of the beautiful Northern Beaches peninsular across the harbour, an astute purchase anticipating the boom in property values once the Bridge was complete. Here, he and Rita could retreat, take in the view of Pittwater to the sound of cockatoos and kookaburras squawking in the canopy of gumtrees, and entertain family and friends. The McNabs were among the visitors.[305] Percy and his uncle Malcolm,

---

* Bert Hinkler went on to further success and acclaim, awarded the Seagrave trophy, the Britannia challenge trophy, the gold medal of the Royal Aero Club and more. He was killed in 1933 when attempting another England to Australia flight. Hinkler, Herbert John (Bert) (1892-1933) E.P. Wixted, Australian Dictionary of Biography, Vol. 9 1983

† Vanna's daughter, Georgina Jerrard, now 23 years old, on her second visit to Australia.

away from the pressures of the city, had the time to plan for the fit out, management and operation of the Springwood business, in which Malcolm would take a leading role. They were also in consultation with David over the worrying state of the jewellery trade throughout the country and in New Zealand, not to mention the Regent Street store, which was caught in the downturn of the UK economy.

In November, Percy announced that The Ambassadors would close for two weeks and would re-open

> *November 17, with many special features, including a new electrically-equipped kitchen, which will be installed on the ground floor with the principal dining terrace, inaugurating a high-class à la carte service, which will be at a moderate figure, served in a de luxe manner. A new dance orchestra of ten members … will render all the latest American dance successes.*

The combination of the economic downturn and loss of business to Romano's was biting harder by the day. As well as loss of patronage, a sign of the times was a relaxation (some would say, decline) in dress standards. Evening dress was now optional, reflecting the broadening of the customer base beyond the once-exclusive society set. Just as Brightlights' five and dime store had displaced Stewart Dawson's in George Street, a five and dime clientele would now be welcomed to the restaurant. But Percy and David also had their eye on the commercial value of the property as negotiations for its sale continued. As any real estate agent will advise a seller, a kitchen renovation is one of the more cost-effective ways to attract buyers. In less than four years the state-of-the-art kitchens had become obsolescent, as new technology overtook the traditional gas-only ranges and ovens. Experience had shown that their location on a separate floor from the dining room was impractical; they would be decommissioned and replaced by a brand-new kitchen more conveniently located. The most telling aspect of the announcement, however, was the reference to the "moderate figure" (price) of the dining service. This, more than anything, was an admission that many patrons could no longer afford The Ambassadors and were voting with their wallets when choosing a restaurant. David had never expected The Ambassadors to be more than a vanity project but now that the property was on the market the prospective buyers had a right to expect a commercial return. Due diligence inspection of the accounts of The Ambassadors as future tenant would not inspire confidence without evidence of remedial action.

The deal was almost ready for closing but before it could be consummated David pre-empted it with the announcement of the sale of the now refurbished Collins Street property in Melbourne, for £250,000, to the Manchester Unity Independent Order of Oddfellows.* He had realised a gross profit of £160,000 on his 1913 purchase price of £90,000. The Oddfellows proposed to demolish the entire building, replacing it with a new building for its own purposes with shop fronts. Stewart Dawson's were not to be evicted, however. David retained the right, which he promptly exercised, to lease a shop for his own business.

The rumours about David's property sales now had substance so there was little surprise when, in March 1929, the Pitt Street block sold to Strand and Pitt Street Properties Ltd., a consortium comprising Woolworths Ltd. and a group of prominent Sydney businessmen. On March 31st, The Sunday Times announced† the "Greatest Sale on Record," with a price tag of £770,000, ("the greatest price ever realised in Australia by the sale of city property in one lot")‡ as the buyers exercised the option granted to them. The delay in closing the deal reflected the hard negotiation of the final terms and closer examination revealed a more complex arrangement than a simple cash transaction. Stewart Dawson Strand Property Ltd would receive a deposit of £150,000, payable in instalments over one year, with a first mortgage over the property for £620,000, to be paid over 25 years at 6½% interest. Stewart Dawson's would lease The Ambassadors and the Pitt Street shop, but The Sydney Morning Herald reported that the buyers intended eventually to convert the basement into a cash and

---

* The Oddfellows was a friendly society founded in 1810.

† Sunday Times 31st March 1929 P.11 "Huge Wealth in Property". The article took the opportunity to promote The Ambassadors yet again: *"pronounced by American and Continental travellers to be the most magnificent dance restaurant in the World."*

‡ £770,000 was nearly 30% of the total of all city property sales for the year.

carry store (another Brightlights), a dismal fate for the still fashionable cabaret and that, accordingly, the lease would only extend for one year.[306] So much for the expensive kitchen re-fit. The buyers' due diligence had forecast total annual rent revenue of nearly £90,000, outgoings of about £63,000, for a surplus after tax of £20,000, equivalent to 11.4% annual return on paid-up capital of £175,000. Such an attractive deal for what many claimed to be "the show shopping block of the Commonwealth"[307] should have been quickly oversubscribed but this was 1929, the first signs of nervousness in the market were emerging, the great crash only months away. The share offering was underwritten by The Australian Investment Company Ltd., which found itself having to make up a considerable shortfall in funds to reach the full capital raising.

David was relieved to unburden himself of what was becoming a millstone, as he grappled with impending loss of rents and the need for a capital injection to bring the precinct into the twentieth century. His skyscraper had remained a pipe dream and other plans for extra arcades had gone nowhere. The Ambassadors had seen its best days in less than five years and now was the time to move on. Harriet's call to return to Europe could be answered and he could leave Percy to conclude the deal. He knew that he was taking a risk as mortgagee that could have been avoided if he had secured a cash sale, but he was realistic and could take some pride in the headline price obtained. Together with the Collins Street sale, he had made over £1million, on paper, in a few months. Yes, he had over-spent on The Ambassadors, but he had made his point about style and sophistication. What's more, the profit on the two deals would silence his critics and cement his reputation for business acumen for all time. As the news spread about the sales and newspapers tallied the value of his other holdings at well over another £1million he told an interviewer in a room adjoining The Ambassadors: "I will sell the lot, provided I can get fair value".[308] He added that, at 80, he was tired of working hard all his life.

> *I have been a busy man all my life – ever since I built that stone fence around my father's farm in Scotland. The sale of these properties does not mean that the retail jewellery businesses of Stewart Dawson will come to a stop. They will go on, I suppose, for some time yet. For these properties, I don't mind telling you, I am getting – or asking – a lot*

more than I paid for them. This block brought me something like two and a half times what it cost me. The site in Melbourne, which I sold last November for £250,000 and received spot cash for the full amount of it, showed a substantial gain.

Noting that he also had the Lambton Quay corner site in Wellington on the market, he surmised:

The willingness of buyers to pay such high prices as I have received for the two properties I have sold recently are evidence, in my opinion, of my judgement, in selecting central shop sites in the principal centres for my business purposes. The growth of the cities has enhanced the values, and not any effort on my part, except, perhaps, a little foresight.

Others soon credited him with supernatural foresight in liquidating so many assets with moments to spare before the Crash but, though he had without doubt a canny eye for the economic climate it was rather a fortuitous coincidence, brought about by his loss of interest in his once-beloved jewellery business and a desire to end his life on a high note. He concluded:

I admit that the jewellery trade is not what it was some years ago – before the outbreak of the war – but as long as there are love, courtship, and marriage, and all their incidental arrangements, jewellery will be wanted by the people.

On April 23rd, after a grand farewell party at The Ambassadors, hosted by the committee of St. Margaret's, the couple set sail on the Orama for London via Melbourne and Perth, on what was billed as a six months' business trip.[309] Sydney's "Truth" observed:

Mrs David Stewart Dawson, smothered in flowers and the usual impediments that is (sic) imposed on travellers, sailed by the Orama during the week. Almost up to the last minute she held a dark suspicion that her spouse would baulk the trip. She got him away, however.[310]

Even now, as his health declined, and Harriet urged him to retire into domestic comfort in her care, his business concerns and his love of his adopted home retained their hold on him.

20. Hugh D ('Huge Deal') McIntosh

21. Davesta, David's Springwood home, with the Bon Accord extension beyond.

22. The Spinney and its sister house. Bonnie Doon is behind the trees to the left, Davesta off right.

23. *The gardens at Clarens ('Wilga'), Potts Point.*

24. *(Above) Feature in 'Construction and Local Government Journal' (Sydney) Dec. 22nd 1919, celebrating the record sale of The Strand Arcade to Stewart Dawsons.*

25. *(Right) The Wentworth Ballroom. the Prince of Wales standing, centre.*

26. *Hannah Macluran*

27. *Bert Ralton's New York Havana Band at the Savoy Hotel,1921.*

28. Photo spread from The Sunday Times, December 23rd 1923, celebrating the opening of The Ambassadors. David's portrait centre.

The Ambassadors—*The Main Dining Hall and Ball Room*

29. The Main Dining Hall and Ballroom.

The Ambassadors—*The Palm Court*

30. The Palm Court

31. The Kitchen

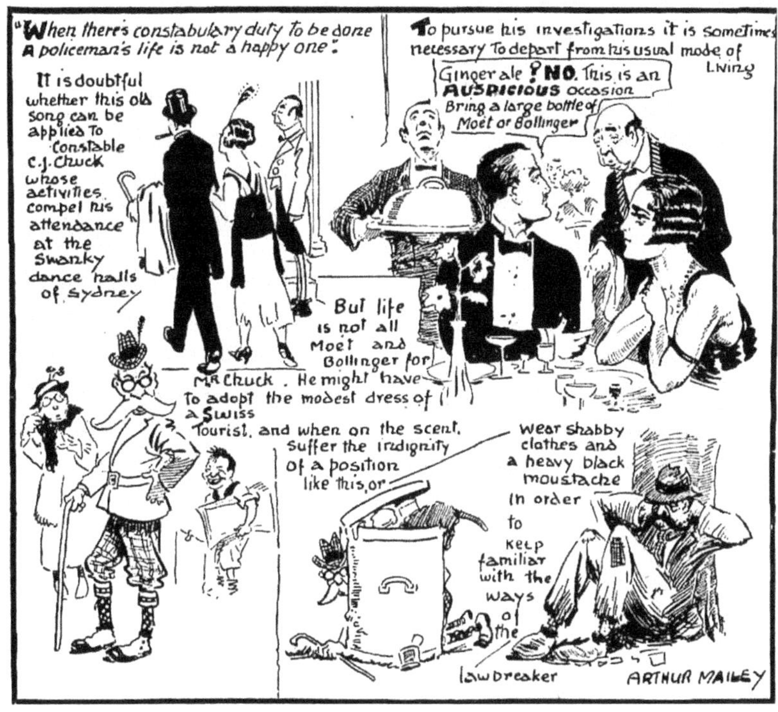

32. Cartoon by Arthur Mailey depicting Constable Joe Chuck hard at work on a 'sly grog' sting. Published in The Sun, 6th July 1924

33. Josie Melville

34. Harriet at the time of her 'Wives of our famous men' interview, 1925.

35. Rita Stewart Dawson, aged 24, when she was President of St Margaret's Hospital Committee in 1926.

36. Bertha Stewart Dawson (Verrall) in 1920s.

37. Bon Accord guest house. The roof of the original 'Davesta' bungalow can just be seen on the left

38. Arthur Mailey cartoon of David at the Proud Benefit Ball, October 1927

Part 2: 1929 – 1945.

The Rudderless Ship

Someday, my Prince will come

Harriet set down her cup on the tray, pushed back the chair and rose slowly to cross the room. Pausing to catch her breath, she reminded herself that it had been a long day, what with the morning visitors and the familiar crowd for today's "At Home". Small wonder that she felt a little light-headed and in need of a rest before tomorrow's theatre party. She crossed to the couch and sank into the soft cushions. From her seat she had a clear view through the one large window but there was nothing to hold her gaze; no dazzling harbour where luxury yachts lined the marina or welcomed early evening cocktail guests; no distant islands or shoreline adorned with marble mansions. Just the familiar wall of nondescript office buildings no more than yards away, the monotonous rumble of traffic a reminder of her circumstances even should she close her eyes. It never ceased, as if to tell her: "You are here to stay, no escape." It was true, she had to make the best of the time left to her, even if she never gave up hope of return, of a reunion with Kathleen, of one last visit to the villa. Now that the war was over who knew what might be possible?

Just weeks before, they had dropped those terrible bombs on the Japanese and already passenger liners were filling with Sydneysiders eager to renew friendships and love affairs across the world. Harriet had seen some of them preparing to depart or others arriving in the lobby below. How long it had been since she had last packed a trunk, admired the collection of exotic labels, mementos of happier, exciting times. Apart from that brief and unmemorable trip to Suva back in '41,[311] it had been six worrying years since her frantic dash from Europe had seen her on the promenade deck of a liner. Until then, what a whirl of travel and gay parties she had enjoyed, despite everything. It seemed that she had been insulated, to a great extent, from the troubles of the world and of her poor family. Her poor family! What remained of it now? Apart from young Harriet, who could honestly be counted content and at peace with the world? Percy seemed to have lost hope in recent times, Stuart seldom even pretended sobriety, young David was as spoilt as people claimed and she would never get over the loss of poor, dear Norman, such a cruel blow. To think, how much hope she had embraced as the Orama cast off from the pier and the last streamers dropped from the rails. David and she were going home at last, where she could care for him and embrace her daughter and errant sons. Even Percy might be persuaded to join them once free of Sydney's encumbrances.

Percy, she conceded, had pulled his weight in those difficult times. It wasn't his fault that markets had crashed, and fashions changed, and he'd had more than his share of ill-luck, what with the fires, bad debts, legal fights, the sad business with Rita and even his long run of "also rans" at the racecourse. And Norman, bless him, had tried so hard to make a go of it with Mack's new business. It was a mystery even today that their initial success had not been sustained. Such a winning idea but it seemed, ahead of its time.

At least she had had the grandchildren for company and comfort. Taking them away from the stultification of their narrow Australian childhood and their parents' troubles had been a blessing for them all. Both had benefited from the years in Europe, gaining such self-assurance, even if young David had gone rather further than she would have wanted. But it had been fun to witness their delight and enjoyment as they mingled with the younger set in Mayfair, Paris, and Monte Carlo. Young Harriet had a polish and style about her that she would never have gained in Sydney. The pity was that dear David had not been there to share the good times or to take charge, as he always had, when things turned down. As for the Prince, though there remained a flicker of hope, he was no David, capable and willing to return and resume their interrupted life together. How had it come to this, a lonely existence in exile far from home, chronically short of the needful and confined to this comfortable but dull hotel room? She rang for drinks and as she sipped her champagne ("Careful, Harriet, one glass only; remember poor Peggy.") she pondered the years of loss and decline.

~/~/~

From the moment that they landed in England and the first telegrams arrived from Sydney, the signs were there that fate would not be kind to them. It had started well enough. His parents safely on the high seas, Percy concluded the sale of the property and arranged the ongoing leases of the shop and the restaurant. There was cash in the bank, albeit a tiny fraction of the total due, but by the end of the year there would be £150,000 plus the first year's mortgage principal and interest, with twenty-four more years to come, a comforting thought to contemplate. In other respects, it was business as usual, as he and Rita dedicated themselves to the back office and front of house, respectively, of The Ambassadors. And dedication was more of a watchword, as the worrying downward trend in business continued. There had been the first real signals of international economic unrest in March, when the Wall Street Stock Exchange suffered a minor crash after the Federal Reserve warned of excessive speculation. On March 26th interest rates on at call loans touched 20%, the highest since 1920, as investors scrambled to clear positions. The aggregate value of stocks tumbled by £200 million, and the tickers were an hour behind the market at closing time. Panic extended to the Chicago Grain Market and New York's Cotton Exchange. Local markets in Australia* remained unaffected in the short term but the nation's credit position was becoming fragile and export markets for wool and other commodities were stagnant. Couples and singles on the lookout in Sydney still took the tram or train into town for a night out and the Eastern Suburbs set were chauffeured to the door of The Wentworth, Ambassadors, Romano's or the other popular cabaret, the Cavalier, but Percy knew, from the steady fall off in sales at the jewellery stores,† that money was becoming tighter. His father had been right to cash in his assets when he did; let someone else carry the burden in these uncertain times.

The night of Monday, July 29th was cold and wet. It had rained intermittently all day as winter set in. Attendance at The Ambassadors for the Golden Wattle Ball was good, all things considered. Nearly 200

---

* There were separate share markets in Sydney, Melbourne, Brisbane, and Perth until 1987.

† By 1929 all Stewart Dawson's Australian stores were offering discounts on most items. David seems to have given up in New Zealand, where advertising was infrequent and lacklustre, lacking any of his legendary bombast and exuberance.

patrons, glad to be indoors and underground, were insulated from the showers and wind gusts. Ladies shed their wraps and danced, bare-shouldered, around the bustling dance floor. Just before midnight, word went around that there was a fire next door. The dancers were reassured by an official that there was no immediate danger and were requested to continue dancing. The orchestra played on, and the ball proceeded, but only for a few minutes. Smoke began to seep into the ballroom and in no time was choking thick. There was little panic as the dancers filed through a door leading to the Strand Arcade. So hasty was the evacuation that few of the ladies had time to collect their wraps and were obliged to huddle together on the footpath outside for more than an hour as the rain turned briefly to hail. Inside, firemen struggled to deal with the blaze, resorting to pouring as much water as possible into the building from upper floors of the Strand Arcade and an adjacent building in Pitt Street. The dome above the ballroom was eventually engulfed in flames, collapsing onto the famous dance floor as water cascaded onto it. Fortunately, so much water had already covered the floor that it suffered no real damage from the burning debris. The old kitchen, so recently decommissioned by Percy, was also consumed by the flames, but the refrigeration plant was spared, averting the danger of deadly ammonia fumes filling the premises.

There was no mystery as to the origin of the fire. At 11.40pm, a patrolling policeman, Sergeant Conlin, noticed a small volume of smoke at the entrance to MacNaught's shoe store, on the Pitt Street side of the block. He could see that a wooden fanlight above the doorway was alight and sounded the fire alarm.

> *I could have subdued the fire myself when I noticed it, he said, if I had had a chemical extinguisher. As I watched I saw that an electric fan was in the position where the fire started, and I believe that a short circuit caused the outbreak.*[312]

By the time the fire brigade arrived the fire had taken hold and it was too late to save the shoe store, which was gutted. Other shops suffered fire, smoke, and water damage but the impact on The Ambassadors was the most dramatic. The "desolate scene" made the headlines of all the local and national newspapers, editors lingering on descriptions of *half empty champagne bottles, jugs of untouched claret cup, a dainty lace handkerchief, overturned and broken glasses … the smell of damp, burnt woodwork, ruined chairs and tables, glorious chandeliers smashed to powdered glass …*[313]

Initial estimates of the damage to The Ambassadors were between £15,000 and £20,000 and there was speculation that this could spell the end of the glamorous cabaret. However, Percy was quick to respond; The Ambassadors would be back in business within a week. At first sight, this looked a hopeless promise, sure to be dismissed as the nervous reaction of one still in shock over the devastation of his own creation. But Percy was as good as his word and on Thursday August 8th the Evening News carried a display advertisement:

Unusual Announcement – Extraordinary Achievement. The Directors have great pleasure in announcing to their many patrons the re-opening of The Ambassadors on Saturday afternoon next.

The advertisement was careful to point out: "The Spring Floor for which The Ambassadors is famous was spared by the fire and its aftermath."[314] There was of course, a large element of sleight of hand in Percy's announcement. The magnificent dome was not to be replaced and never would be. Instead, artful draperies of pastel shaded satins concealed the gaping hole, new luxurious lounges upholstered in bronze graced the floor, the orchestra dais was hung with glistening golden tissue and over all new crystal chandeliers shed blue and white light; in other words, the ballroom had become a stage set.* No matter, the recovery was so fast that Sydney barely had time to blink and though a couple of functions were transferred to the old and new rivals, The Wentworth and Romano's, the dancers returned. It seemed the floor was more important to them than the ceiling.

---

* Not for the first time. Following the successful filming of "Joe" in 1925, not long before the fire Percy and Rita had negotiated with the McDonagh sisters to shoot a crucial scene of "The Cheaters" in the dining room of the Palm Court, which served as "The Plaza Hotel" for the movie. The scene survives today.

Percy had got away with a low-cost redecoration in record time, an expedient in which he could justifiably take pride. He was relieved that the fire had not broken out sooner. Only six weeks earlier Stewart Dawson Strand Property Ltd had owned the whole of the affected part of the building. The new owners were now responsible for the costs of repairing the fabric of the shops and arcades, even of The Ambassadors. So long as he kept the doors open at the cabaret, he could collect his share of the revenue and pay his rent. So long as the owners paid the remainder of their deposit and the mortgage instalments, he need worry about nothing. And there was the rub: Strand and Pitt Street Properties Ltd were already behind with their monthly payments and now were confronted with unexpected costs just at the time when the market was turning down. Grossly undercapitalised (they had struggled to raise the initial £25,000 and spent much of that on the first stage payment of the deposit), they could never afford to pay the full cost of restoring the fire damage and were even more relieved than Percy when the patched-up ballroom reopened. However, this was already the beginning of the end for the poorly conceived partnership. After the fire, Strand and Pitt Street Properties made a formal application to the City of Sydney Council to restore the affected portion of the building to its original state. But the Civic Commissioners, keen to exploit this opportunity to launch Sydney into the twentieth century, took the view that the whole building should be demolished, and a more modern structure erected. This was far beyond the means of the consortium and a protracted wrangle ensued that would not be resolved until the following June, when the Council relented, permitting a re-build. The immediate cost was a bond to complete the rebuild in two years but so much rent had been foregone from the still to be renovated shops (at least £10,000) that Strand and Pitt Street Properties were forced to seek a moratorium from Stewart Dawson Strand Property on payments of both the mortgage and the final instalments of the deposit. Percy and David's dream of hundreds of thousands of pounds of income in the first year had gone up in smoke and the headline-grabbing £770,000 "record sale" was nothing more than a line of bold print in a newspaper. Stewart Dawson Strand Property was forced in 1930 to sue for non-payment of the mortgage and obtained a judgement naming them mortgagee in possession. Percy would now collect all rents to cover mortgage and principal owing, remitting only the residual balance to the hapless owners, out of which they paid the operational expenses of the premises.

Everything Must Go

David and Harriet arrived in London at the end of May 1929. They had escaped the winter in Sydney and could hope to enjoy the northern summer, easing David's chronic symptoms of ill-health. They were to be disappointed; throughout May, June, July, and August temperatures were persistently below average. June was cool and mostly cloudy, and it was mid-July before a brief interval of sunny weather warmed the visitors. Harriet fretted, this was not what she had planned or hoped for, David was supposed to be resting in a garden somewhere. His appetite had all but gone, his joints ached, and he complained of headaches, for which his only relief was another dose of powders. But try as she might, he would not be diverted from business matters. It was clear he had decided to wipe the slate while he still had time to do so. Basing himself at The Treasure House, he commenced negotiations to close all UK operations. He had ceased manufacturing in Hatton Garden some years before, as American and Swiss imports displaced the local product, but he maintained administrative and export operations at The Treasure House and the Regent Street store still paid a small margin on his lease costs.

His priority was Regent Street. He held the lease on the property, but it still had 70 years to run, and its prime location commanded a premium regardless of the economic climate. Inquiries soon turned up prospective buyers and in July he cabled Percy[315] that he had sold the lease to House of Fraser for £70,000. The store would close, and he could then focus on the sale of The Treasure House. Once again, he had made what seemed to be a tidy profit on the sale of the lease but, like the Pitt Street deal, this was not what it at first appeared to be. Times were hard and House of Fraser, like Strand and Pitt Street Properties, did not pay "spot cash", as David would have termed it. He was having to compromise when his every instinct was to take the money and run.*

---

* The final sale of the lease didn't take place until 1939. Letter from Harriet to Kathleen O'Connor (undated but probably mid-1939) *"Unfortunately I have to*

By August, Harriet's impatience to escape to her bolt hole on the Riviera persuaded David it was time to acquiesce, for the sake of his health. The London "Season" was coming to an end and, as everyone knew, boredom and the cold, damp climate would drive them south for the winter. He settled in the limousine as they motored through France to the Mediterranean. Here, Harriet wielded her considerable influence, abetted by friends and companions such as the ever-present Jacobsons.* The Franc remained grossly undervalued and by now many desirable properties lay empty or forlornly awaiting foreign buyers. A tour of Monte Carlo revealed several candidates, but one stood out. The Belle Époque villa at 26 Boulevard de Belgique occupied a commanding position with unimpeded views over Port Hercule, the principal harbour. At four storeys, with terraces stepped up the precipitous hillside, it displayed its Romanesque beauty for all to admire. David conceded, with little prompting, that even Wilga, with its glorious gardens would find it difficult to compete with this spectacular edifice. In no time, the deal was struck, and Harriet had her very own villa just where she had always wanted it. Like most of its late 19th century companions, the villa probably had a name, but this was soon forgotten, as a bold, gilded frieze was added to the street level portico: "Bon Accord". Villa Bon Accord was to become the jewel in the family crown. David could relax in the mild Mediterranean climate, enjoying the magnificent view and indulging Harriet as she entertained† and displayed their wealth and success. For a while, the change of scenery and diet eased his ageing body and mind, though he found it hard to be so far away as Percy struggled with the fire and its aftermath.

---

return to London to sign some leases connected with Regent Street, so I can't get there (France) for quite ten days."

* The Jacobsons had "done" the rounds of London's summer events, including the Henley Regatta, before leaving as usual to motor to the South of France. The Stewart Dawson's, on the other hand, did not appear on the closely scrutinised lists of Australians in London.

† Harriet may well have played hostess to Kathleen O'Connor at this time. In later years the artist was a frequent visitor to Villa Bon Accord.

He was also overseeing the disposal and sale of the jewellery business in Australia. As the year progressed, he advertised less than ever, particularly in Sydney. His advertisements were unremarkable, discounts were greater and there was a move towards more costume jewellery. Rhinestones substituted for diamonds across much of the range as Stewart Dawson's, along with most of their competitors, strove to retain a share of the shrinking market. Since the beginning of 1929 there had been a "rebuilding" sale at the Collins Street shop, long after the completion of the actual building works, and this continued to the very end of the year. As November approached, a faint spark of life was injected into the Sydney store, when he advertised an "80th Birthday Sale" with 30% off most lines. It was to be the swan song of the business. The ripples from the Wall Street Crash of October 29th and Black Monday that followed were beginning to lap at the shores of Australia and it would be only months before vital exports found no markets. Though the full effect of the Depression was not to be felt until 1932, unemployment was already increasing by early 1930 and the last thing on the mind of the average wage earner was browsing a jeweller's store.

Other news from Australia during the last quarter of 1929 gave no encouragement. After the initial recovery from the fire, numbers of patrons at The Ambassadors steadily declined. Rita had been overseas, on an extended vacation in California since shortly before the fire and in her absence, Harriet was dismayed to learn that St Margaret's found alternative venues for its numerous fund raisers. In Melbourne, the final nail in Stewart Dawson's retail coffin was punched when Manchester Unity Order of Oddfellows announced the complete redevelopment of Stewart Dawson's corner. The entire building would be replaced with an 11 or 13 storey complex of offices and new arcades. David had no leverage in the decision, which would force at least a temporary relocation even if he should wish to continue the business in the southern city. There would be no grand reopening; what would be the point? The Melbourne business continued to trade, its prices permanently discounted, for the next two years until, in November 1931, Manchester Unity gave all the tenants notice to quit by the end of the year so that demolition and rebuilding could commence. Stewart Dawson's announced a clearance auction of its entire stock, valued at £50,000. It wasn't quite the end, however; Percy rented cheaper premises on the first floor of Howey Court, Collins Street. As if returning to the 1880s beginnings, David advertised:

New Money-Saving Policy – Having removed from a heavily rented Swanston Street shop to upstairs showrooms has effected a big saving, which now enables us to sell on a wholesale basis, below usual shop prices.[316]

Some of the old phrases, the appeals to the back pocket, the implication of unbeatable competitiveness of the business model, were trotted out. The discounts (20%) were trumpeted, the "immense variety" promoted, but the goods advertised were humdrum items: brush and comb sets, folding coat hangers and so on. Where were the diamond rings? What had happened to the once-ubiquitous watches on which Stewart Dawson's reputation had been built? They were indeed still in stock but the market for them had almost vanished, what little that remained being swept up by younger, more vigorous competitors who were prepared to wait out the worst of the Depression and who, for the most part, would survive it.

By April 1932 Stewart Dawson's were advertising to buy old gold, as prices on the open market reached unprecedented highs. Cash-strapped citizens found that they could realise generous profits on rings, bracelets, necklaces and chains whose gold content value alone now greatly exceeded the total original price paid for the item. Jewellers such as Stewart Dawson's would play the middleman in the deal, reusing a tiny percentage of what they bought and melting down the rest for on-sale into the booming bullion market. In the United Kingdom, where the Depression added a further £23 million to the already crushing national deficit in 1932, the Melbourne Age[317] reported:

A big gold rush is occurring in the furnace rooms, Hatton Garden, where thousands of pounds' worth of old brooches, bangles, rings and cigarette cases are being melted daily ... The output in the shape of hundredweights of glistening gold bars is going, some to the Bank of England, some to the bullion brokers and some to France and America.

The same month, de Beers diamond mines in South Africa announced they were closing their mining operations. The major player in the Diamond Corporation, which controlled the output of the world's diamonds, de Beers laid off thousands of workers. The Corporation held and financed over £10 million worth of diamonds unwanted by a depression-ridden public. Hatton Garden was experiencing the biggest slump in living memory. Several of the smaller merchant firms had closed and others were facing bankruptcy.[318] Melbourne's Stewart Dawson's occasionally advertised diamond rings for the next couple of years, but their main business was now in recycling gold and by 1937 the name would disappear altogether as the easing of the Depression and lack of supply combined to make even that not worth the effort.

The Sydney store survived only until the end of 1930. There was one last, half-hearted attempt to clear stock and revitalise interest when, in October, Stewart Dawson's combined with other stores in the Pitt Street block to stage a giant "All Together, Balance the Budget" sale.[319] The almost empty arcades filled briefly with bargain-hunters but, once the banners came down reality ruled once more. Unemployment had reached over 23% in New South Wales, above even the catastrophic national average of 20.5%.[320] Shoppers bought essential items such as table ware but little else left the shelves of the jewellery store. This time there was no retreat to an obscure, upper floor address to trade gold. A plain notice in the Evening News of December 11th announced:

> *RETIRING FROM BUSINESS SALE. Stewart Dawson & Co., having decided to retire from business in Sydney, are offering their entire stock ... at a reduction off original prices of 5/- to 10/- in £.**

The sale over, the remaining stock went to arch-rival Proud's, who had also acquired the surplus left when the Melbourne store relocated. David was also keen to close the Brisbane outlet and sell the real estate but, unsurprisingly, there were no immediate buyers. The remaining Stewart Dawson outlet in Perth, perhaps due to its remoteness from the east coast centre of his businesses and the lack of local competition, was not considered for disposal. The local management was strong and loyal, as were enough customers to keep

---

* Equivalent to 25-50% discount.

the business viable. Across the Tasman Sea, David's other, relatively autonomous business was weathering the economic turmoil better than the larger Australian operation. Unemployment and unfavourable terms of trade were crippling the New Zealand economy as badly as Australia's and the situation was made worse for importers such as Stewart Dawson's when the New Zealand pound was devalued, shortly after Australia was obliged to take that defensive step. However, much as it was in far off Western Australia, Stewart Dawson's had fewer competitors in Auckland, Wellington, Christchurch, and Dunedin. Apart from the growing James Pascoe chain, in the medium term there was little to trouble the established, dominant player.*

---

* For another fifty years, Stewart Dawson's continued to trade until, in 1985, James Pascoe Group, now by far the biggest chain in the country, acquired the entire business. The new owners, who also hold Proud's and Angus & Coote, among others, promote Stewart Dawson's as their premium brand, with thirteen branches across both islands. Today, though the business itself was relocated in recent years, Stewart Dawson's Corner, the iconic listed building at Lambton Quay, Wellington, remains. How many passers-by would be aware of the glory days when fashionable folks arranged to meet and courting couples dreamed in front of the glittering window displays?

Curtains

Throughout the time of his father's sojourn in Europe, as Percy took charge of the sale of the Australian assets and dealt with the delinquent Strand and Pitt Street Properties the realisation dawned that the end was near for The Ambassadors. Rita returned from her American holiday in December 1929.[321] Though she was quick to opine that "Sydney would go crazy for the new, colored 'talkies'", and delighted in informing her interviewer of how much flying she had done, she confided that "she found American night clubs attractive, but Sydney had little to learn." Hotels and department stores, she described as "marvellous, but give me Sydney." Her loyalty was admirable and perhaps genuine, but it was at best a rear-guard defence of what was looking like a final capitulation. Christmas that year was a low-key dinner dance featuring "June and Collette, the very popular Adagio Dancers" and prices were a low 25/-* for dinner and entertainment. New Year's Eve saw none of the former extravagances; no giant cake, no cascading balloons. Instead, while the Wentworth enjoyed the patronage of the stars of current stage shows, and the pace was so hot at Romano's that gentlemen were handed fresh collars,[322] at The Ambassadors it was another evening of June and Collette, with "novelties and gifts for the ladies."[323] The highlight, if there was one, was the celebration of Percy's birthday.

In 1930 there was little reason for Percy to be optimistic. No sooner had the underwhelming New Year's Eve dance been forgotten than he was back in court, charged with selling liquor without a licence. Another raid by the diligent Sgt Chuck nabbed Percy and several of his employees and uncovered a full cellar of whisky and other spirits. Unlike his wayward younger brother, Percy chose not to contest the charge, paid his £30 fine in lieu of six months' jail, surrendered the confiscated alcohol, and got back to work.[324]

---

* 25/- in 1930 was less than £20 in 2018

When Harriet left in April 1929, St. Margaret's appointed a replacement president of its organising committee, Mrs Arthur McNiven, wife of the prominent Bondi hotelier. Mrs McNiven was, if anything, more experienced and successful than Harriet in the fund-raising business and she proved a worthy and popular successor. However, she only staged one event at The Ambassadors, a charity ball supporting Dalwood Rest Homes in October, and to Harriet's distress, all St. Margaret's affairs henceforth were to be held at The Wentworth. Though The Ambassadors was seldom without a booking, and occasionally had over 600 dancers on the floor, the grand balls of yesteryear were now a fading memory. "Feminine Topics" in The Sydney Mail of August 13th observed: "Cabarets this season have been few and far between."[325] Afternoons saw card parties, bon voyage and welcome home soirées, and bridal teas. In the evenings, there were wedding receptions, college reunions, club dances and, in the season, a few debutantes' balls. Notable events of 1930 included a Movie Ball, where talkies were shown, and guests could take a public screen test, and a gala night for the visiting English aviatrix, Amy Johnson. The few "old faithful" events that continued to patronise the premises failed to attract the crowds who once would have blocked Pitt Street. The annual Millions Club Ball, in July, barely filled the main ballroom, when in former years the Palm Court and dining room had overflowed.[326] Perhaps it was another sign of the times that achievement of the Millions Club's mission to see Sydney's population warrant its name was looking more doubtful by the day.

This phenomenon was not unique to Sydney; Melbourne, Brisbane and other Australian cities were equally depressed and, internationally, the Roaring Twenties were accepted as dead and about to be buried. Writing in The Sun on July 6th, Ferdinand Tuohy described Paris as "that grossly over-written din-box." Though Harriet would have disagreed, he lamented:

Compared even with two or three years ago, the night life of La Ville Lumière has as good as ceased to exist.

Observing that:

For years after the Armistice, it was freak riot by the Seine.,

he speculated:

> *... Many proprietors again pitched into things as if all times were going to continue Armistice times. This is the way with such people ... The very glut of idle, spectral halls in Paris today fatally accents what has happened. Too much was provided; the thing thrown at you – quite in the modern style, measure being now démodé.*[327]

He could have been describing the history of The Ambassadors. David's bold experiment had caught the mood of the early post-war years perfectly but now it was little more than an expensive anachronism. Running costs were estimated to be at least £500 per week despite staff layoffs and a reduced menu, bleeding the operating company dry. To make matters worse, contrary to all logic, new, opportunistic competitors were opening their doors with smaller premises and low-cost operations that skimmed the lower end of the market on which The Ambassadors was now dependent. Prince's Cabaret opened at the end of January, only a block away. The more intimate establishment survived long enough, while still novel, to dilute the numbers who otherwise would have patronised The Ambassadors. Adding insult, Peggy Potts, Percy's tireless and skilled publicity manager, announced that, after five years, she had accepted a position at the new cabaret.

By mid-year, despondency set in. Unemployment continued to surge, and not only due to declining terms of trade. Technological change compounded individual misery as even professional musicians found themselves on the street when talkies made cinema orchestras redundant. As ever, some sought to profit by speculating on future price recovery. Diamonds had lost so much value that keen buyers with enough cash and nerve trawled jewellery stores in search of bargains. Stewart Dawson's may have made a few additional sales, but the main beneficiaries seemed to be the likes of Angus & Coote, who had by now achieved enough market share and economies of scale to out-bid the older firm and under-price it. Public opinion was that time was up for yesterday's kings of commerce. Displaying uncommon Schadenfreude, Smith's Weekly published an article on August 16th,[328] entitled: "How the Wealthy Square Accounts – Fortunes that are made and lost on trifling arguments – Costly fads that entertain Australia's rich." The columnist told of the follies of various businessmen who had overpaid or mistimed purchases in the tumultuous twenties. But Smith's reserved its best anecdote for the last:

> *Sydney's most picturesque instance of a man being induced into business by a desire to satisfy a whim was provided by Stewart Dawson when he built The Ambassadors. ... At a time when the Wentworth alone provided the better class night cabaret entertainment Stewart Dawson and his son were very keen dancers and frequently visited Mrs Maclurcan's establishment. At some period a little argument developed and Dawson got the notion that he could provide a better night club, and do himself prouder than Mrs Maclurcan ever had. But the fad proved a very expensive one, for the building cost something like £40,000 more than was at first estimated.*

Here, Smith's missed the point: as David could have told them, cost was never an issue for him, at least when he undertook the project. It was all about vanity and his absolute belief in his own judgement and taste. But now, as the jewellery stores closed, rental income faltered, and the glitter faded, there seemed little justification in propping up the failing enterprise. The stress on Percy was tremendous. Day after day his working hours were consumed by the need to balance the books, retain dispirited but essential and expensive staff, keep the liquor squad at bay, and attract bookings that would sustain and justify The Ambassadors' reputation. Nothing could be taken for granted, least of all customer loyalty. A new, some would say, seedy crowd displaced many of the genteel card parties in the afternoons. Journalist and social commentator, Gwen Marshall, wrote:

> *The Gigolo has found place in Sydney cabarets ... In the great city, the demi-mondaine sits almost shoulder to shoulder with bashful girls in search of their first social thrill. She described a band of lonely girls, lonely but hopeful, who prayed, each and all, that from the passing crowd one young man might take pity on their solitary state, and a cup of tea might lead to new romance.* [329]

Detailing an investigative afternoon's stroll through tea rooms and cafes, she depicted the wan scenes at the once-top-of-the-list venues: Romano's, where *nothing exciting ever happens now in this former money palace, which in its heyday housed Sydney's elite with standing room only.*

She continued:

On then to The Ambassadors! Here I found Sydney's only male gigolos! No highly educated youths with polished manners, perfectly fitting clothes, good looks and poise, as one finds in every restaurant in Europe, but a rather flashly dressed band of out-of-work waiters and musicians willing to spend their afternoon with any unescorted girl who will pay for their tea and cream cakes. They go about their work clumsily. They have no finesse in the art of being professional dancing partners. If they waited for the women who are anxious to dance with anything in a full suit of clothes, to notify their desire to the head waiter, who, in turn, would send a prospective partner to their table, they would still be waiting. Instead, without any form of introduction, they place bare facts before the girl. "For the price of afternoon tea I'll dance four numbers with you."

Percy, it seemed, had little choice if he were to keep the wolf from the door. Desperate, he agreed to The Ambassadors' participation in the great "All Together, Balance the Budget" sale in October. The gimmick was that shoppers who purchased anything, no matter the price, at any of the participating shops would receive a docket which granted them entry to a draw for a free ticket to a performance at Her Majesty's Theatre, on the corner of Pitt and Market Streets. In order to enter the draw dockets had to be placed in a box in the Palm Court of The Ambassadors, thus inducing the shopper to spend a little time and money they might otherwise not have done. Lucky winners would also be inclined to buy a second ticket for a partner, to the benefit of the theatre. Though the promotion continued well into 1931, it had little impact on The Ambassadors' custom, and Stewart Dawson's was not the only store whose terminal decline it failed to halt.

In August, The Ambassadors announced a "new policy" of even lower prices for casual diners:

for 5/- you can step along with the best girl-friend for supper, and dance the hours away to the tune of one of the best bands in town until the chimes of midnight.*[330]

Christmas and New Year's Eve parties were also at discount "special prices to suit the times."[331] And the times were desperate. The Ambassadors was not alone in this "Slough of Despond"; The Sun reported on the New Year's Eve celebrations:

Australia tears out the tattered leaf of 1930, casts out gloom and starts again.[332]

The Ambassadors was mentioned, though only in passing; more attention was paid to the many private or sporting club dances and balls. The only other cabaret featured in the article was Romano's, where "one of the attractions will be a revue of lovely dancing girls in 'A New Year Frolic'." Percy couldn't afford to match his rival on this one night of the year where it mattered. A fortnight later, an announcement was made: The Ambassadors was to close for an indefinite period, ostensibly for yet more renovations.[333] Few were persuaded that this was other than an excuse, a delaying tactic pending final disposal of the business. Once again, the familiar story of David's extravagance was retold, the crippling running costs detailed.[334] "Catty Communications", the popular gossip column in Smith's Weekly, twisted the knife another turn:[335]

No wonder mine host Romano wears a broad smile these days. The closure of The Ambassadors for at least three months has delighted his heart, and he looks extremely affluent in his big black car ... as he drives each day to the Bondi surf. Which reminds me that Mrs Maclurcan must be laughing at the Wentworth, when she thinks of the closing of The Ambassadors. You know the threat story of course.†

The café did open in time for Easter, prices once more reduced. It was not clear what "renovations", if any, were undertaken; more

---

* About £18 in 2016.

† Referring to Percy's alleged words in his altercation with Hannah Maclurcan in 1921.

likely, Percy took the opportunity to reorganise and reduce staff even further and perhaps negotiated cheaper prices for kitchen supplies. Whatever, the respite was short; by mid-year, the last rites were being read. Percy consulted one last time with his father and the decision was taken to close once and for all. The last dance was held on the evening of August 28th. Only about twenty guests saw the evening out. Percy went home early, "indisposed", leaving Rita in charge. Jack Woods, the orchestra leader, usually played extra dance music at the piano after the band finished but this time Rita dismissed him. As "Catty Communications" observed: "it was a dismal finale! But it showed that Rita can crack the whip."[336]

A Quiet, Unassuming Man

Rita and Percy's marriage did not long survive the trauma. At the beginning of October, they were before the divorce court. Percy's "indisposition" and Rita's petulant termination of The Ambassadors' finale demonstrated the breakdown of their relationship to a public that must have had its suspicions for many months before. The pressures of managing the sale and closing of the shops, the fire and its aftermath, the drawn-out dispute over mortgage payments, and the failure of the cabaret had taken a fatal toll. Percy had shouldered an enormous load with little local help. Rita's loyalty was never in question, but she could only offer moral support once her temporary role as President of St Margaret's expired; and though she probably deserved the break when she took her holiday in California, the timing, coinciding with the fire, could not have been worse. Percy's fragile ego, already damaged by his disastrous marriage to Thelma, took a hit from which he did not recover. On August 31st, only three days after The Ambassadors closed, he left her at their flat in Wilga, never to return.

Rita was distraught, though she could not have been as surprised as she later claimed. She sought restitution of conjugal rights, her only recourse under the law, and the case was heard in March 1932. In evidence to the court,[337] she recounted:

> *Trouble began following his return from abroad in 1929.* Anything I said seemed to displease him and he was not so ardent as he had been before. In 1930 the position got worse, though I never gave him any reason to complain.*

She described how they would arrange to go to the holiday house at Newport and at the last moment he would say that he did not wish to go. There was never anything serious, but it would develop into a nasty argument. He would threaten to leave her, saying he was tired

---

* There is no record of Percy's international travel in 1929. He did not accompany his parents but could have made a separate trip. He could not have been away long as there was so much demand on his time in Sydney.

of married life. It came to a head when, in August 1931, as The Ambassadors was about to shut down, he refused to accompany her on a visit to her family, started another argument, and came to her room (they occupied separate rooms by that time) and told her he was going to leave her. Later in the day she went to his room and found his bags all packed. A messenger boy brought a letter, in which Percy pleaded the hopelessness of their case, as he saw it. He had not carried out his threat to leave before because:

> *something prompted me to believe that there might be a chance for us to live happily together.*

He continued:

> *However, things have never turned out that way. You and I have not the temperament that two people living together should have – we just don't mix. I don't blame you, my dear – I don't blame either of us. We have both made a genuine effort, but it is hopeless ...*
>
> *I mean all best wishes honestly.*

Rita wrote in reply:

> *My Dear Percy,*
>
> *I was very grieved yesterday to know that you have decided to leave me. I honestly do not desire to be separated from you, and I am, and always have been, willing to live with you as your wife, in whatever home you make for me, and have always tried to make you happy, and am anxious to do so. I ask you to return to me and live with me as your wife. If you wish to make a new home for us, I am ready to go to it. I will do my part. I do not want to be separated from you.*
>
> *Your affectionate wife, RITA.*

It was too late; Percy left Sydney for Melbourne and the marriage was over. He ignored the court's restitution order and never returned to Rita. When she met him by chance in Melbourne at a friend's dinner party, he confessed to the table at large that he had never been so happy before and was sorry that he had not done it (left her) before. Harriet could imagine Rita's humiliation in the face of these heartless remarks, but Percy's thoughtless outburst perhaps reflected a genuine sense of relief; he had not been coping well for the past three years and was probably speaking the truth when he wrote: "You and I have not the temperament that two people living together should have – we just don't mix." Rita was extrovert, strong willed, a "bright young thing"; Percy, though often described as "a genial host", and "urbane", had lived too long in the shadow of his notorious brothers, suffered his own humiliation at Thelma's hands, and endured years of subjugation to his father's will. Since 1920 he had applied his talents to the challenges of managing, first, the Pitt Street shop and then the construction and operations of The Ambassadors, six days a week with barely a break. Not naturally outgoing, he failed to reach out to Rita when they needed each other most. By the end of 1931 he was mentally and emotionally at breaking point. It did not surprise Harriet that he never remarried.

And while Percy soldiered on through 1929, 30 and 31, how fared his two brothers? Both Norman and Stuart were there to greet their parents upon their arrival in London in 1929. Both were still bankrupt. Stuart and his wife, Peggy were also drinking to excess, which led Harriet to persuade them that it was perhaps best for everyone if they recuperated while she looked after the children for a while. Young David was seven and little Harriet a spritely two-year-old and it was clear to all that Peggy, for one, was not coping. She was seldom without a glass of champagne and too many of her drinking bouts left her "indisposed". David, almost past caring, was easily prevailed upon to continue his generous support of their useless lives, but it was Norman as ever who was the greater beneficiary. In 1930 he entered his new Rolls-Royce Phantom car in the Monte Carlo Concours d'Élégance. The vehicle was a spectacular example of the "super car" of the day. Luxury marques such as Rolls-Royce, Hispano Suiza, Mercedes, and the like were sold as a bare chassis, onto which custom, coach-built bodies were fitted to the owner's specification, making each one unique. Norman's Phantom I had been built in 1925 or 26 but the coupé body, by Carlton,* was almost new. Norman had added

* According to Tom Clarke, (email dated 15th September 2018*) "An Italian researcher quotes Carlton, probably from a period record.... This is his note:*

custom features including a three-valve radio and ice box for the inbuilt bar. As Harriet recalled it now, after the Depression years and the hardships of the recent war, she felt a twinge of conscience that would never have troubled her then. The price paid for this extravagant indulgence was equivalent to many years' salary for the average wage earner and its purchase at this low point in the Depression era insulted the hundreds of thousands of struggling or out-of-work men and women.

Norman, of course, did not spend a penny of his own money on the acquisition; how could he? He was a perpetual bankrupt, pursued by increasing numbers of creditors (his 1927 absconding from his lodgings was still a recent bad memory for them all) and incapable of earning or saving an honest shilling. All he needed to do was to appeal to his mother's generosity in the knowledge that his father was too tired and ill to resist. This was made all the easier when the family secured what may be termed a "package deal" on a second Phantom, for David and Harriet. The Phantom II was brand new, with a 2-door Sports Saloon body by H.J. Mulliner. Finished all in black, it was a more staid and sober vehicle than Norman's cream and black coupé. Nevertheless, it made the kind of statement about wealth and success that Harriet, more than any of them, demanded. The Jacobsons' Daimler would no longer be the yardstick of opulence.

Norman made the most of his new toy, touring Europe throughout 1931 and hobnobbing with other idle rich at concours and car shows in Monte Carlo, Paris, Berlin, and various fashionable venues in England. David and Harriet were content to be chauffeured between Villa Bon Accord and their London hotel or apartment in Park Lane but, late in the year it was apparent that David's health was failing fast. His kidneys were barely functioning, and the prognosis was grave: he had only months to live. If Harriet had had her way, he would have been admitted to an exclusive London nursing home to see out his days, but David had other ideas. His home was not London or the millionaires' playground of the Mediterranean. He had made his real fortune and put down his roots in Australia, and that was

---

'Montecarlo 1931 Gran Premio Giude Interne Rolls-Royce Carlton Dawson Stewart.'"

where he wished to end his life. Reluctantly, Harriet submitted and on February 12th, 1932, they sailed from Tilbury on the new P&O liner RMS Strathaird, bound for Sydney. They were accompanied by Norman and young Harriet, safe from the shambles of her mother's disintegrating life, and in the ship's hold were stowed the two Rolls-Royces. Stuart remained with young David at the Hotel Splendide in Piccadilly, where he made occasional feeble attempts to mitigate the effects of Peggy's drinking.

The family was in good company, the Strathaird counting among its distinguished passengers Lords Deramore and Aylesford and the great operatic contralto, Dame Clara Butt,* about to tour Australia. David, despite his health, was in high spirits, anticipating the return to Sydney. Harriet was preoccupied with concern for her husband and son, as Percy went through the painful divorce proceedings. Norman flirted with any available female and dreamed of bowling along Australia's open roads in his car, a star-struck young woman by his side.

Their first port of call was Fremantle, where David's return to Australian soil was greeted with respect and affection by the local press. Interviewed ashore, he expatiated on the chances of economic recovery across the Empire. Once more, he stressed the familiar themes of hard work and avoidance of debt that had infused his life:

> *For Australia to become really great the majority of workers in every sphere of life will have be content to get into what was termed in the past the working groove. A section of the financial and commercial interests in England attribute some of the trade depression in that country to the collapse in Australia, following the period of prosperity on borrowed capital.*[338]

Behind his last remark lay David's deep aversion to the tactics employed by the Labor Premier of New South Wales, J.T. "Jack" Lang. Lang's radical solution to the economic crisis and mounting unemployment in 1931 had been to repudiate Australia's

---

* Dame Clara Butt had come directly from the Riviera where she had performed at, among other venues, the Monte Carlo Opera. It is probable that David and Harriet had attended one of her performances there.

international loan obligations and to refuse further interest payments to British bond holders, channelling the retained funds into job creation within the state. Ever the imperialist and free-marketer, David was appalled by what he saw as flagrant insubordination and catastrophic socialism. Even as he spoke in Fremantle, Lang's days were numbered, but the crisis had not reached its peak and he was just another, loud voice in the chorus railing against the policy.

By the time they reached Melbourne David was ready for another interview, still optimistic and hinting at further personal ventures, even as his ailments dogged him. The Melbourne "Age" observed:

> *Half a century back Mr. Stewart Dawson opened his first overseas jewellery stores in Sydney and Auckland. Today, in his eighty-third year, he is still alert and mentally vigorous, and delivered a message of cheery optimism regarding the future of the Dominions.*[339]

After reiterating David's observations in Fremantle on the prospects for Australia and New Zealand and his appeals to "vision and hard work" The Age continued, quoting David:

> *[Merely] Because he had anticipated the depression, and changed from an ownership to a rental basis, he had not, he said, changed his opinion that there were just as great opportunities in Australia today as when he bought both properties [Pitt Street and Collins Street]. While he hesitated at his age to embark on new ventures, he might even yet justify his optimism in a practical way.*

David removed his tongue from his cheek as he completed the interview. He had of course not "anticipated the depression", though some sort of writing had been on the wall since the mid-twenties. But more than one admiring commentator had claimed that on his behalf and now was not the time to disabuse the press. As for "embarking on new ventures … in a practical way," well, why not tease readers a little? He had nothing in mind beyond a quiet rest in the gardens at Wilga or, at a pinch, a trip up to Bon Accord at Springwood. Leave it to Percy to pick up the threads once the good times came in sight again. Or maybe not; he had written his will to ensure life-long security and comfort for all the family, regardless of their personal effort. The cash and real estate assets would see to that. He had nothing left to prove and one thing was certain, he had made a name that would outlast them all.

On March 24th, 1932, the Strathaird sailed into Sydney harbour, passing under the just-opened bridge,* the first large passenger liner to do so. Norman was the only family member to give an interview, the local emphasis being the celebrity and glamour of the disembarking passengers, rather than the less frivolous, not to say, stodgy opinions of the older generation. The Sydney reporters remembered Norman for his playboy exploits, and he was happy to oblige them with hints of his social intentions once ashore. He was keen to see the Phantom back on dry land, having made several entries in his diary for dates with unattached ladies on board. However, he had read the news of the bridge opening with more than usual curiosity and felt compelled to comment on the outrageous attempt to disrupt and upstage the ribbon-cutting ceremony. A member of the quasi-Fascist movement, The New Guard, Captain Francis de Groot, had ridden his horse through the crowds to slash the ribbon with his sword before Premier Lang could apply the official scissors. The protest against Lang's extreme policies had no immediate effect, since The New Guard enjoyed little support beyond a close group of middle-class businessmen in Sydney, but it won enormous publicity and would contribute to Lang's dismissal in May. Norman was moved to comment because he recalled that de Groot had served with him in the 15th Hussars back in 1915, before his move to the RNAS. He remembered de Groot as "a quiet officer, not the type one would expect to act as he did."

The family retired to Wilga, less than ten minutes' drive from the quayside. As Harriet surveyed the familiar rooms and strayed onto the terrace she sighed. There was more riding on her shoulders than at any time before. Although she would rather be back at Villa Bon Accord, and knew that it would only be a matter of time before that dream would be sadly realised, she had much to do and little time in which to achieve it. Percy was all at sea, the divorce about to become absolute, Stuart was struggling with Peggy's alcoholism and sooner or later would have to face the consequences of his dissolute life on the two children, while Norman, now on Australian soil, was at risk

* Sydney Harbour Bridge was officially opened on March 19th, 1932.

of a prison sentence over his ongoing bankruptcy. Thank goodness she had prevailed upon David before they sailed. She felt a little guilty for having taken advantage of his ill-health to persuade him but, once done, it had been worth it. He'd seemed relieved to put one more burden away, as he agreed to clear all of Norman's debts and free his son to pursue more worthy ends. While Norman showed off his car, squiring various ladies about town and ensuring his quota of attention in the gossip columns, David contacted the Bankruptcy Court and arranged a hearing for his son's creditors. Within the week, the announcement was made that all creditors would be paid 20/- in the pound. The formal discharge required Norman's appearance once more in court, where the squalid details of his misdemeanours were retailed. Despite David and Harriet's hopes and entreaties, Norman's responses in the witness box displayed all his by now familiar arrogance. Rather than demonstrate to the court a gracious and humble acceptance of his father's generosity he was evasive, dismissive, and sardonic, exasperating the long-suffering Registrar. Asked to confirm that he had been employed at The Ambassadors in 1924 (as he had claimed in the liquor case that year) he replied: "I really forget." "Don't you know whether you were employed by anyone?" asked the Registrar. "Well, I am my father's son. I don't know if that is an answer," was the impudent response. Asked: "What was your income here in Sydney prior to your departure?" he gave perhaps the only honest, and the most revealing answer of the day: "My income is whatever my father likes to make it." Irritated, the Registrar persisted: "You could save a lot of time by answering. What was it?" to which Norman's reluctant response was: "It was about £3,000 or £4,000 a year, I should say." Though he skirted close to a contempt of court charge, Norman was ultimately dismissed, and his bankruptcy formally ended. David had washed his hands of the prodigal playboy and could turn his back once and for all on scandal.

Percy reunited with his parents just weeks after his final, public separation from Rita titillated the popular press. He was still coming to terms with his "freedom" both from marriage and the agony of the last days of The Ambassadors. Fresh from the divorce court in March, he could turn his mind to accepting full responsibility for David's affairs as the old man prepared to hand over the torch. Percy was to be executor of his father's will and administrator of the estate and the two men spent much time discussing the details. David had long relied on the established firm of Perpetual Trustees to manage his many holdings, including the estate at Springwood. His daughter, Estelle, now approaching 17 and about to go up to university in Armidale, in the New England tableland, was the beneficial owner of Bonnie Doon, where she still lived with her grandparents. However, she would not inherit the property until her majority; until then it would be held in trust for her by Perpetual. Now, David co-opted Percy into instructing Perpetual and preparing the trustee agreement for his entire estate, of which the latter would be joint trustee. By June, arrangements were finalised.

It was to be David's last formal action. By now he was confined to his home, missing an important Vice-Regal operatic concert at the Town Hall, and leaving Harriet to fly the flag together with Estelle Jacobson.[340] As Harriet mingled with her friends and acquaintances in the old familiar haunts, Norman cruised around Sydney and the Blue Mountains,* radio crackling and ice blocks cooling the champagne in his car, and Percy busied himself with the ongoing court cases in the Equity Court, David grew weary, his eyesight failing, appetite non-existent, until even a walk to the breakfast room was beyond him. Through the winter months his condition deteriorated, and the family prepared for the inevitable. The McNabs came down from Springwood, Percy supported his mother and even Norman put a temporary limit on his social activities. The last week in July, David drifted into unconsciousness. Nurses attended him and there were daily doctor's visits but beyond relieving the pain and fever that his illness inflicted upon him, they could do little but watch. The doses of morphine were increased until, on the morning of Saturday, August 6th, he died peacefully, surrounded by his family.[341]

David had been overseas for three years and seldom seen in public since 1927. Upon his return, he was too ill to venture outside and if it

---

* Norman was spotted with friends *acquiring suntan* in Leura (Blue Mountains) in June 1932. Sun (Sydney) 12th June 1932 P.28. He almost certainly drove the Phantom up the mountains; the temptation to show off the car's capabilities would have been irresistible.

had not been for Norman's high-profile presence and Harriet's infrequent social appearances, it might be supposed that his passing could have gone unnoticed, no more than a footnote to the daily news. Such was his reputation, however, that his death was reported throughout Australia and New Zealand. Obituaries in capital city and regional newspapers alike told the tale of the rise from humble beginnings to millionaire status, many reflecting native pride in the entrepreneur who had chosen Australia for his home. They remembered the "quiet, unassuming man" who "was always disinclined to speak about himself." Auckland's "Evening Post" wrote:

> *A romantic career ended in Sydney this week with the death of Mr. David Stewart Dawson … He was 81 years of age,* * *and his extensive connections made him one of the most widely known business men in Australia … He was always disinclined to speak about himself, but his intimate friends knew that he began life in a very humble way, and those who knew him best were able to appreciate the many fine points of his busy life.*
>
> *The late Mr. Stewart Dawson was always regarded as an extraordinarily fine judge of human nature, and he confessed that this had aided him greatly throughout his business career … He always said that a man was never done with learning; and every detail having a direct bearing on life interested him …*

After listing David's record-breaking property speculations, The Post reserved its last, admiring words for The Ambassadors venture:

> *Perhaps the most picturesque effort of his career was the founding of The Ambassadors … Mr. Dawson had succeeded in giving Sydney something that only Continental and American cities had known till then, and his enterprise was fully rewarded. He had no idea of monetary gain, but, as he said, he wanted to enhance the colourful life and culture of Sydney … He did nothing by halves, and his orchestra was easily the most famous in Australia …*[342]

---

* David was approaching his eighty-third birthday at the time of his death.

The funeral was held the following Monday, August 8th. Rev. Hugh Paton conducted the service at St. Stephen's in Phillip Street, a short walk from the Pitt Street precinct where so much of David's success had been built. Harriet was supported by Percy and Norman, Agnes, and Malcolm McNab at her side. James McWilliam, old faithful from before the war, made up the chief mourning party. The papers reporting the ceremony noted that it "was largely attended by business and financial men." Septimus Levy, chairman of Tooth's brewery, cricketer Keith Docker, John Mitchell, the ex-Commissioner of Police, and Joseph Jacobson, were present, as were many ex-employees of Stewart Dawson's and of The Ambassadors. Even James Dempster paid his respects. As the cortège moved off to the Crematorium at Rookwood Cemetery it was followed by many cars laden with floral tributes. The Crematorium had been in operation only seven years,[343] and though some, including David's many Jewish friends, retained conservative views regarding the proper disposal of the dead, David's wishes even in death were not to be countermanded. A necropolis was no place for his memorial when all around the name of Stewart Dawson, emblazoned and engraved on countless crafted artefacts, would proclaim the story of his life and achievements to generations yet unborn.

Retreat

Harriet poured another glass of champagne, just a small one. She had to watch the pennies and keep a clear head. As the bubbles rose and twirled to the surface, she missed the pleasurable sensation she would once have enjoyed at the sight. Instead, there was emptiness, a sense of loss and ending, the same feeling that had overwhelmed her as they left the Crematorium all those years ago.

Though there had been little prospect of David's survival beyond the spring of '32 he had seemed to be in charge almost until the end. He had invested so much imagination and attention to detail in every aspect of the family's welfare. Percy was the only one who came close to understanding the complexities of the will, the interwoven companies and trusts, the minutiae of bequests, caveats, and shareholdings. Before he had made his will in October '31 he had set up individual trusts for her and Bertha that guaranteed a more than adequate lifetime income for both[344] and the last thing on her mind was "the needful", as she termed it. Wilga was at her disposal, and he had assured her that Villa Bon Accord was hers alone to keep. All well and good, but without David the light had gone out. Where was she to look for support and comfort?

In the weeks after the funeral, as the last of the visitors delivered their condolences, the pull of the home country and the beloved Riviera grew stronger. Kathleen's letters of support had only increased her desire to return, reawakening her romantic passion for the urbanity she had forsaken in making this last voyage to the dominion, so she had no hesitation in booking her passage on the Mooltan for October 21st. Norman was also fretting for home, thoughts of concours in Europe filling his imagination. And there was the matter of what to do with Stuart and his family. The news from London was discouraging, to say the least. Stuart seemed to have given up on Peggy, taking young David with him to Monte Carlo and relying on staff at the hotel to temper her excesses in his absence. It was time for Harriet to resume her inherited place as matriarch of the family and return his daughter to her youngest son. There was nothing to keep her here in Sydney. The Ambassadors had gone, and signs of the Depression were everywhere. The city often appeared empty these days, so many people had left for the country in search of work. The opening of the bridge had been no more than a brief interlude before the general torpor descended once more. One by one, Stewart Dawson shops were closing their doors and the scavengers were picking at the remains. It was too much to bear. Thank goodness for Percy; he alone of her sons seemed able and willing to take responsibility for managing the disposals and dealing with the estate.

All through the long voyage north, she dreamed of leisurely days at Villa Bon Accord, perhaps an occasional dip in the swimming pool (little Harriet might enjoy a splash about, too), cocktails in the evenings and welcoming the familiar guests once more. She had missed the tables at the Sporting, dressing in her finest for a night at the opera, mixing with visiting royalty (so many of them these days, escaping the humdrum affairs back in London, Paris, Berlin and all those principalities – she'd lost count). And there was Kathleen, of course. She'd left her with open access to the villa, knowing how much she appreciated the gesture, but though they had corresponded while apart, that was a poor substitute for the hours of friendly chats, sharing opinions of fashion and art. She wondered if Kathleen was any closer to staging her own exhibition, what new works she had completed. She seldom produced much while in Monte Carlo, preferring the northern light of her Paris studio and the parks of the city, but there were always the textiles and ceramic decorations to admire and add to her collection. What a time they would have!

Disembarking at Toulon, Harriet made haste for Monte Carlo. The Villa had been kept open and maintained in her absence and as she unpacked and saw her granddaughter to her room, she made her plans for the coming months. Stuart had returned to London with young David but had soon despaired of curbing Peggy's drinking and was agitating to bring his son to the relative calm and safety of the Villa. Harriet had no hesitation in acceding to his wishes. It was time the two children were reunited, and she had missed Stuart these past months. Invitations were sent to Kathleen to join them whenever she wished. She settled in, still feeling the loss of her husband but reassured to be among true friends.

As the population of winter exiles grew, though not perhaps as greatly as in former years, Stuart arrived with young David towards the end of November. He headed for the Sporting as soon as he could, but who could blame him, poor man? He'd suffered enough in the confines of their London residence, pleading with Peggy to heed the advice of their doctor, and drowning his own sorrows alone. Young David's health had also suffered, and it was on the advice of the same doctor that Stuart now brought his son south. Scarcely had they arrived however, when the news arrived from London that Peggy had been found dead in their room at the Splendide. The cause of death was given as acute alcohol poisoning; the last binge had overwhelmed her body.[345] Harriet consoled Stuart: "Leave the children with me while you arrange the funeral." She'd never been close to Peggy, having had little time to get to know her before the couple retreated to London, but coming so soon after David's death, this new tragedy almost crushed her spirit. Alone once more at the Villa, she had only the hope of Kathleen's arrival to sustain her. Norman had left Australia but she'd no idea where he intended to land. Having tired of the Rolls, he was bringing it back with him in expectation of replacing it with a newer vehicle. She supposed he would head for England, where the motor dealers were more numerous. Once he had done the deal, she expected to see him on the Riviera for the spring concours, but his plans remained vague for the time being. There was his position on the board of the United Kingdom company, of course, but she didn't expect that to occupy him for long. The company, what was left of it, was in good hands. The sub-let of Regent Street was holding value and Hatton Garden seemed to be managing the gold recycling business well enough, so Percy told her, while maintaining supply to New Zealand, Brisbane, and Perth.

Sure enough, news arrived from London early in December that Norman was safely ashore. He'd ordered his new car before leaving Australia and now she learned that it had been ready for him to collect upon arrival. He'd been met at Waterloo Station and driven directly to the coachbuilders, stepped into the car and drove away. Such style he had! The vehicle, a Rolls-Royce Phantom II, was a modern version of his former car. Costing £2,500 (he must have used some of his inheritance, perhaps Percy released funds for him) its all-black body seated four in luxury and could be either an open tourer or a close limousine. Norman called it a "Sedanca Coupé", which sounded impressive. Its top speed was 100 miles an hour, but it was the cunningly designed and exquisitely made fittings that set it apart from humbler vehicles. Like the earlier car, it had a wireless set and catered for passengers' sophisticated tastes with an inbuilt refrigerator. However, the wireless now had five valves and there was a complete cocktail bar concealed in the arm rests of the back seats with accommodation for twenty bottles. A picnic outfit for six persons, its tables hidden in the backs of the front seats, could be released at the push of a button. The interior lighting was concealed behind the edges of the roof, the windscreen wipers, when not in use, were also hidden in special slots as were the direction indicators.[346] Harriet could understand Norman's excitement and pride in owning something so modern and stylish. She must take a ride with him once he had time to travel south. Kathleen, too, would enjoy being chauffeured around the Midi in yet another Rolls. Harriet had brought back their own car and for the time being it was at their disposal here in Monte Carlo, though she felt sure that Norman would encourage her to follow his lead and replace it with a new model. A pity, as the car was still quite new and hardly used.

But Norman paid only the briefest visit to Monte Carlo, just long enough to impress Harriet and her friends and take in a few evenings at the Casino before zooming off north again to cross the Channel. He brought his new valet, Archie Falconer, with him. Archie had been employed in Sydney prior to Norman's departure[347] and appeared to be fulfilling his duties to Norman's satisfaction. Harriet could understand a bachelor such as Norman requiring some help with domestic and travel arrangements, though she wondered sometimes how he afforded the expense, on top of his rent, his immaculate wardrobe, lavish entertainments and of course, that car. She supposed his director's fees must be more than adequate, for he never so much as blinked at ordering another round of drinks, flourishing notes at restaurants and casinos or splashing out on silk cravats and gifts for friends. Not a bit like Percy, but then, Percy lacked Norman's flair and style, poor boy, and still seemed to be buried in his work, whatever that was.

Norman to the Rescue

While Harriet held court in Monte Carlo, Norman, back in England, busied himself with preparing his car for the next show. The Royal Automobile Club annual rally held at Hastings in March 1933 attracted the cream of Britain's motor car enthusiasts and competition for the top prizes was fierce. Norman's Sedanca Coupé was up against limousines and luxury sports saloons. He'd entered in the "Occasional four-seaters and two-door sports saloons" class and was confident of a win. However, he was to be disappointed. First prize was awarded to Mr. S. Harris' Phantom II, which pipped Norman's car into second place.

The Rally over, he focussed his mind on business for perhaps the first time in his life. He was forty-two years old, middle-aged, and if he assessed his life he conceded that though he had achieved much, what with his aviation feats and his social successes, there would be little, if anything to leave for posterity unless he found a cause, a project, something to build and grow. His father had done just that, Percy was making a good fist of the transition from retail to property, he'd no idea what Stuart was up to, but he, Norman, was twice the man his brothers were. Opportunity would knock, and he would show the world what a real Stewart Dawson could do. He'd no intention of marrying, so there need be no domestic constraints on his venture. In truth, he had a more pressing motive for action. His father was no longer the infinitely biddable source of his income. The generous allowance he'd relied upon throughout his life had ceased upon David's death, replaced with a notional fee from his director's position and ownership of a parcel of shares in the UK company. The expected large cash bequest was nowhere to be seen. Thanks to his mother's generosity and influence, he'd acquired the first Rolls and, through that, the second, but a chap couldn't survive long on the slow dribble of fees that came from Regent Street. The future looked dim.

But not for long; news arrived from Sydney that Percy had turned up an interesting proposition from no less a personage than old friend, Mack. Hugh McIntosh's helter-skelter life had started its penultimate plunge in 1929, when the failure of JC Williamson's Tivoli Theatres Ltd (the production company) to maintain rental payments to Mack's Harry Rickards Tivoli Theatres forced him to stage quick-fire revues in a desperate attempt to generate income. He was fighting a losing battle as the Depression shrank audiences. He resorted to illegally subsidising the theatres from the accounts of his Sunday Times company, of which he was still managing director, to the tune of over £66,000 but in 1930, hopelessly insolvent, Harry Rickards' Tivoli Theatres Ltd folded. After "Truth" published an article calling him an "erstwhile pieman" who had "drained the lifeblood" from the Sunday Times, Mack successfully sued for libel but was awarded damages of just one farthing* and shortly thereafter declared bankruptcy. This ended not only his commercial life but his tenure in politics. He'd been admitted to the upper house of the New South Wales parliament in 1917 and though he seldom took part in debates he made much use of the honorific "MLC" (Member of the Legislative Council) in his advertisements. Now, as a bankrupt, he was forced to relinquish that position, leaving him adrift in a pile of debt. Never one to say "die", he tried his hand briefly in a version of his old "pieman" business, opening a cake shop in the old Tivoli buildings. But, as Smith's Weekly reported:

> *Like mushrooms, similar cake shops sprang up all over Sydney almost overnight, and the fierce competition forced McIntosh from sitting on top of the world.*

He avoided complete destitution when Percy offered him the position of manager of Bon Accord guest house in Springwood. It helped pay some of the bills and kept him out of town while he got his affairs back in order. And it wasn't quite the rustication that he might have feared, as the venue continued to attract prestigious and influential visitors. Earl Beauchamp, Governor of New South Wales, was a frequent guest and enthusiastic golfer and in February 1933, just

---

* A farthing was worth one quarter of a penny. Though it was legal tender in 1932 it was practically worthless even then.

before Norman entered the RAC Rally, he had performed the opening ceremony of the new Bon Accord golf course, driving the first ball.[348] Mack enjoyed playing the genial and indulgent host to many visitors from the city. He rolled up his sleeves, personally carving the roast of the day while his competent staff looked after the more mundane business of supplying the kitchens, cleaning the rooms, maintaining the gardens, and paying the bills. Advertising for Bon Accord benefited from his touch, as he added illustrated displays featuring "The Rose Garden Guest House".[349] Percy still appeared from time to time and the McNabs, next-door neighbours at The Spinney, made their contribution as hosts of local charity events. Agnes McNab had become friendly with Rose Lindsay, still her husband's favourite model and Springwood's most glamourous, some would say, notorious, woman. The two collaborated on staging fancy-dress balls at Bon Accord and at other venues around the town.[350]

Mack was grateful to Percy for the respite from his troubles but, restless as always, he was constantly on the lookout for the next great opportunity to make his name and incidentally be rewarded for it. He floated a scheme to enlarge Bon Accord, whose popularity in the peak season occasionally found it over-booked; a hundred sat down for the 1933 Easter dinner.[351] Mack's plan was to extend Bon Accord by adding a further fifty bedrooms with ensuite bathrooms, steam heating and air cooling for the summer, and a large swimming pool "fashioned after the latest designs just brought to Australia."[352] But where was the money to come from? Bon Accord Investments was keeping its head above water but, with the economy only beginning a slow turnaround, the risks associated with doubling the size of the guest house and excavating a swimming pool were just too great. They made a half-hearted attempt to call tenders for the design and construction, but it came to nothing.

True to form, Mack soon conjured another bright idea. Milk bars! There it was, staring him in the face, a breakthrough in popular culture and entertainment for which his long experience equipped him better than anyone he could name. In November 1932, Greek migrant, Mick Adams, opened the doors of the Black and White Milk Bar in Sydney's Martin Place. Australia had seen nothing like it, though the soda fountains of The Ambassadors and a few other now-defunct establishments had given them a glimpse of trans-Pacific innovation. The novelty of an affordable selection of non-alcoholic beverages, served in ultra-modern surroundings where you could stand at a bar or perch on a stool was instantly embraced by a public dispirited by the years of depression. Over 5,000 patronised the Martin Place bar on the day of opening and newspapers filled with stories and photographs of people of all ages and backgrounds enjoying the glamour of the sleekly styled, chromium-plated café. The backdrop of angular, bevelled mirrors and the streamlined profile of the booths lining the wall added to the impression of modernity and the promise of a brighter future.

Mack's head filled with ideas and plans. It wouldn't be long before local competition entered the market, and he didn't fancy a repeat of his recent cake shop fiasco. Who would have thought that drinking milk, of all things, could catch on so? Hitherto, few except the very youngest could be persuaded to lift a glass of the unadulterated liquid to their lips. It was fine in tea or coffee, useful for culinary purposes but as a drink in its own right? Therein lay the answer: plain milk wasn't on offer, rather, exotic flavours and "shakes" that mimicked soda fountain beverages. The appeal to adults was obvious; there were no silly "wowser"* restrictions on consumption, while it was fashionable to be seen congregating in such avant garde surroundings: novelty guaranteed patronage. Mac had to snare the novelty, catch the wave, and ride it to success. But he was broke, and by the time he raised the capital to enter the Australian market it could be too late. He had to steal a march on the competition, as he had done with his early successes in sports promotions and with the Tivoli. The obvious choice, in his opinion, was England, specifically, London. He'd spent a lot of time there during the twenties, when he held the lease to Lord Kitchener's Broome Park, near Canterbury. Though he'd been forced to surrender the lease in recent years, he harboured dreams of escaping the stifling life of Sydney to make a fresh start. He was certainly going nowhere in Springwood, despite Percy's generosity. In London, given enough

* "Wowser" – Australian slang for a person who seeks to deprive others of behaviour they deem to be immoral or sinful. It was particularly applied to members of temperance groups.

capital, he could break into an untapped market before others had time to react, a market ten times bigger than that in Sydney. An approach to a likely investor was all it would take.

Percy could be good for a stake, he reasoned. Now that the old man had gone, and the assets were being liquidated, there had to be a lot of spare cash begging to be used. Percy was free of The Ambassadors, and though the ongoing saga of the Strand property was a concern he seemed to have overcome his early disappointment and was getting on with his life. When Mack broached the subject Percy was intrigued, recalling the popularity of The Ambassadors' soda fountain, but he declined the invitation. He had no interest in the British market, least of all London. Unlike his mother and his siblings, Percy called nowhere but Australia home. He'd been here longer than any of them, worn the uniform in defence of country and empire, married twice and formed a large circle of friends and business associates, particularly in Sydney. He had no useful contacts in England, beyond Norman and perhaps his mother. Given recent events, he wanted a quiet life free from business, at least for a while.

All right, what about Norman, then? Percy agreed his brother was as good as a native Londoner, familiar with the social and entertainment scene in the city, but he was less confident of Norman's aptitude for and application to hard work. Mack assured him that Norman's role would be more promotional than organisational and that, together, they would make a real team, ready to emulate the successes of their esteemed father. All that was needed to launch the business was a short-term "investment" loan. If it went as well as it had with the Sydney Black and White business the loan would be repaid in full, with interest, in no time.

And so it was that Norman opened Percy's letter inviting him to consider Mack's offer. All very well, he thought, but he could see no immediate way to raise the funds. He'd inherited a third of the residual estate from his father, as had his brothers, but it was tightly held in shares or within the Trust fund under Percy's management and was still subject to probate. He'd have to lean on his brother to release the money. Time for a visit to Australia to work the charm on Percy. He could take the new car with him for a spin on some of the great open roads. On June 18th, 1933, accompanied by his new valet,

Frank Wakeham, he sailed for Australia,[353] disembarking in Sydney on July 17th,[354] where he was welcomed back into society. As before, his extravagant lifestyle and gorgeous car attracted attention. He became the regular escort of twenty-seven-year old movie actress, Lotus Thompson, who had recently returned from Hollywood after a brief career of minor roles, notable for the focus on her "perfect" legs. She had gained temporary notoriety for supposedly attempting to disfigure those legs with acid, in desperation over her failure to interest directors in her acting abilities.[355] Back in Sydney, and apparently none the worse for the experience, she was a popular guest at various night spots. Norman accompanied her to a dinner dance at The Australia on July 27th.[356] Lotus was again his partner at The Australia early in August and was seen about town as a passenger in his car. Romance was never seriously in the air, Norman not being one to be tied down for long by anyone.

In any case, there was business to transact. Mack's plans were advancing, and all Norman had to offer was a little over £11,000 from the Regent Street account, not nearly enough. Discussions with Percy showed that at least another £45,000 could be released by transferring funds from the Pitt Street company account.[357] That was more like it. Between them, he and Mack would have enough to obtain a lease on a good corner premises in the West End, fit it out, stock it and employ staff. London wouldn't know what had hit it! Reassured by Percy that the cash could be released and transferred to the London account, Mack prepared for his departure and Norman relaxed once more. He rented sportsman and real estate entrepreneur, Bob Walder's house at Bellevue Hill rather than prolong his residence in hotels and to have somewhere handy to garage his car. Such was the size of the Rolls, however, that the driveway had to be widened and the sidewalk moved in order to accommodate it.[358] The Walders raised no objections. Norman availed himself of the facilities, holding "cheery informal parties, including a tennis party"[359] for his wide social circle. A pity he could not combine his proposed business activities with more of this kind of leisure time. On the other hand, if the milk bars were as successful as Mack promised he'd have both the time and the money to get away whenever and wherever he liked. The future looked brighter already.

Housekeeping

Harriet had spent the northern summer in the Park Lane apartment but now that the season was over, it was time to motor south once more to the villa. Stuart had retreated there with young David, in shock over the death of his wife. She could share his grief as she came to terms with her own loss. But just when she sought solace and rest, family business called her back to Australia. David's will passed through formal probate in June, and all calls on it were concluded in August. Percy wrote to say that there had been no additional claims and that he could now proceed to administer the estate. But though Harriet had known the general content of the will since before David's death, now that the details were before them it seemed that there were more constraints than she had anticipated.

It had started earlier in the year, when Lila and Vanna were parties to a case that went on appeal as far as the High Court of Australia, in which they claimed that they had been denied a beneficial interest in shares of Stewart Dawson Queensland Ltd. Though the issue predated the terms of the will, it portended the complexities that were now beginning to be revealed. It appeared that, ten years before his death, David had made a gift of 3,000 shares in the company to each of his first-family daughters and to Bertha's daughter, Joyce. Lila testified that she alone had received income from the shares and then only for the first three years. The case was brought by the Commissioner of Taxation, seeking to recover underpaid income tax under a complex rule governing multiple companies with common shareholders. Lila's evidence was incidental to the central issue, but it brought to light David's determination to manage every minute detail of his affairs. Attempting to prove that David was in fact the sole beneficial owner of all the shares, counsel for the Commissioner of Taxation contended that:

> *the shares which David Stewart Dawson had allotted to his daughters and grand-daughter were not really theirs, but were merely held on his behalf … The clear conclusion to be reached from the evidence was that Mr Stewart Dawson had directed his attention to taxation*

matters, and had made the distribution of shares to members of his family to avoid too great a holding in his name.[360]

James Robb, manager of the Queensland company, testified:

Mr Stewart Dawson gave written instructions that dividends on all shares standing in the names of members of his family except 4,000 shares in the name of Percy Stewart Dawson were to be paid to him. That was done except for three years, when the dividends were paid to Mrs. Arnold (Lila).

Lila herself, when questioned, said:

… apart from 1922, 1923 and 1924, I did not receive dividends on my shares. I had asked for dividends, but my father said, "Oh, no, there are no dividends," and I was to accept that position.

Asked to confirm that, until she arrived from England recently the scrip was not in her possession, she replied:

No. My father would not have liked that. He was a man who liked to have full control.

Lila was a determined woman, long since the active partner of a competent and successful businessman in his own right, and gave no ground, but the court found in favour of the Commissioner of Taxation and the three women were left empty handed. Unlike the women, Percy played an active role in the management of all the family companies. He had been a keen observer of the proceedings and though his own position was secure he sensed trouble in the future administration of the estate, should too much be revealed to the prying eyes of taxmen and interfering accountants. He was particularly concerned and more than a little irritated by the need to share administration of the estate with Perpetual Trustees. He accepted that there was a legal requirement for this arrangement and appreciated the clerical support that relieved him of some of the burden of administering the numerous bequests, but he resented the constraints on his freedom of action. This had become evident upon the full opening of the will, in May.

Despite his involvement in drafting the document, Percy had not paid too much attention to the finer details until now. The value of the estate for probate purposes was £43,000. This was a gross understatement of David's fortune, most of which remained bound up in his real estate and retail interests. He gave Harriet £1,000 and Bertha £250, payable upon his death, adding that he had already amply provided for them. Lila and Vanna received lifetime annuities of £250 and £750 per annum, respectively. Joyce Verrall, Malcolm McNab, grand-daughter Georgina Jerrard, Gus Jerrard, Harry Arnold and his son, Charles all received lesser and still generous amounts. Stuart's children were granted annuities, as were the McFarlanes and a select group of family friends. The balance of the estate consisted of shares in the several surviving companies, which were distributed among the long-serving managers of his shops in Australia and New Zealand. Percy, Norman, and Stuart were appointed directors of the Australian, United Kingdom and New Zealand companies. All would serve on each board, and each was appointed managing director of one: Percy took Australia, Norman the United Kingdom and Stuart New Zealand. They would each receive £1,000 a year in director's fees. The residuary estate was divided into thirds. Half of each third went to the three brothers and the remaining half was to be held in trust to their children. Percy observed that, since neither he nor Norman were likely ever to produce any heirs, it would be Stuart's family who would ultimately reap the benefits of the estate. How ironic! The least active, most feckless of the brood would be in clover simply for having fathered a couple of brats.

The most intriguing surprise, which raised more than one eyebrow, was David's direction to the executors to

> *allow my wife to have the absolute use and enjoyment during her life of my villa and contents in Monte Carlo.*

That was to be expected, David had said as much in the presence of Harriet and Percy, but what followed caused an embarrassed shuffling of feet among the family. David added:

> *If any of my sons and daughters or their respective husbands, wives or issue should dispute that gift to my wife, the disputant shall forfeit all benefit under my will.*

Just who had been in David's mind when he wrote that? Certainly not Percy: he had no desire to while away his time anywhere but in

Australia, as David knew. In any case, he was far too busy dealing with the wind-up of the retail business (the Brisbane store closed in July) and the tedious, drawn-out dispute with Strand and Pitt Street Properties, and in the very month probate commenced he was overseeing the auction of the contents of The Ambassadors, a sad affair.[361] Could it have been one of his daughters? Again, Percy dismissed that possibility. Bertha was his favourite, but she had long settled into the social life of London with Joyce and was undemanding. Vanna and Gus Jerrard were living contentedly in Hampshire, and both were direct financial beneficiaries, as was their own daughter, Georgina. They'd never even visited the villa, to his knowledge. Lila might be a candidate but, like Percy, her interests lay more in Australia, thanks to husband Harry's ties with the country. That left Norman and Stuart. Both were frequent visitors to Villa Bon Accord, Stuart more than ever since Peggy's final decline and demise. Neither had any permanent home of their own, living in hotels or rented rooms around London's West End. Both were skilled at appealing to their mother's generous nature, which somewhat mitigated against any ambition of outright possession of the property. Why risk everything when you had free access to Villa Bon Accord with none of the expense of running the place? On the other hand, who had most to gain or lose through mounting a dispute? Those same two brothers, of course. Stuart's bankruptcy remained undischarged and though Norman was now free from his creditors, thanks to David's last goodwill gesture, both he and Stuart continued to live hand to mouth and would henceforth be reliant on a smaller income than they had enjoyed in their father's lifetime. It could be very tempting to make a claim on the villa with a view to its disposal in a rising market, now that Norman had his eyes on this new venture with Mack, and Stuart's children were reaching the age when education expenses would begin to take their toll.

Harriet's concern as always was to avoid conflict while observing the spirit of David's will. She was also perplexed by what she had heard of Norman and Mack's business plan. She understood that they would require a deal of capital that somehow Norman would raise, and she had learned enough from Percy to realise that the money would have to come from the estate or the business, she wasn't sure which. But now that the details of the will had been published, she could see Percy's point of view: it would be no simple matter of writing a cheque. She booked passage and sailed once more for Sydney, taking young Harriet with her. Stuart stayed behind at Villa Bon Accord, but she would at least have a chance to meet Norman before he returned to take up his position fully in Regent Street.

She disembarked from the Strathnaver on November 15th.[362] Percy and Norman were there to meet her and drive her the short distance to The Australia. Both apartments at Wilga were rented, one of them to old friends, the Levys, and Percy had removed to more modest accommodation at Potts Point. She took in the familiar streets, the bright sunlight glancing down the faces of the buildings. Passing Strand Arcade, she was dismayed at the sight of the shuttered shop fronts. Selfridges* had taken possession of the Pitt Street premises, while the George Street end remained empty after Brightlights' failure. Percy pointed out where hundreds of unemployed men had staged a near-riot back in February (they said that Communists had been behind it), some climbing onto a veranda in the arcade to harangue the crowd. Matters had got out of hand when a stone was thrown through a window and for a while it had looked as if the police had lost control.[363] Peace had been restored and there had been no further public unrest, but the general mood of the working classes remained sullen. Harriet remarked that the disruption and violence that had swept across Europe seemed to have found its way across the world. Ever since Norman's service during the General Strike Britain, France, Italy and now Germany had been in turmoil. Thank goodness a few strong men had taken charge, though she'd heard disturbing things about the way the new German Chancellor, Mr. Hitler, had dealt with opponents. The business with the Jews was ominous. How concerned were friends such as the Jacobsons, Levys, Bruxners† for the welfare of relatives far over the seas?

---

* Not the London Selfridges. Like Woolworths, this was a distinct, Australian entity licensing the name only.

† Harriet was friendly with all three families, frequenting charity events, parties and race days with them.

Settled into her suite at The Australia, Harriet prepared to rekindle old acquaintanceships before dealing with family business. She had announced her visit some time before her departure from Europe, and St Margaret's Hospital committee was among the many to respond with a welcome tea party to take place the following week at The Australia.[364] Invitations to dinners, the theatre and even the odd dance awaited her, and of course, the racing season was in full swing. Her spirits rose, though she soon realised she would have to disabuse many of the notion that she was here to stay. The word was that she had returned from "a tour of the Continent"[365] when in fact, the longer she remained in Sydney, the more she was drawn to her twin homes in London and Monte Carlo. Perhaps she had misled some with her responses to interviews with the press upon her arrival. Among her several reasons for making the journey was to honour David's memory with a permanent memorial. His ashes lay not in an elaborate mausoleum but beneath a simple inscribed plaque in a wall, as he had wished. Though he had dominated the commercial property market in Sydney briefly, he had failed to build the twelve storey Stewart Dawson edifice that would perpetuate his name. The Treasure House remained the chief example of his endeavours in architecture, but it was in Hatton Garden, on the other side of the world. Wilga, despite their sensitive efforts at remodelling, would always be remembered as James Martin's creation and the Springwood houses, even Bon Accord, were no more than a side show. But there was one object, a genuine monument, that had fired her imagination, and on which she had focussed her attention. Sculpted of solid sandstone, it stood in the grounds of Wilga. At over twenty feet in height, the cylindrical tower on its tiered plinth, four Corinthian columns at its circumference, supported a deep coronet adorned with a frieze of scenes from Greek legend and history. It was topped with an elaborate capital of stylised acanthus leaves. It had been David's favourite of all the statues and stone carvings in the gardens. Now that Wilga was only an occasional residence why not make use of this potent symbol of classical style and grace on David's behalf? Sydney would have something permanent on public display by which to remember him. She'd announced her plan even as she landed in Melbourne and now, she approached the State authorities to execute it. She offered to present the "Greek Temple", suggesting it should be placed in one of the public gardens. She was willing to give it away for that purpose "in memory of her husband", provided the state paid the costs of removal. Explaining its significance, she stated:

> *It is a beautiful old temple. It is supposed to be the only one of its kind in the world and to have an amazing history. It was imported to Australia by the owner of the property that we bought.**

Her efforts were unrewarded, the state government having little appetite for "squandering" taxpayer funds on a useless object in a rich woman's garden at a time when dole queues still formed daily. Though Harriet was mildly affronted, she was sanguine, biding her time for a more suitable opportunity. She or Percy could make another approach when times were better, she reasoned. One way or another, David would not be forgotten.

Meanwhile, there was the matter of Norman and Mack's milk bar enterprise. Harriet liked Mack and admired his determination, but she knew that David had been alarmed more than once by his risk-taking. It wasn't for her to say, of course, all business decisions being a male prerogative, but was this proposed use of funds in accordance with David's will? And how on earth were they going to release all that money from the estate? For, on even cursory examination, there was little spare cash to disburse. Contrary to the publicity at the time of David's death, his "fortune" remained essentially illiquid. As Percy explained, they'd effectively received nothing of the £770,000 bid for the Pitt Street property and now that he'd had to exercise mortgagee in possession rights, they were as good as back where they had been in 1928, except that rental income was considerably less than it had

---

* Harriet was mistaken on several counts. The monument was in fact a copy of the Choragic Monument of Lysikrates, in Athens, which dated from 334 BC. James Martin did not "import" it, he commissioned it from local sculptor, Walter McGill, in 1870. Several other copies exist, including the Dugald Stewart Monument on Calton Hill, Edinburgh, which David would have known from his time working in the city. Perhaps nostalgia for the Scottish connection inspired him, or even the coincidence of the name. After the State government declined Harriet's offer, she made no further attempt to persuade them.

been. Strand and Pitt Street Properties had sold off the remaining equipment and furnishings of The Ambassadors only the previous month in another attempt to cover the mortgage payments* but their position looked hopeless. The situation was similar in London, where Stewart Dawson's were still saddled with the lease on Regent Street, at best making a small margin on the sub-let. The store itself was on its last legs. To be sure, there were the funds realised upon the sale of Collins Street, but some of that had subsidised The Ambassadors in its declining years, not to mention the slow-down in retail sales leading to the closing of the stores. The money for Norman and Mack's venture would have to come from cash reserves in the various companies surviving in Australia, New Zealand, and London, or by releasing some of the inheritance entailed for those never-to-be-born children. Harriet was confused; wouldn't Perpetual Trustees veto any tampering with the estate? Percy assured her all would be well. What they didn't know wouldn't harm them and, after all, it was the family's money, not theirs. Percy knew best, she supposed, and Norman deserved the opportunity to make his own fortune. He certainly looked the part, breezing about the city, splashing out on yet more parties, and still dining and dancing with the lovely movie star.

Reassured that her own income was secure, Harriet was free to enjoy what passed for the "Season" in Sydney. First, she needed a residence that was more appropriate to the style of living to which she had become accustomed. The Australia was a fine hotel and her suite one of the best, but it was too confining, no garden to wander in and no view to admire. Where was the local equivalent of Villa Bon Accord to be found? Wilga would have met the bill but now was not the time to evict the tenants. Dependable Percy found the solution, renting the Curlewis' beach-side home at Palm Beach for the holidays.[366] At the northernmost tip of the Barrenjoey Peninsula, the idyllic retreat of Sydney's millionaires had since the opening of the Harbour Bridge

* Sydney Sun 24th October 1933 P.7. Strand and Pitt Street Properties reported a loss of £10,465 for the year ended 30th June 1933. The annual report concluded: "*...there is justification for believing that the company will eventually resume possession of its properties, and with that in view, the board is endeavouring to control expenses within the company's income.*" This proved wildly optimistic.

attracted even more who sought an escape from the city. Percy's home just south at Newport had been surpassed in scale and panache by the "moderne"-style villas and mansions lining the ocean beach or clinging to the steep slopes above. Harriet approved of his choice. They could sunbathe on the beach, while less than an hour away south, across the harbour there were the customary tea parties and dinner dances. She was welcomed back by the ladies of the Dalwood Homes charity, joining them at a children's party held at The Wentworth.[367] Hannah Maclurcan had retired from active management of the hotel the previous year, handing control to her son, Charles.[368] Despite her continuing innovations, including catering for the rapid growth in motor car traffic to the hotel with a vast parking garage and filling station, The Wentworth was suffering as much as anywhere from the effects of the Depression. Nevertheless, apart from The Australia, it remained one of the few places in town where the ladies could meet in comfort and style. Harriet's memories of The Ambassadors notwithstanding, she acknowledged the strength and determination of her erstwhile rival.

She had arrived too late for the Spring Racing Carnival at Randwick[369] and missed the Melbourne Cup[370], but there were one or two meetings held at Randwick in December where she could have a flutter. The Summer Cup, run on Boxing Day, December 26th, attracted a large crowd. As if to defy the persisting economic woes, competition in the fashion stakes was as keen as on the track. Plain or printed crepe or chiffon frocks predominated, while many of the younger set sported the new, tiny jockey caps with a visor-like brim. Harriet, as always, made her own, confident statement, wearing an ankle-length gown of blossom pink, swathed by a black taffeta sash. Eschewing the jockey cap fad, she wore a pink straw hat with a touch of black.[371] Mauves, pinks and greens were her favourite colours, and while she admired others' choice of black and white, she refused to "dress her age" by adopting a more muted palette. "I am like old Queen Mary," she wrote to Kathleen, "a bit of colour for me."*

---

* From a letter to Kathleen O'Connor, about 1939: "*...I think an old piece of brocade, different colours, you know what I like – mauve, pink & greens mixed. You*

With the new year, Norman, now confident of his capacity to invest in Mack's scheme, loaded his car onto the SS Nieuw Zeeland and sailed for California on January 20th, bound for London via New York. Among his fellow passengers was Lotus Thompson, who threw "the gayest of farewell parties" for her many admirers.

> *There she was, bare legged, red lips contrasting with two rows of even white teeth, blue eyes, and cheeky nose, and adorned with more jewels than dear old Queen Sheba herself, when she set out in reply to King Solomon's "you must come up and see me sometimes." Moreover, she was surrounded by thirty or forty young people, who had decorated her long white neck with a garland of frangipani, and who drank her health in cocktails, – cocktails, and more cocktails – yes, and even more cocktails.**

Just when it looked as if the drinks had run out, the party was saved by the arrival of "Frosty", the bar steward, who was "hailed as the man of the moment" by the "bevy of pretty girls and handsome men." Norman, at forty-three, his hair a distant memory, could only stand on the sidelines and recall the times of his own lost youth. But he reminded himself, he could outspend them all, and as if to endorse his opinion, Smith's Weekly ended its report of the event:

> *Lotus is very fortunate in the fact that she will have a fellow passenger in Major Norman Stewart-Dawson. During her stay in Sydney, Lotus was a conspicuous figure in the Major's long, sleeky, black Rolls-Royce.*

---

can pick up a piece at any old second hand shop or old furniture shop very cheap. The hat sounds nice and will suit you as I always liked you in black & white. These days every lady looks her best in black or black & white but I am like old Queen Mary, a bit of colour for me..."

* Smith's Weekly 27th January 1934 P.2. The gist of the article was Lotus' return to "re-join her husband" in the USA, after she had been *"kicked out...for overstaying her permit (visa)."* She had made the most of her stay in Sydney, partying as if the Roaring Twenties had never ended. Norman was one of her most frequent escorts and no doubt flirted with her in the week or so crossing the Pacific. As ever with Norman, the dalliance was superficial and over by the time they landed. They never met again.

Wasn't she, just! Ah, well, he would make the most of the sea voyage but, once back in London, he had bigger fish to fry. He had Percy's and his mother's blessing and Mack's genius set to make his fortune. Mack would need some time to untangle his affairs in Australia but as soon as he could escape it would be "Milk bars! Milk bars! Milk bars!"

Trust, Care and Responsibility

Bertha's daughter, Joyce, married William Clark in London on February 5th, 1934.[372] Harriet was pleased for her granddaughter, who had been a loving and loyal child, supporting her mother these many years, through her troubles with Joyce's father and her widowhood. It had been a shipboard romance, the couple meeting on board the Strathnaver, where William served as electrical engineering officer. Eleven years on, Harriet's heart still warmed to the sheer romance of the affair. So many voyages in her own life, so many encounters or happy memories of her journeys with David and later, the little grandchildren. Sad memories, too: the parting from six-year-old Percy for that first long voyage to Australia; David's weary last journey to the city he called home. Then, there was her meeting with Kathleen back in '26. What were the odds against that friendship ever having started had they not been thrown together on board a liner? On the other hand, there was also the curious and unfortunate business of Ethel Roberts and that disreputable charmer, Mr Abrahams.

She found it difficult, even now, to ponder the hurt she had suffered at the hands of that couple. With David's death had come the realisation of her complete reliance on him, not only in the material sense, but for counsel and support in her social endeavours. As long as she could remember he had been her companion when she needed him. For a while she had feared him lost to her when he sailed off with that young lass to Australia. Who knew what the future may have held had Valerie survived? But fate had returned him to her, and she remembered the last decade of his life as a mostly happy time when he and she shared in life's rewards. My! How they had danced those many nights at The Ambassadors; the parties, the celebrations of another cheque presented to the Hospital, the gracious dignitaries who favoured their table or who honoured them at Wilga or up at Springwood, and always at the centre, even if avoiding the limelight, her dear friend and anchor, David. Where, now would she find someone, anyone, to begin to fill the void left by his passing? Marriage was out of the question, though she never underestimated her powers of attraction nor shunned the company of gentlemen escorts. Dear Lord Beauchamp had always been so kind, notwithstanding the rumours about his private preferences. Harriet considered herself open-minded and, dare she say? "modern" in her views, and Beauchamp was charming and generous. She supposed that there was always the possibility of a chance romantic encounter on the Riviera, considering the plethora of itinerant dispossessed aristocrats, but for the time being her heart was not for the taking. She needed female company, someone on whom she could rely day to day to take care of the minutiae, to manage her diary, assist with her wardrobe, take tea with, in the lonely hour. Kathleen was a good friend but never one to be tied down in that sort of relationship, especially if it should include entertaining a seven-year-old like young Harriet. It would be better to follow Norman's lead and employ a female "valet".

Thus, it was that Ethel had answered to Harriet's notice in the paper. She presented as a vivacious and friendly girl who could be there for Harriet when the guests had left, when Kathleen had returned to her Paris studio, and her sons had tired of her company. Villa Bon Accord was an exceptionally beautiful home and the Park Lane apartment lacked for no comfort, but they could be very lonely places when only the housemaid and cook were about. Having a bright young thing to chat with, share a cocktail, drive with to the casino or favourite restaurant would be just the ticket for a grieving widow. They got along famously and when Harriet announced her return to Australia Ethel, a Melbourne girl, leapt at the chance to revisit her home country. Harriet pointed out that the Australian visit would be brief; as life companion, Ethel would be more often on the road, at sea or anywhere from London, to Paris, Monte Carlo and who knows where? But the young woman's sense of adventure was obvious and who would not have envied her, travelling the world, all expenses paid?

At first, everything had gone swimmingly as they settled into shipboard life. Harriet, though a little peeved at having to interrupt her planned winter sojourn at Monte Carlo, reconciled with her matronly duty to Norman and Percy and consoled herself with the promise of meeting old friends in Sydney. She was in familiar, comfortable surrounds; the first-class suite on her favourite deck, the stewards and officers remembered from earlier voyages, faces recognised among the guests in the lounge. As far as she could tell, Ethel took to life on board with alacrity, joining the foursomes at the card table, relaxed in the company of an older generation. This voyage would be a probation for her and "so far, so good," thought Harriet. It was after they left Fremantle, headed for Adelaide, that she noticed a change in her companion. She was distracted, and occasionally absent when Harriet needed her. She could not have tired so quickly of the good life, could she? Harriet's gentle prompting failed to shed light on the mystery and the brightness returned to Ethel's smile. It was not to last; as they approached Adelaide Ethel confronted her. She had been made an offer of marriage and, regrettably, would be leaving Harriet's employ forthwith. Not even a few days' notice until they disembarked in Sydney? No expression of gratitude for the weeks of well-paid and, it had to be said, undemanding service? No thought for Harriet's feelings, her embarrassment over the suddenness of the announcement? On the contrary, Ethel seemed to have no compunction in severing her ties with her new mistress and Harriet was left to wonder which passionate young bachelor had won her heart. Imagine her surprise and dismay when Ethel revealed the name of her betrothed: Mr Emmanuel Abrahams, he of the "Small Arms Brothers" case![373] She was on nodding terms with the seventy-year-old financier and had read about him some time in the twenties when he and his brothers were at the centre of a drawn-out dispute over undeclared income and unpaid taxes. The brothers had made their fortune in manufacturing small arms for the Great War and turned a successful goldsmith's business into Sydney's, if not Australia's largest private bank. Their wealth overshadowed even David's but there was always something shady about the business, so they said, and Emmanuel had been in exile for several years while the government chased down the missing company records that they believed proved their case against the brothers. Government officials resorted to breaking open the company safe with a blow torch but, despite finding abundant corroborating evidence, settled on a payment of £500,000 rather than prolong the costly investigation. She remembered David's grudging admiration of the brothers' tenacity, even as he voiced his disapproval of their alleged misdemeanours.

And now, here was that same Mr. Abrahams, wooing someone forty years his junior and, worse, the woman in whom she had placed her trust had given her consent to the marriage. Harriet was mortified and, rather than suffer the indignity of accepting Ethel's resignation, dismissed her on the spot. Her generosity of spirit was no reason to consider her a soft touch. She decided to put the whole unfortunate episode behind her and preserve her dignity, keeping her own company for the week or so between Adelaide and Sydney. Once ashore, she had better things to do than fret about an unsavoury and mercenary contract that revived unhappy memories of David's folly all those years ago.

By the time she learned of Joyce's marriage (one made in Heaven, so rare these days) Harriet was once more on the move, this time back to Wilga. Septimus Levy had died suddenly on January 25th and his widow elected to vacate the Strathisla apartment.[374] Harriet could return to the harbourside. Palm Beach was lovely for a summer break, but it was rather remote from the social life of the city. Norman had left, Percy was preoccupied with administering the estate and doing whatever it was that Mack needed for his milk bar venture, but she had a few months to enjoy at Potts Point and was soon back in harness, joining Agnes on the committee of another of Mrs Jack Jacobson's charity fund-raisers and spending as much time as she could with members of the old circle from The Ambassadors' days. She could see out the southern winter, introducing young Harriet to Australia, and return at leisure to Villa Bon Accord just as the Season in London ended.

And then, it was over almost before she realised. She was beginning to find even the mild Australian winter too cool for her and as July ended with grey skies dulling the views of the harbour her restlessness revived. Percy had taken the express train to Perth on business, and she was alone at Wilga with young Harriet. News from Europe was sporadic, yet intriguing. Norman had spent little time in London upon his return, stopping only to have his car maintained and brought back to concours standard before heading back across the Channel. The work on the car seemed to have paid off, for his entry in a concours at Cannes won him a prize. He was now in Monte Carlo, ensconced at Villa Bon Accord for the while.

As to be expected, his social life continued to attract the attention of the popular press. Pamela Murray's "Monte Carlo Asides" column in the August 22nd edition of "The Sketch" made much of the visit of film star, Merle Oberon, and her entourage, fresh from the release of the enormously successful "The Private Life of Henry VIII", which starred Charles Laughton. Among her companions was English actress, Wendy Barrie, who had played the role of Jane Seymour in the film. The Sketch observed:

> *Merle's mermaid scales in scarlet were spectacular ... but among movie girls our English-bred Wendy Barrie is supremely good to gaze at, animated and as yet uncontaminated vocally by studio Americanisms. Sir Victor Sassoon spends his mornings featuring her in moving pictures, with passing bathers as extras and the pool as an ideal set ... Gene Silva, Mrs. Edward Churchill, and Wendy make a three-little-girls-from-school trio escorted by Major Stewart Dawson.**

Harriet's mind was made up; the natural beauty and benign climate of Sydney were no substitute for the glamour of her beloved Riviera. Where in Australia could she mingle, any time she chose, with international film stars, barons, earls, princesses, artists; in short, interesting people such as these? And then there was Stuart who, after spending more time on the Riviera, consoling himself in the company of expatriate friends, was back in London at the very chic Mayfair Hotel. Harriet was concerned that young David's interrupted school life and constant exposure to his father's rather louche circle was a poor preparation for his immature brain. At twelve years old, he had had no proper home life and seen the worst of his late mother's behaviour, while his father's example was not, for the most part, one of which she would have approved. And now, out of the blue, Stuart was about to be married again. While at the Mayfair, he'd met an

---

* The Sketch 22nd August 1934 P.336. Wendy Barrie was born Margaret Wendy Jenkins in 1912. She adopted the stage name "Barrie" in honour of "Peter Pan" author, JM Barrie, who was her godfather. She went on to star alongside actors such as James Stewart, Spencer Tracy and Basil Rathbone. Mrs. Edward Churchill was the wife of Winston Churchill's cousin.

American actress named Audrey Jean Owens ("Jean" to her friends), fresh off the boat from New York, and after the briefest of courtships, they had announced their wedding, to be held in October.* Harriet learned that Jean had recently divorced her older husband, a Mr Moe Solinsky, a tailor of Russian origin, and almost twice her age, after a mere five years of marriage. According to Stuart, the marriage had been one of convenience for the young actress and dancer, who had been struggling to make her way in the cut-throat world of the New York stage and theatre. Harriet had a sense of déjà vu; another of her sons falling for a glamorous actress, and Stuart with two small children in tow. It was difficult to see how he would cope or, more to the point, why his young fiancée would be prepared to take on a ready-made family. There was, of course, the attraction of Stuart's ready-made income, should he bother to take on his New Zealand responsibilities and start earning it. And it looked as if he might do just that, for he announced that, following the wedding, he and Jean would be returning to Sydney to set up home. Harriet would have a mere couple of months with her youngest son, barely time to make the acquaintance of his wife-to-be and to introduce young Harriet to her stepmother. She decided to wait no longer and booked passage on the Orama for herself and her granddaughter.

Sunshine greeted them as they disembarked at Plymouth on September 26th, and the air was unseasonably warm[375] as they took the London train to meet Stuart at the Mayfair. It was time for a talk about the future of the family. Harriet's focus was on the children. The two or more years of separation had left its mark on them; David's self-confident precociousness contrasted with his five-years-younger sister's gentle innocence and though they appeared happy to be together once more Harriet could sense David and Stuart's discomfort and awkwardness in the presence of the little girl. The poignant scene remained in her mind as they sat with Jean, the discussion turning to wedding and travel arrangements. Jean, she observed, was a striking blonde, tall (as tall as Stuart) with a dancer's lithe figure. Though not

* The precise date of the wedding is not recorded but can be inferred from the England & Wales Civil Registration Index for the period October to December 1934.

classically beautiful, she would have turned heads in any room. No wonder Stuart had fallen for her. If Harriet had any suspicion that Jean was a gold digger she was reassured by the obvious affection between the couple. She had the impression that the impending marriage was a genuine love match, though she was less sure that Jean was prepared for the role of stepmother. Her manner was warm and friendly towards the children, but she seemed out of her depth with David's boisterousness and young Harriet's shyness. It was to be expected, of course, but even more reason to intervene, offer a solution to allay concerns. Why not, Harriet proposed, leave the children with her for a while, as the newly-weds settled into their life together in Australia? Stuart had been away from Sydney for ten years, doing little with his life, and would need careful tutoring from Percy if he were to take responsibility for the New Zealand operations. David had tagged along with his father for much of the time, but he should be settled into a good school by now. Little Harriet's life was already a confusion of places and people and to send her back on another long sea voyage so soon after her arrival could risk making things worse for all of them. Far better for Stuart and Jean to have a year or so alone together until they established themselves in Australia.

She sensed that the idea of a period of relative freedom appealed to the couple and for the moment enjoyed the satisfaction of having achieved something for the family on her own initiative, perhaps for the first time. Alas, she was to be thwarted: though young Harriet's face showed her delight and relief at the prospect of life with Grandma, David clung to his father. Why should he forego the opportunity to see "down-under", be separated from his father to satisfy the whim of a fusty old lady? He'd heard too much about Sydney's summer delights, Bondi Beach, Palm Beach and so on to throw up a chance to be there in favour of trailing about with a clutch of old people. Very well, conceded Harriet, she would raise no objection to his accompanying his father and stepmother, provided Stuart kept an open mind about David's future schooling. She had formed strong opinions of the value of a good English or European education; they need look no further than Norman for an example of its benefits. And, so it was that, after the briefest of honeymoons, Stuart and Jean packed their trunks and, David by their side, boarded the boat train to Southampton. December 12th saw the threesome throwing streamers from the deck of the SS Europa as she pulled out from the quay, bound for New York.[376]

Harriet was not at the dockside, having decamped at the earliest opportunity with her granddaughter to Villa Bon Accord, where Norman still occupied a room. Though she was impatient to re-join the "set", which daily swelled with new escapees from the English winter, she first had questions for Norman. What was going on with the milk bar enterprise? Norman had been back in Europe for almost a year and what had he done to advance the opening of the business? Where was Mack? If he wished to strike before competitors awoke, he should have landed and set the wheels in motion by now. Norman reassured his mother; Mack's plans were nearing fruition and he would be sailing for London early in the new year, by which time Norman would be back in London to support his partner. Harriet relaxed; she should have trusted her son, a man of the world such as he would not let "Opportunity" pass by.

News from Australia, via Percy, confirmed Norman's assurances. Mack and Percy were in the process of leasing Bon Accord guest house to a Mrs. Seeley, who seemed a competent businesswoman, thus releasing Mack from his pleasant but hardly lucrative (by his standards) duties. Bon Accord would be in good hands and of course always available for family weekends. The McNabs would be close by to keep an eye on it. Meantime, Mack would arrive sometime in January and unleash his energy on the British public. Percy had managed to release the funds for Norman to put into the business. He had leased Wilga to the Charlemont Private Hospital, which sought to extend its existing premises further down Darlinghurst Road.* Harriet and he had agreed the house was no longer needed. Percy was happier in a smaller flat and she considered Villa Bon Accord to be her home. The money transferred to London, it would only be a

* Wilga was leased sometime between late 1934 and the end of 1935, perhaps as late as the first half of 1936. Percy was still in residence at "Strathisla" (the flat comprising half of Wilga) in 1934 (per Electoral Roll) and Charlemont Hospital was reported in 1937 to have been the tenant for an indefinite period (Sydney Mail 10th November 1937 P.27).

matter of months before the first milk bar opened and the customers flowed in. Norman's face told of his joy and relief, at least, that was Harriet's initial impression; he could be counting his chickens before the eggs were even laid. She was tempted to remind him of his father's well-founded belief in the rewards of patience and dedication to hard work and his disdain for "get rich quick" schemes. Norman's breezy dismissal of her concerns left her unconvinced, but she determined to retain her optimism for the venture which was, after all, not hers to control.

Percy added a postscript to his letter: had Harriet seen the accounts of a breach of promise case that mentioned her name? He enclosed articles clipped from the newspapers. Intrigued, Harriet unfolded the clippings, recognising the names of the parties to the case. Ethel Roberts was suing Emmanuel Abrahams in the Practice Court of Melbourne for £10,000 over his alleged breach of promise to marry her. She claimed that his offer of marriage had induced her to resign her position as life companion to Mrs Stewart Dawson, thus forfeiting years of income and security. Abrahams' defence was that he had never made any such promise, that Ethel had in fact been dismissed by Mrs Stewart Dawson and that she was exploiting him to extort money. His defence rested upon testimony from Mrs Stewart Dawson, should she be found. Percy had not enlightened the court on Abrahams' behalf, and Harriet's response was unequivocal. Of course she had dismissed Ethel, but why should she be dragged into this sordid affair, to face personal and almost certainly embarrassing and hurtful questions from Ethel's counsel? Harriet cared little for Abrahams' welfare or rights and less for Ethel's. It was clear that nobody would ever know the truth of Ethel's allegation. Harriet herself had found it hard to believe that a worldly man such as Abrahams would have been seduced into a proposal of marriage so readily (David might have come close to that back in 1916, but there was a child involved then) but shipboard romance could trump everything, she conceded. She was at heart a caring person, but there were limits, and Ethel had crossed the line. Was this a case of breach of promise or an attempt at extortion? Let them both stew for a while; Harriet was not for turning. However, the entire matter became moot when, in February 1935, Ethel dropped the case against Abrahams in circumstances that confirmed Harriet's suspicions of gold-digging opportunism. "Truth" reported:[377]

> *… the case in which Miss Ethel Wynne Roberts, pretty lady companion, was suing Emmanuel Abrahams, one of the "Small Arms" brothers, and probably the wealthiest Jew in Australia, for £10,000 for alleged breach of promise to marry, will be discontinued …*
>
> *Miss Roberts sailed some days ago on an extended tour of New Zealand, America and England, and her friends expect her to be away for a considerable period.*

It was a further blow to Harriet's faith in human nature. Had there been a pay-off, an out-of-court settlement by Abrahams? How else could Ethel, living hand to mouth, have afforded "an extended tour" around the world? As she read the news Harriet recalled the many times her own family, friends and the minions of the press had disappointed her. She loved Norman and Stuart dearly and for years had forgiven so much of their fecklessness, but she knew in her heart that they would continue to avoid their responsibilities, prevail yet again on her to extract unearned money from the family inheritance; despite her years of dedication to charitable causes, it was clear to her that her appointed successors in Sydney had consigned her to fading history; her support of poor Dorothy Mort had earned her opprobrium in the papers and little sympathy from her social circle; and her generous offer of the Greek Temple to the city of Sydney had been ignored. She missed David's steadying hand, the stern will that dismissed insults, unkindness, and snubs as the mischief of the ignorant or envious. She could hear his voice now, the Highland brogue accentuated by emotion, reminding her that a Stewart Dawson was worth ten of those hangers-on and vipers of the press. If any of them had worked a fraction as hard as he they might have the right to criticise or demean the family, otherwise let them hold their peace. And then he would have consoled her with a surprise gift or a day out at the races and all would have been well again.

The vision faded; she shook herself. "Come now, Harriet, you've no time for self-pity, take David's advice and put this silly business behind you. You have your health, your lovely homes and two grandchildren who need your care." It was true, she had found a good school in Cannes for young Harriet, now seven years old, and as soon as Stuart agreed, she would do the same for her grandson. She was consoled by the knowledge that, upon arrival in Australia, Stuart had enrolled David at Sydney's prestigious Cranbrook School. Founded in 1918 and located in Bellevue Hill, an easy walk from their rented home, the school had a reputation for academic excellence and the building of character in tomorrow's leaders. By Stuart's account, twelve-year-old David had adapted to life at the all-boys school and was an enthusiastic and competitive swimmer at the summer carnival. However, Harriet's concern for the boy's welfare remained; Stuart and Jean appeared to spend an awful amount of time away from home, not much of it in New Zealand, which on business grounds alone might have justified their absence from Sydney. She accepted that Stuart would want to show his new wife the attractions of New South Wales and perhaps Victoria before they settled into their Sydney home, but David seemed to spend too much of his time alone in the care of servants and housekeepers. Harriet hatched a plan, she co-opted Percy's help to keep an eye on David and report back to her on Stuart and Jean's peripatetic life. If it came to it, she would step in and renew her offer to relieve them of David's care and educational needs for the time being. She knew she risked accusations of interference, but it was in her nature and too much was at stake for the youngster for her to abandon him now. She was, after all, the matriarch and when duty called, she could not fail them. Her self-confidence restored, she turned her attention to enjoying the end of the New Year season on the Riviera and planning her social calendar in time for her return to London.

On The Milky Way

On January 15th, 1935, Mack left Sydney on the RMS Barradine for London. As was his habit, he left a trail of hints about his plans and intentions, attracting reporters eager to fill a column. Sydney's affection for "the Big Man" remained strong. The article in Smith's Weekly was typical:

> *On January 15, Mr Hugh D McIntosh departed, quite without ostentation, on the "Barradine" for London … Once on the open sea, however, Mr McIntosh came into his own: he took charge of all the sports and social life of the ship, and even shared the limelight at Divine Service.*
>
> *It is stated that C.B. Cochrane, London's biggest theatrical man, is trying to revive boxing, and has invited Mr Hugh D McIntosh to administer the Voronoff* treatment. Whether he succeeds or not it will be nice for Hughie to revisit the scenes of his social triumphs at Broome Park and the scene of his not-so-triumphant political activities in the Highlands.*
>
> *Anyway, if any man can put the punch back into boxing, it is "the McIntosh." Go to it, Hughie!*†

Nowhere in any of the press was there mention of his opening milk bars, despite Mack having so recently made great play of his ambitions in that direction. And indeed, he had other irons in the fire as he headed north. During his time at Bon Accord memories of his successful sporting promotions had conjured ideas for new ventures. There had to be one more boxing match, perhaps a cycle race to revive

---

* Serge Abrahamovitch Voronoff (c. 1866 – 1951) was a French surgeon of Russian extraction who gained fame for his technique of grafting monkey testicle tissue on to the testicles of men for purportedly therapeutic purposes.

† Smith's Weekly, 23rd February 1935 P.10. "…. *the scene of his not-so-triumphant political activities in the Highlands*" refers to McIntosh's standing unsuccessfully in 1929 as a Labour candidate for the seat of Ross and Cromarty, in Scotland.

his career, and even if nothing came of it, he could divert attention, buying time to surprise London with the grand opening of the first milk bar. His circle of sporting contacts extended to the United Kingdom, and he made good use of it before and after his departure. Upon arrival in London, he kept the gossip columnists occupied with more teasing hints but never any definitive announcement. Smith's Weekly reported:

> *Fleet Street has seen very little of the great man since his unobtrusive entrance into the Metropolis. But he has not been idle. He has been renewing old contacts and making new ones ... Hugh D. has preserved an oyster-like silence about his mission to London, with the result that all his old acquaintances – and he has thousands of them here – have been kept speculating.*[378]

There was a rumour that he would bring the brilliant Australian welterweight, Ambrose Palmer, to London to fight Eddie "The Viking Assassin" Wenstob, the Canadian light heavyweight champion. According to Mack, Palmer turned down the offer ("He could have cleaned up £10,000 by Christmas. Well, he chose not to come, so that's that!"). The distraction served its purpose, as Mack got down to the business of seeking local backers, negotiating with London's Milk Board officials, and teeing up Norman's financial injection into the new company. For his part, Norman had Stewart Dawson business to attend to in the short term. The Regent Street shop was finally closing, and he oversaw the sale and disposal of the fittings and furniture. All the gorgeous showcases, the crystal chandeliers, the polished counter tops and drawers that his father had so lovingly selected, were piled onto trolleys or packed in crates for transport to the auction rooms. Only the ornate ceilings and still-decorated walls remained from the glory days of long ago, forlornly awaiting a new tenant who, ignorant of their heritage, would paint and board them over. In Hatton Garden, Stewart Dawson's had retreated to a couple of floors of the Treasure House, sub-letting much of the rest for offices and small businesses taking advantage of low rents. The building was on the market but there were no bids.

Back in Australia, Harriet learned, Percy seemed to be relaxing for the first time in years. His dealing with the constant pressure of managing the moribund Strand business while juggling the affairs of his family reminded Harriet of an entertainer keeping a row of spinning plates from tumbling. She was delighted to hear that he had purchased a racehorse and was about to plunge into the Sydney season. The colt, which he named "Strathisla", in honour of his father, was well bred, by Brazen from Chattering Maiden. He'd paid a good price: 575 guineas* for the yearling, so must have high expectations. Though he hadn't won, Strathisla had made a good showing on his first outing as a two-year-old in the Nursery Handicap at Victoria Park.† Harriet felt a tingle as she read Percy's account of the day. She must make a point of being at the track should she return to Sydney. A flutter with the bookmakers was still one of the highlights of her life in Europe and England, as was a new-found interest: lotteries. She had bought a ticket once or twice in the Harbour Bridge lottery during the twenties but had not felt the urge to be a regular gambler as long as "the Stewart Dawson Bank" had met her every financial need without question. Here, it was quite a different matter. European lotteries proliferated,[379] with tickets on sale everywhere and prizes that far exceeded any she had seen in Australia. Moreover, though her annuity from the estate should have been more than adequate for her needs, even including the running costs of Villa Bon Accord, she was beginning to feel the constraints of a fixed income, even the necessity for budgeting. Her instinct was to look for alternative sources of funds, and absent the Stewart Dawson Bank, she turned to the racetrack and the lottery ticket sellers, where the potential reward could be an independent fortune. In this she found an ally in Kathleen who, despite her very different upbringing and bohemian character, and notwithstanding Harriet's generosity, craved freedom from financial burdens to pursue her artistic destiny.

The disposal of the Regent Street shop fittings behind him, Norman bent his attention to Mack's grand plan. They had found a suitable site for the first bar in Fleet Street. David would have

---

* 525 guineas (£577/10/-) was worth about £35,000 in 2018.

† Strathisla placed fourth in his maiden outing. Referee (Sydney) 20th June 1935 P.4

approved of the prominent corner location, a vacant shop with large windows and space in back rooms for storage and administration. Negotiations with the Milk Board progressed without a hitch, after Mack blustered his way past bemused receptionists to make his pitch to the officials. Fit out commenced in great secrecy. Refrigerators and dispensing equipment were acquired and installed, the décor was modelled on the Martin Place "Black and White" bar, and the better hotels and cafés were combed to find the most personable young staff. Mack, the showman, made use of his theatrical contacts to find a glamorous "personality" who might be unemployed and willing to lend her attractions behind the bar. His predictions about the popularity of milk bars had proven accurate back in Sydney. By the beginning of 1935, as well as the Black and White, Sydney had The State (at the State Theatre), Burt's at two Pitt Street addresses, the Everest in Martin Place, Potter's in George Street, and the Lyric, two doors from the eponymous theatre.[380] In just the past year, patronage had leapt 200 per cent, as more men transferred their allegiance from the increasingly restricted and ill-maintained traditional bars to smart, modern venues where there was the added attraction of being able to share a drink with female customers. Sydney's "Truth" observed:

> *The odd thing about this new clientele is that men and women are of the well-dressed office type, and a social flair is introduced over the very pretty tables and nooks when groups of friends come together. There are no odors of greasy cooking hanging around milk bars, no long waiting for courses to appear in humid surroundings. The charming uniformed girls work like automats, and the creamy preparations which satisfy the palate so much are so obviously stimulating that queues five and six deep are noticed in the peak hours.*[381]

Fired up by the good news, Mack and Norman applied themselves to the task. By the end of June, the Fleet Street bar was almost ready for opening. Mack could wait no longer, he gave interviews to selected reporters and columnists in London and, for good measure, in Australia. Styling himself "The Milk King", he announced the opening, not of a single milk bar, but of the first of a chain of 500 milk bars in Britain. Harriet was both confused and shocked. Five hundred milk bars in Britain? Hadn't Norman listened to Percy's advice to take one step at a time? There was a lot of Stewart Dawson capital at stake and while she, and she was sure, Percy, had every confidence in Mack's experience in this line of business, wouldn't it have been prudent to wait until the Fleet Street bar had established a reputation before announcing another 499? And what was this "Black and White" business? Had Mick Adams, in Martin Place, given permission to use his now-trademarked business name, including the appended "4d" (a reference to the price of the beverage)? Did he know that Mack planned to copy his drink recipes? Probably not, but what could he do about it from the other side of the world? In any case, the name was only protected in Australia so why not exploit it here in England? It was catchy, sounded up-to-date and, incidentally, it was too late as he had already registered it and decorated the bar to match. Moreover, as Harriet should have known, had she read the news, the Milk Marketing Board had stolen a march on Mack (stolen his idea, to be precise) by staging an event at the Bath and West annual agricultural show, held in Taunton, Somerset, in May of the year.[382] Knowing his plans, the least they could have done was to wait until after Fleet Street had opened. Now, thanks to glowing reports of the Taunton event, word had got around that this Australian craze was coming to Britain. The Derby, at Epson, had followed with its own milk bar in June,[383] and several large catering companies had expressed interest in setting up their own chains of bars. Now that the cat was out of the bag, Mack and Norman had to move fast and decisively to deter early competition.

On August 1st, the Black and White 4d milk bar opened its doors on the corner of Fleet and Whitefriars Streets. In some regards, it was not an auspicious day. Fleet Street was about to undergo weeks of disruptive repairs, causing no end of inconvenience to pedestrians and motorists. Pneumatic drills deafened passers-by who were forced to navigate around piles of rubble left by the pick and shovel men and teeter on temporary plank bridges over muddy trenches. Nevertheless, more than a few had their efforts rewarded upon entering the already crowded interior of the corner bar. The opening ceremony was performed by Canon "Dick" Sheppard, former Dean of Canterbury, who gave a witty and entertaining speech. The renowned pacifist had been partly responsible in 1926 for the annual Festival of Remembrance in the Albert Hall a week before Remembrance Sunday. Thanks to his military connections, Norman was able to approach Sheppard with a persuasive argument that promotion of milk drinking could alleviate production surpluses while encouraging temperance and healthy living habits. Ten waitresses were kept busy serving plain milk and a selection of fifty other beverages containing milk and fruit ingredients. A crowd formed outside as curious passers-by joined those who awaited their chance to sample the fare and stake their minor place in history, for it was apparent that a craze was about to be born. The following day, enthusiastic reports filled the social and gossip columns of London papers, soon to be followed by a wave of syndicated accounts throughout the land. Norman could not believe their luck, though Mack, his eyes on a horizon crowded with hundreds more Black and Whites, preferred to attribute the success to his vision and thorough planning.

By October, business exploded. A constant stream of customers – newspaper workers, typists, roadmen still at work in the street, clerks, and shopkeepers on their lunch break – filled the spacious premises. Milk consumption had rocketed to 150 gallons a day, seven days a week. Mack himself often presided at the bar, studying the customers, watching their reaction to his ideas, always ready to mix a new drink for a colonial or foreign visitor who knew a good recipe. As winter approached, hot drinks and soups appeared on the menu. The quest to find more premises around London had started in earnest and Mack, claiming the availability of £1,000,000 in capital, had sent feelers out into the provinces.[384] Harriet began to feel that Percy's initial reservations might have been exaggerated and, as she prepared to escape the British winter once more, she looked forward to more good news from Fleet Street.

This Sporting Life

The maid brought the day's mail and Harriet shuffled the envelopes in search of familiar handwriting. Nothing from Kathleen, though she was due for another visit, but here was one she'd been expecting, covered in stamps depicting kangaroos, ANZAC, the King riding his horse for the Royal Jubilee.* Percy's determined scrawl spelled out her address and, turning the envelope over, she observed that he remained at the apartment he'd taken at Potts Point. Nothing much changed with Percy. But, no, there on the first page of the letter was interesting news. She was thrilled, and a tiny bit envious to learn that, free of immediate concerns over the family investment, Percy was able to focus on his new love, racing. Strathisla was beginning to attract the attention of the punters and sporting writers and Percy spared no expense in training and preparing him. He had been rewarded on Saturday, September 28th, when jockey Darby Munro pinched the lead on the final turn of the Hawkesbury Maiden to beat Marina by a head. With typical bad luck, Percy was confined to bed with a severe cold and had to be content with listening in on the wireless.[385] Still, it was a start, a promise of good times ahead for the two-year-old and who knew how many seasons of parading in the winner's enclosure? Between his occasional trips to Perth, where the remaining Stewart Dawson shop still kept its head above water, and less frequent journeys north, tidying up the affairs of the defunct Brisbane outlet, he could indulge himself at Sydney's better restaurants in the company of old cronies from as far back as the war years. Stuart and Jean could often be counted on to turn up on social occasions, particularly when they could mingle with the members on race days. Percy noted that his brother had yet to pay a visit to New Zealand and seemed in no hurry to show the flag across the Tasman Sea. It was of

---

* Australian stamps in circulation in 1935 included the well-established kangaroo image, a commemorative issue for the 20th anniversary of the Gallipoli landings by the ANZAC Brigade, and a commemorative issue celebrating the 25th anniversary of the accession of King George V.

some comfort that the local managers in Auckland and Wellington could be relied upon to maintain a profit and the good name of the company, but it would not have surprised him if they felt cast adrift by the parent company. He'd have to have a word with Stuart and get him on a boat to Auckland.

As for Norman, since the disposal of the Regent Street assets he'd set aside his responsibilities as Managing Director of the United Kingdom business, devoting his time to Mack and the grand plan for expanding the milk bar chain. It was now that Percy began to suspect a degree of "flimflam" in the sporadic communications from London. As the months passed with more of Mack's extravagant forecasts of hundreds of new bars (what on earth was this talk of £1,000,000 waiting to be invested?) his concern over the health of the business grew. It was proving difficult, if not impossible, to prise any detailed financial information out of Mack or Norman. Constant reports of booming sales did little to reassure him of the fundamental profitability of Black and White Milk Bars. He was confident the Fleet Street shop could be viable on its own but already competition was emerging in every quarter, and not just in London. At prices that matched Black and White, the many new entrants left little room for Mack to stand out from the crowd. Percy knew that margins were already tight, and profits relied on high turnover. The bars, unlike the Australian prototypes, lacked seats, the theory being that standing encouraged patrons to drink up and vacate the space for the next customer. Proprietors had gone so far as to calculate an optimum drinking time of four minutes during rush hours.[386] It would only be a matter of time before the market became overcrowded, patronage declined from the initial dizzy heights, and pencils would have to be sharpened. He'd seen it all before at The Ambassadors and in the jewellery stores, but those had been substantial undertakings, with plenty of reserve capital, wide margins in the case of Stewart Dawson's, that permitted considerable latitude in discounting, and a "slow but steady" business philosophy, thanks to his father, that conserved retained profits even after their demise. Why, he'd even managed to secure a decent price for the remaining Stewart Dawson shop, in Perth, this very month, thanks to prudent management practice and loyal customers. The local manager, Mr Barker, had been with the firm since the beginning, and his "steady as she goes" philosophy had paid dividends, so that when Percy's father had closed the shops on the eastern seaboard, there had been no question of Perth following suit. Now, as Percy turned to family matters, the time had come to hand over the baton and it was loyal Mr Barker who grasped it, raising the money to purchase the business while retaining the Stewart Dawson name.* Would that Mack and Norman understood the value of patience and frugality, of knowing their competitors and the market before risking all. The problem was, at this distance, on the other side of the world, Percy's appeals for constraint fell on deaf ears and he could only trust in the momentum of the first year building a sufficiently strong base for the proposed expansion.

It was all too much for his mother to take in. Her instinct was to trust Percy's judgment, but her heart still belonged to Norman, and Mack's charm could always beguile her. She put aside her worries for the time being. She had guests to welcome at the villa and her granddaughter to divert her during the winter holidays. Young Harriet was a quick study and had soon found her feet in the school at nearby Cannes. She was becoming fluent in French, far quicker than her grandmother had achieved. Thinking of the little girl prompted further concern for young David. By all accounts he was doing well at Cranbrook, still excelling at sports, and now winning races in inter-schools swimming carnivals, but the word from Percy was that he was very often alone at home, save for a housekeeper. Stuart and Jean's social life left them little time for domestic affairs, and they were often

---

* S J Barker started with the Sydney branch of Stewart Dawson at the turn of the century and was dispatched to Perth when that store opened. He remained in charge the rest of his working life. The Sunday Times (Perth) reported on February 2nd, 1936 (p.9): *"When many of the old customers expressed such concern at the closing of the place where they had bought their sweethearts' gifts, the engagement ring, wedding ring, and perhaps the first gift for the little stranger, Mr Barker felt that something ought to be done to try and keep the name before the Western Australian public. With this end in view West Australian capital was found to purchase the business as a going concern, so the old familiar name will continue at the old address for many years."* Stewart Dawson's, Perth, survived until the 1950s.

out of town at this or that seaside resort. Even as she read Percy's latest letter, they were galivanting in Brisbane while David kicked his heels alone for the Christmas holidays. She would make another appeal, via Percy, to David's parents. Give the lad a chance at a more fulfilling life in Europe, a wider education that would make a real man of him in his grandfather's image. Harriet would be able to reunite the two children and show them the best of Europe and Britain in ways that Stuart could never accomplish. There were signs the Depression was easing, even France seemed to be recovering from the worst of it, and great cities such as London, Paris and Rome welcomed growing numbers of young tourists. Berlin was drawing new visitors, as preparations advanced for the Olympic Games. How could Stuart fail to see the advantages of exposing his son to this cornucopia of culture in his formative years? Harriet relied on Percy to persuade Stuart (Jean would have little or no say in the matter) and started to plan for David's arrival in the new year.

Mack welcomed 1936 with the opening of the second Black and White milk bar in Cheapside, within sight of St. Paul's Cathedral.[387] So, after all, the expansion was under way. Once more, he and Norman staged an opening ceremony, now with Dean Talbot, of Sydney and the businessman/politician, Sir Newton Moore. Moore was a good catch for Mack, due to his peerless reputation both as a former soldier (he had taken charge of the training of all Australian Imperial Force reinforcements in England from 1916) and as a high-profile representative of Australia in British politics. The site of the bar had been chosen to capture custom. Just opposite the busy Central Telegraph Office, it would soon take advantage of the opening of the new Post Office Underground station,* one of whose exits would be on the footpath in front of the bar. Like the Fleet Street establishment, it would suffer the inconvenience of road works for many months, but Mack's gamble was that the benefits would soon outweigh the short-term costs. However, the two partners had scarcely had time to celebrate the opening when they blotted their copybook with a high-handed dismissal of one of their Fleet Street employees that gained

* Now St. Paul's Station. Like the Fleet Street milk bar site, the building in which the milk bar was located was demolished many years ago.

them notoriety in the press. The Daily Worker, Britain's Communist Party daily tabloid, reported:[388]

> *Six months ago the premises of Black and White Milk Bars Ltd., in Fleet Street were formally opened by the Rev. Dick Shepherd. Some weeks ago an employee of the firm was put on night duty, from 8 p.m. to 8 a.m., to cleanse utensils, crockery, etc. He worked six nights a week (i.e. a 72-hour week) for £2 per week. Three weeks before receiving this notice, the worker wrote to McIntosh, the firm's general manager, requesting a rise, and pointing out that he worked 12 hours in a continuous shift. He asked for meal times to be allowed, as was the custom among employees on the day shift. He received a rise, which brought his wage up to £2/5/- per week, but no mention was made of meal times. On this sum he had to keep a wife and three children. On the Monday before his dismissal he again wrote to the general manager asking for a further 5/- rise and repeating his request for official meal times on the grounds put forward in his previous letter. In reply, he received the following letter: –*
>
> *"In reply to your letter, I regret to say that it will not be possible for me to consider any further raise in your salary, and as you seem to take a very keen interest in other people's affairs and their working hours, etc., I will be glad if you will take this as a formal notice to end your employment.*
>
> *We have quite enough to do to make our business pay, without being worried by repeated requests for increases. The work does not justify any more than we are paying."*
>
> The Daily Worker added:
>
> *The Hon. Hugh McIntosh stood as Labor candidate for Ross and Cromarty constituency in 1929 – he was unsuccessful. During the campaign he said that he was so impressed by the appalling conditions in which many of the Highlanders lived, that he broke down. The chairman of the directors is Major Stewart-Dawson, D.S.O., D.S.C. He recently acquired a new Rolls-Royce (cost, £2,500), complete with wireless (five valve), cocktail bar, refrigerator and picnic outfit.*

Imperious behaviour such as this would have been unknown in the Stewart Dawson era. David's employees, whether in the shops or at The Ambassadors, were valued and respected. Yes, many of them worked long hours, particularly in the heyday of The Ambassadors, but it could never be said that they were exploited or taken for granted. Dismissals were rare, and always for good cause. Even the squabbling kitchen hands brought to court in 1924 had retained their positions after suitable admonishment. If word got around that hard work and long hours were no guarantee of secure employment, how could Black and White attract and retain good employees? The case was a gift to the Daily Worker, which seldom missed an opportunity to criticise capitalists who should have known better. But what was more disturbing for the likes of Percy was Mack's "We have quite enough to do to make our business pay …" If it were true that Black and White was feeling the pinch with only two branches open, then how could they expect twenty, fifty or, heaven forbid, five hundred to turn a profit? Percy decided it was time to take a closer look and booked passage to England, sailing from Sydney on the Orion on March 11th.

Percy's trip had a double purpose; accompanying him was his nephew, bound for reunion with the two Harriets and the education his grandmother had always advocated. As expected, Stuart and Jean had raised no objection to Percy's suggestion that David be removed from Cranbrook and the family home. On the contrary, they appeared relieved of the imposition on their frenetic social life. Stuart showed no sign of maturity in business or his personal dealings. He still spent his allowance on entertainment and cars and continued to bet at and off the track. His driving habits were notorious and even as Percy sailed north, he was facing a charge for reckless driving that would lose him his licence for three years. He had been pursued by police and caught speeding at up to sixty miles an hour along one of Sydney's busiest thoroughfares, Parramatta Road, overtaking all traffic and thundering through a shopping area in the centre of the road. After three previous convictions for dangerous driving, the most recent only a month before, Stuart exhausted the magistrate's forbearance ("My duty to the public compels me to take this course." pronounced Mr. Parker, SM) and Stuart was fined £30 and "grounded".* However, he seemed to learn nothing and care less, brushing aside the conviction and the, for him, paltry fine. Jean was a competent driver, and they were seldom out alone, so for the time being he suffered little inconvenience. Within a week he was back behind the wheel, sans licence. Stopped by the police at Penrith, forty miles to Sydney's west, he was asked to present his licence. He panicked: "I haven't got it and anyhow, if I had it, I wouldn't show it to you." When the constable then demanded his name and address, he claimed to be Percy Dawson, of Bellevue Hill (Stuart was then living in Vaucluse). Percy was overseas, oblivious to his brother's attempt to saddle him with the offence but Stuart's foolish diversion, (perhaps recalling Norman's equally flimsy attempt back in 1915) was foiled by the simplest of police checks and he was fined yet again.[389]

Percy and David landed at Villefranche at the end of March and drove the five miles or so to Monte Carlo, to be greeted by a beaming Harriet. What a victory that had been for love and common sense, she recalled. Young David had matured since she had last seen him. Though still short in stature and slightly built, rather more like Percy than his father, he had Stuart's dark, good looks, and Norman's steely gaze, or what she remembered of that youthful demeanour, now blunted by the years. His self-assurance was, if anything, greater than before, though there was less of the childish petulance she had endured when they last met. Those rough edges would need more polish, but he was only fourteen. A couple of years at a good English school would make all the difference. Meantime, he could enjoy the best that Monaco and the Riviera had to offer for a young lad, reacquaint himself with his sister and enliven his grandmother's days.

Percy's errand complete, he boarded the train for Calais and the cross-Channel ferry, arriving in London early in April. He was feeling rather satisfied. Upon arriving at Villa Bon Accord he'd been pleased to announce to his mother the second victory of Strathisla, the Flying

---

* Sun 6th May 1936 P.13, referring to the dangerous driving offence committed on March 28th, when he was fined £20 for speeding at up to 72mph on the Great Western road near Penrith (Labor Daily, 9th April p.16). The road in those days was sealed but narrow, so Stuart's speed would have been excessively dangerous.

Welter at Moorefield, on February 29th. Lucky leap year! they agreed. It looked as if class and breeding were beginning to show in the two-year-old and that a long and successful career lay ahead for the horse and his owner. Harriet couldn't have been more thrilled, and Percy left the villa in high spirits. Upon his arrival in London, his mood darkened when he learned that Mack had announced another of his sporting enterprises, promotion of six-day bicycle races in Great Britain and Ireland. He had gone into partnership with the Australian cycling champion, Arthur Shepherd, obtaining a concession from the National Cyclists' Union for sole rights to run the races. Percy knew that these cycling marathons were popular in America, France, and Germany. They offered the same facilities for a "flutter" as horse- or dog-racing. International professionals would take part in the English races, for prizes up to £500 and Wembley Stadium would be the headquarters. Mack had the concession for ten years and claimed to be forming a company, once private capital had been subscribed.[390] Percy was annoyed. Here was another distraction from the milk bar venture just when Mack ought to be devoting more, not less attention to building its profits. Knowing his propensity to rob Peter to pay Paul, who was to say that, excited by the prospect of sporting fame through staging the cycling marathons, he would not be tempted to divert funds from an already stretched Black and White?

Percy's meeting with Mack and Norman was brief and tense, but though he was tempted to read the riot act, he succumbed to Mack's charm and confidence yet again. First, Percy need have no concern that the cycling races would be a distraction. Mack would only have a part-time involvement and they would be over in a matter of weeks. As for the milk bars, all would be well, a fortune was being built even as they spoke, "just come and see for yourself at Fleet Street." But what about cash flow? Rents in central London were crippling, employment costs could get out of hand if they ran more than one shift per day, buying and storing all those perishable ingredients absorbed a lot of profits. Now they were talking about dozens more bars just as the competition was awakening. Apart from the many temporary bars at fêtes and race days, permanent ones that copied Black and White were springing up as far away as Plymouth, Uxbridge, Skipton in Yorkshire, Dundee, and Northampton. In

Birmingham, the Milk Board had announced plans to open a thousand bars across the East Midlands by mid-summer. The makers of Ovaltine, the popular malted beverage, had cashed in on the craze with a barrage of advertisements encouraging consumption of the drink: "In wintry weather, fortify yourself during the day by drinking Ovaltine at your café, restaurant or milk bar, the surest safeguard against coughs, colds, influenza and other winter ailments." Mack's opinion was that this was proof of the soundness of his vision. All that was needed was time and another injection of capital to establish the next premises, which were to open shortly in Leicester Square. Percy's appeal to Norman to assert his directorial authority was met with a shrug and the assurance that any new cash would be wisely spent and bound to return a dividend. Unconvinced, Percy left without a commitment to risk further Stewart Dawson capital. As he sailed back to Australia in May, his failure to influence the partners weighed upon him. Sooner or later he was sure he would have to deal with another business collapse not of his making.

In Royal Circles

Hindsight, Harriet mused, is a wonderful thing, always infallible, usually clear, and very handy for sweeping away life's embarrassing mistakes. It would be easy to explain the events of nineteen thirty six and seven with a few "If onlys": "If only Percy had remained strong and determined"; "If only Norman had taken charge as he later showed he could"; "If only I had reminded them all of dear David's words: 'Impatience is one of the penalties for doing poor work'. But I didn't speak up, Percy gave in once again, and Norman took the easy way out, more's the pity. Sitting here in Sydney nearly a decade later, I can make sense of it all and forgive the mistakes and foolishness, but I could not in honesty say that I foresaw the future. Everyone (almost everyone; Percy excepted) was so optimistic, and, to tell the truth, I was confused and distracted much of the time, so many things seemed to be happening at such a pace, so much change and such terrible loss."

As Percy prepared to depart from Sydney, early in 1936, the news had broken of the death of the King. George V had been a revered rock of sensible stability throughout his reign, cementing the dignity of the royal family as he maintained Britain's hold on the Empire and her place in European and world affairs. David had held him in enormous esteem, the bastion of imperial power in the face of a rising America, his marriage to the German-born Queen Mary a symbol of the unifying power of dynastic alliances. His presence behind successive United Kingdom governments assured the people that, despite the trials of the war, the hurly burly of the 1920s and the pain of the Depression years, there would always be a guiding light to better times. And now he was gone. They had known of his failing health for some time, of course, but this seemed so sudden, hard to accept. It was as if they had been willing him to survive and preserve that sensible stability until his son and heir proved able to succeed him. For, as Harriet and practically anybody knew, the Prince of Wales showed little sign of being prepared for the role, despite his many years in waiting. Make no mistake, the Prince's glamorous life and loves enthralled Harriet as much as the next woman (or man, for that matter). Ever since his brief visit to Sydney all those years ago, the appeal of the handsome "eternal youth" had been a factor in her growing fascination for English and Continental society. Her Anglophilia had ripened during the war years and his arrival in Sydney in 1920, so soon after her own return, only served to remind her of what she might be sacrificing by re-joining her husband in the land down under. The Prince's appearance at Mrs MacLurcan's ballroom had spurred David and Percy to go one better with The Ambassadors, but it was she, Harriet, who had reigned over the many balls and dances held there, always in the hope of snaring the dashing young bachelor prince, should he grace Australian shores once more. And it had not been an idle wish; on more than one occasion there had been rumours of a return visit and The Ambassadors was prepared at short notice to host the royal party. Alas, the only royals to tour Australia in that decade were the Duke and Duchess of York, not quite the Prince but a nice couple all the same. Such a pity that their itinerary had left no room for late night dining and dancing, as Harriet and Percy discovered, to their disappointment. On March 30th, 1927, The Ambassadors staged the Big Brothers Ball, yet another of the regular charity events for which it was famous. It was one of those rare occasions when Harriet was not present. Had she been, who knows how she would have reacted when, at 10 o'clock, excited committee women whispered together loud enough for many to hear: "The Duke is coming!"? Officials were questioned. They answered definitely: "Yes, he will soon be here." The president of the organising committee, Mrs Hotham, with a bodyguard of two gentlemen, sat upstairs in the entrance hall and waited. The Duke was at least not going to arrive unheralded or unmet. Enthusiasm ran high when General Lloyd, the Aide de Camp, arrived. Surely this was the advance guard. He talked soothingly for a few moments to besieging women who demanded the Duke then, with commendable diplomacy, he disentangled himself, beckoned to Percy, and the two men retired to a corner. After the general left, Percy broke the news: General Lloyd had come to ask if the Randalls, the dance act of the night, would go on to perform at Government House after their appearance, and also to say that the Duke was going to visit The

Ambassadors before he left Sydney.[391] As soon as Harriet and David learned of this, preparations began for the impending gala occasion which, if not a "Prince of Wales Evening", would outshine any vice-regal affair and put Mrs Maclurcan in her place for once. Harriet blushed now as she recalled the lengths they had gone to, the not-so-discreet publicity they had circulated about the forthcoming evening, only to be disappointed once more when, on Saturday April 4th, instead of the Duke (and, they had hoped, the Duchess), The Ambassadors entertained General the Earl of Cavan, the Duke's Chief of Staff, accompanied by the Countess and Miss Elaine de Chair, daughter of the Governor. A substitute for a substitute! She and David were among the guests, as were Percy and Rita, and they had decorated the ballroom with red roses and blue delphiniums. Some noted that the decorations used for the Millions Club dinner dance a few nights before had been allowed to do duty again but conceded that that did not diminish one's regard for their beauty.[392] Harriet had not, after all, pulled out all the stops.

But that was the way with Royalty, they came and went as they chose, bestowing or withholding their aura. Not that this casual attitude to their subjects in any way diminished their appeal: noblesse could choose exactly how to oblige. Harriet was not alone in hoping that, one day, she would be granted access, however brief, to the royal circle. Her residences in London and Monte Carlo gave her a box seat in the theatre of princes, dukes, counts and assorted aristocracy, with its intrigues, scandals, romantic liaisons, and eternal glamour. Monte Carlo and Cannes swarmed with displaced aristocrats, many "on the make" after losing their titles, estates, and hereditary rights in the aftermath of the war. At the Casino, whether seated at the gaming tables or playing some undefined role in the employ of the proprietor, could be seen erstwhile rulers of vast land holdings, lesser sons of ancient families and others of dubious heritage who nonetheless conveyed the right air of patronage and sang froid. As Harriet placed her bets or occasionally collected her winnings, she sometimes wondered at their reaction should it be revealed that this gracious, sumptuously dressed dowager had her origins behind the bar of a Liverpool pub. She had come a long way from that and was ever careful to cultivate and maintain her image as one, if not of the "old monied" class, at least a cut above the vulgar parvenus taking advantage of the undervalued franc.

And then, just as she arrived at Villa Bon Accord for the winter season of '35, the word was that the Prince himself might be seen with his "companion", Mrs Simpson, at any time. The couple had been holidaying in Europe since early in the year and both favoured the Riviera, having cruised the Mediterranean on board Lord Moyne's yacht the previous year. Dividing her time, as she did, between London and France, Harriet deprecated the hypocrisy of the British ruling class over the matter. While the affair was common knowledge on the Continent, openly discussed by European sophisticates (among whom she now counted herself), in Britain a curtain of silence had been drawn. Not a word, not even a hint, of the depth of the relationship appeared in print or radio broadcast, though the Prince's movements and selected photographs of him golfing, skiing, swimming and occasionally performing royal duties were in every newspaper, as they had been for years. Now it seemed that the couple might well make their appearance in the crowded principality where close encounters were practically inevitable. Her long-postponed meeting with the Prince could be days away, with the bonus of a close-up look at the mystery woman in his life. But, no, rumour it had been and rumour it remained. The Prince was next reported back in London with Mrs Simpson by his side. Harriet would have to be patient if she expected a royal encounter.

But the King died and overnight the blindfold was lifted from British eyes when Edward broke royal protocol on the day of his proclamation by appearing at the window of St. James' Palace with Mrs Simpson. It was now open season on the couple, and Harriet, still at Villa Bon Accord, was as caught up in the gossip and speculation as anyone, so much so that, what with her concerns for the two grandchildren, maintaining her almost daily correspondence with Kathleen and Percy, and a niggling uneasiness whenever she checked her bank balance, she failed to take a stronger stand with Norman and Mack. In hindsight, it should have been obvious, had she paid attention to Percy's warnings. It wasn't as if she was some naïve flibbertigibbet. Though she hadn't been privy to David's day to day business decisions, listening to him pontificate and observing successes and failures in retail and real estate had sharpened her senses sufficiently to find her sharing Percy's suspicions. It was just that, at the time, she had been distracted by family and society happenings.

Throughout 1936 the Black and White milk bars were seldom out of the newspapers. Harriet stood at Norman's side for the opening of the Leicester Square branch in May. Perhaps the target of hundreds of bars might be achieved. However, by mid-year, Percy's worst fears were realised when he received an appeal for more money from Norman. Just as he had predicted, the operating bars were generating insufficient surplus cash to invest in the many planned outlets. Mack had applied for another dozen or so licences and found sites for even more future bars without consideration of the immense establishment costs involved. His optimistic "She'll be right!" response to Percy's cautionary inquiries was received with deep suspicion, confirmed by Norman's plea for financial relief. Percy's preference would have been to deny the request, put a stop to the foolishness and wear the losses incurred to the family endowment, but once more, common sense did not prevail. Norman's influence on his distracted mother was still strong and, out of the blue, Stuart leapt to Norman's defence, spotting an opportunity to stake his own claim to an early share of his inheritance. Why not free up idle money from the Stewart Dawson trusts and companies by setting up a new company to invest in the milk bars? "You mean, bail Norman out?" was Percy's weary response. All the same, Stuart persisted, it could work if the venture gained the momentum that Mack predicted and, on the face of it, the market still seemed to be booming. So, exercising his power as trustee of the family estate, on August 1st, Percy registered Stewart Dawson Investments Ltd., nominal capital £10,000, objects: "to acquire and deal in shares, stocks, mortgages &c." Percy and Stuart were principal subscribers and there were five others, including Constantine Don Service, head of the family law firm. Each was granted one share (nominal value: £1). Pressed by Norman to deliver the rescue funds, Percy used his trustee power to draw cash from the family companies and deposit it in Stewart Dawson Investments, from where it was "invested" in Norman's name in the milk bars. Norman received just over £42,000 and Stuart demanded and received nearly £38,500. Percy reasoned that he was owed his share for the risk he was taking and awarded himself a little over £35,000. That would keep Strathisla in oats for a while.

And perhaps that was what the horse needed. After the initial wins, Strathisla had placed second or third in every subsequent race. A place was better than nothing, but the colt seemed to shy from tight competition on approach to the finishing line despite the efforts of his hard-working jockey. He was fit, started, and ran well and had a good temperament but it seemed he lacked true competitive spirit. Poor Percy, thought Harriet. Just when he looked to be on a winner, fate had dealt another weak hand to him. After the gruelling years of The Ambassadors, the let-down of the Strand Arcade sale, and the out of control milk bar "investment" he deserved some sort of reward or relief from business burdens. Instead, it seemed that Strathisla would serve as a reminder of Percy's "also ran" status. Not that there was a lack of sympathy for Percy. Punters and racing commentators agreed that he deserved better luck than this and there was no shortage of support in the betting ring for the two-year-old, to the delight of the bookmakers.

Upon learning of Percy's rescue mission for Norman and Mack, Harriet relaxed, persuaded now that the worst was over for the cash-strapped company. By the end of 1936 twelve Black and Whites were open in London, each new opening attended by much publicity and another interview with Mack in one newspaper or another, replete with colourful anecdotes and reminiscences. Mack's cycle races also kept his name before the public, with the first staged in September. To inaugurate the season, he gave a luncheon at the Savoy. Guest of honour was Sir Malcolm Campbell, the record-breaking car and speedboat driver, who observed: "Cycling is doing a lot to remedy Britain's deficiency in physical fitness." He raised a laugh when he joked: "I realised early in 1901 that wife beating was cheaper than speeding. I was fined 30/- for cycling at 28½ miles an hour, and a wife beater was only fined 2/6."[393] As so often happened with Mack's enterprises, the success of the first race was not repeated and he lost interest as the milk bar business consumed more of his time and resources.

Meantime, Harriet's fascination with royal scandals reached its peak when, in October, Edward announced his intention to marry Mrs

Simpson as soon as she was free from her second marriage. He was to be crowned the following January and suddenly all eyes were on Westminster, the heads of the Church and the peripatetic Mrs Simpson. As one who, unlike most British subjects, had been aware of the early development of the affair, Harriet was not as surprised by the announcement as the general public appeared to be, nor did it offend her. Her own private life, should it have been revealed in the circles in which she moved, would have raised more than a few eyebrows, and yet she and David had enjoyed a long and mostly happy marriage. Upon reflection, she allowed that they had had the advantage of preserving discretion, thanks to the ease with which they had been able to cover their tracks, a convenience not enjoyed by the Royal family. When the scandal became a crisis in December, thanks to a comment from the Bishop of Bradford: "We hope that he [Edward] is aware of his need [of Divine Grace]. Some of us wish that he gave more positive signs of his awareness," Mrs Simpson fled England for the Riviera, just as Harriet was unpacking for another winter season at Villa Bon Accord.

Harriet's spirits were low. Compounding her distraction over other family affairs and her fascination with the unfolding royal crisis, she was shocked and saddened to learn that her beloved brother, Malcolm, had died suddenly on November 15th, at home in The Spinney. He was just 67, enjoying his retirement in Springwood. Popular and respected in the town, he was mourned by a large congregation at the Frazer Memorial church. He was buried in the Presbyterian section of Springwood Cemetery, a few yards from Valerie's grave. The funeral over, Agnes and the girls, Roma and Joy, were already packing their bags to return to Sydney. Their attachment to the Mountains town had never been as firm as Malcolm's and now that he was gone there seemed little purpose in isolating themselves from city life, where their circle of friends remained strong. Within weeks they had moved to a flat in Edgecliff, not far from Percy and Stuart's residences. Roma had a clerical position with a city firm, while Joy stayed home to keep house for her grieving mother. With their departure, the Stewart Dawson connection with Springwood was over or, not quite, as Harriet reminded herself. Estelle Allison, now about to turn twenty-one, remained with Tom and Annie senior at Bonnie Doon. Under the terms of David's will, she would obtain full title to the residence on her birthday.* David and Harriet had kept themselves informed of the young woman's progress and development during her school years and had been intrigued to learn of her aptitude for music, which they were sure she had inherited from her father. Estelle had won many prizes for piano at school and eisteddfods and was at this very moment about to graduate from college with a music teaching degree. Tom was still employed as a handyman and caretaker at Bon Accord guest house, the lessees having kept on most of the staff when Percy and Mack handed over the keys. Despite her preference for the sophistication of European civilization, Harriet retained fond memories of weekends with David at Davesta and later with Agnes and Malcolm, Percy, dear Lord Beauchamp, and friends at Bon Accord guest house after a round of golf. The continuing success of the guest house (word was it still attracted travellers and weekenders from the city in satisfactory numbers) would attest to David's and Percy's good sense and honour the memory of poor Malcolm in some degree. She would have to remember to pay a visit upon her return to Australia, whenever that might be, to lay flowers on Malcolm's grave and make a courtesy call on Tom, Annie, and Estelle.

For the time being, catching up with old acquaintances in Monte Carlo and perhaps a day trip to Cannes could be the pick-me-up she needed. The gossip about Mrs Simpson was rife and it was soon common knowledge that she was the guest of her friends, Mr and Mrs Herman Rogers, at Villa Lou Viei, just outside Cannes. Curiosity overcame Harriet and she summoned her chauffeur, if nothing else the drive along the coast and through Nice would help blow away the cobwebs. Less than two hours later the villa came into view. In normal times it would have been indistinguishable from the many similar two-storey stuccoed houses crowding the hillside, but today it was impossible to miss. For almost half a mile in every direction the streets

---

* The land upon which Bonnie Doon stood was excised from the original estate under separate title when David transferred overall title to himself after Valerie's death in 1918. Estelle inherited the property, but it was held in trust on her behalf pending her majority in December 1936.

leading to Villa Lou Viei were jammed with motor cars and the arched gateway swarmed with photographers and reporters competing for a glimpse of the mystery woman. From time to time an official-looking black limousine drew up and the word went up that this or that government official had arrived. The elusive Mrs Simpson failed to make her appearance. It was all becoming wearisome and the villa itself was a disappointment for Harriet. She had expected something that could compete with, if not outshine Monte Carlo's best, even Villa Bon Accord, but this modest cube (it was the only way to describe it) would not have been out of place in Hampstead or Brighton, such a disappointment.

Ah, well, back to Monte Carlo in time for supper. She had guests to greet, prominent among whom was dear Lord Beauchamp, the most gracious and charming of men, in almost every respect the antithesis of the Prince and his circle. Recently widowed, he was on the Continent for an extended tour. Some said it was a form of exile, brought about by the earl's brother-in-law, the Duke of Westminster, who had publicly accused him of being a homosexual.* Harriet had known Beauchamp since the turn of the century, in the days when he was Governor of New South Wales. They had first met at a vice-regal event in Sydney, and she had been reacquainted with him upon his return to Australia in 1931. Why, he'd more than once enjoyed Stewart Dawson hospitality at Bon Accord guest house, where she had joined him for jolly games of golf. She'd heard all the rumours many times but the earl was the epitome of good breeding and, by any standard, a progressive thinker on social matters, something close to her own heart. Both Harriet and David had admired his stand over improved conditions for workmen during his term as a Liberal member of parliament under Lloyd George and Harriet herself had been inspired in much of her charity work by his example. She'd felt emboldened in her support for poor Dorothy Mort by the many accounts of the earl's generosity and genuine concern for the common man. As she greeted her old friend, she reflected that, at their age (she could pass for ten years younger, couldn't she?) they would make a handsome couple.

---

* It was, and he had. Beauchamp was virtually banned from England when outed by Westminster, his political rival and a staunch Tory.

Swept away by the continuing drama of the royal affair, she incautiously granted an interview with a newspaper columnist, in which she let slip "I am going to marry a title!"* Though she regretted her words, which did not, fortunately, reach the earl's ears, it struck her that such an eventuality was not impossible, given the large pool of eligible candidates in which she swam. In the meantime, she would take the arm of the handsome earl, show him true hospitality and console him in his loss of home and family.

At a distance of nearly nine years, she reflected, the mass hysteria over the royal affair all been a little silly, but somehow there had been a fatefulness about it, when she considered the turn that her own life had taken so soon after. Even as she had shared what everyone believed to be the latest gossip about the Prince and Mrs Simpson, she had been jolted out of any illusion that the couple would be king and queen when the Prince made his sad wireless announcement on December 10th. The couple were not, after all, to be crowned. Harriet and friends were quick to note that this must have surprised Mrs Simpson. As Harriet observed, word was that London and Paris hairdressers had been asked by her to devise a suitable and becoming hairdressing style for wearing with a crown.[394] Nevertheless, the coronation would go ahead, and who should be the new king and queen but the very Duke and Duchess of York who had so nearly graced the dancefloor of The Ambassadors!

But Harriet was destined not to witness the grand event, which took place on May 12th. By then, she had been in Australia for several months, on an errand to return Stuart's children to Sydney. Her youngest son had made prompt and good use of his "loan" from Stewart Dawson Investments Ltd., buying a prime building lot high above Palm Beach, on which he built an imposing house for weekend retreat. The white-painted villa was a striking example, if not as extreme as some, of the new "moderne" style, which had swept the

---

* Richmond River Herald and Northern Districts Advertiser 18th December 1936 P.6 *"Rumour hath it that the new Lady Beauchamp will be none other than our old friend, Mrs. Stewart Dawson. When she was asked recently what she was going to do, Mrs. Dawson replied, 'Oh, I am going to marry a title.' Lord Beauchamp has been staying recently at her beautiful home on the Riviera."*

western world since the late 20's. In Australia, Harriet soon learned, it was known as "modern ship style", after the curved façades and steel balcony rails that mimicked the bridges of ocean behemoths such as the new Queen Mary.* Stuart's house went so far as to sport a ship's life-ring to the right of the front door and a circular "port hole" window on the left. Its enormous, curved front wing thrust forward two storeys of bay windows and above the front porch the canopy had its own steel rail, emulating the wing of a liner's bridge. The views from the upper balcony in the main wing north-eastward over the Pacific Ocean were spectacular and the beach itself no more than a five-minute stroll down the hill (or half a minute by car, Stuart's usual mode of travel). As he planned his first weekend away from Vaucluse, across the Harbour and up the peninsular, Stuart seemed at last ready to settle into a more stable life, one where he and Jean could spend more time with the children. Or so Harriet thought, as she packed her trunk and booked passage from Toulon for young David and Harriet. She wasn't keen on another long voyage to Australia, but the children deserved to see their father and a holiday in the new beachside house might be just the ticket.

---

* Now commonly called "Art Deco", though the term was not coined until the 1960s.

Matriarchal Duty, Filial Chaos

All through the month-long voyage on board the Mooltan, as the children enjoyed the liner's many facilities, Harriet dwelt on the recent events in France and England. The further she sailed away from her real home the greater were her misgivings. She already missed the company of her London and Monte Carlo friends; the many distinguished fellow-passengers were a poor substitute for her gay, sophisticated circle. News from the Riviera was that Lord Beauchamp, to whom she had let Villa Bon Accord in her absence, was seriously ill; cancer had been diagnosed and his very life might be in danger. She should have remained there, by his side to comfort him. The idea of re-marrying, conjured by her throw-away remark to the journalist, grew in her mind as she faced an uncertain future who knew where. She was approaching her seventy-third birthday and though she admitted to no more than sixty-five, she sensed time running out. No one could ever supplant David, but as she watched couples promenading on the Mooltan's broad deck or recalled similar scenes along the shady boulevards or in London parks her thoughts turned to the possibility of a last hurrah with a man of substance. She longed for stability, comfort, and intimacy and, not to put too fine a point on it, a steadier supply of the needful than the meagre allowance she was drawing from the estate. Though David had left her well-provided back in '32, as the years passed, she came to rely more on the odd win at the tables or the never-realised success in a lottery draw to supplement her monthly income. To make matters worse, transfer of funds from Australia to Europe or the London bank had become unreliable, with unpredictable, frustrating delays from one month to the next. She had not as yet been publicly embarrassed but with housekeepers and gardeners, chauffeurs and cooks to pay, rent on the London flat, property taxes on Villa Bon Accord and some frightening bills for car repairs, there were moments when she longed for the days when a simple appeal to her husband would settle all debts in an instant. Marriage to one of the many dispossessed aristocrats drifting through Monaco might be the answer after all. She had assets that many coveted, and, she didn't mind saying, charm, energy belying her years and excellent connections in Europe, England, and Australia. The princes and dukes may have been physically estranged from their ancestral estates, but many retained the incomes from those estates, or claimed to; judging by their extravagant lifestyles there was no shortage of cash in their bank accounts. All in all, a twilight years liaison could be mutually beneficial. Once she discharged her familial duties in Sydney she would hasten back to Europe with a more open mind.

She landed in Sydney on January 21st, 1937, on a hot and humid day. The heat wave across Australia was as severe as many remembered. There had been nothing like it since the end of the war.[395] Coming from the cool of the Mediterranean winter, Harriet felt the effect immediately the Mooltan docked, and the ever-present on-board breeze died. The children peered over the rail at the crowds on the quay, seeking a glimpse of their father and stepmother. Soon enough Stuart, tall and well-dressed, could be seen pushing through the welcomers. As first-class passengers, the trio were ushered down the gangplank with little delay (save for the obligatory photograph for a "celebrity" reporter from the local paper), through the formality of customs and immigration and out into the mass of people hailing cabs or embracing loved ones. The arch of the bridge soared close above. Though Harriet had shipped her Rolls-Royce on the voyage it would be hours before it was swung onto the quay and processed through Customs. Instructing her chauffeur to collect their luggage and see to its safe delivery, Stuart ushered the party to his car, a brand-new Cord.* Harriet had never seen the like of it, all streamlined curves, great pontoons enveloping the wheels and apparently, no radiator, for where she expected to see a conventional grill several rows of chrome bars wrapped around the coffin-shaped nose. It couldn't have been less like the Rolls: where were the running boards? (done away with,

---

* Stuart bought one of the first few Cord 812 sedans imported into Australia in 1937. It was reported to be maroon in colour and Jean was also seen driving it. The 812 and earlier 810 were technically and style-wise years ahead of any other passenger vehicle, the epitome of "moderne". They also cost several times as much as most other luxury cars.

since the car was very low-slung), and where the headlights? (hidden within the front wings, ready to swivel upwards when needed); where was the gear shift? (a tiny lever on the steering wheel for "pre-selecting" the next gear, whatever that meant). Before she could take in her son's enthusiastic explanation the engine roared into life and they swept away, down George Street, cutting left towards Darlinghurst, through Edgecliff, swooping down to Double Bay, before a tyre-squealing right turn, south to Bellevue Hill and thence to Stuart's apartment. Harriet was surprised to learn that he and Jean had moved yet again, from Vaucluse to Fairfax Road, where he had rented a new and very stylish flat. Like the Palm Beach mansion, it was thoroughly "moderne", decked out in fashionable green and off-white, with the very latest in streamlined furniture throughout. Harriet supposed that Jean must have had a hand in the choice of fabrics and furnishings, though it had to be said that both she and Stuart had excellent taste, cutting fine figures in their immaculately tailored suits.

Seated in the flat, a cooling drink beside her (what a well-stocked cocktail cabinet they kept!), Harriet got down to business. The children's welfare was uppermost in her mind. What school had Stuart in mind for his daughter? The nine-year-old had adapted well to European ways, spoke French almost like a native and might have trouble if thrust into a local school without careful preparation. Stuart explained that they had, indeed, been taking serious consideration of Harriet's needs and had been advised by none other than Malcolm and Agnes. The McNab daughters had both attended Springwood Ladies' College, a mile or so from The Spinney, where they had received a well-rounded education in a most genteel milieu. Roma had been dux of the school in 1932, topping her classes in English, French and Science. Why, Harriet was welcome to speak to her nieces any time, should she need reassurance; they lived only a short walk away. Very well, since it was clear that Stuart and Jean were in no mood to change their social habits to accommodate the children at home, Springwood might offer a solution for all. Young Harriet was used to life at boarding school, while her parents' whirling cycle of cocktail parties, soirées, race meetings and restaurants, not to mention Stuart's harum-scarum driving habits, were not for the faint-hearted or a tender young girl. It wasn't as if they were a close family in the first place. The child had never known her stepmother and her father had devoted what time he spared to David, not to her. So, that was settled. At the earliest opportunity they would motor up to Springwood, where they would inspect the school and Harriet could visit her late brother's grave.

Young David was a different kettle of fish. He confessed to looking forward to summer months driving to the seaside in his father's magnificent car and already fretted at the confines of the flat, thinking of days in the Palm Beach house, but Stuart was surprised to see that he had gained much of his grandmother's fondness for European life in the past couple of years. He was determined to return to his school chums in England when the new term began. Harriet was prepared to defend his case against his father's objections, but Stuart accepted his son's wish. David would return to England with his grandmother. In one short conversation, Harriet's hopes had been realised with none of the ill-feeling she had feared. Stuart and Jean could resume their carefree life, unless Stuart killed himself and who knew else on the road one day.

Having checked into the Australia Hotel, Harriet phoned her old friends. The Jacobsons were first on the list. Harriet knew that their daughter, Marjory, now Mrs Eric Strelitz, had returned from London and success writing short stories, and now she and Marjory were invited to a meeting of the Dalwood Homes committee to plan another fund-raising bridge party. Would she like to join the committee?[396] How could she refuse? Before she could catch her breath, a call from the Arts Club invited her to a musicale right there at The Australia, where she would be guest of honour alongside Marjory and none other than Lady Kingsford Smith, widow of the great aviator. Such a flurry of entertainments! She could already hear the snap of cards, the animated chatter of her old circle, the swell of orchestral strings, see the flash from the photographers' cameras as she posed with these important people. Maybe this visit would turn out for the better, after all.

Next to call was Percy, looking neat and nervous as ever, who brought her up to date with other family and business affairs. Did she know that Lila was in town, renting a flat at Adereham Hall? Early last year, she and husband, Harry, had returned from America where their son, Charles, had recently married, and had taken up residence for the time being in the startlingly modern apartment block in Elizabeth Bay.* Harriet had met Lila only once or twice and though she admired her step-daughter's successful marriage she considered her a bit of a trouble-maker. In dear David's later years, she had made a fuss about dividends unpaid on shares in the family companies (Harriet couldn't recall the details) that had upset her father and now Percy informed her that Lila had brought another case a couple of years since. He hadn't bothered his mother with it at the time and, like the first one, it had failed, but it did tend to illustrate the lengths Lila could go to extract money from the estate. She had lodged a petition for the winding up of Stewart Dawson and Co. (Victoria) Ltd., the holding company for the defunct Victorian business.[397] As the holder of over 3,500 fully paid shares she seemed to believe that she would be entitled to a proportionate share of the residual assets. She must have been put up to it by Harry, of course, but the petition failed to deliver what she sought because there was nothing left to distribute. Thanks to Percy's diligent management of the estate, much of the assets of the various companies had been consolidated into one or two more closely held companies under his control.

News from England continued to support Mack's boundless optimism. Sixty-nine milk bars were open in London, of which fifteen were Black and Whites, and there were over 300 across Britain. Mack bragged: "I am on my way to make a million out of milk."[398] He hoped to have opened five hundred bars within five years. He and others now offered more than a hundred different flavourings. Thanks to this, thousands of gallons of strawberry, loganberry, raspberry, and other fruit syrups were giving new life to British fruit farming. To the existing soup items on the menu, Mack had added New Zealand Toheroa oyster soup, which had been an instant success with patrons at fourpence a bowl. British milk bars were taking half the output of

* Adereham Hall, built in 1934, is an outstanding example of Art Deco architecture in Elizabeth Bay. Known familiarly as "Gotham City" it rises nine floors above Elizabeth Bay Road and has commanding views over Elizabeth and Rushcutters Bays.

New Zealand oysters. Mack and Norman might still pull it off, though at £3,000 a time, the setup costs of each new bar were daunting. If they would only moderate the pace of openings, they could stay afloat long enough to maintain overall profitability. Trouble was, Mack saw the business as some sort of race to a finish, where outpacing the competition was everything.

And how was Strathisla faring on the track? The look on Percy's face told Harriet that perhaps she might have avoided asking that question. There had been no more wins for the now four-year-old, who had been rested for most of the summer season. Percy's hopes lay with the upcoming Highweight Welter Handicap at the Hawkesbury races, in March, though he feared that the favourite, Electron would be hard to beat. Still, they could enjoy a day out together at the Richmond track far beyond the western fringe of Sydney, at the foot of the Blue Mountains. It sounded a jolly idea and would fit in well with Harriet's plan to visit Springwood.

Harriet's presence back in Sydney had not gone unnoticed by the press. She had been expecting to be interviewed from the day of her arrival; the Australian fascination with British and European culture, people and events was limitless. Now, she was approached to talk about her trip to Australia and gossip about "The Continent" and the abdication crisis; anything to divert readers seeking relief from local trivia. After the polite, introductory questions about the purpose of her visit (to see her sons and reunite Stuart with his children), the family plans for the children (they would probably continue their schooling in Australia, but David would return to complete his education at Reading University first) and where she would stay (Bellevue Hill, with her son), the reporters focused on the important issue: what did Harriet know about the abdication crisis and Mrs Simpson? Here was her opportunity to display her superior intelligence, her inside knowledge to titillate the readers. She re-told her story about Mrs Simpson's request to her hairdresser and neatly segued from mentioning young Harriet's school in Cannes to: "The villa in Cannes at which Mrs Simpson was a guest was the centre of great activity for some weeks, and it seemed that practically everyone in Cannes" (and some in Monte Carlo, she might have added) "was consumed with curiosity to see it. It is just an ordinary villa, not nearly as attractive as most of your Australian homes."[399] While on the subject of houses and homes, she added a titbit about the forthcoming coronation celebrations. For the occupation of three windows for a few hours, residents of apartments along the route of the coronation procession in London were asking at least £400 and as much as £700 from patriotic sightseers. Harriet could attest to this as the residents were personal friends in James Street and Park Lane, who stood to make enormous sums. Why, one could buy a whole house in Sydney for that much! Privately, she envied those friends, blessed by the fortuitous location of their flats. Her own London apartment was just as luxurious and prestigious, but not quite on the route, rendering it of no value on the coming day. Perhaps to compensate for her sense of financial loss, she was quick to remind the reporter that Monte Carlo, her other home, had "made a wonderful recovery after its unprosperous time. The place is thronged with visitors, and it is very cheap living for Britishers, as the franc is at more than 100 to the pound sterling."[400]

By March she had quit The Australia for Stuart's flat, where her chauffeur found space to park the Rolls. At the end of the month she and young Harriet seated themselves in the plush interior, while David joined the chauffeur in the open driver's compartment, and they headed for the mountains. The journey in the stately vehicle was without incident, which might not have been the case had they accepted Stuart's offer to drive up in the Cord. Ignoring the continuing suspension of his licence, he had been unable to resist the temptation to show off the powerful vehicle to some of his male friends. The drive south from Sydney along the Princes Highway was a favourite weekend outing for the adventurous motorist. Passing the National Park were long, straight sections of well-sealed road enticing the bolder to explore the limits of their vehicle's performance. If the priority was demonstrating the power of the brakes or the grip of the tyres, then nothing could beat the steep and tortuous descent of Bulli Pass to the base of the escarpment. Once at the bottom, the sinuous coast road through Thirroul and Austinmer offered plenty of opportunities to show off the full capability of the car. Stuart was in his element as the Cord's V-eight engine rumbled, the wind whistling past the open windows. On the return journey, back on the straight, his elated yet nervous passengers urged him to greater speed as the needle on the instrument climbed higher until … until the unmistakable shape of a police motorcycle drew alongside as they slowed for a traffic light, bringing an impromptu end to the adventure. Stuart could not believe his luck. Could a chap not enjoy so much as a day on the open road without these narrow-minded, officious blue-coats spoiling it? Apparently not, for the copper claimed to have been pursuing him for miles, timing the Cord at a top speed of ninety-five miles an hour.[401] Ninety-five! Imagine that! No wonder his passengers had gone quiet at the end. Pity he hadn't clocked the magic 100mph (they said the Cord was good for a hundred and ten) but ninety-five would cause a few deep breaths back home, once the press got hold of it. It would be worth the price of another fine and certainly wouldn't put a stop to his driving.

After meeting Percy at Richmond for race day (as feared, Strathisla was beaten by five lengths into second place by Electron) Harriet spent a day or two in Springwood, sufficient to satisfy herself of the suitability of Springwood Ladies' College and enrol her granddaughter for the next term. The elegant, two-storey Victorian building stood among rustling eucalypts and more recently planted pines. The smack of tennis racquets and merry voices could be heard on nearby courts. These would be no cosseted young ladies, she learned. As well as tennis, there were regular outings to the nearby golf course (Bon Accord's very own) and daily callisthenics with the use of balls, clubs, and physical drills. Most impressive! Young Harriet's would be a rounded education in the company of some of Sydney's finest and fittest girls. Over on Hawkesbury Road, she paid a call on the McFarlanes, dropped in to Bon Accord (still a gem of the mountains, with a good table, a full guest list and those splendid gardens) and took the short drive to the cemetery to pay her respects to her dear departed brother. Unlike Valerie, whose walled enclosure a few yards away still dominated the Presbyterian section, he lay in a yet unmarked grave, no headstone in place.* The remains of floral offerings withered on the subsiding mound of turned earth. Harriet

* To this day, Malcolm's grave remains unmarked, no more than a gap between adjacent plots and a number in Springwood burial records.

added her personal tribute, said a silent prayer, and turned to the waiting car. Poor Malcolm had worked so hard for David all those years, nobody had been more loyal. He'd made good in a calling that he could never have imagined or aspired to back in Liverpool, married well and raised two beautiful daughters who would be a credit to any family. He had discharged his responsibilities, not only to the jewellery shops he'd managed, but in helping Percy set up Bon Accord and keep an eye on the place in his absence. Such a pity she had not been here for him in his last days. The trip back down the mountains would likely be her last, she reflected. Memories of happier times in Springwood were being pushed aside by a sense of cumulative loss. She did not doubt that Percy would fulfil his duty to Bon Accord Investments, which still owned half the golf course, and to the guest house, whose lease would fall due sooner or later, but even he had other fish to fry, and she had sensed in him a desire to rid the family of these encumbrances.

She had another, family reason for curtailing her Springwood visit: Norman was back in town. Arriving on the Mariposa on March 22nd, accompanied by his valet, Charles Millions, he had waited only to see his car unloaded before speeding off to Percy's flat, where the two brothers closeted themselves for the meeting that Percy had been expecting for a while. Norman gave his account of the smashing success of the Black and White business, which added little to what Percy already knew from newspaper reports and Mack's infrequent correspondence. Every month more bars were opening, presenting a real challenge to hotels and public houses.[402] Black and White had nineteen, with five more in preparation. So far, so good, but now Norman broke the exciting news that Mack had plans, advanced plans, to open his own ice cream factory to cash in on the supply of the essential ingredient for so many shakes. What was more, the expansion of bars was no longer to be confined to London; thanks to his, Norman's continental connections and knowledge, France was to be the beneficiary of the next new bar or two. The French wouldn't know what had hit them, but the hordes of American and British tourists would soon show them what modern fashions could do for jaded appetites and palates. Percy's head spun. He would not be wrong, he supposed, that this ambitious programme demanded further injections of capital, hence Norman's visit. Not at all, came the reply, they were confident of finding the funds from their accumulated profits and, if need be, from local investors. Norman's own bank account was not empty, and Mack's charisma could always be counted on to open others' wallets when the need arose. All the same, if Percy, that is to say, Stewart Dawson Investments, wanted an even greater return on their initial investment, now was the time to put a little more into the pot. Percy's response was prompt but firm: no further family capital would be risked until Black and White's books showed more black ink.

Norman was left to ponder how he would break the news to Mack. He'd promised to be back in London by June and now it appeared he would be empty handed. He might as well fulfil his family and social duties, take the car for a spin or two and maybe drum up some local support for the business in the time left. Stuart was rather down in the dumps and could do with cheering up. Jean had had a nasty fall at home and been confined to bed for a while, limiting their social activities; young David was rather wearing him down and anxious to return to England; and his creditors were pursuing him for outstanding claims in the bankruptcy court, thanks to the publicity attending the purchase of his house and car. He was also being sued for a new debt incurred with a company of manufacturing jewellers, Gustave Kollerstrom Ltd., which Norman found ironic, considering the ease with which Stuart could have satisfied any need for baubles from the family stock. He supposed he could work his charm on his brothers and dear mother for a month or so before heading north once more.

Harriet's hopes for a short, quiet family reunion with the bonus of starring in her social circle had been upset by the turmoil of Stuart's chaotic behaviour, Percy's constant tinkering with the estate and Norman's sudden appearance out of the blue on another mission from Mack. Life would always bring surprises, but this generation's frantic rushing about without fear of the consequences was beginning to wear her down. How she longed for the old days when David's steady hand was on the tiller and she had been seldom bothered by her sons' shenanigans. The peaceful haven of Villa Bon Accord was looking more attractive by the day. Then the news broke: Bon Accord had burned to the ground.

Ashes and Dust

Harriet sat up with a start. Twilight, and the lighting of the buildings across the street from the hotel had crept upon her in her reverie and now, the sudden recollection of that shocking announcement jolted her awake, as it had done on that May morning in 1937. When she took the call from Percy and heard "Bon Accord", her heart raced and her head whirled with images of the beautiful villa consumed by flames, reduced to smoking ashes in which all her treasures would lie twisted, melted, charred, and splintered. How would she live now? Where would the loss of this spectacular mansion lead her? Half her life was there, in the heart of Monte Carlo, not on the far side of the world, lodging with one immature son or another. As her thoughts and fears crowded together, she at first failed to take in what Percy was saying, but his tone did not match her mood. What was that about Springwood? What had Springwood to do with it? "No, mother, it's not Villa Bon Accord, it's the guest house in Springwood that's gone up." Her relief was such that she found it hard not to laugh, though she suppressed the urge. Composing herself, she listened to Percy's account of the disaster.

Reports were still coming in, but the story Percy told was of a catastrophic blaze that had started around five in the morning of the 3rd and, before anyone could respond or the brigade marshal its resources, the entire building had been engulfed. The wooden structure stood no chance against the flames and all that remained were the two brick chimneys and the outline of the foundations. By the grace of God nobody had been seriously hurt, but almost nothing had been saved. Percy was about to leave for Springwood to see for himself what might be salvaged and to deal with the shocked lessee, Mrs Sealy. Harriet hung up the telephone and let the news sink in. Despite her initially conflicting emotions, she wept for the loss of Bon Accord. He had been gone less than five years but so much of David's legacy had been turned to ashes. First, there had been the fires in the Strand Arcade and The Ambassadors. There had been two more since: Dent's shoe store had been damaged again in 1934 and a photographer's studio had been consumed this very week, several other shops below suffering extensive smoke and water damage. One of the Springwood cottages, The Spinney's neighbour, had gone,* and now, the jewel in the crown where she had shared some of her happiest times with David was a smouldering ruin. She particularly missed Davesta, "the Bungalow", as it lately had been called. The enormous, two-storeyed guest house extension that had transformed it into Bon Accord had been the showpiece, but the Davesta wing would always be her and David's mountain home. Here, long before Bon Accord, they had escaped the city for quiet weekends among the gum trees, where the only sounds were bird calls: the raucous screeches of cockatoos, the "crack!" and echoing "wheep-wheep-wheep!" of whip birds, fairy wrens twitting and darting through the undergrowth. Here, they could restore their strength and spirit between long days of committees, financial affairs, and real estate wrangling; and too many late nights flying the flag at The Ambassadors. Not that she'd minded the parties, dances, and balls, but a body could only take so much without rest and recreation and where better than in the peace and solitude of Davesta? Of all the places she'd lived in Australia, it held the happiest memories, notwithstanding the circumstances of its creation.

Percy was quick to return with a full report. It was as they feared: nothing of the building, not a stick of furniture, not a floorboard, had been spared by the conflagration. Outside, only the rose gardens had survived, though many feet had trampled the beds as guests escaped and firemen dashed about ineffectually. Aside from the forlorn chimneys, the fountain in front of the bungalow was the only structure rising more than a couple of feet. The two stone lions

---

* The cottage built next door to The Spinney in 1920 (twin of Bonnie Doon) burned down sometime between 1932 and 1934. There is a report in the Nepean Times of 2nd July 1932 P.8 *"A weekend cottage at Hawkesbury Road, North Springwood, was burnt to the ground at about 5.45pm on Sunday evening last. The building was the property of Mrs. G. N. Cohen … The fire had a good hold when noticed, and nothing was able to be saved …"* It is impossible to verify that this was The Spinney's neighbour but no other cottages on Hawkesbury Road were reported lost in the 1930s.

flanking the main entrance steps were blackened and smeared with wet ashes. The air stank of burned timber and the sodden remnants of curtains and carpets. Shards from hundreds of smashed glasses, jugs and bowls protruded from the ashes, where dazed staff members poked and prodded to salvage cutlery and kitchen utensils or, if they were lucky, a personal possession. The twisted frame of the pianola lay like a prehistoric skeleton in a corner of what had been the ballroom. Percy made out the shape of the grand chandelier, centrepiece of the ballroom. He had salvaged it from The Ambassadors' fire, but now it was no more than scrap, shattered into a thousand pieces where it had crashed to the floor. Police were interviewing staff and shocked guests, many of whom wore borrowed clothes, some with bandaged hands, singed hair, or cuts to their faces.

From what he gathered, the fire had broken out at about 4.30 in the morning in the storeroom between the bungalow and the main building, waking staff quartered in the bungalow. One of them, a Mrs Smith, rushed out of the house in a nightdress and kimono and with others began to throw buckets of water on the fire. Two of the men played a garden hose, which was all that was available, but it was useless, and they turned their attention to saving the guests, running around the rooms, and telling them to get out of the building. Fortunately, it being a "low" season, there were only thirty guests; Percy shuddered to think what might have eventuated had the full complement of one hundred been in residence. The fire spread so fast from the storeroom to both ends of the building that the lights failed, and the main staircase collapsed. Twelve people were trapped on the top floor, where they were in grave danger of suffocating in the dense smoke. William and Kingdom Smith, the two brothers who had attempted to douse the flames with the garden hose, sprang into action and erected a ladder. Climbing up to the balcony they shepherded the dazed guests to safety. They also saved the belongings of some of the people before returning to fight the fire. The gardener, William Moroney, blinded by smoke, had to be guided out. A guest, Mr Ernest Westrup, unable to reach the ladder, attempted to scale down a rope of knotted sheets, but within feet of the ground he was struck on the head by a piece of burning timber. He fell, sustaining further injuries to his back. He and Moroney were taken to hospital.

Such was the confusion that a girl who had been brought out of the house ran back in to get her clothes and had to be dragged out again by Mrs Sealy and her daughter. It was all over in little more than an hour when the roof fell in. The mass of flames could be seen all over Springwood and other parts of the mountains and there was soon a crowd of onlookers, joining the confused, shivering guests and staff on the road outside. Percy understood that most of the guests had been taken to the Royal Hotel, in the town, some to other guest houses. Several reported the loss of valuable articles: a watch worth £70 and a £50 ring among them. To make matters worse, the weekend takings and all the records had also been destroyed.[403]

Harriet listened, horrified by the images of whirling sparks, timbers crashing to the ground and glass shattering in the heat. She supposed that, yet again, it had been an electrical fault that had started the fire. But the staff confirmed that the storeroom where the fire broke out was neither lit by electricity nor did it have any wiring for power. Moreover, nothing flammable had been kept in it; no kerosene or cooking oils, no cleaning fluids, paint thinners; nothing that could have accelerated the initial spark. The police and fire brigade were mystified. This warranted further investigation, which would delay payout of the insurance on the property. Percy sighed, when would any of the family companies ever be free of these financial losses and defaults? It was bad enough having to deal with Strand and Pitt Street Properties, who were no closer to paying off their debt over the Strand Arcade, and with Mack's constant drain on the estate. Now they had a possibly unrecoverable loss of £25,000 or more on Bon Accord, not to mention the foregone lease payments from Mrs Sealy. Holding property at arm's length had appealed to Percy and his father back in 1930, when rents seemed assured, and tenants could be relied upon to manage the buildings and their contents. Latterly, if they had not been encumbered as mortgagee in possession of the Strand Arcade, how simple life could have been, with over £700,000 accumulating in their bank account. The entire building could have collapsed into Pitt Street, for all they would have cared. If Mack or Percy had been managing Bon Accord, who was to say what extra measures they would have taken to secure the safety of the property? Given Percy's own experience dealing with the fire at The Ambassadors, what might he have done to apply the lessons learned there to the vulnerable wooden guest house? But this was idle speculation, of course. The damage had been done, it was time to clear the ledger once and for all. Mrs Sealy was talking of rebuilding Bon Accord, but Percy had had enough: he would start negotiations to wind up Bon Accord Investments and sell off the entire property, lock, stock, and barrel.

"It's my turn, now"

Once her granddaughter had been installed at Springwood Ladies' College, Harriet had one last pleasant duty to perform, chairing another committee for Dalwood Homes. The Japanese liner, Kitano Maru was visiting Australia. The goodwill flags were out, to celebrate what many hoped would be the end of years of international tension over trade. Continuing Australia's longstanding tariff policies, a regime of imperial preferences had been strengthened in 1935, further penalising imports from Japan and the United States in particular. When the Japanese retaliated in 1936, hitting Australia with punitive tariffs on wool, wheat, beef, butter and tallow, relations hit a new low until an uneasy resolution was reached at the end of the year. The Japanese Consul-General in Sydney put on his diplomatic hat, courting the social set with invitations to cultural events. Few could resist the lure of the exotic East for long and when the Kitano Maru's arrival was expected, Dalwood Homes' ladies required little persuasion to stage a fund-raising ball on board the liner. And who better to chair the organising committee than Harriet Stewart Dawson? There was also the cachet of her "international" reputation, which she was keen to burnish. She never gave up hoping for the antipodean renaissance for which she, David and Percy had sought to plant the seed in 1924. The ball on board the liner was to be on May 27th. Fifty Japanese ladies would attend, dressed in full national costume, and the ship was to be decorated from stem to stern with lanterns and traditional Japanese objects and furniture. Harriet's job was to marshal her team of well-connected ladies to publicise the event and secure as many reservations and pledges for donations as possible. She would attend the ball but, as was her habit, take only a minor part in the celebrations and entertainments. Her greatest pleasure was to bring happiness to others and to preside over the presentation of the cheque to the foundation. As they counted the days to the 27th, she put aside for the moment her enduring concerns for Percy, Stuart, and Norman.

On May 14th news broke that cast another shadow over the family: Rita had died in Melbourne. After the divorce, she had never recovered from the blow to her esteem. She left Sydney, taking a house in Melbourne's stylish Albert Park, where she remained, alone. In 1934 she again visited California. She spent more time in Los Angeles, enjoying the high life of Beverley Hills and Hollywood, and incidentally meeting Percy's nemesis, Ronald Colman, but the respite was brief. She returned to Melbourne where, in March this very year, it was reported that she had suffered a nasty fall that necessitated a spell in bed.[404] She was said to be recovering but her health had rapidly declined, and she had died at her home. Rita was just thirty-five. Percy, who seldom spoke of his former wife, nevertheless retained an affection and great respect for her, as did Harriet. The cause of death was not reported but they speculated that there were complications from the fall, or perhaps the fall was the result of an existing condition. The Barnetts returned her body to Sydney, where she was buried in Randwick Cemetery, not far from the family home. Out of respect for the Barnetts, no Stewart Dawson attended the funeral, but Percy and Harriet grieved for the vivacious young woman whose imagination and artistry had captured the spirit of the jazz age.

Though distressed by the announcement (Rita had been a model daughter-in-law and a willing protégée), Harriet applied her mind to the task at hand. The ball, now titled "A Night in the Orient" was much anticipated. On the night of the 27th the gangways of the Kitano Maru were crammed with party-goers eager to share the exotic delights of the East. The ship was decked with cherry blossoms, many-hued lanterns, and hundreds of twinkling lights. Captain Aizawa, the commander of the vessel, wore traditional dress, on his head an elaborate wig. He led the dance of seven Japanese ladies, all guests, who wore their national costumes, bright with embroideries. Supper was in the captain's room, where a peony tree in full bloom was the principal decoration. Made by the ship's cook, it was entirely of sugar. The blooms were of a rosy hue, and tiny yellow butterflies rested on the green leaves. The scene was reminiscent of the spectacular displays that had once been the pride of The Ambassadors. Inspired by their hosts, the ladies of the committee wore their most fashionable and colourful gowns. Capes of white ostrich feathers mixed with pea-green chiffons and rose taffetas. Subduing her preference for "a bit of colour", Harriet wore black satin in mourning for Rita, and took a background seat, from where she admired the style and panache of the festival she had helped to promote. Dalwood homes would once more be the grateful recipient of many hundreds, if not thousands of pounds.

Just a fortnight before, another charity event had been staged in the Blue Mountains. To aid members of Bon Accord staff who had lost everything in the fire, a dance had been held in the Roxy Theatre. Some hundred persons attended and danced to the music of Sheridan's Orchestra. With Mr. Bear as MC the success of the night was assured. A spot dance was won by Miss Dot Kelleher and Mr Lindsay O'Hara. A lucky number competition, the prize being an open order for drinks, was won by Mr Bill Honeysett. A fine supper was provided by the committee. The function was a huge social success and terminated at 2.30am. With donations it was expected that an amount of £40 would be realised.[405]

As the end of May approached, heralding the southern winter, Harriet prepared for her return to Europe with her grandson. Having accomplished her principal aims in Australia, she again considered her own future. A couple of months in Sydney had confirmed her belief that, should she consider remarriage, the candidate suitor was not to be found here. Back home, Earl Beauchamp might on the face of it be her choice, but she was not as naïve as she might have portrayed herself in her incautious interview. The Earl's sexual proclivities were now an open secret and besides, his health had declined alarmingly, it could only be a matter of months before the cancer claimed him. She owed her friend one last visit for old time's sake, but it would be from the ranks of his European cohort that her future husband would emerge. She booked passage on the Oronsay from Sydney to Monte Carlo on June 19th, accepting that this could be her final farewell to Australia. She would miss Percy and Stuart, but she doubted the feeling would be mutual. Stuart was too consumed by his hedonistic needs to show more than a passing interest in his mother's welfare, which he seemed to take for granted. Percy was, well, simply consumed. Harriet had long since given up fathoming her eldest son's passionless existence. Seldom had anyone worked so hard for so little emotional reward. Even as she prepared to embark, he had suffered more disappointments at the track. After another two second placings in a month, Strathisla was being talked of as one of the unluckiest horses in Sydney. Of his latest failure, his jockey observed:

> *Strathisla is not really an honest galloper, and I had to ride him hard all the way. He had just consented to do his best, and was going on fast, when 100 yards from the post Brazandt came out a little, and Kaylah veered right in. Strathisla put his ears back and would not stretch out.*[406]

Though Percy was a man about town, he preferred the circle of male acquaintances to which he had belonged almost since his bachelor days. From time to time he escorted a lady-friend, but Harriet knew nothing would ever come of it. He had his father's determination to "get on" but lacked the imagination and boldness that had characterised David's life and success. Worst of all, he seemed unable to relax and let his hair down (Harriet smiled to herself: there was precious little to let down these days, as Percy competed with his brothers for the title of shiniest pate in the family). However, when all was said and done, Percy was perhaps the most resilient and unquestionably the most capable of the brothers. He could manage quite well without his mother at his shoulder.

But, enough of the Stewart Dawson boys; Harriet was consoled by her friend, Estelle Jacobson's acceptance of her invitation to Villa Bon Accord for the summer months. Though the Jacobsons still frequented the Riviera they had never established a base there. Estelle would be good company and support for Harriet in her quest for the elusive title. Dalwood Homes held one final party for her at the Australia, where she was farewelled in English, Japanese and Hebrew by grateful ladies of the committee and the Consulate, and on a rainy morning in June she boarded the Oronsay with David and Estelle and waved goodbye from the shelter of the promenade deck. Sydney was quickly left astern, and she had retired to the comfort of the saloon long before the Bridge disappeared into the drifting mist. As the seas rose beyond the heads of the harbour and the Oronsay turned southwards for Melbourne, Adelaide, and Perth she wondered, would she ever see these ports again or would they, and David's last resting place, soon fade from memory?

The voyage north was uneventful. Young David was by now a seasoned traveller and, at fifteen, beginning to feel his way in the adult world. Impeccably turned out, thanks to Harriet and his parents, he cut a fine figure. He was keen to be back among his English friends but made the most of the on-board entertainments and deck games for the three weeks at sea. As the air lost its winter chill, Harriet and Estelle were content to recline on deck chairs, reminisce, and make plans for the season in Monte Carlo. Now that the Coronation was over* balance and sanity would be restored as international visitors returned to the continent. The casinos would fill with the regular crowds and hangers-on, queues for restaurants would lengthen, the new summer fashions would be on parade. Harriet anticipated Kathleen's arrival for another break from her Parisian garret. And how fared Earl Beauchamp, who languished still at the Villa?

By the time they disembarked at Toulon, Harriet was refreshed and ready for the fray. Beauchamp was cheerful as ever but clearly not at his best. His peripatetic life had taken a toll and now he was on the move again, to Germany, Italy, Austria, who knew where? They bid him "au revoir", with an open invitation to escape the hurly burly at this very private retreat. Young David had the summer break, until the new school term in September, to hone his skills as a juvenile bon vivant. Estelle and Harriet were caught between indulging his youthful high spirits and safeguarding him from the hazards abounding in this most cosmopolitan community. Harriet already suspected him of smoking, a habit easily acquired from the moving pictures he loved to watch. His parents were notoriously free with alcohol about the house so, who knew whether he had been inducted into their bibulous habits? Best to give him a long leash, with one of the servants as companion. As it happened, Norman was expected in Monte Carlo within the month. His fruitless quest in Sydney over, he was sailing back via New York and was due in London by the 28th, whence he planned to drive to the Riviera. As was his custom, he

* King George VI and Queen Elizabeth were crowned on May 12th, 1937.

would be accompanied by his valet, Charles Millions. Millions was a youthful twenty-five and could be counted on to look after David's best interests, thought Harriet. She and Estelle could relax, confident the young man would be in safe hands.

Norman brought news from London. Black and White milk bars were flourishing. The ice cream factory was well on the way to completion, to be opened for business in September. Mack's energy was inexhaustible, it seemed. While Norman had been away, his relentless pursuit of the press for free publicity had not abated, while he divided his time between managing the bars and organising more cycling races. Against all expectations, interest in the sporting events was still strong and money continued to flow into the business. When pressed, Norman still could not say if either Black and White or the cycling was making a profit, but he remained ever optimistic. Sooner or later his and Mack's fortune would be assured. In the meantime, he would fly the flag for the milk bars on the continent, incidentally, showing his car at concours and mingling with influential men and attractive women. And, by the way, could Harriet spot him for a little cash to tide him over in Monte Carlo? It had cost a packet to ship the car to Australia and back and he had to consider his valet's wages and keep. Harriet, already feeling the pinch from her own travelling and housekeeping expenses, was reluctant to accede but she was persuaded by his argument that Millions would be providing a service to her by looking after David.

The summer and early autumn months were spent at Villa Bon Accord, where she could maintain a presence among the eligible gentlemen and refine her selection of potential mates. David was back in England by September, to start the new term at his school in Reading, and Norman's stay on the Riviera was cut short when he joined Mack for the opening of the ice cream factory. Mack was euphoric as he presided over the opening ceremony:

> *The milk bar boom has only just begun. In London alone we serve a quarter of a million customers a week. One bar serves 5,000 milk drinks a day. Why, the business has become so vast that it attracts visitors from all parts of the world. From France, from Switzerland, from Poland. I have had inquiries, even from America, which is supposed to be the home of milk bars!*

When I started a bar in Paris seven weeks ago, I thought that the English visitors there might just manage to keep it going. But already it has beaten all records for business – even in London – and seventy percent of the customers are French!

Now a chain of bars is to be opened right across France and I have already completed arrangements to open five bars in Switzerland.[407]

Transported by the genius of his ice cream factory initiative, Mack announced:

By next year I plan to have a number of modern dairy farms, fully equipped and stocked, to supply the bars with milk. And by the end of the summer one thousand Black and White milk bars will be open.[408]

It seemed that the dreams of the two partners would, after all, be realised. Mack's vision and drive would be vindicated, and dividends from Norman's investment would release him from his debts to Percy and his numerous creditors. Alas, before he could enjoy the fruits of the venture, Norman was obliged yet again to go cap in hand to Harriet for more of the needful. In late November he crashed his car, miraculously escaping with only severe bruising to his chest as he was thrust forward onto the steering wheel. The Phantom was towed to the Rolls-Royce workshop, where the damage was assessed. The entire front half of the vehicle's chassis and bodywork, its steering box, front wheel case, radiator and silencer had to be replaced.[409] The bill for repairs was shockingly high, even by Stewart Dawson standards. After Stuart's law-breaking exploits behind the wheel, and now Norman's near-death experience in his mammoth car, Harriet prayed for the day when her two younger sons would restrain their impulse for speed. If Norman needed an excuse to leave the herd behind, why not choose an aeroplane? But it had been many years since he had taken to the skies. Unlike Percy, who was a frequent passenger on air services in Australia, Norman, as far as she knew, never once boarded an aircraft either as passenger or pilot these days. She would have admired him had he volunteered for the International Brigade in the war in Spain, where he could have shown the younger fliers a thing or two. Could success with the milk bars be the anchor Norman so desperately needed?

Prince, Pauper, Scoundrel?

What with the milk bar business and Norman's car problems, it was December before Harriet could focus on her own marriage prospects. As she later recalled to her Australian friends, she had an extensive field to play. Her frequent visits to the Sporting brought her into contact with many distinguished gentlemen and not a few of a shadier nature. Though the flux of the seasons brought constant change to the throng, there was a core whose regular presence at the tables, in the dining rooms or at the opera could always be guaranteed. She was seldom unescorted thanks to the social contacts she had forged over the past decade and the open house she kept at Villa Bon Accord. As "The Tatler" reported:

> *In an age which defies youth, Monte Carlo has made a corner in and for the elderly who lead cosy lives in the sun and the Sporting, with mild flutters, much harmless gossip and sometimes a gay little story such as this, told by a youth of eighty. A friend said to a much-married belle, "I hear you've got married AGAIN," to which she replied, triumphantly, "Yes, but this time he's got one foot in the grave and one hand in Cartier's."*[410]

Not that she would have cast herself in that light. On the contrary, several of her escorts were many years her junior. In February, she took the arm of Lord Robin Innes-Ker, youngest son of the Duke of Roxburghe, to a party at the Sporting. Innes-Ker was of a similar age to her own daughter, but Harriet as was her habit was careful to edit her autobiography to suit the times and circumstances. Her origins and her age were not subject of enquiry in these circles; the Stewart Dawson wealth and social prowess were enough to establish her status. She was blessed with a youthful complexion, her dark hair remained, with help from her hairdresser, free from tell-tale strands of grey, and though she had gained weight since her svelte middle years, she could pass for less than sixty. To gossip columnists, she now "admitted" to fifty-seven, peeling a further eight years from her most recently stated age. She sometimes wondered how she got away with the fiction when in the company of her middle-aged son, who looked every one of his forty-eight years. Innes-Ker had divorced musical comedy actress, Josie Collins, in 1935 and was celebrating his freedom with a younger set that included the Actons, the Durhams, the Edward Comptons ("she, tall and infinitely distinguished, wears the correct chrome yellow for a brunette," opined The Tatler), and Sir Jock Delves Broughton.* It was a "fast" set, where breeding and rank excused any amount of louche living and where extending credit had become an art form, where the likes of Norman hovered and circled in search of money-making opportunities. Delves Broughton was in the throes of selling off most of the 34,000 acres of his family estate in Cheshire to pay gambling debts, which were not relieved by his activities in Monte Carlo.

Norman himself, meanwhile, had been recalled from England by his mother, on a mission that would appeal to his restless nature and innate self-belief. Among the Sporting crowd, one spare, gaunt figure had caught Harriet's attention. Prince Michael Radziwill, known as "Rudy", on account of his red hair and beard, had been associated with the casino since the early twenties, when he had been employed in some undefined capacity by the then owner, Sir Basil Zaharoff.† Born in 1870 in Berlin, he had served both Germany and, post-war, Great Britain in diplomatic and military roles, before returning to the Second Polish Republic in 1926, assuming Polish citizenship that year. He had been back in Monte Carlo for several years. Rumours about Radziwill's shady past and doubtful character abounded but the man himself dismissed such arrant gossip with a wave of the hand. He had

* This was the same Jock Delves Broughton who, in 1941, was accused of murdering his wife's lover in the notorious "Happy Valley" ("White Mischief") case in colonial Kenya. He was acquitted but soon after committed suicide in a Liverpool hotel after being ostracised by the Happy Valley set.

† Radziwill subsequently claimed to have bought the Casino from Zaharoff, and both Harriet and Norman repeated the falsehood. At most, the Prince may have held a position on the board of management for a short time.

been married twice, first, to Greek beauty, Maria de Bernardaky.* That marriage had produced two children but had ended in divorce in 1915. In 1916 he married his second wife, Maria Henrietta Martinez de Mendinilla de Santa-Susana, but that marriage, too, soon foundered and, so Harriet believed, had ended in 1929. When they first met, in January 1938 at a luncheon party given by the Countess of Winchester,[411] though it was no more than a brief encounter, the story told by the Prince changed Harriet's life in an instant. He had just returned from Poland, after a failed attempt to regain the rights to his family estate and to clear his name of accusations of mental incompetence and bad faith. It had started earlier in the year, when he had announced his engagement to thirty-five-year-old Mme Jeanette Suchestow, and his intention to adopt her six-year-old son. The former wife of a wealthy oil magnate and daughter of a successful perfumier was expected to accompany her fiancé to his family estate at Antonin, in western Poland. Harriet had read of the romantic affair and had been at once intrigued and envious; the Prince's fiancée, a sometime mannequin, was a handsome woman and, by all accounts, generous and warm hearted, but the man himself would have fit Harriet's bill in a trice. He was reputed to be worth millions, with an income of at least £50,000 and a magnificent chateau with its own hunting grounds. His family pedigree was impeccable and included the late Kaiser as a cousin. Mme Suchestow had landed a prize, despite her being Jewish at a time when antisemitism was making some very disturbing headlines throughout Europe.

The Prince's engagement had had immediate tragic consequences when Mary Atkinson, his long-time nurse and housekeeper at Antonin, shot herself in a London hotel. They said that the poor woman had formed an emotional attachment to her employer and lived in the hope that her feelings would be reciprocated. The sudden

---

* According to Bartosz Borkowski (*Michał Radziwiłł. Polish magnate who signed his property as a gift … to Hitler,* quoted in Cziekawotski historyczne.pl (Historical Curiosities) 17th January 2018) Maria de Bernardaky was said to have been the lover of Marcel Proust immediately prior to her relationship with Radziwill. The Prince was often violent towards her, breaking her leg on one occasion.

announcement left her alone and, as she saw it, abandoned. Though the Prince paid due respect to Miss Atkinson for her long and dedicated service, his reputation suffered when it was revealed that the nurse had been penniless when she left Europe for London. They said that the Prince had owed her unpaid salary and had even borrowed from her but had promised to lend her his Rolls-Royce motor car and give her enough funds to buy herself a house. While he remained in Monte Carlo, she awaited at Antonin, but neither car nor money arrived, until she outwore her welcome and was evicted from the chateau. She moved to Danzig, on the Baltic coast, from where she wrote pleading letters that went unanswered. The Prince claimed not to have received the letters, which was understandable, Harriet thought, given the unreliability of the postal services in those regions. Miss Atkinson's final move to London and lonely death in a Bayswater hotel had taken the Prince and his fiancée by surprise. As they told it, far from pining for his love, she had taken her life when the man she really expected to marry jilted her upon her arrival in London.

Radziwill's troubles had only begun, however. Prior to announcing their formal engagement, Mme Suchestow had accompanied the Prince to Poland to be baptised, and to view the wedding gift he had promised, a palace of her own. Family antagonism towards the young woman was immediate, but the Prince was undeterred. Returning with his bride-to-be via Czechoslovakia, he proclaimed his intentions to formally adopt her son. This proved a step too far for his brother, Prince Janusz and the greater family. The official reason given for their objection to the marriage was that the Prince was technically still married to his second wife, the divorce never having been finalised. The unspoken fear was that, should the marriage be allowed to proceed, the six-year-old Jewish lad would become heir to the family fortune and estate and given the Prince's age and uncertain health, would inherit sooner rather than later. Radziwill was already regarded as unstable, having been persuaded by the late Miss Atkinson not so long before to lease land and sawmills on the estate, a poor business decision. He'd also acquiesced in her push to replace Polish officials and servants with English or German staff, to almost universal dismay.* Moving swiftly, the family brought a case to court in Warsaw declaring the Prince mentally unfit and appointing a trustee-cum-guardian over his assets. Radziwill, short of ready money, was left to fume impotently in Monte Carlo, asserting:

Despite everybody, I will marry Jeanette ... I am completely sane. To prove that I am capable of managing my affairs I have been examined by an eminent Paris psychiatrist, Senator Domaszkiewicz, who certifies that I am in full possession of my faculties.[412]

He explained further:

I did not consider, nor did Mme Suchestow consider, adopting her son. That would not even be possible, because the father of the child, M. Suchestow, would not agree. In any case, it would not be legally possible for Emanuel Suchestow to become my successor, because the successor of the title can only be a flesh and blood descendant of a Radziwill. The Radziwill statute makes this clear.

In an obvious allusion to the recent abdication crisis, he added:

I demand for myself the same rights as an English Lord. Let me give my heart to the person of my choice without fear of public denunciation![413]

His defiance was unavailing, obliging him to rely on the charity of friends while he fought for his rights. His fiancée was fortunate to be able to borrow on his behalf from contacts in France but her hopes of a title, estate and endowment dwindled daily. It was now that chance presented Harriet the opportunity to intervene. She had left Monte Carlo for Paris, where she could reacquaint herself with Kathleen's bohemian circle and pay a visit to the new Black and White bar. There

---

* Dariusz J. Peśla Prince Michał Radziwiłł "Rudy" 1870-1955 Women "antonin maharaja". Peśla's opinion is that Mary Atkinson and the Prince conducted a love affair for several years leading up to his divorce from his second wife, and that Atkinson exerted undue influence over him. Taking advantage of his poor health, she obtained enough power of attorney to decide the fate of Antonin's assets. The combined incompetence of the couple accelerated the decline of Antonin. When the authorities refused to extend Atkinson's residence and work permits there were few who regretted her departure.

were also the familiar haunts at the higher end of town, where the Riviera set paused on their way to and from London, and it was here that fate brought her to the Prince. He had seldom spent more than a few nights in one place since the debacle of his disinheritance had commenced, seeking support and validation wherever he could. Now he was in the French capital on a lone mission to appeal to his trustee and guardian, while Jeanette Suchestow awaited his return to Monte Carlo. When Harriet heard from his own lips the tale of injustice and family cruelty, she was spurred to action. A phone call to Norman was all it took to set her on a course that few, least of all she, could have imagined. She would rescue the Prince from the evil clutches of his jealous and misguided family. Norman's answer to her appeal was prompt and positive. Of course, he would help! This was the sort of mission he had been cut out for, in which he had proven himself time and again in the war and the Russian campaign. He would drive immediately to Poland to act as the Prince's emissary, making a direct appeal on his behalf to the Polish court. How dare they deprive this noble gentleman of his estate and income, his right to marry whomsoever he chose? Fear not, a word from an acknowledged hero of the great war would be all that was needed to restore the Prince's fortune. And without further ado, Norman set forth for Warsaw.

It was now mid-April. Europe was entering a period of tension and fear. Hitler's annexation of Austria seemed to confirm his ambitions to threaten the peace; the Spanish war, after see-sawing back and forth for two years, had taken a dramatic turn when the Nationalists launched a major offensive towards the Mediterranean; and now Hitler had turned his attention with renewed venom to the Sudetenland in Czechoslovakia. Everywhere there was talk of rearmament, just as France and Britain, battered by the excesses of the Great War and the slump of the Depression, were beginning to look forward to new prosperity. Even as Norman motored across Germany towards Warsaw, the Poles were threatening neighbouring Lithuania and joining the Nazi push to claim parts of Czechoslovakia where ethnic Poles were in the majority. Britain and France seemed to be the only nations willing to take a stand against international aggression, as Mr Chamberlain and M. Daladier doubled their efforts to preserve peace. Norman's mission could be a close-run thing.

Radziwill was running out of options. An attempt to formalise his divorce from Maria de Santa-Susana in Poland had failed, when he unsuccessfully approached the Calvinist church in Vilnius, notorious as the "Vilnius Factory" for granting divorces on request, contrary to law. He had toyed with the idea of converting to Judaism when the family and the hierarchy of Poland's Catholic church refused to recognise Jeanette's baptism. By March, Mme Suchestow had become desperate. She had not seen Radziwill for weeks and suspected his ardour had already cooled. Gossip in the French and British press did nothing to reassure her. Now, as Norman arrived in Warsaw, the Prince was in urgent need of money and a place to live. He was close to being evicted from his Paris hotel and had outstayed his welcome in Monte Carlo for the time being. Why not be Harriet's guest in England? She could put him up at a hotel near her Kensington Gardens apartment while Norman completed his mission. He needed little persuasion. After returning to Monte Carlo to pack his belongings, he arrived in London at the beginning of May. No sooner had Harriet welcomed him before he was off once more, pursued by rumours and a swarm of reporters, to a small hotel in Brighton, where he locked himself in his room and refused all calls save those from Harriet. The news was out that he had abandoned Jeanette Suchestow and switched allegiance to Mrs Stewart Dawson. The Prince had parted from Jeanette in Monte Carlo with a vague promise to obtain money so that they could finally marry, but this had only served to increase her suspicions, and news of Harriet's welcome in London had convinced her of his betrayal. Then Norman's cable arrived at Kensington Gardens: under no circumstances would Jeanette Suchestow be acceptable as the wife of a Radziwill, nor would her son be granted any rights over the estate. The courts had spoken, and the verdict was not to be overturned. Moreover, as Norman had soon discovered, the very ownership of the estate by the family was at risk. The Polish government's radical agrarian policies threatened to confiscate many ancient landholdings from their historical owners and redistribute the land among the peasantry. This was especially so in the central and western regions closer to the German border, where the fertile land had enriched many dynasties, including the Radziwills. The family's action against the Prince was not so much an expression of distrust of his personal motives (though there was deep animosity toward him) as a defensive move to forestall dispossession by a socialist, antisemitic government for whom Jewish inheritance of the estate was anathema.

If Harriet expected Radziwill to respond to the news with apprehension or resignation she was immediately and shockingly disabused. Rather than rage at the injustice of the decision before accepting a life in exile with his bride-to-be, he proposed a radical alternative that, he maintained, would restore his fortune and secure his inheritance: he would marry Harriet instead. She would never forget the moment when he made the outrageous proposition. But, how could it be possible? He was promised to another. Hadn't he said, when news of the Polish court's decision broke: "Nothing can stop our marriage, tell that to the world?" No, no, didn't Harriet see? Warsaw had been right all along, its verdict annulled any unconsummated contract of marriage, and in any case, he had never legally committed to take Jeanette as his wife, merely shown sympathy for her and her son after her divorce. She might object or even go so far as to contest his decision, but she would have the weight of Polish law against her, backed by his family. He would find means of compensating her for the inconvenience incurred by her misunderstanding his intentions but that was as far as he was willing to go. Marrying Harriet was the most elegant of solutions. Radziwill was sufficiently realistic to acknowledge the inevitable sequestration of the estate at some time in the future. The government had already begun seizing land that had lain untenanted or under-utilised and would take an early opportunity to pounce on Antonin when he departed this life, with or without an heir. Marriage with Harriet would be a mutually serendipitous arrangement. Two mature, Christian adults with no possibility of producing an heir would be invulnerable to the assaults of envious and corrupt socialists. They could enjoy the rest of their life together, sharing their wealth and happiness. If, "après nous, le deluge", then so be it. The family would welcome them, his past would be forgiven as the new Princess Radziwill entered the chateau on his arm.

The mention of the title was all that it took to convince Harriet of the logic of the Prince's argument. Hadn't she foretold this destiny? And who, among the many aristocrats she had met, was more exotic, "mad, bad and dangerous to know"? Where, but in the melting pot of Monte Carlo, could she ever have met the likes of this fascinating gentlemen? She recognised the expediency of the proposal, of course, but if life dealt one a good hand at the end of the game, who, but a colourless mouse, could decline to play it? Hadn't she always been willing to step over the threshold where other, more timid women feared to tread? Her life with David had started not with their stolen moments in Crown Street; even at the age of twenty-one she had been nobody's fool, making the most of what would likely be a brief affair before her lover found other arms to embrace him. What had set her apart was the alacrity with which she undertook the role of wife and mother, life partner and social champion of David's long career. Her high profile in charitable works and even her support for poor Dorothy Mort had not come about by chance but because of her determination to step forward from the crowd. Now that David, her rock, was gone, and her children were absorbed with spending their inheritance, her instinct was to take the plunge. Bertha, long since independent and distrustful of any man, and Percy, should they hear of it, would be bound to object on the grounds of the Prince's reputation. Norman would see the marriage as a further source of funds for his schemes, while Stuart would laugh and order another case of champagne. She would disregard them all, for once. She had a decade left if her health held out. She had sought female companionship with mixed success. She could count on Kathleen's and Estelle's friendship but both women had lives of their own to lead in Paris and far away Sydney. Her attempts at enticing a younger woman to be her companion had been embarrassing failures. Though she was reluctant to admit it, her decision to leave Australia had already begun to cut her adrift from the old Sydney circle of influential ladies and she had formed few equivalent relationships in France or in London society. The more she considered it, the more determined she was to marry the Prince. On May 10th she accepted his proposal.*

---

* Or thereabouts, the date is inferred from the reports of rumours of the engagement. It was almost certainly before 13th May, when Harriet was interviewed by The Daily Herald and denied the rumours.

Despite his initial surprise, Norman rallied to support his mother's decision. Emboldened by his confrontation with the Polish authorities, he had extracted what he believed was a concession toward the Prince's former fiancée. The family would release funds to compensate Mme. Suchestow for the financial advances she had made to the Prince, on the condition Radziwill disavowed her. Well, he'd done that, hadn't he? And what better way to confirm his freedom than to celebrate his marriage to Harriet without delay? Jeanette Suchestow's supposed plight was the talk of London, Paris, and Monte Carlo. It was time to put an end to the gossip. While the Prince remained incommunicado in Brighton, Harriet faced impertinent reporters on her doorstep. Mme Suchestow, now back in Paris, had consulted a lawyer with the intention of bringing a case of breach of promise in the French courts:

I gave the Prince help and money, she said, I changed my religion and left my country and now I am alone. One night in Monte Carlo I saw the Prince's trunks being packed. He told me he was going to London to get money so that we could be married. I have not seen him since.

So, what did Harriet have to say?

I met him six months ago in Monte Carlo, and he is altogether delightful. But, I suppose, because we were seen about together as friends, people talked. But as for marrying him (she laughed) I think that from that point of view, he couldn't settle down. I believe that while he was in Monte Carlo some money was sent to him, and he gave some of it, I think, to a woman friend.

She turned to Norman, at her shoulder. He would soon see off the impudent pressmen.

The Prince is very much misunderstood, he said. I wish I could tell you the whole story, but at present I can't. At the moment I am acting, with unlimited powers, on behalf of the Prince, trying to get some of his money, and he has an income of £50,000 a year at least in Poland, out of that country. I have just returned from Warsaw, where I have been consulting with solicitors. Already I have been able to arrange for some of his debts to be paid. Any question raised by Madame Suchestow will probably come up for discussion.[414]

That should keep them at bay for a while. They would see that there were two sides to this story and that the Prince's intentions were honourable. On Wednesday, May 19th, they announced the solemnisation of their marriage one week later at Caxton Hall Registry Office. Jeanette Suchestow's reaction was immediate. She gave notice of a formal claim against Radziwill for breach of promise, seeking damages of £50,000. She exclaimed:

It is impossible! Only nine days ago the Prince wrote, calling me "Dear Jeanette". He asked me for papers, the production of which was a necessary preliminary to our marriage.[415]

The die having been cast, while Norman diverted the press the Prince returned to London at the last possible moment, and on Thursday, May 27th, they married at the Registry Office in the briefest ceremony. Apart from Norman, there were few guests, though the official announcement had attracted curious onlookers and a contingent of press photographers as they emerged onto the street. Harriet, still in a state of mild shock, posed briefly in her ermine and sable cape as flashbulbs popped around them. The Prince addressed the crowd:

I am, naturally, very happy. English hospitality is truly great. We are going to stay here for a long time. There are no plans for the future yet. We will soon take a church wedding as a confirmation of the civil ceremony.

Questioned about his abandonment of Mme Suchestow, the Prince shrugged his shoulders and turned to Norman's waiting car. The new Princess Radziwill added:

We will spend our honeymoon touring by car in England. Then we will return to London, where we will settle permanently.[416]

before hastening away with the Prince to the haven of her apartment. Or so she believed; like a baying pack of hounds, the reporters laid siege to the building. Jeanette's accusations were widely circulated, gaining her enormous sympathy, and titillating a public seeking relief from the grim news of international tensions. Any plans for a honeymoon were set aside. Remaining in the apartment was also out of the question, so with Norman's help they played cat and mouse around small hotels and spare rooms in friends' houses and apartments, one step ahead of the vigilant press corps. It was going to be a long, difficult game if they were to be free.

Trapped

Night had fallen, the streetlights casting yellow pools onto the sidewalks along Martin Place. If she craned her neck, Harriet could just see around the corner into Castlereagh Street, where an occasional pedestrian paused to glance at the shop window displays. There was not much to attract their attention, despite the lifting of war time restrictions. Nothing to match the good old days of boundless hope and innocent gaiety, when David's offerings would see young lovers pointing to the latest in engagement rings and well-to-do matrons appraising new arrivals of silver plate. "The good old days", how she longed for those times. But with every passing week her hopes withered. There would be no happy ending, no reassuring embrace from dear departed David, and no dashing prince to rescue her from her loneliness.

Things had gone wrong from the very beginning of the hastily arranged marriage. The Prince had made clear his priority to reclaim Antonin. He'd spoken of accompanying his new wife to Australia or taking some sort of grand tour of Great Britain and Europe, but Harriet quickly learned that in the Prince's world, nothing was quite what it seemed. At his urging, she had initiated acquisition of Polish citizenship, persuaded that it was mandated for the title of Princess to be officially sanctioned. This would have meant renouncing her British birthright, something she'd never contemplated during her years in Australia, but needs must, she would obey. She would also require a visa for entry to and residence in Poland. What she expected to be a mere formality turned into a cycle of form filling, visits to consulates, and lodging of bonds.

By August 1938 they were no closer to resolving the visa question, as they shuttled between hotels, fending off the relentless reporters. For a brief interlude, they had escaped to the comfort and privacy of Villa Bon Accord, but by July they were back in London. Jeanette's breach of contract case had been launched that month, demanding the Prince's attendance despite his promises to recompense her without prejudice. This alone kept the gossip-mongers busy and Harriet on the defensive. Cornered by columnist Elizabeth Ayliffe at the Mayfair Hotel she was asked, not for the first time, to comment on the Prince's scandalous dealings with Mary Atkinson and Jeanette Suchestow, and the claims about his mental state. Her response, when she found the words, was not quite as she had intended:

> *It is all nonsense to say that he is not fit to manage [the estates]. The poor fellow is not half as bad as he is painted. He can't help all those silly women surrounding him with notoriety. The fact is all that trouble about that poor nurse who committed suicide has estranged his family. She came to London to marry another man, not the Prince at all. Ours has not been an auspicious set of circumstances for a happy marriage but we will be happy all the same. I understand the Prince. He is not half as black as he is painted.*[417]

"Not half as black"; that had been an unfortunate slip, damning Radziwill with faint praise. But even then her doubts had been mounting, as she tried and failed to keep pace with the Prince's feverish quest for restitution of his rights. The Polish authorities were now asserting that her own marriage to Radziwill would not be recognised, for the same reason they had blocked his nuptials with Jeanette. As far as they were concerned, Polish law mirrored the Spanish on the question of the legality of his divorce from his second wife. If Spain refused to sanction the divorce, then he was still married under Polish jurisdiction. Despite this, Harriet had succeeded in obtaining a temporary Polish passport within days of the wedding (sans visa for travel to Poland) but in the meantime the Prince's own passport expired and the Ministry of Foreign Affairs refused its renewal until the legality of their marriage was clarified. Radziwill had made efforts to have the second marriage annulled under French law, having been advised by his solicitor of a form of reciprocity between the French and Polish legal systems, but this, too, was problematic and remained unresolved. Harriet was now well and truly tangled in the Prince's web of subterfuge and bluff; at risk of criminal prosecution should she venture across the German border into Poland. For the time being, she was trapped. Having surrendered her British passport in May, by October she found her new Polish passport had expired. Now, neither she nor her husband could leave

England. They could neither escape to Antonin, nor winter at Villa Bon Accord. The villa would remain shuttered over the season while they continued to evade the hostile British press. Deprived of his income from the estate, the Prince was by now entirely dependent upon Harriet, as he faced the prospect of a judgment against him in the breach of promise case. Harriet's faith that all would turn out for the best was being tested daily as her own expenses mounted in London, where they entertained friends at the Dorchester Hotel and kept a box at the Opera,[418] and in Monte Carlo. On the other hand, if they worked out the passport and visa problems it should not be long before they would have three arrows to their quiver, in London, Antonin and Monte Carlo, and access to Radziwill's fortune. Meantime, they would have to sit tight in London while the lawyers wrangled.

Norman had been rather quiet. He had enjoyed his day in the limelight as spokesman for the couple, styling himself as personal secretary to the Prince, but lately he had been closeted with Mack somewhere in the city. Harriet had lost track of Black and White's progress, though she recalled seeing figures of over a thousand bars across the United Kingdom. Then, in late October, just as her problems with passports reached their climax, the announcement came like a gust of icy air: Black and White Milk Bars was in liquidation. As Percy had predicted, Mack's ambition had outstripped his abilities. Though the bars remained popular and all generated good revenue, he could not cover his mounting debts.

> *We went ahead too fast,* he said. *The responsibility is mine, we didn't have enough capital. Every one of our centres has made a profit this year, despite the bad summer and last year we made £11,000.*[419]

Percy, when he heard the news, was beside himself. Hadn't he warned them, time and again, to be patient, to protect their capital while it grew? Hadn't they learned from others' mistakes? What about the cautionary tale of Strand and Pitt Street Properties, the millstone around his own neck all these years? And what about the loan? How did Norman propose repaying that? Didn't he realise how far out on a limb Percy had gone on his behalf, risking who knew what penalty over his management of the family trust? Norman resisted talk of crying over spilt milk but, with typical insouciance, deflected his brother's ire and retreated to his club. Mack, on the other hand, was his usual ebullient self:

> *I'll be back,* he declared. *I'd put my heart and soul into this business, and plenty of my money, too, and now I'm finished with it all. But I can take it on the chin. I've got plans running through my head for something which I think will give everybody a surprise. No! it's a secret. But I hope that when I disclose my ideas it will catch on as milk bars have done.*
>
> *When I opened England's first milk bar over three years ago, I founded a new industry in the face of amused incredulity. There are now 1,300 milk bars in this country, of which I had seventeen. Thousands of people are being given employment through that idea of mine.*[420]

Percy observed, wryly, "'Plenty of *my* money'? He was bankrupt when they launched the business, all the money came from us! As for 'thousands of people' in employment, what about the hundreds of Black and White employees now in dole queues?" And if Mack had a "secret" plan for a new business, he could whistle for capital in whatever hare-brained scheme that turned out to be.

There was a further blow in November, when reports arrived from New York of the sudden death of Earl Beauchamp. He had been in transit on his way to Australia, where he planned to stay for six weeks at his home in Bellevue Hill. Now estranged from his British family, save one loyal daughter, Lady Dorothy Lygon, and in the final stages of cancer, he sought the peace of isolation and the goodwill of the Australian people for his last days. The voyage across the Atlantic took its toll and, no sooner had he arrived in New York, where he was to attend a reunion of the American branch of the family, than he was admitted to hospital. The prognosis was grave, yet he discharged himself and returned to his suite at the Waldorf Astoria, abhorring the prospect of a hospital deathbed. He died on November 15th, Viscount and Viscountess Elmley and their daughter, Dorothy, at his bedside. Harriet was devastated by the news. Her true friend had been an exemplar of kindness, honesty, and old-fashioned chivalry through the worst of times. He had suffered terrible opprobrium in silence and with dignity.

Comparison with the secretive, superficially charming Radziwill was unavoidable and gave fresh perspective to Harriet's choice of spouse.

Nevertheless, she stiffened her resolve. She had made her bed and now she must lie in it. Christmas saw the couple still at the Mayfair. For the first time since 1919, Harriet was unable to join the exodus to the Riviera. Bitterly cold east winds in the run up to a white Christmas produced heavy snow over parts of southern and eastern England. There was some consolation in the knowledge that most of northern Europe was suffering even bleaker weather, which seemed to match the mood across the continent. In November, Nazi-led mobs had indulged in a night of terror against Germany's and Austria's Jewish population, destroying more than 1,000 shops and synagogues, arresting 30,000 and killing nearly forty.* Thousands of unaccompanied Jewish children were offered sanctuary in Britain as panic spread across Austria, Czechoslovakia, Poland, and Hungary. The hopes generated by Neville Chamberlain's declaration of "Peace in our time" after the Munich agreement had evaporated and everywhere were signs of preparation for war. Parts of London had already tested night-time blackout precautions against bombing attack, and army, navy and air force reserves were put on alert. As he had done in the Great War, Norman was one of the first to volunteer for reserve service. He was too old for active flying duties but on the strength of his sterling service record he was accepted with the nominal rank of Pilot Officer.

By January, Hitler's attention turned to Poland. Danzig, where Mary Atkinson had fled less than two years before, was a free state run by the Nazis under the auspices of the League of Nations, but Hitler pressed the Poles to cede all control over the port city, insisting "Sooner or later, Danzig will return to Germany." Polish protests to the League and nominal allies, France, and Great Britain, were deflected as Chamberlain, Daladier and their cabinets desperately played for time. Norman and his circle were disdainful of this weak-willed response to the crisis though even the most belligerent among

---

* Later to be known as "Kristallnacht" (Night of Broken Glass).

them were sobered by the daily newsreels from Germany of marching stormtroopers, columns of tanks, and armadas of bombers filling the skies.

And still there was no good news for Prince and Princess Radziwill. In January, the Prince was finally granted a new passport, again limited to six months, but Harriet's was once more denied pending ratification of the marriage. Radziwill left London as soon as the passport was delivered, with a promise to return and escort Harriet to Antonin a soon as she was able to travel. While he headed for Monte Carlo with Villa Bon Accord at his disposal, Harriet was left holding the fort. She had dwindling expectations of ever freeing herself from the west end of London and increasing concern for her financial wellbeing. The Prince had left behind his elderly Rolls-Royce, which was in a poor state of repair, with instructions to have it ready for travel to Antonin without delay. He would pay for all mechanical restoration once they regained control of his assets but, for the time being, would Harriet see to any bills arising? This was bad timing on his part. News came of another legal case brought against Radziwill in Paris. A Madame Hirsch was suing him for money she alleged she had lent him. One of the witnesses was Jeanette Suchestow, who stated that, while living with her in Monte Carlo, the Prince had to ask her for money when he wanted a drink or a shave. She had had to pawn her jewellery to pay his bills.[421] Loath to believe the testimony of a disaffected lady, Harriet submitted Radziwill's instructions to Norman, who arranged for the vehicle to be taken to the Rolls-Royce workshop. Once more, Harriet faced the prospect of paying hundreds of pounds for no personal benefit and, she feared, slim chance of repayment.

February, and her concerns for and about the Prince had grown. He'd moved to Italy, where relatives had offered yet more temporary accommodation, but she'd heard nothing from him since his departure from England, her passport application was stalled, and her expenses frequently outstripped her sporadic income. She moved from the Mayfair, whose long-term residents included Ladies de Freece, Davies and Samuel, and Randolph Churchill, son of Winston,[422] to the cheaper Hotel Splendide, in Piccadilly, and redoubled her efforts to extract more cash from her bequest. She often wished David had left part of her endowment in a British bank. March came and went with no reply to her letters to the Prince. She felt sure he would soon return with news about the estate and that his silence could be explained by his preoccupation with legal and financial matters. And then, out of the blue, an official letter from the Polish Consulate arrived in April, followed by an envelope containing her new passport, and finally, a brief note from Radziwill. He had permission to travel to Antonin, so could she arrange for his car to be delivered to Paris, from where he would drive to Poland? He would send for her once he'd arrived and organised her accommodation. At last! But there was still the matter of her visa. The letter from the Consulate had hinted it would be granted "soon", perhaps in a matter of weeks. She could only wait.

She had had little to occupy or console her during her confinement in the Splendide. There were occasional glimpses of Bertha's name in the papers and even fewer meetings face to face. Bertha and Joyce still lived close by in their Park Lane apartments. Both were accomplished horsewomen, frequent award winners at show jumping meets, but their busy lives left little time for socialising outside their immediate set. Harriet's lifeline had been the almost daily letters between her and Kathleen. Her artist friend had kept up their correspondence through months of separation, finding time to encourage Harriet and provide a window into the Parisian scene from which Harriet had been excluded. Now, if only her visa came through, she could escape to Antonin, with a side trip to Paris to collect Kathleen, and claim her title once and for all. That is, if Hitler did not follow up his most recent threat to Poland. At the end of April, he had torn up the non-aggression pact he had signed in 1934. The United Kingdom responded by introducing conscription for men aged 20 and 21, the first ever in peacetime. Norman's advice was to stay in London until the situation was clearer, but she had come too far to surrender now. For the time being, she could at least use her new passport to break the monotony and enforced solitude of London with a trip across the Channel, perhaps even as far as Monte Carlo. Kathleen found a small hotel for her in Paris, the Windsor on Rue Vital. They could share a room for a few days while Harriet prepared to reunite with her husband and hand over his car. She got as far as Le Touquet and was about to take the Paris train to meet Kathleen, when a message came from Norman: she was needed back in London to sign over the lease of the Regent Street shop. Freed from his involvement with the milk bars, Norman had applied his mind to realising the value of the remaining sixty years of the lease and had secured final settlement with the House of Fraser. However, the deal could not be sealed without Harriet's signature. She cancelled her rail ticket and packed for the return across the Channel. She wrote to Kathleen:

> *Dear Kathleen*
>
> *I like the look of the Windsor and it seems bright and central so when I come over book there.*
>
> *Unfortunately I have to return to London to sign some leases connected with Regent Street so I can't get there for quite ten days or two weeks as the car will not be ready till next Monday. I mean the Rolls-Royce belonging to the Prince. I do wish you could see your way to come over and we could return and motor to Paris together as the car is so large for one person …*[423]

Her frustration mounting, she hurried back to London and suffered through the tedious sign-over of the lease. It appeared that Norman had not had to concede much to House of Fraser, restoring the health of Stewart Dawson's London accounts. Very well, but Paris still called, and the Prince's car was almost ready for shipment. Now, if the man himself could join her, (avoiding his creditors in the French capital) he could take possession of the Rolls, make his way to Poland, and claim some of that fortune he had promised her. She was already scraping the bottom of her local account to foot her own and his bills, not to mention the cost of the car repairs, which was not far short of £200. It was about time he made good on his promise; she could only extend credit so far, as Kathleen kept reminding her. Something would have to be sacrificed in the short term and with sadness she opted to close the Villa, paying off all the staff. She seldom used it during the summer, though it was occasionally let, but who knew how long she would be away in Poland? Best to keep it under wraps until matters were settled at Antonin. As was her habit she had fallen back on the hope of a win in the lottery, sending whatever spare cash she could scrape together to Kathleen for the purchase of more tickets.

Towards the end of May, she wrote:

Ma Chère

If you have at any time brought me luck you will be the first to benefit by it, so hurry up and send your prayers out. Hope to see you early next month. Will let you know the date, but, in the meantime when I release money from Australia will send a bit on for more tickets and a bit for yourself, so send on the papers when you get them for last lottery.

Love

Harriet Dawson.[424]

The breakthrough came on the first day of June, when her visa arrived in the post. Radziwill had not waited for his car but had travelled directly to Poland, where his erratic behaviour upon his arrival had done little to mend relations with his family. Harriet's letter to Kathleen that day expressed her mixture of relief, confusion, frustration, and hope:

Dear Kathleen

Just got your letter posted on to London and my visa for Poland arrived today so in two weeks' time I go down to the Prince's palace at Antonin unless I hear from the Prince that he won't stay there. He arrived there I hear from Leo [Radziwill's valet] yesterday and he was supposed to stay at a nursing home but wouldn't do that – went to some relatives and wouldn't stay with them, only one night and now I don't know what he is going to do or what I am going to do. However, if I go will you come also as I hate going alone. However, I shall be here for a week or ten days and if you could come over do so and I shall pay all expenses here on travel. I know you are very careful in your wants and don't forget to send me the lottery ticket and I will also pay you for that. I get some money next week …

In haste always

Harriet[425]

Later the same week she scribbled another note to Kathleen, repeating most of her previous letter. She was still in the dark over the

Prince's movements but remained determined to make the journey while still in possession of passport and visa.

> ... *No use crying over spilt milk,* she wrote, *as I feel sure the day will come when once I get things put right and a little more of the needful.*

Once again, she appealed to Kathleen to accompany her on the journey, with a promise to pay all her costs and share the expected hospitality of Antonin with her friend:

> ... *Plenty to eat and plenty to drink, I hear a good bed to sleep on. I shall take the big car [the Prince's Rolls-Royce] and Norman will go in his own car – but I must know as I must take someone and would prefer you to a stranger. Will send for the ticket in a couple of days when I get some money. I am keeping the hotel [the Windsor, where she hoped to meet Kathleen in Paris] and prices seem to be nice.*
>
> *Au revoir*
>
> *Harriet*[426]

Her hopes of meeting with Kathleen either in London or Paris, and of Kathleen's accompanying her to Antonin were not to be realised. Though the artist kept up a lively correspondence, replying by return post to Harriet's letters, she deflected every attempt to persuade her to leave Paris with light-hearted chat. It was just too difficult at present, she had exhibitions to arrange or visit, commissions to finish, dealers and agents to see; in short, a life of her own to lead. Still, she found time to search out bargains in dress fabrics for Harriet, who was always on the lookout for something to freshen her décolletage. On June 5th, Harriet wrote:

> *Dear Kathleen*
>
> *I think an old piece of brocade, different colours, you know what I like, mauve, pink and greens mixed. You can pick up a piece at any old second hand shop or old furniture shop very cheap. ... The numbers as you know are 17-36-0. You remember poor old Lord Beauchamp and the bracelet. I still wear it, he was such a dear and a gentleman to his finger tips, wasn't he?*

She made a last attempt to persuade Kathleen to come to London, hoping that this initial step might weaken her friend's resistance to accompanying her to Poland:

You needn't have let your people know you had been here and we could have returned in a week or ten days' time together. I am only waiting for the Prince's big Rolls car to be finished and then off to Antonin.

But Kathleen was not to be moved, and by the time of her departure from London Harriet had accepted that she would be travelling alone:

I leave here on Thursday for Dresden so shall not be staying in Paris. Will be going over in the new boat train arriving in Paris too early for you to come down see me otherwise I should ask you to do so, then we will motor on to Dresden.

I shall try and give you the money for the ticket. I will also wire you when I get there my address to send it on to me. I am not a bit anxious about going. I would prefer a holiday in Paris but I must see about what's doing and my future plans with the Prince

Au revoir, memories

Harriet.[427]

There was one, final exchange of letters, when Kathleen passed on word from Anne, Harriet's former housemaid at the Villa. Anne had stayed on to the last, when other staff were let go, and had been on hand to cook and clean for the Prince and his valet as they passed through on the way to Italy. Now unemployed, the maid remained nearby, in the hope of finding a position in one of the many other mansions in the Principality. She expressed her concerns that the unoccupied Villa would deteriorate in the damp winter months without constant maintenance and pleaded with Kathleen to intercede on her behalf with Harriet to employ at least a caretaker staff. Harriet dashed off a note to Kathleen as she packed her bags for Poland:

Yes, once I get my Villa into my own hands I shall never let it again. I will run it on cheaper lines, good cook, house parlour maid and woman coming in daily to do the heavy work such as steps, kitchen

> *floors etc. Am not sure about Anne, will see when I see her. I want useful workers these days, not ladies who want to sit around and do what they want to do etc.*

She added a postscript that revealed her growing concern over the Prince's bona fides:

> *I shall try to get the car in my name. It's in his at present and if I take it he could say it's his and take it back and it's cost me nearly two hundred to get it done up at the Rolls-Royce Co.*[428]

On June 15th Norman's Phantom drew up outside the Splendide behind the Prince's car. Harriet stepped from the foyer and took in the sights and sounds of the busy traffic in Piccadilly one last time, as the chauffeur held open the door to the rear compartment of the Rolls-Royce. With a nod from Norman the engine rumbled into life and the two vehicles commenced their stately convoy through St. James's, along streets that recalled David's and her past lives, down the edge of Green Park, then south towards Victoria Station, where the Boat Train waited. Despite her bravura assurance to Kathleen, Harriet was more than "a bit anxious". Her journey would be long and tiring, through France and Belgium, across Germany into the very border country where, every day, tensions rose between Poland and its western neighbour. Thank goodness for Norman. His black Phantom would be her escort and reassurance, a visible reminder of British strength and resolution that would see them reunited with the Prince.

A Close-Run Thing

For most of the drive across Europe, Harriet paid little attention to the passing scenery, preferring the privacy and security of the Rolls' spacious passenger compartment. To relieve her boredom and loneliness she joined Norman in the front seat of his car from time to time, but as they drove through Germany his running commentary on the political crisis became too much for her and she retreated to the Prince's car. The further east they motored, the more signs of preparation for war were apparent. Grey columns of army transports, ammunition carriers, tracked vehicles sprouting machine guns, and towed artillery pieces lined the roads or ranged in fields or forest clearings. Squads of grey-uniformed infantrymen marched through towns and villages or climbed aboard open-topped lorries. Unusual numbers of aircraft with bright blue undersides, black and white crosses on wings and sides, droned overhead. More than once they were halted by armed guards for inspection of passports and visas. They were always waved through until they reached the Polish border, near Görlitz, where the wait seemed interminable while officials dealt with jostling queues of anxious travellers. Once they reached the head of the line, their own crossing was prompt and polite thanks to Norman's fluent German and his practised self-assurance. Inspection of Harriet's documents on the Polish side of the border raised a few eyebrows among the harassed officials but rubber stamps were applied, and they were off, on the final leg to Antonin.

After a short stop in Wroclaw for rest and refreshment, where Polish troops congregated in numbers that rivalled the opposing Germans, Norman announced that they should be at the palace within an hour. The vehicles refuelled, oil reservoirs and radiators checked and topped up, they set off to the north-east, through more nondescript towns, into open countryside covered with summer crops. Forests of conifers displaced the cultivated fields in the last twenty miles, and numerous small lakes shimmered in the June sunlight. As they motored beside yet another lake, the trees on their left opened to reveal a winding driveway, its curve concealing their destination. One last turn and there was the palace of Antonin. Harriet was taken aback at the sight. She had imagined a grand chateau or English stately home, but this edifice resembled nothing she had ever seen before, certainly not a palace. Instead of the expected stone or brick, it appeared to be constructed of unpainted wood. Its proportions were odd: three or more storeys high but hardly as wide as it was tall. It looked to be cruciform in plan, with two short wings protruding from the central tower. The tower was crowned with a conical roof from which a tall, cylindrical chimney extended. They alighted from the cars and were greeted by courteous members of the Prince's staff, whose command of English put them at ease. There was no sign of the Prince, but it was explained he would not be far away. Harriet stood on the steps before the tall, embossed front door and took in the surrounding gardens. Unlike the palace itself, they had an English look, with beds of annual and perennial plants cut into well-kept lawns. To her delight, she recognised her own name planted in blossoms in one of the more prominent beds. What a touching tribute! After months of isolation in London, fearing she had been forgotten, to think that the Prince had gone to this trouble to welcome her home.

Stepping inside, the English couple were unprepared for the exotic interior. Rather than a foyer or entrance hall and grand staircase, with chandeliers hanging from a plaster ceiling, this was one great room, surrounded by galleries on three or four levels and dominated by the colossal, cylindrical chimney at its centre. The ornate, fluted chimney was painted white, with coloured friezes at the level of the two galleries. Mounted hunting trophies hung from the friezes. Dark-stained exposed beams radiated from where the chimney penetrated the conical roof, the green painted ceiling between them adorned with gold leaf. The major-domo explained that the palace had been built as a hunting lodge for an earlier Radziwill in 1824. Frederic Chopin had stayed here more than once, and it had always been popular with the Radziwill family and friends. Harriet followed the major-domo across the room, where a door led to one of the adjoining wings. Here, the layout was more conventional, with private rooms looking out to the gardens. So, this was to be her home. Not exactly Villa Bon Accord or Wilga, but what tales she could tell once back in London or Monte Carlo. For she was in no two minds: Antonin would be at most a summer retreat, or perhaps an autumn one, it would depend on their commitments in London for the summer season and how soon the cooler weather drove them south once more.

When the Prince arrived, he seemed pleased to be reunited with his new wife, was affable towards Norman and grateful for the delivery of his car. He had little to say about the events of the past months and Harriet was too tired to press him for details; they had time enough for that when she recovered from the journey. But neither that evening, nor in the weeks that followed, did he explain his long silence or dwell on the past. He was absent on the estate or in lawyers' offices much of the time, leaving his Princess to her own devices in and around the palace. She was looked after well by the household staff and came to enjoy the Polish cuisine served in the dining hall. Menus featured hearty soups, many meat dishes, pork, veal, and beef predominating, crumbed or in rich sauces, plenty of excellent steamed vegetables, and rather rich pastries for desserts. After Norman left, Harriet's days at Antonin were long and for the most part solitary. Radziwill charmed her when at home, but conversation was superficial and soon over as he retired to compose yet another letter of protest or supplication or disappeared on a further mission to his family. They entertained from time to time, but she knew few of his local circle and every occasion reminded her of how far away she was from her old friends and acquaintances. She explored the house, wandered the gardens, wrote letters home, but boredom set in. Antonin was miles away from the nearest town of any size, half a continent from Paris or London. She started to count the days to when they could return to Monte Carlo and reopen the Villa.

Not six weeks since her arrival, she suffered a bad fall, injuring her knee. She was in need of medical attention. The Prince summoned his own physician. She was put to bed under his care, but her injuries were more serious than at first thought. A stay in a nursing home was recommended but there was none nearby. After much discussion, with Norman weighing in from a distance, it was decided to repatriate her as far as Dresden,* where high quality care was to be found.

* Probably Dresden. The city of Harriet's nursing home stay was not explicitly identified but Dresden is the closest city of any size to the Polish border.

Relieved to be that much closer to her real homes and in a real city, Harriet took stock of her situation. She was in the dark concerning the Prince's plans, still footing many of his bills with no sign of repayment of past loans, far from friends and familiar haunts in the middle of a Europe that daily grew more unstable and threatening. A speech by Britain's Foreign Secretary, Lord Halifax, had warned Hitler that Britain was "ready to fight at once" to resist aggression against Poland. In Danzig, the Nazis ordered fifty thousand men to join the so-called Free Corps, stoking fears of an internal coup. Paris reported German troop movements on the western frontier, up to 60,000 German reservists were called up and Italian troop trains were seen on the Brenner Pass. Radziwill remained behind at Antonin, assuring her of his love and support but refusing to leave the palace for fear of losing it again. What would she do when she was back on her feet? Returning to Antonin might be a step in the wrong direction but would she face obstacles if she attempted to enter Britain on her Polish passport? The situation resolved at the end of July. By then, it was clear that Hitler would find some pretext to attack Poland within weeks. The war of words was reaching a climax as leaders threatened ultimatums and sabres rattled in every land. As Harriet recovered and took her first steps, Norman cabled that he was on his way to rescue his mother from potential internment in a hostile country. He arrived at the beginning of August, saw to her discharge, made her comfortable in the rear seat of his car and whisked her away on the road to Paris.

By the time they arrived at the French coast Harriet needed no convincing that war was imminent. Royal Airforce bombers passed overhead on training flights, and there was talk of a British Expeditionary Force to help the French defend the Maginot Line. No sooner had they settled into their London hotel when a test began of five hundred barrage balloons above the city. A trial of the largest air raid black out in Britain's history was announced for August 10th, from midnight to 4 a.m. News came that Berlin had already staged a full-dress practice, lasting for four days.[429]

With no news from Antonin, Harriet was desperate. There was no question of her returning to Poland now, and travel to Monte Carlo was impractical and probably unsafe. In any case, the Villa was shut down, reopening it now would be difficult. But would she be any safer in London? The entire city was on a war footing, with sand-bagged doorways, windows criss-crossed with tape to mitigate the effects of bomb blasts, lights dimmed or extinguished. Already people were evacuating to supposedly safer towns and villages further north. She had no desire to rusticate in some rural backwater, she'd had quite enough of that life at Antonin. Then there was young David to consider. He had gone up to Reading University but at less than sixty miles from London that was no guarantee of his safety should the bombers arrive. She consulted Norman. Percy and Stuart were urging a return to Australia, reuniting the whole family. Norman agreed that his mother and nephew should make the journey while they could, but he was committed to serve the mother country and would remain in London. Bookings were arranged with P&O, David's plans to return to Reading at the end of the summer vacation were cancelled, and as August drew to a close, Harriet and her grandson joined hundreds of other anxious travellers aboard the Oronsay for the long voyage south. She had little hope of seeing the Prince until the war, if it came, was over. In her haste to leave Antonin most of her personal possessions, including some of her treasured jewellery had been left at the palace. She had exhausted her available funds paying for the hospital in Dresden, the journey to England, the London hotel and now the fares to Australia. There was plenty in reserve to replenish her Australian bank account but very little of the needful to hand. She even had unpaid debts in London and would have to trust Norman to see to them.

The Oronsay powered down the Channel and into the Bay of Biscay. On board, every ear was tuned to the radio broadcasts and all eyes on bulletin board summaries of British newspapers. Hitler's rhetoric had reached new extremes and with the signing of the Nazi-Soviet non-aggression pact all hope of peace in Europe ended. On September 1st German troops crossed the Polish border and swarms of dive bombers obliterated resistance on the ground. British and French reaction was swift, invoking their treaty with the Poles, but the die had been cast and Hitler's army rolled on. Neville Chamberlain's ultimatum to the Nazis expired unanswered on September 3rd and war was declared. The Oronsay's passengers willed their captain and crew to squeeze every knot of speed out of her and bring them safely to the southern oceans. Only when the port of Freemantle hove into sight did they relax, as a line was thrown to a friendly tugboat.

Harriet had kept to her cabin for most of the voyage, still recovering her strength from the accident and worrying over daily reports of the disastrous capitulation of the Poles. She did not doubt that Antonin had been overrun but she dared not imagine the fate of its household and of the Prince himself. Had he not said that he would stay on to defend his rights? But it was one thing to brazen out a legal contest with family rivals, quite another to man the barricades against an invading army. Had he escaped to France or Italy, where he could still rely upon the charity of more sympathetic relations? It was pointless to speculate, she knew, but what else could she do? Hope was all she had left.

On November 1st they docked in Sydney. Harriet's feelings were mixed. She had left Australia behind, perhaps for good, when she arrived in Monte Carlo in '37. With the marriage to Radziwill she had taken a further step away, loosening the ties to her antipodean past. She had missed her Australian family, particularly young Harriet, but lived in hope of a reunion in one of her northern hemisphere homes someday. She was getting too old for long sea voyages, preferring the easy two-day drive through France each season. She could even have accepted periods at Antonin under those circumstances, had fate allowed. On the other hand, as she felt the warm sun on her face and glimpsed the splashes of purple from jacaranda trees on the far shore, she admitted that Sydney had its compensations. Nothing compared with the natural beauty of the harbour, and the benign climate contrasted with damp, gloomy London, and often outshone Monte Carlo, where drizzling rain could keep her indoors on winter days. She returned to her cabin, collected her handbag and wrap, pinned on her hat, and with a last look in the mirror to powder her face, closed the door behind her and walked the few yards to the gangway, where her grandson awaited. Percy or Stuart, she wasn't sure which of them, would be on the quayside, and she'd have to endure their questioning when all she wanted was a quiet room of her own for a while. There would be time enough for all that once she had settled in.

"This B... War"

Harriet no longer had a home of her own in Sydney. Percy's bachelor apartment and Stuart's Bellevue Hill flat were convenient for the city, but neither offered the space and privacy she needed. The Godhards had offered part of their harbourside apartment, which would be ideal accommodation for the Prince, should he ever escape Europe, but Harriet for the time being opted to occupy her old suite at The Australia. She preferred not to be a burden on her friends and family while she awaited news from Norman or the Prince. It wasn't long in coming. The Polish consulate in London informed Norman that the Prince was alive and well in Italy. So, he had escaped the Nazis, after all. Indeed, he had but, as Norman told it, not before he had shown his true colours. When the Germans occupied Antonin, he had pledged his allegiance and offered them the palace. He also offered to renounce his Polish citizenship in favour of his German birthright, reminding them of his service to the Kaiser. The Germans were not in a bargaining mood, pointing out that he was in no position to make an offer of a property they had already occupied, and, after a brief internment in Berlin, he was allowed to leave for France and thence to somewhere in Italy, nobody was sure exactly where. "That German swine", as Norman called him, had betrayed his family, his country and everything Harriet had married him for.* Harriet was stunned. She had been taken for a fool, giving her trust and far too much of her wealth to a charming trickster. She should have seen the warning signs when Mme

---

* Dariusz J. Peśla Prince Michał Radziwiłł "Rudy" 1870-1955 Women "antonin maharaja" op. cit. Peśla and others contend that Harriet called Radziwill "a German swine" and instituted divorce proceedings, but her letters to Kathleen O'Connor and her statements to the Australian press show that she remained publicly loyal to him to the end of her life, whatever her personal feelings might have been. The appellation is much more likely to have been coined by Norman (the language is typically jingoistic, not Harriet's style), as the first recipient of the news, reflecting his disgust and embarrassment over the Prince's betrayal of trust.

Suchestow made her claims against the Prince, but she had been blinded by glamour and romance. Things could have been worse, she could even now be wasting away in a German internment camp or pining for home in some dingey Italian town, abandoned by her husband now that her usefulness as his banker was over. Under the circumstances, her accident had been fortuitous, providing the excuse for her escape to freedom. Nevertheless, she would face social humiliation if word of Radziwill's perfidy got about. She would preserve her dignity by maintaining the public face of one desperate for news of a husband who was an innocent victim of the war. He would be the gallant exile, dispossessed by evil invaders, his fate in the balance. She would be his Penelope, faithful and patient until his return.

In January 1940, she had the first test of her assumed role, when news came of the fate of other members of the Radziwill family. Cousins in the east of Poland had been executed by the invading Russians and another cousin, John, who was also a captive of the Russians, was said to have been released to the Germans. It was said he would occupy the position of Premier of Hitler's puppet Polish government. Harriet recognised the similarity of John's behaviour to her husband's and sprang to his defence:

*I do not believe a word of this cable. During the occupation of Poland, the family were robbed of their estates and were allowed to leave their country with only the barest of personal possessions. I heard two and a half months ago that my husband, Prince Michael, was a "prisoner" of the Nazi Government in Rumania. We planned, in the short time we were together, after the Nazis invaded Poland, to meet again in Australia. I have established a little home here, in Billyard Avenue, Elizabeth Bay, and I go to town every day in the hope that there will be a message from him to say he is coming. But now I feel like giving up all hope of ever seeing him again.**

She concluded:

The Poles are an intensely patriotic people. They will remain true.

---

* Daily News (Sydney) 3rd January 1940 P.5. Harriet had by this time taken up the Godhard's offer and moved to their home in Billyard Avenue, Elizabeth Bay.

She continued her correspondence with Kathleen, who intended to sit out the war in Paris. Like many in France, Kathleen was confident the Maginot Line would withstand any German advance. When this proved to be a vain hope, she took the advice of the British consul in Paris, gathered as many canvasses as she could and, rolling them into an African rug, walked out of her apartment and caught the first train to the coast. Days later, hungry and frightened after Luftwaffe aircraft had swooped and shot at the train, she boarded the ferry at St. Malo and crossed to the safety of Southampton. Unlike Harriet, she was too late to make the voyage to Australia, even had she wished to do so, and would see out the war in England.[430] Harriet's letters to Paris were forwarded to Bath, more than a hundred miles northwest of London, where Kathleen hoped to escape the bombing of the capital when it came, and they kept their friendship alive as both contemplated the bleak years of separation ahead. On April 9th, 1940, Harriet wrote on stationery that bore Percy's Bellevue Hill address:

> *Dear Kathleen*
>
> *Your letters are always welcome and I only wish I were near you instead of writing. Your news seems very cheery and I appreciate your sending me the fashion plates. Yes, I love reds, yellows and greens. I have some lovely clothes that I brought out but so few places to go and show them off – only one theatre and the rest of amusements pictures* etc. I go through agony when I begin to think of all the nice people I left behind including you, dear. Always your kind self, always anxious to give a helping hand but some day you will be rewarded and when I get a bit more of the needful I shall send you a bit and start my lottery tickets again.*
>
> *Oh, how I wish the B… war would end so that I could get back to the Villa and how I shall appreciate and live there always winter and summer with a week or two in Paris with yours truly … I hope you are keeping well and that we shall meet in Monte Carlo very soon as I shall return immediately.*

---

* "Pictures" – cinemas

Write soon and give me all your news. None from the Prince as yet so don't know if I am a widow or a grass one.

My love

Harriet[431]

Her relief upon arrival in Sydney having subsided, she felt as if she were in a waiting room, where little changed from day to day and somewhere else life, the life she once had, went on without her. Elsewhere people weathered the dangers of war but responded with a brave, gay face. She'd read of the spirit of the British in this time of adversity and with the benefit of hindsight would have preferred to join them in the thick of it than to sit out the conflict in dull Sydney. She'd managed perfectly well in the first war, even as the Zeppelins' bombs burst nearby. It couldn't be any worse this time, with the precautions for public safety on the ground and all those guns and barrage balloons to keep the bombers away. Sydney would never suffer bombing, life would go on with little to show there was a war somewhere, though she was dismayed when it was announced that the Navy had requisitioned land at Potts Point to expand its facilities around the dockyard. Several homes, including Wilga, which was still occupied by Charlemont Hospital, were to be taken over and turned into quarters for WRANs.* She had no illusions that the Navy would treat the old house with the respect it deserved. Meanwhile, her routine would comprise daily trips to the city for morning or afternoon tea with her dwindling circle of friends, theatre outings or an hour or two in the dark watching the latest Spencer Tracy or Myrna Loy film. She would lunch in town or with Stuart and Jean, young David, occasionally Percy. Stuart had little to occupy him beyond short meetings of the board of the New Zealand business and spent much of his time up at Palm Beach, where his son seemed to have settled into a life of parties and surfing. Young David had shown no interest in resuming his interrupted education. He claimed to be studying accountancy but had instead fallen into his father's footsteps, appearing at Sydney's best restaurants, escorting eligible

---

* WRAN – Women's Royal Australian Navy.

young ladies. He was not yet nineteen, but his matinee good looks made him the target of gossip columnists and photographers eager for a diverting article in the popular press. Stuart and Percy had appointed him "property manager" to assist the latter with the Pitt Street business, where he had little to do while Percy oversaw the moribund operation.

Percy still worried Harriet. Since 1937 he had been extricating the Stewart Dawsons from Springwood. After the fire that destroyed Bon Accord the site was cleared of rubble but left otherwise untouched, the rose beds soon infested with weeds and the terraced slopes behind crumbling and overgrown. An attempt to auction the site in 1938 saw no buyers. Bon Accord Investments was ready for winding up. Blue Mountains Shire Council had its eyes on the two golf courses, with a plan to consolidate them into a single, eighteen-hole course under its management. Percy was ready to sell, accepting the Council's offer of £2,500, but J.T. Wall, the owner of the other nine-hole course, held out for a better price. The Council considered his demand for £6,000 extortionate and threatened to resume the land if he failed to accept a reasonable offer. The negotiations dragged on through 1938 until Wall capitulated and the deal was sealed in September, when Percy initiated the liquidation of Bon Accord Investments Ltd. Even that proved to be a drawn-out affair. All the land comprising David's original purchase was under title to Bon Accord Investments and had to be released for sale to complete liquidation. The exceptions were the lots on which the two remaining houses stood. The Spinney would be retained for rental, and Bonnie Doon had since 1936 been the property of Estelle, now in residence with her husband, her two children, and her parents. There had been little local interest in the other vacant portions of the property, which had been sub-divided for the sale, and by 1940 only a couple of lots had been sold, the overgrown site of Bon Accord a dismal reminder of the Stewart Dawson heritage. The albatross of Bon Accord Investments would hang on Percy's neck a while yet.

Percy's luck at the track had not improved while his mother was away. Strathisla ran second time after time despite the best efforts of trainer and jockey. There was an occasional first place proving the horse's ability, but every time Percy's hopes were raised Strathisla would disappoint at the next outing. The meagre prize money for placings did nothing to offset Percy's expenses but, he reasoned, what else did he have to spend his cash on? And it was true, his tastes were modest compared to his two younger brothers'. He dined alone or only with close male friends, drove a good but modest car, and kept a low profile in Sydney society. When Thelma paid a surprise visit to Australia early in 1940 Harriet accepted her invitation to lunch at Romano's. Percy was nowhere in sight,[432] but a fortnight later Harriet persuaded him to join her for a reprise, and the threesome exchanged pleasantries. Thelma's marriage to Ronald Colman had ended in acrimony and, her career in movies over, she had returned, chastened and "short of the needful", to make the best she could of her life. If Thelma expected a reconciliation and second chance from Percy, she was to be disappointed. Twice bitten, though he remained on cordial speaking terms, he made no attempt to resume their relationship.

Rumours of the Prince's fate and whereabouts broke from time to time but the reports, coming from numerous uncredited sources, were confusing and often contradictory. In February, not long after Harriet had scoffed at the report of John Radziwill's defection to the Nazis, she was obliged to respond to another garbled account, which claimed the Prince was imprisoned in the town of Posen. Interviewed by a reporter from Sydney's "Truth", she took advantage of the newspaper's predilection for verbatim reporting to set the record straight, as she wished it. "Truth" reported:[433]

> *... Her persistent efforts to discover whether her husband had been killed or imprisoned or had managed to escape, were not until this week rewarded by any reliable information, and even now, with the knowledge that the Prince has been captured and held prisoner in Posen, the princess is still crippled by anguish as to his subsequent fate.*

The source of this information was a letter from Princess Marie Radziwill, another of his cousins by marriage, forwarded via the American Consulate in Rome, in which she wrote:

> *... I have been trying to obtain exactly the information you request. They told me first that my cousin, Prince Michael Radziwill, has been interned in his former estate, Antonin, in the dependency of Posen.*

Yesterday, they assured me that he had been interned in the town of Posen. Unfortunately, I have been unable to obtain any more definite information.

"Truth" noted:

Supplementary to this note, the American Consulate in Rome writes that the above news does not agree with information received through the Polish Consul General, and the American Consul in Berlin is being asked to obtain further particulars ... Swift changes in European politics and popular hostility towards many aristocratic families increase [the Princess's] deep concern for the safety of her prince-husband.

The reporter gave Harriet her chance to tell her story:

Goodness knows where he can be. He may be in a poorhouse for all I know. I have called and written to the Polish Ambassadors in every country, asking for news of him, but can hear nothing. Perhaps he was shot, murdered like his brother by those dreadful Russians. And the authorities won't tell me.

I blame myself now for the whole dreadful business. Six months ago the Prince asked me to take him to Australia to see my lovely country and I put off doing it so we had gone to the palace at Antonin from the South of France, where I have a villa.

My son, Major Norman Stewart Dawson, was staying with us. When I first saw the palace I thought it was something out of a fairy story. It was beautiful. Such grounds, such beauty, such silver and furniture and carpets! And the fisheries and greenhouses, dogs and horses! I loved it.

After six weeks, just when I was beginning to learn a few simple Polish phrases, I slipped and hurt my knee. Prince Radziwill insisted that I go to Germany for treatment and my son, the Major, motored me there. Then came the war. I was only just able to reach London safely. I said to my son, "I must go back to the Palace." But he said, "Mother, you'll only be caught and put into a concentration camp." I'm sure he saved my life. But I shall go on blaming myself that I didn't come to Australia earlier, and bring the Prince with me.

Revealing perhaps more than she intended about the Prince's character, Harriet concluded:

He is a magnificent looking man, tall and handsome, with exquisite manners. He had been for years in the diplomatic service. All the women fell in love with him when they met him. I expect he has been rather wicked where the ladies are concerned, but it wasn't his fault. Women all liked him so much. He is a great bridge player and a great reader, and he speaks six languages. Now if he is alive he must be a very sick man, penniless and perhaps in the workhouse.

On reflection, she should have toned down Radziwill's lady-killer traits, and had she said: "in the workhouse"? That rather dated her, didn't it? She was supposed to be fifty-seven and here she was talking like the septuagenarian she really was. She steered the interview toward the safer and more appealing topic of her new apartment, describing

the big sun verandah, bright with seagrass furniture in vivid colors, and a separate dining room and drawing room where he can have his bridge parties and where he can read. The view is right over the Harbor to the Heads. I think he will be happy here, if only Fate has allowed him to escape from his broken country. So I watch the arrival of every foreign ship, especially those from Italy, with hope still in my heart.

In her reference to Italy, she hoped to allay once and for all speculation that the Prince was still somewhere in occupied Poland or locked away in a German or Rumanian prison. All in all, she was satisfied with the interview. She had played for sympathy, maintaining her public loyalty to Radziwill while she suppressed her feelings of humiliation and betrayal. He had indeed been "rather wicked where the ladies are concerned" and she was just another of his foolish victims.

She was also having to deal with the consequences of her hasty departure from England. At the end of January, Manley Estates Ltd., of London served her with a bankruptcy notice for unpaid accounts. Wasn't Norman supposed to have dealt with all her bills? It seemed he or she had overlooked one for a couple of hundred pounds and her creditors had opted to sue her rather than permit a period of grace. She was miffed, had they forgotten there was a war on? Even in the lead up to the declaration her payments from Australia had become irregular and now, with currency restrictions in place, it could take weeks for wire transfers to be executed, they knew that. Percy stepped in:

> *We still lack details of the petition, but presume it resulted from a matter Princess Radziwill inadvertently overlooked when she left London. Our solicitors in London were as surprised as we were when we heard the news. They are attempting to clear up the matter as quickly as possible.*

And there the issue rested, but Harriet was hurt, nevertheless. Preserving her dignity was becoming a challenge. Her comfort was that her friends, especially the Godhards and Jacobsons, were loyal and always there to support and divert her. She accepted an invitation to chair a committee to raise money for a bronze plaque dedicated to Count Paul Strezlecki, the discoverer of Mount Kosciusko, Australia's highest peak.[434] She presided at a meeting of the Dalwood social committee to organise the Leap Year Fashion Parade, where she announced that, as Gladys Moncrieff was to be guest of honour, she had arranged for a special orchestra to play musical selections from the popular plays in which Miss Moncrieff had appeared.[435] In April, she was a guest at a charity fashion parade in the Wentworth ballroom.[436] Concerned that her grandson was adopting Norman and Stuart's indolent habits, she introduced him to Dalwood Homes' committee. He was a regular diner at Romano's, where the committee was to stage the annual Flower Ball on April 18th. The Stewart Dawsons retained a lasting friendship with Romano, whose reputation for quality and good taste was by now second to none in Sydney. He had taken up the baton from The Ambassadors for providing a venue for Dalwood Homes' and other charitable committees to stage fundraisers. The scale of the events might be smaller but what they lacked in size they made up for in style. Now, Harriet proposed David be given the chairmanship of his first committee. As she had done with Rita, she would be his mentor, but her hope was that he would find his feet and a real purpose in life beyond dining and dancing. She needn't have worried. David's self-confidence and easy charm carried him through. The event was judged a success and he won the admiration of ladies of the committee. Romano was impressed; he would keep an eye on the young man who might have inherited his grandmother's talent for enticing the punters and his uncle Percy's skill for organisation.

Winter came, the news from Britain was grim. In May, France and Norway had fallen; the British Expeditionary Force had been driven to defeat and escaped piecemeal from Dunkirk; the air above the Home Counties was filled with the rumbling of engines, rattling machine-gun fire and the smoke trails of doomed aircraft. Winston Churchill's call to arms in "the Battle of Britain" foretold worse times than any had feared. The First War had stripped layers of historic privilege from society, but British tradition died hard and even through the Depression crowds had flocked to great public events where fashion, class and breeding could be displayed. Now, there would be no house parties in the country over Ascot week, for this year there would be no Ascot. There would be no tennis at Wimbledon, no rowing at Henley, no Derby at Epsom, no Tattoo at Aldershot, and no flowers at Chelsea. London's night life continued, though uniforms took the place of top hats and tails and evening frocks for women were almost non-existent. Harriet's determination to return wavered. As the threat of bombing raids grew, she feared for Bertha and Joyce, somewhere in the West End, and for Norman, who was "flying a desk", vexed that age kept him from defending his country in the air. And still there was no word from Prince Michael Radziwill. Despite early rumours of him in Italy, which Harriet followed up with letters to consulates and such members of her Riviera network as she retained, the confused message passed on from Princess Marie was all she had. Not so much as a note, no newspaper report or fragment of gossip hinted at the Prince's whereabouts or fate. As the months passed and local interest in Harriet's lost hero evaporated, she turned first with resignation and gradually with a sense of relief to home comforts. She had her two sons and most importantly, her grandchildren, close at hand. She had her memories of life here with a real husband who, apart from that one unfortunate affair, had been her strength and refuge. It was time to move on. She had to put her chaotic interlude with the Prince into perspective and focus her attention and love on her family. Percy, and through him, Norman, and Stuart, were in trouble with the law again.

In April, Perpetual Trustees commenced proceedings against Percy, charging breach of trust in the administration of David's estate. Perpetual alleged that in order to pay death and succession duties, Percy had obtained a loan from Stewart Dawson Strand Property Ltd. and executed a charge over shares in other Stewart Dawson companies. Since then he had not made a distribution to any of the beneficiaries named in the will, nor set aside a fund to answer annuities bequeathed to the likes of Estelle and her parents. The administration of the estate appeared to have come to a standstill, Perpetual alleged, and Percy, without its knowledge or consent had borrowed on behalf of the estate from the several companies and applied the money to making payments to "certain of the pecuniary legatees and annuitants." It sought to restrain Percy from collecting any part of the income and assets of the estate, and the appointment of a provisional receiver with power to become registered as the holder of shares in the companies and to petition for the winding up of all or any of them.[437]

It looked as if the chickens had come home to roost for Percy. Harriet had had no idea and still found it hard to believe that her income and that of Bertha, Lila, Vanna and all the others named in David's will had come, not from the sound investments David had made in the family companies but via a convoluted and perhaps illegal chain manipulated by her son. No wonder her "regular" payments had been anything but. And what about the other annuitants? Had they been left without a penny all these years? She recalled the case brought by Lila and wondered how much more would come to light if Perpetual dug deep. And there were those loans to Norman and Stuart. At the time, Percy had assured them all that it was above board. The pressure brought by Norman and Mack to provide capital for the milk bars had pushed him over the line further than he had admitted. It was only due to his persistent refusal to supply Perpetual with information about the transactions, in fact, any information at all, that he had got away with it until now. At least, that was Perpetual's assertion. Percy had another view of the matter and despite the whiff of scandal surrounding the case, he remained confident his innocence and probity would be demonstrated. He would marshal his defence and fight the case.

Through the winter months and into August, Percy was seldom seen, closeted in the offices of C. Don Service, the family solicitors. It was fortunate that Harriet's bankruptcy case was to be answered in London, where Norman retained control of the English estate, from which he could pay the debt. When it came to court, the silly affair was settled without fuss, as it should have been in the first place. The Sydney case was quite another matter. In the last week of July, all adjournments having been exhausted, Percy faced his accusers at the Court of Equity. Perpetual's barrister, Mr. Mason, KC, attacked with forensic precision.[438] Percy, he alleged, had "dissipated and wasted the assets" of the family estate. He should be excluded as trustee.

> *From 1932 Percy Stewart Dawson has not done a single thing urged by the Perpetual Trustee Co., a co-executor and trustee of his father's estate. The shares of the Dawson companies have not been registered since the death of David Stewart Dawson. The reason is easy to find in the fast and loose manner in which the Dawson companies have been managed.*

Apart from complete denial of all the charges, Percy asserted that Perpetual had knowledge of and acquiesced in his actions, and that there was ample security for advances. Percy's defence was that Perpetual had had many opportunities to discuss and approve or deny payments over the years and had failed to raise objections at any time. Mr. Mason asserted that the brothers had plundered the companies in 1936 for "loans" that Percy had no authority to grant. Norman owed the Pitt Street company £45,000, the New South Wales company £3,000, and the London company a further £11,200, despite being an undischarged bankrupt.[439]

It was becoming clear that Percy's management of the estate had been, at best, unorthodox, yet his defence team argued that nothing illegal had occurred. Perpetual's attempts to prove its case were undermined by relentless cross-examination of its witnesses, whose evidence was picked apart in detail. Since Perpetual had made no payments to the beneficiaries, how had they in fact been paid? When Dorothy Goodman, the bookkeeper of the companies, took the stand, she told Mr. Mason the directors had instructed her to make the payments to annuitants. She didn't know who kept the minutes of the companies. She had never kept the minutes or attended a meeting, and she couldn't name anyone who had prepared the minutes.

Perpetual's case was that the Stewart Dawson companies should be wound up under the "just and equitable" rule of the court if they were being run for the benefit of the directors, that an independent director be appointed and payments to the brothers must cease. But Percy was not yet ready to admit defeat and he knew his brothers relied on him to retain control of the trust and the companies. Mr. Mason could assert:[440]

> *Percy Stewart Dawson has looked after the Dawson family and himself, but has made no provisions for future generations of the Stewart Dawsons. The machinery of Company Law has been used for a swindle. Authorities should investigate these matters. The history of the Dawson family reveals that two sons, Norman and Stuart, are bankrupt, and that Percy is up to his ears in debt.*

but Percy's barrister submitted:

> *No case to remove Percy Stewart Dawson from the administration of the estate has been presented. Everything he has done was with the permission of the Perpetual Trustee Co., or with its subsequent agreement. Because of the complicated nature of the estate, the trustees should continue to manage it together.*

Mr Justice Roper adjourned the case to consider his judgement, which came not four weeks later. Having described the administration of the estate as "irregular and perplexing", he ruled:

> *On the application of the Perpetual Trustee Company, I grant an order restraining Percy Stewart Dawson, co-executor of the estate, from doing anything in his capacity as director, shareholder or otherwise as an officer of any of the companies in which the estate holds shares, or in his personal capacity to permit any advances or other payments without the consent of the court. I also direct that the affairs of the estate be inquired into by the Master-in-Equity. I believe the particular fault of the defendant has been to indulge the wants of himself, the testator's widow, and the two other sons, apparently thinking that their interests in the estate, and in the various companies, would be sufficient ultimately to permit the balancing of their accounts.*[441]

Percy's cosy arrangement to keep Perpetual at arm's length was over. He had hoped to play for time when the sale of the Strand Arcade to Strand and Pitt Street Properties failed to deliver the promised £700,000 windfall. His father's wish had been that the money received would be placed into the trust for honouring the conditions of his will. Instead, for over ten years as mortgagee in possession Percy had waited for the purchasers to show some sign of honouring their debt, but he knew in his heart this would never happen. He collected declining amounts of rent each year as tenants in the arcade closed their doors and shops remained vacant. Strand and Pitt Street Properties struggled to pay the bare minimum to cover the mortgage as their other businesses failed. There was little left over to maintain the arcade, which became shabbier year by year. And there was nothing, not a penny, to deposit in the trust account. He'd had to find cash to pay the death duties from the other companies, but when the court sanctioned this it became all too easy to extend the loans to pay the annuitants and to raise the additional loans to himself and his brothers. He had let things get out of hand, but it would all work out if he could find a buyer for the Strand Arcade. He'd said as much to Perpetual in 1937, when he believed there was still value in the property, but no new buyer emerged. He re-doubled his efforts, hatching plans for restoration of the family fortune.

Harriet might have been relieved that the court had tempered its judgment on Percy but even as the case ended, she was prostrated by the appalling news that Norman had been killed in a motor accident. Just weeks before he had been dealing with her bankruptcy case and corresponding with her in his inimitable way, keeping her abreast of London life. Now he was gone. News of the accident was sketchy, but it appeared he had lost control of his car (described as "a high-powered sports car") while driving in the blackout.* The

* Tom Clarke's opinion is: *"I somehow doubt that this was the Rolls-Royce Phantom. He wouldn't have had a petrol ration anything like big enough for such a car, most Rolls-Royces were decommissioned, and it was too big to be called a sports car. Had it been this car then there'd be evidence on the R-R records for parts and*

imposition of headlight masks might have made cities safer from night bombers but the dim, narrow beam they threw was barely adequate, even at the war-time speed limit of 20 miles per hour. In the first month of the war alone, over a thousand drivers, passengers and pedestrians had been killed in night-time accidents. Knowing Norman, he would have disregarded the speed limit. He was a more competent and less reckless driver than his younger brother, but his imperious, over-confident nature had been his downfall on more than one occasion. Perhaps a night out with his cronies, dining and drinking, had left him short of time to return to his RAF quarters. The official report was cryptic and brief. Bertha was left to deal with the funeral and cremation at Golders Green crematorium. Harriet's grief was profound; her favourite son had proved his valour in the first war and saved her life only a year before. He had lived a colourful, adventurous life, risking his neck in Africa, over the Channel and in Russia, taking on Percy's front-of-house duties at The Ambassadors, doing his bit for Britain in the General Strike, and lending his talents to the Black and White business. He had been looking forward to a reunion with his mother after the war, when he would have made it his business to track down the missing Prince and demand justice for Harriet. Percy and Stuart commiserated, but they were no substitute for dear Norman, they would never fill the void in her heart.

She had to get away, anywhere to cope with her sorrow. She had been planning her annual excursion to Melbourne for the racing season. She would make the journey south, retire to her suite at the Hotel Australia and grieve for her son, alone. A day at the races might serve to divert her; she would keep her options open. Coincidentally, Thelma was down for the season as well and was one of the first to call on Harriet to offer her condolences. Harriet was touched by Thelma's warmth and empathy. Her former daughter-in-law, a

---

repairs – it would have been a big smash to end in death and thus more likely the vehicle concerned was written off" [it wasn't – there are post-war records of the car]. It is also possible that he was driving or being driven in a borrowed car. I can find no official record of the accident (15th October 1940) that might provide the missing information (GN).

youthful fifty, offered the female companionship she craved. It was a pity they had not met during Percy's brief marriage to the star. Their friendship might have compensated Thelma for Percy's forced absence at the front and seen a happier future for the marriage. For now, it was enough to have a shoulder to cry on, away from the depressing, empty apartment in Sydney. Thelma accepted her invitation to share her suite at the hotel and the two women reminisced about the good times abroad they both hoped to re-live when the war was over.

But the war was not over, not then nor for another four and a half years. Harriet's enforced exile in Billyard Avenue grew wearisome. She continued her "at homes", dropped into Dalwood committee meetings where she took more of a back seat as younger women stepped forward, and waited, waited for news from Europe. The entry of Japan and the USA into the conflict at the end of 1941 raised the stakes for native Australians. Now it could be young David's turn to face the enemy somewhere in Europe, the Middle East or nearer home. The thought of losing her grandson, the bearer of the family name, pained her almost as much as the inconsolable loss of Norman. As things turned out, Stewart Dawson honour was to be upheld not by the younger generation but by the oldest of her children and the least likely candidate. In May 1941, Harriet received a cable from London, signed "Andrews, Ashley Gardens":

> *Mrs. Verrall fully recovered. She is a very, very brave and conscientious member of the firewatching unit I command. She and her daughter have been recommended for the George Medal for extreme bravery under gunfire.*[442]

Bertha and Joyce had themselves been bombed out of their apartments, but this had not deterred them from their nightly patrols as searchlights swept the skies and bombs whistled down. Though high explosive bombs brought instant death and destruction where they fell, it was the thousands of incendiaries, no bigger than a policeman's truncheon, that spread the conflagrations consuming whole districts. Filled with magnesium powder, they burned fiercely for up to a quarter of an hour, hot enough to melt steel. Throwing out sparks, they ignited everything flammable for yards around them. They were especially dangerous when trapped in gutters on roofs or if they happened to drop into a building through a hole pierced by shrapnel. Volunteer Firewatchers were expected to get close to the flaming sticks, often in confined spaces, where they directed jets of water pumped by hand onto the flames, or shovelled sand onto the bomb itself. They had to be agile and alert for falling debris. Smoke and embers could quickly overcome them if the wind changed, or a door opened unexpectedly. Bertha was now fifty-four but by any standard she was fit and athletic, thanks to years of vigorous exercise as a competitive horsewoman. Joyce, who lived nearby with her husband and young daughter, had followed in her mother's footsteps and they made formidable partners.

There were other losses. The Navy occupied Wilga and demolished most of the terraced gardens to make way for an electricity sub-station. The "Greek temple" that Harriet had tried without success to donate to the nation in 1933 was one of the few objects to survive the bulldozers. The Sydney Morning Herald mounted a campaign in December 1940 to save the monument. In an article headlined: "A Masterpiece. Sydney should save this", F. S. Burnell wrote:

> *Among the various properties at Potts Point resumed in connection with the new naval dock is Charlemont Hospital, and in the grounds of Charlemont, overlooking the water, is [a] beautiful little building … As an example of ancient Greek art unique in Sydney, and perhaps in Australia, one naturally asks what is to become of it?*

Burnell described the monument for his readers, concluding:

> *In its present position the Lysikrates monument … is probably unseen by and unknown to at least nine-tenths of the population of Sydney. An opportunity now for the first time apparently presents itself of transferring it to a site in which it may be beheld and admired by the general public, the Botanic Gardens, let us say, or the grounds of Sydney University.*[443]

Except that there had been such an opportunity. Not only had Harriet's generous offer been rebuffed, but Sydney had also completely forgotten it and she was to receive not a word of credit then or later for her gesture. By now she was almost past caring. She had come to terms with the closing of the last happy chapter of her life in Sydney. Let others claim kudos for saving the temple; she would always remember it as David's monument.*

Another chapter came to an end in 1942, when Mack died in London, at the age of sixty-five. After the failure of Black and White he had attempted a final comeback, somehow finding capital to open a cake and pie shop, but his nostalgic return to his commercial origins was soon over and, penniless, he ended his days alone and forgotten. He had been Harriet's last link with Norman. Had he survived she was sure her son would not have allowed his friend to sink without trace. Between them they would have found a new venture on which to rebuild their fortune, despite Percy's wings being clipped and the Australian funds cut off. There was never a dull moment with Mack, and he had given Norman a reason to live when he might have continued to drift and waste his talents.

Her correspondence with Kathleen somehow kept up, though some letters went unanswered. There were just too many places for the mail to be lost or diverted by harassed postal services. Bath had not been as safe as Kathleen had been led to believe and she was bombed out of her lodgings in 1942. She hadn't a penny to her name, her income from Australia having ceased upon her mother's death at the end of 1941; the few possessions she had brought from France had been lost in the bombing, and she had nowhere to go. Harriet was powerless to intervene, but Kathleen was to find a local benefactor in nearby Wiltshire, Father Duggan Coates, who accommodated her with other refugees in the large rectory. Grateful as she was, she was restless to escape rural England. Though her aim was to return to her beloved France this would be impossible until after the liberation and in early 1944 she toyed with the idea of a spell in Australia. Harriet was delighted:

---

* It was moved to the Royal Botanic Gardens, where it remains to this day, facing Farm Cove. It fell into disrepair over the years until it was restored by John and Patricia Azarias, with funds raised through their creation of the Lysikrates Foundation. A plaque commemorating Martin and the restoration was affixed. There is no mention of Harriet or David Stewart Dawson on the plaque nor in any contemporary reference to the monument.

Just received your letter and do so wish you could come out – as we always get on so well together and I could take a small flat until peace and then return to Monte Carlo. Am sure Ruby [Kathleen's agent] *would help sell one or two pictures and a few introductions from me.*

Happy memories and love

Harriet Radziwill[444]

She had quit the Billyard Avenue apartment, accepting she would never see the Prince in Sydney, and was back in her old suite at The Australia. But if Kathleen were to escape to Sydney a flat overlooking the harbour would be a perfect spot for a small studio, almost as good as the Villa. Peace wasn't far off, everyone said, and when the day came, they could sail back to the Mediterranean and reclaim Villa Bon Accord together. Kathleen's reply was encouraging, she was open to the idea of a short spell in Australia before peace returned to France. But when the Allies landed in Normandy in June 1944, and it seemed it would only a matter of time before Paris was liberated and the evacuees could return, she grew cool on the idea. Her letters to Harriet remained friendly and full of the gossip they loved to share, but she avoided discussion of any plans to travel to Australia. Harriet clung to hope. In January 1945 she wrote again to Kathleen. There was a scheme whereby orphans and dispossessed children in Britain were to be sent to Australia and other colonies for a new start in life. Adults who volunteered to accompany the children were granted special passes on board the ships. Kathleen could apply and save the cost of the fare. Once ashore she would be free to join Harriet, they would regain their strength and, who knew? be back in Monte Carlo by the end of the year. Harriet wrote:[445]

My dear Kathleen

I am always pleased to get news from you and hope you are looking well … and am still hoping to see you out here and have spoken for a two berthed cabin for our return and you can help to look after me can't you? All I want to do is sit on the deck in a comfortable chair and bask in the sunshine and a real rest cure as I feel tired, brain weary and worn out and I don't care how soon it comes and if this does not happen write to Mr. Charles Woolrich, English lawyer, and let him know I will be on my way as soon as peace is declared but for choice would rather you came out here. Passports, luggage etc. would be a great help to me as I am such a helpless traveller, never having it to do when dear Mr. Dawson was alive. Am wondering if you could [book] a passage by looking after some of the orphans as I read they are sending such a lot to this country. Anyhow write your plans soon as I am longing to get back and find the Prince who I hear is with the Royal family in Italy and well cared for.

I think I have given you all my news this time so will conclude with loving memories. Your old time friend,

Princess Harriet Radziwill

Overcome with emotion, Harriet appended two verses she had clipped and kept from the "In Memorium" column of the newspaper:[446]

Courage

To feel that your heart is breaking
And there is nothing left to live for
And the faith you believe is fading fast
Hold on to the end and you will win at last.

Long live friendship
May the spot be green where it commenced
May every place bloom where it grew
And when all the bloom is over
And the trees withered and fallen
May love and friendship still continue.

Harriet

ps I think these words are lovely and so true. Don't you, Kathleen?

She had reached her eighty-first year, almost David's age when he died. Tired and lonely, she had no genuine expectation and little desire to reunite with the Prince. Her initial sense of betrayal had softened, and she felt sympathy for his plight as an exile, but she had learned a lesson: keep your heart for your true friends. But fate could keep even true friends apart, for Kathleen did not come. She had learned that the S.N.C.F., the French railway company, had expropriated her apartment at 52 Avenue du Maine in 1942, and was preparing to demolish it to make way for the new Montparnasse railway station.[447] She was in for a long fight for compensation, which became all-consuming as the months passed. If Harriet sought a reunion it would be on French soil or not at all. She would be obliged to travel alone, with no Norman to greet her and take care of her onward travel arrangements. She had no idea of the state of the Villa or even whether she could still gain access to it. Her London lawyer, Mr. Woolrich, could help but there was only so much he could do and, so Percy said, he was occupied with the disposal of the last London assets of the company, including The Treasure House. The landmark building had survived the Blitz but had ceased to function as Stewart Dawson's centre of operations. Like the Sydney properties, the sooner it was sold, the better. Harriet accepted the inevitability of the sale, but it broke her heart that David's signature building was to be swallowed by landlords ignorant and uncaring of his heritage and creative genius.

So, here she was, sitting in the dark in her depressingly familiar hotel suite, contemplating another day, tomorrow, of the same parochial round of teas and theatre, as far away from Paris, London, and Monte Carlo as ever. If she could find the energy and a little more support from her family, she would be on the next ship out of Sydney. But Percy and Stuart were preoccupied with their own lives, young David was his own man, launching into business of sorts, and she wondered if she had the strength, any longer, to travel across the world. She'd become quite breathless lately, the least effort leaving her weak and dizzy. Best get a good night's sleep if she was to be ready for tomorrow's play. She rang for room service to clear away the supper tray and, placing her jewellery in the familiar Stewart Dawson cases, prepared for bed.

39. The ballroom of The Ambassadors after the fire. Debris from the collapsed dome covers the dance floor.

40. Villa Bon Accord, 26 Bvd de Belgique, Monte Carlo.

41. Part of a cartoon in Smith's Weekly, by DH Souter, illustrating the 'Army of Social Leeches' displacing traditional patrons of Sydney's cafes and dance halls.

42. Norman in his Rolls Royce Phantom I in Berlin, 1931.

43. Norman on his return to Sydney in 1932.

44. Stuart with young David and a lady friend in Cannes, shortly after Peggy's death.

45. Harriet with grandchildren, David and Harriet, on their return to Sydney in 1937.

46. The smouldering ruins of Bon Accord after the fire. The Spinney is behind, between the chimneys, right.

47. Cartoon in Smith's Weekly, 1935, by Virgil, satirising Mack's milk bar venture and Australian 'Black and White' life savers.

48. Prince Michael Radziwill and Jeanette Suchestow in Monte Carlo at the time of their engagement, 1938.

49. Harriet and Radziwill marry in London

50. Antonin Palace, Poland.

Part 3: 1991.

The London Interviews

The twilight of the Stewart Dawson family

Day Two: The War Years

"Come in, find a pew. Sorry about the clutter, we had a couple of friends round last evening and they've left a bit of a mess behind. Haven't got around to tidying up. There you go, just put those magazines in the rack. No, on your right. D'you want some tea? There's some left in the pot, help yourself.

"Bloody awful weather. Typical English winter. I can't seem to keep the drafts out. Doesn't bother the wife, but she's younger and fitter than me, as you've probably noticed. That's one thing I do miss about Australia, even the winters there were quite tolerable. You could still swim and surf off Palm Beach well into May, June, even. Not that I could do that now. I'm lucky if I can walk to the end of the street; emphysema, I'm afraid. An easy chair with a good bottle of red would be more my style. That's if I was allowed a drink."

"Thanks, David. Yes, it is rather nasty weather, even for this time of the year. I hope you're feeling better. Are you up to a chat, today? I could leave it a while if you prefer. No? OK, we were talking about your childhood and how you'd spent your early years in London. Perhaps you could take me through the period after you returned to Australia before the war."

"The war? I joined up, well, I tried to, in '41. I wanted to be an airman, so I took flying lessons at Mascot Aero Club. I tried three times to join the R.A.A.F., but they turned me down. Same thing with the regular army, the A.I.F.; didn't want me. In the end, in December, I was drafted into the First Australia Division CMF as a signalman but I only lasted five months. I spent more time on my back in hospital than on the parade ground. Discharged unfit." [448]

"What was the CMF?"

"Citizens Military Force, Australia's reserve army. There was a hell of a fuss over conscription when war broke out. We didn't have it in World War One, did you know that? Nearly tore the country apart for a while, white feathers and all that nonsense. So, when we went in in

1939 there wasn't much appetite to try it again. Everyone thought the war would be over in months, they always do. Our regulars would do their bit for king and empire and be back for Christmas. No need for back up. Cut a long story short, by the time of the fall of France and the start of the North African campaign they were having second thoughts. Big debates in parliament, same arguments as before and they settled on calling up all able-bodied men from eighteen to thirty-five as long as they didn't serve outside Australian territory. I was considered 'able-bodied' enough for the CMF. Bloody boring. I mean, it wasn't as if there was much going on in Australia. Once the Japs had bombed Darwin and a couple of other spots up north, we sort of battened down the hatches on the home front. The regular army blokes were on the ships off to Papua and the Indies or trundling up to Brisbane and Cairns once the Yanks came over. Except for the division that fought on the Kokoda track, (not my lot) we in the CMF basically swanned around various training camps and bases for most of the time.

"I think, well, I know Dad was relieved when I was discharged. Uncle Percy had seen a lot of action in the first war and of course Uncle Norman had earned all those medals fighting the Red Baron, which was what had inspired me to fly. So, the Stewart Dawson family honour had been served and I was just a postscript. When I was in Sydney, being in uniform, even CMF, I could get better service in restaurants and so on. The regulars didn't like it much, they called us 'Chocos': 'Chocolate Soldiers', but the average man in the street, or woman, more to the point, didn't really make the distinction. I used to turn up at Romano's and Prince's all togged up in khaki and take Patricia for a turn around the dance floor, feeling quite the lad, I must say.

"But I'm getting ahead of myself. By this time, I'd got engaged to Patricia Fitzgerald as she was. We met in July or August '41 before I was called up. I'd been out on the town with another girl, can't remember now who, it was probably Joy McArthur. Joy and I had been dating for several months. We used to call it 'walking out' then.

It was she who got me to cut down on my smoking.* I used to smoke up to eighty a day. Everybody did those days. I mean, not as much as that, perhaps, but plenty by today's standards. I started when I was at school in England, peer pressure. It was considered very grown up. All the top film actors smoked like crazy on screen and there were cigarette adverts everywhere. That's what got me kicked out of the army; as soon as we started training, anything strenuous and I was out cold. I had what they used to call 'effort syndrome'. You get breathless, heart palpitations, with the least bit of heavy exercise. I even had a bout of pneumonia; it was that bad. Mind you, I still smoke, even though it's killing me. Can't give it up at my stage of life.

"Anyway, I saw Patricia 'across a crowded room', and it was love at first sight. She was a stunner; smile like a film star, hair like Betty Grable, legs to go with it. And sharp, vivacious, always a smart remark but not pushy, if you know what I mean. I was pretty confident in myself by then. I'd been around the Sydney scene for a good two to three years, thanks to Dad and Jean and Grandma, bless her, so even though I was still only nineteen I could handle myself well enough in company. I remember when Loudon Sainthill, Harry Miller and I got our names in the paper when we went out on the town wearing black suede shoes with our tuxedos.[449] You laugh, but that was considered avant garde daring back then; we revelled in it. Anyhow, there I was, smitten by Patricia's looks, and the next thing I know I'm asking her out. Easier than I'd imagined. She was game and before you knew it, we were announcing our engagement. We were both terribly young, but those days people thought nothing of marrying in their early twenties and, with the war on, there was a sense of urgency to grow up, more commitment to relationships than you see nowadays. We were passionate about each other and just having an affair didn't feel like enough at the time.

"Then, there was the money aspect. It didn't occur to me 'til later but we were of course a wealthy family that was bound to appeal to a girl with her eye on the main chance. We still as good as owned half

---

* Truth 25th February 1940 P.37. *"And David Stewart Dawson has cut down on his smoking. Used to smoke 80 cigarettes a day, no less. Indeed. But Joy has persuaded him to cut down to three per diem. Sweet, isn't it?"*

the Strand Arcade and other properties and Uncle Percy had been in the news off and on for years, particularly with the Perpetual court case; some very large figures were bandied about there. I'm talking hundreds of thousands of pounds in the estate and maybe half a million tied up in the Pitt Street properties alone, not to mention the villa in Monte Carlo. That may not sound a lot these days but back then it was a fortune. I always had plenty to spend, despite the fact my actual income wasn't huge; I got £6 a week allowance from the estate and a wage from Percy. But Dad was good for a handout and I lived rent-free at his flat or Grandma's place, had the full run of both. We entertained on a pretty lavish scale, at Palm Beach or around town. Some of those parties up at the house would have broken the bank with many of my friends. The booze bill alone could have fed a family for a month. God, we put it away! So, yes, even though I'm sure Patricia thought me a handsome devil, it didn't hurt that I was sitting on a pile of the readies. Remember, I was the sole male heir to the estate. Norman was dead and gone a bachelor, Percy had no children, there was my cousin Joyce in England and of course my sister, Harriet, but I would be the only Stewart Dawson once Percy and Dad died. At the time I didn't think about it much. I sort of took everything for granted and lived for the moment. Percy had got me into the business managing part of the Pitt Street properties but, to be honest, there wasn't a lot for me to do and I didn't fancy being his rent collector for the rest of my life. I'm not sure I was happy. I've been looking at some old society pages photos of me in those days and I must say I look pretty serious in most of them. Maybe I was putting on an act for the photographer with my 'cool' demeanour. Those forties film actors have a lot to answer for! But you'd think I might have cracked a smile just occasionally, wouldn't you?

"I shouldn't say this but, though I'd been born with a silver spoon in my mouth I didn't feel as if there was much to look forward to. I'd been terribly spoiled as a boy, specially by my grandmother, but now I look back on it, my parents neglected me and Harriet for most of our childhood. My mother was a drunk, let's not beat about the bush. She had so many 'unwell' days when we were in London. We children were shooed away when the doctor arrived or just left in the hotel suite while Dad disappeared, probably off drinking somewhere else on his own. Harriet was shielded from more of this than I was. She's six years younger than I and then Grandma took her under her wing and got her into a succession of good schools. I tagged along with Dad back and forth to Europe. I didn't know from one day to the next whether we'd be at the Villa with Grandma's arty friends, on the Lido with another of his girlfriends or flitting from one hotel to another in the West End. Dad seemed always to be just a step ahead of the bailiffs; at least, that's how I understand it now. At the time I didn't pay much attention, but there was always a sense of urgency and a furtiveness about our moves that I think must have been due to his fear of the knock on the door. Dad and Grandma must have felt guilty about it; they spared no expense on me. I got anything I wanted without question. Actually, Dad might have done it out of guilt, but Grandma was just kind-hearted. She was the most generous person I've ever known, would've given the coat off her back. That was her weakness, of course; she got taken advantage of time and again.

"When Dad married Jean (good move, by the way, Jean was a lovely woman, much stronger than Mum, much stronger than Dad; just what he needed) and they went back to Australia, it didn't take much to persuade me to accompany them. With hindsight, I might have been better off staying on at my school in Reading. I was just twelve, I needed some stability in my life, but the idea of sun and surf and sailing on the Harbour won me over. There was no contest, really. As a matter of interest, I'm not sure Dad was that keen on me joining him and Jean so soon after their marriage. I think he would have preferred some sort of extended honeymoon with her before I arrived. In the end, it turned out alright for them because he parked me at Cranbrook, which was and is a damned good school, I admit, while he and Jean toured around the country. So, on the one hand, I had all the comforts I needed, and more, and the best education in the country, but no home life to speak of. In later years Dad settled down a bit and I spent more time with him and my stepmother, mainly at Palm Beach. We used to surf-ski off the beach. Dad bought one of the early skis (they were hollow plywood affairs, not too heavy) and we all got quite good at it, even Jean. She was a sight to behold; blonde hair, she had a collection of gorgeous swimsuits. She'd turn heads up and down the beach, but you should have seen the looks she got when she stood up on the ski.[450]

"So, Patricia and I were married. That was at the end of 1942. The war was not going well, we'd had the Jap submarine attack in the Harbour and a few shells, mostly duds, lobbed into the Eastern Suburbs. That brought it home to the general population, that we were in it for the long haul."

"After you were discharged, did you go back to work with Percy?"

"I did. The family business took another turn in '41. Strand and Pitt Street Properties threw in the towel, accepted Percy's offer to release them from all mortgages, for £6,000 cash.[451] This meant we owned the property free and clear once more but by then it was run down. It definitely wasn't worth the £700,000 my grandfather had sold it for. Percy decided to sit on it for the duration. We did some minor remediation, enough to keep it ticking over, kept the tenants happy and waited for the war to end."

"You had some trouble with one of the tenants, didn't you? Wasn't there a court case brought against the Rex Cabaret?"

"Oh, that. No, they didn't give us any trouble. On the contrary, they were always on time with the rent. That was John Spooner. He'd taken over what was left of the old Ambassadors on a five-year lease from us and fitted it out as a cabaret. It was much smaller than The Ambassadors and not in the same class at all, but it did good business for a while. When the Yanks started to arrive in '42 some of them found their way into the place. They didn't all stay around King's Cross and Darlinghurst. So, business picked up. Problem was, we still had the ridiculous liquor laws, same ones that got my uncles into trouble in the twenties. Spooner got nabbed for serving or allowing too much liquor to be brought onto the premises. The law was open to interpretation, and he was probably a bit lax. The police did a raid and there were a few people worse for wear. They had him up for running a disorderly house. I seem to remember they alleged he allowed criminals onto the premises because he had an ex-boxer working as a doorman. Apparently, he'd been on the wrong side of the law, the boxer, that is. Being 'declared' sent him out of business. He'd had hundreds in the place before the raid but that dropped to about fifty a night and he had to close.[452] Pity, really. Percy let him off the lease but of course that meant even less income for our company. The irony was, once Spooner had gone, Percy put in his own manager, and in August 1943 they rescinded the order. Poor old Spooner had done the hard yards and lost everything. Percy wasn't that interested in running another cabaret, so he sold it on. I think he'd been burned out by The Ambassadors. He pretty much stood back."

"What about Percy? He seems to have been the least flamboyant of the brothers. How do you remember him?"

"Uncle Percy was a funny old stick. I don't mean 'funny-amusing', more 'funny-odd'. He had no sense of humour, wasn't terribly sociable. He wasn't unkind; I got on OK with him and he did try to teach me the business, but it was hard to get close to him. He always gave the impression of having a great weight on his shoulders, which I suppose he did in a manner of speaking. He'd worked his arse off running The Ambassadors, I think that almost finished him, then he took on Grandfather's estate and I think it was more than he could handle, particularly when The Ambassadors closed after all the work he'd put in. The will was devilishly complicated, Grandfather had tied up so much in the various companies and there were so many loose ends when he died. It was right in the middle of the Depression and Percy didn't seem interested or have any ideas of what to do with the estate. He wasn't what you'd call adventurous, wouldn't have taken a punt like Grandfather did. He was more the king in his counting house, doling out our allowances and keeping Perpetual at arm's length. Dad and Uncle Norman exploited him awfully. Once Norman got his claws into him, Percy was lost. Grandfather had kept such a tight leash on everything and everyone. With him gone, all bets were off. I don't think Norman and Dad had a lot of respect for Percy. Norman was a hopeless playboy. Money went through his hands like water; there was always another 'get rich quick' scheme that was going to make him the toast of the town. You've heard the expression 'she'll be right!'? Well, that was Norman all over, not that he'd have ever used those words. Percy was more of a 'We'll all be ruined!' type."

"How about his relations with women? He seems to have had some unfortunate experiences with Thelma and then Rita. Did he ever speak about that; why he suddenly left Rita; why he never remarried?"

"No, he didn't, not to me at any rate. I suppose I was too young at the time to be taken into his confidence. But he wasn't good with close relationships, so I suppose being tied down in a marriage was too much for him. I have some sympathy for him. After all, I did the same thing with Patricia as he did with Rita. I don't think he was queer or anything like that, if that's what you are implying, just very inhibited. He got on fine with his mates, he'd known some of them since the first war, and he liked going to the track. That horse of his gave him a lot of pleasure despite its embarrassing record. He gave it away to the trainer in 1940, did you know that?[453] Strathisla was well past it by then of course. Maybe he should have held on to him; his son, Strathdarr, won first up, fifty to one.[454] But, no, to answer your question, all I can say is Percy preferred male company to female and his own to anyone else's."

"You mentioned your walking away from your own marriage to Patricia. Care to talk about that?"

"Well, as I said, we were very young. Patricia was, shall I say, a good time girl. Nothing wrong with that, but she didn't sit around playing solitaire, if you know what I mean. I'd become frustrated with myself. When I got kicked out of the army and couldn't get into the air force, I had no real sense of direction, purpose, and I know I took it out, not just on her but on my family and friends. I felt especially bad about Grandma. She was so lonely those last years, waiting for that damned prince of hers to show up. I'd taken advantage of her. I used to dine with her a lot; she was such good company, but I think I became so absorbed with my own problems I stopped calling her. I just assumed she was getting along with her little old ladies' circle and would be gone, back to Europe, once the war was over. But of course, she never made it. Died all alone in her hotel room in October '45. At least, she didn't suffer. Heart attack just after she'd come back from the theatre.* And I like to think that if her life flashed by, she had the satisfaction of knowing that Polish bastard wasn't getting a penny from her. She left him out of her will, y'know. I found out he came back from Italy once the war was over but of course there was no way he could go back to Poland; the Russians were in control. He drifted around Europe for a while, but everyone was wise to him. He went broke and ended up in Tenerife, that's where his second wife came from. Last I heard he died there in 1955.[455]

"But you asked me about my split with Patricia. As I said, we'd drifted apart. It turned out we hadn't much in common after all. In '45, I went into business with her as co-director of Dawson Realty Company Ltd.[456] I thought it would give us both something to build on, so I set up the company and for a while we did quite well. We dealt in city, commercial property exclusively. Basically, I was just following in Percy and my grandfather's footsteps. I had Percy's blessing and I had learned a bit in my time working with him, so it wasn't as if I was a complete novice. Our biggest coup was the sale of the entire Pitt Street block, Strand Arcade and all, in 1949.[457] We did it in conjunction with LJ Hooker. Sold it to Coles for £850,000. Our swan song, you might say, and I can't take any credit for it, for reasons I'll explain. Anyway, Patricia was my silent partner in the business. It bored her. I'd thought the fact of my being a real businessman in my own right might have re-kindled the flame, but I was mistaken. Over the war years she'd made new friends, kept up with the night life, and so on. She was seeing a lot of the Garvans, Pat in particular."

"The Garvans? Not the family associated with the Garvan medical research Institute?"

"No, well, not closely. There were an awful lot of Garvans around, y'know. Pat and his brother, Denis were near contemporaries of mine from Bellevue Hill, a bit older than I. I didn't know Denis all that well.

---

* Harriet suffered a heart attack and died in her room at the Hotel Australia on Friday 12th October 1945, after returning from a theatre performance. Sydney Sun 14th October 1945 P.5

He joined the RAAF early in the war, got himself a DFC and married (another Patricia, those Irish didn't have a lot of imagination when it came to names). Pat Garvan and I met now and then at Romano's or Prince's, but I wouldn't say we were close friends. He was still single at the time. I think he took a fancy to Patricia from meeting the two of us. Then it was supposedly chance encounters when she dined out, that sort of thing.* I had my suspicions but couldn't bring myself to confront her. It came to a head in October '45.† We'd gone to Bowral for a holiday, the Grand Hotel. I had this idea that getting her alone, away from Sydney and the Garvans for a week or two, we could try a fresh start. I could see as soon as we got there, she was restless, distracted. She kept making excuses to go back to town, so back we went, just for the day. I thought it was a complete waste of time and got pretty irritable, I don't mind saying. We didn't actually do very much once we got there. I kept thinking, 'What's going on? What's her game?' We'd booked the return train from Central at 9.30 in the evening. It was only a five-minute cab ride from our flat in Elizabeth Street, but she fiddled around so much packing her bag that, by the time we got to the station the train was pulling out. That put the tin hat on it for me. I'd had enough. I called a cab, shoved her in, took her back to the flat and dumped her there. I said, 'If that's what you want, good luck, I'm off' or words to that effect. She said, 'What do you mean?' I said, 'You know what I mean. You can go back to your boyfriend, for all I care.' And I jumped into the cab and got him to take me back to Bowral. You should have seen the look on her face as I drove off."

"So, what happened after that? Did you make any attempt at reconciliation?"

"God, no! I stewed all the way back to Bowral. It's a good couple of hours' driving, you know. I still hadn't got over my anger when she

---

* Sydney Daily Telegraph 1st November 1945 P.20. *"Happy reunion on Tuesday night, when Mrs. Peter Russo, over from Melbourne, danced with a party of friends, including Mrs. Stewart Dawson, Alec Murray, and Pat and Dennis Garvan."*

† The account of the events leading to David and Patricia's divorce is taken, in part from the report of court proceedings (Patricia's testimony) in the Brisbane Truth, 24th February 1946 P. 21

arrived on the doorstep two days later, right there at the hotel, all contrite and weepy. By then I'd made up my mind. She'd made it plain she was bored with me and I felt I was being constantly compared with the older men she met around town, such as Pat Garvan. I was younger, by a few years, and I looked younger. Pat stood taller than me and was, not exactly a bruiser, but very 'masculine', if you know what I mean. His nickname was 'Butch'. He'd served in the 'proper' army, unlike me, so he held all the cards. So, when she started to turn on the tears I just said, 'Forget it, I don't want to live with you again. I don't love you anymore.' And that was that. She went straight back to Sydney with her tail between her legs. I must say, I felt better for having made my point. I returned myself a couple of days after. She was in the flat when I arrived, but I was not in a mood to talk. I repeated what I'd said before. I didn't want to discuss anything, and I told her to leave, which she did. She went back to her mother's and that was the end of it for us."

"Did she just give up, accept what had happened?"

"She wrote to me a few weeks later. I could tell it was one of those letters lawyers get wives to write to set up a divorce.[458] You know the sort of thing: 'I am writing to you to ask you to give up the ridiculous attitude you have adopted to me …' 'You told me that you could not live with me again and did not love me anymore, but I do not believe that this was a true expression of your feelings …' 'I can assure you that I have done nothing whatever to justify this …' '… you made some wild charges against me, which I denied, and which you must know are entirely without foundation …' And so on. She finished off with the obligatory request: 'I hope that you will do as I ask and come back to me.' As if I would. I thought it significant that she signed off: 'Yours affectionately'. No 'love' there. I should have ignored it, but I wanted it over with. I wrote back. I kept a copy of my letter:

> *'Dear Patricia*
>
> *I have your letter of November 9 and am sorry to tell you that I have nothing more to add to what I have previously told you, except to repeat that I do not intend to resume married life with you. Yours truly …'*

"She took me to court in February '46 to get a restitution order. I didn't bother to show up. It was more or less a formality, but it did get her a lot of sympathy because they only heard her side of the story. I was past caring by then. I'd had several months to get over the split and we'd resumed our separate lives. She was still seeing Pat and his friends,[459] I'd settled back into bachelorhood, and that was pretty much the end of it. She got her decree nisi in October. Funnily enough, we did bump into each other on occasion, both before and after the divorce, and it was quite civilized. Once she started proceedings, I felt a great burden had been taken off my shoulders. I don't know about her."

"You'd met Beverley Atkinson by then, hadn't you?"

"I can see you've been doing your homework. Yes, around New Year I first saw Bev at Prince's (where else?) dining with a couple of girlfriends. She was a fashion model, picture in the papers all the time. Another blonde, fabulous complexion, and a terrific figure. She did a lot of work at fashion parades, even swimsuits. We took up some time in April, as far as I remember. I could see immediately she was more my type. Someone once wrote: 'Beverley Atkinson is really my gel, she is unspoilt, unaffected, has that necessary something above the ears besides hair, and can turn up exhausted from modelling chores looking like a million dollars.'[460] And that about sums her up. But that's another story. Enough for today, I'm tired."

Day Three: The Palm Beach Incident

"I'd like to talk, today, about the incident at the Palm Beach house in September 1946.[461] *So much was said at the time, it was such a scandalous affair, if I may say so, that perhaps the truth was lost in the telling. I wonder if you feel any differently about it with the passage of time. Has the pain of it all lessened for you?"*

"To be frank, no, the pain is still there after forty odd years. More a feeling of injustice. Yes, there was blame on both sides but there were some who got off scot free while I came out of it rather poorly. More to the point, the family never really recovered from it. That's my biggest regret. Some awful things were said about the Stewart Dawsons. It was as if all we'd stood for was somehow for nothing; resented, sneered at, even. As if people had been looking for an excuse to bring us down. There was a degree of envy among some. Others stayed loyal but we were never the same afterwards. Thank God my grandparents weren't around.

"Where do I start? I suppose, with the Sunday lunch. I'd agreed to accompany my sister to lunch with a couple of acquaintances at Gleneagles restaurant.* That was up at Potts Point, long gone now. She'd met Mary Ann not long before and I think my name had come up in conversation, something like that."

"Mary Ann?"

"Mary Ann Verspoor. American girl not long out from the U.S.A. She was in Sydney on her own while her husband was doing business in Papua.[462] She was twenty or so, a bit older than Harriet. Brunette, attractive and typically forward for her age. A lot of American women at the time had that self-confidence you saw in the movies of the day, the Katherine Hepburn style that rather took you aback at first. It took

---

* Pat Garvan was part owner of Gleneagles Restaurant, which had a reputation for supplying illegal liquor, as many venues still did in 1946.

quite a few years for local girls to catch up. And she was 'Mary Ann', not just 'Mary', as she would remind you. She came from Kansas, and she had her infant son with her, though that didn't seem to slow her down at all. She seemed to manage very well, got herself a modelling job and had plenty of friends around town.

"And there was George. That's George Rankin McKay. He was Mary Ann's escort on the day, though I suspected early on that they were rather closer than casual. I'd known George for about a year. We would bump into each other at private parties. He was British, ex-RN, Fleet Air Arm, like Uncle Norman. He'd got a position as an indent agent in Sydney when the war ended. I think he'd made business contacts from when he'd been stationed in the Far East and was exporting various things from Australia, mainly to Singapore. He was doing OK but not as well as he made out. He played on his supposedly upper-class Britishness and his looks. He was one of those chiselled, steely-eyed types, the kind you see in James Bond films; quite tall, well set-up. He was very full of himself, charming but quick to put you in your place.

"We finished lunch at about three o'clock and that's where it might have ended. Pity it didn't. But I made the mistake of throwing out a spur-of-the-moment invitation to come up to Palm Beach for supper at my parent's house. I'd been planning to go up anyway and it seemed natural and courteous to invite them to join us. To be honest, I had felt a bit out of it during the meal. George held the floor a lot of the time and I could see he was going all out to impress the girls. I suppose I thought I'd show him how the other half lived, get him onto my home territory. So, I phoned for a hire car, and we drove across the bridge and up the peninsular to Palm Beach. I remember it was an unseasonably cool day; they'd had snow up at Katoomba, very unusual for that time of year, so we all rugged up in the car and I was looking forward to getting to Dad's house, which was quite modern and cosy. I'd phoned ahead and Jean answered. She said they had five other guests, but they ran a very 'open house', so the more the merrier. We were in a good mood on the way up, laughing and singing.

"We arrived at five-ish and things went well for the early part of the evening. We had supper at about half past seven and then the other guests left, so there were just Dad and Jean, we four and a Mrs.

Hefti, friend of Jean's. I'd served drinks before supper, but nobody drank very much. Well, Dad had his usual tipple and we got through a few bottles of wine with the meal but, for the most part, it was a pretty unremarkable evening. Mary Ann didn't drink at all, just Coca Cola. We sat or stood around chatting after supper. The radio was on, playing the usual Sunday evening background music, dance tunes, that sort of thing. I didn't serve any more drinks myself. There was a bar in the corner of the room, and they could help themselves. I noticed that George was getting stuck into it. He actually said, 'I'm going into training next week, so I'm going to get very drunk.' He boxed, fancied himself as handy in the ring. I thought at the time 'Good, that'll throw him off his game a bit with the ladies.' I felt better with myself, on home ground and quite clear headed. Then, about ten o'clock, someone suggested we get a lobster or two to finish off the evening. You could get good fresh ones down at Palm Beach or Newport, so Jean offered to go and buy a couple. She and Mrs. Hefti left in the hire car. While they were away George got progressively drunk and sort of slumped in the corner, looking sullen and belligerent. He was four sheets to the wind. To give you an idea, he went out to the backyard and threw up twice. Mary Ann said to me, 'He needs help.' I said, 'That's obvious.' She just gave me a look and said, 'Never mind, I'll go myself.' The rest of us tried to ignore him, listened to the music, and chatted. Jean and Mrs. Hefti got back just before eleven and buzzed off to the kitchen to prepare the lobsters. Then the anthem came on and that's when things fell apart."

"The anthem? You mean, the national anthem?"

"That's right. They used to close the evening radio broadcast at eleven o'clock, none of this late night, all night programming. As far as I know, they don't bother with it these days. Anyway, on came 'God save the King'. I was in the mood for more music and maybe dancing, putting on a record or two, so I walked over to the radio and switched it off in the middle of the anthem. I said, 'To hell with the bloody King.' Dad tut-tutted and I was about to say I meant the anthem, not the king himself, when George lurched across the room, pushed me aside, and switched the radio back on. He shouted, right in my face, 'To hell with you, you disloyal little bastard!'"

"What did you do?"

"I pulled myself together. He'd spilt drink over the radio, and everyone was looking a bit stunned. I said I hadn't meant it in a disloyal way, and if he hadn't been so drunk, he'd have known it. I pointed to the picture of Uncle Norman in uniform and said he'd been a major in the Middle East and been decorated. I meant to show we were a patriotic family. He was having none of that. He said, 'You have done nothing in this war, you miserable little rat. You bought your way out of the Army.' He must have known this was untrue. I told him I'd been discharged because of ill-health and had volunteered for the R.A.A.F. He gave me a sneering look and picked up Norman's photo. He said, 'So this is the family hero. I hear he bought his commission in London.'"

"He said that? Why on earth would he make that accusation?"

"You tell me. It was plain he resented our wealth and status. I thought at the time it was the drink speaking, which it was to some extent, but he'd been spoiling for a fight ever since supper. He came across as an arrogant Pom who couldn't bear the thought of Australians being his equals. Maybe something had been said earlier that pushed him over the edge, I don't know. But he'd gone too far with the slur on Norman. It was one thing to have a go at me but quite another to slander the reputation of a dead hero. Dad had been hanging back but now he exploded. He said, 'How dare you pass a remark like that about my brother.' Jean had come into the room while this was going on. She walked over to George and said, 'Young man, I cannot have you behaving like this in my house. You must all go now.' That should have been the end of it. She'd been quite restrained until then, despite George's obvious drunkenness (he'd dropped cheese and biscuits on the carpet and trampled them in. I knew she'd seen him do it, but she said nothing) but she'd had enough. She was polite, as polite as one can be in the circumstances, but firm, and he should have done the gentlemanly thing."

"But he didn't?"

"No. He said to Jean, 'I have been in the homes of the English nobility. I have never been requested to leave anybody's home before.' Jean wasn't about to stand for this, she ordered him to leave, but by now you could see he was bent on insulting the whole family. He shoved his face towards her and said, 'No well-bred hostess would ever dream of asking a guest to leave, but perhaps it is too much for you to be aware of that.' There was a ghastly silence and then Dad started yelling, 'Get out! Get out! You English swine, you insulted my wife!'. George just turned on him and said, 'You keep out of this, you old bastard.' Dad was speechless. George filled up his glass, right to the top, downed it in one gulp, and went over to Jean. He took her hand as though he was going to kiss it. His entire manner was insolent. Jean said, 'Young man, I advise you not to get so drunk in anybody else's home.' But he said, in that sneering way, 'I have never been so drunk in anybody else's home, my dear would-be lady.' Then he turned and walked out the door. Mary Ann and Harriet followed him. Dad went to the doorstep and shouted after him, 'Get out of here! You disgraced my family here at Palm Beach, you filthy reserve. You are so bloody conceited about your Naval career.' I was a bit disappointed that my sister didn't stay behind but she was very young, and I could see she was scared, on the verge of tears. Maybe she felt Mary Ann needed support. They would have a long trip back with a very drunk, angry George in the car."

"So, you were left wondering what this had all been about. How were your father and step-mother?"

"We were stunned, as I said. Jean was magnificent, calm. Dad was anything but. He was always a bit on the nervous side, easily upset and not very good in a tight corner. This had really got to him, the slight on Norman and George's insolent behaviour towards Jean. I'm sure he regretted not taking a firmer line when George first attacked Jean, but it all happened so fast I suppose it caught him off balance. He wasn't a well man, you know; high blood pressure and diabetes. So, there we were, behind the door, trying to regain our composure and waiting to hear the car drive off. But it didn't, of course. I learned later from Harriet that, as they walked to the car, George stopped and said, 'I will not take that from the Stewart Dawsons. They have been getting away with that sort of thing for years.' I've no idea, to this day, what he meant by that. He wanted to go back and demand an apology. Mary Ann told him to drop it, Dad could apologise later. George ignored her. He took off his coat and said, 'No, he's going to apologise to me now, and you can pick up the pieces.'

"The next thing we heard, inside the house, was someone running up and banging on the door. It was Harriet. She sounded hysterical. She was shouting, 'Look out, Daddy, he's going to kill you!' I opened the door. She was standing on the step with George right behind her. He pushed past, went straight up to Dad and said, 'You bastard! I'm going to make you regret what you've done to me tonight!' Dad sort of staggered backwards and picked up an empty gin bottle on the telephone table. He was shaking. He said, again, 'Get out! What the hell did you come back for?' George must have felt he was in control. He wasn't shouting any more, just said in a menacing voice, 'I came back to show you and your upstart wife that you cannot insult an English naval officer and get away with it.' Well, that got Dad going again. He lifted the gin bottle as if to strike George. George picked up an empty ginger ale bottle and said, 'Go on, hit me. It will be the last thing you do in this life.'"

"Was there really a ginger ale bottle? Didn't the case hinge on whether McKay threatened your father with a bottle?"

"Let's say George became extremely threatening. He was a big man; he'd boxed and played first grade rugby. Dad was incapable of defending himself against anyone. I could see matters had got out of hand and any moment George would physically assault one or both of us. He was capable of inflicting enormous injury with his bare hands, his fists. I genuinely thought he would kill Dad, and I was no match for him. I mean, look at me, I was about half his size."

"So, that's when you went and got the gun?"

"It was all I could think of to do. Jean said, 'Get the police,' but, by the time they got there, it would have been all over. I went inside and got my pistol from my coat pocket. Before you ask, it was common knowledge that I carried a gun on my rounds inspecting our properties. There was always the risk of encountering someone with a criminal intent on the premises after hours, which is when I made my rounds. I'd never had cause to use it, thank God, until now. Anyway, when I got back to the porch, George was standing looking down at Dad, who was at the bottom of the steps. I was sure he would kill Dad if he'd touched him. I stood in front of him and raised my arm, not very high but enough for him to see that I had the gun in my hand. I said, 'I'm going to shoot.' He made no move away from Dad. He said later he didn't see the pistol. I was about five feet from him, and I thought I'd shoot at his feet to scare him, to show him I was serious. The gun went off before I'd expected it to. I'd forgotten it had a rather soft trigger. George yelled out, screamed like a woman. He stood there for a moment, then he said, quite quietly, 'You shouldn't have done that, David' and sat down on a stone flowerpot on the porch.

"Everyone was looking at me. I thought, 'What happened?' I'd never seen anyone shot except in films. In westerns they always stagger backwards or fling their arms up, don't they? George didn't do anything like that, so I figured he was just reacting to the sound of the shot so close to him. After a couple of seconds, Dad came up the steps and pulled me inside the door. George got up and I thought he was going to attack one or both of us, but he fell on the floor at Dad's feet. Dad kicked out at him a couple of times, and it was then I realised he really had been shot. There wasn't any blood, but he'd gone very pale, and you could see he was in pain. I said, 'I meant to miss him.' The chauffeur and Mary Ann helped him up. He screamed again and they half-carried him to the car. Harriet was flapping about in tears. She followed them and they all got in. It was all over in seconds."

"What a shock it must have been. How did the family cope after they'd left?"

"How do you think? Jean was white and shaking, Dad was in a complete funk. I pulled myself together as best I could, ushered them inside and closed the door. I'd hardly had time to turn around when there was another knock. It was the chauffeur. Mary Ann had left her handbag, and could I fetch it? I told him I'd return it tomorrow and to get them back to town as quickly as possible. I watched them drive off. I picked up Dad's gin bottle and another bottle on the porch, that was the ginger ale bottle, had a last look around in case there was any blood on the floor (there wasn't, as far as I could see) and joined them in the living room. Dad said something about having to sort things out with George, find out how badly he'd been hurt. They both agreed it was George who was at fault and that I'd had no alternative, but we were nervous. We'd no idea where he'd been hit. I said Harriet was our best bet to fill us in and that I'd phone her in the morning. I actually thought Mary Ann would be more useful. She'd kept her head and taken charge when they left. We got Dad to bed, and Jean fetched Mrs. Hefti (she'd made herself scarce when George first blew up) and called a cab for her. I had intended to go back to my city apartment in the hire car but now I was marooned at Palm Beach, so I went to the guest room. I thought I'd try to get some sleep, I kept going over what had happened, memorising who said what. I knew it wouldn't be long before someone called the police."

Day Four: Plots and Schemes

"That was quite a story you told, yesterday. I can see why the memory of it would still be fresh after forty-odd years. Did you eventually get to sleep on the night?"

"No, I don't think any of us did. Just after midnight the police telephoned. Someone, a neighbour, had witnessed the shooting and reported it to Mona Vale station, down the road. They sent a patrolman to take down a statement. He arrived at about half past midnight. I told him the bare facts, emphasising that I hadn't intended to shoot George. I made it plain that he'd left us, left me no alternative. Another officer arrived and I had to go through the whole thing again for him. There was a bit of a fuss over the gun. Did I have a licence? Yes, in the name of Stewart Dawson Estates. Could I let them take the gun? No, I didn't have to since I was a JP with rights over it to protect our property. That was a bit of bluff, but they didn't pursue it at the time. They had a look around, made much of there not being any broken glass where I'd said the ginger ale bottle had been smashed. I said that maybe it wasn't smashed but it had been in George's hand. They left it at that, but they insisted on driving me to Manly Police Station to give a signed statement.

"When I got to Manly, I was interviewed by a third officer, so I had to start again from the beginning. I suppose it was so they could compare my stories, but I hadn't given much away at the house, and in any case, I was confident I could show I'd acted in self-defence. I mean, in Dad's defence."

"Had you discussed what you would tell the police with your father?"

"If you mean, had we concocted a story? no. The more we went over the night's events, the more we were sure that I'd had no choice. George's behaviour was outrageous, deliberately offensive and provocative. He reminded me of the worst kind of bullies I'd seen at school or one of those 'standover' men in a criminal gang. No, Dad and Jean agreed I'd done the right thing to use the gun, just that it was a pity my warning shot had gone home. We decided it would be best to own up to the police but to make it clear it had been an accident. I think that helped my case in the end if anything did. It turned out the police had only confirmed that George had been wounded just after I arrived at Manly. Apparently, when the patrolman was sent from Mona Vale, he met the hire car on the road. The witness who phoned had described it. He stopped the car and asked George if he'd been injured, shot. George denied it. I didn't know then why he did that. I put it down to his stupid bravado. Either that or he was in shock and didn't know what he was saying. So, when the patrolman arrived at the house and asked me what had happened, and I volunteered that I'd shot him, I suppose I showed right away that I wasn't trying to hide anything."

"How did the police get confirmation of the shooting, then?"

"Ah, now we come to the heart of the matter. This all came out later, you understand. When they left in the car, George must have sobered up a bit and the initial pain of the shot could have worn off. Maybe he was more comfortable sitting down. By the time the motorcycle policeman stopped them he'd decided to keep quiet about the shooting. He said later he wanted to protect Mary Ann's reputation, but that was a pretty lame excuse. He must have known the police were suspicious, why else stop the car? I believe he'd already hatched his plan."

"What plan?"

"I'm coming to that. They drove into the city but didn't go to George's hotel, that was too public. Instead, they went to Patricia's apartment. That's right, my soon-to-be ex-wife. And guess who was there with her? Pat Garvan. They'd been living together since the time of our split-up. It goes without saying that there was little love lost between her and me. As I'd suspected, George and Mary Ann were having a fling, too. George started talking about damages. He mentioned £10,000, £15,000, £20,000; the sky was the limit. I heard that, later, he asked Mary Ann, 'How would you like the Stewart Dawson home at Palm Beach?' He had his eyes on the prize, alright. Patricia probably put him up to that. The so-called damages first mentioned was £2,000. She said, 'You can get more than that out of them.' George's eyes must have lit up. He was chronically short of money, lived on commission from his export business but never had much capital. He borrowed a lot. Pat Garvan lent him a sum not long before the shooting. It explained his resentment of our family. He couldn't stand that Dad and I, colonial upstarts, lived well while he, the great hero of World War Two, the English gentleman, had to work to make ends meet. 'Gentleman', that was a joke. His plan involved getting Mary Ann to do his dirty work. Not that she wasn't a willing accomplice."

"How do you mean?"

"After the interview at Manly, I went back to my city apartment. The police hadn't charged me, but they'd spelt out the possible charges, and it didn't look good. Malicious wounding could get me five years in prison. I didn't think it would come to that, but I was expecting at least two years if found guilty. On Monday evening, there was a knock at the door. It was Pat Garvan. Say what you like about him, he was a decent chap. Not the sharpest, he didn't banter terribly well, but a good heart. I didn't hold it against him that he was seeing Patricia. He must have felt guilty about the previous evening's conversation with George and the others. He said, 'It looks bad, David. It looks like a shakedown, they're talking £15,000.' I said, 'A shakedown can only go on lies.' He said, 'I know, it's a risky thing to do.' I said, 'What's a risky thing to do?' and he said, 'Well, settle out of court.' I could see where this was going, so I said, 'It's not a question of settling out of court. It's straight out blackmail, in other words, £15,000 or else.' He seemed a bit flummoxed. He just said, 'But it's risky for him, too,' and stood there, waiting for me to answer. I wasn't in a mood to negotiate, not with him, so I said I'd think about it and he left. It occurred to me that he must have come on his own account. He looked most uncomfortable talking about the money and I was pretty sure the others didn't know he'd visited me. The next day, Tuesday, I was sitting, staring at the wall, feeling depressed, when who should call but Mary Ann. Could I come over to her flat? She had something we needed to talk about. This was just before noon, I remember. I said, 'Why not?' I figured this was the start of the shakedown. I'd prepared my response, my counteroffer if you will. I'd make a formal apology, maybe some sort of compensation for the hurt, hospital expenses and so forth. I went to her flat. She got straight down to business, no preliminaries. She said, 'I want to know what you are prepared to do about George. He's pretty badly hurt and unless you're prepared to help him, things can be made awkward for you.' Then she said, 'I've dodged the police for about forty-eight hours, and I can't hold them off any longer. If I tell a certain story you will probably go to jail.' I thought, 'Here we go.' I said I didn't know what she meant but if George needed financial assistance I could help. I offered her £2,500. That was probably more than he earned in a year. She came right back, 'We were thinking £15,000 damages.' I said, 'You can call this damages if you like, but I think there's a better name for it. Had George behaved himself this would never have happened.' I said, 'I always believed George was financial. He must have bought many hundreds of pounds worth of goods to send to Singapore.' I suspected he wasn't, but I didn't want to appear a pushover. She said, 'Don't be a fool. You know that's borrowed money. George wants £15,000, and it's that amount or else. You're lucky he's not asking for the Strand Arcade.' I said, 'Don't be ridiculous, I haven't anything like that amount of money and under no circumstances has George any claim on me.' She was so transparent; if I'd had any doubts about her and George being in cahoots I certainly didn't now. It confirmed they didn't know about Pat's visit or that the police had told me at the Monday morning interview that they'd spoken to George at the hospital, and he'd admitted to having been shot by me. He changed his story from when he was in the car. I thought, 'They won't get away with it.' There were plenty of witnesses who, if they were honest, would back my story. Harriet could be counted on to give a truthful account of what happened outside the house and in the car."

"Can I interrupt you? When did the police speak to McKay at the hospital? You said they all went to Patricia's apartment."

"They did, but once they'd hatched the plot, they took another look at George's wound. George had told Pat that he thought it was only a graze, but Pat saw the bullet hole and decided to take him in to Sydney Hospital. I believe he was admitted at about four in the morning. As soon as the surgeon saw it was a bullet wound (it was in the right side of his groin) he called the police. No choice, really. They came right away and interviewed George. He was a bit groggy because they'd given him morphine, but he told them what had happened, his side of it. So, that's how I knew.

"As I was saying, I thought the facts of the case were straightforward, so I figured they were threatening to embellish them to make sure I was convicted and got a long sentence. I said to Mary Ann, 'If you think you and your boyfriend can extort money from me with some cock-and-bull story you've got another think coming.' She just shrugged, said, 'You know very well that by putting in a word here and there, by stressing words and by intonation, you can make black look white.' I'd had enough. As I was leaving, she gave it another try. She said, 'Well, to start the dice going, let me have some sort of an offer. I'll take it to George and see what he says.' She'd ignored or forgotten my own offer, I could see. I said, 'No, Mary Ann. Apart from not having the money, the whole thing is despicable.' She didn't give up. She said, 'Start the dice rolling at £5,000 as an offer. Your word is good enough for George. If you say you'll pay him he will accept that, even if you pay him over a period.'"

"So, let me get this straight, she'd gone from demanding £15,000 'or else' to £5,000 in instalments?"

"Yes, see what I mean? I felt on surer ground, so I point blank refused. As I was leaving, she said, 'Don't say you haven't been warned. If you go to jail, I don't care if you get five years or 25.' I wasn't sure if there might be someone else listening in the apartment and I didn't want to be trapped into saying something I might regret. But it gave me an idea; two could play at that game. I knew it would be no use appealing to Mary Ann again and talking to George was out of the question, so I singled out Pat for my scheme."

"Why pick on Pat?"

"Pat had already as much as admitted the shakedown plan, so I thought I'd trap him into providing solid evidence they were out to blackmail me. If I could succeed the case against me would look very weak. It took a couple of weeks, during which I was in and out of police stations a lot. Oh, and I had another call from Mary Ann. She said she'd made her statement to the police and asked me 'before it was too late' to ask my solicitors to see George or his solicitors. I refused. I said it couldn't be done. She got quite angry. She said, 'You've been warned. If you go on like this George will see to it that you get life or swing, if possible.'"

"It sounds like they were holding out to the last."

"Well, that was the last I heard from them. I thought they hadn't played a good hand from the start. Anyway, in that couple of weeks, I got one of our maintenance electricians to wire up my apartment with a microphone hidden in the living room, leading to headphones in one of the bedrooms. I hired two shorthand writers. Then I phoned Pat and asked him over for a drink. I said I was feeling a bit down and needed company. I set up a party in the flat, got the two stenographers to pose as guests. He arrived, we had a couple of drinks, and the girls made an excuse to leave. They nipped off into the bedroom instead. Pat and I were alone, as far as he knew. I played it casual to start with. I said things like, 'I don't care about going to jail, I could do with a change from the food at Prince's and Romano's,' that sort of thing. He said he didn't think I was taking it seriously; I was in big trouble. George was going to sue me for enormous damages even if I got off going to prison. I said, 'Damages? You mean blackmail, don't you?' I said, 'You as good as told me last time you were here. Right from the first night it's all about money, then you get blackmailing straight away.' He said, 'No, the next morning.' I thought, 'Got him!' but of course I needed him to say 'blackmail', so I carried on a bit more. I said, 'Well, look, old boy, this is bad; it looks like a shakedown.' He said something like, 'That's my opinion, George is not game to come out in the open.' Well, George would want to keep it quiet that he was extorting money from me, but try as I might, I couldn't get Pat to say the word 'blackmail'. I could see that I was pushing my luck, and our friendship, such as it was, as far as it could go. After another couple of minutes, I let it drop and he left. I felt a bit sorry for him, but it was my life, my freedom and reputation that was on the line, after all. I thought I probably had enough to prove their intent, should they try that tack in court."

"And that was where you left it?"

"Yes, things went quiet after that. I didn't hear from any of them again, but I knew they were talking to the police. From the questions I was being asked in successive interviews I could tell they'd been feeding a line, playing down George's behaviour. Then, on September 28th, I was called to Manly police station and charged with malicious wounding. I went to Manly court and got £200 bail and they set the trial for October 14th. There was a second charge concerning the gun. The police claimed the licence wasn't valid after all. They decided to combine the two to save the court's time. In the scheme of things, the gun charge was just a formality. We briefed Jack Shand, KC. He was the best defence counsel of the day, bar none. But that's enough for today, re-living it has quite upset me."

"I'm sorry, David. If you'd like a break for a while, we can come back to it another day."

"I'll be alright, thanks. Same time tomorrow?"

Day Five: The Hearing

"Yes, the trial. It's not true you sit there in a daze as the defendant, you know. I didn't, my mind was focussed on every word. The court itself was a bit intimidating when I first was led in, but it wasn't one of those with a dock for the accused; I sat in the body of the court with my barrister and solicitor, so I didn't feel terribly exposed. I could communicate with them, and they passed comments back and forth, sotto voce, so all in all I was in good hands. What I hadn't realised until it was explained to me was that this wasn't actually the trial, it was the preliminary hearing. Before this I'd no experience of courts, the law and so on, apart from what I'd seen at the pictures, and those were almost always American court rooms. I was being called before a magistrate, no jury, to determine if there was a case to answer. In theory, I could have got off there and then, never gone to full trial."

"The charge was malicious wounding. Did the prosecution go all out to get the maximum sentence from the start?"

"Well, that was the strangest thing. They had to prosecute me, but for most of the hearing I got the impression the police were, if not sympathetic towards me, not terribly disposed towards George and his cronies. They didn't gloss over his loutish behaviour and though they contested my account of the blackmail attempt they allowed evidence of what you might call the conspiracy over damages."

"What was the prosecution case, then?"

"The facts, for the most part, weren't disputed. The first witnesses were the police. Constable Jenkins, he was the patrolman, described what happened when he stopped the car. I knew some of this from earlier interviews, but what I didn't know was that when Jenkins asked George if he'd been shot, George didn't just deny it, he said, 'Why? Has there been trouble? Has there been an accident?' I don't know whether that constitutes withholding evidence. Does it when you're the victim? Anyway, it came across as suspicious, to say the least. I could see eyebrows raised and a lot of scribbling among the court reporters at that point. Constable Jenkins gave his account of what happened when he interviewed me at the house. I thought it was quite accurate and professional, no hint of bias or suspicion. The only thing he said that upset me was that I'd said, after I denied deliberately shooting at George, 'You know, a man ought to have pumped the five into his guts. He screamed like a woman.' I'd forgotten I'd let that slip out. More scribbling and eyebrow-raising. Then he mentioned that I'd said, 'He came at father with a broken bottle – I think it was broken,' which I did remember. There was more evidence from the other officer who interviewed me at the house and from my interview at Manly, pretty much as I've already told you. The bottle was mentioned several times."

"Did the prosecution follow up this line of evidence? Did they try to pin down whether there had been a bottle in George's hand? That must have been critical to determining the extent to which you were justified in shooting at George."

"It was interesting, I thought, that the prosecutor never followed up on this question. They never asked the police if they'd searched for a bottle, whether they thought there had ever been a bottle. They seemed more intent on showing that Dad or I, or both of us, could have fought off George with our bare hands. I could see the magistrate looking at me and Dad and he must have seen pictures of George, so he could make his own comparison. I thought, 'We're on safe ground. I'll bet he wouldn't have been game to take him on unarmed.' Think about it; if he was dangerous without a weapon, imagine facing him in his state with one. There was no dispute over Dad holding the gin bottle and one of the subsequent witnesses, a chap from across the road, did say he saw me pick something up from the ground after George was carried away."

"Forgive me, but didn't another witness contradict that evidence?"

"The only other independent witness was a fellow called Bakker. He'd been riding past on a motorbike, pillion passenger. He saw the shooting and said George was standing still with his hands on his hips immediately before the shot. He wasn't asked whether George had anything in his hand so, no, he didn't contradict the evidence, in my view.

"That was it for the first day. I asked Shand how he thought it had gone. He was noncommittal, said we should concentrate on the next day, and he was right, because that was when George was called to the stand."

"So, George was out of hospital by then?"

"He was. They hadn't got the bullet out, but he was on his feet and not looking any the worse for it. I was expecting him to play up a bit, walk with a cane or something like that, but he came in practically bouncing. Probably didn't do him any good with the magistrate and made Mary Ann look a fool for telling me he'd been seriously injured. He gave a highly edited version of the events, of course. He left out everything that put him in a bad light, never so much as mentioned his insults to Jean and Dad and Uncle Norman. It was as if it all hinged on my offending him when I turned off the radio and nothing else had happened until I shot him. He claimed I'd meant it when I said, 'To hell with the bloody King'. You have to remember, back then there was a lot more reverence for the royal family, the King and Queen. The King won a lot of sympathy for having been thrust into the role after the abdication and then he and the Queen behaved magnificently during the blitz. George was putting me in a very bad light. Oh, and for some reason he claimed there'd been two shots. No idea why, unless he was trying to imply I'd really intended to hit him and needed two goes at it. I knew how many shots I'd fired and there were no other witnesses to support him, but the court heard it all the same.

"I was uncomfortable, listening to his so-called testimony, but my KC gave me a reassuring glance, didn't even bother to take notes. Then he was on his feet, cross-examining. He took George apart, though George didn't help his case. Shand referred to when George took off his coat and returned to the porch. He said, 'You were going to fight?' I thought, 'Here comes the denial,' but he blurted out, 'That was my intention.' I can only speculate but it struck me he'd been trapped by his own bully-boy bravado, because, when Shand tried to get him to clarify for the court that that was his intention, he said,

'Yes'. Then he must have realised the hole he'd dug, because he said, quite po-faced, 'That is untrue, that answer I have just made. I went back to the front door with the intention of getting an apology and was prepared to demand it from David Stewart Dawson.' Not a good start.

"Shand held up George's bloodstained shirt, very dramatic gesture, and said, 'This mark here, is that Mrs. Verspoor's? How did it get there?' There was lipstick on the back of it. George was taken by surprise. He thought he was going to be asked about the bloodstains. He waffled. He said, 'I have no idea at all. Wait a bit, I think it may have got there while I was dancing but I had my coat off.' Shand was cool as you like, he pointed to the marks. They were right on the back. He said, 'A lady would have to be a giraffe to get her lips around the back here.' Snickering all over the court, I had to hide my face. George was right off-balance but, I'll give him his due, he recovered enough to say, 'That probably got there while Mrs. Verspoor was assisting me to the car.' But Shand had only just started. He'd planted the idea that George and Mary Ann were more than friends, next he threw George off with questions about how drunk he'd been on the night. George fended him off, he'd been 'slightly drunk' or 'a little more drunk' at various times on the night. He must have thought he'd survived that line of questioning but, right out of the blue, Shand, shot at him, 'You've been drinking heavily for eighteen months, haven't you?' George was still reeling from that when Shand said, very clearly, 'You know what blackmail means?' George muttered something, and Shand got straight to the point. He said, 'I suppose you will agree that if a person were asked to give a false account of an occurrence such as a shooting, with the idea of extorting £15,000 to £20,000 from the other person concerned, that would be blackmail.' The prosecutor tried to object, told George not to answer, but Shand ploughed on. He said, 'I'm going to establish this man and this thing.' George had no choice but to answer. He said, 'It would be blackmail.' I looked at the magistrate, he had sat up. Shand didn't have George on the ropes yet, but he was going in hard, and George knew it. Shand said, 'And more so if you used a woman friend as an intermediary?' George said it would be despicable, and Shand came right back at him, 'Will you deny you sent Mrs Verspoor to see David Stewart Dawson?' Of course, George did deny it, but he didn't sound very convincing. I was beginning to enjoy this. Shand said, 'You know Mrs Verspoor went to David Stewart Dawson?' George hardly had time to say, 'No' (which was a lie), before Shand went for the jugular. He'd done his homework on George and Mary Ann, had times and dates, everything. He said, 'Will you deny that on October 4 from 11.30pm until 4.46am your car was outside her flat? Will you deny your car was outside Mrs. Verspoor's flat on October 8 from 9.45pm to 5.15am?' I loved the precision of the times: '4.46am, 5.15am', it was priceless. George was reduced to 'I can't remember.' His counsel objected but Shand spelt it out for the magistrate in case he hadn't cottoned on. He said, 'It will be established Mrs. Verspoor visited the defendant with a certain proposition and this witness says he knew nothing about that visit.' So, the magistrate allowed the question."

"Where did you think the questioning was heading? Had your barrister discussed it, the details of it, with you?"

"I knew he'd go hard on the blackmail. He didn't put his list of questions on the table if that's what you mean. But as he went on, I could tell where he was scoring a hit with the magistrate. I tell you; it was better than Hollywood. I almost forgot I was the accused, had to remind myself I was the one who could end up in prison. Shand's skill was in opening up a line of questioning and then leaving the court to draw the conclusion. He would say he was going to establish such and such, get the witness to react to his questions, assertions, but where I might have been tempted to sum it up, say, 'So, that proves you were blackmailing,' or suchlike, he would move on to the next topic before you knew it. You were left to think, 'Well, it must have been blackmail.' Brilliant stuff.

"He brought up the money again, asked George to confirm that he'd said on the night of the shooting he was going to get ten, fifteen, twenty thousand from the Stewart Dawsons. George admitted it but said it was for damages. Shand kept coming back to the idea that George had been very quick to talk about damages on the night, that he'd co-opted both Mary Ann and Pat to put the squeeze on me. No matter how many times he denied putting them up to it, Shand would come at him from another angle. It was like a bombardment. Then he changed tack again. He said, out of the blue, 'Were you responsible for taking off a brideship* a lady married to an American?' George first said 'No', but Shand, calm as you like, said, 'Did you go down to the boat and walk off with her carrying her child?' George was not happy with that question. He said, very cagily, 'I went down to the boat.' I thought my KC was asking him about Mary Ann; she had a child. But she was married to Dutchman, so it must have been another woman, because Shand said, 'You were associated with her continually for some time?' He said he was going to put George forward as a man of no morality whatsoever, an adventurer. He passed a slip of paper to him and asked whether he knew the woman whose name he'd written. George, I could almost see his clenched teeth when he said it, said, 'Yes, she's married to an American.' And that was it for him."

"And was that it for the day? It sounds like a long day for anyone to be on the stand."

"It was. You should have heard the chatter as they cleared the court. The reporters were falling over themselves to get outside. George went straight over to his supporters. I couldn't hear what they were saying but there was a lot of patting on the back, more commiseration than congratulation, I thought. I was about to do my own bit of back patting on Shand, but my solicitor gave me a warning look, as if to say, 'Not here, not now, it's not over yet.' And of course it wasn't. The next day we had the chauffeur's evidence, which I thought didn't do us much harm."

"How do you mean? He was a prosecution witness, wasn't he?"

"Yes, but it was rather like the police evidence. He'd seen and heard pretty much everything that happened outside the house and he was, if you like, impartial, so the court paid close attention to him. The bad

---

* Brideships transported Australian women who had married mostly American servicemen based in Australia to the United States or, less frequently, American wives of Australian servicemen to Australia.

part of it was, he was the one who said, quite positively, that he'd not seen a bottle in George's hand, nor heard glass breaking, nothing like that. But he did agree with our KC that George was the trouble causer, that he was full, he'd been threatening to fight, and so on. He said one thing I thought would go in my favour. He said after the shot he'd asked me whether I'd hit George and that I'd replied, 'I don't think so.' And when you remember that, though George was yelling and screaming as they led him to the car, he quietened down once he was in it, it's not surprising most of them there would have agreed with me. It was only after George fell over when he went for Dad that it dawned on me that I hadn't missed. The others, Mary Ann and Harriet and the chauffeur, were down on the lawn when that happened. They were more concerned with getting George away and off to town."

"So, the chauffeur's testimony didn't hurt your case as much as you'd expected?"

"Neither hurt nor helped, or perhaps a bit of both. But he wasn't the main act that day. That was Pat Garvan. He started strongly with the account of my phoning him on the night but though he stuck to his side of the blackmail story I could see he was being pummelled by my KC."

"Hang on, what was that about you phoning him on the night? I thought you first spoke to him a couple of days later. I'm confused."

"Sorry, I should have mentioned earlier. I did phone him almost as soon as the car had left, and we'd gone back inside and tidied up. I thought I'd overheard Mary Ann, or it might have been George himself, tell the driver to go to Patricia's place in town instead of to George's hotel, so I thought I'd get in first with my story before they arrived. I called Patricia and asked for Pat. I knew he'd be there. I said, 'There's been a bit of trouble down here. McKay has got himself shot. There's been a row and I had to use a gun. This friend of yours is a nice one, he's played up badly.' Then I told him how George had come at Dad with a bottle, and I'd had to shoot him. Pat didn't say much, so I left it at that.

"Pat told how he'd been the one who first saw the bullet wound and had insisted on taking George to the hospital. That was basically the end of his evidence. I could see how the prosecution would want to avoid bringing up all the talk of blackmail, the meeting I'd had with Pat, but Shand of course went straight to that in his cross-examination, and it wasn't long before he had poor old Pat on the back foot. He got him to admit to having the conversation with me and to learning later that I'd had it recorded. Then he said, 'I may assume that what you told David Stewart Dawson was the truth?' You'll never guess Pat's reply. He said, 'That's rather a big assumption. It was not on oath.' It was all downhill from then. Shand said, 'What you told him was what you genuinely believed to be the truth?' Pat was fidgeting. He couldn't look Shand in the eye. He said, 'Not altogether.' Shand said, 'Might you on any occasion have deliberately lied to him?' Pat was caught. I could see, and he must have seen, that he was being led into a dead end, but he had to answer, so he said, after a bit of a pause, 'I suppose that's possible.' Shand led him on a bit more. He said, 'I suppose you would have some pretty strong reason?' and Pat started on about getting the impression I was taking the whole business too lightly (that was my deliberate ploy to throw him off, you remember?) and that he'd said one or two things to shock me into a more reasonable state. Shand let him ramble on for a bit. Pat must have thought he'd got away with it, then Shand said, 'Was one of the deliberate lies to the effect that McKay was trying to blackmail him?' and Pat gave his smartest answer of the day. He said, 'I didn't say that to him.' Think about it; he was telling the truth, inasmuch as he never used that word despite all my efforts, so in a way it didn't matter that he'd admitted to lying about other things. Mind you, the inference of blackmail was still strong. I wouldn't say it was all we had, but it would have gone a long way to demonstrating a conspiracy against me. Shand tried every way he could to trap Pat but the best he could do was to lead him through our conversation, where we had both talked about a shakedown. Pat dodged and weaved, kept saying things like, 'It's possible I said that. I would not like to swear that I used those exact words. I cannot deny and I cannot affirm.'

"It looked like we were in the dead end now, but Shand wasn't finished. After I'd seen the notes of our recorded conversation, a day or so later, I'd phoned Pat. I'd told him everything we'd said was on the record and that he'd better let George know the game was up because we had solid evidence of his blackmail. Shand said to Pat, 'Will you agree that you and McKay decided to say it was really damages McKay was after and not blackmail? McKay said, "Don't worry about it. You can expect that sort of stuff."?' Shand didn't wait for an answer, he went straight on to questions about George and Pat setting up Mary Ann to trap me. Pat had played the 'I must have forgotten' card so often by now that he was sounding like a broken record. He first said he'd forgotten whether they had arranged for her to see me (this was supposed to have happened when they were all at the hospital together), then, when Shand challenged him, he said, 'I don't remember that occasion. It may be my stupidity. I believe they have seen each other.' Shand let that word, 'stupidity' hang for a good few seconds, before letting Pat off the stand."

"So, that was the end of the hearing?"

"God, no. Just as I was thinking we'd come out of it well, after Pat's woeful performance, they called Mary Ann to the stand. She was a completely different act from the start. She gave her evidence of the night, the argument and the shooting, in much more detail than George had. For the most part, it sounded accurate, I thought. She'd remembered details of the argument between George, me, Dad and Jean pretty much verbatim. Naturally, she was biased towards George, saying things like, it was my fault as much as George's that the argument started, but she said, for example, that she agreed it was reasonable that Jean had been annoyed and was right to ask them to leave when she saw the drink spilled on the carpet. Mind you, she claimed she'd said to Jean, 'I have been asking to go home earlier all the evening. It's just as much David's fault that the drinks are spilled as George's.' She said that after they'd been asked to leave, she'd apologised, but it was a very qualified apology, I must say."

"How do you mean, 'qualified'?"

"She said, 'I apologised for the simple reason that I had never been asked to leave anyone's home in my life, and I did not appreciate being asked to leave.' I thought, 'She's using George's words. The magistrate is bound to see that.' The rest of her account, the part about the actual shooting, didn't add much to the evidence, apart from her saying I had a very determined, sadistic look on my face. She actually said, 'sadistic'. She'd no idea how frightened I was. Then, she made a lot out of when Dad kicked out at George, made it look as if he'd deliberately kicked a wounded man in the face and groin when he was down. She made it sound even worse, going on about how Dad was screaming and running around like a madman. I know, he was quite hysterical by this time, but I still maintain that neither he nor I thought George had been shot until just after then. As far as we knew, he was still intent on giving Dad a thrashing.

"Shand cross-examined her. He went in hard, as we'd expected, but she was no Pat Garvan, she was a lot tougher. Shand tried to establish she was having an affair with George. She admitted to visiting George every day in hospital, but he couldn't budge her on the question of George's overnight visits to her flat. She just denied everything, quite hotly. She admitted seeing her solicitor, she said, to secure advice, to protect herself after reading accounts of the affair in the papers. Shand wanted to know which papers she'd read and there was a lot of to-ing and fro-ing gathering various editions into evidence. Mary Ann said there was one missing, a clipping from 'The Sydney Sun'. She asked her counsel for it and when Shand said, 'Give it to me,' she really upset him. She said, 'I would rather his Worship saw it first.' Shand was normally very controlled but she'd got to him with that. He said, very sharply, 'You will give it to me. You are not conducting this court, see!' I thought, 'Whoops! She's in trouble now,' but, no, she gave him a big smile, insolent as you like, and handed the clipping to a court constable.

"Shand was off his stride for a good couple of minutes, but then he got onto the blackmail conspiracy. She admitted they had discussed what she insisted was damages but wouldn't concede that it had been more than £5,000, though she got a laugh from the court when she mentioned Patricia's saying, 'You can get more than that out of them – £20,000.' When Shand said, 'And £15,000?' she said she didn't recall that sum being mentioned. I thought, 'You liar, that was your opening bid with me, and George has already admitted you all talked about it.' Shand got to the point, saying he was inferring she was a party to blackmail. She didn't play with words, like Pat, she just said, flat out, 'That's an absolute lie.' She said the same thing when Shand asked her to deny putting off seeing the police until she'd seen me. She said, 'Why do you not call it bribery. I was offered money and I didn't ask for that.'

"She was getting cockier by the minute. After denying having said, 'If I tell a certain story you will probably go to jail,' she admitted having said George was badly hurt and his business would suffer. Shand asked her, 'After that you suggested the sum of £15,000?' She wasn't falling for that. She said, 'I did not. David suggested the sum of £2,500 to me.' We were going around in circles. Shand wasn't going to crack her. He said, 'You have told us that once,' and she came back bold as you like, 'Well, I am saying it again.' I'd never seen anything like it, not in a woman. I know it wouldn't raise many eyebrows these days, but back then that was shocking behaviour for a young woman, on the stand, in front of an eminent KC, a man old enough to be her father. I certainly wouldn't, couldn't have carried it off the way she did, especially as I knew she was hiding so much. To give you another example, when Shand was cross-examining her on her account of the shooting, he asked her to show how George was standing before the shot. She made a tremendous fuss; she couldn't do it without a suit of pants. I mean, really! Shand said, 'Are you shy? Do your best,' but she just stared at the floor. Shand asked her why she refused. She said because he'd accused her of being an exhibitionist. The magistrate was getting irritated by this time. He said, 'I think you are under a misapprehension,' and Shand, I'll never forget it, said, 'I am not sure that she is.' And when she was being very obtuse answering questions about Dad's kicking at George, the magistrate intervened again. He didn't do this with any other witness, mind you. He said to her, quite sternly, 'You must put down the right line.' She looked straight back at him and said, 'Your Worship, if you notice ('if you notice'!) Mr. Shand rushes me.' She'd sailed very close to the wind. The magistrate snapped at her, 'Well, don't you rush him!'

"You're a woman. Do you think that was unusually forward for the time? Would you have stood up to Shand and the magistrate the way she did?"

"I'm not sure I can offer an opinion on that, David. She does sound very sure of herself, though. And she was the last witness?"

"She was. They must have kept her last because she was the strongest. And it told against us. The next morning, it was Friday, I turned up at Manly, with Jean and Dad. The court was packed to overflowing, we had to push through the crowd outside to get in. Lots of shouted questions from reporters, some well-wishers too. Inside, shuffling and coughing, waiting for the magistrate. He came in, it was over before we knew it. He committed me for trial. He'd not only found there was a case to answer, he'd upped the charge from 'malicious wounding' to 'malicious wounding with intent to do grievous bodily harm'. That carried a longer sentence, up to life. I was shocked. I'd been convinced that the charge would either be dropped altogether or reduced to some sort of misdemeanour. I was so disappointed that the magistrate hadn't been swayed by the blackmail argument. The only concession he made was to deny the police prosecution request to lock me up on remand. They claimed I would leave the country otherwise, but the magistrate opted to increase my bail to £800 instead. So, I was free for at least a few more weeks. We had a lot of work to do if we were to win before a jury."

Day Six: The Trial

"You had several weeks to prepare for the trial, didn't you? How did you feel, going into court? Had the mood of your family improved?"

"We had about six weeks between the hearing and the trial itself. We could see there were a couple of threads, I suppose you could call them, that ran through the case. This was the value of the hearing. It didn't just help the prosecution; we learned their strategy from the evidence they gave most weight to. We also got to know what we would be up against with George and Mary Ann on the stand."

"And what were the threads, David?"

"The main one, the critical one as far as we were concerned, was whether I had been justified in thinking that Dad's life was in danger. My defence team pointed out that, if we could prove to the jury that I'd genuinely feared for Dad's life, I could, in law, take extreme measures to protect him, to defend him. Shand explained that the prosecution would play dead on George's obnoxious behaviour; there was too much evidence of that, even from Mary Ann. They would dodge questions about the money, try to tie us up and confuse the jury, and they would go all out to blacken me as irresponsible and intent on doing serious harm to George."

"What was the other thread? You said there were a couple."

"Oh, that was the bottle. It was supplementary to the main issue but a critical bit of forensic evidence. If the jury believed the prosecution, there never had been a bottle in George's hand, only in Dad's; we'd made up that part of the story to justify my firing the gun. Shand and my solicitor thought there was enough evidence of George's violent attitude to persuade the jury, with or without proof of the bottle. The problem for us was that, once it had been introduced into evidence, it couldn't be ignored. The jury would have to decide which side was lying about it."

"So, what was your defence strategy?"

"To attack George and Mary Ann as opportunist fortune hunters. Everyone could see that George was recovered from the injury and he'd admitted himself that he didn't realise he'd been shot until Pat took a look at the wound. Yet, we had solid evidence that he'd started talking so-called damages almost as soon as he got back to Sydney. It was the sheer scale of it, the fifteen, twenty thousand pounds they were after, that could clinch it for us. As my solicitor pointed out, if it was damages he was after, why didn't he bring a civil case against me?"

"But the shooting was still a criminal matter, regardless, wasn't it?"

"Yes, it was just that the attempted blackmail, if we could prove it, would mitigate in my favour. If we could persuade the jury that there'd been a malicious plot against me, they might see me as more victim than culprit. At any rate, that was the idea."

"So, you must have spent many hours with your solicitor and counsel during those six weeks."

"Not that many. I was on bail so I could go pretty much anywhere I liked in Sydney. We had a few meetings, to coach me for when I would be cross-examined by the prosecution. I hadn't had to take the stand at the hearing, and in theory I could have avoided it at the trial proper, that was my right. But my team took the view that we should tell our side of the story to the jury, so that meant I would testify, and Dad and Harriet, too. So, they put us through the questions that the prosecution might ask, to make sure our defence was strong and consistent. It boosted our confidence, though Dad was shaky. He was a very emotional chap, not a bit like his brothers. But we couldn't not have him give evidence, he'd been central to the argument on the front porch.

"I made the most of my freedom. Actually, I was freer at that time than I'd been for a while; Patricia got her decree nisi right in the middle of the hearing.[463] I'd started going out in public with Beverley and, once the divorce came through, we dined and danced most evenings. We hadn't any firm plans for marriage, but we were quite serious about each other. I was enormously grateful for her loyalty."

"I was going to ask about that, about loyalty. Did your friends stick by you after the hearing?"

"It's times such as that when you find your true friends. We all expected, well, hoped for an acquittal at the trial. It goes without saying, I'd lost the ones who took George's side, including Pat Garvan. But George was more of an outsider, and he had a reputation that didn't win him many friends. There was a lot of sympathy for me, a sort of 'There, but for the Grace of God …' sentiment. I think it was to some extent a sign of the times. The attitude towards Great Britain had changed during the war. Don't misunderstand me, there was no less loyalty to the Crown, the mother country, and there was still a lot of cultural cringe about, but on a personal level, things were different. We'd seen lots of Yanks during the war, more than ever before, and we'd got to like their openness. It was such a change from stuffy British standoffishness. They weren't class conscious, never dreamt of putting you in your place. Then, the war ended, and we had Brits like George swanning in, lording it over us as if nothing had changed. We resented that and the more people heard of George's behaviour, his insulting words on the night, the more they came to our defence. It was reassuring for us.

"The trial opened on December 12th. It was in the old court building in Darlinghurst before Justice Holt. I'd expected a full house, after all the publicity, and it was a bit of a letdown when I looked around. There wouldn't have been more than half a dozen in the public gallery. I had to formally enter my plea and we went through the jury selection. You're allowed to challenge, as you probably know. We went through six, I recall, rejected them because Shand thought they would be biased in one way or another. I couldn't have told which might be for or against us, but I suppose he knew best. There was a lot of formal procedure before the real business got under way. They had C V Rooney KC prosecuting. He had a formidable reputation, Shand knew he was in for a fight. Rooney was what they call 'a colourful Irishman'. He wore a monocle, reminded me of Charles Laughton, squinting through it.

He used to let it drop out of his eye for dramatic effect.[464] Very stagey but effective, all the same.

"Rooney confirmed our expectations when he opened. He said one of the most important issues of fact would be whether George had threatened Dad with the jagged end of a bottle. If he had done so, I would have been justified in taking steps to protect Dad. He said the evidence of six eyewitnesses would negate any suggestion he had had a bottle in his hand or had threatened Dad with one. Then he called George and we went through the whole of his story once more. Same line about how insulted he'd been, how awfully we'd behaved. No mention at all of the insults he'd thrown at Jean. The way he told it, he accidentally knocked over the drink on the radio when he was 'furious', he said, with me over the anthem. I remember he said, 'I knocked over two glasses which had liquor in them. Mrs. Verspoor then suggested that we go home. We went to the car. After reaching the car, I took off my coat and went back to the front of the house.' Then he described the altercation with Dad and the shooting. Not a word about the awful things he'd said to Jean. As far as the jury knew, she'd played no part in it. Nor why he'd taken his coat off and gone back, which must have sounded strange to them. He made a big thing about not having a bottle in his hand 'or any weapon, at any time', said he was standing with his hands in his pockets and next thing he heard two shots (two), felt a shock in the stomach, didn't actually see the shot fired, got up, fell over, was helped back to the car: end of story. Oh, he repeated what he'd said before about concealing the incident to protect Mary Ann from publicity."

"I suppose Shand opened up the background, the things George had omitted."

"Of course, he did. He quoted all the insults to Jean: 'Didn't you say to Mrs. Stewart Dawson in a very affected voice, "My dear lady, I shall go home when I bloody well like"?' and so on. George flat out denied every instance, said they were all lies. Shand got him to admit that he now appreciated that what I'd said at the radio wasn't said seriously. He brought up the cosy relationship with Mary Ann and how quickly George had got onto talk of money with her. George must have been coached since the hearing because he denied having mentioned specific sums. Now, remember, he'd admitted all this at the hearing, so what was the jury expected to think? It wasn't as if they weren't aware of what he'd previously said; it had been reported in all the papers and only a fool would believe they hadn't read the reports. I could tell he hadn't fooled some of the jury members from the way they reacted. Shand left him hanging at that point, to let it sink in with them."

"It sounds as if George wasn't on the stand as long as he'd been at the hearing. Was he the only witness that day?"

"I honestly can't recall how long he was up. By this time, I'd heard it all, so I wasn't paying as much attention as I'd had at the hearing. It was the anomalies, the changes in his evidence, that made me sit up. Also, it took longer, what with all the preliminaries, for the testimony to get started. It was well past lunchtime when George got down. They only had time for Bowden, the hire car driver, in the afternoon session, which, by the way, was packed. Word must have got around, and the gallery was full. Bowden had nothing new to say, though it helped when he said he thought things were looking a bit sticky when George took his coat off and went back to the house. He also repeated what he'd said at the hearing, that he'd only heard one pistol shot. On the negative side, he said George didn't have any weapon and didn't offer violence to Dad. So, that was it for the first day."

"I expect you had another family conference that evening, to digest the day's events."

"I was in Long Bay jail that evening, my first night locked up. I was advised not to apply for bail; they would have set it very high, and the trial would be over in a matter of days. I was in the remand centre. All the same, I had an awful sinking feeling as they led me out of the court. I could see Dad's face. He looked terrible. Jean was supporting him, and Harriet was there, too. And best of all, Beverley was in court. She gave me a little wave, mouthed something affectionate. I could have kissed her there and then. So, off I went in the prison tram. The police and prison officers were quite civil, and I was admitted at Long

Bay without a fuss.* I had my own cell, a bit bare but clean. I'd slept in worse quarters in the army. It was when the lights went out that it sank in. I had to reassure myself that, chances were, it would all be over before I knew it; I'd be home and free.

"Being on remand they let me wear my own clothes, though they took my belt and tie away, and I had to wear clogs because they'd removed the laces from my shoes. I wasn't in any danger of topping myself but, those were the rules. It was quite a noisy place, lots of clanging doors, shouting, some very colourful language, as you might expect. The worst thing was the food. Talk about monotonous! Porridge and black tea for breakfast; soup, meat and vegetables and pudding for lunch; more porridge and tea for supper. Same every day, same meat, vegetables and pudding. I was already regretting my throw-away remarks to Pat about needing a change from Prince's and Romano's. No, I wasn't. The fact is, I had very little appetite for anything. They could have fed me on bread and water, for all I cared."

"Did you mix with other prisoners on remand?"

"Oh, yes. I wasn't in solitary confinement. Most of the day was spent in the common area. It was quite a crowded place. I was one of the lucky ones to have a cell to myself. At first, I was nervous being among some very hard old lags and a few rough looking younger blokes. I thought I'd be just the type they would pick on. But they left me alone, for the most part. Some were curious as to how I'd got myself into this mess, but the general mood, the code of behaviour, seemed to be to live and let live.

"We were back in court the next day, Friday, and Mary Ann gave her evidence. She was on her best behaviour. Rooney must have warned her not to repeat the prima donna performance at Manly,

---

* The description of conditions in Long Bay gaol is taken from an article published in Sydney's Daily Telegraph on 29th December 1946 P.7. titled: "Two men (from two worlds) meet in Long Bay". It contrasts David's background and likely fate with that of one Alexander Mitchell, a 17-year-old unemployed youth convicted of shooting a policeman and sentenced to ten years' hard labour.

because, when Shand cross-examined, she was polite, firm but no backchat. I won't bore you with the detail, there was nothing we hadn't heard before, even Shand's attempts to prise open the discussion we'd had about damages was the same, with the same results. I kept having to remind myself that this was for the benefit of the jury and impressions counted for a lot.

"We knew they only had the minor prosecution witnesses to come and that their case would be finished some time on Monday. I had the weekend to prepare for my testimony. Shand visited me at Long Bay. He warned me to watch out for Rooney's attacks on my character and to keep my answers short and to the point. I told him not to worry; I wasn't Mary Ann. We had a bit of a laugh at that. All the same, I wasn't prepared for what Rooney threw at me when he started his cross-examination."

"You mean, he introduced new evidence? Brought something in from left field?"

"Precisely. The Crown witnesses had finished. We had the police, the chap on the motorbike, I think that was all. The gist of it was that I'd admitted to the shooting, said I hadn't meant to hit George, that though I'd spoken about the bottle none of them had seen anything in George's hand. Shand didn't challenge much of what they said, just enough to get them to concede I hadn't behaved like a monster. Then it was our turn. I'd given my evidence-in-chief, point by point. I admitted to the joke about the anthem, but I was able to give all the details of George's foul insults and menacing attitude. Shand had counselled me not to lay it on but to leave the jury in no doubt as to the seriousness of the situation, which I think I managed to do. I did mention that when I went into the house to get the gun, I heard what I thought was a bottle being smashed. Shand took me through the shooting. I had to demonstrate how I fired the shot and Shand asked, if I'd meant to miss George, how come I'd hit him? I said, all I could think was I didn't know how hard to pull the trigger, and I must have jerked it before I meant to, and it went off too soon. Then we covered all the conversations I'd had with Mary Ann. I hoped this would clinch it for us. Then Rooney got up, and, out of the blue, said, 'Do you frequent the society of gunmen? Are you on familiar terms with any of them?' I said I didn't, wasn't. He said, 'On Thursday last at this court did you greet somebody on the bench outside?' I said I knew his face. Rooney said, 'Did he say, "Hello, David. Good luck, mate"? I said I thought he had. 'What was his name?' I said I thought it was McKenzie or McDonald, and Rooney said, 'Do you know a man called Rolls?' at which point Shand leapt up and objected. He approached the bench, and the judge told the jury to ignore what had been said while he considered whether it was admissible."

"What was that about? Who was this McKenzie or Rolls person?"

"His real name was Rolls, Cecil John Rolls. I had met him once before, at a private party, actually the first party where I'd been in George's company, as I remember. It was at Patricia's flat. I didn't know him from Adam. He was about my age, sharp looking. He had a second-hand goods business in town, did a bit of pawn-broking. I must have been introduced to him, but I didn't recall having more than a few words. I had forgotten about him until he called out to me at the court. As I said to Rooney, he was introduced to me as McKenzie or something similar, definitely a Scottish name."

"So, what was it about Rolls that caused Rooney to bring him up like this?"

"I found out at the end of that day. Shand sat me down and said, 'David, tell me honestly, have you ever had any dealings with this Rolls person?' I told him, no, I'd only met him once and had never heard the name 'Rolls' before today. And, anyway, who the hell was he? Shand said, 'He's a known gunman, he's up on a charge of carrying an unlicensed pistol even as we speak. That's why he was at the court last week. The Crown is trying to paint you as an associate of criminals.' I thought, 'My God! What's this coming to?' Shand explained that Rooney would hammer at me over the gun, give the jury ideas that I'd obtained it illegally for nefarious purposes, that I was reckless with it and ready to use it on anyone. He said it already looked bad that I'd been in the habit of carrying a pistol. He understood my reasons, but many wouldn't, could suspect my motives. He thought there was a better than even chance that the judge would allow Rooney's line of questioning, so I'd better be prepared for it, keep my head and stick to short, simple answers. And, by the way, Shand was right to warn me about Rolls; he was arrested a couple of months later for an armed robbery at Fairfax and Roberts jewellers. They said he'd taken over £8,500 worth of rings and bracelets, and that was while he was out on bail for the gun charge.[465] He got ten years for the robbery and another two for the gun."

"Fairfax and Roberts; wasn't that one of Stewart Dawson's main rivals?"

"Yes, it had been. Imagine if we'd still been in business in Sydney. It could have been our shop he robbed. That would have been ironic!

"When the case resumed the next day, the judge allowed Rooney to continue, as Shand had said he would. He said it went to my character. I was trying to look calm, but I was seething. I was determined not to fall for this smearing campaign. Rooney asked me the same opening questions, about whether I knew Rolls. I gave him the same answers as before. He asked me if I knew him as a convicted gunman and I said, quite honestly, that I'd only found out last night. He tried to push me into speculating why Rolls might have called me 'mate', but I played a straight bat, so he changed tack again. He put it to me that the pistol had been 'my constant companion', that I'd fired it at Patricia's flat. I explained that it had gone off as I was transferring it from my pocket. Then he did the monocle dropping trick. He said, 'I suggest you deliberately fired this pistol between Garvan and McKay on that occasion.' I didn't think that was worthy of an answer. I just said that was nonsense. He wasn't giving up. He said, 'Have you ever poked the pistol on another occasion into McKay's ribs and said "Stick 'em up"?' I thought, 'This is ridiculous, where has he got this rubbish from?'"

"I'm guessing it was from George himself."

"Well, it must have been. What had happened was, people knew I carried the gun; someone mentioned it in George's presence; he made a remark about me being a danger to society, something like that, and I prodded him in the ribs with my finger, not the gun, and said, 'Stick 'em up'. Rooney was determined to paint me as a real danger to society, though. He asked me whether I'd ever shown the pistol to the employees at Prince's. Yes, they had seen it; I used to leave it with the doorkeeper when I went in. He was implying I waved it around in the restaurant. I thought the questioning was getting very tiresome and I could see that Shand's patience was running out, but Rooney had one last try, and it was then I knew he was grasping at straws. He said, 'Have you ever been called by intimates "Trigger Dawson"?' Shand had had enough. He got up and said, 'This has become intolerable!' Rooney said he was suggesting I had a familiarity with this type of firearm, but Shand shook his head. He said, 'The harm has been done. How can you get material evidence from whatever anyone calls him?' Poor old Shand. He hadn't been prepared for that last question because, of course, it had never occurred to me it would be asked."

"Why was that, David?"

"Because, as I explained to Rooney, I had been called 'Trigger' on one occasion, but that was after the shooting. He gave up at that point. I had a feeling he hadn't gone down well with the jury. I expected a lot of questions then about the shooting but there were very few. Instead, he pushed me about my dealings with Mary Ann. He tried to make out that I was the one to initiate the meetings, using the pretext of returning the handbag she'd left at Palm Beach, that I'd broached the matter of paying for her silence, and so on."

"What about the blackmail question? Were you able to address that?"

"In a roundabout way. Rooney was never going to use the word, and he phrased his question carefully. He said, 'When the question was raised that McKay may be suing for damages you said to her you had another word for it?' I thought, 'Here's my opening.' I said, 'When she mentioned the fifteen thousand pounds.' He said, 'Did you mention what the other word was?' Well, I hadn't, so I just said, 'No,' and that was it.

"I was about to step down when the judge said he had a couple of questions. He focused on the actual shooting. I could see where he was going, and it was quite encouraging. He wanted to know if, before I went for the gun, I'd been certain that Dad was in peril. I said I was; and had I made any remark to George before I fired. I said I didn't remember. He said, 'Did you call on McKay to desist?' I said I didn't think I had, and he said something that made me sit up. He said, 'Take your mind back. Surely you can assist the jury on that, can't you?' I couldn't. I said, 'The whole thing was so hectic I can't remember.' He asked me if I'd said I was going to shoot George. I said I might have said 'I'm going to shoot', meaning 'at the ground'. Then he said, 'What were your feelings to McKay when you fired?' I said I didn't think I'd had any. I thought, 'That was for the benefit of the jury. He's trying to help me summarise my case for them.' When I sat down again, I felt, what's that expression? Quietly confident."

"Did your father and sister speak on your behalf?"

"Both of them did, and Jean. Harriet wasn't up for long. She did very well. She was only eighteen, remember, and she'd been caught right in the middle of the argument. Little wonder she'd become hysterical on the night. But, on the stand, she was composed; quiet, but composed. Shand kept her to the events outside the house and when she recounted how George had said, before he turned back, 'This has never happened to me before. I should have killed him. It's not only an insult to me, but to the British Navy. Be ready to pick up the pieces,' there was a lot of rustling and muttering in the court. The judge had to intervene. Rooney was very unpleasant toward the poor girl. He asked questions she couldn't answer because she hadn't witnessed the event or had been too upset to take it in, then he said, 'You say your brother's remark about the King was made in a joking manner. Can you give us an illustration of how "To hell with the King" can be said like that?' I thought, 'Why is he asking Harriet that, when George himself has conceded that it must have been in jest?' Poor Harriet had a couple of attempts. Rooney dropped the monocle and said, very sarcastically, 'So that's a joking manner, is it?' I could have punched him.

"Jean started off well. She gave a good account of the insults inside the house and at the door but made a bit of a blunder when it came to the point where Dad picked up the gin bottle. Having said that George picked up the ginger ale bottle and said, 'You hit me with that bottle, you old bastard, and it will be the last thing you do,' when Shand prompted her 'What happened then?' she said, 'My husband started to strike him with the bottle.' I groaned, and Shand made his own blunder. He said, 'Well, you thought he was going to.' Rooney's monocle practically shot out. He objected to Shand's leading the witness, he'd never heard a more flagrant breach, etcetera, etcetera. Of course, it was too late, the damage had been done. Rooney, when he cross-examined, asked Jean if she didn't think it her duty to placate a guest who had taken offence, that the laws of hospitality work two ways, a standard for the guest and one for the hostess. Jean said she thought she'd been very patient. Rooney, as seemed to be his habit, went on a bit too much about Jean's supposed duty to soothe George's feelings. He gave up after a few more silly questions and Jean got down.

"That left Dad, for the last. And, I must say, he surprised us all. He was dignified, spoke clearly, and only raised his voice when he recounted the moment when George did the insolent hand kissing. He admitted he'd lost his temper from the moment George insulted Norman's memory. He admitted he was so angry that he would have hit George after the 'it's the last thing you'll ever do in this world' taunt. But he was very clear and precise describing George's attitude and the exact words he'd used. Very consistent and compelling, I thought. Rooney concentrated on whether and where Dad had kicked George when he was down. The judge cautioned Dad that he needn't answer if he thought it would incriminate him, but he said he preferred to answer; he hadn't kicked George, hadn't even touched him. He said he'd been wearing old sandals, not what you'd call kicking instruments, he'd just been fending George off when he lunged at him.

"I think that's enough for today. I'm tired. I may need rest tomorrow if you don't mind."

Day Seven: The Verdict

"The jury were taken to Palm Beach to inspect the house and garden on Wednesday, so we had a day off. On Thursday they recalled a couple of witnesses. George was asked some more questions about the alleged kicking. He admitted to Shand that he'd been going after Dad, meaning to tackle him, when he fell. Mary Ann came back. She had amazing recall, it seemed. Now she remembered Dad saying, after the first alleged kick, 'Haven't you had enough?' She should have been a script writer. They recalled me, too. Did Dad kick at George's face or thigh? I said he might have kicked at his hands. The prosecution called a medical officer who'd attended George at Sydney hospital, to tell the court that George had pointed out a yellow bruise on his thigh. Back and forth, back and forth it went. I suppose it must have made an impression on the jury, but I was thinking, 'OK, so let's say Dad did kick him when he was down. That was after the shooting. What's it got to do with my guilt or innocence?' We had our own medical witness. Dad's doctor confirmed that Dad had high blood pressure and that he'd advised him in August to avoid any excitement.

"Friday was the last day. The court was already full when I arrived. I was relieved we went in via a back door. I didn't fancy running the gauntlet outside the front entrance. Christmas was coming up, the weather was lovely, I remember, a perfect early summer's day. I wondered if I'd be out for the weekend to celebrate with the family at the beach, or back in the remand centre."

"Had you any firm expectation of the verdict?"

"Look, I had a good feeling about the judge, and the jury, for that matter. I felt there was a lot of sympathy for me, that they accepted I'd been in an impossible position. On the other hand, from a strictly legal point of view, I was on shaky ground. The judge was bound to instruct the jury on that, despite anything else he might say. I was looking at up to life, with hard labour, but I don't believe any of us thought it would come to that if I were found guilty.

"Shand got first crack at the jury. The gist of it was that the law says that when a son thinks his father is in peril he can shoot to kill and he's not guilty of any crime. He asked the jury if they would expect their own son to act as I had done. He said, 'Consider the personalities. A young, powerful man (George), a mere stripling (me), and an aged man who has been insulted. I submit that the accused acted as any normal man would.' He attacked George and Mary Ann's evidence. He said, 'McKay and Mrs. Verspoor obviously gave much thought to preparing their evidence. They are intelligent people and knew exactly what to say. They put their heads together to produce a story that would give the impression of a deliberate, cold-blooded shooting. They told a wicked story, with the objective of prejudicing the jurors' minds.' He called George a drunken lout who strutted about the house as if he owned it, reminded the jurors that both Mary Ann and Harriet expected violence when George went back to the house. One of the best bits of his address, I thought, was when he pointed out that though both George and Mary Ann had omitted any reference to the arguments inside the house, had implied that the incident at the radio caused the trouble, they had remained in the house half an hour afterwards, and the radio incident had completely passed off. In other words, George's insults and affected accent were calculated to provoke us.

"Rooney's address was, in my opinion, the worst kind of distortion of the facts. He said, 'The defence suggests that David Stewart Dawson was justified in firing the gun because McKay threatened Stewart Dawson, Senior. But the first gross provocation and the first gesture of violence both came from the Stewart Dawson family. Yet they have the effrontery (he actually used that word) to suggest that they were the innocent victims, and that McKay was the bully and attacker.' His main objective seemed to be to put Dad in a bad light, justifying anything George might have intended or done. He said, 'When Stewart Dawson, Senior seized a gin bottle and threatened to hit McKay, he was guilty of conduct upon which Woolloomooloo or Surry Hills would frown."

"What and where are Woolloomooloo and Surry Hills? Are they places in Sydney?"

"Sorry, I should have explained. They're both in Sydney. Woolloomooloo is right on the Harbour, between Potts Point, King's Cross to the east, and Hyde Park, on the city side. Surry Hills is a bit to the south of it. They're both quite gentrified these days, but back then they were slums, with a reputation for crime, sly grog shops, gambling and prostitution. That's what Rooney meant. He said, 'Was this the behaviour of a poor sexagenarian* invalid, who was too ill to travel from Palm Beach to his office, and who must be spared any shocks, because they might cause his death, or was it the action of a drunken commando?' He said George had returned to the house with the intention of obtaining an apology (no mention of 'picking up the pieces' you notice), he had not threatened any of us in any manner (oh, yes, he had) but 'Stewart Dawson, Senior came out of the house with a bottle and behaved like an emotional old Pantaloon.'"

"What did he mean, 'Pantaloon'?"

"Pantaloon? It's a character from the old commedia dell'arte: an old, foolish man. Thought you'd know that. Anyway, Shand interrupted at that point. He said, 'It was a drunken commando a minute ago.' Rooney, he was at his worst by now, just snapped back, 'Well, take your choice.' He wrapped up then. He made a mild concession, said George's actions were blameworthy and he was afterwards ashamed of them, but he said, 'This is not a court of morals or manners. Even if all the allegations about McKay's rudeness were true, no insult, however gross, justifies the deliberate use of a firearm.' So, you see, he made it a matter of an insult rather than a threat to Dad.

"Then it was the judge's turn. He instructed the jury that they had to be certain there had been an element of intent, otherwise they were to bring in an alternative verdict."

---

* Stuart was fifty-three years old at the time of the trial, but in poor health.

"What might that have been?"

"Not guilty. I was just on the one charge. He said that though there had been a great deal of evidence relating to events before the shooting, they were to be treated only as history, that though the behaviour of all three of us men had been deplorable, they shouldn't let that prejudice them. So much for Rooney's slanderous comments. He chided Rooney for bringing up the 'Trigger Dawson' thing and for implying I was an associate of gunmen. He finished by saying they should acquit me if they believed I had reasonable grounds for believing Dad's life was in peril or that he was in danger of serious bodily injury. It was all over by three o'clock and the jury retired. I, we thought we'd be back in court on Monday, that the jury would need the weekend to deliberate. But they were back in less than two hours. We had to rush to collect my things from the holding cell, almost ran along the corridor, up the stairs and into the dock. Then, the wait for everyone to be seated, quieten down, let the judge take his seat. I was wetting myself; I don't mind telling you. The jury filed in. I was trying to read them, but they weren't giving anything away, kept their heads down. My immediate feeling was that they must have found me not guilty, must have decided I deserved the benefit of the doubt. I thought, 'Don't show emotion, no matter what.' My hands were trembling, and I didn't want the court to see that, so I gripped hold of the rail at the front of the dock to steady myself. And I felt a sort of detachment. So, I wasn't focused on what the foreman said. It was as if it came out of a bad radio play, when he said, 'We find the accused guilty as charged.' I hardly had time to react before he added, 'We ask for leniency in view of the age of the accused.' I looked around. Dad had gone white; Jean and Harriet were already in tears. I still felt detached. If I had any thought, it was, 'So, it may not be life. Don't move, don't give George and Mary Ann the satisfaction of seeing you break.' They were both looking very smug. I kept hanging onto the thought that any discount on the sentence I might get would be some sort of vindication. Sounds pathetic, I know, but you've not been there."

"No, I haven't, David. But I think I see what you mean. It must have required a lot of self-control, particularly when your family was so visibly upset."

"I felt worse for Dad than anyone. He was frail, that wasn't an act. He'd been caught in the middle of the affair. I don't know whether George would have gone off the way he did regardless of my flippant remark; I still believe he would have found a reason to pick a fight on some pretext. But it probably wouldn't have got out of hand the way it did. Who knows? But it did and, once George insulted Norman there was no going back, I see that now. I felt guilty for having precipitated the fight, Dad must have felt the same for letting it get to the point of no return on the doorstep. He was shattered. They almost carried him from the court. I had to stand there and watch. It was humiliating. Apparently, he collapsed outside on the grass. Jean and Shand, plus a couple of kind press reporters, looked after him and helped him to the car. After he'd gone, we had an odd consensus from both counsels and the judge, none of which made me feel any the better. They all said my behavior might be explained by my having been spoilt as a boy by over-indulgent parents. That was all I needed!"

"So, what happened next? Did the judge pass sentence?"

"No, I was remanded over the weekend; more porridge, meat, and veg., while he considered the sentence. I had two full days to contemplate my fate. Shand and my solicitor visited, said they would still try for a bond rather than a custodial sentence, but I could tell they weren't optimistic. I asked Shand what he thought was the worst case, but he wouldn't be drawn. So, there we were, back in court on Monday. The judge started by saying my actions had been arrogant, unjust, and ruthless: bad news. He said Dad and I had allowed George to get drunk and had incited him by insults: worse news. He didn't overlook the fact that George's conduct was contemptible in the extreme: starting to sound a little better. Then he said to me, 'It is not your doing that McKay is still alive. Due mainly to lack of parental control and over-indulgence, you have been allowed to form an unwarranted opinion of yourself and your duties to the community.' By this time, I had no idea how many years he would give me. But then he said he'd considered as extenuating factors George's provocation and unpardonable conduct and (and this was what clinched it) the jury's recommendation for leniency and the fact that I had no previous criminal convictions. He thought hope could be held out to me. I thought, 'Here it comes.' He said if my conduct in jail were exemplary (so, I was going to jail) I should be given the opportunity to petition for an earlier release. He sentenced me to ten years hard labour with a two-year minimum."

"You could be out in two years with good behavior?"

"Yes, two years. I could have got life, so this was about the lightest sentence he could have given me. It said a lot about the court's feelings towards my accusers. They might have had the satisfaction of seeing me locked up, but public opinion was on my side, I knew. When they led me out, the last I remember was Beverley; she was almost swamped by the spectators and reporters squeezing towards the exit. I could see her blonde head among all the trilbies. The babble was deafening, so I wouldn't have heard anything she said. I just kept the image in my mind as I went back down the stairs. And, yes, I was handcuffed this time."

Day Eight: Goodbye to All That

"David, I want to thank you for opening up the way you have. It must be very hard to bare everything and to re-live those painful times. I suppose this was the low point of your life."

"Low point of my life? Not at all. Being sent to jail may sound ignominious for someone from a good family, but there are far worse things than jail, I can assure you."

"You spent your time in the Emu Plains Detention Centre, didn't you?"

"Is that what they call it now: 'Detention Centre'? What have we come to? It was the Emu Plains Prison Farm in my day. No, I was only there for the last six months. I started my sentence at Goulburn. But that was just a temporary stay while they found a place for me in Long Bay. The hardest thing right then was parting with my family. I'd been kept in the remand cells overnight, after the sentence was pronounced. The next morning, we said our farewells at Long Bay before I was shipped off to Goulburn. They all came, Dad, Jean, Harriet, Beverley and dear old Uncle Percy. There were lots of tears. I felt duty bound to keep a stiff upper lip, though I came close a couple of times. I said, 'I'm going to take my medicine, as a gentleman should. Don't worry, Dad, everything will be all right. It's not your fault. I made a mistake, a foolish one.'[466] Uncle Percy was a surprise. I knew he'd been following the trial, but I don't think I'd ever before appreciated how fondly he thought of me. I realise now I was the son he'd never had, and to be honest, he might have been a better father to me than Dad. So, I was really touched when he showed up. What I wasn't prepared for was his state of mind."

"You mean, he was angry with you, disappointed?"

"He was devastated, shattered, by the whole affair. I'd never seen him so upset. He aged almost overnight. It was frightening. I'd expected Dad to take it badly, that was his nature, but he came to terms with my fate, I suppose because he saw me taking all the blame, while all he suffered was some name-calling. Percy, on the other hand, behaved just as I thought Dad might have. He was agitated, kept going over and over the 'injustice', as he saw it. I didn't know what to do to calm him down. I kept telling him I was OK, public opinion was with me, but it made no difference. He'd had no end of troubles in the past few months, quite apart from my case, so I guess it piled up in his mind."

"What else was he having to deal with?"

"He'd finally given up on his plans to redevelop part of the Strand Arcade precinct, after spending too much time and money on the project. He wanted to revive Grandfather's old scheme to build a skyscraper on the corner. Grandfather had this idea back in the twenties to put up a twelve-storey building on the King Street side, I think, but it came to nothing. Once we got the property back in forty-one Percy waited for the war to end to take advantage of the expected post-war boom. In 1944 he bought more frontage on King Street. That closed the gap in our holding. Then, he announced his plan for an eleven storey 'fashion centre', as he called it.[467] It would have been his signature achievement. But he couldn't get past 'go'; there was an acute shortage of labour and materials. By early forty-six he still hadn't made any progress. He'd budgeted upwards of £700,000 for the project but there were no takers, so he kept it on hold. By the end of the year he'd put it off so much that I think he lost heart. Time was passing him by. He was only in his late fifties, but he'd always compared himself with his father and, in his mind, I believe he saw his life as a failure.

"Then, to cap it, just as my trial was about to start, his half-sister, Lila, sued him over non-payment of a dividend from the family company.[468] She was rather prone to litigation; this wasn't the first time she'd taken us to court. The amount involved was trivial, less than £200, and Percy was in the right, but it caused him no end of trouble to fight it. He was having to dig up paperwork from London and our Sydney archives going back to 1937. He was in a terrible funk, Dad said. I suppose it was the last thing he wanted to deal with just as the family honour was being threatened by my case. By the time of my sentencing he was not coping well at all.

He said he couldn't stand the strain of staying in Sydney, he had to get away from everyone. I never saw him again. He went down to his place in Melbourne and the next thing, he was dead, just like that. They found him at the foot of the stairs, got him to hospital but they couldn't do anything for him: he'd had a stroke. He lingered for a couple of weeks but didn't regain consciousness. He died on January 25th.[469] Dad and Jean went straight down to Melbourne. There had to be a post-mortem due to the circumstances, but they found it was by natural causes, so they released the body. Dad organised the funeral in Sydney. Of course, I couldn't attend, which made me very sad."

"So sudden. And Percy wasn't even sixty. It was a shame you were never able to re-build your friendship with him after your release."

"Well, as I said, I only came to appreciate how much he cared for me when it was too late. I would have looked forward to getting closer to him once I was released, I know he wanted me to go back into business with him. Now, do you see what I meant when I said going to jail wasn't the low point in my life?

"Dad's composure suffered from Percy's death. He became quite depressed. He was the last of the brothers still standing. Norman was fifty when he was killed, Percy should have survived another twenty years, at least. I think Dad had intimations of his own mortality, what with his poor health. Not long after Percy's death he put the Palm Beach house on the market, couldn't live there with the associations of that night. That didn't go well for him. There was so much malicious gossip about it in the papers that the agents advised him to take it off the market for the time being.[470] He was at sixes and sevens. Jean would have been his rock, but she wasn't well, just when he needed her. Things kept piling up on us and by the middle of the year we'd reached a low point."

"Was that the 'drinks in the cell' incident?"471

"It was. What a kerfuffle! I suppose it never would have happened if it hadn't been for the other case, the money matter, that brought me back to Sydney. What happened was, I'd got into a bit of financial trouble at about the time of my trial. I'd run up an account with a chap called Berg, David Berg. He owned a lingerie business in Little Strand Arcade, but he was always good for an advance to fellow businessmen."

"So, this wasn't a debt for ladies' underwear?"

"Good God, no! Berg's sideline was money lending. I'd borrowed a total of £305 from him, he said I still owed him that, but I didn't. I'd repaid well over half, and by my reckoning, there was only £150 outstanding. He'd got a judgement against me for the full £305 and I was appealing it."

"If you don't mind my asking, why would you need to borrow from anyone in the first place? And why would it have been necessary during your trial?"

"First, it's none of your business as to why I needed the money. Suffice to say, it wasn't for personal use. Second, I borrowed it in '43, not the end of '46. It's just that things came to a head then. He'd been after me to step up repayments, I'd got the balance down to £100 by November '46, then he advanced me another £50 to tide me over during the lead up to the trial. I wasn't earning from our real estate business, and I had a lot of expenses, so I turned to him. Once I was sent for trial, he must have thought it was 'goodbye' to the rest of my repayments. My solicitors had been negotiating to settle the account, but the ball was rolling so we were obliged to appear at court. And that's how we had, what you called 'the drinks in the cell' incident.

"It was the middle of June. I'd been brought to Sydney from Goulburn but when I got to the court there was so much legal argument between counsels, they made me wait in a witness room. I didn't mind; it was a lot more comfortable than my cell, and, best of all, my family and friends could join me. We must have been there four or five hours, Dad, Beverley and I. Jean was still unwell. Dad was in a good mood. He'd brought cigarettes (good jail currency, as well as a welcome gasp) and a few bottles, to liven up the proceedings."

"How did he get liquor past the prison and police guards? Wouldn't they have questioned or searched him?"

"You'd think so. But you don't know Dad. He could wheedle his way around most people or put on a bit of bluster if he chose. Anyway, there we were, smoking and drinking, having a pleasant chat. We must have got through three or four bottles of champagne and one of scotch. When I was called, I felt very mellow. The two counsels had tied each other up so much the case was deferred, so my being there was superfluous, but I'd had a good day out. I thought nothing more of it, until a few days later I heard that Dad and the prison warder were in trouble over what turned out to be a gross breach of regulations."

"That was the prison warder with you while you were drinking?"

"It was. Roy Kelly, I'll never forget his name, didn't deserve to be treated so badly for what he did. He was the prison officer who'd escorted me to the court. After I'd been sent to the witness room, Dad and Beverley arrived and asked if they could bring lunch in for me. Kelly was a good-natured fellow, so he allowed it, but he couldn't leave us alone, so Dad asked him if he'd like to join us for a bite. When Dad brought out the champagne, he looked a bit askance, but Dad plied the charm, and he accepted a glass or two. I don't think he had more than that. But someone, don't know who, ratted on him. I suppose they were jealous of him. They turned up the empty bottles after we'd gone and pinned it all on poor Roy, in some sort of conspiracy with Dad to pervert the course of justice."

"What did that imply?"

"That we'd conspired to get Roy drunk so that I could escape. Ridiculous, of course. I hadn't even bothered to lodge an appeal against my sentence, and can you imagine how we might have expected to get away with an escape? Where would I have gone? What would have happened to Dad, and Bev, for that matter? So, though there was scurrilous speculation it came down to Roy being dismissed from the service for dereliction of duty. The poor man had a wife and sick child to care for, he'd lost his job and his superannuation. I must say, though, he was very philosophical about it. He said afterwards, 'It was because, in my capacity as a warder, and trying to be a human being, I permitted a father to see his son.' He said he'd done it for us and the girl I was in love with. I heard later he'd taken on his sick brother's business so, good luck to him. Incidentally, they dropped the charge against Dad, so no harm done there."

"So, by this time, you were in Long Bay. You mentioned a couple of days ago your time on remand there, the 'old lags' and the living conditions. How did you cope with these over the long term?"

"Well, you have to, don't you? The first few weeks were the worst, when it dawns on you that you're here for the long term; it was by no means certain that I'd be out in two years. I could see that, if I didn't keep my head down, I could either run afoul of one or more of the real criminals or get myself into trouble and lose my good behaviour record. Or both! Fortunately, I suppose it was fortunately, my old health problems cropped up again. It could have been the cold and damp in the place, but I had a recurrence of my heart trouble that landed me in the prison hospital.[472] That meant I was out of general circulation and, incidentally, in considerably more comfort than in my cell. I wore a clean, white shirt each day, changed my prison coat and trousers regularly and slept in a proper bed, with sheets and pillows."

"Didn't all prisoners have equal privileges?"

"No. Outside the hospital you got one shirt, a rough, grey one, that had to last you a whole week without washing. You kept the same pair of trousers and coat until they wore out, and you slept on a mattress on the floor, no pillow. You were locked up from four in the afternoon until seven the next morning; ate the basic menu I told you about; couldn't even write a letter without permission. On top of that, they were rather strict about contraband: money, cigarettes or even pens. We, on the other hand, had lights out as late as 9 pm, we could play cards, cook extra meals on a primus, write letters. I remember having butter, biscuits, condensed milk, chocolate even. And any amount of cigarettes: Phillip Morris, Craven 'A', Chesterfield. There was a lot of resentment, a lot, outside the hospital, over what they considered special favours given to us. And the longer I was in the hospital, the stronger it got."

"So, you were at risk from the general prison population?"

"Not as long as some of them were in the hospital with me. Cliffie Thomas and Harold Price were my 'mates' for quite some time and, with them on my side, I was pretty safe. Cliffie was in for murder and Harold was doing twelve years for a big fraud, £35,000, as I remember. They knew the ropes, had their tame screws and loyal mates to count on. Cliffie was supposed to have TB and Harold was asthmatic. We were three coughing stooges, you might say."

"How long were you in the hospital?"

"On and off, about four months. When they released me back into the prison proper, I had a note from the doctor exempting me from heavy labour, and I was fortunate to be given a job in the prison library,[473] which was right up my street. I still had to sleep in a cell and lost some of the privileges I'd had in hospital, but I managed all right. It's amazing what a little spare cash will get you once you've worked out the rules."

"What happened to George and Mary Ann afterwards? Did you ever hear?"

"Mary Ann didn't stay around for long after the trial. She divorced her husband and went back to Kansas early in '47.* So much for her and George's cosy relationship. George tried to sue me for damages in September '47. He wanted £5,000. Far cry from what he was after when he sent Mary Ann to me. His case was all over the place, almost as if his heart wasn't in it."[474]

---

* Sydney Daily Telegraph 7th January 1947 P.7. George McKay was on the dockside to farewell Mary Ann. She never remarried, dying in 1967 at the age of 41.

"Did he not seem serious?"

"Well, he served the claim on me, directly, but I wasn't going to roll over, not after what I'd gone through in the trial, so I lodged an application with the Supreme Court for further particulars. I wanted to flush him out. He'd had his chance of a private settlement and I wasn't going to give him a second one. When it came to court, he didn't appear. They wouldn't release me for it so neither of us was there. They had to read out his claim and it made little sense. He said I'd assaulted and beaten him (no idea where that came from), causing him to be grievously wounded, to suffer permanent injury and great pain of body and mind. He said he'd incurred expenses for surgical and medical attention, was unable to go about his business, and lost money and profits he otherwise would have made. All this would have been more than covered if he'd accepted my offer of £2,500 but now it was too late. I'd closed the book on that and wasn't about to reopen it. The judge ordered him to supply particulars of his medical expenses, how he'd been wounded, and the permanency of his injury. A reasonable request, you'd think, but George's counsel prevaricated. He said he couldn't provide George's exact medical expenses and the question of the permanency of the injury couldn't be answered for perhaps another two years. The judge practically threw it out of court. He ordered George to supply the particulars and pay the costs of my application. It was 'put up or shut up' and George shut up. We never heard from him again.*

"I fell into the routine of prison life, but I wanted to keep my mind alert. You could see how easy it would be for a working-class chap to slip into criminal ways of thinking after a few months, listening to the bragging about 'easy money' outside. But this was where my upbringing rescued me. I was determined to make something of my life once I was free and I knew my education, my connections and of course, my family, would serve me well. I occupied my time in the library reading and doing a little studying, and time passed. I had my regular visitors, unlike some of my fellow

* George McKay recovered from his wound, married in 1954 and lived an uneventful life out of the headlines.

prisoners, and I could keep up with the news. That's how I learned that Mary Ann had left Sydney.

"The rest of '47 was uneventful. Dad really was the last one standing by July. His sister, Bertha, died in London that month.[475] I remembered her from the thirties, when we lived there, and I'd heard the stories about her bravery in the blitz (she was up for the George Medal, you know), but apart from the odd letter from her or my cousin, Joyce, we'd lost touch. In September, Grandma's probate was sealed.[476] That was how we found out she'd left nothing to Radziwill. I got £6 a week for life and a full-length portrait of her done by Sir John Longstaff. She looked young in it, so it must have been done about the turn of the century, I'd guess. There were lots of other bequests, to Harriet, my cousins, various friends. Dad came off best; Grandma released him from all debts to her. I didn't even know he owed her, but I wasn't surprised. He was already better off than he'd been at the beginning of the year: he'd finally sold Palm Beach, made a good return on it. So, though he'd lost Percy and Bertha in the space of a few months, he was feeling less stressed by the end of the year than I'd seen him for some time. He'd also got our London agents to dispose of the villa in Monte Carlo, I think at about the same time. It had been sitting empty for the duration of the war. I believe it was in a pretty poor state by then. They got about £60,000 for it; not bad, considering the state of the market. I suppose Dad could have repossessed and refurbished it, but he had no real interest in Europe anymore and it just became a burden for the family. No doubt it's worth a fortune today if it's still standing but, there you go.

"By the beginning of '48, I had no expectation of release for at least another year, so I kept my head down, best behaviour etcetera. I was still running the library, with occasional stays in the hospital. Cliffie had got an early release on account of his TB and there had been quite a turnover in the general population, so I had a deal of seniority. I wasn't anyone special, you understand, not one of the high-ups in the hierarchy, but I'd earned a degree of respect and they left me alone. Outside, life went on. Jean recovered, but she needed a good rest. She and Dad were back in Bellevue Hill. There was talk about a trip to the USA, to see her family, but she wasn't up to it, so they put it off. Patricia and Pat Garvan got married in July.[477] He was throwing money around, had an enormous yacht built. Patricia launched it. I believe it was the largest of its kind at the time, something like ninety feet long. It was built in Newcastle, a good hundred miles up the coast from Sydney, so they chose to sail it down to the Harbour for their honeymoon. I had some satisfaction reading that they were both seasick most of the voyage.*

"We submitted our petition for my early release in December, exactly two years into the sentence. I don't know what I expected, but there seemed to be an awful amount of heel-dragging."

"What, from the courts, or the prison authorities?"

"Both, really. As I said, I'd kept my nose clean, and we had the same judge, Justice Holt, who'd sentenced me, to consider the release. But Christmas came and went, New Year, and still nothing. It was a low point, as I'd been counting the days and the family was convinced I'd be back home soon. Harriet had announced her engagement and was to be married in January, but it looked a slim chance I'd be there for it."

"She married Hugh Denison, didn't she?"†

"That's right. He was the grandson of the other Hugh Denison, the one who founded Macquarie Radio. He was studying to become an architect. Brilliant mind and a real catch for Harriet. They were the perfect couple, couldn't have found better. I was so pleased for her, all the more reason to be disappointed to miss the wedding. Instead, I learned early in the month that I was to be transferred to Emu Plains. They said it was to be temporary and I'd be out, free, in a month, but it didn't turn out that way, as you probably know. Emu Plains, by the way, isn't some out of the way place in the boondocks. It's right on

---

* Pat Garvan and Patricia's marriage was short. Patricia left Pat in 1951 and they divorced the following year. Both later remarried. Patricia died in 2002, while Pat survived to the age of ninety, in 2009.

† Sun 26th January 1949 P.14. Harriet married Hugh George Denison in Sydney on 27th January 1949.

the western fringe of Sydney at the foot of the Blue Mountains. We used to pass through it on the way up to Springwood when Percy was still running the guesthouse up there. It was all orchards and smallholdings in the forties. Nowadays it's more suburban, I'm told. The prison had been an actual dairy farm, a commercial enterprise, back in the day. They kept a herd of dairy cattle and most of the inmates helped with the milking, bottling and so on, or looked after the cows. It wasn't at all grim. We slept in what you might call a barracks. The food was better than in Long Bay, lots more variety and of course fresh dairy produce. It could have done with being a little warmer in winter and certainly cooler in summer, but otherwise it was quite OK."

"Why? Was the weather in Emu Plains that bad?"

"The climate to the west of Sydney is more extreme than on the coast. It was as hot as Hades in summer, and we had frequent winter frosts. There was no such thing as air conditioning, and we relied on a single stove for winter heating. By and large, we managed, though."

"All the same it must have been tough getting up to milk the cows on a winter's morning."

"I wasn't involved with the dairy, actually. I was put in charge of the chickens. We had a good-sized run that produced eggs that we sold to local and Sydney markets. I learned a lot about breeding and handling chickens, got to like them. I found that I could let my mind drift while I was cleaning out the coops or collecting eggs. I could forget my troubles."[478]

"So, you were there for six months?"

"About that. I was released at the end of June. I can't tell you how happy I was when I got home. I thought, 'All I want is a normal life, out of the spotlight.' I took a taxi, went straight to my hairdressers for a proper haircut and shave, and bought some decent clothes, before I felt able to face my parents. Afterwards, I drove over to Beverley's home in Double Bay. The silly things you do; I spent that evening polishing my car, it was a nice, red MG, just because I could. The next morning, it was a lovely, crisp winter's day, I put the top down in the MG, threw a bag behind the seat, and drove to Cowra to spend a few days with friends.[479] The feeling, driving along the Hume Highway, with the wind in my hair, I can't begin to describe it. I was making plans as I went, and none of them involved city life. I had to break away, find my own way in life. The idea that everything was preordained for me was wrong."

"Do you mean, continuing the family business? You were the third generation Stewart Dawson in Australia. Your grandfather built an enormous legacy for you all. Didn't you want to preserve it?"

"You misunderstand me. Of course, I recognise, recognised then, that Grandfather had made our name and deserved our eternal respect for it. But Stewart Dawsons' the jewellers was how we'd become famous, and by 1949 who in Australia remembered? There was one shop left, in Perth, that we'd sold to a local syndicate, and for a short time there were another two West Australian branches, in Geraldton and Albany, but that was it for Australia. There were the New Zealand outlets, but they were just ticking over and out of sight from Sydney. Dad kept an eye on them, but I never got involved. We were out of most of our real estate business, sitting on an enormous pile of cash, thanks to the Pitt Street sale. All the same, there was this unspoken belief in the family that, somehow, I'd resurrect the Stewart Dawson name. I think Dad hoped to take a back seat and let me run everything, find a use for the capital. If that meant in retail or real estate, I was having none of it. I didn't know the first thing about retail, and it looked as if I'd lose my real estate licence to practice thanks to my jail term. "

"But you did go into business, didn't you?"

"After I got back from Cowra I was still determined to get out of the city. That's when our old friend, Romano, came up with an idea. I'd known him for years. He'd bought a farm out in Baulkham Hills, about twenty miles to the north-west of Sydney. He ran chickens, ducks and pigs there for his restaurant and general sale, but he was getting on and was thinking of selling. He was about to leave on an extended trip overseas and wanted somebody to look after the farm while he was away. Dad told him about my enthusiasm for doing something on the land, my experience with chickens, and so on. He let me stay on the farm as a resident manager. I couldn't have asked for more. It was a lovely spot, well set up. There were several cottages for live-in workers, as well as the main house, so it almost ran itself. I could live life as a gentleman farmer, learn the ropes, without committing any capital. And I could be in the city in half an hour if I wanted."

"Didn't you say you wanted to get out of the city?"

"Well, not entirely. I needed time to adjust after my release and couldn't face the prospect of landing right back in the night life of the Eastern Suburbs. At Baulkham Hills, I worked in the open, got my hands dirty, went to bed early. Then, if I felt like it, I could visit my parents and look up a few good friends in my own time. I was also seeing a lot of Beverley, of course, so that meant weekly visits to Double Bay. It was shortly after I'd taken up residence at the farm that I proposed to her. It was a foregone conclusion; we'd made up our minds to marry before I went to jail. We agreed to keep the wedding a secret, or at least as private as possible. We knew the gossips would have a field day and were both sick of having cameras thrust at us. So, we organised a very small ceremony on November 17th at St. Stephens, in Macquarie Street, immediate family and just a few friends. We made a quick dash to the church; the door was closed with someone on watch. They opened the door as we got out of the car, we nipped in and 'bang!' it was slammed shut. Despite everything, the press had got word of it. They didn't catch us going in, but they were waiting when we came out. We didn't stop for photos, so the ones published in the papers were not what you'd call flattering. I had on my serious face, though Beverley looked happy. Mind you, she could dazzle you with a smile any time. Maybe it was her training as a mannequin. I prefer to think it was her natural personality. We drove back to Beverley's flat in Double Bay, with the press in tow, so we had to give them a few words to get rid of them. They knew I'd recently been to Cowra, so I told them that's where we planned to honeymoon. It wasn't, but it was all they were going to get from me."[480]

"You weren't going to Cowra, so where did you go?"

"We were going to Surfers' Paradise, the opposite direction from Cowra. I thought I'd put them off the scent but, that little scheme backfired almost immediately."

"How was that?"

"We strapped our suitcase onto the luggage rack of the MG and set out after lunch. I drove over the bridge and up the Pacific Highway through Sydney's North Shore suburbs, feeling pleased I'd given the reporters the slip. We'd just passed through Hornsby, pretty much on the fringe of the city, when we hit a patch of rough road. In those days, the surface wasn't anywhere near the standard you'd expect now. If it rained, there would be potholes and lots of loose gravel. I came around a slight bend and there was this potholed stretch ahead of me, water everywhere. I had to tighten up the steering to avoid the worst of it and that's when the back wheels let go. Next thing we knew we were heading for the other side of the road. There was quite a bit of traffic, and I could see a car approaching. I was sawing away at the wheel, but it was all over before I could regain control. Fortunately, nobody was hurt, but the MG was rather bent, couldn't be driven. The other driver was an understanding chap. His car was driveable and after we'd exchanged details he drove off. That left us in the rain, car-less, not even out of Sydney on our supposedly secret trip."[481]

"What did you do?"

"We had a bit of luck because the garage owner who came to tow the MG away had a hire car business. He hired us another car and we were on our way before five in the afternoon. But the cat was out of the bag, because the police who attended the accident had to report it. The press kept an eye open for these reports and, by that evening, the papers were full of it: 'Dawson and Bride in Smash.' We were still on the road. We stopped over in Newcastle that night, then pressed on. I drove all day and it wasn't until we arrived in Surfers' and read the papers that we saw we'd been sprung."

"Did you really escape the press in Surfers'?"

"Yes, they thought we were somewhere in New South Wales. We had our privacy after all. It was just that I'd wanted to keep out of the news and here we were on the front page again. Anyway, we enjoyed our time at Surfers'. This was before the boom, you understand. It was still a quiet retreat in those days, none of your high-rise hotels and apartment blocks. That came later, in the fifties and sixties. It was while we were there that I completed my plans for Romano's farm. As soon as we got back to Sydney, I made an offer to him, called him long distance, in Italy, which he accepted. I got the whole ten acres for £18,000, walk-in, walk-out. I even kept the live-in workers on. It was a bargain. The house was quite modern, beautifully finished, lots of cedar furnishings. There was a tennis court and a bowling green. Beverley was already planning parties before we'd even signed the deeds. She read a lot of American magazines, so her head was full of ideas for improving the property. I agreed, we could make it the show farm of the Hills, so we dug deep to extend the house, add a swimming pool (not many private houses had one back then), and double the livestock. That was going to take another £15,000 and six months, so we didn't move in right away.[482] I suppose I should have stuck to my guns, kept my promise to myself to stay out of the city for a while, but, once the decision was taken it seemed quite logical to move into a flat in town while the building work was done. Before we knew it, I was back into the old, familiar routine, as if nothing had changed since Palm Beach. The farm was still operating, of course, and I spent as much time as I could on site, but evenings saw us dining out at Romano's, Prince's, Gleneagles. My resolve was being tested; I can tell you."

"Didn't I hear that you planned to go overseas at the time?"

"We talked about it, but the terms of my parole were quite restrictive. Travel outside Australia was never a serious proposition. If we had gone, taken a few months' break, things might have turned out quite differently. Instead, by the time the work was complete, Beverley had gone cool on moving 'to the country', as she thought of it. We did spend periods at the farm, which I'd renamed 'Stuart Lodge', and it's true, it was a fabulous place for entertaining, but I suppose we treated it more as a holiday home. At the time of the birth of our son, in June 1950, we were still using it and the farm was doing well, but within a year or so we hardly ever drove out to it.

"The times were changing post-war. Sydney was expanding but the infrastructure wasn't keeping pace. Our journey time to and from Baulkham Hills was already longer than when I'd first taken up residence. Dad was busy winding up various Stewart Dawson companies after the sale of our city property, and I had to abandon my moribund real estate business when I lost my licence. I kept up the farm for a couple of years but, after the birth of our second son, at the end of '51, the strain was beginning to tell on our marriage. We were renting an apartment in Elizabeth Bay, a nice one at Ashdown Penthouse,[483] but Beverley was feeling the pinch. She insisted we move to a proper house for the sake of the children, so I put Stuart Lodge on the market. It sold in no time. I'm not sure we got our money back, but we had enough to look around for a decent house in the city. We bought the house in Eastbourne Road, Darling Point.[484] I was on the market too, so to speak, once I handed over the farm. We put our heads together and came up with the idea to set up a travel agency business."

"Why a travel agency? Didn't you say you weren't interested in running a retail business"

"Well, it wasn't retail in the sense that I would have to stock shelves; it was a service business. I thought I had good experience of real travel from my younger days, albeit before the war, and both overseas and local travel were booming. Flying was attracting people away from ocean liners and, as I mentioned before, places like Surfer's Paradise were gaining popularity. Beverley wanted a challenge, so we announced we'd be opening up in King's Cross."[485]

"What name did you give to the business? Was it another Stewart Dawson venture?"

"It wasn't anything. Before we'd even registered a name, we realised we'd bitten off more than we could chew. The competition was too strong, too entrenched. David Jones Travel, Orbit, Reynolds; they had a stranglehold on Sydney. I'd thought by setting up in King's Cross we would be on the doorstep for well-heeled Eastern Suburbs types. They wouldn't have to go right into the city centre to make bookings. It turned out they didn't mind taking a few extra minutes to see a trusted agency. As it happened, I'd canvassed our ideas with local acquaintances before we committed to a lease on premises. They put me right and we abandoned our scheme.

"I'd got the bug, though. I still wanted to get into travel or hospitality if I could, so I took the opposite approach to running an agency for outbound travellers. Australia in general and Sydney in particular were opening up fast to international visitors and there was an acute shortage of good accommodation for them. Not far from our new home Glen Ascham Hotel was up for sale."

"Ascham is a private girls' school, isn't it?"

"Not the same place. The school is in Edgecliff, a mile or so south of the hotel. Glen Ascham was at the northern end of Sutherland Crescent, at Darling Point. It had only been operating as a hotel since the beginning of the year. Before that, it was a private house, owned by the Kelly family. Roy Burnstein bought it from them in 1951, turned it into a guest house, and made a reputation for attracting millionaires and celebrities.[486] Before you knew it, at the beginning of '53, he wanted out. He was a larger-than-life character, literally. I don't suppose you've seen pictures of him: he was almost spherical, great paunch sticking out, trousers hiked to the armpits, flashy tie hanging down to his knees. He was a cartoonist's dream. He'd made his fortune selling furniture and then got into horse breeding. That was his forte and I don't know what made him dabble in the hotel business in the first place. I heard the rumours of the sale on a visit to the track, so I got in fast. I made him an offer and was surprised he accepted so quickly. I should have seen the warning signs, I suppose, but after the failed go at opening the travel agency I was itching to strike a deal."

"You were able to tap into your inheritance, then?"

"Not exactly. You've no idea how tightly the estate was tied up. It would be a while before I could get my hands on anything substantial, in my own name. The thing was, it was common knowledge that Harriet and I stood to inherit well over a million between us, so I was considered good for extending a loan, some sort of credit. Burnstein advanced me about £56,000, by way of mortgage, and I borrowed another £28,000 from Stewart Dawson New Zealand."[487]

"None of your own money?"

"No. As I said, I expected to be able to pay the lot off in one instalment as soon as the funds were cleared. In the meantime, I'd service the debts from the hotel's revenue. Debt, really; Dad waived the interest on the New Zealand loan."

"Sounds like a quick purchase. How did Beverley take it?"

"She was thrilled to bits. Couldn't wait to move in. I say, 'move in', she wanted to get involved in managing the hotel, had heaps of ideas for smartening it up, improving the menu, and so on. She was keen on developing the publicity, too. I thought, for the first time, I'd found a real partner. The future looked bright. I announced plans to spend a further £32,000 on a new wing for sixty more guests.[488] I started negotiations with an airline company to throw open the whole hotel to them for three months a year as a block booking for tourists. Beverley worked on cutting costs of meals in the restaurant to attract more casual diners. We recruited Marcel Le Blond, one of Grandfather's chefs from The Ambassadors.[489] But running a hotel was a lot tougher than we'd bargained for. Bookings weren't nearly as high as Burnstein had led us to believe and we'd underestimated the day to day operating costs. I know, I should have exercised better due diligence and I'm sure there would have been no end of advice from the sidelines if I'd listened, but we'd committed to the venture, so we had to make the best of it. Problem was, I couldn't pay the staff if I was to keep up the repayments to Burnstein and New Zealand. Dad was easy to deal with; he gave me a moratorium on the New Zealand loan until things turned around. But Burnstein wanted his money, or rather, his wife did. She was the financial head of that household and very hard-nosed, started rattling the can right away. And then I did a foolish thing. I was in a corner, a real fix. I had the hotel debt hanging over me and still hadn't paid off our house. I needed cash, lots of it, fast."

"So, what was the foolish thing you did?"

"I can scarcely bring myself to speak about it, haven't spoken of it for over thirty years: I gambled on it. There, I've said it. And I lost, lost everything."[490]

"Oh, I see. Were you a regular gambler, then?"

"No, that's just it. I used to bet a little on the races or at the fights, but nothing big, nothing I couldn't afford to lose. I broke even, it was just for fun. But the crowd I moved in included a few harder characters. We'd go on after a race meeting or on a fight night for drinks at King's Cross. There were lots of clubs opening there after the war, where chaps could meet, drink and gamble. I got into one or two baccarat games, moderate stakes, and kept up my break-even streak. I still wasn't a heavy gambler, though. But one thing led to another. I knew there were poker schools where big money could be won so, when I was invited to join one, I saw my chance to wipe the slate clean on my debts. On the night in question, in July, I was playing against a chap called Roth. I should have known better but, when I lost a couple of hands and could see the stakes getting higher, I put the lot on what I thought was a winning hand. I stood to win thousands. You can guess what happened."

"How much did you lose, if I may ask?"

"Twenty-two thousand pounds. That would have been about ten years' earnings for a manager, twice that for a working man. Shocking, isn't it? I had to break the news to Beverley, which was the last straw for her. We had the mother of all rows, lots of door slamming, and I stormed out, went to ground, in my private room at Glen Ascham. I had run out of options, so I sold the house, quick sale. That paid off part of the hotel debt, and covered some of my day-to-day expenses, but I was still deep in the hole, and I'd crossed a line with Beverley."

"I guess she didn't approve of the house sale. She must have resisted when you put it on the market."

"She didn't know. I kept it under my hat until I'd signed the contract of sale. I knew what she'd say if she got wind of it. Time was of the essence, and I couldn't afford, couldn't face arguing over it."

"You didn't tell her? But she was still living in the house, wasn't she?"

"She was, and that rather complicated things with the new owners. The Falsteins wanted to move in when the contract was finalised in October. But Beverley made no effort to move out. She said she had nowhere else to go, needed time to make arrangements for her and the boys. The Falsteins said, OK, they'd accommodate her. They would move into part of the house, and she could stay for a while, until she sorted things out. It was a big house, so there shouldn't have been a problem. But Beverley dragged her feet and pretty soon war was declared. She got an injunction against the Falsteins, a writ of attachment, to prevent them from evicting her. They took her to court and got the writ overturned, so out she went.[491] She got an order against me for maintenance costs and moved into a hotel at Point Piper, the Buckingham, but though I kept up the payments for a few weeks I was struggling to cover the hotel bills. She had two rooms, one for herself and the children and another for the nurse, which added up to more than I was prepared to pay. She told everyone she wanted a house or flat up the peninsula, at Palm Beach or Newport, but she knew I couldn't afford that. By November it had come to the crunch. And that's when 'the siege of Glen Ascham' started."

"I think I heard about that. Was that when Beverley barricaded herself inside the hotel?"[492]

"That's it. She waited until I was out at a fight, came over with her mother, the boys and their nurse, grabbed plenty of food from the kitchen, the keys to two rooms on the top floor, and locked herself in. When I got back from the fight there were reporters and staff milling around in the lobby. The reporters wanted my reaction to Beverley's sit-in. I said I had no idea what they were getting at, so they took great delight in informing me and seeing the look on my face. I dashed up to the top floor, but she'd locked the door and refused to come out. She was demanding I pay her two, three times the maintenance costs, the ones I already couldn't afford, before she'd come out. So, we had a standoff. I decided on a two-pronged approach: I hired security guards to watch the rooms twenty-four hours a day, so that she couldn't sneak out, and I called in the Welfare Department to rescue the children from their confinement. I was determined to win, to starve Beverley and the other two women out. Business was bad enough without this farce."

"What about the children? Wouldn't they have suffered first?"

"I allowed food in for the boys, but none for the adults. I trained searchlights onto the outside of the rooms, to keep her awake and to scare off the reporters and photographers who were climbing onto the roof to interview her through the window."

"Couldn't you have negotiated, resolved your differences without all that drama?"

"She started it. It wasn't my fault she went to extremes. If she'd waited a few days, I could have sorted out the accounts at the Buckingham and none of this would have happened. She went behind my back while she knew I was out, to sneak in and occupy the rooms. She did immeasurable damage to the business; got us all the wrong kind of publicity; I was the laughingstock of Sydney. For a fortnight, I was in my own room, and she was locked up in the same hotel. I'd run out of ideas, to be honest, and she knew it. In the end, she wore me down; I agreed to increase the alimony to a little over £70. That covered the room at the Buckingham and a further £35 a week living expenses. I couldn't afford it, but she was making all kinds of legal threats. She wanted a written agreement and money to redeem her jewellery that she'd pawned, but I wouldn't go that far.[493] She came out, left with the boys and the nurse, and I tried to restore Glen Ascham to normal. We had Christmas coming up and a lot of tourists arriving for the summer season. I thought the worst was over."

"But it wasn't, was it?"

"Of course not. I was getting deeper in debt by the day, still owed Roth for the card game, and most of what I'd borrowed to buy the hotel. Now, I was expected to pay £71 a week on top of that. I appealed the judgement in April '54 and got it reduced, back to £35, which was still beyond my means.[494] I undertook to increase the amount when things turned around, but things didn't turn around. By the middle of the year, we were doing a little better and I could pay the regular bills, but not much more. Beverley and I still saw each other, and I think we both realised things had to change. She was bored being cooped up with the children at the Buckingham and she could see her stake in Glen Ascham going nowhere. She was itching to try out her ideas for boosting custom and, I must admit, she hadn't lost that sparkle that had attracted me to her. But there was no question of me taking her back as my wife; it had gone too far for that. Entre nous, I was having a fling with another woman by then, and Beverley knew about it. So, we agreed that she would move back into Glen Ascham and take over management. I'd run out of energy and lost interest in the business, but she had plenty to spare. To keep the press happy, we announced we'd reconciled,[495] but I didn't want to be on the scene any longer. After she moved in, I left; went to a rented apartment.

"Does the name, Lee Gordon, mean anything to you? Thought not; you're too young. If you were in Sydney in the fifties and sixties, you'd remember him. He was an American, about my age, who almost single-handed introduced Australia to modern jazz, big name US entertainers, rock n' roll. He was the one who brought The Beatles to Sydney in 1964. Yes, that's him. We took over Glen Ascham in April '53 and that was the first place he stayed when he arrived in Sydney. Terrific chap; had a great personality, and very well-connected. We all got along famously. I played cards with him. Lost again, I'm sorry to say.[496] Beverley made the most of the relationship, though. Almost as soon as she took over the hotel in July '54 she found out that Lee was organising a tour of American entertainers to Australia, starting in Sydney. She offered the hotel at a good bulk rate, and he signed on. It was a genuine coup. Don't care what you say about our relationship, she had an eye for opportunities that I never had. The tour included

Artie Shaw, Buddy Rich, Ella Fitzgerald, and several other band members.[497] It was a massive windfall for us. She booked Johnnie Ray a couple of months later, even bigger hit."[498]

"Sorry, I've heard of Artie Shaw, and Buddy Rich and of course, Ella Fitzgerald, but who was Johnnie Ray?"

"Johnnie Ray? Before Elvis Presley, he was the top popular singer. Some people call him the father of rock 'n roll. He was amazingly good-looking, put a lot of emotion into his singing, literally threw himself into it. Teenage girls swooned over him; they used to rip his shirt off. I'm surprised you've never heard of him. He died last year, I heard; you must have seen it in the papers. Well, he was another Glen Ascham guest, thanks to Beverley.

"But by then I was out of the picture, not even in Sydney. I'd gone up to Surfers'. I had to get away from my creditors, give myself breathing space, so I moved in with my lady friend, Pat Beerlein. She owned a café there. I paid my way waiting tables for her.[499] It was such a relief, being in that lovely place, far from my troubles. Of course, I knew they'd catch up with me sooner or later, but I thought I'd solve it all in one swoop. I put an advertisement in the Sydney papers offering Glen Ascham with possession, fully furnished, walk-in, walk-out."

"Don't tell me; Beverley was caught by surprise again."

"'Fraid so.[500] She couldn't see beyond the immediate successes of the American tours. I'd looked at the books and, though things were on the up, I could see no way out of the debt trap. She would never have understood and, anyway, it wasn't her decision to make; I was the titular owner, not she. But before there were any offers, I was served with a foreclosure writ on the hotel, courtesy of Lee's American agent, Arthur Schurgin. It came about because of some minor overpayment they'd made on their bookings that we'd not been able to reimburse; something less than two thousand pounds. I might have played for time (I didn't have two hundred, let alone two thousand) but, as soon as I saw the details of the writ, I knew it was over. They gave me until November 23rd to pay or they would force the sale of everything I owned. The writ listed all the loans and mortgages outstanding, reminding me of the hole I'd dug for myself.[501] It was the final straw. I couldn't meet the November deadline, so I just stood back and waited for the inevitable."

"So, that was it, then? Glen Ascham sold from under you."

"It wasn't as simple as that; nothing in my life was simple, come to think of it. Prior to the day of the sale, our old friend, Romano, made an offer of £52,000, but it was out of the money; the Burnsteins wanted at least £60,000, so they refused the bid and took possession of the hotel for themselves until a genuine buyer showed up.[502] On the sale day, a chancer by the name of Freame made the only bid: two pounds, for my entire interest in the property and business, and the auctioneer accepted it! He explained to Freame, who was a clerk working in the Registrar General's department, that he had taken on all my debt with the purchase. Freame obviously hadn't thought it through. It must have 'sounded like a good idea at the time'. He hadn't two pennies to rub together and a good couple of weeks were wasted while he cast about for someone to rescue him. For a while, it looked as if his great aunt would step in, but it was all talk and in the end they let him off the hook; bloody fool![503] Meantime, Beverley was still in residence and, you guessed it, she tried another sit-in. Burnstein turned up to take possession and she'd barricaded herself into a room, the same room she'd gone to previously. Burnstein's people got into a terrible row with the staff; I believe punches were thrown before they saw sense. Practically all the guests left, so things were fraught for a while. Burnstein said all he wanted was to sell up and get out. He said he wasn't going to throw Beverley out, but she had to accept that time was up, which she did the next day, to everyone's relief. There was another nasty moment as they were packing up to leave. Beverley's mother got into a shouting match with Burnstein's dragon of a wife over rights to various personal items; all very distasteful.[504]

"Beverley left, moved back into the Buckingham, and I was recalled from Queensland to answer a summons over my debts. That didn't go well, either. I'd hardly arrived at Dad's house in Bellevue Hill when who should turn up but Beverley, with a divorce petition in her hand. We had another row, right there on the doorstep, there was a bit of shoving when I tried to eject her, and next thing she's called the police. They arrested me for assaulting her, and booked me at Paddington Police Station, but she must have had second thoughts because she withdrew the accusation.[505] The police let me go, but I still had to face my creditors. There was an amount outstanding for furnishings at our house. I'd forgotten all about it, but they tracked me down, there was another court hearing and I had to find over £600 'or else'.[506] I felt as if the world was closing in on me. Beverley took me to court again over alimony and I had a minor win when I was able to convince the magistrate I couldn't pay more than £20 a week and he agreed her expense claims were exaggerated, but I was only staving off the inevitable. On March 10th she was granted a divorce on the grounds of my adultery. It was another irony: I'd broken up with Pat Beerlein, but I was past caring; I didn't defend the action."[507]

"You'd lost a lot in a short time, hadn't you?"

"Everything. And it wasn't over. In May '55 I was taken to the bankruptcy court by another creditor, the printer we'd used at Glen Ascham. I was, genuinely, bankrupt.[508] My assets amounted to less than £50,000 in the Stewart Dawson estate and I owed far more than that to the Burnsteins and, I can't remember how many other creditors."

"I thought you said you and Harriet together stood to inherit almost a million pounds. How could your assets be so much less than that?"

"Most of the estate was tied up in the remaining Stewart Dawson companies, entailed until Dad died and they could be liquidated. I could no more get my hands on it than fly to the moon. I'd run out of options, at least in Sydney. I'd lost my wife and children, had only the clothes I stood in, not even a car. I couldn't face Sydney anymore, so I took the first opportunity to leave town. I went back to Surfers', thought I could make a go of it with Pat again, but that didn't work out either. I was so desperate for cash I stupidly pawned her diamond ring and she found out. She chucked me out and I had yet another court appearance. I was still on parole for the shooting but, fortunately, none of my subsequent brushes with the law were for violent crimes, otherwise I'd have been back inside for the duration."[509]

"And then you came over here, to England."

"Not right away; I had to wait for my parole to be over, so I kept a low profile in Surfers', doing odd jobs. Dad subbed me just enough to keep my head above water. As soon as I was able, in early '57, I booked a ticket for Liverpool and made my way to London. I was able to stay in a spare room at our Hatton Garden premises, so I could save on hotel costs."*

"Didn't you say that the Hatton Garden building had been sold in the forties?"

"We put it on the market then, but it didn't sell. Most of it was sub-let by the time I arrived. We had been using some of the storerooms for export goods for New Zealand and the Perth store, but that had dried up, so the building was surplus to requirements. Dad asked me to push the sale when he learned I was going to London. I must say, it was still an impressive edifice after half a century; all that Art Nouveau décor, Grandfather's monogram engraved on the front doors. I had little memory of it from my childhood, but I did know it was Grandfather's pride and joy, so it was rather a sad occasion, having to let it go like that. We did find a buyer and Dad released some funds for me.

"The rest, as they say, is history; very boring history as far as I'm concerned. I've been here thirty-four years, never went back to Australia. I gave up all my ambition to be a businessman. I don't think I ever had it in me, to be frank."

---

* UK Incoming Passenger List, RMS 'Port Adelaide' arrived Liverpool, 4th April 1957. David, one of 12 First Class passengers, gave his address in the UK as 20 Hatton Garden and his occupation as *"Company Director"*. He stated the purpose of his visit was *"Visitor/Business"*, presumably because he was on a mission for his father to dispose of The Treasure House.

"What did you do for a living, then?"

"I drove a cab. That's right, I've been a London cabbie, retired a couple of years ago.[510] My health was never that good, as you know, but I was able to sit behind the wheel and, once I got, 'the knowledge', as they call it, they gave me my taxi licence and I never looked back. I married my third wife here.* We make no great demands on each other. On the contrary, she's looked after me terrifically well, as my health declined. I rely on her entirely now. I don't know how much longer I've got; I suspect not long, but I'll try to enjoy every day."

"Any regrets?"

"Too many. I had it all and I threw it away. Stewart Dawson was once a name to inspire people. I should have been the one to carry it forward, but what's left of it today? My sons are estranged; I believe Beverley changed their family name when she took off to America. She's lived there almost since we broke up; married at least five times since then; I'm pretty sure it's five. I've lost count and lost touch years ago.† My sister, Harriet, is a good egg. She's the one who took on Dad's responsibilities, even before he died. He passed away in 1961 but she'd been looking after most of the family businesses for some time before. She and her husband used to fly over to New Zealand to attend board meetings and she organised the final sale of the New Zealand business to James Pascoe Limited just a few years ago.[511] That's the only remaining place anywhere where you'll find Stewart Dawson jeweller's stores; Pascoes kept the name as their premium brand. Otherwise, we're history.

---

* It is not clear that David legally married a third time. The informant named on his death certificate is listed as *"Widow of the deceased"* but there is no record of a marriage.

† Beverley left Australia for the United States no later than May 1956 and married/divorced at least five times after divorcing David. Settling in Florida, she made a late career in politics, being elected Sarasota County's first woman commissioner in 1971. She died in Sarasota, on April 6th, 2004.

"I sometimes wonder what Grandfather would make of it. He would never have imagined a woman taking charge the way Harriet did. But, when you look at us, it's the Stewart Dawson women who've been the stronger. Apart from Percy, who else was ever worthy of the name? I certainly wasn't, Dad coasted through life and Norman was a disappointment. But think about the women: Grandma was an inspiration to thousands, never lost her dignity despite the Radziwill business; Aunt Bertha and my cousin, Joyce, were two of the bravest people; Jean held Dad together for years; I'm told Percy's wife, Rita, was an absolute gem at The Ambassadors; even Beverley left me for dead when it came to managing the hotel; she never would have run up debts the way I did. If were allowed a drink, I'd raise a glass to the Stewart Dawson ladies!

"And that's it. I'm exhausted. That's all you're getting from me. No more 'mea culpa' soul baring. Remember our deal: no publishing until after I've gone (that won't be long, now) and keep my wife's name out of it; she's no part of my Australian story. I've not told it before and I'm not sure I should have now. But, there, it's done."

"David, I can't tell you how grateful I am for your frankness and openness over these past days. Your story, the Stewart Dawson story, is worth preserving and telling, and I promise to be faithful to the spirit of it. I know how hard it's been for you to relive those memories, and the toll it must have taken on you. Thank you, once more."

~/~/~

51. David Stewart Dawson jr.

52. Patricia Ann Fitzgerald, David's first wife.

53. The Stewart Dawson home at Palm Beach.

54. George Rankin McKay

55. Mary Ann Verspoor

56. Stuart Stewart Dawson

57. Stuart's wife, Jean

58. David's sister, Harriet, at Manly Court.

59. Owen Patrick 'Pat' Garvan

60. Stuart and Jean at Manly Court.

61. Beverley Atkinson, David's second wife

62. Last known photo of Percy, 1946.

63. Sale of the last Stewart Dawson Sydney property, June 1949.

64. David and Beverley's 'secret' wedding, July 1949.

65. Glen Ascham hotel.

66. Beverley's sit-in with her sons at Glen Ascham.

Epilogue

David Stewart Dawson died at home, in Brompton Road, South Kensington, on February 28th, 1998. The cause of death was congestive heart failure, brought about by chronic obstructive pulmonary disease; David's lifetime of smoking had caught up with him.[512] With his death, the Stewart Dawson name disappeared from local memory.

David's sister, Harriet, enjoyed a long and happy life married to architect, Hugh Denison, raising three sons in a Sydney that had been transformed during her lifetime from colonial entrepot to cosmopolitan metropolis.

Yet, many of the landmarks of Harriet's youth remain. The Strand Arcade has been meticulously restored to its Victorian glamour and style, though the basement that once housed The Ambassadors is now a home electronics store, the only clues to its origins being fragments of the ornate cornices, half-hidden behind stairwells. The remains of the terraced gardens belonging to Clarens/Wilga are a protected archaeological site at Potts Point. In Springwood, Bonnie Doon and The Spinney, after decades of neglect, now have owners who cherish and preserve them. Up the road from the latter, the terraces, retaining walls, fountain bases and arbours that once made Davesta/Bon Accord one of the Blue Mountains' showcase gardens are being respectfully preserved.

The Treasure House, at 19-21 Hatton Garden, stands as a testament to Edwardian style. Though its interior has been modernised, the elegant façade is untouched, a permanent memorial to its creator's energy and vision.

In Monte Carlo, Villa Bon Accord survived World War II and the depredations of Monaco's Consultative Committee on Public Works, which viewed Belle Epoque villas such as this as social anachronisms, demolishing scores to make way for high-rise apartments. It stands, today, proudly displaying its name above the entrance, the owners doubtless ignorant of the Scottish origins of that name.

And in a field in Scotland, not far from Kininvie, might a curious visitor, pushing aside the ferns and thistles, stumble upon a low, stone wall, dried sprigs of heather peeking out of the cracks?

Photo Credits

1. Young David builds the wall. *"The Boy and the wheelbarrow 1858, The Man and The Ambassadors 1924." P.8*
2. Buchanan Street, Glasgow. *www.glasgowhistory.com*
3. Two Stewart Dawson watches. L. *Illustrated in Antiques Reporter (Australia) Sold at auction by Bonhams & Goodman in 2006.* R. *For sale, eBay, saved by Suzy Kelly on Pinterest*
4. Prescot watch factory workers. *Prescot Museum. www.prescotmuseum.org.uk.*
5. SS Chimborazo. *State Library of South Australia, Item No. B11786 Used with permission*
6. First known Stewart Dawson advertisement in Australia. *Melbourne Leader, 3rd January 1880*
7. Stewart Dawson defensive advertisement. *Riverine Herald, 19th December 1884 P.4*
8. 1908 Franco-British Exhibition at White City. *From a postcard in public domain*
9. "The Treasure House", 19-21 Hatton Garden. *"The Boy and the wheelbarrow 1858, The Man and The Ambassadors 1924." P.12*
10. David in 1908, aged 59. *New Zealand Times, 11th April 1908, P.12*
11. 1905 portrait of Harriet, by John Longstaff. *The Australasian, 10th June 1905 P.27. Originally published in Pall Mall Magazine.*
12. Interior of Stewart Dawson's Regent Street shop. *"The Boy and the wheelbarrow 1858, The Man and The Ambassadors 1924." P.21*
13. Norman Stewart Dawson in 1915. *Great Britain Royal Aero Club Aviator's Certificate No.1758, 17th September 1915*
14. Thelma Raye in 1917. *Unknown, probably London (Dover Street Studios) Image taken from postcard in public domain*

15. Percy Stewart Dawson in about 1930. *Truth, 12th June 1932 P.18*

16. Annie McFarlane (Valerie Allison) in 1916. *McFarlane family collection, courtesy Alexis Dailey*

17. David in 1923. *"The Boy and the wheelbarrow 1858, The Man and The Ambassadors 1924." P.20*

18. McFarlane family at Taronga Zoo in 1917. *McFarlane family collection, courtesy Alexis Dailey*

19. Annie's grave in Springwood Cemetery. *Author's photo*

20. Hugh McIntosh. *Public domain image, per Library of Congress*

21. Davesta, David's Springwood home. *Springwood Historical Society*

22. The Spinney and its neighbour in early 1921. *Springwood Historical Society, per Susan Hamill*

23. The Strand Arcade when Stewart Dawson's acquired it. *Construction and Local Government Journal (Sydney) 22nd December 1919*

24. Clarens (Wilga) garden, Potts Point. *State Library of New South Wales (Mitchell Library)*

25. The Wentworth Ballroom. *John Maclurcan*

26. Hannah Maclurcan. *John Maclurcan*

27. Bert Ralton's New York Havana Band. *Published in Vintage Jazz Mart, edition 166, 2013, courtesy Jack Mitchell and Nick Dellow.*

28. Photo spread of opening night of The Ambassadors. *Sunday Times 23rd December 1923*

29. Main dining hall and ballroom of The Ambassadors. *"The Boy and the wheelbarrow 1858, The Man and The Ambassadors 1924." P.24*

30. Palm Court of The Ambassadors. *"The Boy and the wheelbarrow 1858, The Man and The Ambassadors 1924." P.22*

31. The Ambassadors' kitchen. *"The Boy and the wheelbarrow 1858, The Man and The Ambassadors 1924." P.38*

32. Arthur Mailey cartoon of Constable Chuck sting. *Sydney Sun 6th July 1924*

33. Josie Melville. *State Library of South Australia Cat. Item No. B62365*

34. Harriet in 1925. *Sunday Times 25th July 1925*

35. Rita Stewart Dawson in 1926. *Sydney Sun 12th August 1926 P.19*

36. Bertha Stewart Dawson (Verrall) in the 1920s. *The Herald, Melbourne, 31st August 1928 P.8*

37. Bon Accord guest house. *Springwood Historical Society, courtesy Susan Hamill*

38. Arthur Mailey cartoon of David in 1927. *Sydney Sun 19th October 1927 P.9*

39. Ballroom of The Ambassadors after the fire. *Sydney Morning Herald 31st July 1929 P.16*

40. Villa Bon Accord, Monte Carlo. *Baptiste Rivière 2007. Used with permission.*

41. DH Souter cartoon of 'Army of social leeches' *Smith's Weekly 13th December 1930 P.8*

42. Norman in his Rolls-Royce Phantom in 1931. *Rolls-Royce Owners' Club of Great Britain, per Tom Clarke*

43. Norman on his return to Sydney in 1932. *Sydney Morning Herald 26th March 1932 P.12*

44. Stuart with young David in Cannes. *Table Talk (Melbourne) 28th September 1933 P.4*

45. Harriet with grandchildren in 1937. *Sydney Sun 21st January 1937 P.35*

46. Ruins of Bon Accord after the fire. *Sydney Sun 3rd May 1937 P.1*

47. Black and White milk bar cartoon. *Smith's Weekly 10th August 1935 P.6*

48. Prince Michael Radziwill with Jeanette Suchestow. *Public domain*

49. Harriet and Radziwill's marriage. *Telegraph (Brisbane) 4th June 1938 P.14*

50. Antonin Palace. *Poloniae Amici polska-org.pl. Used with permission*

51. David Stewart Dawson Jr. *Sydney "Truth" 22nd December 1946 P.26*

52. Patricia Ann Fitzgerald. *Sydney "Truth" 16th February 1941 P.27*

53. The Stewart Dawson home at Palm Beach. *Sydney Sun 9th September 1946 P.1*

54. George Rankin McKay. *Sydney "Truth" 22nd December 1946 P.26*

55. Mary Ann Verspoor. *Ibid.*

56. Stuart Stewart Dawson. *Ibid.*

57. Stuart's wife, Jean. *Sydney "Truth" 6th April 1941 P.35*

58. David's sister, Harriet *Sydney Sun 15th October 1946 P.1*

59. Owen Patrick Garvan. *Sydney Sun 16th October 1946 P.1*

60. Stuart and Jean at Manly court. *Sydney Sun 14th October 1946 P.3*

61. Beverley Atkinson. *Sydney Sun 29th June 1947 P.1*

62. Last known photo of Percy. *Sydney "Truth" 26th January 1947 P.1*

63. Sale of the last Stewart Dawson property in 1949. *Sydney Sun 10th June 1949 P.5*

64. David and Beverley's "secret" wedding. *Newcastle Sun 18th November 1949 P.3*

65. Glen Ascham hotel. *Sydney Sun 24th November 1954 P.1*

66. Beverley's sit-in with her children. *Sydney Sun 20th November 1953 P.2*

Notes and References

The illustration on the fly leaf is the coat of arms of Aberdeen, with the motto: "Bon Accord", which David Stewart Dawson appropriated for his family and businesses.

All newspaper/journal sources accessed via the Australian National Library Trove website are quoted under Australian Creative Commons licence:

https://creativecommons.org/licenses/by-nc-sa/2.1/au/legalcode

---

Introduction: Heights and Depths

[1] England and Wales Civil Registration Death Index Ref. C8C/2391C/18

A Long Way from Scotland

[2] Melbourne Argus 13th March 1884 P.4 A detailed account of the voyage of the SS Chimborazo, praising the skills of Captain Ruthven in weathering the storm in the English Channel.

[3] Ship's manifest, SS Chimborazo, departing London for Adelaide, Melbourne and Sydney, 23rd January 1884, per Victoria, Australia, Unassisted Passenger Lists, 1839-1923

[4] The Scotsman 11th December 1906

[5] Brisbane Courier, Friday 8th April 1910, P7

[6] 1871 Scotland Census, Roll CSSCT1871_139

[7] Scotland, Select Marriages, 1561-1910 FHL Film No. 6035516

[8] England and Wales, Civil Registration Birth Index 1872 Q3 D

[9] "Kaltenbach of Cardiff" Wales and Marches Horological Society *https://www.walesclocks.org.uk/kaltenbach-of-cardiff*

[10] Advertisement: Baner ac Amserau Cymru 21st August 1872

[11] "Railway Time" Wikipedia *https://en.wikipedia.org/wiki/Railway_time*

[12] Advertisement, Gippsland Times 13th June 1884:

"About seven years ago Stewart, Dawson & Co, Liverpool introduced a new system of business in the English watch trade, viz. instead of continuing to sell their watches on credit with long accounts they resolved to go direct to the public themselves and sell their manufacture for cash."

[13] Wikipedia "Pryce Pryce-Jones" *https://en.wikipedia.org/wiki/Pryce_Pryce-Jones*

Catching the Second Wave

[14] This episode, which lasted from 1873 to 96, was labelled the "Great Depression" at the time, and it held that designation until the Great Depression of the 1930s … Nevertheless, profits generally were not adversely affected by deflation although they declined (particularly in Britain) in industries that were struggling against superior, foreign competition. That foreign competition was particularly damaging in the watch making industry, where large scale factories in the USA, such as Elgin and Waltham, not to mention the rapidly automating Swiss watch industry, rendered the English hand-made articles uncompetitive, driving most out of business by the turn of the century. Manufacturing Time: Global Competition in the Watch Industry, 1795-2000 P.85. Amy Glasmeier, Guildford Press 2000

[15] Liverpool University op. cit.

[16] Advertisement, Melbourne Leader, 3rd January 1880

[17] Brisbane Courier 8th April 1910. Interview with DSD

[18] ibid

[19] 1881 England Census ref: 85/362/18/P.29

[20] Houses for Sale advertisement, Liverpool Mercury 19th September 1890

[21] 1881 England Census op. cit.

[22] 1881 England Census op. cit.

[23] Weekly Times (Melbourne) 25th October 1884 P.5. Advertisement

[24] Section 17 of the act read: *"In any question between husband and wife as to the title to or possession of property, either party… may apply … to any judge of the High- Court of Justice in England or in Ireland…and the judge … may make such order with respect to the property in dispute…"*

[25] England and Wales, Civil Registration Death Index, Deaths Registered in October, November and December 1882, ref. Vol 8b Page 242

The Plunge into Retail

[26] Illawarra Mercury 13th January 1882 P.3 Advertisement

[27] Clarence and Richmond Examiner and New England Advertiser 9th December 1882 Advertisement

[28] Burnley Express and various other newspapers. Advertisement. 5th January 1884

[29] Burnley Gazette and numerous other newspapers 27th September 1879 Advertisement.

---

[30] Wrexham Advertiser 16th December 1882 Advertisement

[31] *"Is there a company to be got up to stock the wilds of Western Australia, or to form a railway on the land-grant system in Queensland, to introduce the electric light, or to spread education among the blackfellows, the promoters belong to Melbourne, or go there for their capital. The headquarters of nearly all the large commercial institutions which extend their operations beyond the limits of any one colony are to be found there. If you wish to transact business well and quickly, to organise a new enterprise – in short, to estimate and understand the trade of Australia, you must go to Melbourne and not to Sydney."* "Town Life in Australia" R.E.N. Twopeny, London, 1883. Reported in the Sydney Mail and New South Wales Advertiser P.5 5th January 1884.

[32] Passenger list, SS Chimborazo, Depart London 23rd January 1884. Maitland Mercury and Hunter River General Advertiser Shipping Arrival Notice 13th March 1884

[33] Southern Argus 5th April 1884 P. 8 Advertisement announcing DSD's arrival and gift offer.

[34] Australian Town and Country Journal 9th May 1885 P.17

[35] Advertisement in the Mount Alexander Mail (Victoria) on 19th December 1884. Similar advertisements were printed in many other Australian and New Zealand newspapers around this time

[36] Australian Town and Country Journal (Sydney, NSW: 1870 – 1907), Saturday 7 June 1884, page 17

[37] Hawkes Bay Herald, 8th April 1884 Advertisement *"Important Announcement – Messrs Stewart Dawson & Company, Liverpool, beg to announce to their thousands of customers and to the public throughout New Zealand, that they will open a branch Establishment within the colony within the next fortnight for the sale of their World-Renowned English Lever Watches…"*

[38] New Zealand Herald 24th April 1884 Advertisement

[39] Gippsland Times 13th June 1884 P.2

[40] ibid

[41] 1881 England Census, Ref. 3628/25 P.5

[42] Lancaster Gazette 29th October 1887 Advertisement

[43] 1891 England Census, Ref. 456/86/ P. 58

[44] Australia WW1 Service Record. Service No. 34086. Also, Truth 5th January 1930, P.18, relating New Year's Eve party where Percy celebrated his birthday. Actual birth date could therefore be December 31st or January 1st.

---

[45] Wellington Times and Agricultural and Mining Gazette 17th January 1891. Advertisement

[46] Clarence and Richmond Examiner 3rd January 1891. P. 8 Advertisement

[47] Stewart Dawson's NZ "About Us" *https://www.stewartDawson's.co.nz/about*

[48] "The Boy and the Wheelbarrow, 1858, the Man and The Ambassadors, 1924" P.4 "*Hereunder are a few of Mr Stewart Dawson's Business Maxims*" There follows a list of 14 maxims extolling the virtues of hard work, from which this one is extracted.

[49] Houses for Sale advertisement, Liverpool Mercury 19th September 1890 Op. Cit.

[50] London Electoral Register 1890 P. 298

[51] Great Britain, Royal Aero Club Aviator's Certificate 17th December 1915 Item 1758

[52] "The Boy and the Wheelbarrow, 1858, the Man and The Ambassadors, 1924" P.4 ibid

[53] Australia WW1 Service Records. Service No. 93425. Stuart lied about his age, reducing it by 5 years (claimed birth year was 1898)

[54] Passenger manifest, SS Himalaya, August 1884. Victoria, Assisted and Unassisted Passenger Lists, 1839-1923.

[55] Australian Town and Country Journal 15th August 1894. Report that the manager and staff of the Sydney shop expected David's arrival later that month.

[56] Australian Town and Country Journal 15th August 1894. Account of the staff of the shop presenting silverware to JM Dempster on the occasion of his marriage, which mentions David's impending arrival in Sydney

[57] Strand Arcade: Design and Construction 1891 from "Strand Arcade – Our Story" *https://www.strandarcade.com.au/our-story/6-design-and-construction-1891*

[58] Warragul Guardian and West Gippsland Advertiser 12th October 1894 P. 2 Advertisement

[59] Australasian 10th November 1894 P.41

[60] Australian Star 13th December 1894 P. 5

[61] Evening News (Sydney) 19th December 1892 P.3 A Christmas "advertorial" (one of David's specialities) promoting the George Street store

[62] Warragul Guardian and West Gippsland Advertiser 23rd November 1894 P. 2

[63] Australian Star 22nd January 1895 P. 6

64 Sunday Times (Sydney) 16th August 1896 P.3, Kalgoorlie Miner 25th August 1896 P.3

65 'The Boy and the Wheelbarrow, 1858, the Man and The Ambassadors, 1924' P.40

66 Age (Melbourne) 15th January 1895 P.6

67 Age (Melbourne) 8th January 1895 P.7

68 Age (Melbourne) 23rd January 1895 P.6

69 Evening News 5th February 1895 P.3

70 Age (Melbourne) 23rd January 1895 P.6 op. cit.

71 Australian Star 24th April 1895 P.5, Evening News (Sydney) 22nd June 1895 P.5, Truth (Sydney) 23rd June 1895 P.5, Australian Star 5th July 1895 P.6

72 Argus (Melbourne) 17th October 1895 P.6, Evening News 13th November1895 P.4

73 Freeman's Journal 20th June 1895 P.9 Woman's Column

74 Traveller (Melbourne) 19th December 1896, quoted in the Portland Guardian 7th May 1897 P.2 "An Enterprising Firm of Jewellers".

75 The Age (Melbourne) 24th July 1897 P.9

76 Table Talk (Melbourne) 25th June 1897 P.13 "A Melbourne "Tiffany's"

77 Bowral Free Press and Berrima District Intelligencer 22nd January 1898 P.3 "Visitors to Bowral – Grand Hotel – Mr and Mrs Stewart Dawson, family and nurse."

78 Evening News (Sydney) 15th April 1898 P.7

79 West Australian Sunday Times (Perth) 24th July 1898 P.11

80 West Australian Sunday Times 10th July 1898 P.8 "Through a Woman's 'Pince-Nez'" (By "Silvia")'

81 Western Mail (Perth) Christmas Number 16th December 1898 P.106 "Kalgoorlie"

82 Kalgoorlie Miner 23rd July 1898 P.4

London or Sydney?

83 Table Talk 8th September 1899 P.19

84 1901 England Census Ref. 239/15/P.21

85 1901 England Census Ref. 77/34/P.60

86 Table Talk 8th September 1899 P.19 op. cit.

87 Aberdeen People's Journal 2nd December 1899 Notice of relocation

[88] Australian Town and Country Journal 9th November 1901 P.44

[89] Australian Town and Country Journal 2nd November 1901 P.43 *"It seems but fitting that a special 'Melbourne Cup' costume should be illustrated in this number, although the design is one which would be appropriate for almost any smart summer function. It is composed of a fine muslin, trimmed profusely with lace edging and insertion, and may be entirely white or combined with any color preferred."*

[90] The Sydney Morning Herald 6th November 1901 P.9

[91] Referee (Sydney) 6th November 1901 P.2

[92] Freeman's Journal 4th January 1902 P.24

[93] Punch (Melbourne) 6th March 1902 P.10

[94] Freeman's Journal 4th January 1902 P. 24 Op. Cit.

[95] "The Boy and the Wheelbarrow, 1858, the Man and The Ambassadors, 1924" P.40

[96] Evening News (Sydney) 18th November 1902 P.6

[97] Geelong Advertiser 13th December 1902 P.2

[98] West Australian 4th March 1903 P.3

[99] Punch (Melbourne) 12th February 1903 P.20

[100] Freeman's Journal 4th January 1902 P. 24 Op. Cit.

[101] Art Gallery of NSW Collection *https://www.artgallery.nsw.gov.au/collection/works/5864/*

[102] Advertiser (Adelaide) 6th June 1905 P.5

[103] Historic England: Treasure House List Entry 1378738 https://historicengland.org.uk/listing/the-list/list-entry/1378738

[104] Derived from information compiled by and/or copyright of Dictionary of Scottish Architects: Niven and Wigglesworth, Courier Building 1901 *http://www.scottisharchitects.org.uk/building_full.php?id=213459* Used with permission

[105] Ibid Bio Notes

http://www.scottisharchitects.org.uk/architect_full.php?id=100248

[106] Evening News (Sydney) 1st January 1908 P.9

[107] Both quoted in "The Boy and the Wheelbarrow 1858, The Man and The Ambassadors 1924"

[108] Sunday Times (Perth) 20th December 1908 P.6

[109] Pall Mall Gazette 14th November 1907 P.9 "Stewart Dawson has something more to say about the Philosophy of Business Success."

[110] Sydney Morning Herald 11th September 1907 P.13

[111] Truth (Brisbane) 8th November 1908 P.7

[112] Daily News 16th December 1908 P.9

[113] West Australian 16th October 1909 P.4

[114] "The Boy and the Wheelbarrow 1858, The Man and The Ambassadors 1924" P.16-17

[115] Quoted in "The Boy and The Wheelbarrow, 1858, The Man and The Ambassadors", 1924 P.19

[116] Punch (Melbourne) 6th March 1902 P.10

[117] Huon Times 30th November 1910 P.2

Hints of Mortality, Changing Times

[118] Table Talk (Melbourne) 27th July 1911 P.16

[119] Marriage Certificate Verall/Dawson 17th July 1907

[120] Divorce Petition Ref. J77/1096/3248 Verall vs Verrall 14th November 1912

[121] Ibid.

[122] 1911 England Census Paddington South District Ref. 17/85

[123] Sunday Times (Perth) 21st April 1912 P.30

[124] Sunday Times (Perth) 11th August 1912 P.1

[125] The Argus (Melbourne) 4th March 1912 P.13

[126] Daily News (Perth) 27th November 1912 P.3

[127] Evening News 31st December 1912 P.4

[128] Sun (Sydney) 26th January 1913 P.21

[129] Sun (Sydney) 4th February 1913 P.6

[130] Dominion 13th February 1913

[131] Sun (Sydney) 21st March 1913 P.6

[132] Sun (Sydney) 23rd March 1913 P.19

[133] Sydney Morning Herald 9th April 1913 P.14

[134] Age (Melbourne) 6th February 1914 P.9

[135] Daily Mail 13th February 1914

[136] West Australian (Perth) 4th February 1914 P.7

[137] Passenger List SS St Louis departure Liverpool for New York November 25th, 1916. David's and Annie's appearance are described in the passenger manifest.

[138] Great Britain, Royal Aero Club Aviator's Certificate 17th December 1915 Item 1758 Op. Cit.

[139] Age (Melbourne) 5th September 1917 P.8

[140] The Daily Mirror (London) 29th November 1917

[141] How WW1 Made Wristwatches Happen. BoingBoing 4th March 2015 *http://boingboing.net/2015/03/04/how-wwi-made-wristwatches-happ.html*

[142] 1911 England Census Ref.24/26/1894

[143] London Church of England St John the Evangelist, Ladbroke Grove, Banns of Marriage 31st July 1915

[144] Calling card: "Mrs Allison" 1916, Estelle Allison Birth Certificate 14th December1915

[145] Estelle Allison Birth Certificate 14th December1915

[146] The Scotsman 26th January 1916

[147] Table Talk (Melbourne) 8th January 1920 P.6

[148] Passenger List SS St Louis departure Liverpool for New York November 25th, 1916, Op. Cit.

[149] Honolulu Passenger and Crew List SS Makura 25th January 1917

[150] Geelong Advertiser 13th December 1902 P.2 *"The name of 'Stewart Dawson and Co' has become a household word in Australia."*

[151] Honolulu Star Bulletin 20th January 1917 P.14

The Fatal Shore

[152] The Dominion 16th February 1917

[153] Ibid 13th February 1917

[154] Australia WW 1 Service Record. Service No. 93425

[155] Truth (Brisbane) 1st April 1917 P.2

[156] Photograph (annotated) Tom, Annie McFarlane, Valerie, Estelle at Taronga Zoo

[157] Photograph (annotated) Valerie with Estelle in Sydney Royal Botanic Gardens

[158] Sydney Evening News "Of Interest to Women" 3rd February 1918

[159] England and Wales Civil Registration Death Index June 1917 Christchurch Hampshire Vol 2b P.833

[160] Australian Dictionary of Biography: McIntosh, Hugh Donald (1876-1942) Chris Cuneen *http://adb.anu.edu.au/biography/mcintosh-hugh-donald-7373*

---

[161] Table Talk (Melbourne) 8th April 1915 P.17

[162] Arrow (Sydney) 24th March 1917 P.3

[163] Australian Dictionary of Biography: Lindsay, Norman Alfred (1879-1969) Bernard Smith *http://adb.anu.edu.au/biography/lindsay-norman-alfred-7757*

[164] New South Wales Certificate of Title Vol. 2229 Folio 60 and Folio 184

[165] Blue Mountain Echo 22nd February 1918 P.5

[166] Photograph annotated by Annie (Valerie) sent to Maggie

[167] Barrier Miner (Broken Hill) 21st October 1918 P.1

[168] New South Wales Death Certificate: Valerie Allison, 30th November 1918, Ref. 1918/014262

Loose Ends

[169] "Time of Tension – Trust in Leaders" Melbourne Argus, 11th November 1918. Full account of speeches given at the Lord Mayor's dinner, attended by representatives from all the victorious powers.

[170] Devon and Exeter Gazette 9th June 1915 P.3

[171] Warwick Examiner and Northern Times, 21st October 1918 P.1

[172] Sydney Morning Herald 27th February 1919 P.5

[173] Sun (Sydney) 20th August 1919 P.5 and various other newspapers

[174] Melbourne Age 12th September 1919 P.9

[175] Melbourne Age 6th January 1920 P.8

[176] Farmer and Settler (Sydney) 7th March 1919 P.5 advertisement

[177] The Australian Dictionary of Biography, Vol 11, 1988 William James (Bill) Proud (1871-1931)

[178] Evening News (Sydney) 26th March 1919 P.1 advertisement

[179] Sun (Sydney) 23rd August 1917 P.5

[180] Table Talk (Melbourne) 8th January 1920 P.6

[181] Sun (Sydney) 14th March 1920 P.12

[182] Daily Examiner (Grafton) 10th April 1920 P.5

[183] Sunday Times (Sydney) 23rd May 1920 "Social Notes from The Wentworth"

[184] The Mirror (Sydney) 27th April 1919 P.6 "Through the Eyes of a Woman"

Joining Sydney's Establishment

185 Smith's Weekly 9th October 1920 P.11 "Gossip from Here, There and Everywhere"

186 The Times, 24 June 1893, issue 33986, page 7, *"Terrible naval disaster"*.

187 Sun (Sydney) 13th June 1921 P.9 Building, Industry and Machinery Private Contracts

188 Blue Mountains Echo 19th November 1920

189 Blue Mountains Echo 11th March 1921 P.6

190 Blue Mountains Echo 6th January 1921

Percy Steps Up

191 Sun (Sydney) 12th April 1921 P.2 "Just in Time – Roof in Flames"

192 Brisbane Courier 10th September 1921 P.3

193 Sydney Morning Herald 20th October 1921 P.6

194 £233,000 in 1921 is worth about $18m today

195 £50,000 in 1921 is worth a little under $4m today

196 Australian Dictionary of Biography, Volume 10, 1986 – Theodore John Marks. By Martha Rutledge.
http://adb.anu.edu.au/biography/marks-theodore-john-7491
Robertson and Marks were to go on to greater success with the Head Office of the Bank of New South Wales and the Prince Edward Theatre and are in business to this day.

197 Blue Mountain Echo 2nd June 1922 P.1

198 Nepean Times 11th March 1922 P.5

199 Brisbane Courier 21st October 1921 P.5 Trade and Finance. Announcement of the registration of Stewart Dawson, Queensland. Malcolm is listed as a director, resident in Springwood.

200 The Sun (Sydney) 22nd December 1911

201 Hannah Maclurcan (life story and family history) by John Maclurcan 2013

202 John Maclurcan family reminiscence 2017

203 The Brisbane Worker 13th October 1936. Hannah Maclurcan obituary

204 Strand Arcade: Our Story – The Ambassadors Cafe, 1920s
https://www.strandarcade.com.au/our-story/the-ambassadors-cafe

205 Wentworth Hotel brochure, 1913

206 Sunday Times (Sydney) 10th July 1921

207 Perth Daily News "Chit-Chat" 4th November 1922

208 Sun (Sydney) 20th December 1920

209 The Boy and The Wheelbarrow 1856, The Man and The Ambassadors 1924 P.39

210 The Australasian 27th October 1923 P.32

211 Bert Ralton and his Havana Band by Jack Mitchell and Nick Dellow, published in Vintage Jazz Mart, edition 166, 2013

212 Sunday Times (Sydney) 14th October 1923 P.24

213 Sunday Times (Sydney) 4th November 1923 P.12

214 Table Talk (Melbourne) 20th December 1923 P. 8

Happy New Year

215 Sunday Times (Sydney) 16th December 1923 P.6

216 Sydney Morning Herald "Near and Far" 2nd January 1924 P.4 and Telegraph (Brisbane) "Gossip from Sydney – Notes for Women" 5th January 1924 P. 16

217 Sunday Times (Sydney) 6th January 1924 P.14

218 Telegraph (Brisbane) op. cit.

219 Telegraph (Brisbane) op. cit.

220 Sunday Times 6th February 1921 P.5

221 "The Boy and the Wheelbarrow 1858, The Man and The Ambassadors 1924", P.30

222 Evening News 8th January 1924 P.11

223 Sun 18th January 1924 P.7

224 Sun 1st February 1924 P. 7

225 Labor Daily 1st March 1924 P. 6

226 Mirror (Perth) 16th February 1924 P.4 and Sun 7th March 1924 P.7

227 Sun 14th March 1924 P.7, Evening News 14th March 1924 P.9, Sun 25th March 1924 P.9

228 The Australasian Op. Cit.

Roaring Along

229 Sunday Times 30th March 1924 P.14

230 Sunday Times, 23rd March 1924.

---

[231] Sunday Times 9th March 1924 P.17

[232] Sun 17th June 1924 P.13

[233] Truth 7th September 1924 P.12

[234] Truth op. cit.

[235] Truth 21st September 1924 P.6

More Family Business

[236] Sunday Times 21st[th] September 1924 P.18

[237] Sunday Times 28th September 1924 P.24

[238] Op. cit. P.17

[239] Sydney Morning Herald 13th May 1924 P.6

[240] Sun 9th June 1932 P.15

[241] UK Incoming Passenger List 11th April 1924 London arrivals, RMS Mooltan

[242] Sun 2nd November 1924 P.24

[243] Evening News 5th February 1924 P.8

[244] Evening News 9th December 1924 P.1

[245] Sun 29th October 1924 P.14

[246] Op. cit. P.14

[247] New South Wales Certificate of Title Vol.2289 Folio 184

[248] New South Wales Certificate of Title Vol. 2229 Folio 60 and Folio 184

[249] Sunday Times 29th March 1925 P.4

[250] Sunday Times 26th April 1925 P.5

[251] Truth 25th January 1925 P.7

Re-Grouping

[252] National Advocate (Bathurst) 22nd November 1924 P.2

[253] The Blue Mountains Echo 17th April 1925 P.6

[254] National Advocate (Bathurst) 16th June 1925 P.2

[255] Freeman's Journal, 21st May 1925 P.20

[256] Sun 22nd May 1925 P.9

[257] Quoted from Sancta Sophia College: History. *http://www.sanctasophiacollege.edu.au/about-sancta/college-history/* Used with permission of the Principal, Fiona Hastings.

[258] Salmon Ponds Heritage Hatchery and Gardens – History: Trout and Salmon from England. *https://www.salmonponds.com.au/history/* Salmon released into streams swam out to sea, never to return.

[259] Sun 14th October 1925 P.13

[260] Advertisements placed in November and December 1925 in Sydney Morning Herald, The Sun and Sunday Times.

[261] Sydney Morning Herald Financial and Commercial Supplement, 8th February 1927, P.2. Quoted from "INDUSTRIAL DEVELOPMENT IN AUSTRALIA 1920-1950". Thesis Submitted for the Degree of Doctor of Philosophy at the Australian National University, Colin Forster, August 1959.

Cads and Bricks

[262] Evening News 23rd March 1926 P.8. The voyage was described as "via ports", in the language of the day.

[263] Sunday Times 18th July 1926 P.14

[264] Sun 8th May 1926 P.7

[265] Barrier Miner (Broken Hill) 9th November 1950 P.3

[266] Yorkshire Evening Post 3rd June 1927 P.12

[267] UK Incoming Passenger List, RMA Ormonde, London, 4th April 1922. Joseph is listed as "Merchant" and gives his intended address as "SH Lock & Co. Ltd., Mark Lane, EC."

[268] Evening News 4th October 1926 P.10

[269] Ibid

[270] Geelong Advertiser 22nd July 1926 P.1

[271] Quoted with permission from "Kathleen O'Connor – Artist in Exile" PAE Hutchings and Julie Lewis, Fremantle Arts Centre Press 1987 Pp 60, 61 and following.

Bon Accord

[272] Sunday Times 19th September 1926 P.17

[273] Sun 16th October 1926 P.8

[274] Brisbane Telegraph 6th November 1926 P.12

[275] Brisbane Telegraph 8th May 1926 P.12

[276] Cairns Post 21st April 1926 P.11

[277] The Telegraph, Brisbane, 29th March 1926 P.2. The Queen Street property was described as "The Acme of Value".

[278] Melbourne Argus 13th November 1926 P.34 Op. cit.

[279] Blue Mountains Echo 14th August 1925 P.6

[280] Sydney Morning Herald 27th November 1926 P.12

[281] Blue Mountains Echo 1st January 1927

[282] Ibid 11th February 1927 P.6

[283] Brisbane Courier 1st February 1927 P.2

[284] Sunday Times 6th February 1927 P.2

[285] Sydney Morning Herald 17th February 1927 P.4

[286] Sydney Morning Herald 1st July 1927 P.6

[287] Sunday Times 31st July 1927 P.21

[288] Truth 12th June 1927 P.19

[289] Blue Mountains Echo 1st April 1927

[290] Northern Star (Lismore) 7th April 1927 P.4

[291] Sun 15th March 1927 P.14

[292] Sun 17th October 1927 P.6

[293] Keith, Alexander (1987). A Thousand Years of Aberdeen. Aberdeen: Aberdeen University Press.

[294] Sydney Morning Herald 11th October P.5

[295] Construction and Local Government Journal, 1st January 1928

[296] The Blue Mountains Echo 16th March 1928 P.6

[297] Blue Mountain Echo 22nd June 1928 P.1. The article is headlined: "The Dawson Road".

[298] Sunday Times 13th March 1927 P.14

[299] Sydney Mail 15th November 1933 Advertisement.

[300] Sun 18th January 1928 P.18

[301] The Armidale Chronicle 9th June 1928 P.12

[302] The Hinkler recording is preserved at the Mitchell Library to this day. It can be heard on YouTube at https://www.youtube.com/watch?v=rwvZB8d1J4E

[303] Evening News 12th April 1927 P.12, Truth 23rd October 1927 P.19, Truth 30th December e1928 P.16

[304] Evening News 31st January 1928 P.12

305 Truth 4th March 1928 P.18

306 Sydney Morning Herald 28th March 1929 P.15

307 Smith's Weekly 19th July 1930 P.8

308 Hobart Mercury 18th April 1929 P.8

309 Sun 1st April 1929 P.10

310 Truth 28th April 1929 P.22

Someday, my Prince will come

311 Sydney Daily Telegraph, 1st March 1941 P.8. "Tea Parade of Fashions". *'Princess Radziwill, who recently returned from a trip to Suva, was present.'*

312 Sydney Morning Herald 30th July 1929 P.11

313 Sun 30th July 1929 P.16

314 Evening News 8th August 1929 P.7

Everything Must Go

315 Sydney Morning Herald 6th August 1929 P.10

316 Table Talk (Melbourne) 26th February 1932 P.25

317 Age (Melbourne) 2nd January 1932 P.9

318 Australian Worker 13th April 1932 P.18

319 Sun 16th October 1930 P.15, Melbourne Argus 18th October 1930 P.20

320 Otago Daily Times 22nd November 1930 The Industrial World, J.T. Paul

Curtains

321 Sun 21st December 1929 P.7

322 Daily Advertiser, Wagga Wagga, 3rd January 1930 P.3

323 Sydney Morning Herald 31st December 1929 P.2 advertisement

324 Evening News 20th January 1930 P.5

325 Sydney Mail 13th August 1930 P.30

326 Sun 10th July 1930 P.29

327 Sun 6th July 1930 P.17.

328 Smith's Weekly, 16th August 1930 P.6

329 Smith's Weekly, 13th December 1930 P.8 *"Army of Social Leeches – Men and Women, Boys and Girls"*

[330] Truth 24th August 1930 P.14

[331] Sydney Morning Herald 19th December 1930 P.2

[332] Sun 28th December 1930 P.1

[333] Sydney Morning Herald 16th January 1931 P.2

[334] Sun 14th January 1931 P.9. *"To Close – The Ambassadors Café – Cost £140,000 – End of Night Life"*

[335] "Catty Communications", Smith's Weekly 31st January 1931 P.9

[336] "Catty Communications", Smith's Weekly 29th August 1931 P.47

A Quiet, Unassuming Man

[337] Sun, 5th March 1932 P.9 *"P. Stewart Dawson to Go Back – Court's order – Temperament to Blame."*

[338] Northern Times (Carnarvan, WA) 24th March 1932 P.3

[339] Age (Melbourne) 22nd March 1932 P.7

[340] Sun 12th June 1932 P.3

[341] Sun 6th August 1932 P.5 and many other newspapers.

[342] Auckland Evening Post, 18th August 1932

[343] Rookwood Crematorium opened on May 28th, 1925.

Retreat

[344] Sydney Morning Herald 26th May 1933 P.7 *"Late Mr D. Stewart Dawson – Bequests to Family".*

[345] Dundee Evening Telegraph 29th November 1932, West Australian 1st December 1932 P.17

[346] Evening News (Rockhampton) 9th June 1933 P.6 and numerous other accounts. The Australian reports of the car immediately preceded and followed Norman's return with the vehicle, in July 1933.

[347] UK Incoming Passenger List, SS Berengaria, arriving Southampton ex New York via Cherbourg, 2nd December 1932. Archibald Falconer, c/- Stewart Dawson, 73 Regent Street, London (the London store address), age 27, occupation: Valet, country of last residence: Australia.

[348] Nepean Times 11th March 1933 P.6

[349] Sydney Mail 15th November 1933 illustrated advertisement.

[350] Blue Mountain Star 4th May 1929 P.4 and 29th June 1929 P.8

[351] Nepean Times 22nd April 1933 P.4. *"Bon Accord, the late home of Stewart Dawson, was a popular resort. It is reported that 100 sat down to Easter dinner."*

[352] Sydney Morning Herald 7th October 1933

[353] UK Outward Passenger List, SS Bremen, 18th June 1933 ex Southampton for New York. Norman Stewart-Dawson, Company Director, Mayfair Hotel W.1, and Frank Wakeham, Valet, same address. Both travelled first class.

[354] Sydney Sun 17th July 1933 P.8

[355] Lotus Thompson (1906-1963) *https://en.wikipedia.org/wiki/Lotus_Thompson*

[356] Sydney Daily Telegraph 28th July 1933 P.4

[357] Taken from a detailed account of the court case brought against Percy by Perpetual Trustees in August 1940, Sydney Truth 4th August 1940 P.19.

[358] Sydney Daily Telegraph 31st August 1933 P.13.

[359] Ibid.

Housekeeping

[360] This and following references to the case: The Argus (Melbourne) 22nd February 1933 P.9

[361] Auction notice, Sydney Morning Herald, 21st June 1933 P.19

[362] Melbourne Herald 13th November 1933 P.14. Harriet's arrival date in Sydney is inferred from the date of her arrival in Melbourne, here reported.

[363] Sydney Morning Herald 28th February 1933 P.9

[364] Sydney Daily Telegraph 29th November 1933 P.15

[365] Melbourne Herald 13th November 1933 op. cit.

[366] Australian Women's Weekly 23rd December 1933 P.23. *"As it is in Beach Road, with lawns sloping down to the water, and is particularly well furnished…the Stewart Dawsons are quite happy to pay eighteen guineas a week for the Curlewis' home at Palm Beach, which they have taken for the Christmas holidays."*

[367] Sydney Morning Herald 21st December 1933 P.3

[368] Beverley Kingston, "Maclurcan, Hannah (1860–1936)", Australian Dictionary of Biography, National Centre of Biography, Australian National University, *http://adb.anu.edu.au/biography/maclurcan-hannah-13070/text23641*, published first in hardcopy 2005, accessed online 22 September 2018.

[369] The Spring Racing Carnival is held in October

[370] The Melbourne Cup is run on the first Tuesday in November

[371] Sydney Morning Herald 27th December 1933 P.3 'For Women'

Trust, Care and Responsibility

[372] Dundee Courier and Advertiser 6th February 1934

[373] Truth (Brisbane) 18th November 1934 P.13 (republished from Truth, Melbourne). An account of Ethel Roberts' breach of promise case against Emmanuel Abrahams, which includes history of the Abrahams brothers (the 'Small Arms Brothers').

[374] Maitland Mercury 10th February 1934 P.4.

[375] Monthly Weather Report of the Meteorological Office (United Kingdom) September 1934

[376] New York, Passenger and Crew Lists, SS Europa, passengers sailing from Southampton December 12th, 1934. The Stewart Dawsons were in transit through New York for the west coast of the USA and thence to Australia.

[377] Truth (Brisbane) 3rd February 1935 P.14

[378] Smith's Weekly 27th April 1935 P.10

[379] Cited from The History of Lotteries, Gerald Willmann, Department of Economics, Stanford University Stanford, CA 94305-6072, U.S.A. gerald@willmann.stanford.edu August 3rd, 1999

[380] Truth 24th February 1935 P.10

[381] Ibid.

[382] Yorkshire Evening Post 27th May 1935 P.6 and several other regional newspapers

[383] Sheffield Independent 6th June 1935 P.6

[384] Smith's Weekly 18th October 1935 P.5

[385] Truth 29th September 1935 Pp.2 and 5

[386] Tweed Daily 1st February 1937 P.3 reporting from London.

[387] Smith's Weekly 11th January 1936 P.10

[388] The Daily Worker, quoted in Truth 26th January 1936 P.14

[389] Nepean Times 9th May 1936 P.3

[390] Cairns Post 31st March 1936 P7, from a London correspondent, dated March 14th, 1936

In Royal Circles

[391] Sun 31st March 1927 P.21

[392] Sunday Times 3rd April 1927 P.14

[393] Sydney Morning Herald 16th September 1936 P.16

[394] Perth Daily News 12th January 1937 P.2. An interview with Harriet upon her arrival in Perth on the RMS Mooltan, bound for Sydney. Her opening words were: *"It is common talk in London that Mrs Simpson had hoped to star at the Coronation."*

Matriarchal Duty, Filial Chaos

[395] Stormy Weather: a century of storms, fire, flood and drought in New South Wales. Australian Government, Bureau of Meteorology, 2009.

[396] Labor Daily 25th February 1937 P.9

[397] Daily Telegraph 11th January 1935 P.8

[398] Grafton Daily Examiner 10th March 1937 P.3

[399] Sydney Sun 21st January 1937 P.35

[400] ibid

[401] Richmond River Herald and Northern Districts Advertiser 2nd April 1937 P.3 Headline: *"Speed Crazy – Doing 95mph."*

[402] Brisbane Telegraph 1st April 1937 P. from a London report dated 31st March.

[403] Sydney Sun 3rd May 1937 P.1, Sydney Morning Herald 4th May 1937 P.11 and various other newspapers. There were also reports of the inquest, which found no proximate cause of the fire.

"It's my turn, now"

[404] Truth 14th March 1937 P.27. The article mis-names her as "Jean Stewart-Dawson". Jean was Rita's unmarried younger sister.

[405] Nepean Times 20th May 1937 P.2

[406] Sun (Sydney) 23rd May 1937 P.17.

[407] West Coast Sentinel 10th September 1937 P.5

[408] ibid

[409] Royce Foundation archives for chassis number 74MY, Gurney Nutting sedanca coupé. Supplied by Tom Clarke.

Prince, Pauper, Scoundrel?

[410] The Tatler, 2nd March 1938 P.371

[411] Daily Telegraph 14th October 1945 P.5 Account of Harriet's death.

[412] Daily Telegraph, 20th May 1938 P.2, reporting a statement by the prince at the time of the court application.

[413] Ilustrowany Kurier Polski, Bydgoszcz, 19th December 1937, p. 5. R. dell'Ombra, Prince Michał Radziwiłł speaking about his intention to marry. Quoted by Dariusz J. Peśla *Prince Michał Radziwiłł "Rudy" 1870-1955 Women "antonin maharaja"*

[414] London Daily Herald, 14th May 1938 P.11

[415] Sydney Daily Telegraph, 20th May 1938 P.2

[416] Dziennik Ostrowski No. 120, May 6th, 1938, P. 2. *London sensation with the marriage of Fr. Michał Radziwiłła*

Trapped

[417] Labor Daily 25th August 1938 P.6 *Harassed Couple's Hidden Honeymoon.*

[418] Australian Women's Weekly 12th November 1938 P.3

[419] Northern Star (Lismore) 23rd November 1938 P.4 Syndicated from UK sources

[420] Ibid.

[421] Daily Telegraph 28th January 1939 P.1 *Lent Prince cost of a shave*

[422] London Electoral Register, City of Westminster, 1939 Pp 134-135

[423] Letter from Harriet to Kathleen, sent from the Westminster Hotel, Le Touquet, 23rd May 1939

[424] Letter from Harriet to Kathleen, probably 29th May 1939

[425] Ibid.

[426] Letter from Harriet to Kathleen, probably 1st June 1939

[427] Letter from Harriet to Kathleen, probably 12th June 1939

[428] Letter from Harriet to Kathleen, probably 12th or 13th June 1939

[429] Courier Mail (Brisbane) 28th July 1939 P.7 from an AAP report of war preparations.

[430] "Katherine O'Connor, Artist in Exile", PAE Hutchings and Julie Lewis, Freemantle Arts Centre Press 1987 Pp 77-78

[431] Letter from Harriet to Kathleen, 9th April 1940

[432] Truth (Sydney) 7th January 1940 P.3

[433] Truth (Sydney) 25th February 1940 P.29

[434] Sun (Sydney) 6th February 1940 P.11

[435] Sydney Morning Herald 29th February 1940 P.16

[436] Daily Telegraph (Sydney) 11th April 1940 P.16

[437] Sydney Morning Herald 29th April 1940 P.11

[438] Daily Telegraph (Sydney) 3rd August 1940 P.6

[439] Truth 4th August 1940 P.19

[440] Daily Telegraph (Sydney) 6th August 1940 P.7

[441] Sun (Sydney) 9th September 1940 P.3

[442] Sun (Sydney) 23rd May 1941 P.10

[443] Sydney Morning Herald 28th December 1940 P.5

[444] Letter from Harriet to Kathleen 13th February 1944

[445] Letter from Harriet to Kathleen 5th January 1945

[446] "Long live Friendship" from Melbourne Argus 31st January 1938 P.10. The author was "E. Goode". Harriet mis-quotes in part. The last two lines should be:

And its leaves withered and fallen away
May friendship still continue.

"Courage" source unknown. Harriet may have composed it herself.

[447] "Kathleen O'Connor, Artist in Exile", PAE Hutchings and Julie Lewis, Freemantle Arts Centre Press 1987 Pp 83-84

Day Two: Patricia Fitzgerald

[448] World War II Service Record, David Stewart Dawson (Service No. N214459)

[449] Truth 8th June 1941 P.29

[450] Sydney Daily Telegraph 4th February 1940 P.33

[451] Sydney Morning Herald 26th November 1941 P.7

[452] Truth 29th March 1942 P.20

[453] Newcastle Sun 2nd August 1940 P.8

[454] Sydney Daily Telegraph 16ht January 1944 P.10

[455] Dariusz J. Peśla Prince Michał Radziwiłł "Rudy" 1870-1955 Women "antonin maharaja" op. cit.

[456] Sydney Sun 25th July 1945 P.11

[457] Sydney Sun 10th June 1949 P.5 and many other newspapers

[458] Patricia's letter and David's reply are reported in full in Sydney Truth, 17th February 1946 P.17

[459] Daily Telegraph (Sydney) 1st November 1945 P.20

[460] Sydney Sun 15th September 1946 P.17

Day Three: The Palm Beach Incident

[461] The account of the events leading to the Palm Beach shooting is taken from several reports of court proceedings, including in Smith's Weekly, Brisbane Telegraph, Sydney Sun, and other publications.

[462] Sydney Daily Telegraph 24th May 1945. 1st Lt Paul Verspoor was an officer in the Netherlands Army.

Day Six: The Trial

[463] Patricia was granted a decree nisi on the grounds of David's desertion on October 10th, 1946. The divorce was made absolute six months later.

[464] Beyond Victor's Justice? The Tokyo War Crimes Trial Revisited, Edited by Yuki Tanaka, Tim McCormack, Gerry Simpson. Martinus Nijhoff, Leiden, Boston, 2011. Forward by Sir Gerard Brennan. CV Rooney was Chief Prosecutor at the war crimes trial. Gerard Brennan was his Clerk of Court.

[465] Sydney Daily Telegraph 18th February 1947 P.1

Day Eight: Goodbye to All That

[466] Sydney Daily Telegraph 24th December 1946 P.1.

[467] Newcastle Sun 16th August 1944 P.3

[468] Truth 8th December 1946 P.24 *"Wealthy Businessman sued for £165"*

[469] Truth 26th January 1947 P.1

[470] Sydney Daily Telegraph 30th January 1947 P.13

[471] This account of the "drinks in the cell" incident is based on several reports, including in the Sydney Daily Telegraph (29th June and 6th July 1947), The Sun (29th June) and Truth (29th June).

[472] Details of David's life and conditions in Long Bay prison hospital are from an article: *"Special Prisoners pampered in jail"* printed in Sydney's Daily Telegraph on 22nd August 1948. A recently released prisoner (un-named in the article) claimed David, Cliffie Thomas and Harold Price had bought privileges to which they were not entitled and that none of them were as ill

as they claimed. His statement was offered to the Minister of Justice but there was no response from the minister.

473 Sydney Sunday Herald 3rd July 1949 P.4

474 Truth 28th September 1947 P.49

475 NSW Index to Deceased Estate Files: Bertha Verrall. Ref. B825 of 1949.

476 Truth 7th September 1947 P.46

477 Sydney Daily Telegraph 2nd August 1948 P.4. The article covers the wedding and the maiden voyage of the "Estrellita", Garvan's yacht, on which the couple celebrated their honeymoon.

478 Sydney Sunday Herald 3rd July 1949 P.4 op. cit.

479 Sun 30th June 1949 P.3

480 Sun (Sydney) 17th November 1949 P.1 and Newcastle Sun 18th November 1949 P.3

481 Sydney Daily Telegraph 18th November 1949 P.5

482 Sydney Daily Telegraph 10th February 1950 P.1

483 Truth 24th August 1952 P.11, reporting yet another court case in which David was sued over a debt.

484 Ibid.

485 Sun 8th May 1952 P.38

486 Truth 9th November 1952 P.44

487 Government Gazette of the State of New South Wales 22nd October 1954 Notice of forced sale of Glen Ascham, which includes details of all of David's debts on the property and contents.

488 Construction (Sydney) 29th April 1953 P.11

489 Sun 30th April 1953 P.29

490 Central Queensland Herald (Rockhampton) 22nd September 1955 P.9 Account of David's bankruptcy hearing in Sydney

491 Truth 11th October 1953 P.58

492 Sun 20th November 1953 P.2, Newcastle Sun 23rd November 1953 P.2, Sydney Morning Herald 23rd November 1953 P.4, Sydney Daily Telegraph 29th November 1953 P.7

493 Sun 28th January 1954 P.1

494 Sun 30th March 1954 P.2

495 Sun 2nd July 1954 P.3

---

[496] Melbourne Argus 22nd April 1955. Reporting David's £22,000 loss to Roth and incidentally a further £1,200 to Lee Gordon while at Glen Ascham

[497] Truth 18th July 1954 P.56

[498] Sydney Morning Herald 20th September 1954 P.4

[499] Sydney Daily Telegraph 26th September 1954 P.9

[500] Truth 26th September 1954 P.42

[501] Government Gazette of the State of New South Wales 22nd October 1954 op. cit.

[502] Sun 16th November 1954 P.3

[503] Sun 24th November 1954 P.1, Newcastle Sun 24th November 1954 P.5

[504] Sun 23rd November 1954 P.5, Sydney Morning Herald 24th November 1954 P.3

[505] Sydney Morning Herald 24th November 1954 P.1, Newcastle Sun 25th November 1954 P.5

[506] Sun 24th November 1954 P.3

[507] Central Queensland Herald (Rockhampton) 17th March 1955 P.9

[508] Canberra Times 20th September 1955 P.5

[509] Central Queensland Herald (Rockhampton) 10th November 1955 P.29

[510] Death Certificate Ref. QBDAB 412851 David Stewart Dawson 28th February 1998. Occupation: "Taxi Driver (Retired)".

[511] Recounted by Anne Norman, Managing Director, James Pascoe Ltd. 2019

Epilogue

[512] Death Certificate Ref. QBDAB 412851 David Stewart Dawson 28th February 1998.